D-DAY
LANDING CRAFT

D-DAY
LANDING CRAFT

HOW 4,126 'UGLY AND UNORTHODOX' ALLIED CRAFT
MADE THE NORMANDY LANDINGS POSSIBLE

ANDREW WHITMARSH

The
History
Press

Cover illustration: *Front*: Landing Craft, Assault (LCA) of 557 Assault Flotilla, carrying the Royal Winnipeg Rifles to Juno Beach, D-Day. The flotilla's ship, MV *Llangibby Castle*, can be seen in the background. (Canada Dept of National Defence/Library and Archives Canada/PA-132651) *Back*: Royal Navy LCAs loaded with US troops, with US Coast Guard LCI(L)s behind, at Weymouth before D-Day. (Photo: US Coast Guard)

First published 2024

The History Press
97 St George's Place, Cheltenham,
Gloucestershire, GL50 3QB
www.thehistorypress.co.uk

British Library Cataloguing in Publication Data.
A catalogue record for this book is available from the British Library.

ISBN 978 1 80399 445 1

Typesetting and origination by The History Press
Printed and bound in Great Britain by TJ Books Limited, Padstow, Cornwall.

MIX
Paper from
responsible sources
FSC® C013056
www.fsc.org

Trees for LYfe

Contents

Acknowledgements		7
Glossary		9

Introduction: 'Ugly and Unorthodox …'		17
1	Landing Craft Types: Origins, Design and Construction	23
2	Allied Strategy and Landing Craft Production	65
3	Forging the Weapon: Landing Craft Crews, Bases and Training	85
4	The Plan	99
5	Embarkation, Departure and Crossing	109
6	Utah Beach	149
7	Omaha Beach	179
8	Gold Beach	227
9	Juno Beach	267
10	Sword Beach	317
11	After D-Day	355

Order of Battle	361
Roll of Honour	389
Notes	391
Bibliography and Sources	439
Index of Landing Craft	451
Index	455

Acknowledgements

The author wishes to acknowledge and thank the following:

The many landing craft veterans and their families who I have interviewed or communicated with over the years, primarily through my work as curator of The D-Day Story, Portsmouth (before 2018 this was known as the D-Day Museum).

This book was written outside paid employment, but I wish to thank my employer, Portsmouth Museums (part of Portsmouth City Council), for the experience and knowledge that I have gained in over twenty years in that post. I also wish to thank all involved in the restoration, display and operation of LCT 7074, now available to visit at The D-Day Story, Portsmouth (particularly, project director Nick Hewitt and project historian/archaeologist Stephen Fisher).

I acknowledge the work of the many historians who have written on aspects of this topic, both in publications and online. I particularly wish to recognise the role of the late Tony Chapman, archivist of the Landing Ship, Tank (LST) and Landing Craft Association in the UK, who played an important role in gathering so many British landing craft veterans' accounts into the association's archive, now held by The D-Day Story, Portsmouth.

I thank Dr Simon Trew, formerly of the Royal Military Academy, Sandhurst, and a leading expert on the Normandy campaign, for his support and encouragement over the years on a variety of projects, and for showing me how good history is done. Dr Michael Whitby, Senior Naval Historian at the Canadian Directorate of History and Heritage, kindly helped with information about Canadian landing craft crews. Robert von

Maier and his team enabled me to present a paper based on a chapter of this book at the 'Normandy 75' conference in Portsmouth, in July 2019.

For making archival resources and other information available online, or providing access to archival material in person, I particularly thank: Library and Archives Canada; Fold3.com (material from the US National Archives); the Ike Skelton Combined Arms Reference Library at the US Army Command and General Staff College; Mike ('Trux'), Michel Sabarly and others who have posted information on landing craft at the WW2Talk.com forum; and The National Archives, UK.

For use of photographs: Conseil Régional de Basse-Normandie (photos from flickr.com/people/photosnormandie/); Evansville Museum (Indiana, USA); Imperial War Museum; Library and Archives Canada; National Museum of the Royal Navy; The D-Day Story, Portsmouth (photographs of LCT 2130 courtesy of Leslie Fowler and John Ellis; photograph of LCT 574 courtesy of Brian Bernet); US Coast Guard; US National Archives; US Naval History & Heritage Centre; Veterans History Project, American Folklife Center, US Library of Congress. Thank you to the staff from these institutions who have assisted with the preparation of this book.

Amy Rigg, Commissioning Editor – Specialist History at the History Press, and her colleagues for their encouragement and support.

My brother Mike for his assistance with setting up the website accompanying this book: ddaylandingcraft.net.

And finally, I wish to thank my wife Bryony for her love, support and patience over the many years of this project.

Glossary

A note on landing craft numbers: In the Second World War, landing craft and LSTs were so numerous that they were only given numbers rather than names, such as 'LCT 7074'. For British and Commonwealth vessels, this is known as the pennant (or pendant) number; the US term is the hull number. Officially, British landing craft numbers were preceded by 'HM', and US numbers by 'USS', but that was often omitted in everyday usage. In some cases, both a British- and a US-built craft existed that had the same pennant number, but they were different marks and were not connected in any way. US minor landing craft carried on board a ship had numbers derived from the hull number of that ship: for example, the LCVPs on USS *Thurston* (APA-77) were numbered 'P77-1' to 'P77-24'. Also see LTIN and mark number.

APA:	'Auxiliary Personnel, Attack', a troop transport ship (US Navy).
AVRE:	Armoured Vehicle Royal Engineers, a British Churchill tank converted for specialist engineering roles.
Beach/Beach Area/ Beach Sector:	In 1944 terminology, Utah and Omaha were areas rather than beaches; a beach was much smaller, such as Uncle Red in Utah Area. However, this book follows the now commonly accepted usage of describing five landing beaches and referring to smaller areas as beaches or sectors.

Bow door:	Another name for the ramp at the front of landing craft, which was dropped to allow the troops on board to go ashore. Ramp is generally used here.
Breaching team:	On Anglo-Canadian beaches, specialist tanks which were landed around H-Hour to clear routes through beach obstacles and off the beach, working with obstacle clearance personnel on foot.
Broach-to:	When a vessel is swung side-on to a beach by wind or currents, in which position it might need assistance to get off the beach again.
BUCO:	Build Up Control Organisation.
COSSAC:	Chief of Staff to the Supreme Allied Commander.
D-1, D+1 (etc.):	One day before or after D-Day.
D-Day:	The day on which a military operation begins. Here, it is of course used to mean 6 June 1944.
DD tank:	An amphibious tank, used on all five beaches on D-Day.
DSOAG:	Deputy Senior Naval Officer, Assault Group; the naval commander controlling a section of the landings. At Gold Beach, King Green and King Red each had a DSOAG.
DUKW:	A US-designed amphibious truck.
Eastern Task Force (ETF):	The naval forces for Gold, Juno and Sword beaches.
ETOUSA:	European Theater of Operations (US Army).
FDT:	Fighter Direction Tender; an LST converted for controlling fighter aircraft.
First lieutenant:	The second-in-command of a British or Commonwealth landing craft; a role rather than a rank.
Flotilla:	In the Royal Navy and Royal Canadian Navy, a unit of typically up to twelve craft (or up to sixteen for those not involved in the assault). A flotilla was led by a flotilla officer, with a small support staff. In US forces, a flotilla was a larger unit, formed from two or more twelve-craft groups.
FOO:	Forward Observation Officer (British); an artillery officer and his team controlling gunfire.
Force:	Forces U, O, G, J and S were the naval forces that delivered the assault troops to the five beaches. The

initial of each force matched the first letter of each beach: Force U was for Utah Beach. Forces B and L were the follow-up forces for the western (US) and eastern (Anglo-Canadian) beaches respectively and arrived later on D-Day.

GAT: Gap Assault Team. A combined US Navy and US Army team for beach obstacle clearance.

Group: This term was used with a variety of meanings: a convoy of landing craft that crossed the English Channel together (sometimes one convoy was divided into multiple groups); an Assault Group was a larger formation of all craft operating off a beach sector; for US forces, a unit of around twelve craft.

H-1, H+1 (etc.): The time before or after H-Hour, for a particular beach. Unless stated, the time is in minutes.

H-Hour: The time at which the assault landings began, which varied across the five D-Day beaches.

HQ: Headquarters.

Kedge anchor, kedge hook: The anchor on the stern of a landing craft, dropped as the vessel approached the beach and used for unbeaching.

Knots: Nautical measure of speed, in nautical miles per hour. A nautical mile is 1.15 miles; one knot is 1.15 miles per hour.

Launching Position: The location at sea at which amphibious DD tanks were to be launched from the LCTs carrying them.

LBE: Landing Barge, Emergency Repair.

LBF: Landing Barge, Flak.

LBK: Landing Barge, Kitchen.

LBO: Landing Barge, Oil.

LBV: Landing Barge, Vehicle.

LBW: Landing Barge, Water.

LCA: Landing Craft, Assault.

LCA(HR): Landing Craft, Assault (Hedgerow).

LCA(OC): Landing Craft, Assault (Obstacle Clearance). A craft carrying British LCOCU obstacle clearance personnel.

LCC: Landing Craft, Control.

LCE:	Landing Craft, Emergency Repair.
LCF:	Landing Craft, Flak.
LCG(L):	Landing Craft, Gun (Large).
LCH:	Landing Craft, Headquarters.
LCI(L):	Landing Craft, Infantry (Large).
LCI(S):	Landing Craft, Infantry (Small).
LCM:	Landing Craft, Mechanised.
LCOCU:	Landing Craft Obstacle Clearance Unit (an obstacle-clearance team, not a type of landing craft).
LCP(L), LCP(Sy) or LCP(R):	Landing Craft, Personnel (Large), (Survey) or (Ramped).
LCS(L):	Landing Craft, Support (Large).
LCS(M):	Landing Craft, Support (Medium).
LCS(S):	Landing Craft, Support (Small).
LCT:	Landing Craft, Tank. Where there is a number in brackets following, the number indicates the 'mark' of the variant of LCT. For example, LCT(3) means LCT Mk.3 (Mark 3).
LCT(A):	A modified LCT(5) with additional armour in places – hence 'A' for Armoured – and a ramped platform near the bow so two tanks could fire from the craft.
LCT(AVRE):	Landing Craft, Tank (carrying Churchill AVRE tanks and other obstacle clearance forces). This was a role determined by the load carried, not a type of LCT.
LCT(CB):	'CB' stood for 'Concrete Buster', which referred to the Sherman Firefly tank carried by each craft on a ramped platform near the bow on D-Day, so the Firefly's 17-pounder gun could be fired from the LCT to destroy concrete bunkers. Like the LCT(A), it was a modified LCT(5), but lacked the former's extra armour.
LCT(DD):	Landing Craft, Tank (carrying DD amphibious tanks). This was a role determined by the load carried, not a type of LCT.
LCT(HE):	Similar to the LCT(A), it was an LCT(5) with a ramped platform near the bow, from which two tanks could fire. It lacked the additional armour applied to

	the LCT(A). 'HE' indicated that the craft carried high explosives for use by the obstacle clearance teams.
LCT(R):	Landing Craft, Tank (Rocket).
LCT(SP):	Landing Craft, Tank (carrying self-propelled artillery guns). This was a role determined by the load carried, not a type of LCT.
LCVP:	Landing Craft, Vehicle, Personnel.
Line of Departure:	An imaginary line around 4,000 yards off the beach at which control craft oversaw the despatch of waves of landing craft to the shore.
Lowering Position:	The location at sea, up to 11 miles off the Normandy coast, where the troop-carrying landing ships would anchor and unload the troops into smaller craft. Known to the Americans as the Transport Area.
LS:	Landing Ship – used here to describe troop transport ships used in the assault, such as British LSI types or American APA types.
LSD:	Landing Ship, Dock.
LSE:	Landing Ship, Emergency Repair.
LSH:	Landing Ship, Headquarters.
LSI(S), LSI(M), LSI(L) or LSI(H):	Landing Ship, Infantry (Small), (Medium), (Large) or (Hand-Hoist).
LST:	Landing Ship, Tank.
LTIN:	The Landing Table Index Number (US: Army Serial Number), a number identifying a specific load of troops, where appropriate, including vehicles and/or stores, for a single landing craft, which was used in planning and was displayed on the craft.
LVT:	Landing Vehicle, Tracked, also known as amtrac, Alligator or Buffalo. A tracked amphibious vehicle, not a landing craft, which was available for use at Normandy but was not used in significant numbers.
Mark:	The version of a landing craft is indicated by the number in brackets following the abbreviation: e.g. LCT(3) means LCT Mark 3.
ML:	Motor Launch. A relatively small, fast vessel, used in the Normandy campaign as a navigational leader or escort.

MOVCO:	Movement Control Organisation.
MT:	Motor Transport, meaning support vehicles, mostly wheeled. For example 'MT Ships' were merchant ships with the main role of carrying such vehicles.
NCDU:	Naval Combat Demolition Unit, a US Navy unit with US Army engineers attached, tasked with clearing German beach obstacles. The British equivalent was the Landing Craft Obstacle Clearance Unit (LCOCU).
NL:	Naval Lighter.
Obstacles, beach obstacles:	Metal, concrete or wooden obstructions placed by the German forces on the Normandy beaches to impede and sink Allied landing craft.
Oerlikon:	A 20mm anti-aircraft gun which was widely used on British- and American-built landing craft; also used against other targets including enemy defences ashore.
Officer in charge:	The commanding officer (CO) of a US landing craft. On a larger ship he would have been known as the commanding officer, but US landing craft were not commissioned as individual ships.
PC:	Patrol Craft (US Navy vessel type).
QORC:	Queen's Own Rifles Canada.
RA:	Royal Artillery (British Army).
RAC:	Royal Armoured Corps (British Army).
RAMC:	Royal Army Medical Corps (British Army).
RANVR:	Royal Australian Navy Volunteer Reserve.
RAOC:	Royal Army Ordnance Corps (British Army).
RASC:	Royal Army Service Corps (British Army).
RCA:	Royal Canadian Artillery.
RCN:	Royal Canadian Navy.
RCT:	Regimental Combat Team (US Army). An infantry regiment accompanied by attached troops from other arms.
RE:	Royal Engineers (British Army).
Relief officer:	The second in command on a US landing craft.
REME:	Royal Electrical and Mechanical Engineers.
Rendezvous Area:	A sea area where landing craft wait until it is time for them to depart.
Rhino:	A Rhino Ferry was a large, powered pontoon, particularly designed for landing vehicles from LSTs.

	Rhino Tugs were similar, smaller vessels which helped the larger ferries manoeuvre.
RM Commando:	Royal Marine Commando. In 1944, there were both Army Commandos and Royal Marine Commandos.
RNR:	Royal Naval Reserve; civilian Merchant Navy sailors who had received some Royal Navy training in peacetime.
RNVR:	Royal Naval Volunteer Reserve; included most personnel who had volunteered or been called up into the Royal Navy in wartime.
SC:	Submarine Chaser (US Navy vessel type).
SOAG:	Senior Naval Officer, Assault Group.
Tank deck:	The large well deck of an LCT, used for carrying vehicles.
Tankdozer:	A standard Sherman tank, fitted with a bulldozer blade for engineering tasks.
Tellermine:	A powerful German anti-tank mine, which was attached to some German beach obstacles to increase their deadliness.
Time:	The time used in all Operation Neptune orders, war diaries and reports was Double British Summer Time, also known as B Time or Zone Baker Time. This was two hours ahead of Greenwich Mean Time and was, in fact, the same time zone used in German-occupied France.
Transport Area:	See Lowering Position.
Transports:	US term for the troop-carrying ship type known to the British as a Landing Ship, Infantry.
TURCO:	Turn Round Control Organisation.
Unbeaching:	The act of withdrawing a landing craft from a beach.
USCG/USCGR:	US Coast Guard (Reserve).
USN/USNR:	US Navy (Reserve).
Wave:	A group of landing craft scheduled to land together at a single time. Throughout D-Day there would be twenty or more waves at any particular beach.
Western Task Force (WTF):	The naval forces for Utah and Omaha beaches.
WN:	*Widerstandsnest* (German defence).
WPB:	War Production Board (US).
XAP:	Auxiliary Transport, a type of landing ship.

Introduction

'Ugly and Unorthodox ...'

Without the work of the landing ships and craft victory would not have been possible ... Naturally, the 'Blue Water' school of the Royal Navy found it very hard (with certain honourable exceptions) to endure the existence of such strange newcomers among the King's ships. Not only were the landing craft ugly and unorthodox, they were manned largely by hurriedly-trained 'hostilities only' ratings commanded by RNVR officers who, by training and tradition (or the lack thereof), were sometimes as unorthodox as the craft they commanded. None the less, by their native seamanship and determination, they wrote a bright enough chapter in naval history.[1]

These are the words of Commander Rupert Curtis DSC RNVR, written as a retired naval officer. On D-Day, Curtis was in command of LCI(S) 519, and as flotilla officer of 200 LCI(S) Flotilla, commanded ten more of those craft which would land Lord Lovat's commandos on Sword Beach. Curtis spent the decades after the war gathering information about D-Day, particularly about the role of the LCI(S) – Landing Craft, Infantry (Small) – and the commandos, and giving talks on these subjects. His words capture the nature of the many types of landing craft and their crews, who were rarely professional sailors but dedicated to their essential but unglamorous duties.

This book aims to tell the story of landing craft on D-Day. 'D-Day' in the title is used as shorthand for the Normandy Landings as a whole, though strictly speaking, it refers to a single day – 6 June 1944. Partly because of space limitations, the book's focus is D-Day itself.

While it would be an exaggeration to say that the role of landing craft in this operation has been forgotten, it certainly tends to be overlooked. That was not the case at the time of D-Day. In late 1943, Chief of Staff of the US Army General George C. Marshall is said to have remarked that before the war he had not heard of any landing craft except a rubber boat but now he thought about little else. Supreme Allied Commander for D-Day General Dwight D. Eisenhower is said to have commented, 'When I'm buried, my coffin should be in the shape of a landing craft, as they are practically killing me with worry.'[2] Landing craft and Landing Ship, Tanks (LSTs) were regularly discussed by the top Allied political and military leaders, starting with US President Franklin D. Roosevelt and British Prime Minister Winston Churchill.

Of course, this book's focus does not mean to imply that other types of shipping were unimportant. In telling the story, this book combines wartime official documents, including plans for D-Day and after-action reports, with archive photographs, veterans' memoirs, historians' analysis and other sources. It aims to combine a record of the succession of waves of landing craft on each beach, with more anecdotal descriptions of the experiences of the crews and the troops they put ashore. Errors and inconsistencies are not uncommon in all these sources. Mistakes have no doubt been made by the present author too, despite his best efforts: constructive criticism and corrections will be welcomed.

The British Naval Official History states that Allied naval forces for the Normandy Landings were formed from 6,939 vessels, including 4,126 landing ships and landing craft. The latter figure is used in the title of this book, and it is worth considering this subject briefly.

The figure represents not the total number of landing craft that crossed to Normandy on D-Day, but the total number involved in Operation Neptune (6–30 June 1944), and therefore includes reserves and craft that were not yet ready for operational use but which joined the campaign later. The report of the Allied naval commander-in-chief on the invasion of Normandy gives a different figure of 4,266, while the US official history of Operation Neptune uses the figure of 4,021.[3]

Digging into the 4,126 total also requires consideration of what is meant by a landing craft. The figure includes 310 landing ships, including sixty-eight LSIs and LSHs, which were not landing craft, and over 230 LSTs which, strictly speaking, were not landing craft but wartime documents did sometimes describe them as such. The number also includes seventy-two Rhino Ferries, 424 landing barges of all types and thirty-five fuelling trawlers (minesweeping trawlers converted for refuelling landing craft).

All these vessels fall outside the strict definition of landing craft but were intimately connected to their operations and so feature in this book. The purist might say that the true figure for the number of landing craft involved was just over 3,500: this includes those carried on board larger ships as well as those that crossed to Normandy under their own power.

A further distinction is that Operation Neptune was only the first assault phase of Operation Overlord, the plan for the landings in north-west Europe, which is usually summed up as the Battle of Normandy. That campaign began on D-Day, but its end date is less agreed upon: popular candidates include the Allied armies crossing the River Seine on 19 August, the liberation of Paris on 25 August or General Eisenhower taking command of Allied ground forces on 1 September.

These dates have a bearing on that total number. For example, LST 921 did not participate in Operation Neptune and is not included in John de S. Winser's excellent *The D-Day Ships*. The vessel was built in the USA and commissioned on 23 June 1944, so was not available to Allied forces before that operation ended. On 14 August, LST 921 was torpedoed by a U-boat while crossing from the UK to the Normandy coast, with the loss of forty-three US sailors: few would doubt the ship's contribution to the campaign.[4]

If nothing else, perhaps this brief consideration of that number will serve to point to some of the variety, complexity and rich detail to be found in the story of D-Day landing craft.

If a ship's name is given after a flotilla number, it indicates the ship that carried that group of smaller landing craft on its davits or decks: for example, 551 Assault Flotilla (SS *Empire Javelin*). When first mentioning a group of landing craft, the mark number is generally included, for example 'LCT(4)'. For reduced unwieldiness in a book that is already full of abbreviations, the mark number is omitted on later mentions. The plural is indicated by adding an 's' after the entire abbreviation: for example, LCS(M)(3)s is the plural of LCS(M)(3). The book uses the more modern phraseology of calling ships and landing craft 'it' rather than 'she'.

Five chapters look at events on D-Day on each beach, as seen from the point of view of the landing craft and their crews, as well as through the eyes of the troops that many of these craft carried. For clarity, successive waves of landing craft are usually described separately. However, individual craft or whole waves were sometimes delayed or may have been held back by control craft if conditions were judged to be unsuitable for them to beach. In such cases, waves often became intermixed, so the scene would have seemed less clear cut in practice. Where wave numbers applying to the entire beach are known, these are sometimes included. In some cases, craft landing simultaneously on adjacent sectors of one of the five beaches had different wave numbers, in which case, referring to waves does risk confusion. Documents contain many other references to waves or flights, which apply only to craft from a single troop transport ship and are therefore not included here.

The planned time and location to beach for each group of landing craft is often mentioned. In practice, there were many variations in both, and where possible, these changes are indicated. Often, that information is not known in full or else space would not permit the inclusion of every detail. Both wartime documents and veterans' recollections often contain some contradictory details. For example, some after-action reports appear to use the planned times for when certain events should have taken place, rather than the actual times. These have been cross-checked as much as possible.

Robert D. Blegen was one of the US Navy crew of LCT(5) 149, and wrote after the war about the actions of LCTs in his flotilla at Omaha Beach. He commented wisely on the sources available:

> I find myself questioning the accuracy and the veracity of everything, including the action report for my own boat, LCT 149. I'm sure my memory is faulty. There are things in the report I don't remember at all. But there are things I do remember quite clearly that don't match the action report. I suspect the people who wrote these reports didn't realize that they were writing valuable history. I suspect at least one was bucking for hero status. Others may have been protecting themselves against criticism or serious discipline. We may never know.[5]

By mixing in more anecdotal accounts from veterans or wartime documents with a description of the waves of craft, the intention is to represent both aspects of the story. There is sometimes a greater or lesser amount of detail on different groups of landing craft, depending on a variety of factors, including the availability of sources. Where certain groups or types of craft do not feature so fully, it is hoped that accounts relating to other, similar craft will help represent their role.

Details of the personnel, vehicles and/or stores carried by landing craft are sometimes included. Particularly in the case of larger craft such as LCTs and LSTs, their cargoes were so extensive and varied that it is impossible to mention more than a handful of details. At the time of writing, excellent resources listing the planned craft loads in detail are available on the WW2Talk.com forum. Similarly, although some mention is given of the role and objectives of the units put ashore, particularly as they affected landing craft, it is not possible to go into detail and the reader is directed to other sources for more information: the *Battle Zone Normandy* series is a good starting point.

Where the identities of individual craft are known such information is included in either the text or the endnotes, but information is often not available. Sometimes, craft identities have been deduced from a variety of sources and where there is an element of doubt in these identifications, this is noted. In the case of minor landing craft that crossed to Normandy on board larger ships, the ship's name is given after the flotilla: for example, 524 Assault Flotilla (SS *Empire Arquebus*). The limitations of space do not allow descriptions of the many other parts of the Allied fleet, from escorting warships to merchant vessels, but they clearly also played vital roles.

All times are given in a twenty-four-hour clock. The Allies used current UK time – British Double Summer Time – for the operation, which also matched the time used in France. This was known to the Allied military as Zone Baker time. Unless otherwise stated, times given (expressed as H– or H+ and a number) are in minutes and relate to H-Hour on the beach in question. Unless otherwise stated, all landing craft on Gold, Juno and Sword beaches had Royal Navy crews and US Navy crews at Utah and Omaha (the many exceptions to this will be specifically noted as being from the US Navy, Royal Navy or Royal Canadian Navy).

Please visit ddaylandingcraft.net for additional information on this subject, including a Roll of Honour of landing craft crewmen who died in the Normandy campaign.

1

Landing Craft Types:
Origins, Design and Construction

For the first time in our history we have had to begin every major campaign in this conflict by amphibious operations.

George Mowry, policy analyst for the US War Production Board[1]

A rule of thumb to distinguish landing craft from other vessels was that they were designed to be driven ashore onto a beach and then withdrawn after unloading. However, not all types of landing craft had a bow ramp or were intended to land personnel or vehicles, since some had support or control functions. The wartime British convention was to separate major and minor landing craft types. The US Navy instead tended to use the terms landing boats (or small boats) and landing craft.

Major landing craft were distinguished from ships by being under 200ft in length, while landing ships were larger, oceangoing vessels. Even for shorter journeys, such as crossing the English Channel, landing craft tended to be in groups led by another vessel as navigational leader. Unlike the smaller types, major landing craft had at least simple accommodation on board for the crew and could not be hoisted onto a larger vessel in normal use.[2]

Earlier in the war, British landing craft type names ended with the word 'craft': for example, Assault Landing Craft. After the USA joined the war, the names were standardised with the American terms, all of which began with 'landing craft': for example, Landing Craft, Assault. While 'landing barges' is sometimes used to mean minor landing craft, in official terminology barges were converted from civilian use and were not used in an assault role, whereas landing craft were designed for that purpose.

This section explores the history and characteristics of the main types of landing craft that were most widely used in the Normandy Landings. Most of these were developed during the course of the war. 'Every class had to go into production straight from the drawing board,' one British naval officer recalled. 'This gave us many anxious moments, not only from the design aspect, but also from the operational point of view.' From an American perspective, 'emphasis was always on rapid production rather than on perfection in designs that might cause delays in construction'.[3]

A Note on Landing Craft Specifications

Specifications are given below for the main types of landing craft mentioned and do not necessarily represent all the variations in design of a particular landing craft that were used throughout the Second World War.

The number in brackets after a landing craft type indicates the 'mark' of the variant: LCT(3) means LCT Mk 3 (Mark 3).

Length is overall length, including propeller guards if they projected beyond the stern.

Beaching draught is at the bow, with the craft fully loaded and adjusted for beaching (with the vessel trimmed such that the draught at the bow was reduced as much as possible). Certain types of landing craft would not typically beach as part of their role, in which case this figure is less relevant.

Displacement is essentially the weight of the landing craft. The displacement is given for both unloaded and loaded where known, in other words without and including cargo. It has been standardised as long tons or Imperial (British) tons, rounded up or down: 1 long ton = 1.12 short tons (US) = 1.02 metric tonnes.

Speed is the typical speed used on operations when loaded, not the maximum speed. A knot is a measure of speed, in nautical miles per hour. A nautical mile is 1.15 miles; 1 knot is 1.15 miles per hour.

Crew size given is typical and does not include one officer per three to four minor landing craft where relevant. Additional personnel such as command or flotilla staff were sometimes carried.

Capacity relates to fully equipped troops in an assault role. More men could be packed on board a landing craft, but that would be inadvisable in an assault, though capacities were sometimes exceeded even on D-Day. More heavily loaded craft would beach much further from the shore and therefore in deeper water. Seagoing vessels would often carry a larger cargo than indicated here when making a long sea voyage, rather than an amphibious landing, as beaching draught was not a factor.

Weapons: The main weapon types were not always fitted. Supplementary weapons such as Parachute and Cable (PAC) are not listed but were carried on some larger craft. Also not listed are the small arms carried by many craft or the smoke pots carried by some, for generating a smoke screen.

Engines: Where multiple types were fitted, they may not all be listed. Engine choice was often more about what was available than what was ideal. Diesel engines were usually favoured as they posed a lower fire risk, but petrol engines were used in some cases.

Armour: Many landing craft were fitted with limited armour protection on what were judged to be the most vulnerable parts of the vessel, such as the wheelhouse, bridge and gun positions. Full details are not given here but suffice it to say that while such armour generally gave protection against small arms, no craft were armoured to the point of invulnerability to enemy fire, particularly from anti-tank guns. Most landing craft did not have overhead protection. Armour was not the only means of protection: it increased the vessel's weight, and a lighter landing craft was more likely to unbeach rapidly and escape the danger zone at the water's edge.[4]

MINOR LANDING CRAFT

LCP(L), LCP(Sy) and LCP(R): Landing Craft, Personnel (Large), (Survey) & (Ramped)[5]

Designed by Andrew Higgins of New Orleans, the wooden LCP(L), or Eureka Boat, was the original 'Higgins Boat' before that name became more commonly applied to a later model from the same designer, the LCVP. The US Marines and the British were both firm advocates for this craft. The first fifty LCP(L)s were acquired by the Royal Navy in October 1940, with raiding enemy coasts in mind. The US Navy later caught up, ordering a modified version with greater troop capacity. Some of both types had limited armour protection.

While it was fast and strong, it did not have a ramp, so troops had to clamber over the side. The LCP(L) was initially used for delivering personnel in assault landings, but by 1944 it only had an auxiliary role, including as despatch boats or for smoke-laying.

The LCP(Sy) was a navigational leader for landing craft. It was an LCP(L) fitted with extra equipment including radar. On the Anglo-Canadian beaches they led the LCTs, carrying DD tanks, and if the DD tanks launched into the water, they led the tanks as they swam. This type was later used for carrying out hydrographic surveys, for example, for setting out the Mulberry Harbours and Gooseberries, and laid buoys to mark wrecks.[6]

Modified to include a narrow bow ramp, this craft became the LCP(R). Though considered outdated by 1944, these craft were still present in the D-Day fleet, as they were carried by LSTs as despatch boats. The next Higgins design, the LCV, had a larger ramp but an exposed coxswain's position so it was unsuitable for use in the assault.

LCVP: Landing Craft, Vehicle, Personnel[7]

This type was an alternative solution to the same problem that the LCA aimed to meet – how to land a relatively small group of troops or a light vehicle on an enemy shore. It was commonly referred to as the 'Higgins Boat', after its designer and builder, Andrew Higgins, of New Orleans. Former Allied Supreme Commander Dwight D. Eisenhower famously described Higgins as 'the man who won the war for us', since without the ability to land on an enemy beach that the LCVP provided, 'the whole strategy of the war would have been different'.[8]

The 'V' part of LCVP indicated that the craft could carry a light vehicle: a 3-ton lorry, for example. The ramp – wider than on its predecessor, the LCV – enabled troops to disembark at speed, though it reduced speed compared to craft with a more streamlined bow. Veteran Robert J. Dolan recalled that LCVPs were 'fun to drive'.

US commanders seem to have favoured the LCVP over the LCA, often describing the latter as 'unseaworthy', while British commanders were critical of the LCVP. Both types shipped considerable water in the rough seas, but the LCVP had an automatic bilge pump which seems to have been considerably more effective than the pumps on most LCAs.[9]

The LCVP's engines had more power than those of an LCA, and the coxswain could operate them directly rather than sending signals to a second crewman who controlled them. The LCVP was certainly well able to beach in strong surf. By keeping the engine in forward gear at low speed while the troops disembarked, the coxswain could keep the craft at right angles to the shore and then unbeach using engine power alone. Unlike the LCA, LCVPs did not use a kedge anchor to aid in withdrawing from the shore. The craft did, however, require skill to handle, and was vulnerable to being swamped at the beach when the ramp was lowered. The LCVP had greater draught than the LCA, so troops typically had to wade ashore through deeper water.[10]

The LCA provided better protection for the personnel on board – it had 3,810lb of armour, compared to 1,700lb on the LCVP – but the American craft had armoured sides and the ramp provided protection against small-arms fire. LCVPs used in the assault sometimes carried two .30in machine guns on the rear of the craft, which could be fired in support of the troops as they landed. Some assault craft were not equipped with these guns as commanders feared that indiscriminate firing by the crew posed a risk to Allied troops.[11]

During the Second World War, 23,358 LCVPs were built by a total of eight firms. Around 500 of these craft were used at Normandy, nearly half of them by Royal Navy and Royal Marine crews of the Build-Up Flotillas, who arrived off Normandy late on D-Day or on subsequent days to help unload larger ships.

LCA: Landing Craft, Assault[12]
The LCA was designed both to offer some protection to the troops on board and to land soldiers in stealth on an enemy coastline. Its size was a balance between carrying a useful number of personnel while still being small and light enough to be carried on board ship using (strengthened) davits. One feature making the LCA easily recognisable were the raised crew positions either side of the bow: the coxswain's position to starboard and Bren gunner's to port.

Plans for the craft that became the LCA were afoot even before the outbreak of war, and it was designed by the Southampton firm of Thornycroft and the Admiralty Department of Naval Construction. Many were built by small boat-building companies, railway engine manufacturers and even furniture-makers (as the craft was of wooden construction). Originally the Royal Navy wanted to keep the weight of the LCA below 10 tons, so that it could be lowered from standard lifeboat davits, but the addition of armour and other modifications took it well over that figure, to about 13½ tons.

From the troops' point of view, the LCA had the advantages that it had three benches for troops to sit on, rather than sitting on the deck, and (in later boats) the armoured side decks partly overhung the cargo deck, providing some protection from both enemy fire and sea spray. The LCA was also fitted with ¼in-thick armour on its sides.

The craft was designed for night attacks, beaching at lower speed using its quiet engines. It had a low silhouette for stealth, which meant a low freeboard (the distance from the water to the top of the craft's side) and a greater chance of shipping water over the side. In a daylight attack in rough seas on D-Day, the LCVP had some advantages over the LCA, but the latter undoubtedly played an essential role in the landings.[13]

The British built 1,929 LCAs during the Second World War. Around 500 standard LCAs took part in Operation Neptune, carried by forty-six different British and Canadian landing ships. A small number were designated LCA(OC), which simply meant they were carrying LCOCU obstacle clearance personnel and their stores but did not indicate any modifications. Others had been converted into LCA(HR) Fire Support craft.

LCM: Landing Craft, Mechanised[14]

'LCM' refers to both the British-built LCM(1) and the US-made LCM(3). Reflecting the original concept for this craft, it was sometimes referred to as a 'tank lighter', meaning a flat-bottomed vessel used for transferring cargo (a tank) from ship to shore. Both types played essential roles in the D-Day Landings, not least because they had a much more generous capacity than smaller craft like the LCA and LCVP, and were also less easily damaged than those boats, but they were smaller and more manoeuvrable than LCTs.

The LCM(1) had its origins in pre-war prototypes. It was a simple design: essentially, a floating pontoon with sides added to it. Although the LCM(3) had a number of advantages, including better stability, the LCM(1) was lighter and therefore could be lowered by davits or boom with personnel or crew on board.

The British built 536 LCM(1)s during the Second World War. Many were built by the Great Western Railway Works at Swindon and the Southern Railways Works at Eastleigh, as well as by structural engineering firms.

Originally known as a 50ft lighter, the LCM(3) was a new design by Andrew Higgins. The pontoon origins of the LCM(1) meant that its cargo deck was above the waterline. Higgins lowered the cargo deck of the LCM(3), which increased the craft's stability and therefore the load it could carry – up to a Sherman tank. However, it was too heavy to be lowered from davits. A British mission visiting the USA in late 1941 immediately saw the potential of the LCM(3).

Some 464 LCMs of both types were used in Operation Neptune, the greater number being LCM(3)s. Some were carried across the English Channel on board larger ships, but the majority crossed under their own power or under tow. The Americans used some LCM(3)s early on D-Day, such as those which landed obstacle clearance teams at both American beaches in the first thirty minutes after H-Hour. They could cope with rough seas and survive damage from beach obstacles that would have sunk a smaller craft. A few LCMs were used in a similar role on the Anglo-Canadian beaches, but the majority were part of the Build-Up Flotillas that helped unload larger ships after the assault.[15]

After D-Day, many LCMs remained at Normandy unloading larger ships. They were most useful for disembarking personnel – they could hold 100 troops for short distances – but vehicles were best landed using larger craft. A small number of LCM(3)s were fitted out by the Americans as LCM(Salvage), with pumps and towing equipment. They acted in units of three vessels, two of which had bulldozers to help refloat beached craft.[16]

Other Types

A handful of LCE (Landing Craft, Emergency Repair) were present. This was an LCV that had been converted for repairing other craft.

Specifications: minor landing craft

	LCP(L)	LCA	LCVP	LCM(1)	LCM(3)
Hull	Wood	Wood	Wood	Steel	Steel
Length	36ft 8in	41ft 6in	36ft	44ft 8in	50ft
Beam	10ft 10in	10ft	10ft 5in	14ft	14ft 1in
Beaching draught	3ft 6in	1ft 9in	2ft 2in	2ft 6in	3ft
Displacement (unloaded/ loaded)	6 / 8 tons	10 / 13 tons	8 / 12 tons	21 / 35 tons	23 / 46 tons
Speed	8–9 knots	7 knots	9 knots	7.5 knots	8 knots
Crew	3	4	3	6	4
Capacity	24–36 troops	35 troops	36 troops or one 3-ton truck	1 vehicle under 16 tons or 100 troops	1 x 30-ton tank or 60 troops
Weapons	1–2 machine guns	1 x light machine gun	2 x machine guns	2 x machine guns	2 x machine guns
Engines	Various	2 x Scripps 65hp V-8	Hall-Scott 250hp petrol, or Gray 225hp diesel	2 x Chrysler 120hp petrol	2 x 110–225hp diesels

(This is a simplified summary and does not represent all the variations that were used.)

MAJOR LANDING CRAFT

LCT: Landing Craft, Tank[17]

'[T]here never can be enough of these craft to carry M.T. [motor transport] and stores,' the Joint Planning Staff reported to the British War Cabinet in May 1943. If the success of Operation Neptune as a whole was dependent on the Allies having enough LSTs to transport vehicles in bulk, one could argue that the success of D-Day depended on having enough LCTs to land the tanks, artillery and other vehicles that would be essential to blunt the expected German counter-attack.[18]

The LCT was created by the British to land tanks on a beach in the early hours of an amphibious landing, but its cargoes were much more diverse than that name suggests. Early in the war, it was apparent that in the coming years, tanks would grow in size and weight to the point that they could not be lowered from a transport ship into landing craft, and craft were needed specifically for carrying such vehicles.

The British types of LCT were designed by Rowland (later Sir Rowland) Baker of the Royal Corps of Naval Constructors. Pressed by British Prime Minister Winston Churchill for a solution, he came up with the basic design in three days, soon after the 1940 Dunkirk Evacuation. Baker went on to design most of the other British types of landing craft used in wartime.

The main types used in the Normandy campaign were the British-built LCT(3) and LCT(4), and the US-built LCT(5) and LCT(6). The LCT(1) – first trialled in November 1940 – and LCT(2) were built in relatively small numbers but their use in the Mediterranean proved their value. The LCT(3) was introduced in 1941 and was the first mature variant of the design, able to carry eleven Sherman tanks or five of the larger Churchill tanks.

The 235 LCT(3)s that were built included seventy-one craft of the LCT(3★) type and nearly half were used in Operation Neptune. The latter had US-supplied Sterling Admiral petrol engines fitted to resolve the British shortage of the usual Paxman diesels, and unusually, these were built by shipyards that had spent most of the war building naval or merchant vessels.

After the LCT(3) was in production the British realised that the typical gradient of the French beaches – a likely landing site for D-Day – was too shallow for that craft. The LCT(4) was born out of this realisation. Compared to the LCT(3), it had a shallower draught, so could beach on a 1:150 gradient beach rather than the LCT(3)'s limit of 1:33.

On D-Day, the LCT(3) was generally used to carry amphibious DD tanks – which meant that, in theory, they would not need to beach – or were set to arrive once the assault was over, when it would be less problematic if they dried out on the shore. The LCT(4) was found to be more prone to breaking its back in rough weather or if it dried out on an uneven beach. Some LCT(4)s were strengthened ('stiffened') as a precaution, but they could still break in half from accumulated stresses and damage. Coming into service from September 1942, in total, 731 LCT(4)s were built, and about 400 were used at Normandy.

Construction of the LCT(5) began in May 1942. It was later updated in the form of the LCT(6), and both types had the same basic features as the British LCTs but were built to quite a different concept. In fact, they originated as an idea by the British designer K.C. Barnaby of Thornycroft. Many were built in the inner regions of the USA and made long river journeys to reach the sea. While the British types were primarily intended for cross-Channel invasions, these two US types were intended to work in tandem with an LST(2). Most importantly – so the craft could actually reach the UK in the first place – the LCT(5) and LCT(6) could be transported across the Atlantic on the deck of an LST.

Many LCT(5)s were designed so that their bulwarks (sides) could be removed in order to 'marry' with an LST at right angles and load vehicles from that ship while at sea. The LCT(6) was double-ended, meaning that vehicles could load from an LST via the stern doors and then go ashore via the bow ramp. In total, the USA built 1,435 LCT(5)s and LCT(6)s and over 350 were used at Normandy.[19]

Both US types were less than two-thirds the length of the British-built LCT(3) and LCT(4). As a rule of thumb, thirty-two LCT(5)s could carry a load equivalent to twenty-four LCT(3)s or (4)s. While the British used many LCT(5)s – and a mere two LCT(6)s – under Lend-Lease, the only use the Americans made of British-built LCTs was a relatively small number that had been converted for fire support purposes. Under the original US numbering, LCT(5)s had pennant (hull) numbers up to 500, and LCT(6)s were numbered 501 and upwards.[20]

The pennant number of LCTs used by the British indicates the type: those numbered 300 to 499 and 7001 to 7150 were LCT(3)s, those numbered 500 to 1364 were LCT(4)s. An LCT(5) or LCT(6) in British service had 2,000 or 3,000 respectively added to the pennant number allocated by the US: for example, LCT 2 became LCT 2002. Confusingly, both British- and US-built LCTs took part in Operation Neptune with the same pennant number: for example, LCT(4) 650 was crewed by the

Royal Navy and part of Force S, while the US Navy's LCT(6) 650 was in Force O.

LCTs were converted to create a variety of fire support craft. Those whose conversion was essentially temporary and easily reversible are considered here, and more extensively modified types feature later.

The LCT(A) was a conversion of the LCT(5), which was widely considered by Allied commanders after D-Day to have been unsuccessful. A temporary wooden ramped platform was built at the front of the tank deck, on which two tanks could be positioned so that they had a good field of fire as the craft approached the beach. The 'A' in the craft's name stood for 'armoured' – 75 tons of extra armour was fitted around the bow of the craft and to protect the engine room, fuel tanks and wheelhouse. During the crossing to Normandy, many of these craft took on water because of leaks around where the armour had been fitted. Many were delayed as a result, and some even sank.[21]

There were two more types that were also LCT(5)s in special roles, but with minimum modifications. Some of the craft used for the LCT(A) role with the platform-mounted tanks were designated LCT(HE), which indicated that they were carrying high explosives for use by the obstacle clearance teams, but they did not have the extra armour fitted.

On the Anglo-Canadian beaches there were also a handful of LCT(CB), which also had the tank platform but no additional armour (an earlier experiment of fitting a tank turret over an LCT's tank deck had proved too unstable). They carried a Sherman Firefly tank, which had a powerful 17-pounder gun that was judged to be particularly effective in penetrating concrete bunkers. These tanks had only been issued to the British Army in mid-April 1944.[22]

Wartime documents often refer to the LCT(A), LCT(HE) – and LCT(CB) if present – collectively as LCT(A), and it is not always clear how many of each type took part. All these types were 'a makeshift arrangement', in the words of a US Navy report. At the British Army's request, they were substitutes to replace the Landing Craft, Gun (Medium), a new type equipped with two 17-pounder or 25-pounder guns which was not produced in time for D-Day.[23]

Reference is sometimes made to LCT(DD), LCT(AVRE) and LCT(SP). In these cases, the designation in brackets simply indicated the main type of vehicle that they were to carry in the assault: amphibious DD tanks, Churchill AVRE engineer tanks, or self-propelled artillery.

LCTs that were to launch amphibious DD tanks at sea had a 'DD ramp extension' fitted. These were a pair of metal channels extending out from the LCT's ramp, matching the spacing of the tracks of a Sherman tank. When the tank launched into the sea, its propellers would not be damaged by catching on the edge of the ramp.

LCTs played a vital role in the Normandy Landings. They were second only to LSTs in the number of vehicles they could carry and were considered small enough to be risked on the beach earlier on D-Day. Around 870 LCTs of all marks were used in the operation – or some 960, if the various LCT-derived fire support variants are included. While a number were lost or so badly damaged that they were written off, it is also surprising how much damage some absorbed while at least still getting their crews safely off the beach again.

LCI(L): Landing Craft, Infantry (Large)[24]

In many ways closer to a ship than a landing craft, this design originated with a British requirement for a so-called 'giant raiding craft' which could carry 200 men for two days at sea. It was intended for making long-distance raids on German-occupied coasts, which was a major focus for Combined Operations Command at this time. Whereas its smaller cousin the LCI(S) was made of wood, a steel hull was essential to ensure that the LCI(L) had a shallow enough draught to land troops on a beach.

Only the US had the capacity to build these craft from steel. More than 900 were built during the Second World War, of which over 200 were present at Normandy with American (Navy and Coast Guard), British and Canadian crews. To the Americans, they were simply known as the LCI – the British-built LCI(S) was not used by US forces and was only present in small numbers – or more informally as the 'Elsie Item', a play on the abbreviation and the phonetic alphabet.

Many LCI(L)s were built at yards with giant production lines established on sites set up specially for the purpose, sometimes run by firms without pre-war shipbuilding experience. As with LST production, these sites were often inland on major American rivers. Many parts were made by off-site subcontractors. As the hull moved along the production line, each prefabricated section was welded into place.

The first craft was commissioned in October 1942, ready for their first operational use in the North Africa landings the following month. Being US-built had its perks for the crew, compared to the privations of British-built LCTs, for example, including showers and bunks not just for the officers but also for all ratings, a large galley, cold storage room and refrigerator.

The LCI(L) was fast – for a landing craft – and oceangoing, but still had a relatively shallow draught. It carried personnel only, but a good number of them. Its performance at sea was partly derived from its ship-type bow, which was similar to those of a more conventional warship, but this came at the cost that troops would land via a pair of 36ft ramps lowered on either side of the bow. These ramps could be easily damaged or lost, in which case the troops had to disembark using scrambling nets along the side of the craft. LCI(L)s numbered 351 onwards had a modified design, recognisable by the rounded rather than rectangular bridge, and had a slightly larger troop capacity of 209.

Those LCI(L)s in Royal Navy service were sailed across the Atlantic by Royal Navy crews. While waiting for the vessels to be completed, the British sailors stayed in impressive New York hotels; wealthy American civilian supporters made curtains for the bunks on board, and had to be dissuaded from providing a piano for each craft. Lieutenant Commander Alan Villiers RNVR brought a group of LCI(L)s across the Atlantic. He recalled that these craft 'were hurriedly welded together … using metal so thin that to walk across the decks in places was to give one the willies, for the plates gave'. They used two groups of four General Motors diesel bus engines, because those were not in demand by other naval vessels. The craft's designer, John C. Niedermair, of the US Navy's Bureau of Ships, later recalled that sheet steel was in such short supply that the grade of steel rolled for automobiles had to be used in building LCI(L)s.[25]

LCI(L)s were generally recognised as making a valuable contribution to Operation Neptune, not just on D-Day but for embarking troops from larger ships off the beaches. They proved to be less suitable for landing on flat beaches – instead, one craft could unload all its troops into three LCMs – but they were effective when the beach had a steeper gradient at high tide. Though hard to sink, the troops on board proved vulnerable to mines or enemy fire. The craft did have limited armour, including on the forward third of the sides and bulwarks.

Some LCI(L)s were modified as LCHs (Landing Craft, Headquarters), with space for sixty-two staff from an army battalion or brigade group/regimental combat team. After D-Day, LCHs were control craft for the ferry service vessels putting forces ashore from larger ships.

LCI(S): Landing Craft, Infantry (Small)[26]
This craft was designed in parallel with the LCI(L) and inspired by a similar concept. Three key differences were that it was smaller, built in the UK (to a design by Fairmile) and made from wood (it was the largest wooden landing craft). With its speed and more elegant lines, it almost resembled a more conventional warship, and new officers greatly preferred to be

appointed to an LCI(S) rather than an LCT. Like an LCI(L), troops landed by a pair of ramps, one of which was lowered either side of the bow; in practice, the ramps were easily damaged.

The main role of the LCI(S) on D-Day was to land commandos, not long after the assault troops had gone ashore. Therefore, it is surprising that these craft had only limited armour fitted to the sides, deck and bridge. Critically, they lacked self-sealing fuel tanks, and in the worst D-Day loss, LCI(S) 524 blew apart through what was said to be a direct hit off the beach after having landed its commandos on Sword Beach.

Thirty-nine LCI(S) were used in the assault on D-Day, some as reserve or hospital craft, and many were left badly damaged. The Commander, Eastern Task Force concluded after the operation that LCI(S)s were best used in their original role of surprise night attacks, or for landing follow-up waves in the aftermath of an assault and ferrying troops ashore over subsequent days.[27]

Specifications: Major Landing Craft

	LCT(3)	LCT(4)	LCT(5)	LCT(6)	LCI(S)	LCI(L)
Hull	Steel	Steel	Steel	Steel	Wood	Steel
Length	191ft 11in	187ft 2in	114ft 2in	120ft 4in	105ft 1in	158ft 4in
Beam	31ft 1in	38ft 9in	32ft 9in	32ft 9in	21ft 5in	23ft 3in
Beaching draught	3ft 10in	3ft 6in	2ft 11in	3ft 4in	3ft 8in	2ft 8in
Displacement (light / loaded)	350 / 640 tons	200 / 586 tons	120 / 253 tons	128 / 276 tons	63 / 110 tons	173 / 384 tons
Speed	9 knots	8 knots	8 knots	8 knots	12.5 knots	14 knots
Crew	2 officers 10 men	2 officers 10 men	1 officer 12 men	1 officer 11 men	2 officers 15 men	3 officers 21 men (later 4 and 24)
Capacity	300 tons	350 tons	134 tons	134 tons	102 troops 18 bicycles	188 or 209 troops
Weapons	2 x 2-pounder or 20mm guns	2 x 2-pounder or 20mm guns	2 x 20mm guns	2 x 20mm guns	2 x 20mm guns	Up to 5 x 20mm guns
Engines	2 x Paxman 920hp diesel	2 x Paxman 960hp diesel	3 x Gray 675bhp diesel	3 x Gray 225hp diesel	2 x Hall-Scott 1500hp petrol	8 x lorry 1440bhp diesel

(This is a simplified summary and does not represent all variations that were used.)

Fire Support and Control Landing Craft

A range of support landing craft were used at Normandy. Several types were converted by the British and supplied to the US Navy in Reverse Lend-Lease, including fourteen LCT(R)s, eleven LCFs, nine LCG(L)s, twenty-six LCT(A)s or LCT(HE)s, and forty-eight smoke-laying LCP(L)s. The Americans received them at a late stage, with two LCT(R)s only delivered to their crews a few days before D-Day, which did not help them overcome their suspicions of these craft.[28]

The LCT(A) and LCT(HE) were also considered support craft – with the fire support coming from the embarked tanks rather than the vessels' own guns – and are covered in the LCT section.

LCA(HR): Landing Craft, Assault (Hedgerow)

This variant of the standard LCA carried twenty-four spigot mortars in the space normally used for troops. The mortars were adapted from the Hedgehog anti-submarine mortar, which was designed to be fired ahead of a ship. In its new role, the mortar bombs were intended to make a path for the assault troops through barbed wire and minefields. These mortars were fired in four salvos in quick succession, with the craft close to the beach.

On D-Day, the craft were towed to France, and some did not make the crossing: at Sword Beach, all but one of the nine LCA(HR) were lost. Where they were able to get into position to fire, they did earn praise from naval commanders. There was no questioning the bravery of the crews, but some after-action reports suggested that a longer-range mortar should be fitted to LCT(AVRE) instead, not least because the weapon would then clear mines directly in the path of the tanks coming ashore from that craft.[29]

LCS(M): Landing Craft, Support (Medium)

These were small craft intended to get close to enemy defences, spot potential targets through the dust and smoke and directly support friendly troops ashore. They could be carried by the same ships as the LCAs that they would accompany, providing close-in fire support with machine guns and mortar while the other craft beached.

On D-Day, some were towed across the English Channel. Those used at Normandy were all LCS(M)(3)s, referred to here simply as LCS(M). The craft mostly had Royal Marine crews, though a few had Royal Navy personnel on board too.

This type was used at Gold and Juno beaches on D-Day. Another two LCS(M)s accompanied the LCA carrying 2nd Rangers to Pointe du Hoc, at Omaha Beach. No LCS(M)s were available for use at Sword Beach: they used LCP(L)s instead. The LCS(M)s also carried artillery Forward Observation Officers (FOOs), who controlled the fire of the self-propelled artillery regiments during the run-in shoot from as little as 500 yards off the beach: their work was judged to be very effective.

LCS(S): Landing Craft, Support (Small)[30]

This was the American equivalent of the LCS(M): the size difference was not as great as the craft names might suggest. They were carried across to Normandy on larger ships. Based on an LCP(L) hull, the LCS(S) had ¼in armour and a variety of weapons, including twenty-four rockets in projectors mounted on the sides of the craft. Another twenty-four rockets were carried which could be quickly reloaded.

Naval commanders seem to have been critical of the D-Day actions of LCS(S)s at Omaha, but praised their use at Utah. The Commander, Force O judged that the ability of the LCS(S) to deliver rocket fire from close to the beach made it 'a weapon of considerable power', but if the crews were not sufficiently trained, 'they are not worth the davit space they take away from LCVPs'.[31]

Some LCS(S)s were operated by US Navy Scout and Raider units, which functioned as control craft to guide the first assault waves to the correct landing site. After the assault, LCS(S)s were used as despatch and control craft.

LCS(L): Landing Craft, Support (Large)[32]

Both the LCS(L)(1) and LCS(L)(2) were used by the British at Normandy in small numbers to target enemy strongpoints: in total, fourteen craft, all but one of those that were built. The first variant had the primary armament of a turret-mounted 2-pounder gun, which by 1944 was outdated.

The LCS(L)(2) had a 6-pounder gun in a turret, plus a 4in smoke mortar, two 20mm guns and a ½in turret-mounted machine gun. The second type was based on the wooden LCI(S) hull and had little protection against enemy fire.

At Normandy, these craft were praised for providing fire support at close range to the shore, which could suppress enemy pillboxes and machine-gun posts. On King Red sector of Gold Beach, two LCS(L)s joined with LCG(L)s in suppressing enemy defences in support of the 5th East Yorkshires, who were pinned down on the beach. After D-Day, they were one of the types used to defend the eastern flank of the anchorage on the Trout Line.

LCF & LCG(L): Landing Craft, Flak and Landing Craft, Gun (Large)
Both types were converted from standard LCTs, meaning those craft were not available for carrying troops and vehicles. Nearly thirty LCFs were used in the Normandy Landings, providing additional anti-aircraft defence as well as firing on enemy coastal defences around H-Hour. About a third were operated by the US Navy and the remainder by the Royal Navy.

A British concept, most of these craft were based on the LCT(3) or (4) and were designated LCF(3) or (4) accordingly. The LCT's tank deck was decked over, with anti-aircraft guns placed on top. These craft were usually fitted with eight 20mm Oerlikon guns and four 2-pounder guns. The space below the gun deck was used for accommodation for the Royal Marine gun crews, as well as for ammunition storage. Though they were used for fire support as the troops landed, Force G observed that the gun crews were in exposed positions and would have suffered had there been significant return fire.[33]

The LCG(L) was widely praised for its role at Normandy. It had similarities in design to the LCF: the LCG(L)(3) and (4) were British developments based on the LCT(3) and LCT(4). Two 4.7in guns were placed on the decked-over tank deck, a type fitted to many destroyers. The craft was intended for battering enemy coastal defences at close range as the assault force landed and was regarded as less vulnerable, or perhaps more expendable, than a destroyer. The LCG(L)(4) was given an improved bow for better seagoing ability and armour that was 1–2in thick protecting vulnerable points.

Thirty-three LCG(L)s were built in wartime and twenty-five of them took part in Operation Neptune, roughly half of each variant. Of these, nine were operated by the US Navy and the remainder by the British. Once the Allied armies had advanced a short distance inland, LCG(L)s were no longer needed in their conventional role.

Allied command of the air meant that LCFs were of limited use in their standard role, even on D-Day, and there was no shortage of anti-aircraft guns among the rest of the Allied fleet. However, both types were used nightly in forming the Trout Line, a defensive line of landing craft on the eastern side of the landing beaches to defend the anchorage against nocturnal attacks by E-boats, human torpedoes and other German small craft.

Some craft were also on watch in the daytime. They certainly earned their keep in this role, but at a cost. For example, on 17 August 1944,

LCF 1 – the sole LCF(2) present – was sunk by a German explosive motor boat while on this duty, with great loss of life among the crew.

Lieutenant J.G. Lloyd RM reported that the LCF and LCG(L) crews lived on army 'compo' rations for eleven weeks, with hardly any vegetables or fresh meat and no bread for the first six weeks. The crew were affected to the point that eventually some had severe stomach trouble or fainting fits.[34]

LCT(R): Landing Craft, Tank (Rocket)

Perhaps the most memorable fire support landing craft, the LCT(R) was another British conversion from the LCT(2) – not used at Normandy – or LCT(3). The craft fired around 1,000 3in rockets to a range of 3,500 yards, in a series of quick salvos, rather than all at once, to avoid damaging the craft. The rockets were mounted at a fixed 45-degree angle and could not be aimed other than by the direction of the ship, whose crew used radar to ensure the bombardment fell on target. In normal use, the rockets would cover an area something like 700 yards deep by 150 yards wide. The scars left on the earth by these rockets can be seen in many aerial photographs from D-Day.[35]

The craft were scheduled to fire their rockets in the final minutes before the assault troops went ashore. Individual rockets were not aimed at specific targets: it was an area-effect weapon, relying on the volume of fire to encourage enemy troops to keep their heads down. Each craft carried a second load of rockets on its lower deck and it typically took sixty men (some provided from another ship) four hours to reload one craft.[36]

Thirty-five out of the forty-three LCT(R)s built took part in Operation Neptune, with fourteen transferred by the British to the US Navy for use on Omaha and Utah beaches. Generally, the LCT(R)s were praised for their effectiveness, though in some cases they were judged (not always fairly) to have fired too close to friendly forces.[37]

LCC: Landing Craft, Control – and Other Control Craft

As the name suggests, control craft were used to ensure that waves of landing craft beached at the desired time and place. Some types were not considered landing craft at all.

The British LCC was a converted Fairmile B motor launch, while the US-built LCCs were specially built. These types were fitted with a variety of communications and navigational equipment.

Specifications: Fire Support and Control Landing Craft

	LCA(HR)	LCS(S)(1)	LCS(M)(3)	LCS(L)(1)	LCS(L)(2)
Based on:	LCA	LCP(L)	LCA, modified	Motorboat	LCI(S)
Hull	Wood	Wood	Wood	Wood	Wood
Length	41ft 6in	36ft 8in	41ft 2in	46ft 11in	105ft 1in
Beam	10ft	10ft 10in	10ft 1in	12ft 7in	21ft 5in
Beaching draught	1ft 9in	42in	1ft 9in	2ft 4in	3ft 8in
Displacement (loaded)	13 tons	10 tons	13 tons	24.5 tons	116 tons
Speed	7 knots	10 knots	7 knots	10 knots	12.5 knots
Crew	4	6 crew 3–4 gunners	1 officer 10 men	1 officer 12 men	2 officers 23 ratings and Marines
Capacity	n/a	n/a	n/a	n/a	n/a
Weapons	24 x spigot mortars	2 x rocket projectors 1 x .50in 2 x .30in machine guns	2 x .50in machine guns 2 x light machine guns 1 x 4in smoke mortar	1 x 2-pounder gun 1 x BESA machine gun 2 x .50in machine guns 1 x 4in smoke mortar	1 x 6-pounder QF gun 2 x 20mm Oerlikons 2 x .50in Vickers machine guns 1 x 4in smoke mortar
Engines	2 x Scripps 65hp V-8	1 x Hall-Scott 250hp petrol	1 x 130bhp	2 x Gray 330bhp diesel	2 x Hall-Scott 1,1400hp petrol

	LCC (US)	LCC (British)	LCF(3)	LCG(L)(3)/ (4)	LCT(R)(3)
Based on:		Motor launch	LCT(3)	LCT(3) / (4)	LCT(3)
Hull	Steel	Wood	Steel	Steel	Steel
Length	56ft	112ft	192ft	192ft / 187ft 2in	192ft
Beam	13ft 7in	18ft 6in	31ft	31ft / 38ft 9in	31ft 1in
Beaching draught	n/a	n/a	n/a	n/a	n/a
Displacement (unloaded/ loaded)	30 / – tons	– / 75.5 tons	470 / – tons	491 / 570 tons	– / 560 tons
Speed	10 knots	17 knots	9 knots	9 knots	9 knots

	LCC (US)	LCC (British)	LCF(3)	LCG(L)(3)/ (4)	LCT(R)(3)
Crew	14	14	RN crew: 2 officers, 10 men. RM gunners: 2 officers, 48 men.	RN & RM: 3 officers, 44 men / 3 officers, 48 men	2 officers, 15 men
Capacity	n/a	n/a	n/a	n/a	n/a
Weapons	2–3 x twin .50 machine guns	1 x 3-pounder, 2 x 20mm guns	12 guns: mix of 2lb pom-poms and 20mm Oerlikons	2 x 4.7in QF naval guns, 2–4 x 20mm Oerlikons	1,080 or 936 rockets (Mk1 or Mk2 projectors)
Engines	2 x 125hp diesel	2 x petrol	2 x Paxman 920bhp diesel	2 x Paxman 920bhp diesel	2 x Paxman 920bhp diesel

(This is a simplified summary and does not represent all variations that were used.)

Landing Barges[38]

Although minor landing craft such as LCVPs are sometimes informally referred to as 'invasion barges', these were the true landing barges, and strictly speaking, they were a separate category from landing craft. Being slower and more vulnerable, they were not designed for use in the assault but for the build-up period that would follow. However, their function was so similar to landing craft that they are featured here. The landing barges did not make repeated crossings to Normandy but crossed later on D-Day or on subsequent days, and remained off the French coast as part of the ferry service, unloading large ships or supporting such work.

The majority were converted from unpowered barges used on the River Thames, typically around 70ft in length. As it was judged to be too difficult to find enough towing ships, many were fitted with engines, as well as a bow ramp for unloading vehicles. For protection they were also given a 4in-thick cement belt around the inside of the cargo hold, up to 4ft high. Around sixty contractors, mainly in the Thames Estuary area, worked on converting some 500 barges of all types.

Over 400 barges were used in initial stages of Operation Neptune and the remainder may have been used later to replace losses. Landing barges were used at all five beaches, always with British crews, most of whom had considerable experience in civilian life in operating barges and similar craft on the River Thames and were now enlisted in the Royal Navy.

Some barges had crews from Inland Water Transport units of the Royal Army Service Corps.[39]

The most numerous type was the LBV (Landing Barge, Vehicle), 240 of which were converted and formed into LBV flotillas. Some were used to transport vehicles and stores to Normandy, and on arrival were beached so they could be unloaded, while others crossed empty and were put to work unloading larger ships. The report of the Allied Naval Commander-in-Chief stated that LBVs 'did excellent work', unloading stores from ships off the beaches into small ports, such as Courseulles, but were less suitable for unloading over open beaches for long periods.[40]

Supply and Repair flotillas were formed using a mix of the other types, which were towed to Normandy by fuelling trawlers rather than crossing under their own power. The LBOs (Landing Barge, Oil) were designed specially rather than converted. Each held a 30ft-long cylindrical tank holding either petrol or diesel fuel for refuelling landing craft and any other vessels. Similarly, the LBWs (Landing Barge, Water) carried water.

LBEs (Landing Barge, Emergency Repair) were mobile workshops for repairing damaged landing craft. Each had a workshop lorry on board, which could be landed via the barge's ramp if necessary. Many craft received damage from repeated beaching, and particularly in the great storm that began on 19 June, so there were certainly plenty of candidates for this work.[41]

Many minor landing craft would be working off the Normandy coasts for weeks after D-Day, but the crews had no means of preparing hot food. The LBK (Landing Barge, Kitchen) was designed and built in rapid time at the start of 1943 to meet this need. Each had an ungainly looking structure topped with ventilation funnels, built up on the barge to accommodate food storage and cooking facilities. Each was intended to feed 800 men, though at Normandy some fed double that number per day, sometimes also including personnel ashore. They were widely praised for their work. The LBF (Landing Barge, Flak) carried two 40mm Bofors guns for escorting other barges in convoy and additional anti-aircraft defence during the Channel crossing and off the Normandy coast.

Some large dumb (unpowered) barges were also used after D-Day. Sixteen 1,000-ton barges (which had been towed across the Atlantic) were used by US forces to deliver an initial load of ammunition, food and fuel and were then used as ferry craft. Bolted section-steel cargo barges were designed and built by the American Steel Dredge Company and assembled in the UK. These unpowered barges were, at first glance, visually similar to a Rhino Ferry, but constructed by bolting steel components together, rather than welding, as with a Rhino. Unlike a Rhino, which carried its cargo on its upper surface, they were designed to hold cargo inside their compartments. The US Navy towed eight barges containing ammunition across the English Channel after D-Day and beached them so they could be unloaded at leisure: these may have been this same type of barge.[42]

LANDING SHIPS

LST: Landing Ship, Tank[43]

'The destinies of two great empires ... seem to be tied up in some God-damned things called LSTs,' British Prime Minister Winston Churchill is said to have despairingly remarked. The LST arose from a need for an oceangoing ship that could also land vehicles directly on a beach. The first LSTs were three British-designed ships based on shallow-draught oil tankers used on Lake Maracaibo in Venezuela. They had bow doors and a ramp and demonstrated the potential of this vessel but still had too great a draught for landing vehicles on a beach. Still the three – HMS *Misoa*, HMS *Bachaquero* and HMS *Tasajera* – did arrive at Normandy as part of Force L, carrying a cargo of vehicles, and remained off the French coast to act as depot ships for Rhino Ferries.[44]

The first production LST was the LST(1) or 'Winette' (named after Winston Churchill), which began to be built in the USA in late 1941; none of this type were used at Normandy as they were unsuitable for the gently sloping French beaches. Around the same time, the British asked if the Americans could build an improved version of the LST, along with an LCT suited to be carried on its deck across the Atlantic.

John C. Niedermair of the US Navy's Bureau of Ships made a quick design sketch for what would become the LST(2). Many were built on the banks of the great rivers of the USA, and the first LST(2)s were ready in September 1942.

The complexity of these vessels – they had 30,000 parts – is demonstrated by the fact that an LST took longer to build than a Liberty Ship, although the latter was five times larger. The LST(2) used a pair of diesel railway locomotive engines, rather than the power-plants that were in demand for other ships. It had a flat bottom so it could beach in just over 3ft of water at the bow, but when the ship's ballast system was flooded it gave it stability at sea. Vehicles were landed using a ramp which extended from behind bow doors that gave better sea-keeping abilities than an LCT.

The design had an internal tank deck, which could be used for carrying tanks and other heavy vehicles. An upper deck, which was open to the elements and could take vehicles up to 10 tons in weight, was reached via a lift (or a ramp on later LSTs).

An LST could carry twenty Sherman tanks on its main deck, an average of fifty-five vehicles – or forty for the US LSTs, whose capacity was reduced due to extra davits and anti-aircraft guns on the upper deck. When configured for a beach landing, the ship carried a cargo totalling 500 tons – only a quarter of its potential load, but this ensured it had a draught of only 37in at the bow. The vessel had up to 130 crew and a cruising speed of around 9 knots.[45]

LSTs were fitted with up to six davits, each of which could carry a minor craft such as an LCVP, LCS(S) or a DUKW. At Omaha and Utah beaches, the craft provided by LSTs made a significant contribution by landing assault troops loaded from landing ships. Some LSTs were 'medically equipped', with a capacity for transporting over 450 wounded. They carried additional medical staff and had brackets fitted along the sides of the tank deck that could be used to carry several rows of stretchers, in addition to stretchers laid on the deck itself. Other LSTs, without these additional facilities, were also called upon to carry casualties back to the UK.

The LCT(5) and LCT(6) were designed to be transported across the Atlantic on the upper deck of an LST(2). The LCT could be unloaded either by using a giant crane or causing the LST to list and side-launching the LCT into the sea.

The initials were sardonically said by its crews to stand for 'large, slow target'. The vessels had almost no armour and were not intended to be used in the assault, but LSTs did prove surprisingly tough. It was found that LSTs could be safely beached, unload their cargo of vehicles, once the tide had receded, and refloat with the rising tide, although Allied naval commanders were reluctant to attempt this at first.

Initially alternative means of unloading LSTs were used: Rhino Ferries and NL Pontoons. However, the vulnerability of these ships was illustrated on 28 April 1944 when German E-boats attacked shipping taking part in Exercise Tiger, a landing exercise off Slapton Sands, Devon, sinking LSTs 507 and 531, and damaging LST 289.

The USA built over 1,000 LST(2)s during the Second World War. Of that total, 236 took part in Operation Neptune. Around sixty LST(2)s that served at Normandy were crewed by the Royal Navy, over 160 by the US Navy and eleven by the US Coast Guard.

If reference here is made simply to an 'LST', it means an LST(2). In 1944, a new type, the LST(3), was under production in the UK and Canada for use in the Far East, but these ships were not available for the Normandy campaign.

LSI(S), LSI(M), LSI(L), LSI(H): British Landing Ship, Infantry (Small), (Medium), (Large) and (Hand-Hoist)

APA, XAP: American Auxiliary Personnel, Attack and Attack Cargo Troop Transport Ship[46]

Large ships were needed that could transport hundreds of troops and many small landing craft to the enemy coast. These ships were not landing craft but played a key role in transporting most of the smaller types of craft used in the assault. They were much more than simple troop transports, which were designed to ferry personnel from one quayside to another.

There were over fifty LSIs involved in the Normandy Landings. Most of the vessels were adapted from merchant ships rather than being built specially, so their specifications varied greatly, even within each type of landing ship. They ranged from the smaller LSI(H), around 300ft in length and with a gross tonnage of around 2,500 tons, to the largest LSI(L) at some 500ft long and 13,000 tons or more. Despite their differences, however, they did have many common features.

A variety of modifications were required to convert a ship into an LSI. Additional accommodation was installed for troops, landing craft crews and other support personnel of the landing craft flotilla, with cooking as well as sleeping facilities – those extra personnel might be on board ship for days at a time. Even the smaller craft, like the LCA or LCVP, were too heavy for standard lifeboat davits, so stronger davits had to be fitted, which carried the boats suspended from the ship's sides and could also lower them into the water. The most effective davits, which were used on many of the larger LSIs, were Welin Machlachlan luffing davits. These held one craft ready to be lowered, with two more stored adjacent that could be lowered with the same set of davits.

If a ship carried one or more LCMs, their larger size meant that they had to be lowered into the water by a derrick (a type of crane), rather than by davits. Ships needed extra ballast to counteract the destabilising effect of the weight of the small craft carried on the upper parts of the ship. Extra armament for anti-aircraft defence and extra storage space (from food for the additional personnel to fuel for the small boats) were also required.

The most numerous craft they carried were LCAs on British ships and LCVPs on US ships, but they also carried many other types, such as LCP(L)s to lead the waves of minor craft, LCMs for their greater capacity of equipment and vehicles, or LCS(S)s and LCS(M)s to accompany the troop-carrying boats and provide fire support.

Before the outbreak of war, the British Inter-Service Training and Development Centre (ISTDC) in Portsmouth had identified three Glen Line ships (511 ft-long, 9,880 gross registered tons), which could be converted to carry troops and landing craft. That conversion work did not begin until April 1940.

The converted ships were designated LSI(L), and two of them – HMS *Glenearn* and HMS *Glenroy* – were both present at D-Day. As configured in 1944, each could carry over 1,000 troops, twenty-four minor craft and over 600 crewmen for the ship and the landing craft on board.

Another group of British-manned LSI(L) were conversions of US-built merchant ships, supplied under Lend-Lease, such as SS *Empire Halberd* or SS *Empire Spearhead*. These were so-called Red Ensign ships (operated by British Merchant Navy seamen). They had eighteen small craft with Royal Navy or Royal Marine crews and could carry over 1,000 troops.

The US equivalent of the LSI(L) was the US Auxiliary Personnel, Attack (APA), which typically carried 1,200 to 1,400 troops. This type was also known as an Attack Transport to distinguish it from a standard troop transport ship (AP), which did not have the ability to land troops with its own small craft. Some troop transports were designated XAPs, meaning that they had to lower their LCVPs from the ship's deck using derricks, rather than being able to despatch them from davits on the ship's sides.

Ferries were another type of ship converted by the British into LSIs. Several Belgian cross-Channel ferries were converted into LSI(S)s, such as SS *Prince Baudouin*, whose LCAs landed the 5th Rangers on Omaha Beach. These were smaller vessels, carrying eight landing craft on davits and some 230 to 340 troops depending on the ship. LSI(M)s such as HMS *Queen Emma* (eight small craft), which took the Canadian Scottish Regiment to Juno Beach, were converted from Dutch cross-Channel ferries. They were slightly larger, with a capacity of around 400 troops. LSI(H)s, such as SS *Duke of Argyll* (six small craft) had hand-hoisted davits, hence the 'H' in the designation.

Other Landing Ship Types

Three LSDs (Landing Ship, Dock) took part in Operation Neptune. These ships had a huge open hold that could be flooded to let landing craft on or off. As a concept, by 1944 this had been superseded by other types of landing ship. On D-Day, HMS *Oceanway* carried twenty LCMs to Omaha Beach, each with a single Sherman tank on board, while HMS *Northway* took forty-six DUKWs to Juno Beach. HMS *Eastway* crossed to Normandy after D-Day. LSDs were sometimes used for returning damaged landing craft to the UK.

Thirteen LSHs (Landing Ship, Headquarters) participated in the campaign. These were command and control ships, extensively fitted out for this purpose. They were conversions of merchant ships or warships and almost all did not themselves carry significant numbers of troops. The most notable exception was USS *Bayfield*, the headquarters (HQ) ship of Force U, which carried twenty-seven small craft and over 1,000 troops.

LST(2) 13, 216 and 217 had been converted into Fighter Direction Tenders (FDTs), retaining the same numbers in their new capacities. These vessels were used for controlling fighter aircraft in support of the landings until units had been put ashore that could carry out this role, and they were not used for landing personnel.

Several LSEs (Landing Ship, Emergency Repair) took part in the operation: a type known to the US Navy as a type known to the US Navy as a Landing Craft Repair Ship or ARL. This was a converted LST(2) with workshop facilities on board for repairing landing craft.[47]

Naval Lighter Pontoon Equipment, Rhino Ferries and More

The following equipment types were not landing craft but were used extensively alongside them. Although Naval Lighter (NL) Pontoons and Rhino Ferries were used for different purposes, they were made from the same components: rectangular all-welded steel boxes or cells, 5ft long, 7ft wide and 5ft deep. These were connected in modular fashion to create equipment for specific roles.

Both NL Pontoons and Rhinos addressed a similar problem: how to bridge the gap between an LST and the shore. It was likely that LSTs would not be able to beach far enough up the flat Normandy beaches – in shallow enough water – to put their cargo of vehicles ashore without them being swamped. The Allies were reluctant to depend on drying out LSTs on the beach, although in practice, they found that this was possible without risk of damage.[48]

NL Pontoons or causeways were two cells wide and thirty long and were to be used in conjunction with LSTs. They were transported to

Normandy with one slung from either side of an LST. Launched into the sea off France, the pontoons were towed towards the shore and arranged end to end, with one end fixed on the beach. The causeway thus formed enabled an LST to safely unload its vehicles and was also then used by LCTs.

After the success of NL Pontoons in the 1943 invasion of Sicily, British Combined Operations Command lobbied for what became the Rhino Ferry, thirty cells long like the NL Pontoons, but six cells wide, forming a self-propelled lighter that could load vehicles from an LST (or other vessel) several miles offshore and take them to land, thus greatly reducing the risk to the LST from enemy artillery fire or damage while beaching.

In practice, in the rough seas on and immediately after D-Day, the crews found it difficult to 'marry' Rhinos to LSTs. Many Rhinos were soon out of action due to damage at the beach. Smaller Rhino Tugs were also used to aid in manoeuvring the larger ferries. Both types were towed across the Channel behind LSTs, and several of the tugs were lost in the crossing.[49]

The DUKW amphibious truck played a vital role on D-Day and afterwards, making use of its ability to move cargo on both water and land. DUKWs worked closely alongside landing craft and could carry a 5,000lb load in rough seas at a speed of up to 5.5 knots in calm water. Many DUKWs crossed to Normandy on board LSTs.

One piece of equipment that could perhaps have been widely used on D-Day was the LVT (also known as the amtrac, Alligator or Buffalo). From late 1943, these tracked amphibious vehicles were used in the Pacific to enable troops to cross the danger zone at the water's edge as quickly as possible. They could carry up to twenty-four troops (depending on variant) and could be launched from an LCT or LST. They were not perfect, with a speed through the water of 4 or 5.6 knots (compared to around 7 knots for an LCA or LCVP) and no ramp (meaning troops had to clamber over the sides in the face of enemy fire). Depending on the variant, they had little or no armour.

The Allied armies did consider their use on D-Day, including a remotely controlled version for obstacle breaching. In May 1944, there were 300 LVTs available in the UK, all but a handful of which were left unused. Perhaps the Allies judged that there was insufficient time before the operation to train on these vehicles, or their potential use was not understood. Whether LVTs might have reduced casualties at Omaha Beach, for example, as some have suggested, is debatable.[50]

Line Drawings

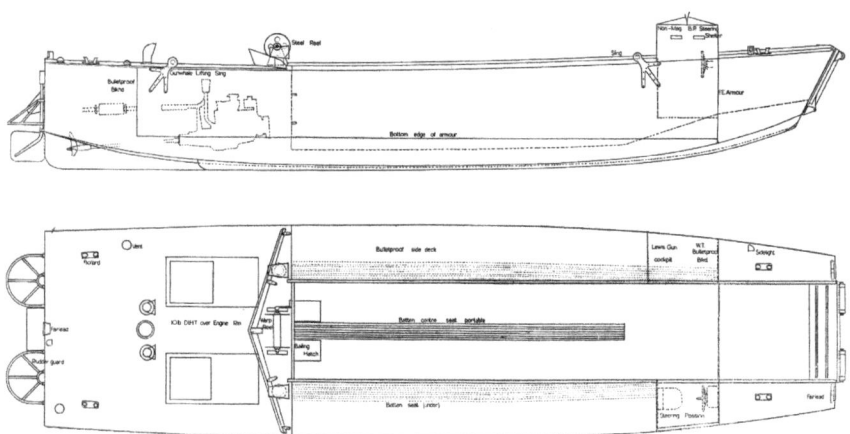

LCA: The craft had a distinctive steering shelter near the bow and three benches for the troops. Bulletproof side decks and side armour (which did not extend to protect the engine room) provided some protection for the men on board. (Baker, 'Notes on the Development of Landing Craft' in Duckworth (ed.), p.230.)

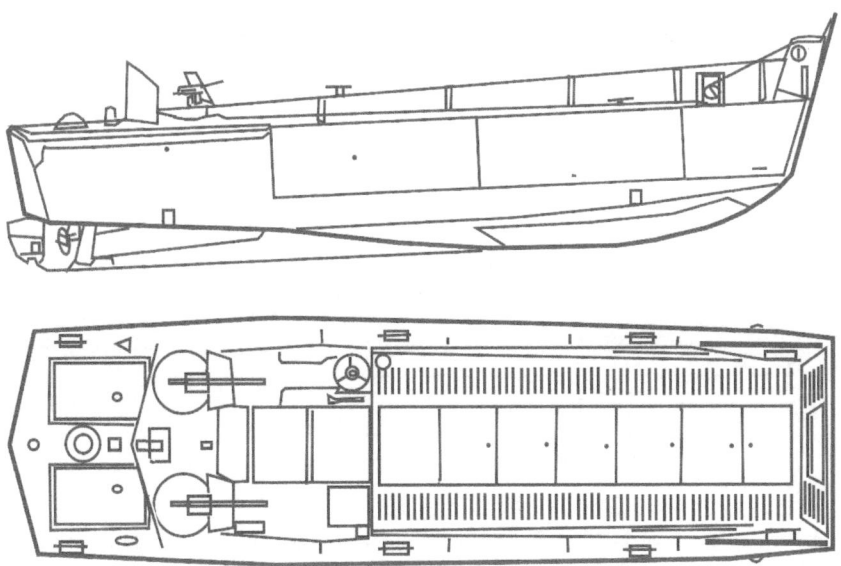

LCVP: The coxswain's position was to port, behind the troop compartment. A pair of machine guns are shown just further aft so the crew could provide fire support as troops landed, but these were not always fitted. The skeg under the craft protected the propeller and rudder against damage while beaching.

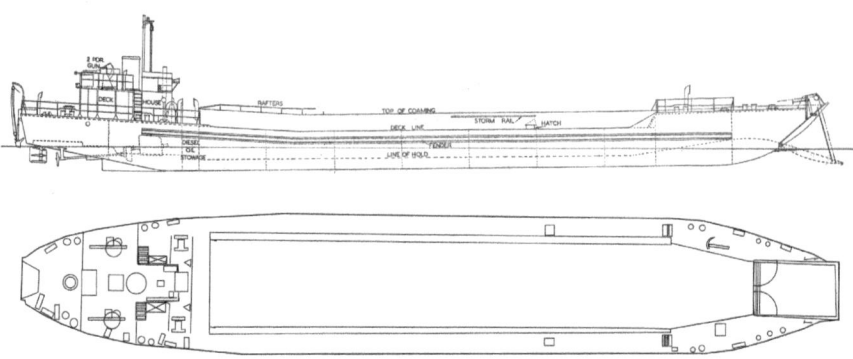

LCT(3): On this mark of LCT, the tank deck was below the water line. A curved 'whaleback' section just aft of the ramp reduced the chances of water flooding the deck. A pair of 20mm Oerlikons were often used in place of the 2-pounder Pom-Pom guns illustrated here near the stern. (Baker, 'Notes on the Development of Landing Craft' in Duckworth (ed.), p.238)

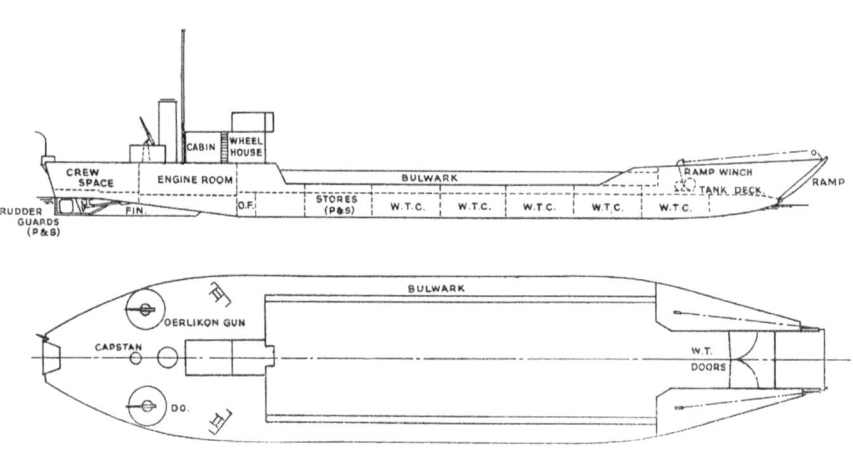

LCT(4): This mark of LCT carried its cargo higher in the water than an LCT(3) and could land on more shallow beaches. 'WTC' marks the water-tight compartments under the tank deck, which could keep an LCT afloat despite considerable damage. (Baker, 'Notes on the Development of Landing Craft' in Duckworth (ed.), p.239)

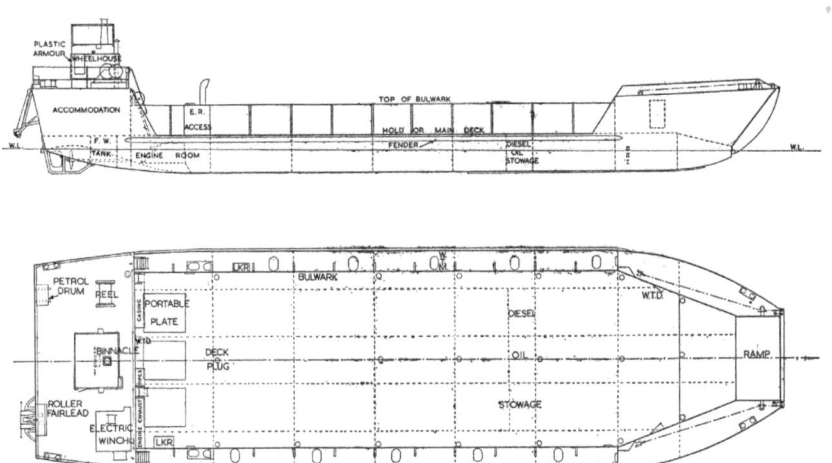

LCT(5): Though this had a different design from the British types, all marks of LCT had many common features including the open tank deck and large ramp at the bow. Some of the LCT(5)'s bulwarks were removable so it could 'marry' sideways to an LST(2) for unloading vehicles. (Baker, 'Notes on the Development of Landing Craft' in Duckworth (ed.), p.240)

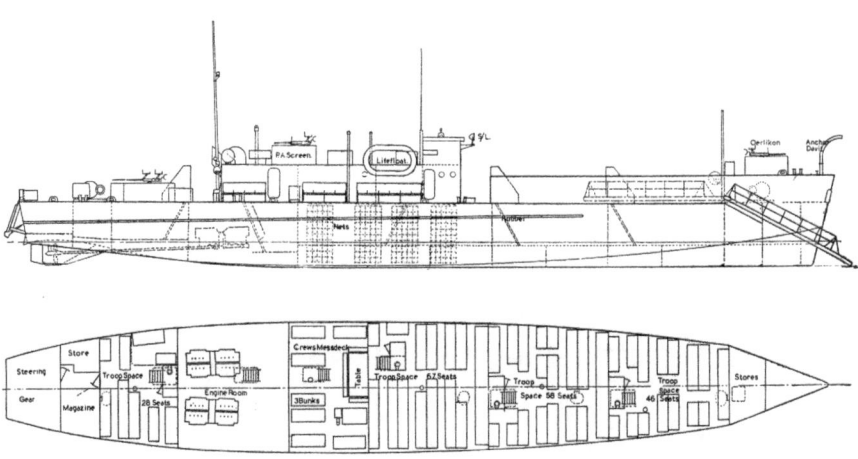

LCI(L): Troops usually landed by the moveable ramps either side of the bow, but scrambling nets were also fitted (as illustrated) and were useful for passengers transferring to smaller craft alongside. The plan view shows below decks: four troop spaces, which could hold 188 troops in total (209 on later variants), plus the engine room and crew mess. (Baker, 'Notes on the Development of Landing Craft' in Duckworth (ed.), p.234)

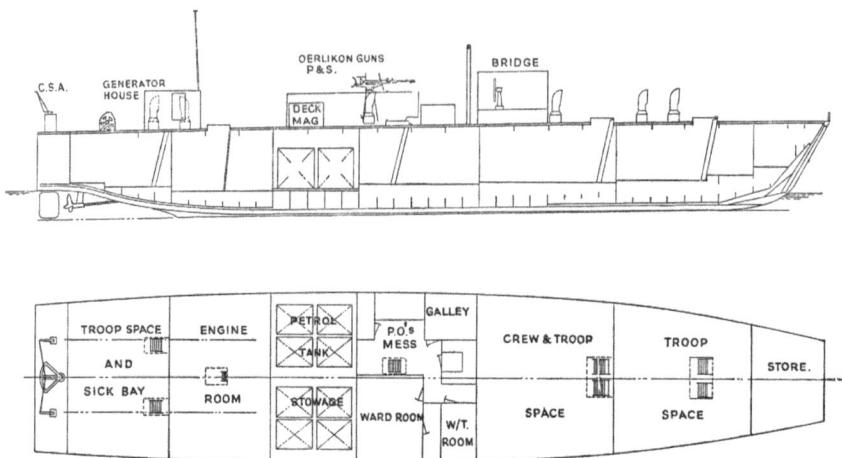

LCI(S): The craft's three troop spaces are shown with a total capacity of 102 men. Not illustrated are the ramps either side of the bow, used for landing troops. The relatively vulnerable fuel tanks can be seen. (Baker, 'Notes on the Development of Landing Craft' in Duckworth (ed.), p.234)

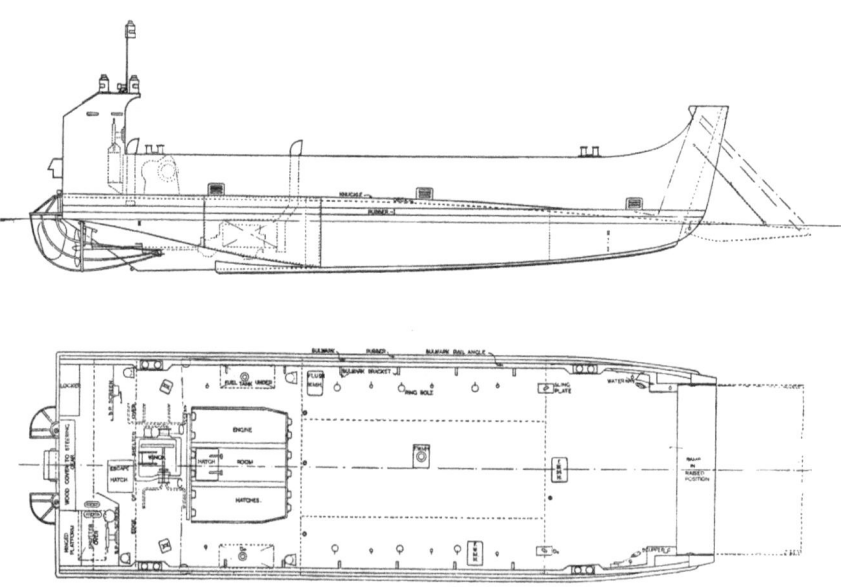

LCM(1): This British-designed craft carried its load just above the water level, which was not optimal for stability. (Baker, 'Notes on the Development of Landing Craft' in Duckworth (ed.), p.235)

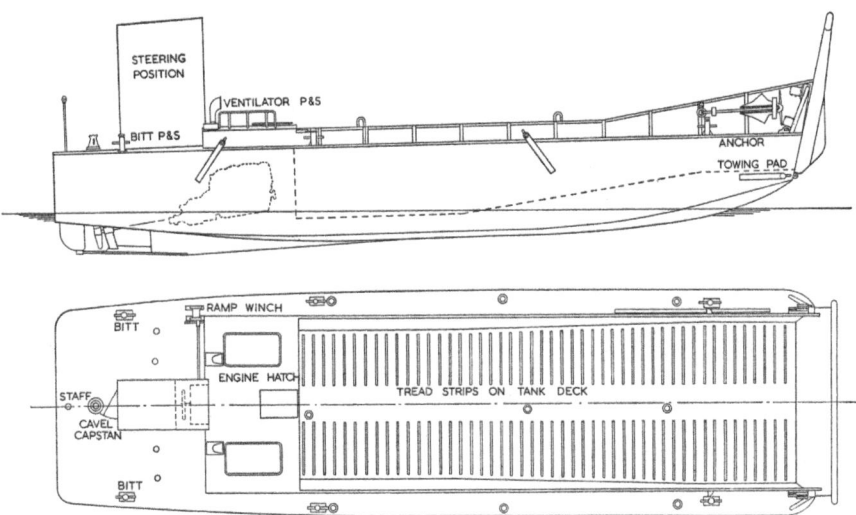

LCM(3): The different design of steering position was one way to distinguish this craft from the LCM(1); another (not shown here) was a grille-style top to the LCM(3)'s ramp. The LCM(3) carried its load lower in the water than the LCM(1), giving greater stability. (Baker, 'Notes on the Development of Landing Craft' in Duckworth (ed.), p.236)

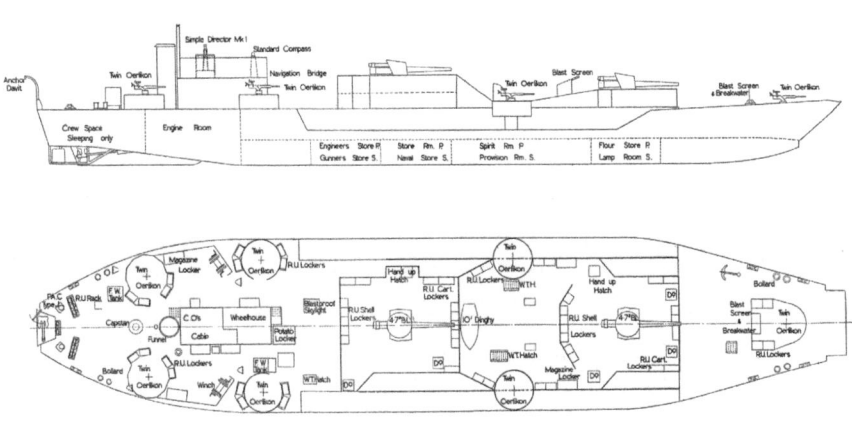

LCG(L)(4): Both LCT(3)s and LCT(4)s were converted into an LCG(L). This shows a converted LCT(4). Two 4.7in guns were mounted on the decked-over tank deck. The space below included magazines storing ammunition for the guns, as well as accommodation for the gun crews. (Baker, 'Notes on the Development of Landing Craft' in Duckworth (ed.), p.247)

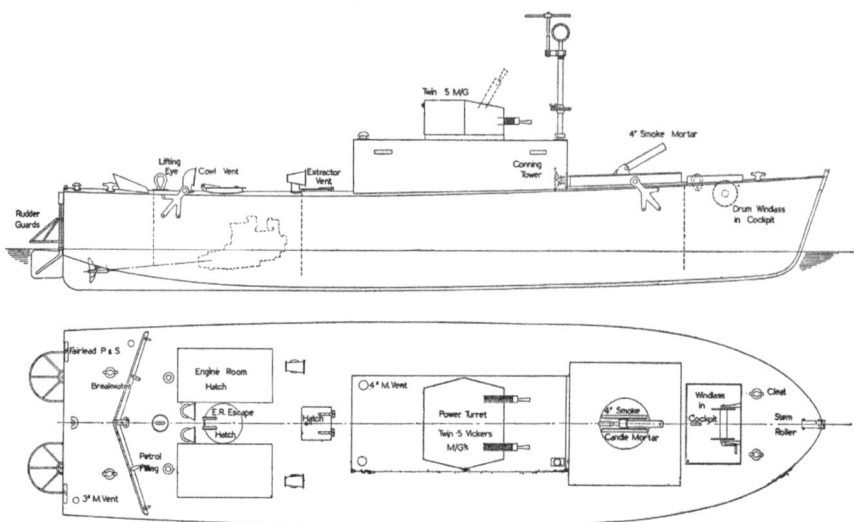

LCS(M)(3): The craft's twin .50in machine guns and 4in smoke mortar could provide useful fire support from close inshore. These craft were also used by FOOs for controlling fire from artillery regiments aboard LCTs before H-Hour, known as the run-in shoot. (Baker, 'Notes on the Development of Landing Craft' in Duckworth (ed.), p.243)

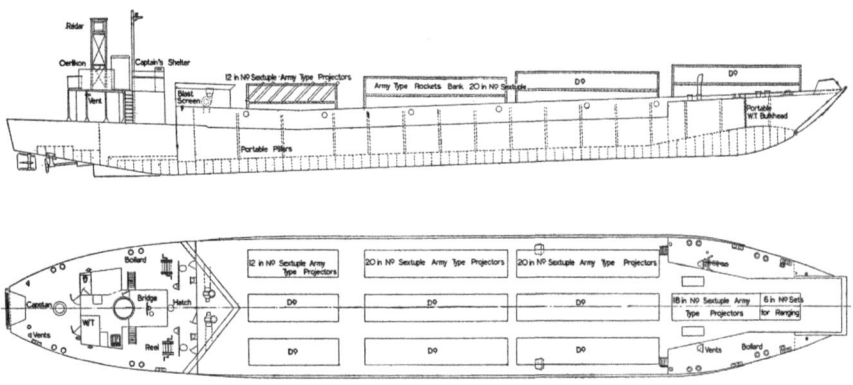

LCT(R): This modified LCT(3) was fitted with banks of rocket projectors on the decked-over tank deck. The blast screen in front of the bridge provided some protection to the craft's superstructure when the rockets fired. LCT(2)s were also converted into this role. (Baker, 'Notes on the Development of Landing Craft' in Duckworth (ed.), p.248)

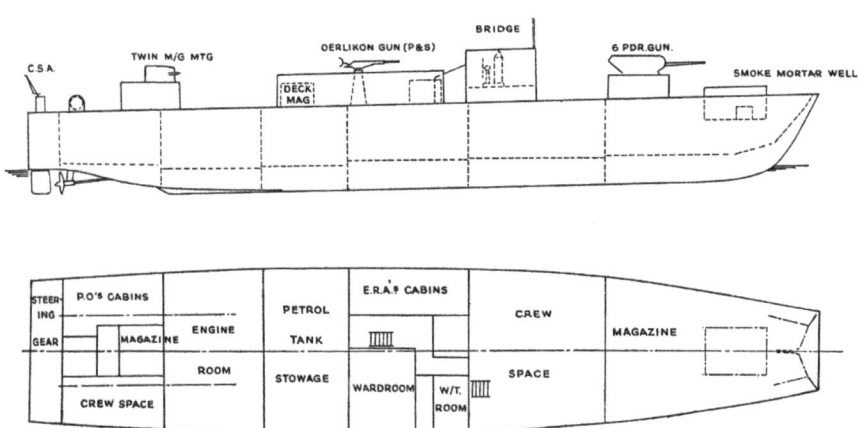

LCS(L)(2): This craft's main weapon was a 6-pounder gun mounted in a turret near the bow. The LCS(L)(1) was also used at Normandy but had a much smaller hull and carried a 2-pounder gun. (Baker, 'Notes on the Development of Landing Craft' in Duckworth (ed.), p.245.)

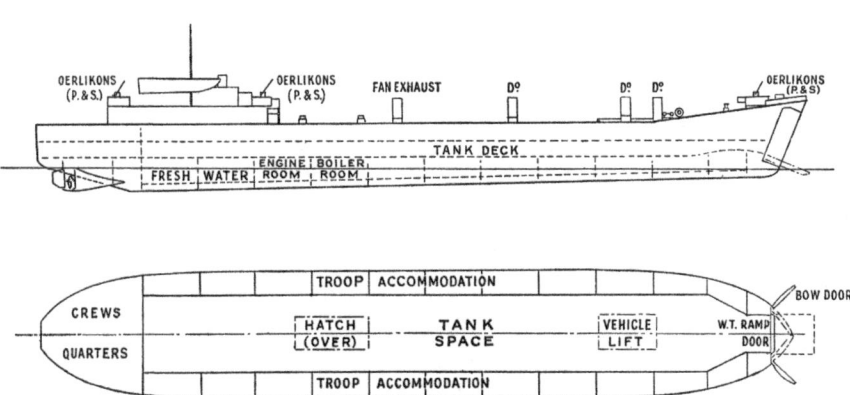

LST(2): This simple diagram shows the LST's key features, including the long lower tank deck, with the main deck above (accessed by a lift, or a ramp on later vessels). Up to six small boats such as LCVPs could be carried on davits near the stern. The ship was nearly 328ft long. (Baker, 'Ships of the Invasion Fleet' in Duckworth (ed.), p.64)

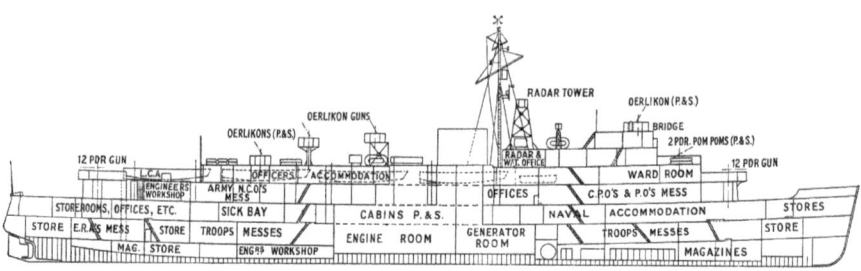

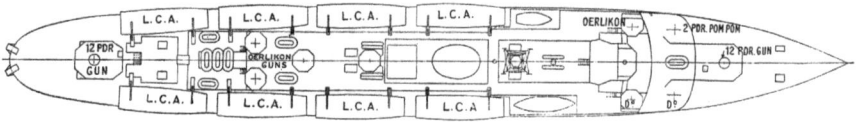

LSI(S) HMS *Prince Baudouin*: At 370ft in length and shown here carrying eight LCAs on davits, this was one of the smaller types of LSI. It was part of a group of converted Belgian cross-Channel steamers. Accommodation was provided for the crews of both the ship and the LCAs, as well as the troops on board. (Baker, 'Ships of the Invasion Fleet' in Duckworth (ed.), p.53)

Sources for Line Drawings

Unless stated, the sources are:
Baker, Rowland, 'Notes on the Development of Landing Craft' in Duckworth, A.D. (ed.), *Transactions of the Institution of Naval Architects*, Vol. 89 (London: Institution of Naval Architects, 1947), pp.218–58.
Baker, Rowland, 'Ships of the Invasion Fleet' in Duckworth, A.D. (ed.), *Transactions of the Institution of Naval Architects*, Vol. 89 (London: Institution of Naval Architects, 1947), pp.50–72.

Landing Craft Construction

The landing craft used on D-Day were built at dozens of locations on both sides of the Atlantic. Shipbuilding was a vital industry in the Second World War. The main construction firms were supported by other companies who were building components, some of whom had changed over to war work from peacetime work, such as making wooden furniture.

In 1943, the entire British shipbuilding industry employed 264,600 workers. At its peak in the USA, 1 million workers were involved in building ships of all types, based at 325 yards, with a further 2 million workers in supporting industries. There were many other calls on this capacity besides landing craft. In particular, the Battle of the Atlantic resulted in huge demands for merchant shipping and escort warships (also essential to ensure that American troops and equipment could safely reach the UK ahead of D-Day).[51]

The decisions of Allied military and political leaders on whether landing craft should be prioritised over other types of shipping will be covered in the next chapter. Even if individual vessels could sometimes be built in a matter of months, ship construction required long lead-in times. Civilian contractors needed to ensure they had the yard space and skilled workers required to carry out the work and had to order the raw materials from their suppliers. None of these were easily available due to high demand, including competition from the other services. Components from radios to ball-bearings to engines had to be made in good time.[52]

Traditionally, the UK had several types of shipbuilders. The Royal Dockyards almost exclusively built warships, although in wartime they mainly dealt with repairs. Larger commercial naval yards like Harland & Woolf usually specialised in building either warships or merchant shipping. For much of the war, these yards were not involved in landing craft production because other shipping construction was judged to be more urgent.

Landing craft construction at major British yards peaked at two points: in late 1940 to early 1941, when no other firms had yet been found to build these vessels, and in early 1944, when all possible means were used to maximise the output of landing craft, meaning that major yards fitted in small numbers of landing craft between the construction of larger warships. Smaller firms, including traditional yacht builders, in wartime built smaller warships, merchant ships and a range of other vessels (such as many of the smaller, wooden types of landing craft). Ships were designed centrally by the Admiralty, unlike in the British aviation industry, for example, where civilian contractors designed as well as produced aircraft.[53]

Additional measures were required, and from 1941 some of the shipyards that had been closed during the years of the interwar depression were reopened for building LCTs. These sites had been stripped of equipment such as cranes, but LCTs could be assembled using only basic facilities. Sections of hull were prefabricated off site and then brought to the construction site for assembly.

The manufacturers were structural engineering firms that normally built structures such as bridges because even if they were not shipbuilders, they were accustomed to working with steel. The LCT(4) was, in fact, specifically designed with these makeshift shipyards in mind. Minor landing craft, such as the LCAs or LCMs, required little infrastructure compared to major landing craft like LCTs, and could be built at a much wider range of locations.[54]

The concept of prefabrication – then a relatively new concept in industry – was that engineering firms would make units which could be assembled into a finished ship at another location, increasing the productivity per slipway and for a given dockyard labour force. The yard used by Fairfield (a Glasgow company) at Chepstow in Wales had been set up in the First World War as National Shipyard No.1, with eight slipways intended for building merchant shipping. By the Second World War, its slipways were still intact and it had workshops suitable for steel fabrication, which enabled Fairfield to build sixty-one LCT(4)s there, at a rate of three per month.

Two engineering firms on the River Tees in the north of England, Stockton Construction Company and Teesside Bridge & Engineering, built 211 and 179 LCTs respectively (Marks 2, 3 and 4). At Meadowside, in Glasgow, the structural engineering firms Sir William Arrol, Redpath Brown and Motherwell Bridge & Engineering constructed ninety-five, seventy-five and fifty-seven landing craft respectively, mostly LCTs (and not all were used at Normandy).[55]

Early 1944 was the high point of the UK shipbuilding labour force. With a limited number of people available to join the workforce that year, the government chose to prioritise recruitment to the armed forces rather than the munitions industries. However, improvements and efficiencies meant that British munitions production rose to its highest output in the first half of the year.

Landing craft were also built in the Dominions, notably in Canada, though Canadian production only ramped up in 1944–45. No Canadian-built landing craft were used on D-Day, although Canadian-made MINCA barges were transported across the Atlantic, reassembled in the UK and used for moving supplies to France at some point after D-Day.[56]

Landing craft construction in the USA was also an enormous effort, which cost around $1 billion during the whole war. The USA had great industrial potential, including space to build factories and yards and a large population, but it was just that – potential, which had to be developed.

Efficient management of the wartime naval expansion and the huge programme of landing craft production was a new experience for the US Navy. Between July 1940 and the USA's entry to the war in December 1941, the number of US shipyards undertaking new construction had already grown from twenty-nine to 156, in large part funded by British orders, and would eventually reach a high point of 332 yards.[57]

Many US-built landing craft were ordered from firms based inland on major inland waterways such as the Mississippi, Missouri, Ohio and Tennessee rivers, as well as in the Great Lakes region, including at Manitowoc on Lake Michigan and North Tonawanda, near Buffalo. These included so-called 'cornfield shipyards', which were not literally built on farmland but in states that were known more for agriculture rather than industry. As the crow flies, these inland yards were some 700 miles from the sea, but the LST(2)s, LCT(5)s and LCT(6)s built there had to make even longer river journeys to reach the ocean.[58]

The British could not simply copy American methods because US shipbuilders had several advantages over their British counterparts. In the USA there was plenty of space for setting up shipyards and it was easier to obtain labour. There were no restrictions caused by enemy bombing, whereas in the UK the blackout meant that outside work could only be done in daylight. The Americans also had more opportunity to prepare for and scale up production before entering the war, whereas the British had to improve output through increasing the efficiency of existing factories. In the UK, local housing shortages (often worsened by the impact of enemy bombing) made it difficult to bring labour into the area from elsewhere. It was not the case that the British simply lacked the imagination to use mass production.[59]

New yards were no use without workers. In the UK, the structural engineering firms were lent some 1,000 men from existing shipbuilders to kickstart the construction process, but primarily had to rely on unskilled workers who had been quickly trained in a specific task – this was known at the time as 'dilution'. These included women, who often did hard physical work that only a few years earlier they would have been considered unsuitable for. By the end of 1944, nearly 6 per cent of ship construction workers in the UK were female.

The introduction of women workers happened simultaneously with the introduction of new processes such as welding, much of which was done by women. The British Official History states that women were said to often be adept at learning welding due to 'the delicate and painstaking character of the work'.

Lilly Errington worked as a driller and spot welder at R & W Hawthorn, Leslie & Company's shipyard at Hebburn, which mostly built conventional warships but did construct six LCT(3★)s in early 1944. She later recalled, 'The drill was bloody heavy ... it was hand drilling and I had to do thousands of holes with it ... over me shoulder ... I had big muscles like that ... I've still got the muscle; it's never gone away really.'[60]

The demand for workers meant many changes in the USA as well. At Evansville, Indiana, the Missouri Valley Bridge & Iron Company cleared an undeveloped site on the banks of the Ohio River to create a yard, where from June 1942 they built 167 LST(2)s, many of which took part in the Normandy campaign. At the high point, the yard had nearly 20,000 workers, working in three eight-hour shifts per day. Additional housing had to be built for this influx of workers and the beds were rented out to three different people, who slept as well as worked in three shifts.[61]

British landing craft crews often collected their craft from the builder's yard, which might provide useful opportunities. Paul Motte Harrison was first lieutenant of LCT(3★) 7069:

Daily, we would go down to the yard to check on the building progress, to cajole the various foremen into providing odd fittings and bits and pieces – to enhance the comfort of ourselves and the crew ... Ultimately the nearly completed craft slid down the slipway for fitting-out ... Engine trials followed and then, to make space for other new-builds, we were ordered to secure alongside a fast mine-layer which was moored mid-stream, awaiting re-fit. I cannot recall the name of this ship ... I don't think that she even had a watchman on board. Our coxswain took advantage of this, and LCT 7069 was the only craft of the 17th LCT Flotilla ... which had teak gratings and double the official establishment of ropes, lines and coir matting.[62]

The Impact of Earlier Campaigns on Landing Craft Design and Use

Whether the Allies incorporated into their D-Day plans any lessons from earlier amphibious landings (notably in the Pacific and the Mediterranean) can only be touched on briefly. Not all lessons were directly relevant. Pacific landings were often preceded by a long sea journey, which had a bearing on the types of landing craft that could participate. At relatively small and isolated objectives, the attacker often had little to lose in sacrificing the element of surprise in favour of a days-long naval bombardment; this was not the case at Normandy, where a rapid assault was essential before the Germans brought up reserves.[63]

Attempts were made to circulate lessons, such as in British Combined Operations' monthly progress reports. Much of the equipment used on D-Day, from LSTs and pontoon causeways, to DUKWs and British-designed fire support landing craft, had been trialled in earlier operations. Fire support craft in part originated from lessons learned in the unsuccessful Dieppe Raid of August 1942. Some of the most important lessons related to more 'mundane' elements, such as the rapid unloading of supplies: often a problem in 1942 and sometimes still in 1943, but one that had been improved for D-Day. Understanding a particular lesson did not automatically confer the ability to put it into action: in the time available, it might not be possible to source the desired equipment or trained personnel.[64]

Some participants were certainly aware of the benefits of experience. The D-Day report of USS *Charles Carroll* (Force O) stated that 'The experience gained in three other assault landings under combat conditions have ironed out most of the technical difficulties in amphibious landings ... The experience of the personnel in the boats, veterans of previous landings in Africa and Mediterranean, stood them in good stead ...'[65]

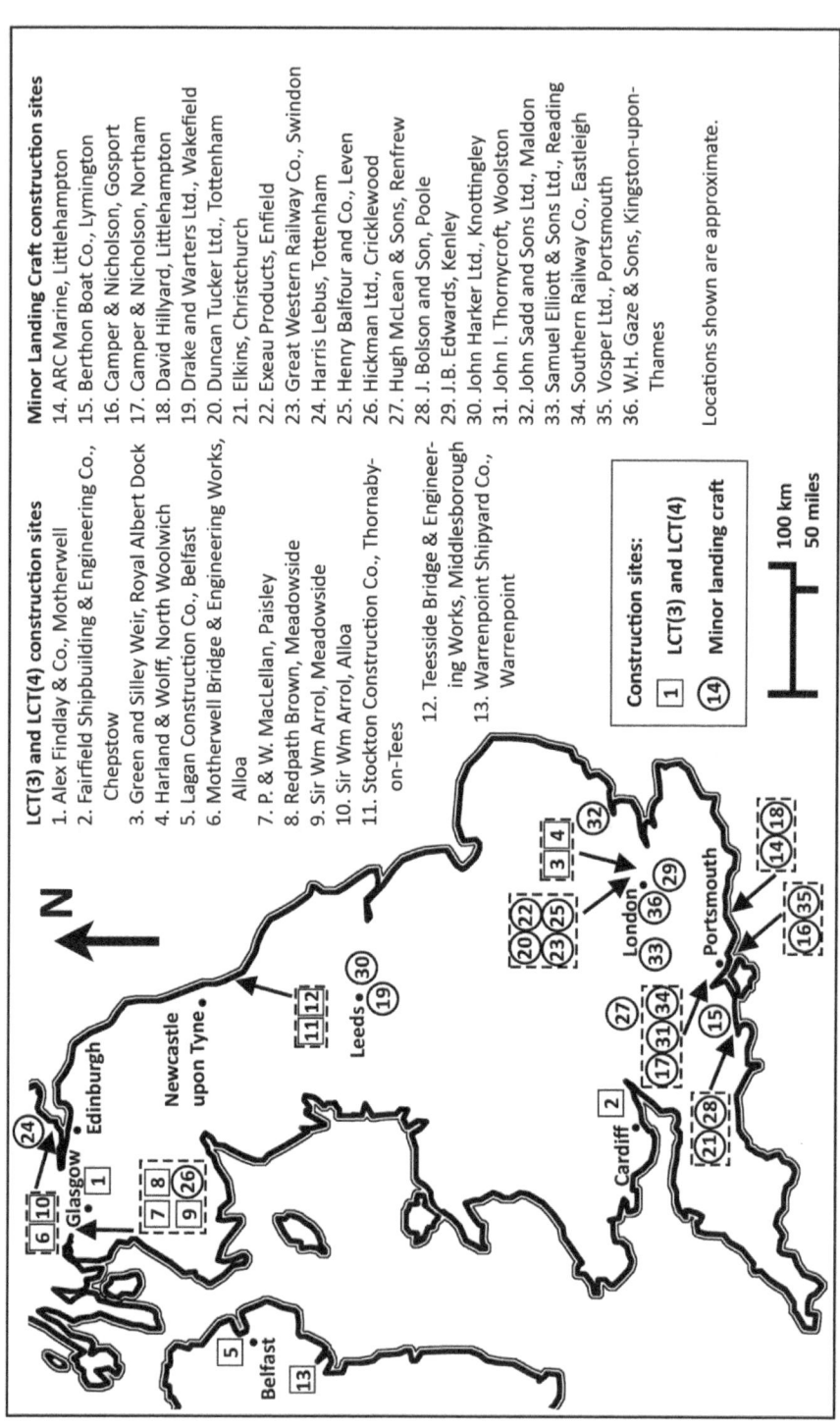

Minor Landing Craft construction sites

14. ARC Marine, Littlehampton
15. Berthon Boat Co., Lymington
16. Camper & Nicholson, Gosport
17. Camper & Nicholson, Northam
18. David Hillyard, Littlehampton
19. Drake and Warters Ltd., Wakefield
20. Duncan Tucker Ltd., Tottenham
21. Elkins, Christchurch
22. Exeau Products, Enfield
23. Great Western Railway Co., Swindon
24. Harris Lebus, Tottenham
25. Henry Balfour and Co., Leven
26. Hickman Ltd., Cricklewood
27. Hugh McLean & Sons, Renfrew
28. J. Bolson and Son, Poole
29. J.B. Edwards, Kenley
30. John Harker Ltd., Knottingley
31. John I. Thornycroft, Woolston
32. John Sadd and Sons Ltd., Maldon
33. Samuel Elliott & Sons Ltd., Reading
34. Southern Railway Co., Eastleigh
35. Vosper Ltd., Portsmouth
36. W.H. Gaze & Sons, Kingston-upon-Thames

Locations shown are approximate.

LCT(3) and LCT(4) construction sites

1. Alex Findlay & Co., Motherwell
2. Fairfield Shipbuilding & Engineering Co., Chepstow
3. Green and Silley Weir, Royal Albert Dock
4. Harland & Wolff, North Woolwich
5. Lagan Construction Co., Belfast
6. Motherwell Bridge & Engineering Works, Alloa
7. P. & W. MacLellan, Paisley
8. Redpath Brown, Meadowside
9. Sir Wm Arrol, Meadowside
10. Sir Wm Arrol, Alloa
11. Stockton Construction Co., Thornaby-on-Tees
12. Teesside Bridge & Engineering Works, Middlesborough
13. Warrenpoint Shipyard Co., Warrenpoint

Construction sites:

[1] LCT(3) and LCT(4)
(14) Minor landing craft

100 km
50 miles

N

Edinburgh
Glasgow
Newcastle upon Tyne
Leeds
Belfast
London
Portsmouth
Cardiff

Landing Craft Builders in the UK: Showing selected locations only: those where fifteen or more LCT(3)s or LCT(4)s, or thirty or more minor landing craft, were built during the Second World War. Craft built at most if not all these sites were used at Normandy. Many other firms built a smaller number of craft or supplied components. (Map primarily based on: TNA, CAB 102/539)

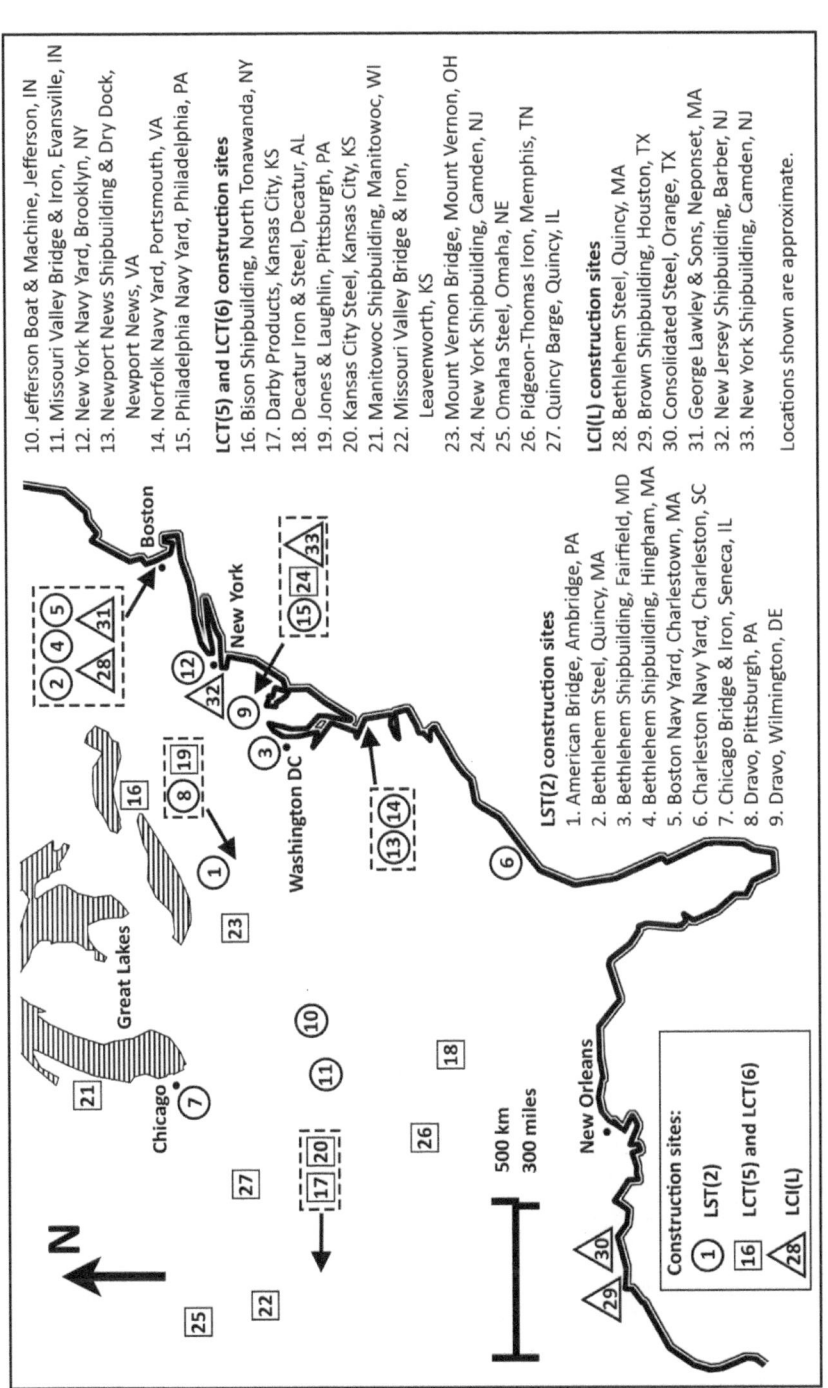

Landing Craft Builders in the USA: Construction locations in the USA for LCT(5)s, LCT(6)s, LCI(L)s and LST(2)s that were used by Allied forces at Normandy. There were other firms and yards in western USA (not shown), which built major landing craft and LST(2)s that were only used in the Pacific theatre. The many builders of minor landing craft, such as the famous Higgins Industries of New Orleans, are also not marked on the map. (Map primarily based on: Doyle, *US Landing Craft*, Vols 1 & 2; shipbuildinghistory.com)

The following text appears within the map image:

LST(2) construction sites
1. American Bridge, Ambridge, PA
2. Bethlehem Steel, Quincy, MA
3. Bethlehem Shipbuilding, Fairfield, MD
4. Bethlehem Shipbuilding, Hingham, MA
5. Boston Navy Yard, Charlestown, MA
6. Charleston Navy Yard, Charleston, SC
7. Chicago Bridge & Iron, Seneca, IL
8. Dravo, Pittsburgh, PA
9. Dravo, Wilmington, DE
10. Jefferson Boat & Machine, Jefferson, IN
11. Missouri Valley Bridge & Iron, Evansville, IN
12. New York Navy Yard, Brooklyn, NY
13. Newport News Shipbuilding & Dry Dock, Newport News, VA
14. Norfolk Navy Yard, Portsmouth, VA
15. Philadelphia Navy Yard, Philadelphia, PA

LCT(5) and LCT(6) construction sites
16. Bison Shipbuilding, North Tonawanda, NY
17. Darby Products, Kansas City, KS
18. Decatur Iron & Steel, Decatur, AL
19. Jones & Laughlin, Pittsburgh, PA
20. Kansas City Steel, Kansas City, KS
21. Manitowoc Shipbuilding, Manitowoc, WI
22. Missouri Valley Bridge & Iron, Leavenworth, KS
23. Mount Vernon Bridge, Mount Vernon, OH
24. New York Shipbuilding, Camden, NJ
25. Omaha Steel, Omaha, NE
26. Pidgeon-Thomas Iron, Memphis, TN
27. Quincy Barge, Quincy, IL

LCI(L) construction sites
28. Bethlehem Steel, Quincy, MA
29. Brown Shipbuilding, Houston, TX
30. Consolidated Steel, Orange, TX
31. George Lawley & Sons, Neponset, MA
32. New Jersey Shipbuilding, Barber, NJ
33. New York Shipbuilding, Camden, NJ

Locations shown are approximate.

Construction sites:
1. LST(2)
16. LCT(5) and LCT(6)
28. LCI(L)

500 km
300 miles

Boston
New York
Washington DC
Great Lakes
Chicago
New Orleans
N

2

Allied Strategy and Landing Craft Production

We've got to get to Europe and fight ...[1]

> Brigadier General Dwight D. Eisenhower, War Plans Division,
> US Army, in early 1942

By May 1945, total US production of landing ships and craft had exceeded 82,000, which were used in theatres all over the world besides Normandy. The UK built 4,300 landing ships and craft, while also benefitting from 2,600 other amphibious vessels produced by the USA and the Empire: figures that only seem less impressive in comparison to the American totals.[2]

The ability of the western Allies – particularly the USA – to mass produce weapons and military equipment is so much part of the way the Second World War is remembered. Yet the landing craft used on D-Day were only obtained in competition with other theatres, and in some cases, only at the last minute. Allied planners and military and political leaders paid close attention to the production of amphibious vessels. Strategy and plans had to take account of the available amphibious forces, and leaders with an interest in D-Day had to constantly strive to secure enough craft.

Both production and strategy had their own complicated internal tensions and contradictions, and each constantly influenced each other. The composition of the naval forces used at Normandy was the result of this interplay. The portfolio of amphibious vessels used on D-Day was not built up solely for that operation.

The expression 'Allied strategy' could obscure the fact that multiple competing strategic plans existed, each stemming from different national or service perspectives. In a global war, it was unsurprising that D-Day was always considered in a wider context. However, it was a safe bet that whichever theatre of war was chosen as the priority, the Allies would need amphibious forces to put their troops ashore in enemy-held territory.

Before 1939, there had been limited trials of amphibious landings in both the UK and the USA, leading to the development of the LCA and Andrew Higgins' Eureka boats (predecessor of the LCVP). Initially, the British primarily thought of amphibious operations as small raids – rather than permanent landings – made against a lightly defended beach, and relying on surprise and stealth to get ashore. Landing craft were simply not the priority in British shipbuilding at this point.[3]

While the evacuation of British forces from France in May–June 1940 increased the likelihood of future amphibious operations, at first the greatest concern was that those operations would be a German invasion of the UK. The British Army and RAF had priority over the Royal Navy for steel, armour and guns. Around the same time as famously calling for the establishment of what became the commandos, British Prime Minister Winston Churchill demanded the craft that became the LCT(1). The first of what became Combined Operations' landing craft bases began to be established ashore, including HMS *Northney*, HMS *Helder* and HMS *Tormentor*. These bases could maintain craft and train crews but could also support future amphibious raids.[4]

The first major period of British landing craft production took place between September 1940 and around March 1941. Supported by orders from Churchill that the construction of larger warships that could not be completed in 1941 should be paused in favour of smaller craft, over 200 landing craft were under construction simultaneously during the period September 1940–March 1941. This made it the wartime peak for British landing craft construction. The Admiralty's target was 369 minor landing craft, carried on fifteen landing ships, plus 180 LCTs. In October 1940, the Admiralty approved an order for ten Winettes (the first version of the LST), seven of them from the USA. In the same month, the LCT(1) was undergoing trials.[5]

Still, the Royal Navy was ahead of the US Navy, which showed little initial enthusiasm for amphibious vessels. While the USA would not enter the conflict until the end of 1941, the US armed forces understood they might soon be at war, but different services had varying ideas on amphibious warfare. The US Marine Corps anticipated making attacks on small islands and therefore favoured smaller landing craft. The US Army wanted more substantial vessels that could be used in larger-scale landings in Europe.[6]

By November 1941, the UK had constructed less than ninety LCTs and planned to build another 100 in the coming year, but the Admiralty judged that well over 1,000 would be needed for a landing in north-west Europe. LSTs were in even shorter supply.

The solution lay in the USA, but the existing designs of LCTs were not sufficiently seaworthy to cross the Atlantic. At British prompting, John C. Niedermair of the US Navy's Bureau of Ships sketched the design that became the LST(2). It could carry across the Atlantic on its deck a new American design, the LCT(5). The UK placed an order for 200 LST(2)s and 200 LCT(5)s – soon to be increased to 300 and 400 respectively.

The US approved the order for LSTs on the day before the Japanese attack on the American fleet at Pearl Harbor. Churchill visited the USA in December, shortly after the Pearl Harbor attack, and took the opportunity to make the case for American construction of LSTs for the British.[7]

As the USA entered the war, its munitions output – including landing craft – was a pale shadow of what it would become. Interest in landing craft among the US armed forces was still tentative. This was important, because the UK could only purchase items from the USA under the terms of the March 1941 Lend-Lease Act if there was a need for them in the US armed forces, meaning that in theory, the items could be later returned for US military use.

As 1942 dawned, the strategic situation was not looking promising for the Anglo-American alliance. Both countries had agreed on the strategy of 'Germany First': eliminating the threat from that country first, before turning to the Pacific. However, they did not agree on how to achieve this. The US Navy favoured an offensive in the Pacific, while the US Army preferred a landing in Europe as soon as possible. It was also becoming clear that the Americans had been overoptimistic in estimating their own munitions production. The USA had planned to spend $42 billion on munitions production in 1942 (compared to a 1942 GDP of $166 billion), but had actually spent only $9 billion.[8]

'Germany First' officially remained Allied policy throughout 1942. Yet by the end of that year, the USA was committing at least half its forces and production resources (including landing craft) to the Pacific, rather than the Atlantic, European and Mediterranean theatres. Rather than the British being able to rely on US production for most of its landing craft, British industry would also need to do its share. Over the winter of 1941–42, the British ordered a 500 per cent expansion in naval assault forces, including landing craft, over two years (admittedly from a low starting point).[9]

What were the initial plans for landing in north-west Europe? Some American commanders even hoped for an invasion in 1942. 'We've got to get to Europe and fight,' as Brigadier General Dwight D. Eisenhower – the future Supreme Allied Commander for D-Day – of the US Army's War Plans Division, put it in early 1942, when advocating for an amphibious landing in Europe that summer.

Before long, the US Army proposed a plan that would require a fleet of 8,100 minor landing craft, which at most could carry a single tank. This fleet comprised 1,400 LCP(L)s, 3,200 LCVs, and to carry vehicles, 3,500 LCM(3)s – not an LST or LCT in sight. Under these US Army plans, the whole assault force – at that point considered as two infantry divisions and two tank regiments – would cross the English Channel in a single trip, using the craft almost as single-use equipment. These troops would capture a port, which the follow-up troops would use to land in conventional shipping. The British pointed out the problems of co-ordinating such a swarm, and the strain on the troops of making such a long cross-Channel voyage in small craft.[10]

In early April 1942, the US War Department asked the US Navy to provide all 8,100 craft in the UK by 15 September that year, a near-impossible task, even ignoring the needs of other theatres of war. This helped to convert the USA to the use of major landing craft – LCTs, LCI(L)s and LSTs.

It was in June 1942 that the UK ordered its first LCI(L) from the USA, and an order of the same type of craft for the US Navy soon followed. However, at this stage the US Navy was mainly interested in 'combat loaders', such as attack troop transports (APAs) and the small craft that those ships would carry and that would be used to unload them, rather than major landing craft such as LCTs.[11]

In spring 1942, General George C. Marshall – US Army Chief of Staff – proposed an April 1943 D-Day involving forty-eight divisions, which the US Army judged would need 7,000 landing craft. US President Franklin D. Roosevelt had to intervene to increase LST production as the US Navy and Army were not giving the programme enough urgency. Only in mid-1942 did the US armed forces begin to accept that LSTs would be vital to amphibious operations in north-west Europe.[12]

In April 1942, the Allies agreed to a series of plans, which had been drawn up by Eisenhower while leading what was now the Operations Division of the Army Chief of Staff's office. First was Operation Bolero, the build-up of US troops in the UK. Second was an 'emergency' landing in Europe in 1942, Operation Sledgehammer, to be launched only if it seemed that the USSR was about to collapse under German attack. Sledgehammer was sometimes described as a potentially 'sacrificial' operation, in the sense that the troops might not survive but it could still achieve its strategic objective of aiding the Soviets. The British were not keen on this plan, not least because it would take time for the USA to move troops to the UK, so for the moment, Sledgehammer would involve primarily British troops.

A plan for a landing at a time of the Allies' own choosing was developed as Operation Roundup, a landing by eighteen British and thirty US divisions in northern France, but this would still only be possible with a significant increase in landing craft production. Details of both operations, including the size of the forces and the planned landing sites, sometimes changed over time with different incarnations of each plan.[13]

Another plan, Operation Skyscraper, was developed by a pair of planners – American Brigadier General Ray Barker and British Major General John Sinclair – on their own initiative and out of frustration that the Roundup plan was unrealistic. Unlike the weakened German opponents featured in the Roundup plan, Skyscraper envisaged intact German defenders and therefore used an Allied assault force of ten divisions, plus four or five airborne divisions and accompanying specialists such as commandos and engineers: a force which would need a substantial invasion fleet to transport it. They urged the British Chiefs of Staff to decide if such resources could be obtained, so it would be known if the plan was possible, rather than staying in limbo.[14]

There was no shortage of invasion planners, even if workable plans were in very short supply. In the UK, Combined Operations felt they were the experts on amphibious operations, a position that seemed to be strengthened after Admiral Lord Louis Mountbatten was appointed Director of Combined Operations, with a seat on the British Chiefs of Staff and simultaneously holding the ranks of Vice Admiral, Lieutenant General and Air Marshal. The Commander-in-Chief Home Forces, the Air Officer Commanding RAF Fighter Command and the Royal Navy's Commander-in-Chief, Portsmouth – known as the Combined Commanders – were also tasked to develop plans.[15]

In April 1942, President Roosevelt and members of the US armed forces attended a key conference at the White House. This led to an immediate order for 600 LCM(3)s for US use, yet the target date of 1 September proved to be an impossibly tight deadline. Any of the LCM(3)s that were built in time would end up being used in Operation Torch that November. The fault lay not with industry but with the Bureau of Ships' planners who had put the order in so late.[16]

In fact, Roosevelt had initiated what in retrospect can be identified as the first surge in US landing craft production, which ran from around April 1942 until it tailed off in May 1943, with the most productive period being November to February. Craft built included LCTs (first ordered in April 1942) and LCI(L)s (first ordered that June). In this period, the USA built 8,719 amphibious vessels of all sizes, including 214 LSTs, 302 LCI(L)s and 470 LCT(5)s, plus nearly 8,000 minor landing craft. Rather than hoarding these landing craft for what would become D-Day, many were used in Operation Torch, the Allied landings in north Africa in November 1942.[17]

A substantial number of the LSTs and landing craft built at this time were used on D-Day. In June 1944, LCT(5) 27 was serving with the US Navy in Force O. That craft had been completed in October 1942 and then took part in landings in north Africa, Sicily and at Salerno. Many of the LCT(5)s converted by the British to LCT(A)s were also built in this period and were transferred straight to Royal Navy service.

Although the final totals were respectable, the word 'programme' implies a much more measured rate of production than was the reality. By July and August 1942, the US landing craft programme was at least 50 per cent behind schedule. In the second six months of the programme, landing craft construction had to be increased by more than twentyfold to meet the final targets. The equivalent British programme also ended in May 1943, by which time around 1,050 major and minor landing craft had been built.[18]

By mid-1942, it was apparent that a cross-Channel attack that year was impossible. From a purely military point of view, it made sense to stockpile invasion forces in the UK, and this was certainly the view of the British and American Chiefs of Staff. However, both domestic and international politics would not permit this. Roosevelt and Churchill felt that it was essential to launch an offensive somewhere in the European theatre, which included the Mediterranean and north Africa. This led to the decision to launch Operation Torch, the Allied landings in north Africa in November 1942, even though – as the US Joint Chiefs of Staff pointed out – this was probably the final nail in the coffin of a 1943 landing in France.[19]

Unlike the future Operation Overlord, Torch was mounted at a great distance from friendly bases. This meant that the types of landing craft used were different from D-Day, with more landing ships required and fewer small craft. In fact, Torch diverted effort from building up craft for the main attack (Roundup), and meant that in the near future there would only be enough assault shipping and landing craft to land some four to six brigades.[20] The requirements of Torch even took over shipping that would otherwise have been used to move US troops to the UK as part of Operation Bolero, which incensed the US Joint Chiefs to the extent that they (unsuccessfully) demanded that imports to the UK for civilians be reduced to free up shipping space for moving troops.[21]

In January 1942, landing craft had been eighth in priority for naval construction in the US Navy's Shipbuilding Precedence Groups; by July, they had risen to the highest priority. However, by mid-November 1942, greater demand for merchant shipping and escort warships for the Battle of the Atlantic meant – following Operation Torch – they had fallen back to twelfth in priority.

Although in this early period landing craft production often suffered due to the need to focus on other campaigns, this was not a situation unique to landing craft. The Allied war effort involved constant reassessment of the priorities for munitions production according to both short- and long-term strategic needs.[22]

Contrasting American and British approaches to strategy were evident at the January 1943 Casablanca Conference. The Americans wanted a clear Allied plan mapped out for winning the war, so that production could be directed accordingly. The British attitude was that there were too many variables to create such a master plan. As long as the Allies always followed the approach of weakening Germany, they should constantly review their plans in the light of the most recent events. At future inter-Allied conferences this British approach maddened the Americans, who saw it as the British looking to renege on past commitments to the invasion. General Frederick Morgan (architect of the draft plan for D-Day) summed it up as 'the Churchillian theory of trying everything else first' before launching Operation Overlord.[23]

One reason for the American desire for strategic planning was that the potential of US war production was huge, but not unlimited: that potential had to be focused in the right direction. Led by Donald Nelson, executive vice president of the department store Sears Roebuck, the US War Production Board (WPB) was set up in January 1942. It had the role of directing American industrial production for the war effort and removing any inefficiencies and blockages.

Unlike in the UK, where production was often limited by labour shortages, in the US the availability of raw materials and components were more significant brakes on war manufacturing. Engines were a common bottleneck, and shortages of diesel engines (despite a 100 per cent increase in production during July–September 1942) led to 100 of the planned 490 LSTs to be built in the USA being cancelled – six out of seventeen shipyards building LSTs were switched over to building merchant ships instead.[24]

Only in August 1942 was the WPB brought in to assist with US landing craft construction. The board arranged for Bethlehem Steel Company to set up an office in New York to co-ordinate materials for the landing craft programme. Every WPB regional office now had a landing craft specialist, who would resolve any hiccups in the flow of raw materials or components: components should not be stockpiled or ordered too far in advance so they sat around unused.[25]

After Operation Torch, the additional vessels required by the Allies for a 1943 D-Day were assessed to include 172 LSTs, 300 LCI(L)s and 295 LCT(5)s. Yet at the January 1943 Casablanca Conference, the Allies decided that rather than turn to a cross-Channel offensive that year, campaigning should continue in the Mediterranean, as strongly championed by the British. To many American commanders, particularly the Commander-in-Chief of the US Navy, Admiral Ernest King, it appeared to be an attempt to avoid the agreed focus on the defeat of Germany.

Following the conference, 90 per cent of the US Navy's new shipping, including many landing craft, began to be sent to the Pacific. Historian Phillips Payson O'Brien argues that had they focused naval forces (including landing craft) on north-west Europe, rather than the Pacific and Mediterranean, the Allies could have gathered enough to launch a 1943 D-Day in France.[26]

In addition, shipping losses in the Battle of the Atlantic continued to be a worry, and the construction of escort warships had to take priority over amphibious craft. Monthly deliveries of US-built landing craft to the British peaked in February 1943 – by which point, the Americans had delivered 115 LCT(5)s to the British. During the period June 1942–May 1943, the British had expected to receive from the USA 260 LCT(5)s, 750 LCM(3)s and 300 LCI(L)s. The actual numbers received were 150, 496 and 150 respectively.[27]

In 1943, planning for what would become the Normandy Landings became more detailed and focused. However, the same disconnect between plans and available landing craft continued. In March 1943, Lieutenant General Sir Frederick Morgan was appointed as COSSAC – Chief of Staff to the (yet to be appointed) Supreme Allied Commander – to lead the planning staff for D-Day.

Much of the COSSAC staff's time involved making calculations based on the number of landing craft required under different scenarios: for example, reflecting different states of weakness of the German forces in France. COSSAC reported in May 1943 that for an assault in the first half of 1944 the Allies needed to start building naval forces that summer. For an assault landing, one infantry division would need thirty-six LCI(S)s, 100 LCAs, twenty-four LCI(L)s, 120 LCT(5)s, 144 LCT(3)s or LCT(4)s and twenty-eight LSTs. The British Chiefs of Staff asked the USA to supply by 1 April 1944, nine LSI(L)s, one LSH, 122 LST(2)s, six LSE(2)s, 125 LCT(5)s, 280 LCM(3)s and 140 LCI(L)s. The British programme for 1943 was for 1,050 landing craft, later increased to 1,900. A significant increase would be needed in the allocation of new personnel to the Royal Navy, for crews and supporting staff.[28]

Towards the end of May 1943, following that month's Washington Conference (Trident), the Combined Chiefs of Staff (the British and US chiefs of the two countries' armed forces) set a precise date for the invasion: 1 May 1944. Both US and British planners had a ten-division assault in mind, but whereas the Americans calculated this would require 4,600 landing craft, the British figured that 8,500 craft would be required.

The different figures partly reflected the fact that there was no agreement on how many vehicles a division should be able to land in the assault. After discussion, a target figure of 4,500 craft was reached, to land three assault divisions in assault landing craft, plus two follow-up divisions in types not suitable for the assault.[29]

Yet the Washington Conference had also confirmed the upcoming US advance across the central Pacific, which required more amphibious vessels. The conference confirmed that US landing craft production levels would be maintained or even increased, but where would those craft go? By January 1944, the USA had 144 LSTs in the Pacific and 138 in the Atlantic theatre respectively; for LCTs, the balance was 213 to 206; and for LCI(L)s it was 152 to 148.[30]

The other decision taken by the Combined Chiefs of Staff at Trident – and later confirmed and continued at subsequent conferences – was to agree to focus on a Mediterranean strategy for the rest of 1943. This was reluctantly agreed to by the USA and led to a series of amphibious operations that diverted (or delayed) landing craft and associated personnel from assembling in the UK ahead of a cross-Channel invasion: Operation Husky (the landings in Sicily in July 1943), Operation Avalanche, at Salerno in September 1943, and Operation Shingle (Anzio, January 1944).[31] Husky even required the transfer of US Navy ships from the Pacific.

While these operations did have many negative consequences for D-Day, in other ways they did promote landing craft development, which was of benefit at Normandy. For example, as Husky drew closer, LCTs were converted into LCT(R)s and LCG(L)s to provide fire support. Both types were tested in action in Husky, as was the LST(2) for the first time in significant numbers.[32]

The COSSAC plan had to be ready by 15 July 1943 to allow time for the plan to be reviewed first by the British Chiefs of Staff then by the Combined Chiefs of Staff, ahead of the August 1943 Quebec Conference (Quadrant), where it would be discussed in detail. This was a tall order since Morgan had to create his staff from scratch, and give a renewed sense of purpose to those existing planners who had been working so long on a succession of plans that they 'had ceased to believe in the reality of their work'. Ironically, although the Americans had consistently wanted D-Day to take place much sooner than the British did, most of the planning work at this stage was being done by the British.[33]

A key part of the creation of the COSSAC plan was Operation Rattle, a conference for over seventy senior officers and planners from multiple Allied countries, held at the end of June 1943 and into early July at HMS *Warren*, a Royal Navy shore base at Largs, Scotland. This provided a genuine opportunity for all parties to air their ideas on subjects such as the optimum location and time of day for the assault. Critically, it also ensured that a consensus was reached on such matters, rather than letting debates continue.

One important decision involved an aspect of D-Day that we now take for granted: rather than the landings beginning with a predawn assault by infantry, it should take place after sunrise and with tanks, engineers and other forces supporting the infantry. This mixed landing force posed new challenges for the Allied navies in determining how different types of landing craft would best work alongside each other.[34]

Earlier invasion plans had calculated a desirable force size without any reference to whether that was possible. Morgan had taken a different approach in demanding to be told what force size was available for the invasion and then creating a plan on that basis. The answer he was given was four and a half divisions landing on the beaches, plus two-thirds of an airborne division.

That did not mean that Morgan did not make the case that a larger force would be preferable. The Combined Chiefs of Staff were not unsympathetic to COSSAC's demands but were also considering the needs of other theatres, and the need for other ship types. In considering the requirement for landing craft, the COSSAC staff prepared detailed tables to account for factors such as the expected losses and damage to shipping in the initial assault and on subsequent days, as well as the rate at which damaged craft could be repaired and returned to service. The Quebec Conference confirmed COSSAC's plan.[35]

A few months later, demonstrating his capacity for lateral thinking, Morgan asked the US Army Air Forces about the possibility of landing most of the invasion forces by air, with amphibious forces supporting, rather than the other way round. This concept was studied in detail, but the planners concluded that the most seaborne troops were needed in order to deal with the most powerful German units in France.[36]

One of the major results of Quadrant was that the Allies agreed a definite date for Overlord: 1 May 1944. Yet many other details were still to be confirmed.

Meanwhile, in the USA, landing craft production had stagnated to the point that by spring/summer 1943, some yards that had previously been used for landing craft construction were standing empty. The US Joint Chiefs of Staff appreciated that a major effort was needed and ordered that the US Army, US Navy and Maritime Commission (responsible for US merchant shipping) surrender a third of their allocation of carbon/alloy steel in the period from September 1943–March 1944. The Detroit Diesel Engine Division of General Motors and Pontiac would be expanded to ensure additional engines.

The US War Production Board lamented, however, that the types of landing craft that would be required had not yet been defined. This made the Board's job of co-ordinating the achievement of production targets much harder. WPB recommended a 25 per cent increase in landing craft production at the expense of other construction projects by the US armed forces.[37]

The second US landing craft programme began in late August 1943 – although it would have a slow start – and ran until the following May, when it peaked. It would be natural to assume that, building on the lessons of the first programme, the second would have faced fewer problems and run more smoothly. According to a 1944 study, however, 'the obstacles that the 1943–44 landing craft program had to surmount were immeasurably greater than those that the first program had surmounted'. This time, more than twice the tonnage of craft had to be built in about half the available time, and there was more competition from other projects for manpower, materials and components. Although US production capacity had increased, demand had increased still further.[38]

In September, Donald Nelson, head of the WPB, visited London to speak to British and US planners directly about what equipment was needed for the invasion. US General Charles Bonesteel was Chief of Plans to Lieutenant General Jacob Devers, in command of ETOUSA (US forces building up in the UK). He later recalled:

> The number of landing craft available ... was just unbelievably inadequate ... I got together with an American admiral who was Commander, Amphibious Craft, or whatever he was called ... We spent about 36 straight hours with Mr. Nelson, the American Chief of War Productions, in a hotel suite near Grosvenor Square. We convinced him of the essentiality of bucking up production and diverting as many landing craft as we could from the Pacific to the European theatre ... Well, we succeeded in Normandy and damn, he did unbelievable things. He almost doubled the production of landing craft in something like six months.[39]

Nelson's conclusion was that the production of LSTs and landing craft needed to be brought forward by at least one month. Before leaving the UK, he cabled Charles E. Wilson, WPB's Executive Vice Chairman:

> I am convinced, after detailed discussion with American and British military authorities, that landing craft, particularly LCT and LST types, is the most important single implement of war from the point of view of the European theatre. It is my belief that the requirements have been grossly understated and that we should, without fail, advance the whole landing craft program by at least one month. Furthermore I am convinced that 25,000 or more lives will depend on our doing this.

However, Nelson did not have the level of influence that Bonesteel attributed to him.[40]

Fortunately, his was not the only voice raising this issue. In the same month, Churchill demanded that the British aimed to increase the forces for Operation Overlord in size by at least a quarter and attempt to tackle 'the landing craft bottle-neck'.

The British Minister of Production, Oliver Lyttelton, Churchill's production trouble-shooter, had been given responsibility for 'solving' the landing craft issue. In response to Churchill's message, the Admiralty and

Ministry of Production judged that the shortage of LCTs (as required for a three-division assault) could be resolved through several means. For example, thirty-six LCT(4)s could be found from craft that were currently in use for training (meaning that training with the army would need to stop on 1 February to allow time for refitting); twenty-four would return from the Mediterranean (time would need to be allowed for these to be re-engined, due to the wear and tear of past operations); twenty LCTs would be built before March, and a further thirty during March, so they could be available for follow-up landings if not for the assault.[41]

At this point, it was planned that most landing craft would have British crews. Three divisions of assault troops – two British and one American – would be carried by predominantly British naval forces. Two more naval forces – one British, one American – would carry follow-up formations. A further naval force including eight LSI(H)s and four LSI(S)s would carry commando forces. In addition to the minor landing craft carried by the assault forces, the landings would also be supported by 240 landing barges and over 1,200 minor landing craft.[42]

If a fourth assault division was added – and an extra landing beach – it would need many additional landing craft and ships (exactly how many varied, depending on the exact calculations used). The British Defence Committee (Supply) believed that 'to include in the assault an additional division would be to increase the gap beyond any chance of provision in the time'. This was the situation some seven months before the actual date of D-Day, and with hindsight, we know that not four, but the equivalent of five assault divisions landed on that day.[43]

★ ★ ★

In October 1943, steps began to be taken in the UK and the USA to ensure more landing craft would be available. The Bureau of Ships increased the US landing craft programme by 25 per cent compared to August's plan. Landing craft that could be delivered from the USA to the UK by 1 June 1944 (meaning that they would be available for the later stages of the operation that was still scheduled to start a month before that, even if they were not ready for D-Day) were given the very highest production priority of 'AAA'. This applied to craft which would be built by 1 June 1944, including the following types: LST, LCI(L), LCT(6), LCM(3), LCVP and LVT. Other landing craft construction was given the slightly lower priority of 'AA-1'.

The Materials Coordinating Agency was set up to ensure the flow of materials and components for landing craft. The WPB urged all component manufacturers (and through them, their subcontractors and suppliers) to report any issues that might impact landing craft production, such as shortages of labour and raw materials or conflicts with other orders. WPB resolved half of such conflicts within twenty-four hours. Critically, Admiral King agreed that all landing craft produced in the USA from November 1943 would be allocated to Europe rather than the Pacific.[44]

In the UK, means had to be found to significantly increase landing craft production. This topic was discussed in the British War Cabinet as well as at the highest levels of the Admiralty. The Admiralty planned to build seventy-five additional LCT(3)s in time for D-Day. These craft would be fitted with US-built Sterling Admiral petrol engines, rather than the usual Paxman diesels, as the British were struggling to reach their production target of twenty-five engines per week. They were designated LCT(3*), with the star indicating modifications to the standard Mk3 design, such as the non-standard engines.

It was proposed that the LCT(3*)s be built at commercial shipyards rather than at existing LCT construction yards, which were at full capacity. However, the 70,000 workers at the LCT yards were paid more than those at shipyards. If naval shipyards built LCTs, the workers there would insist on being paid at the higher rate. In a heavily unionised industry, having significantly different rates of pay for two different sets of workers on the same site would be likely to lead to industrial action. The result could be that the pay of all workers at all British Naval shipyards would have to be increased, making shipbuilding much more expensive. The Ministry of Production feared that this disturbance could cause a 10 per cent reduction in ship production. Fortunately, this delicate situation was successfully negotiated.[45]

The seventy-five additional LCT(3*)s were due to be completed by March–April 1944. This batch of LCTs would need 22,000 tons of steel, which would otherwise have gone to larger warships and – of greatest concern to the War Cabinet – merchant shipping. Even though sinkings by German U-boats in the Battle of the Atlantic had improved, merchant shipping still absorbed around 44 per cent of the shipbuilding labour force, with two-thirds working on construction and the other third on repair.[46]

The Allied leaders met again in November 1943: first Churchill and Roosevelt held talks at Cairo before they travelled on to Teheran to meet with Stalin. As ever, both Western countries came with a variety of objectives besides D-Day. No agreement was reached at Cairo, but subsequently at Teheran, Roosevelt and Stalin forced Churchill to focus on Overlord and Anvil (the landings in the south of France).[47]

On the second day of the Cairo Conference, Roosevelt sent a cable to James Byrnes, Director of the Office for War Mobilization, asking if landing craft production could be increased, as the president put it, 'on [the] assumption that landing craft takes precedence over all other munitions of war'. Byrnes organised a hurried conference between the WPB, US Army and US Navy, which resulted in the decision to undertake 'accelerated construction'.

All landing craft being built in the USA with a completion date of June to August 1944 would be finished early, by the end of May. This amounted to an additional eighty-one LSTs, 129 LCI(L)s and 149 LCTs. In addition, all landing craft built before D-Day would be allocated to north-west Europe rather than the Pacific. In December alone, an additional 39,000 tons of steel plate would be transferred from other munitions to landing craft construction. However, the accelerated programme did not mean the UK would get any craft faster than originally planned.[48]

On 9 December, US LST manufacturers were given contracts for the delivery of LSTs by 1 May 1944. LSTs began to be built at coastal yards, not just at the inland yards that had been used up to this date. The US Navy asked the WPB for assistance with achieving the new deadlines. By the end of the year, sixty-seven yards in the USA were building landing craft and amphibians. A US admiral, quoted in the *New York Times*, stated that one out of every four dollars spent by the US Navy on ship construction was now being spent on landing craft. Yet still the US landing craft programme was behind schedule.[49]

These production difficulties were not simply the result of Overlord losing out to the demands of the Pacific theatre. In late 1943, while working out how to produce the necessary craft for Overlord, the Allies were also planning production of amphibious forces for the invasion of Japan, which was forecast to take place in 1945 at the earliest. Lack of diesel engines for British-built LSTs destined for that operation – and which would not be ready in time for Overlord – meant that they would be fitted with frigate engines instead. The consequence was that this vessel type – designated LST(3) – would have a draft 18in deeper than the LST(2), so they could not unload on shallow beaches without using other equipment.[50]

By the first weeks of 1944, with D-Day still planned for May, on any particular slipway or construction site there would almost certainly only be time to build a single major landing craft, allowing a little time for its crew to 'work it up' before D-Day was likely to have arrived. There was little room for change or error. The US Chiefs of Staff suspected that the British could have found ways of increasing their landing craft construction output but did not appreciate quite how much the UK's resources were being strained by the preparations for Operation Overlord.

Incredibly, in the first quarter of 1944, US landing craft production rose to such importance that it was given the same priority level as the Manhattan Project (the codename for the construction of the atomic bomb), synthetic rubber, 100-octane gasoline and certain aircraft (groups 1–4). If it clashed with these other priority projects, landing craft construction could – with the agreement of the Army, Navy, Maritime Commission and Petroleum Administration for War – be given overriding priority. Despite this, for the first months of 1944, US landing craft production was behind schedule compared to the programme set out on 1 December 1943, only catching up at the end of April 1944.[51]

Soon after General Eisenhower and General Sir Bernard Montgomery were appointed in their command roles for D-Day at the end of December 1943, they focused on the question of the size of the landing force for Overlord. Eisenhower asked both his own Chief of Staff Lieutenant General Walter Bedell Smith and Montgomery to consider the issue. Eisenhower and Bedell Smith had, in fact, seen the COSSAC plan at the end of October, and their immediate reaction was that a larger, five-division assault force was essential. Bedell Smith later recalled that when he first heard the size of the assault force, 'I nearly fell out of my seat. After all, we had more than that for our landings [in the Mediterranean].'[52]

In the first days of January 1944, the COSSAC planners briefed Montgomery and emphasised their preference for at least one more assault division than they had been allocated and extending the frontage of the landings to the west and east to include Utah and Sword beaches. Montgomery asked about additional landings on the west side of the Cherbourg Peninsula or in Brittany, but these were recognised as impractical. Thus, when Montgomery presented an expanded version of the COSSAC plan, few among the planners and commanders would have disagreed with him. It was agreed that COSSAC's three assault divisions and one follow-up division – which Monty described as 'quite theoretical and un-practical ... not in any way a sound operation of war' – would be expanded to five and two respectively, with the two follow-up divisions preferably landing on the second tide of D-Day. This would create a broader front, 50 rather than 25 miles across, make German counterattacks more complicated, and enable the Allies to seize ground more quickly.[53]

On 23 January 1944, Eisenhower reported to the Combined Chiefs of Staff that the assault must be strengthened and given a wider frontage. He advised that this expansion meant an additional requirement of forty-seven LSTs, 216 LCTs and one HQ ship, plus extra landing ships or attack transports. He proposed a one-month delay to the date of Overlord so that additional landing craft could be acquired or constructed. He also asked for more transport aircraft, so that the airborne landings could be increased from two-thirds of a division to three.[54]

Discussions continued over several months on whether Anvil should be cancelled. Montgomery favoured cancelling the operation to free up landing craft for Overlord. Allied troops remaining longer in Italy would aid Overlord by continued pressure on the Germans there. Eisenhower was conscious that Anvil could allow the Allies to make use of Mediterranean-based troops that could not be deployed against the enemy in the confined battlefields of Italy. The decision also had a diplomatic dimension: it was vital that the Free French divisions in north Africa be used in the liberation of their own country, and transporting them to the UK to take part in Overlord was not practical. The decision on Anvil was delayed until 20 March 1944.[55]

As land forces commander, Montgomery was concerned with the specifics of available landing craft. As he set out to Eisenhower in a letter on 23 February 1944, 'It is probably impossible to make use of any additional craft on the first and second tides [meaning on D-Day] owing to beach and loading limitations.' The main shortage was in LSTs and LCI(L)s, which could land forces on the third, fourth and fifth tides (D+1 and the morning of D+2), in the period before the expected arrival of any craft that had returned to the UK to collect a second load. If more craft were not available in this period, the same troops would have to be landed from personnel and motor transport ships. As well as the unloading process being much slower, personnel and vehicles would have to be 'married up' after landing. This would greatly limit the Allies' ability to build up forces in Normandy and maintain the offensive momentum created on D-Day.[56]

In a briefing to his army commanders (Generals Dempsey, Bradley and Patton) on 11 February, later famous for his emphasis on simplicity, Montgomery emphasised the need to land all the fighting troops of the five assault divisions on D-Day, while taking 'the bare essentials in vehicles only'. He emphasised the need for fire support, identifying LCGs, LCT(R)s, LCT(SP)s and LCFs. He was not in favour of fire support from LCA(HR)s and from Centaur tanks on board LCT(A)s, judging that it was more important that they could carry additional troops: an argument he would lose.[57]

As this increase in the size of the landing force is a well-known part of the story of D-Day, it is perhaps easy to forget how relatively last minute these demands were and how significant an increase in naval forces this represented. For the ground forces, the change in plan simply meant that many units would leave the UK a few days earlier than under the previous plans. However Allied naval forces needed the capacity to lift a significantly larger force of troops, as well as needing to find the other supporting vessels which included fire support landing craft, as well as the landing craft and landing barges of the ferry service. The changes could only be achieved through facilities that already existed and craft that were already under construction. It was also far from straightforward to muster the additional warships and merchant shipping.[58]

It further complicated matters that the US Joint Chiefs of Staff were working from different assumptions to the staffs of the Allied Naval and Supreme Commanders. The former worked on the basis of the maximum capacity of craft, whereas the latter used a figure that they judged to be more realistic for campaign conditions. This led to disagreement on whether there would be sufficient landing craft. The planners in London believed that one further LSI(H), forty-two more LSTs and fifty-one more LCI(L)s were required in order to carry the remaining 20,000 personnel and 2,200 vehicles. In February, two planners from Washington visited the UK to discuss this.[59]

The larger naval forces were only achieved through a range of measures. The number of vehicles landed per division on D-Day would have to be reduced from 3,000 to 1,450. This reduced the 21st Army Group's requirements by seven LSTs and thirty LCI(L)s. After a month of discussions, on 20 March 1944, Eisenhower recommended that Operation Anvil (the landings in the south of France) be postponed until August 1944 rather than happening simultaneously with Overlord, which made available an additional twenty LSTs and twenty LCI(L)s for the latter. The naval planners also agreed to aim for higher serviceability rates for US landing ships and craft, which were achieved. Slightly more vehicles were carried on each LST (referred to as 'overloading').[60]

Overlord was postponed by nearly a month, from 5 May to 31 May 1944, to gain the benefit of an extra month's production of landing craft. This also allowed more time for shipping, especially LSTs, to reach the UK from the Mediterranean. This was an issue that had been discussed extensively, all the way up to the British War Cabinet. LSTs were still particularly useful in Italy, and as late as March 1944, the Anzio bridge-head was still dependent on supply by sea, in which LSTs played an essential role. Time had to be allowed for these vessels to be serviced before Overlord.[61]

Three LSTs allocated to Force B – LST(2)s 197, 326 and 381 – in fact arrived from the Mediterranean too late to cross with Force B for D-Day and took their assigned loads to France at a later date.[62]

The expansion in assault forces meant that significantly more US Navy vessels were required, drawn partly from ships originally designated for Operation Anvil (later renamed Dragoon). However, when the decision was taken on 20 March 1944 to postpone Anvil, these US naval assault forces only had seventy days to make the journey from the Mediterranean to the UK, carry out maintenance and refitting (which could be substantial), and take part in training.[63]

The landing forces that could be put ashore in the first lift of Operation Neptune now totalled nearly 177,000 personnel, over 20,000 vehicles. Not all would necessarily be ashore by the end of D-Day.[64]

Before D-Day (and in fact, as early as mid-1943), the planners were already looking ahead to the next major amphibious operation, against the Japanese mainland. Exactly the same issues around availability of landing craft arose as for Operation Overlord: production of certain types fell behind schedule, refitting craft for Overlord delayed the production of LST(3)s and LCT(8)s for use against Japan and there were delays moving craft to the region from other theatres.[65]

'Getting to Europe and fighting' – to adapt Eisenhower's 1942 expression – was never going to be easy. Most of the Allies' plans for landing in north-west Europe before mid-1944 were almost certainly never achievable due to shortages of landing craft and landing ships, which, in turn, were due to many other factors described above. It seems debatable whether the Allies could have taken any other course of action, given the resources demanded by other theatres, such as construction of merchant shipping and escort warships for the Battle of the Atlantic, and because of the need to be seen to be taking offensive action somewhere in Europe in late 1942 and 1943 – which, in turn, acted against the build-up of a sufficient number of craft.

The Admiralty concluded that the programme of landing craft construction for Operation Overlord had been completed on time.[66]

3

Forging the Weapon: Landing Craft Crews, Bases and Training

To many of the officers, Combined Operations does not represent the
Navy of their imagination.[1]

Report on Canadian Combined Operations Training in the United
Kingdom, 1942.

The vast story of the recruitment and training of the Allied landing craft
crews and the establishment of the shore bases in the UK that supported
them and enabled them to launch Operation Neptune can only be summarised here. Naturally, each landing craft crew was composed of individuals
with varied backgrounds and personalities. The crew of LCT(5) 2235,
for example, included a Royal Navy regular who had previously served
on a cruiser; a Canadian who had made substantial winnings with trick
handgun shots at the Calgary Stampede; and a man from southern Ireland
who had been wounded while serving in the International Brigade during
the Spanish Civil War.[2]

Some crewmen were already seasoned veterans of amphibious operations or had prior service on other types of ships. Reg Deighton, an able
seaman on LCT(A) 2345, recalled that the average age of his crew was
28½. He was the youngest at 18½. He had a 45-year-old skipper and five
men on board were aged 30 or older. In contrast, when LCT(3*) 7086
was commissioned, its commanding officer Sub Lieutenant Raymond
Shone RNVR was the oldest crew member at 22 years, 11 months.
He was also the one with the longest service: twenty-three months,
during which time he had been an ordinary seaman on a destroyer

in the Russian convoys and a first lieutenant on another LCT for three months.[3]

In the early days of Combined Operations, the skippers and skipper lieutenants of the RNR provided a backbone of officers, serving, for example, as instructors and as deck officers on LSIs. More experience was contributed by 'T124X men' – former Merchant Navy personnel, who came under Royal Navy discipline and wore the service's uniform, but kept their Merchant Navy pay (these included engineer officers and ratings on LSIs).[4]

Some of the lower ranks could also have considerable experience. In 1944, Alan Higgins was serving on LCI(L) 111. He had joined the Royal Navy in 1939 as a boy telegraphist. In mid-1942, he was serving on the light cruiser HMS *Edinburgh* when it was sunk while escorting a convoy returning from the USSR. He spent four months in the Soviet Union until he could return home. On D-Day, Robert Thompson was a signaller on board LCH 187. He had three and a half years' experience, having joined the Royal Navy aged 16. He had served on the cruiser HMS *Jamaica* on convoys to Russia, saw action against Vichy French destroyers in Operation Torch in November 1942, and the following month participated in the Battle of the Barents Sea off the coast of Norway against the German heavy cruisers *Admiral Hipper* and *Lützow*.[5]

Some were volunteers, some were conscripts. Paul Motte Harrison, later an LCT officer, volunteered for the Royal Navy as he feared he might be drafted into the army as 'cannon fodder' for the Second Front. Buck Taylor, who later served on LCF 24, was a 16-year-old office boy when, on the spur of the moment, he went into a recruiting office while on a trip into Bristol. He discovered that he was too young for the Royal Navy but could join the Royal Marines at age 17. He had never heard of the Royal Marines but joined with his parents' permission. In August 1942, one month past his 17th birthday, he was called up.[6]

For British, American or Canadian sailors, training usually involved attending several training establishments in turn. The opening and closing of bases over time meant that various paths were possible. Officers and other ranks were trained separately. Most British landing craft crews did their training under the auspices of Combined Operations Command, which originated in mid-1940 with Prime Minister Winston Churchill's desire to begin preparations for returning to continental Europe.

For Royal Navy officers, a typical path began with initial training at the shore bases of HMS *King Alfred* or HMS *Lochailort*. The former trained future sub lieutenants and midshipmen for the whole Royal Navy. The latter was specifically for men who were destined for Combined Operations and was preceded by another six-week class in Scotland in preparation. Those who attended the *Lochailort* course would, after spending time at sea, get a watchkeeping certificate marked 'in Combined Operations ships and craft only'. Some on that course had failed the *King Alfred* course; were men considered more suitable for Combined Operations because their strengths were seen as more physical than intellectual; and 'Y-Scheme' entrants from schools aged 17 to 18, who could get a commission without sea time.[7]

At *Lochailort*, there was less 'flannel' (formal discipline) than at *King Alfred*, perhaps as befitted the environment that landing craft officers typically worked in, but there was a greater emphasis on physical training, fighting and 'guts' to toughen up the men. Paul Lund, who did not pass the *King Alfred* course but did pass the *Lochailort* training, felt that while both courses were tough, at *Lochailort*, at least the instructors seemed to be trying to ensure the cadets passed, while at *King Alfred* they appeared to be aiming to fail them.[8]

Raymond Oram, later an officer on LCI(L)s and LCTs, went through a five-month officer training course at *Lochailort* covering topics such as navigation and pilotage, ship handling, pay and allowance, ship routine, morse and flag signalling, knowledge of small arms and demolitions and hand-to-hand combat. On arrival, he recalled:

> The training officer, a short fierce-looking officer, addressed the new entry informing us that training, both physical and mental, would be hard, top results were insisted upon and every Saturday those who were unable to keep up with the set standards, for any reason, would be weeded out and sent back to base. No truer words were ever spoken.

The trainees were only allowed to cross a nearby river by bridge on Sundays, whereas on other days they had to swim or ford the river. A boxing evening once a month was used to assess aggression. He next went on to HMS *Dundonald* at Troon to practise on LCTs.[9]

Many potential and newly trained officers (though by no means all) were ambitious to rise through the ranks. Some believed that Combined Operations offered the best prospects of an early command. This was not always the case. Many who trained at HMS *Lochailort* became boat officers on minor landing craft in a flotilla attached to a landing ship. However, when many of those craft were taken over by Royal Marines as a measure to alleviate the shortage of Royal Navy personnel, those Royal Navy officers affected were then trained to serve as first lieutenants on major landing craft instead. As a result, they sometimes found themselves serving under their contemporaries or even officers who had been commissioned after them.[10]

Royal Navy ratings also trained at a sequence of camps. Typically, this would begin at HMS *Northney* for initial training, followed by further training according to the individual rating's specialism. During the training, ratings would be formed into crews. After completing their training, crewmen often went to a suspense base where Combined Operations personnel were held until it was time for their first posting: there might be a delay due to shortages of landing craft or of officers.

Many did some of their training at HMS *Quebec* at Inveraray in Scotland, which was also the location of the Combined Training Centre, established for combined army–navy training. Some men were starting with little or no experience. Eric Holderness, later in the crew of LCT(4) 568, did a training course on diesel engines at HMS *Shrapnel*, Isleworth, 'Up to that time I had never seen under a bonnet of a car and had no idea as to what did what!'

HMS *Manatee* and HMS *Medina* were both used for training ratings who in civilian life had worked on Thames barges. They did a four-week course that was mainly disciplinary training, since they already had boat-handling skills, and then carried out two weeks of training on LBVs.[11]

It was not just the landing craft crews who were trained. Members of the Hard Parties (who would operate the embarkation 'hards', where landing craft would load for D-Day and subsequent crossings) were given special training at the Hard Party Training School, Stokes Bay (HMS *Porcupine II*) to ensure the most efficient loading process.[12]

On the other side of the Atlantic, in March 1942 the Amphibious Force, US Atlantic Fleet had been created: a recognition that the growing numbers of landing craft and associated personnel needed their own command. In the summer of 1942, ahead of Operation Torch (the landings in north Africa in November 1942), amphibious training bases were set up in the USA at Solomons, Maryland and Little Creek, Virginia. However, that operation demonstrated that US amphibious training needed to improve. From before the USA's entry to the war, the US Army and US Navy both had responsibility for amphibious warfare training and operations. This led to duplication of effort, until in early 1943 the navy finally agreed to carry out amphibious warfare training in the USA to meet army requirements.[13]

Many US Navy officers were 'ninety-day wonders', having done a mere thirteen-week training course before joining their craft. In theory, there would be the chance to do more training once crews reached the UK, while waiting for D-Day. Some of the US gunfire support craft, which were supplied to the US Navy by the British, did not arrive until shortly before the operation. Multiple crews had to train on those craft that were available, although work such as fixing defects could eat into training time. In an extreme case, this meant that on some of the US Navy's LCT(A)s and LCT(HE)s, 'the captains of many of these craft beached their ships for the first time on the Normandy coast of France'.[14]

Once a major landing craft had been commissioned, there were various stages before it was ready for operational use: trials to confirm all was operating as expected; degaussing to reduce the craft's magnetic field as protection against sea mines; then several weeks of 'shake-down training'. This was also an opportunity for the crew to get to know each other.

Alan Villiers commanded a group of LCI(L)s that Royal Navy personnel collected from Norfolk, Virginia, USA, and brought back across the Atlantic. Before making such a long journey, the mostly inexperienced crews familiarised themselves with their craft in the crowded waterways of New York Harbour. This sometimes led to accidents:

> ... most of them had made trial runs, to the great consternation of the Staten Island ferries and all the pilots in New York Harbour, for the steel shoulders where the ramps ran were effective battering rams. The little ships were already notorious for wild and unpredictable manoeuvres in the paths of most vessels which came near them ... they split one another open like sardine cans ... a gang of welders – mostly girls – was kept busy patching them up again where they'd knocked one another about.[15]

Naturally, not all crews received a brand-new craft. Able Seaman Edward Zealley recalled how the Royal Canadian Navy took over LCI(L)s from the Royal Navy at the end of February 1944. The craft had seen previous service in the Mediterranean and although they had been refitted, they were still short of spares. The Royal Navy had cannibalised parts from some of these craft for vessels operated by their own crews.[16]

Given the small size of most landing craft crews – around twelve on most LCTs, for example – the men on board tended to work closely together, with fewer formalities than on larger warships. In the Royal Navy, most new officers joining major landing craft went to LCTs. A lucky few joined an LCI(S), 'considered by many to be the cream of all the landing vessels' due to their faster speed and better lines. Certainly, in British and Canadian forces, most major landing craft had at least two officers (more on an LCI(L), for example).

In the Royal Navy, the commanding officer (CO) or 'skipper' was in charge, and typically had the rank of sub lieutenant, but could also be a lieutenant, bosun, skipper RNR or midshipman. The second in command was the first lieutenant (a position, not a rank), who might be a sub lieutenant or midshipman.

The skipper was naturally in overall command of his craft, with responsibility for its safety and navigation. The first lieutenant had the role of passing the CO's orders to the crew, allocating crew duties and ensuring the neatness of the craft. Popular orders were often credited to the CO, unpopular ones to the first lieutenant, 'who, as in most ships, was [known as] "the bastard"'. The first lieutenant was also traditionally known as 'Jimmy the One', or behind his back as 'F★★★★★g Jimmy'. Many first lieutenants would in time progress to command their own landing craft.[17]

In the US Navy, the commanding officer was instead known as the 'officer in charge', because LCTs were commissioned not as a single ship but as a flotilla and the flotilla commander was known as the commanding officer. US LCTs often had only a single officer on board. If there was a second in command, he was titled the 'relief officer'.[18]

A sensible officer knew how to draw on the experience of the older but more junior crew members. D.G. Woodford, coxswain of LCT(3★) 7070, served under a first lieutenant who was:

> … tall, fresh faced, well-spoken. He had been to University, joined the Navy and came straight from Dartmouth to take up his commission in LCT 7070. He was keen as mustard and knew his King's Regulations and Admiralty Instructions inside-out and backwards but readily admitted that his training had been short on practical seamanship. When he was stuck he would come and ask and gratefully accept a cox'n's practical demonstration.[19]

Not every landing craft crew was a happy family, however. Stan McGowan, wireman on LCT(5) 2053, felt that his skipper was 'rather class conscious and there was no rapport'. He also turned down McGowan's request to apply for a leading wireman's course. He viewed the first lieutenant as 'a midshipman still in nappies and wet behind the ears'.

On LCI(L) 415, the officer in charge, Lieutenant (j.g.) John Forby Schereschewsky, had been a headmaster in peacetime and was in the habit of praising his crew with the words, 'Good job, sonny!' Representatives of the crew pointed out to him that they found this condescending, and he altered his turn of phrase, which the crew greatly appreciated.[20]

There was some variation in the ranks held by the rest of the crew. On British craft, the motor mechanic (in charge of the engine room) and the coxswain were usually more senior ratings. There was some variation in the exact crew roles, probably simply according to the skipper's preferences. On some LCTs, for example, one seaman was designated the 'second coxswain', whereas on others there was no such role.[21]

As was traditional in the British armed forces, many crewmen addressed each other by nicknames. As D.G. Woodford, on LCT 7070, later recalled:

I do not recall the other ratings' names – probably because names were unimportant on board and in the NAAFI or the pub. We always addressed the officers as 'Sir' and everyone else was where they came from or what they did. Paddy came from Ireland and Sparks looked after the electrics.

The signaller was often known as 'bunts' after 'bunting tosser', referring to his use of signal flags. The wireman (electrician) was 'wires', the stokers were 'stokes', the motor mechanic was 'mack' (short for 'motor mack', or motor mechanic), the coxswain was 'cox'.[22]

One of the seamen was appointed cook, but generally this was not a reflection of any particular skills or training. As Reg Dean of LCI(L) 177 put it, they would continue as the cook 'if the water didn't burn'.

Despite the less formal arrangements on landing craft, the officers were clearly separated from the rest of the crew in certain ways, such as having slightly better accommodation on board. While at sea, the two officers would typically alternate four-hour watches, while the other crew were on duty for four hours then had eight hours off. However, 'off watch' time did not translate to hours of leisure, as duties such as cleaning and cooking had to be done in this time.[23]

Crewmen found themselves carrying out varied tasks. As Bill Havill of LCT(3) 323 observed:

Whereas on board a 'big' ship all I would have done would have been the telegraphy work. But on these craft with small crews, it was expected that you mucked in wherever possible. So I learnt how to man the guns, loading the magazines and firing, lookout, to take a turn … on the wheel steering by compass, reading and sending signals by the flashing light.

The signaller was often stationed on the bridge, so he was to hand for sending or receiving signals. In this role, E.J. Loseby of LCT(4) 821 found that he would often hear about the craft's planned movements and the rest of the crew would regularly quiz him about what he had heard.[24]

As Harry Eddy of LCT(4) 944 describes, the duties of a wireman were varied:

> … maintaining all the electrical installations which included firing mechanisms on fast aerial mines and parachute and cable for aerial defence … also in charge of an anti-dive bombing barrage balloon and responsible for the de-gaussing gear for protection against magnetic mines. When at sea he was also expected to take his turn as Able Seaman on deck duties including helmsman and gunner.

In addition, he was the regular 'buoy jumper':

> … an unenviable job which was necessary each time the craft was moored to an anchoring buoy … it meant that the Seaman who carried out the operation had to stand on the cat walk outside the guardrail with a light heaving line, and on approach had to jump from the ship to the buoy, then pull across a heavy steel hawser and attach it with a heavy duty D shackle. Not too bad in calm conditions but when the sea was rough or the tide was flowing it was extremely hazardous as the ship could, and did, overrun the buoy on occasions and I have seen the buoy disappear under the ship and come up on the other side, alright if you know when to jump or not to jump.[25]

Smaller craft naturally had fewer crew. An LCVP had a three-man crew: coxswain, engineer and deckhand. Norman Moss's LCA had four crew: a coxswain, a stoker and two deck hands. 'We all had to work as a team, it was important to communicate with each other at all times, all our lives depended on it.' Given its additional role of firing mortars accurately against the enemy beach defences, an LCA(HR) had on board an officer in addition to the other crew carried by a standard LCA.[26]

For the Royal Navy, where to find more personnel to crew landing craft was a constant struggle, given the requirement to regularly increase the size of the Royal Navy's landing craft forces. Staff to support the operations of those craft were equally important: personnel numbering roughly an additional 25 per cent on top of the number of the crews. To make matters worse, trained personnel were regularly removed for operations elsewhere, such as in the Mediterranean. Some help came from the Royal Marines, who provided 1,200 officers and men for landing craft: many would be used for manning guns on support craft.[27]

In October 1941, the Royal Navy asked for Canadian help in manning landing craft. Over the remaining years of the war, a total of about 830 officers and ratings of the Royal Canadian Navy Volunteer Reserve served in Combined Operations, though not all were at Normandy. They saw operational service in 1942–43, including in the August 1942 Dieppe Raid, Operation Torch and Operation Husky (the invasion of Sicily in July 1943) as well as in smaller raids. The Canadian Government preferred that they would serve in exclusively Canadian flotillas, which was not always possible.

By the time of D-Day, Canadian flotillas comprised 858 men serving in three LCI(L) flotillas totalling thirty craft, and 144 men in the two LCA flotillas (total sixteen craft) attached to HMCS *Prince David* and HMCS *Prince Henry*. The Canadians were sourced both from personnel already serving in Combined Operations and from men who were specially recruited for the role, some from the Fishermen's Reserve. Initially, the Admiralty asked that the Canadians operate flotillas of LCTs, but with an eye to the future, the Royal Canadian Navy preferred LCI(L)s because these craft were more suitable for Canadian waters. In fact, the Royal Navy found Canadian engine room ratings very useful in LCI(L)s as they were more familiar with the American engines and equipment of these craft than British personnel.[28]

Still more personnel were needed for Combined Operations: the matter was discussed by the British Chiefs of Staff and the War Cabinet. There was even a proposal that the British Army would have to provide the number of troops equivalent to one or more divisions for use as additional landing craft crews. An alternative solution was found in June 1943.

Prior to this date, Royal Marines had manned the guns of support craft, but in future they would also operate some minor landing craft. This freed up trained minor landing craft crews and flotilla staff to be transferred to major landing craft instead. This was a process that took place over a long period of time and continued into 1944. For the forces involved in D-Day, no further transfers took place in the final three months before the operation, to avoid last-minute disturbances, which, in fact, created a surplus of unallocated Royal Marine landing crews before D-Day.[29]

Operation Neptune required not just landing craft and their crews but a series of shore bases in the UK and support staff to operate them. Just like the craft and the crews, it took time to develop these bases, which were in addition to the training bases referred to above.

Planning for setting up bases on the south coast of England began in late 1941, as surveys were carried out to determine the capacity of harbours and creeks as bases for craft and associated accommodation ashore and maintenance facilities. Lord Louis Mountbatten's appointment that October as Chief Adviser on Combined Operations – from April 1942, he was promoted to Vice Admiral and Chief of Combined Operations – provided increased focus. While Combined Operations Command grew the number of personnel available, the Combined Operations section of the Naval Staff focused on the logistics build-up in the south of England, which was carried out by local Royal Navy Commanders-in-Chief.[30]

Bases known as 'assault stations' were those that would be used to launch an amphibious operation. When these facilities were beginning to be developed along the south coast of England, Normandy had not yet been selected as the landing site for D-Day. In Portsmouth Command, HMS *Cricket* at Bursledon and HMS *Turtle* at Poole were built for this purpose. Bases for landing craft maintenance and the provision of supplies to their crews were essential to keep as many craft serviceable as possible at any time. In each command in the south of England, one main maintenance base was set up, with other maintenance facilities at the suspense and assault stations. Slips or grids were also built at shipyards and boatyards for use in repairing craft, using plant from the yard but with the work done by personnel of the Royal Navy (or in the south-west, the US Navy). Each command had one central base for stores and food, plus subsidiary depots, as well as fuel storage locations.[31]

Embarkation hards would also be vital for troops and especially vehicles to load onto landing craft. As a starting point, Portsmouth Command was ordered to build around thirty hards between Portland and Dungeness by 1 July 1942. As construction began, the Royal Navy and British Army debated where the responsibility for construction lay. In the end, the War Office agreed to take responsibility for roads linking to the public highway, while the Admiralty would build the hards themselves.

The specification for the hards was that they could support a 60-ton tank, have a minimum width of 20ft, and be at a slope of between 1 in 10 and 1 in 30. On land, there needed to be hardstanding for vehicle parking and turning, concrete slabs on the beach to prevent it from being churned up by vehicles, three dolphins (mooring structures not connected to the shore) in the water and two mooring bollards on shore. Each hard also needed stores of fuel and water for the landing craft and accommodation for reserve crews. Work on embarkation hards continued through to the time of D-Day.[32]

Some of the early landing craft base facilities were used in August 1942 by the naval forces taking part in the ill-fated Dieppe Raid. This demonstrated the need for a commander and staff who could deal with all issues unique to landing craft, and that October, the post of Commodore Landing Craft Bases, was created in Portsmouth Command. The post holder oversaw both landing craft bases and hards in the command, and until summer 1943 was also the representative of the Chief of Combined Operations in the command.

Minor landing craft could not simply be held in reserve awaiting forthcoming operations, so were continuously used for training. This required extensive facilities for repairing and maintaining the vessels, and some bases were specified as landing craft maintenance bases, examples being HMS *Tormentor*, HMS *Northney I* and HMS *Squid*.[33]

Under the earlier version of the Operation Overlord plan, involving three assault divisions, one naval assault force (carrying one assault division) would be based in Portsmouth Command, plus 60 per cent of the Build-Up craft, which would arrive after the assault. The other two naval forces – Force S, from the area east of Southampton, and Force O, from Portland – would also be concentrated in the command before the operation.

This all changed when the plan was modified in early 1944 to a five-division assault. Forces G and J would train in Portsmouth Command and they would be joined by Force S for the final assembly before D-Day. Force O and its Build-Up Flotillas would have their final assembly in the Portland and Poole area.[34]

Base facilities in Portsmouth Command consequently had to be revised, with more berths alongside being created in Southampton, as well as more moorings (trots) in Southampton Water and Portland. Additional accommodation was needed, including for 2,000 personnel in Southampton. Accommodation for the Build-Up Flotillas was rearranged so those serving the Anglo-Canadian beaches were in the eastern area. More maintenance facilities were added.

At first, it was planned that Forces G and S would arrive in Portsmouth Command one month before D-Day and be accommodated afloat. Force S had to be assembled and trained at Rosyth in Scotland, as there was insufficient space to do so on the south coast. However, in March 1944 it was announced that both those forces would arrive in April and would need accommodation ashore instead. At the last minute, places needed to be found for headquarters for two force commanders and six assault group commanders, as well as accommodation for 10,000 additional personnel. By D-Day, in Portsmouth Command, there were berths for 3,000 landing craft, including 2,300 moorings; thirteen maintenance bases with slipping facilities for 110 craft; accommodation for 29,000 Royal Navy and WRNS personnel; and 172,000 square feet of storage space. WRNS personnel included 413 Wrens working in wireless and telephone communications at landing craft bases.[35]

What the records of Combined Operations describe as the first 'full scale combined exercise' took place in September 1941: Exercise Leapfrog. This involved eighty-six landing craft, including three LSIs (at this stage known as IASs, or Infantry Assault Ships) and two LCTs. Many more large-scale training exercises were to follow.

The Naval Commander Eastern Task Force later judged that this training had more than proved its value off the coast of Normandy. Forces J, S and G had been formed eighteen, seven and two and a half months respectively before D-Day. He judged that Force J's long period of training without carrying out an operation had a detrimental effect, although admittedly in the meantime, it had also taken part in the Dieppe and Sicily landings.[36]

Force S trained for five months, which seemed to be enough time. This force began training with British 3rd Infantry Division in December 1943, and by the following March had carried out five major exercises. However, its experiences were not without problems, such as shortcomings in training facilities. For example, it was only in late March 1944 that assault and fire support could be practised on the same beach. Only formed in March 1944, Force G did not have enough time for training and consequently, the focus had to be on the initial landings not the build-up. Still, Force G did four brigade-size exercises in March–April 1944.[37]

The US forces began training for amphibious operations in January 1944. American exercises such as the Duck series involved a few dozen LSTs and major landing craft, which put troops ashore. Exercise Duck 1 highlighted flaws in basic training and organisation of some of the troops. This was perhaps understandable, as US 4th Infantry Division had still been in training in the USA when Utah Beach – where that unit would come ashore on D-Day – was added to the D-Day plan. Some of the division's troops had to complete their weapons training in England.

Exercise Fox even featured six APAs (landing ships). Light relief was provided – for staff officers at least – in the form of Exercise Trousers in March 1944, in which the Eastern Task Force and part of the Western

Task Force participated. This prompted a series of code names: 'Trousers Down' and 'Trousers Up' were signals to start or stop loading troops, and so on.

The US 4th Infantry Division took part in Exercise Muskrat in late March 1944, in which soldiers loaded onto transport ships in Scotland and then made an assault landing in Devon: the journey by sea was a useful rehearsal. The British 3rd Infantry Division undertook similar rehearsals from Scotland.

By early April, all the assault forces had completed their individual training and it was time for major exercises. These included Exercise Tiger in April 1944, which was infamously intercepted by German E-boats with considerable loss of life among US personnel. Exercise Fabius, in early May, consisted of six separate exercises for Forces S, J, G, O, B and L respectively.[38]

Around the same time, individual landing craft flotillas were also training, either alone or with the army. This included practice in hoisting and lowering from LSIs in rough weather. Coping with poor weather was not simply a matter of developing toughness. Norman Moss, an LCA crewman in 537 Assault Flotilla, recounted:

> One of our first jobs was to land our troops as safely and comfortably as possible, it has to be considered it's of no use to land a platoon so badly bruised and sea sick on the beach ... Our crew's job was to make this happen as best we could, slowing down the engines in bad weather if necessary to avoid everyone being thrown around like rag dolls.[39]

In contrast, the flotilla officers of three Royal-Marine-manned LCVP flotillas (805, 808 and 809 Build-Up Flotillas) all reported after D-Day that their crews had insufficient experience in open or rough seas. In one flotilla, 70 per cent of crewmen were seasick during the crossing to Normandy.[40]

Memoranda for Force L (the British follow-up force) indicate the range of topics that were rehearsed. These included rapid loading at hards; station-keeping and manoeuvring in large groups of craft; defence against surface or air attack; proceeding down a narrow, swept channel in formation, with a strong cross tide; and marking time in the waiting position. Areas in the East Anglia region, where Force L was based before D-Day, were identified for training use. These included a dan-buoyed channel that could be laid on request off Harwich or Lowestoft and Great Yarmouth for practice in making passage with a cross tide between two lines of dan buoys, as would be done in the approach to the Normandy beaches.[41]

The process of recruiting, training and forming the landing craft forces that would be tested in action on D-Day was not always perfect, but generally proved its worth on D-Day. Royal Marine Roy Nelson served in an LCVP flotilla:

> ... no amount of training (and we had plenty) can prepare you for actual warfare – I was 18 years of age and in charge of a landing craft and crew which was a lot of weight on young shoulders. In fact, I would think that the majority of landing craft crews were aged 18 to 20 years and H.O.s [hostilities only] – and we certainly found the hostilities we had joined for.[42]

4

The Plan

... the voracious demands of the Army were not always in its own interests ...[1]

Admiral Sir Bertram Ramsay, Allied Naval Commander-in-Chief

Although Operation Neptune was probably the most extensively planned military operation of all time, many details were adjusted or finalised at a relatively late stage. Aspects of what became the multifaceted Operation Neptune plan had been under discussion for years by a range of headquarters, staffs and committees too numerous to list here. Naturally, much of that planning related to landing craft.

Admiral Sir Bertram Ramsay had first been appointed as the Naval Commander-in-Chief for a possible invasion force in early 1942. He left to command the amphibious landings in north Africa and Sicily, before returning to the UK in mid-1943 to resume the same role ahead of D-Day. Combined Operations Command was also deeply involved in the early planning, most notably under the leadership of Vice Admiral Lord Louis Mountbatten, and particularly concentrated on manpower, training, equipment and techniques. So, too, were the Combined Operations section of the Naval Staff at the Admiralty and the local Commanders-in-Chief for the UK's naval commands (such as Portsmouth Command), whose concerns included the logistics build-up in the south of England that would support the operation.

In March 1943, Lieutenant General Frederick Morgan was appointed as Chief of Staff to the Supreme Allied Commander, or COSSAC, leading a staff that would create a workable plan. The British Army, US Army and US Navy were involved to varying degrees, depending on other pre-occupations at the time. The Rattle Conference in late June 1943, under the chairmanship of Mountbatten, brought together Allied planners to discuss questions such as whether the assault should be made in daylight or darkness, methods of obstacle clearance, naval and air support, and the use of airborne troops alongside the seaborne landings. Delegates also inspected landing craft and ships.[2]

The early months of 1944 were a fraught time for Allied planners. All naval planning had to proceed in triplicate until it was confirmed whether there would be a three-, four- or five-division assault. A Wren staff officer at COSSAC described this period:

> Any major adjustment made by any one of the authorities concerned sent repercussions shivering down through the others which were felt down to the smallest planned detail. Oh! the changes, adjustment and endless detail. The hours of work put in on plans that had to be scrapped soon after owing to a change of policy made by someone else ... Each day brought the invasion date nearer and still there was no decision. We were in a pitch-black tunnel of nightmare.[3]

The Initial Joint Plan for a five-beach assault was issued by the Allied commanders on 1 February 1944. This provided a starting point for individual services to finalise their specific plans, and included details such as the fact that H-Hour would be around three hours before high water. The document outlined the allocation of landing craft types to the seven naval forces (including the two follow-up forces). For example, it stipulated that there would be 110 LCTs for each of the five beaches, around thirty carrying DD and engineer tanks, leaving another eighty to land vehicles between H+90 and H+360.[4]

Admiral Ramsay issued the 241-page Naval Plan on 28 February, enabling subordinate commanders to start firming up their plans. On 10 April, Ramsay's staff issued the operation orders for Operation Neptune. In twenty sections and at around 600 pages in length, they included orders for the assembly of naval forces in UK ports, the embarkation of troops, crossing the English Channel and actions leading up to landing. These orders also covered all the other essential components of the operation, such as minesweeping, bombardment forces, air support, the Mulberry Harbours and the build-up period after D-Day. Next, the Western and Eastern Task Force commanders finalised and issued their orders, followed in the final week or two of May by the orders for the seven naval forces.

Many US Navy commanders complained after the operation that they preferred the US custom of allowing subordinates the freedom to decide how they would achieve the objectives that they had been set over the British method of superior commanders issuing more rigid orders. However, a high level of co-ordination was arguably essential for such a complex operation. In Admiral Ramsay's words, 'The timing of the approach of the Assault Waves, and the deployment from the "cruising" to the "assaulting" formations, required a degree of efficiency and seamanship never attempted hitherto with landing craft.'

Lieutenant Commander William Leide USNR, commander of LCT Flotillas 12 and 26 at Omaha Beach, felt that his LCT officers did not have time to read all the printed orders. He argued that flotilla and group commanders should condense orders for their subordinates.[5]

The capabilities and limitations of landing craft and landing ships naturally had a considerable bearing on the plan. The Allies decided to land before German beach obstacles were covered by the tide: in other words, one to three hours after a low tide, as the tide was coming in. This would provide the greatest opportunity to clear lanes through the obstacles to aid larger landing craft in the following waves. Landing soon after dawn and a low tide also meant that a second high tide period would fall in daylight during the first day. This was important as a way of maximising the number of troops landing on D-Day, given that an incoming tide was the most suitable period to put forces ashore without the landing craft being stranded in the process.

These tidal conditions needed to be timed so they occurred thirty to 135 minutes after dawn, allowing enough daylight for accurate naval and air bombardments before H-Hour, but also allowing the Allied naval forces to cross the final part of the English Channel under cover of darkness. Add in the need for at least a half moon, to aid the airborne troops in their night-time landings, and there were only six days in June 1944 that were suitable: 5–7 June and 18–20 June.

The two US beaches had a wider tidal area of beach than the others, and as a result, the Germans had installed more rows of beach obstacles there. This factor and the slightly earlier tide times in the west meant that US commanders decided on an earlier H-Hour. The latest H-Hour was at Juno Beach, to ensure that there would be enough water over the rocky shoals off parts of that beach so that landing craft could pass over them without grounding.

The planners needed to know not just the times of high and low tide, but the height of the tide at any time throughout the day on each beach. Without sufficient historic data, this had to be specially predicted. Calculating the beach gradient at different tidal states helped planners assess which types of landing craft could beach or dry out at that time. The potential impact of currents and the weather were also factored in.[6]

The complex question of which troops would be carried on which vessels was a significant part of the planning. The naval planners allocated units of landing craft to each of the naval forces. The craft available varied between each naval force. For example, LCT(3)s were only used in the assault forces on the British and Canadian beaches and not by the USA. Force J was the only naval force in the Eastern Task Force that had LCT(5)s, leaving aside those converted as LCT(A)s, LCT(HE)s or LCT(CB)s, and used them to land obstacle clearance (breaching) teams. Forces S and G instead used LCT(4)s to carry their breaching teams. Since the LCT(5) could carry fewer vehicles than the LCT(4), a team that, on the other two beaches, was carried by one craft had to be embarked in two LCT(5)s in Force J.[7]

In many cases, landing craft carried troops of the same nationality as the vessel's crew, but this was certainly not always true. Nearly 100 craft manned by the Royal Navy or Royal Marines landed US troops at Omaha Beach and Pointe du Hoc on D-Day, and more than 100 British-manned barges also operated there. Seven Royal Canadian Navy LCI(L)s of 264 LCI(L) Flotilla and fifteen US Navy craft of LCI(L) Divisions 61, 62 and 70 carried British troops to Gold Beach. Around 40 per cent of the more than 170 US Navy- or US Coast Guard-manned LSTs in the assault and follow-up forces sailed to Gold, Juno or Sword beaches.[8]

Allocating units to ships and landing craft was the responsibility of the Allied armies, who began planning how they would use the allocated number of ships and landing craft for each beach. The navy checked these plans, which often would have left many landing craft overloaded, meaning that they would sit too low in the water to safely land their cargoes far enough up the beach. As Admiral Ramsay later noted, 'As in previous operations, it appeared to the Naval Officer that the voracious demands of the Army were not always in its own interests …' To complicate matters, the number and type of craft available regularly fluctuated, requiring the army to make changes in response.[9]

When deciding which troops should land when, factors that the planners considered included the likely level and location of enemy resistance at that point in the landings. For example, LCTs carrying self-propelled guns were near the beach at H-Hour because they had been conducting the 'run-in shoot', firing at targets ashore. However, these vehicles were unsuitable for use in the first waves of an assault and were not put ashore until several hours later.

In the first hours of the landings, there was a much greater risk to landing craft from enemy fire or defences such as beach obstacles. Larger and more vulnerable vessels, such as LCTs, LSTs or LCI(L)s, were therefore usually held back until the level of threat was reduced. Even so, some of these craft did beach relatively early and suffered casualties and losses as a result. One of the notable exceptions to this principle were the LCTs used to land engineering or fire support tanks around H-Hour. Some were fitted with additional armour, but many suffered considerable damage, loss and crew casualties, because their greater size compared to adjacent minor landing craft made them an obvious target for enemy gunners.

Before the detail had been worked out, the Neptune Initial Joint Plan had envisaged that each wave of landing craft would consist of one or more complete flotillas. Before long, the army 'shattered' (as a US Navy narrative put it) the group and flotilla organisation, dividing landing craft from these units between separate waves or even beaches, and mixing different types of craft landing at the same time. At the navy's insistence, the plan was revised to keep navy units intact where possible, due to its importance for administrative and tactical control.[10]

Twelve craft was generally seen as the largest number that could be controlled by a single officer: as one senior US Navy LCT officer put it when discussing the subject, 'The ocean is a big place'. The smallest unit for landing craft operated by the Royal Navy, Royal Marines and Royal Canadian Navy was a flotilla. This was typically around twelve craft or eight LSTs, although support craft flotillas were often smaller. Flotillas of minor craft carried by landing ships could be larger: in Force J, MV *Llangibby Castle* carried eighteen LCAs from 557 Assault Flotilla. Build-Up Flotillas of LCVPs or LCMs, or landing barge flotillas, were also larger, presumably because tactical control was less of a concern, given that they were not used in the assault. Two to five flotillas, usually but not always of a single type of craft, were grouped together into a squadron.[11]

The US Navy and US Coast Guard had a comparable unit structure. A group consisted of twelve landing craft or LSTs, which was divided into two divisions. A flotilla was usually formed from three groups, and thus, a US flotilla was a larger unit than in the Commonwealth forces. All these units were, however, primarily for administrative purposes, such as overseeing crew training and other preparations for the operation. After

D-Day, landing craft units often became dispersed, for example, due to maintenance issues.

Creating a loading schedule which would embark all those units – mostly soldiers, but including some sailors, Royal Marines and airmen – onto the correct ships was the joint responsibility of the naval force commander, the army landing force commander, and the commander of the relevant Royal Navy home command, who was in charge of the ports and other naval facilities being used.[12]

The document that the army used for planning which personnel and vehicles would be on which landing craft was known as a landing table. This divided the sequence of each unit's landing in Normandy into a series of craft loads, and therefore was equally important as a means of planning how the vessels would be loaded. Far ahead of the operation, it was impossible to say exactly which individual craft would be available.

Each craft load was identified by a Landing Table Index Number (LTIN), taken from a run of numbers issued to their parent army unit. The table detailed precisely how many men and vehicles from each unit would be on board and any quantity of stores. The time at which the craft would be ready to beach was also indicated. While troops were loading, LSTs, LCTs and LCI(L)s displayed a 3 x 5ft black-painted board marked with the LTIN. Many craft were still displaying these on D-Day. If a landing craft made multiple trips to the shore, it would carry a different LTIN's load each time.[13]

The landing tables were frequently revised, including at the moment of loading, and the final versions do not necessarily survive. There were many reasons for such changes. In Force O, some DD tanks were loaded onto the wrong LCTs (within the group of LCTs equipped to carry that type of tank). Rather than offload them, the paperwork was altered instead. Force S dealt with the problem of three overloaded LCTs by redistributing some vehicles to other craft, and in extreme cases, by moving tanks to reserve LCTs. One of the LCTs in 28 LCT Flotilla, Force G, which was due to carry obstacle clearance personnel, had engine trouble. Two commanding officers of other available LCTs drew cards to see which would take its place. According to Bill Kiss of LCT(4) 647, his commanding officer, Lieutenant Ron Davies RNVR lost, and his craft became the replacement.[14]

Although accounts of D-Day may mention that a particular Royal Navy flotilla (or the US equivalent) landed a particular unit, often this did not involve the entire naval formation. Similarly, it was rare that a single landing craft or a small group of craft only carried troops of a single unit.

Units being landed were divided between multiple craft for several reasons. In most cases, the whole unit would not fit on a single vessel. Space on board had to be allowed for landing elements of other units of equal priority at the same time. Often, a unit could begin performing its role when only a proportion of its personnel were ashore and so-called 'residues' might be landed even days later. Dividing up units also ensured that an entire unit would not become casualties with the loss of a single craft.

Many army units did not neatly fit into available landing craft. US infantry worked in forty-one-man rifle platoons, but only around thirty-six men could fit into an LCVP. Infantry companies were therefore reorganised for the landings into six boat teams in which each man had a specific role. This also allowed sufficient space to add an additional engineer, signals and medical personnel to each craft.[15]

Even at a very late stage, a few critical errors in the plans came to light. About twenty-four hours before SS *Empire Javelin* (Force O) was due to sail, commanders on board realised that the limits of their landing beach did not match exactly on army and navy maps:

> As it was, neither the flotilla nor the troops knew exactly to which section of the beach they were going until the evening of June 4th and this information could not be relayed to the Primary Control Vessel, P.C. 567, until after the first wave had actually beached.[16]

Intelligence gathering is generally regarded as one of the outstanding successes of the planning for D-Day. In 1942, the Allies had so little information about potential landing sites on the Continent that the BBC was asked to issue a public appeal for British citizens to send in their postcards and holiday photographs which might provide useful clues. An enormous amount of information was available by D-Day.

While waiting on board an LST, Captain Oscar Rich of the US 5th Field Artillery Battalion inspected a rubber map of the Omaha Beach area in the ship's briefing room. As the pilot of one of the battalion's L-5 spotter aircraft, he noted that it even showed an apple orchard behind Easy Red, where it was planned that the first airstrip would be created.[17]

Generally, the navy and army praised the intelligence they had been provided with. Material available to officers commanding major landing craft and groups of minor craft included a range of maps, photographs and extensive descriptions of the coast of Normandy. A special booklet, the *Neptune Monograph*, was produced by US forces, with a condensed summary of intelligence information relevant to Utah and Omaha beaches. US forces also produced Shoreline Sketches for both beaches, which were annotated panoramic drawings of the beach to help landing craft coxswains or navigators.[18]

'Photographic shoreline panoramas' were also issued for landing craft crews. These consisted of multiple photographs taken by a low-flying reconnaissance aircraft, which were joined together to create a continuous view along the beach. They were intended to give a similar perspective to that seen from a landing craft approaching the shore. They were also a means of indicating targets to fire support craft. It was judged to be more effective for this purpose than a map reference. By laying a transparent

Allocation of the Main Landing Craft Types to the Assault and Follow-Up Forces.

Force	LSH	LSI or APA	LST	LCT (all types)	LCM (inc. ferry craft)	LCI(L) and LCH	LCI(S)	Support Craft	A=LCA V=LCVP (extra ferry craft)
Force S	4	6	24	141	48	54	28	34 major, 29 minor	92 A (96 V)
Force J	4	20	24	150	96	27	11	44 major, 72 minor	168 A (144 V)
Force G	4	10	29	148	96	27	–	41 major, 72 minor	148 A (150 V)
Force L	–	–	53	48	–	19	–	–	–
Force O	1	15	24	144	151	37	–	39 major, 62 minor	76A, 124 V (172 V)
Force U	1	3	30	158	73	49	–	21 major, 30 minor	18 A, 65 V (88 V)
Force B	–	–	52	48	–	14	–	–	–
TOTAL	14	54	236	837	464	213	39	–	474 A, 189 V (650 V)

The table only includes the most numerous types. The figure for landing ships (LSIs and APAs) is potentially misleading as the largest of these vessels could carry several times as many troops as the smaller types. Force J had many smaller LSIs, for example. Forces S and U have a far larger number of LCI(L)s than the other three assault forces, presumably because they were the last two added and those craft were the main means of providing additional personnel-carrying capacity. As follow-up forces, arriving when there should have been a reduced threat from enemy defences, Forces B and L naturally had more LSTs than the five assault forces. The table does not reveal every feature of the use of different types of craft. On the Commonwealth beaches, for example, most LCMs arrived as ferry craft later on D-Day or on the following days, whereas on US beaches they played a more significant role in the early hours of the landings.

template over the relevant photograph, the user would obtain a grid reference that could be used to locate a small target such as a pillbox.[19]

Compiling and then updating the huge volume of intelligence information that the Allies possessed was no straightforward matter, not least because the Germans were concealing as much of their defences as possible and were also continuously adding to them. Senior naval officers on Gold and Omaha beaches reported that there were more beach obstacles present than they were expecting. Along most of Jig and King sectors of Gold Beach, there was a strip of soft peat or clay 50m below the high-water mark, which caused problems for vehicles crossing it. This had been seen on aerial photographs but not identified for what it was. The commander of Force U's gunfire-support craft reported that intelligence on the locations of small-calibre guns and machine guns was often not accurate.[20]

One of the greatest Allied intelligence failures concerned missing the presence of a battalion of the German 352nd Division at Omaha Beach, rather than 20 miles away in reserve. They were not there on exercise, as is sometimes said, but were stationed along the coast. Historian Joseph Balkoski has discovered that Allied intelligence only sent information on the location of these troops to the top US army commanders while they were crossing to Normandy. By that point, it was too late to make changes in the plan even if they had wished to. The presence of these troops would make landing at Omaha Beach even harder for the US troops and the landing craft crews carrying them there.[21]

Despite the exhaustive planning process, not everything could be foreseen by Allied planners and commanders. Success or failure of the landings on D-Day would also depend on the bravery, endurance and resourcefulness of the many Allied personnel at the sharp end.

5

Embarkation, Departure and Crossing

The assault will be pressed home with relentless vigour, regardless of loss or difficulty.[1]

From the naval orders for Force J

As the date for D-Day drew nearer, preparations intensified. Many vessels needed maintenance after long periods on campaign or rigorous use in training exercises to maximise the number that would be serviceable on D-Day.

Mechanical problems with landing craft engines were a frequent issue, and flotilla staff overhauled engines that were due for their regular servicing. The staff of landing craft bases and dockyards assisted with more complicated maintenance issues. Maintenance was often delayed because essential parts took so long to arrive or there were insufficient slipways, and this, in turn, could reduce the time available for training. After great efforts by maintenance personnel, over 99 per cent of US Naval vessels were operational; the equivalent figure for the British was nearly 98 per cent: both were much higher than planners had anticipated.

Some craft required modifications for their D-Day roles. Many LCTs had additional equipment fitted, such as Mulock ramp extensions. These were three hinged sections that were attached to the end of the ramp, normally folded inwards so as not to obstruct the view forward from the bridge and turned outwards before beaching. By increasing the length of the ramp, they produced a shallower angle that was easier for vehicles to descend. Sixty US LSTs were also fitted with Welin-McLachlan davits so they could carry more LCVPs.[2]

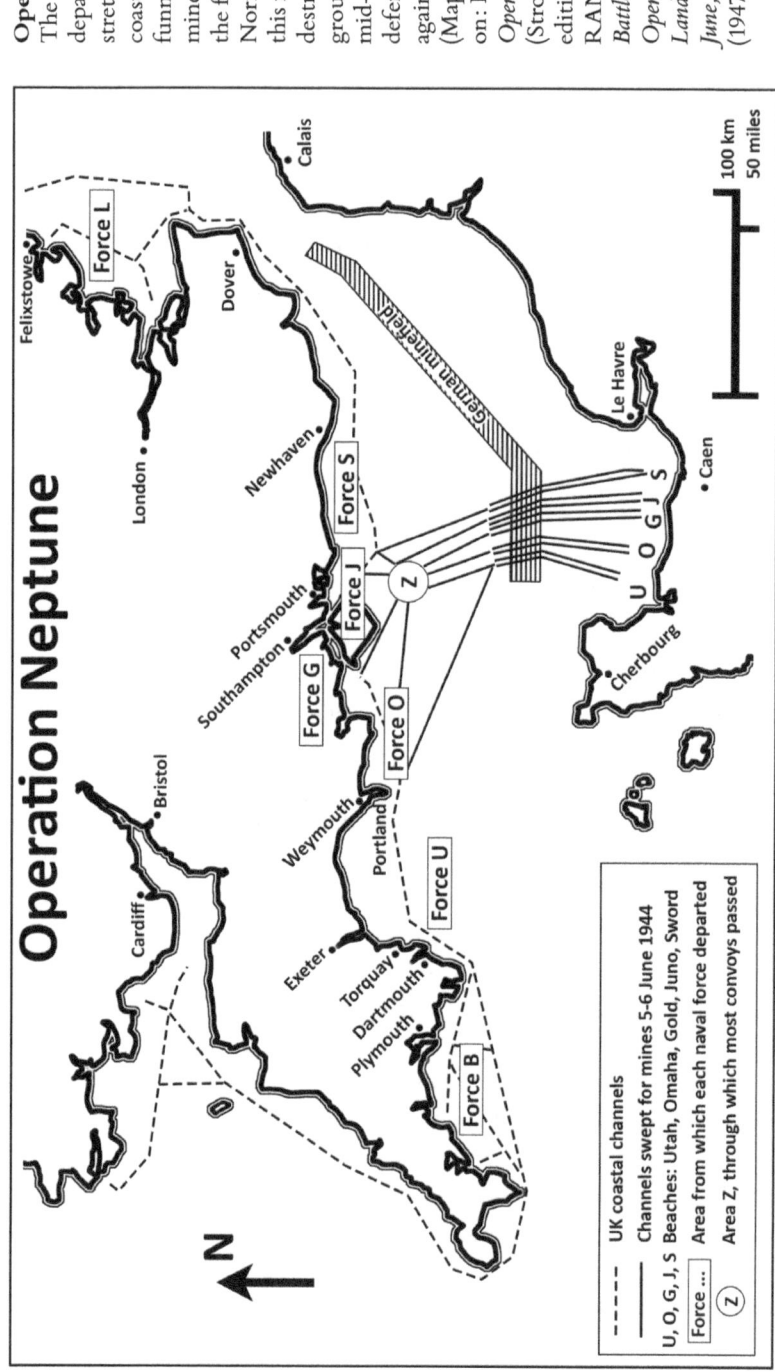

Operation Neptune:
The Allied fleet departed from a long stretch of the British coastline before funnelling through ten mine-swept lanes for the final approach to Normandy. For clarity, this map omits the many destroyers, coastal forces groups and aircraft in mid-Channel which defended these routes against enemy attack. (Map primarily based on: Edwards, Kenneth, *Operation Neptune* (Stroud: Fonthill, revised edition, 2013), p.107; RAN, Admiralty, *Battle Summary No.39, Operation 'Neptune'. Landings in Normandy. June, 1944. CB.3081.* (1947))

Convoys crossing to Normandy as at H-6 on D-Day

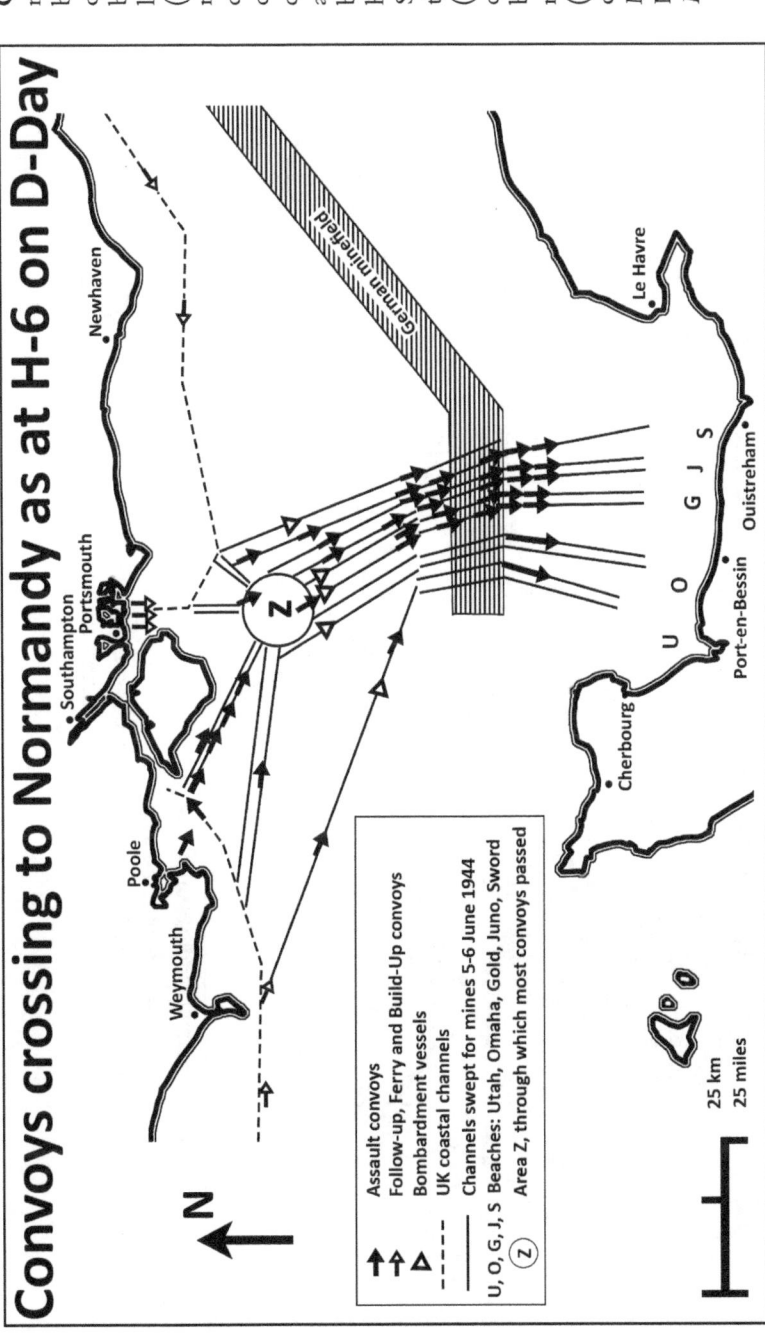

Key:
- ↑ Assault convoys
- ↑ Follow-up, Ferry and Build-Up convoys
- △ Bombardment vessels
- --- UK coastal channels
- U, O, G, J, S Beaches: Utah, Omaha, Gold, Juno, Sword
- ||| Channels swept for mines 5-6 June 1944
- Ⓩ Area Z, through which most convoys passed

Map labels: Weymouth, Poole, Southampton, Portsmouth, Newhaven, German minefield, Cherbourg, Port-en-Bessin, Ouistreham, Le Havre

Scale: 25 km / 25 miles

N

Convoys: Allied convoys make their way to the beaches, as at H–6 (0030 on D-Day, six hours before the first troops landed). Minesweepers (not shown) are operating nearest to the French coast. In mid-Channel, convoys of landing craft and ships, as well as warships of the bombardment groups, head for the French coast. Several convoys from the follow-up forces (Force B and L), ferry craft convoys and two build-up convoys are nearer the English coast. (Map primarily based on: DDS, 2005/1000, Mickey Mouse Diagram No.4; RAN, Admiralty, *Battle Summary 39*, Plan 4)

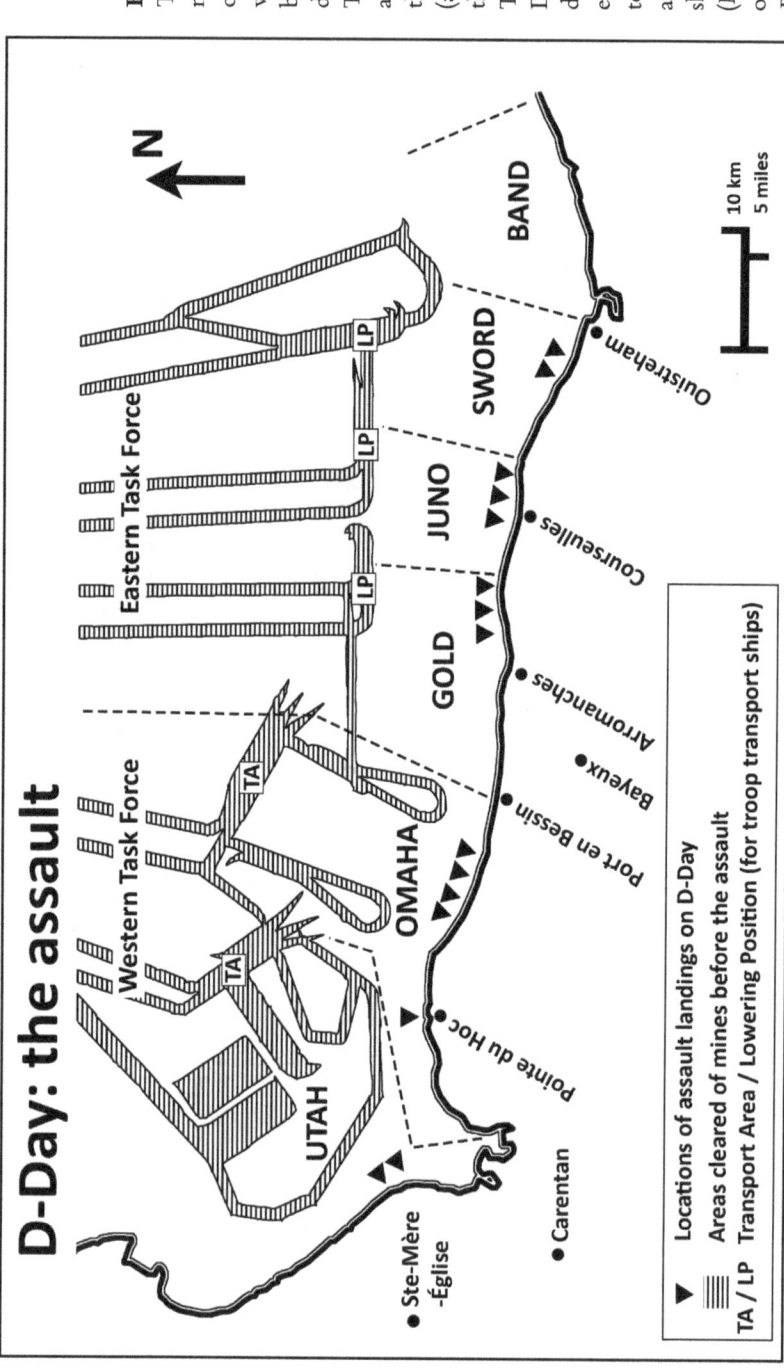

D-Day: the assault

N

Eastern Task Force

Western Task Force

BAND

SWORD

JUNO

GOLD

OMAHA

UTAH

LP

LP

LP

TA

TA

Ouistreham

Courseulles

Arromanches

Bayeux

Port en Bessin

Pointe du Hoc

Ste-Mère-Église

Carentan

10 km
5 miles

▶ Locations of assault landings on D-Day

▥ Areas cleared of mines before the assault

TA / LP Transport Area / Lowering Position (for troop transport ships)

Beaches and Sectors:
The map shows the mine-swept areas off the beaches which were used by the Allied fleet during the assault. Troop-carrying LSIs and APAs anchored at the Lowering Positions (at the US beaches, these are known as Transport Areas). On D-Day, Allied troops did not land on the entire coastline due to unsuitable terrain and the limited shipping available. (Map primarily based on: RAN, Admiralty, *Battle Summary*, Plan 1)

Vessels had to ensure they had all their authorised stores, particularly items that might be hard to obtain once overseas. Midshipman John Lund, on LCT 354, later described how ahead of the operation, 'the stores position was absolute chaos'. Ordered by their commanding officers to secure coal supplies for the galley stoves at any cost, first lieutenants resorted to stealing from the Southern Railway's coal dumps along the Southampton dockside, with railway staff chasing them off. Force J reported that in the Solent area, the Royal Clarence Yard at Gosport and the Naval Store Department at Portsmouth seemed to be 'rather overwhelmed' ahead of D-Day because so many ships needed reprovisioning with food and drink.[3]

Meanwhile, the Allied forces who would land in Normandy had been going through their own preparations. The full story of the complex and extensive programmes and infrastructure created by the Allied armies to ensure that all troops arrived at the right place and time, ready to board the vessel that would take them to Normandy, is beyond the scope of this account. The coastal areas, mostly along the south coast of England, where troops gathered in anticipation of departing for France, were known as marshalling areas. Assault troops were sealed into camps in these areas to preserve the secrecy of the operation and were grouped into craft loads. Final preparations included applying the final stages of waterproofing so that vehicles could wade through deep water.

The Luftwaffe made a rare appearance, which threatened to intervene with the preparations for D-Day. Around twenty German aircraft raided the Portland–Weymouth area on the night of 27–28 May 1944. The transport USS *Thurston*, which on D-Day would carry twenty-six LCVPs and LCM(3)s, reported that one bomb missed the ship by 30 yards. The explosion damaged *Thurston*'s propulsion system, and only by a determined effort was it repaired in time to sail on 5 June. Among other ships affected, seven LCTs were damaged, two of them to such an extent that they could not be used for D-Day.[4]

In outline, the Allied naval forces were to load as follows:

Force U: at Torquay, Brixham, Dartmouth and Plymouth.

Force O: at Weymouth, Portland and Poole.

Force B: at Plymouth, Falmouth and Fowey.

Force G: at Southampton and Stanswood Bay in the New Forest.

Force J: at Southampton and Gosport.

Force S: primarily at Portsmouth and Gosport, but Group S2 at Newhaven and Shoreham.

Force L: at Tilbury and Felixstowe.[5]

Ferry craft: assembled at Shoreham, Newhaven, and in the Solent area.

This is a broad description, and embarkation often took place over a wider stretch of coastline than just at that specific town or city. Ships of these naval forces had assembly points near to the embarkation points, where they would wait both before and after loading with troops. LCTs of Force S anchored in the Solent, for example, while LCTs of Forces G and J tied up in the Southampton Docks. Ferry-service craft mostly assembled in Chichester and Langstone harbours for the Eastern Task Force and Poole for the Western Task Force.[6]

Loading of certain non-perishable stores, including explosives, took place on 1–18 May, onto 162 LBVs and a handful of LCTs. Embarkation of troops began on 31 May 1944, which since D-Day was set for 5 June, was D-5, or five days before D-Day. Ships like LCTs and LSTs that took longer to load tended to be loaded first. Transport ships often remained at anchor and were loaded by either their own small craft or other larger vessels ferrying personnel out to them. Craft that could be loaded rapidly, such as LCI(L)s and LCI(S)s, which only carried personnel on foot, tended to be loaded on D-1. In at least some cases, such as some Force S craft, once tanks or self-propelled guns had been loaded onto LCTs, only three soldiers per craft remained on board and the remainder returned to camp for a few more days.[7]

Given the vast size of the forces involved, it was unsurprising that there were some problems, most frequently involving overloading. Force S reported that the extra weight of the Porpoise sleds (holding additional tank ammunition) that some tanks were towing had not been factored in. The cumulative effect of many additional stores brought by the troops all added up. In Force U, eighteen LCTs were overloaded, the worst having a forward draught of 5ft rather than 3ft 6in. In the most extreme case, Royal Navy LCT(5) 2498 of Force U is said to have capsized on 4 June due to overloading, although without loss of life.[8]

There were issues on transport ships too. The US Coast-Guard-manned transport USS *Samuel Chase* was to carry 1st Battalion,

16th Infantry. Despite being a veteran unit, when the battalion's troops came on board they were still in standard subunits, and they had to reorganise into boat teams within the limited space on board. Army personnel placed heavy and light loads in the same ship's hold, meaning that when unloading, the ship's crew would have to use heavier duty – but slower – lifting equipment. These issues should not be exaggerated, however: out of the several thousand vehicles to be carried by Group G-1, only one (a tank) did not turn up for loading as expected and a lorry took its place.[9]

The Royal Navy's Portsmouth Command (responsible for the area in which Forces G, J, O and S loaded) reported after D-Day that the assault forces had left behind four LSTs, forty-four LCTs and six LCI(L)s which were not required for the assault. Instead, these craft were loaded on D-Day and sailed to Normandy soon afterwards. Given the huge efforts to assemble LSTs and major landing craft ahead of the operation, this is particularly surprising. The explanation may simply be that fewer craft were out of action for maintenance reasons than the planners had allowed for, unexpectedly leaving some additional craft to spare.[10]

What was this period like for the crews of landing craft and landing ships? Sub Lieutenant Alf Twelftree RNVR was Communications Officer for U LCT Squadron:

> The run up to D-Day was a long round of work in preparation driven by an immense feeling of elation that, at last, after almost four years of being largely on the receiving end, watching ships blown up in convoys and good seamen drown, followed by months of training others for the invasion, we were really going to do it.[11]

Landing craft personnel knew that a major operation was in the offing and tension mounted. 'The air was pretty well electrified, anticipation, when will it be? How soon?' Charles Bruce of 506 Assault Flotilla recalled. 'The talking was done in quiet tones in case anyone overheard, looking at each other wondering what was in store for us all.'

Officers learned of their part in the upcoming operation first. For Ensign Eugene Pendleton Banks USNR, officer in charge of LCT(6) 765, his D-Day briefing was a dramatic moment:

> When I saw the chart on the stage with all the channels clearly leading to the coast of France I felt a thrill of fear mixed with excitement; it was the only time in my life when I literally felt my knees shaking.

For others it was less dramatic. Stoker Ken Hawkins was on board LBO 35 when, on 5 June 1944, the flotilla officer came alongside in a small boat and said, 'Right lads, we are all off to France'. Hawkins says this was all the briefing his crew received before D-Day.[12]

More senior commanders such as flotilla officers were the first to be briefed, followed – just before loading began – by the commanding officers of major landing craft, officers commanding Royal Marine contingents on LCFs and LCG(L)s, and flotilla officers of minor landing craft. Once briefed, officers were still not yet allowed to read their orders. As one LCA flotilla officer pointed out, unfamiliarity with the written orders made it hard for the officers being briefed to ask questions.[13]

Some senior officers miscalculated in their attempts to raise morale. The officers of the LCI(L)s of Force S were at first pleased to hear they were being rewarded for their service in four previous amphibious landings in the Mediterranean. Their 'reward' turned out to be that they had been given the 'honour' of landing troops at Sword Beach on the far eastern flank of the Normandy Landings, which was described to them as expected to be the 'most hotly contested'. At this, there was 'a storm of protest ... notably from the rear, and this continued for some minutes'.

Midshipman Roland Tracey, of LCT(4) 981, attended another Force S briefing at which a senior officer asked all officers of 45 LCT Flotilla to stand up:

> When we were stood up he looked at us and said, 'I am having a good look at you gentlemen as you have the honour of leading the advance and I do not expect to see many of you again.' Not a very encouraging send-off.[14]

For security reasons, commanding officers could not let the rest of their crews in on the secret immediately. At Southampton, the skipper of LCT(A) 2052 went ashore to be briefed. On his return, he would not respond to the crew's questions about the date of the operation, except that 'he pointed to a bag of potatoes and said [D-Day would be] "before that lot is eaten"'.

In one case, multiple ships' companies attended what was billed as an aircraft recognition lecture, which was actually their D-Day briefing. More often, each commanding officer briefed his own crew.[15]

Once they were allowed to open their orders, most landing craft commanders spent several hours reading the documents and implementing the various amendments, which was done either by writing corrections by hand or sticking in strips of paper with the updated wording. Some commanders burned the sections of the orders that did not apply to them. Most shared the orders with their first lieutenants, the exceptions perhaps being a few who had not reflected on their own chances of surviving the operation unscathed.

Norman Moss and his fellow LCA crewmen on SS *Empire Battleaxe* were briefed on the main deck of their ship on 2 June 1944, the day the ship embarked troops. The briefing featured a scale model and aerial photographs. At midnight on 5 June, only hours before their craft would be lowered into the sea off Normandy, they were given photos of their exact landing spot. Landing craft personnel were instructed to wear clean underwear to reduce the risk of infection if they were wounded. On LCT(4) 571, Ron Wilson's commanding officer advised the crew:

> We must be in uniform or we could be shot on the spot, if we were taken prisoners of war, and we were also informed that the chance of not making it was odds on, such a prospect for an almost twenty year old.[16]

Some crewmen were not briefed until they had begun the journey to France. On board LCI(L) 94, Motor Machinist's Mate 1st Class Clifford Lewis of the US Coast Guard described how after setting off for Normandy at 17.00 on 5 June, the commanding officer gathered most of the crew in the crew quarters and showed them some of the intelligence material about Omaha Beach. Men received the news in different ways. For 18-year-old John Andrews of LCT(3*) 7065, his reaction was, 'I was on a real adventure with a great bunch of shipmates'. The wording of General Eisenhower's message to the forces, which was distributed at the end of the briefing, hit home for John Lambourne, on the crew of LCS(M) 102 on HMS *Prince Leopold*, 'It was at that point that I began to realise the importance of what we were required to accomplish.'[17]

The time waiting on board ship or landing craft did not necessarily mean idleness for the troops. On transports, the troops exercised or practised loading into the small assault craft that would take them to the shore.

On some larger vessels, there might be menus of unaccustomed variety. The US Navy cooks on LST 522 in Force L, for example, offered a breakfast of cold oranges, bacon, eggs, cereal and milk, with lunch including breaded pork chops, candied yams and spaghetti, while dinner featured steamed frankfurters, sauerkraut and rice pudding.[18]

There were many examples of comradeship between naval personnel and the embarked troops. Royal Marine Buck Taylor recalled how the crew of LCF 24 helped men from Canadian tank crews who were embarked on an adjacent LCT. They guarded the Canadians' tanks so the men could go ashore for a shower, the LCF's crew cooked them egg and chips and the troops were allowed to sleep on the LCF's mess deck for one night, so they were under cover rather than in the open air.[19]

Being on board the landing craft could be difficult, even before departing for Normandy. Midshipman Derek Brightman recalled the period when LCT(4) 809 was anchored in the Solent:

> An L.C.T. is an absolute bitch in any sort of rough sea, and at anchor she rides and pitches like the very devil. The Army Personnel were dreadfully sick … At first with sea sickness you fear you are going to die, but you then become afraid that you might live.[20]

Royal Navy officer John Antony Crawford Hugill was one of the passengers on board LCT(3★) 7073 at anchor in a more sheltered spot on the River Orwell in Suffolk. He described the three days he spent on board and the conditions created through the presence of a large number of men in a confined space, 'Days of apathy and indigestion, of struggles against the dirt of an LCT, of fits of depression, of laying in stores of sleep.' How much longer would it be?[21]

Whatever their nationality or branch of service, most individuals in the Allied fleet must have had similar thoughts as they departed for Normandy: of home, loved ones and their future. D-Day was famously postponed by twenty-four hours from its intended date of 5 June 1944 due to poor weather. When the signal was sent round the fleet at 05.15 on 4 June to indicate a delay, many vessels assigned to faster convoys, those travelling a shorter distance and those due to land troops later than the initial assault had not yet departed. Some convoys of Force U had been at sea for some time already, because they had further to go. The postponement meant that they had to backtrack for twelve hours.

Several hundred landing craft had to shelter in Weymouth Bay, arriving between 17.00 and 21.00 on 4 June. When the new date for D-Day was confirmed at 23.00, commanders had only a few hours to round up the scattered vessels in the dark before they had to get under way. Convoy U-2A of Force U did not receive the postponement signal and had to be intercepted by two destroyers and a seaplane.[22]

The crew of LCT(4) 808 were not fazed by the delay as they were used to exercises, bad weather and 'being messed about', in the words of Rex Eye. In contrast, Ken McCaw on LCT(4) 974 was ready for the operation and felt that the delay was 'simply a terrible let down'; his crew also assumed that the delay would mean that the Germans would be alerted.[23]

With D-Day rescheduled to 6 June, the Allied convoys departed again. The timings and routes for the fleets leaving UK waters for France were planned to the same level of detail as other aspects of Operation Neptune.

Crossing the English Channel was a complex part of the operation. The departure of shipping from anchorages such as the Solent had to be carefully timed or chaos would ensue. Each group of vessels had to arrive off its designated beach on time: too early, and they could hinder the landings through congestion. For those taking part in the initial assault, the time of H-Hour was a factor: 06.30 on the two US beaches, 07.25 on Gold and Sword, and 07.35 and 07.45 on the two halves of Juno. Dawn was around 06.00.[24]

To avoid strain on engines, vessels travelled at a cruising speed rather than their maximum speed. Typically, the troop-carrying transports and LCI(L)s were in 12-knot convoys, while LSTs, LCTs, LCMs and similar craft crossed at 5 knots. Landing craft, therefore, did not necessarily depart the UK in the sequence that they would beach, or with all the other craft that would be alongside them on the far side.

The vanguard of the Allied fleet would arrive off the beaches before dawn, but given the short hours of darkness in June, much of the crossing would be in daylight. During the crossing, ships were strung out in long lines and were more vulnerable. Each force bound for the Anglo-Canadian beaches was divided into sixteen or more convoys. Forces U and O crossed in fewer, much larger convoys, up to 20 miles in length.[25]

The US Commander Gunfire Support Craft, 11th Amphibious Force, worried about the vulnerability of convoys as large as O-2 (comprising some 300 ships and landing craft):

If we persist in these tremendous lumbering convoys of great length, consisting of cumbersome, lumbering, unmanoeuvrable, slow landing craft, loaded with vehicles, personnel and equipment and inadequately protected, we are not going to be lucky every time. The spearhead of the attack was in this convoy. It could easily have been totally disrupted by a determined enemy surface attack during darkness.[26]

As had been demonstrated by the loss of two LSTs during Exercise Tiger, the sinking of a large ship could have led to heavy loss of life and disrupted the landings. Mines were a significant threat, and the convoys therefore followed routes that had been swept by minesweepers. Most passed through 'Area Z', also known as Piccadilly Circus, about 5 miles in diameter and to the south-south-east of the Isle of Wight.

Force U was travelling so far from the west of England that its ships took a more direct route, which was also swept for mines.

The main role of Piccadilly Circus was to help convoys to enter the mine-swept channels radiating southwards towards the beaches. Each was marked by lines of buoys: green lights along the centre line, red to starboard and white to port. In the words of one British LCT skipper, this made the crossing 'as easy as walking down Piccadilly and less expensive'. Two channels had been swept to each beach which, ahead of the assault, were to be used by fast and slow convoys respectively.[27]

In mid-Channel there was a known German minefield 5 miles wide, but Allied minesweepers only found a few mines there. Allied commanders feared that had the Germans got wind of the coming invasion, they might have added to this minefield.

Most landing craft had no navigational equipment and were simply following a dim blue light on the ship ahead, visible at up to around 600 yards away. As Eric Loseby of LCT(4) 821 put it, 'For most of the night it was just another monotonous journey, following the very dim blue stern light of the craft ahead and occasional increase or decrease of engine revs to maintain a safe distance.'[28]

Many landing craft had a difficult crossing. LCT(A)s and LCT(HE)s often experienced water flooding into their engine rooms or onto their tank decks. LCT(HE) 2229 never reached Omaha Beach as it sank during the crossing. As survivors recalled, in the evening of D-1, the bulwarks (the sides of the craft along the tank deck) began to detach. This sent water flooding into the craft. At 05.55 on D-Day, the officer in charge had to give orders to abandon ship using a life raft. By the time they were rescued by a British minesweeper at 09.15, six sailors and three soldiers had died from exposure. The deceased included the officer in charge, Ensign Virgil Eugene Wilkerson USNR.[29]

Many larger vessels had smaller craft in tow, such as LCMs, LCP(L)s or LCA(HR)s, for which there was no space on the decks or davits of a larger ship. The towing craft were often fire support LCT variants – LCT(A)s, LCT(R)s, LCG(L)s and LCFs – and the situation was often unsatisfactory to both parties. Tow lines repeatedly broke and towing shackles were ripped off the towed craft.

The nine LCA(HR)s of 592 Assault Flotilla (Force S) were towed by LCT(AVRE)s. Only one craft, LCA(HR) 976, managed to cross on time, five were swamped by the sea and sank, and three came adrift and had to be abandoned. In such cases, there was often time for the crew of the smaller craft to transfer safely to the towing vessel. Sub Lieutenant Michael Irwin RNVR of 591 Assault Flotilla (Force G) was – perhaps somewhat harshly – critical of this, pointing to craft in his flotilla whose crews were so determined to fulfil their D-Day mission that they unhitched from their tows and proceeded under their own power, at the cost of several crewmen drowned during the crossing.[30]

Often conditions were little better for troops on larger craft. Signalman Mike Crumpton recalled the seasick tank troops on board LCT(5) 2331:

> They had no shelter on the open tank deck and were soon soaked with spray and vomit … They were not permitted to shelter in their Tanks in case of capsize or collision and thus existed in these conditions for best part of two days. They were then expected to start fighting! We felt sorry for them.[31]

Many men must have been too ill to consider eating, however, and the seasickness pills that had been issued were widely reported not to have worked. Naval personnel were affected, as well as their passengers. The crews of major landing craft were expected to look after the soldiers on board. The orders for Force L noted that this was the troops' last period of rest and relative comfort before what might be weeks of battle, 'Generally speaking, no effort is too great for [the crew] to take to ensure that the military are put ashore fighting fit'.

Improvisation was required in some circumstances. LCT(3) 354 was carrying Canadians of the Fort Garry Horse with their DD tanks. Able Seaman Bennett reportedly used the bowl from the Elsan Closet – a portable toilet, intended for use by the troops on board – as a container for making stew for the army from tinned foods, steak and tomatoes, as the crew had nothing else that was large enough.[32]

Orders issued to troops of British XXX Corps, which commanded troops landing on Gold Beach, covered several issues involving the relationship between sailors and soldiers, particularly on LCTs:

> The Commanding Officer of the Craft, irrespective of his rank, is in absolute command of all personnel, including military personnel, in his

craft. He is responsible for the safety of his craft and may take it off a beach, or refuse to beach it against the wishes of a unit, if he considers it necessary.

The craft's bridge was the best place for the naval and army officers to liaise; however, 'It is ... to be understood that the bridge is for the Naval control of the craft – it is NOT a watch tower for the use of the Army'.[33]

There were many differences in the course of events at each of the five beaches, due to variations in the timing of the assault, the sea conditions, the composition of Allied naval and military forces, the German defences and the topography. There were also many common features, and to reduce repetition in the following chapters, the typical elements of the assault will be described here.

There were several designated areas and control lines off each beach. The big landing ships (troop transport ships) anchored in what the Americans called the Transport Area and the British knew as the Lowering Position. Larger vessels had to remain within the comparatively confined area that had been swept for mines. Transports and fire-support warships were timed to arrive and anchor before the LCTs of the slower convoys began appearing, lest congestion cause delays.

Based on exercises held before D-Day, one senior US Navy officer later remarked about the Transport Area, 'It was not a question of whether there would be confusion but whether the confusion would become chaos'. If a group of landing craft had to pause to allow vessels ahead to get into position, they tended to drift and become dispersed.[34]

At the Transport Area, troops on the transport ships loaded into the smaller boats that would take them to the beach. For troops landing close to H-Hour, those boats probably came from the ship that they were on board, but if beaching later, it was equally likely that troops would load into the small boats that had crossed the English Channel on another transport or on an LST. Alternatively, they might embark onto an LCI(L) or LCT that had crossed under its own power and had already delivered its first cargo to the beach.

Ensign Lemuel C. Laney described returning to the Utah Transport Area after H-Hour. His LCS(S) had arrived ahead of most of the fleet, so he was struck by the number of ships, 'It looked more like a city than anything else. That was one of the greatest thrills in my entire life, to see all those ships anchored there.'[35]

If possible, troops would load into small craft that had been hoisted onto the ship's davits. Known as rail-loading, this meant the heavily loaded troops simply had to step down into the craft which, once loaded, would be lowered into the water with them aboard. Marine Edward Neale of 535 Assault Flotilla described launching his craft from HMS *Glenearn*:

> The waves ran under the keel lifting them up and causing them to fall back onto the hooks with a shuddering jolt … The Davit hooks had to be released at exactly the same moment, if not, the craft would be left hanging by one davit and everything would have been thrown into the sea. Finally by the grace of God we managed to release the craft and were smashed against the side of the ship before being hurtled forward and on our way; all soaked to the skin and looking a very sorry bunch of humanity.[36]

The other option was net-loading: troops would climb down the side of the transport using a net or debarkation ladder, risking a broken ankle or worse.

US transport ships carried some boats on their decks, often on top of the hatches that gave access to the ship's holds containing light vehicles. These boats, up to the size of an LCM, were lowered by a boom suspended from a mast. An unusual method of loading used by certain British ships was a canvas chute known as the 'helter-skelter' after the fairground ride that it resembled; however, they were easily damaged if used for troops rather than stores.[37]

Once in the water, the small craft would circle nearby until ready then proceed towards the beach, in theory, simply following a compass course. As they drew near the shore, they would need to look out for landmarks identified in their orders.

Strong currents could drag craft off course, dust and smoke could obscure landmarks and other vessels could get in the way. Leading Seaman Reg Hodgson was the signaller on LCA 733, carrying troops who would land on Gold Beach soon after H-Hour:

> We took along with us hot soup and coffee in thermos containers sufficient for everyone in the boat … the troops were not interested one little bit … which left plenty for the crew who took full advantage of the rum-laced coffee, and by the time we got to the beach we were all quite merry.[38]

Due to the danger from enemy fire, the minesweepers had not swept the final distance to the beach. Some of the first LCTs to arrive had been fitted with simple mine-clearing sweeps, each of which could clear a path 75 yards wide for following craft. In the chaos of D-Day, it seems that few if any of them deployed this equipment.[39]

Running parallel to the beach and much closer to it – some 3,500 to 4,500 yards out – was the Line of Departure. Landing-craft waves could be reassembled or paused here for a short time before being sent to the beach. A variety of control vessels tried to ensure that all craft landed in the correct place. Any vehicles on board the craft would be running their engines to warm them up before going ashore. In the accounts that follow, waves are described one at a time for clarity. In practice, waves were often muddled together, but if the personnel on board were landed at roughly the correct location, often they could still carry on as planned.[40]

Further off the coast, there were larger headquarters (HQ) ships carrying the naval force commander and his army equivalents. HQ ships took an overview of the landings and were not so concerned with the progress of individual waves. Battalion HQ personnel from the assault infantry and naval commanders such as the Senior Officer Assault Group and his deputy were often in LCHs, so they could get close to shore for a better view of the action. The control organisation did not always work smoothly, particularly due to congestion.[41]

A boat group commander or flotilla officer led each wave of up to about twelve landing craft. He might make tactical decisions such as directing the craft to a specific part of the designated beach, depending on enemy fire or gaps in the beach obstacles. The control-and-command craft were equipped with radios, and once radio silence had been lifted, they could report on progress. However, there were complaints in after-action reports that there was so much radio traffic, much of it unnecessary, that radios could not be used for control purposes.

A craft commanding a wave might have a radio that could only receive but not transmit, so it could be used to listen for orders. Most of the craft had no radios, so orders were issued by loudhailer or flag. Most landing craft did not have navigation equipment either, except for a few such as transport or HQ vessels, as well as some fire-support craft such as LCT(R)s. A few of the leading landing craft also carried radio counter-measure equipment to hamper the range-finding radar of German coastal gun batteries. These included around half the LCT(A)s and most of the LCG(L)s in Force G, for example.

The point where an individual landing craft beached would be determined by its commanding officer or coxswain, often based on where there was a space between beach obstacles. The orders to landing craft were generally that if there was no other option, they should force their way through any remaining beach obstacles and ensure they delivered their troops. Orders for Force J stated, 'Do not worry too much about how you are to get out again, the first and primary object is to get in and land your load without drowning the vehicles.' The orders issued by HMCS *Prince Henry* stated that craft should beach at full speed to get the troops as far up the beach as possible. That speed would cause the craft to plane, meaning that the bows would start to lift out of the water, but the stern would correspondingly sink. To avoid hitting the bottom too early, the troops could move their weight forward to level the craft out.[42]

During an amphibious landing, the whole crew would be at the action stations. On an LCT the first lieutenant's station was at the bow, where he would supervise the raising and lowering of the ramp according to klaxon or hand signals from the skipper on the bridge. On smaller craft, the crew had similar roles, but scaled back to the size of their vessel. The senior army officer had to tell the craft's commanding officer what was the maximum depth that the vehicles on board could wade in. The skipper was responsible for taking depth soundings and confirming to the army whether the water was shallow enough for them to go ashore. The army officer could refuse to go ashore if he was not satisfied that the water depth had been checked.[43]

On landing, a sailor might be sent ashore with a 'lifeline', which troops could use as a handrail as they landed. He could also check for any holes in the seabed that might cause vehicles or troops to drown as they disembarked.

Soldiers' accounts sometimes mention landing craft crewmen who were said to have been too afraid to drive their craft well up the beach and give the troops a safer landing. It was natural for the troops to blame the coxswain for any difficulties with the landing, regardless of whether it was his fault. Martin J. Perrett, coxswain on one of USS *Bayfield*'s LCVPs, described the behaviour of the soldiers carried on his first trip to Utah Beach:

These 36 [soldiers] are standing there and instead of looking out front … every one of them are in the boat staring me down eyeball-to-eyeball not saying a word to each other … it kind of unnerved me … And finally one of them piped up and said, – Look Cox, we landed at Sicily and Salerno a few months ago and the coxswain put us off in about three or four feet of water, and we're telling you, you better not do that today.

Eyeing up the Thompson submachine gun held by the speaker, Perrett promised he would do his best.[44]

Sub Lieutenant Jimmy Green RNVR commanded craft of 551 Assault Flotilla, which landed GIs at Omaha Beach. He responded to accounts by American historians who had described how, as he put it, 'reluctant British coxswains had to be persuaded at the point of a Colt .45 to land their soldiers on the beach', by pointing out that on an LCA, the coxswain was enclosed in an 'armour-plated turret ... well clear of any Colt-toting mutineer intent on assuming command'. Landing craft crewmen were human beings, and it would be remarkable if there were not at least some incidents where they were at fault. There were also cases of army personnel being too hesitant in landing in the face of enemy fire, exposing craft and crews to damage and casualties.[45]

Another issue that caused confusion on D-Day was whether landing craft crews should evacuate the wounded from the beach. US Army reports from Omaha Beach express frustration that they did not, which the commanding officer of 3rd Battalion, 16th Infantry blamed for there being a 1:1 ratio of killed to wounded on that beach, rather than the more usual 1:7 (no doubt, this was not the only factor). This was interpreted by the army as the crewmen being more concerned with saving their own skins than helping the wounded.

The crew had to get their craft off the beach as fast as possible. This cleared space on the beach for subsequent waves and made the vessel available for landing more troops. On many craft, unbeaching was meant to be done using the kedge anchor as well as the engines. Sometimes, crews did not deploy their kedge anchor, had the anchor cable severed by other craft or cut it themselves in the hope that they could unbeach faster. However, this could cause craft to swing to the side as they unbeached and broach-to. Sometimes, landing craft were stuck on the beach due to hull damage or because they had 'dried out' by the outgoing tide. In such circumstances, crews might go ashore, either to seek shelter from enemy fire or to seek souvenirs.[46]

The larger warships anchored on the flanks of the Transport Area and the boat lanes so they could fire their guns in support of the troops ashore. A variety of fire-support landing craft also played a significant but often overlooked part. What was described as 'beach-drenching fire' was aimed at an area to disrupt enemy morale and communications, keep enemy troops in their shelters and possibly damage enemy weapons. This could give the assault troops a chance to cross the exposed beach and close with the enemy. This fire support before the assault troops landed was particularly effective if it was directed by a forward observer in a craft just off the coast.[47]

A major 1945 study attempted to compare the bombardments on all five landing beaches. On the British beaches, rocket-firing LCT(R)s and LCTs carrying self-propelled artillery were judged to have provided 52 and 36 per cent respectively of the volume of fire (by weight of explosive delivered on targets).[48]

Other support craft had point targets, such as individual bunkers or other German defensive positions, both ahead of H-Hour, when the enemy troops were probably sheltering, and after H-Hour, when the gunners might be fighting back. These craft included LCG(L)s equipped with 4.7in guns, LCS(L)s with a 6-pounder gun, and LCFs with anti-aircraft guns that could equally be turned against the beachfront defences.

Within minutes of H-Hour, tanks were due to land from LCT(A)s, LCT(HE)s or LCT(CB)s. These were all modified LCT(5)s, fitted with a humped platform near the front of the tank deck so that a pair of tanks – Centaurs on the Anglo-Canadian beaches, Shermans for the Americans – could also fire for the final few thousand yards. Despite their contribution, the strength and design of many German beachfront bunkers meant that they could only be fully silenced by ground troops. Many naval force commanders agreed that most fire-support craft had proved their worth. On Gold Beach, for example, LCG(L)s and LCS(L)s played a critical role when the assault infantry were pinned down on the beach and suffering heavy casualties.[49]

The Allied naval plan for landing troops on each beach naturally related to the army's plan for advancing inland. On each beach, the army's part was co-ordinated on D-Day by a single infantry division (a unit of around 15,000 to 18,000 personnel), which would begin the landings on a frontage of either one or two infantry brigades, each supported by attached units such as tanks and engineers: known to the Commonwealth forces as an infantry brigade group. The American equivalent of a brigade was a regiment, which along with the attached units formed a regimental combat team (RCT). Each brigade group or RCT put either one or two infantry battalions ashore first. If two brigade groups were landed side by side, an additional brigade would be attached to the division so there was a reserve brigade to follow up behind each assault brigade.

The first stage of the landings was the assault, timetabled to begin around H-Hour. Assault infantry would be supported by swimming DD tanks and tanks landed directly ashore. Their objective was to gain control of the German beachfront defences, which centred on strongpoints known in German as a *Widerstandsnest*, or WN. Each strongpoint included bunkers and shelters constructed from concrete or wood and earth, and where available, often incorporating the remains of pre-war seafront buildings, all interconnected by trenches and tunnels. Barbed wire and minefields surrounded these strongpoints and plugged the gaps between them.

There were numerous German obstacles both on the beach and inland. The beach obstacles included wooden ramps to capsize landing craft, Element C (Belgian Gates), which could physically block the beach, wooden stakes, steel hedgehogs and concrete tetrahedra, which could hole vessels. Many obstacles had Tellermines (anti-tank mines), artillery shells or other explosive devices fitted to them, one of which could wreck a smaller landing craft and cause significant flooding to the larger types.

Engineers and other obstacle clearance personnel were vital to deal with these obstacles and landed from around H-Hour onwards. Supported by armoured vehicles, they would play an essential role in making it easier and safer for later waves of landing craft and troops to come ashore, as well as creating or improving exits so that vehicles could clear the beach area as quickly as possible.

Commanding some of the obstacle clearance units, but also many other formations, were the beach groups (Anglo-Canadian) or engineer special brigades (US). Their general role was to organise the beachhead and ensure speedy and efficient landings, including ensuring that exits off the beach were suitable for vehicles. They were also responsible for marking the most suitable points where landing craft should beach. They were primarily army but included associated naval personnel, including the Royal Navy Beach Commandos (British) or Naval Beach Battalions (US).

On all beaches except Utah, British Commandos or US Rangers landed by sea to attack special objectives near the beaches or further afield (inland from Sword and Utah Beaches, troops landed by air played a similar role). After ninety minutes or so, troops would begin to land who were intended to support the assault troops as they advanced inland: for example, by providing artillery or logistical support. After several hours, the reserve brigade would begin landing. Allied planners presumed that by this stage,

German resistance along the beach would have been overcome and these newly landed forces could advance inland as fast as possible before the defenders had a chance to reinforce. As the day went on, further army logistical personnel came ashore. Before the end of D-Day, supply dumps would be set up just behind the beach to ensure that the army could restock with essentials such as ammunition and fuel.

Even once the German defensive positions along the beach had been captured, the beach remained perhaps the most dangerous place because of German mortar and artillery fire: the defenders knew that whatever the specifics of the Allies' plans, everything had to pass over the beach. It was too risky for larger units such as infantry battalions to land en masse until enemy fire had slackened. The same was true for larger landing craft.

The landing craft beaching on D-Day were divided into two 'tides', referred to as First Tide and Second Tide. H-Hour was about ninety minutes after low tide. The next low tide, at very roughly 18.00 on D-Day (slightly earlier in the west than in the east), imposed a pause and marked the beginning of the Second Tide period. The Third Tide began after the next low tide, roughly 06.00 on 7 June. The hours of darkness did not necessarily bring the landings to a halt, though they greatly slowed progress. On D-Day, there were more than seventeen hours of daylight, which was to the Allies' advantage in maximising the landing of troops.[50]

Some landing craft were not intended for the assault but were scheduled to arrive later on D-Day or the following day to form part of the ferry service. This naval organisation oversaw landing craft that would remain off the Normandy coast for weeks or months, continuing to unload larger ships that could not themselves beach. Their role came into play as the landings moved from the initial assault phase to the build-up phase: putting the maximum quantities of troops, vehicles and supplies ashore. They were still landed over the beaches, but in theory at least, with much reduced chance of enemy interference. Craft, therefore, did not need to be combat-loaded, as they had been for the assault.

The ferry craft included LCM(1)s, LCM(3)s and LCVPs on the British-Canadian beaches. A proportion of landing craft that had been used in the assault also transferred to the ferry service rather than returning to the UK immediately, as did Rhino Ferries that had been towed over by LSTs.[51]

Vessels that were not part of the ferry service would return to the UK, if not on D-Day then soon afterwards. Minor landing craft that had crossed to Normandy on board transport ships sometimes made only a single trip to the beach but might make several journeys before being rehoisted on board. Although one might expect that, for the crews of such craft, their first beaching would have the most difficult experience of the day, this was not necessarily the case. By the time they returned to their transport ship, crews would have experienced the physical drain of being on board the landing craft in rough seas for four to six hours, as well as the physical and emotional trauma of putting their troops ashore.

Many craft suffered damage on the beach from enemy fire or beach obstacles that made the return journey extremely difficult. Able Seaman Thomas of LCA 557 (526 Assault Flotilla) sat in a hole in the bows of his craft for the entire journey back to HMS *Queen Emma* and was judged to have saved the LCA as a result.[52]

The process of recovering the craft involved the crew manoeuvring it under one of the ship's davits and connecting the lifting eye that was lowered down on a cable to a hook on the deck of the craft. No.557 Assault Flotilla had two men injured when hit by the lifting eye during this manoeuvre. Bob Bradshaw recalled that on returning to SS *Empire Crossbow*, it proved impossible to recover his craft, LCA(HR) 671, which had been shipping water. As the ship's crew tried to hoist the LCA(HR), the lifting eye pulled away, along with part of the smaller craft's deck, as the water on board meant that it was too heavy to lift. In a 14ft swell, Bradshaw told his crew to jump for the scrambling net on the side of *Crossbow*. The coxswain fell into the sea but survived.[53]

The big landing ships could not disembark their entire load of troops in one go using the ship's own craft. MV *Llangibby Castle* in Force J, for example, carried eighteen LCAs, which together could land 630 troops (thirty-five per craft), but that was around a third of the 1,587 troops that the ship carried for D-Day. Other minor or major landing craft, including LCTs or LCI(L)s, would come alongside the transports to load up with remaining troops (this sometimes delayed the LSI in recovering its LCAs).[54]

Towards the end of D-Day and into the next day, the first landing barges would arrive to remain off the Normandy coast as ferry craft. Some LBVs were loaded with stores and were first beached to be unloaded. Other types of barge, such as LBWs, LBOs, LBKs and LBEs, were not meant to land but would resupply and support minor landing craft and barges (particularly those of the ferry service).

Nearly 133,000 Allied personnel landed from the sea on D-Day, but the total first lift for Neptune was nearly 177,000 troops. As the difference between these two numbers indicates, at the end of D-Day, a significant portion of the Allied land forces were still embarked on ships and landing craft waiting off the French coast. Many were carried by the craft of Forces B and L, the two follow-up forces. These troops were not expected to take part in the assault, but as the name suggests, to follow up behind the assault forces and continue or support the advance inland.

Force B carried troops destined for the US beaches and Force L would land forces on the Anglo-Canadian beaches. In total, each force had around fifty LSTs, over forty British LCTs and a lesser number of LCI(L)s. Both forces were divided into various convoys, which would begin arriving from the late afternoon or evening of D-Day onwards.[55]

Although Forces B and L were less likely to face enemy attack than the assault forces, there was nothing routine about their D-Day experiences. D.G. Woodford, coxswain on LCT(3★) 7070 in Force L, recalled how as his craft approached the French coast in darkness, a German Ju-88 swooped low to attack them. On their return to the UK, the LCT's commanding officer (who was well regarded by the crew) was hospitalised because he had been on the bridge continuously for seventy hours.

Once the follow-up forces were ashore, the build-up began. As the name suggests, this involved building up Allied forces in Normandy so they could sustain and expand the beachhead.[56]

★ ★ ★

So far, this account has been almost exclusively from the Allied perspective, but their opponents had a say in the matter too. The Allied planners were certainly conscious of German naval forces which, although weakened, were still a potential threat, especially to slow and poorly armed landing craft. The German naval forces near the Allied landing area included three torpedo boats, one minesweeper, twenty-nine E-boats (fast torpedo boats), thirty-six R-boats (coastal minesweepers) and forty-nine other small vessels. These were particularly expected to be a threat during the hours of darkness and when there was low visibility.

Early on D-Day, three German torpedo boats from Le Havre sank the destroyer HNoMS *Svenner* and came close to threatening some of the Force S landing ships. However, Allied naval and air forces were so strong that the German navy could only harass rather than stop the Allies.[57]

For their part, the Germans had at least basic knowledge of many types of Allied landing craft. *Erkennungstafel Landungsboote Feindmächte*, a printed guide issued in October 1943, listed the characteristics of various types of craft, including the LCA, LCVP, LCT(5), LCF and LCG(L). Field Marshal Erwin Rommel had predicted that the Allies would use 'submergible' tanks: in other words, DD tanks, one of the Allies' most secret weapons. The Germans thought the Allies had eighty army divisions in the UK and enough landing craft to put twenty divisions ashore at once. It would have amazed German intelligence officers had they known about the Allies' discussions only a few months earlier, on whether to use three or five assault divisions.[58]

LST(2)s under construction on 22 May 1943 at Evansville, Indiana, on the Ohio River. Many built here, by the Missouri Valley Bridge & Iron Company, took part in Operation Neptune. The wartime workforce peaked at 19,500 men and women. (Collection of the Evansville Museum of Arts, History and Science)

Eight LCT(6)s being built by the Pidgeon Thomas Iron Co., Memphis, Tennessee, on 1 April 1944. Engines, ramp motors and other equipment sit on their tank decks, ready for installation. Both LCT(5)s and LCT(6)s built here were used at Normandy. (US Naval History & Heritage Command, NH 91512)

Wooden-hulled LCAs under production in 1942 at the Harris Lebus Factory in north London. Like many other civilian companies in the UK, this furniture manufacturer adapted to build equipment for wartime use. Thornycroft of Southampton were the main builder of this type of craft. (IWM A 9836)

Wrens check a 20mm Oerlikon gun on an LCT. No Wrens sailed with the invasion force on D-Day, but they played an important part in preparing the fleet and in aiding crews as they returned. (IWM D 18179)

LCT(5) 2130's crew, probably more smartly dressed than usual, in late June 1944. Sub Lieutenants Leslie Fowler and John Ellis (middle row, third and second from left) were the commanding officer and first lieutenant. On D-Day, this LCT was in the H+175 wave at Utah Beach. (The D-Day Story, Portsmouth, 2005/74)

A potato-peeling session by crewmen on an LBK off the coast of Normandy on 11 June 1944. By the look of it, some of their 'customers' were participating too. The mostly informal but practical styles of dress were typical on smaller landing craft. (IWM A 24015)

The LCA(HR) was fitted with twenty-four spigot mortars to clear minefields and barbed wire from the beach. Here, only four spigots have their mortar bombs mounted. A crewman is in the coxswain's position in the left foreground. (The National Museum of the Royal Navy)

SS *Monowai* was an LSI(L) that on D-Day carried nineteen LCAs – visible on davits on the ship's side – and over 700 troops. These craft landed the Queen's Own Rifles of Canada and the Régiment de la Chaudière on Juno Beach. (IWM A 23740)

LCS(M)(3) 202 did not take part in Operation Neptune, but many others of this fire-support craft type did. The Royal Marine crew demonstrate the LCS(M)3's weapons: a 4in smoke mortar, two stripped-down Lewis guns and twin .50in Vickers machine guns in a power-operated turret. (IWM A 28452)

Rocket projectors cover the deck of this LCT(R). The light-coloured heads of several of the 5in rockets can just be seen on the left. LCT(R)s converted from LCT(3)s were used on all five beaches, fitted with around 1,000 rockets. (The National Museum of the Royal Navy)

Over 400 barges such as this LBV were used in Operation Neptune. LBVs carried additional stores on D-Day, then acted as ferry craft over the following weeks, unloading larger ships that could not beach. Other barges were in supporting roles. (The National Museum of the Royal Navy)

Seen during a training exercise, these two LCI(L)s illustrate slight differences between earlier and later types. Both were at Omaha Beach on D-Day. The left-hand craft was converted to an LCH (LCH 87) for the Deputy Assault Group Commander O-1. (US Coast Guard 190424-G-G0000-7016)

USS *Samuel Chase* was a US Coast Guard-crewed APA landing ship that carried thirty landing craft to Omaha Beach on D-Day. In this photo, LCVPs can be seen on the ship's davits, and other craft including an LCM are on its deck. (US Naval History & Heritage Command, NH 107712)

An LCI(S), a type used on D-Day for landing commandos, is flanked by a pair of LCS(L)(2) fire-support craft. The LCS(L)(2) was based on the LCI(S) hull, with extra weapons, including a 4in mortar in the bow, and a 6-pounder gun turret. (The National Museum of the Royal Navy)

The LCP(L) was originally designed as an assault craft by Higgins Industries of New Orleans. By 1944, it was used in other roles, such as navigational leader, hydrographic survey or smoke-laying. (The National Museum of the Royal Navy)

LCCs were used by the Americans to direct landing craft to the correct beach. LCC 70, seen here off Normandy on 10 June 1944, was the Tare Green tertiary control vessel at Utah Beach on D-Day. (US Naval History & Heritage Command/US National Archives, NH 80-G-252686)

A pair of American LCS(S)s off Utah Beach on 10 June 1944. They used rockets and machine guns for close-in fire support around H-Hour on the US beaches, hence the crafts' armoured cabins. The craft on the left has the markings of its parent ship, USS *Bayfield* (APA-33). (US Naval History & Heritage Command/US National Archives, NH 80-G-252688)

African American personnel transfer rations and other stores to a US LCI(L) before D-Day. The photograph shows the distinctive ramp of the LCM(3) on the right and illustrates its considerable carrying capacity: a Sherman tank or sixty troops (even more for short distances). (US National Archives 12003996/80-G-251869)

Only lighter vehicles such as these British trucks, many marked with the Allied recognition star, could be carried on the upper deck of an LST(2), as seen here. Heavier vehicles including tanks, travelled on the lower deck. (US National Archives 176887804/111-SC-190059)

Men of the 6th Green Howards sit on the three benches of LCA 1000 on 5 May 1944 during large-scale practice landings (Exercise Fabius). On D-Day, this craft landed the same battalion on Gold Beach soon after H-Hour but was later lost with the deaths of two crew. (IWM H 38229)

At Gosport on 3 June 1944, Sherman tanks of the 13th/18th Hussars and other vehicles reverse onto LCT(4) 610, scheduled to deliver them to Sword Beach at H+45. The Landing Table Index Number (LTIN) is displayed on the LCT's bridge, identifying this cargo of troops and vehicles. (IWM H 39000)

Another view of LCT(4) 610, now with tanks and men of the 13th/18th Hussars on board and in the Solent before D-Day. The image illustrates the crowded conditions on the LCTs. Camouflage netting, a precaution against enemy reconnaissance aircraft, has been folded back for the photographer to reveal a Sherman Firefly tank. (IWM B 5105)

6

Utah Beach

Were you shot at? ... You're darn right we were shot at ... maybe like a city block from the beach I'd see out ahead of me the machine gun bullets hitting the water and cascading ten feet high ...

Martin J. Perrett, coxswain on LCVP from USS *Bayfield*[1]

Utah is often mentioned only briefly and dismissively when summarising the five D-Day beaches. However, the fact that many aspects of the Utah landings proceeded according to plan did not mean that executing that plan was always straightforward or without danger.[2]

Around 4½ miles off Utah Beach, a shoal ran parallel to the shore known as the Banc du Cardonnet. This shallower water provided the Germans with the perfect place to lay a minefield. On the northern side of the landing area, the shoal broke the surface to form two small islands, the Îles Saint-Marcouf. As the assault forces would pass right by these islands, Force U had to plan for their early capture on D-Day. The naval orders for Force U emphasised that there would be a strong cross-current and, indeed, this did come into play on D-Day.[3]

The whole of Utah Beach was nearly 10,000 yards long, but the initial landings would take place across roughly a quarter of that distance: on Tare Green (the more northerly of the two assault beaches) and Uncle Red. The planners had divided this part of Utah Beach into Tare and Uncle sectors. As will unfold below, the beaches where the troops really landed were more southerly than these planned locations.

The beach had a shallow gradient, particularly at low water when the slope was as gradual as 1:140 or less. At low tide, some 1,000 yards of beach were exposed, three times more than at Omaha. At high water, the gradient could increase to 1:30 or steeper, by which time the depth of the beach would have decreased to a mere 25 yards. Seen from the sea, the coastal terrain was low lying, with few distinctive terrain features.[4]

There were ridges and furrows (runnels) running along parts of the tidal section of the beach which, when covered by the tide, created hidden ditches that could act as traps for troops or vehicles wading ashore. Behind the beach were dunes stretching some 150 yards inland with virtually no buildings in sight. A further mile or more inland had been flooded by the Germans as a defensive measure to slow the potential advance of Allied troops.

Like Sword Beach, the other beach added in early 1944 when the COSSAC plan was expanded from three to five assault beaches, the assault at Utah would be made by one Regimental Combat Team (RCT, the equivalent of a British brigade). That RCT was drawn from the US 4th Infantry Division, US VII Corps, with supporting troops attached. In contrast, at Omaha, Gold and Juno, the attack would be launched on a two-RCT/brigade frontage, meaning roughly double the number of troops in the assault.[5]

One factor limiting the frontage of the assault was lack of attack transports or landing ships. The troop capacity of these vessels could vary considerably, so this question is more nuanced than simply the number of ships. Like Force S at Sword Beach, Force U had only four of these key ships, compared to nine at Omaha (not counting those tasked to land Rangers, including at Pointe du Hoc). There was a limit to how fast troops could disembark from such ships. The issue was not a shortage of minor landing craft such as LCVPs, LCAs and LCMs to land troops on the beach, since Force U was relatively well provided for in that respect. When it came to LCTs, Force U had around 156 of these landing craft, slightly more than any of the other naval assault forces.

H-Hour was set at 06.30, earlier than on the eastern beaches, to maximise the time available to deal with German beach obstacles. Having secured the beach, the troops would advance inland along a limited number of causeways leading through the flooded area behind the beach, to link up with US 82nd and US 101st Airborne Divisions, which had begun landing in the first minutes of D-Day. For the assault, US 4th Infantry Division had been strengthened with two further battalions of infantry from US 90th Infantry Division.[6]

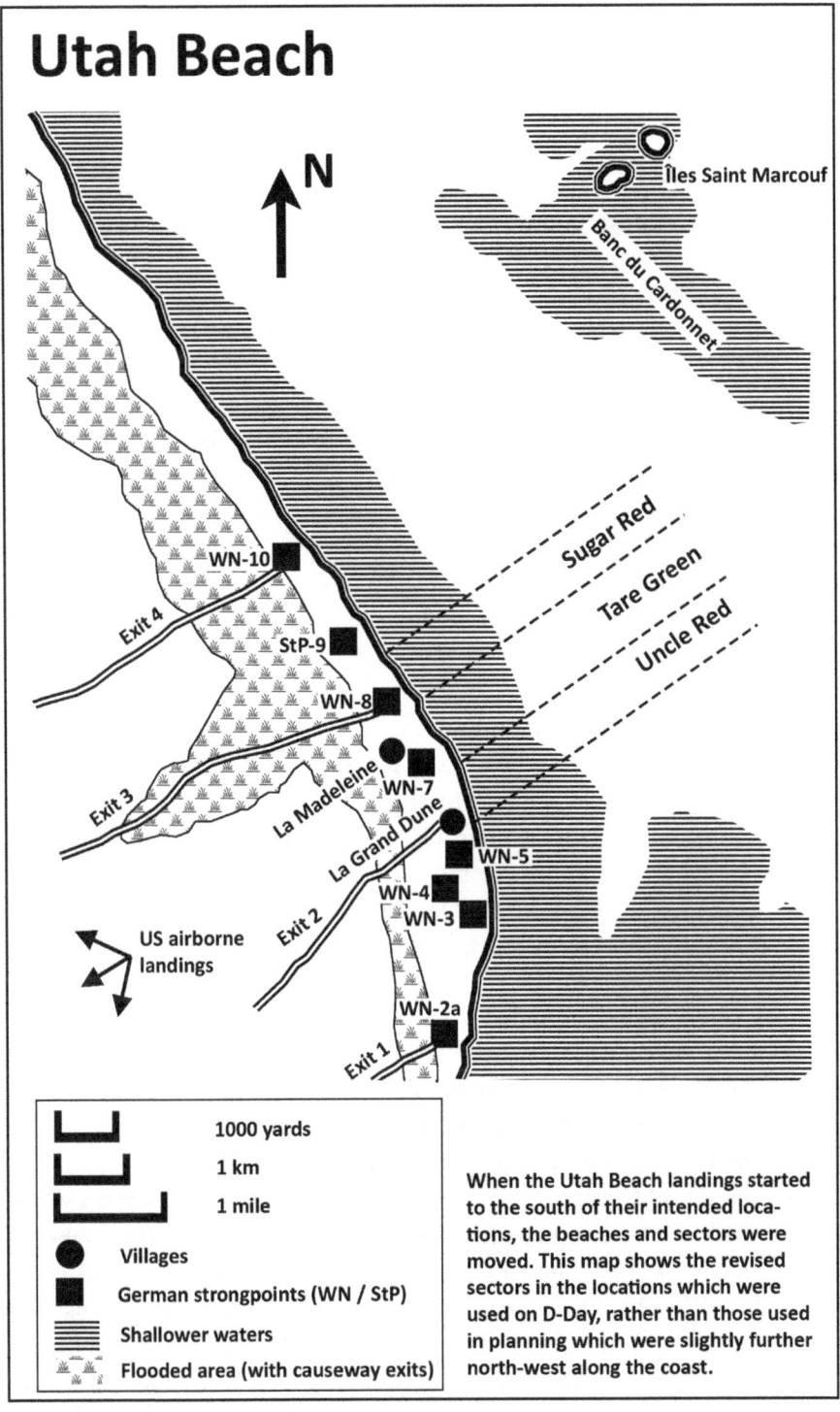

Utah Beach

N

Îles Saint Marcouf

Banc du Cardonnet

Sugar Red

Tare Green

Uncle Red

WN-10

Exit 4

StP-9

WN-8

La Madeleine

WN-7

La Grand Dune

Exit 3

WN-5

WN-4

Exit 2

WN-3

US airborne landings

WN-2a

Exit 1

1000 yards	
1 km	
1 mile	
● Villages	
■ German strongpoints (WN / StP)	
≣ Shallower waters	
Flooded area (with causeway exits)	

When the Utah Beach landings started to the south of their intended locations, the beaches and sectors were moved. This map shows the revised sectors in the locations which were used on D-Day, rather than those used in planning which were slightly further north-west along the coast.

Utah Beach: Map approximately to scale. Some details omitted for clarity. (Map primarily based on: Badsey, Stephen, *Utah Beach* (*Battlezone Normandy*) (Stroud: Sutton, 2004); Chazette, Alain et al., *Atlantikwall Utah Beach* (Vertou: Histoire & Fortifications, 2012).)

It was probably not on the minds of most landing craft crewmen on the day, but at a strategic level, the landings on Utah Beach were a calculated risk. The beach was separated from the remainder of the Allied landing beaches. The Vire and Douvre rivers and estuary formed a natural barrier to movement on land towards the adjacent Omaha Beach. On the other hand, the addition of Utah Beach meant that Allied forces would be ashore at a point closer to the port of Cherbourg, a key objective for the weeks after D-Day.

Today, the German defences at Utah Beach are often summarised as weak, but the Allied plan did not dismiss them lightly. In fact, the plan for the naval assault here was closely shaped by those defences, particularly the presence of many gun batteries, often protected by reinforced concrete casemates, to both the north and south of the approach to Utah Beach by sea. As a precaution, the planners chose to locate the Transport Area, where the landing ships would deploy their small boats, 13 miles out to sea, compared to 7 miles out for the eastern beaches. This increased the journey time to the beach for landing craft crews and the troops on board.

The German defences along the beachfront itself had similarities to those on the other landing beaches. Compared to Omaha, at Utah there were no bluffs rising at the rear of the beach, and many coastal strong-points had to be sited along the back of the beach. Thus, they had more limited fields of fire and were more vulnerable to amphibious assault troops than most strongpoints at Omaha. Without high ground, it would be more difficult for German artillery observers to direct artillery fire.[7]

At 02.00 the first convoy of Force U arrived at the Transport Area: Convoy U-2B, which included five LST(2)s, each towing a Rhino Ferry. The Rhinos would not start landing vehicles until the afternoon, but the early arrival of the LSTs was essential because each carried obstacle clearance personnel. In addition, the LCVPs on board these ships would play a significant part in landing some of the assault troops.

Around 02.30 Convoy U-1A began anchoring in the Transport Area, having made the crossing at a much faster speed then the LSTs: 12 knots compared to 5 knots. The core of this convoy was four troop transport ships: the APAs (American attack transports) USS *Barnett* and USS *Bayfield* carried troops for Uncle Red beach, while the APA USS *Joseph T. Dickman* and the British Merchant Navy landing ship SS *Empire Gauntlet* were loaded with assault forces for Tare Green beach. *Bayfield* was doing double duty as the HQ ship for Force U.[8]

Rather than the troops on board simply embarking in that ship's own landing craft, in each pair of landing ships one vessel sent many of its empty boats to the other, so that vessel would be unloaded first. Additional craft also helped with this process. For example, at 02.26, USS *Barnett* anchored in the Transport Area and began rail-loading troops onto its own craft. By 02.33, the first wave of *Barnett's* own boats (ten out of twenty-seven LCVPs) was clear of the ship's side. Those soldiers would spend around four hours on board the LCVPs before they went ashore.

About an hour later, all of *Barnett's* boats, which probably also included two LCM(3)s, had been loaded. The ship was now ready to begin loading into other craft, including twelve of USS *Bayfield's* LCVPs, as well as LCVPs sent from some of the LSTs. By 06.33, all personnel of the assault waves and nine priority vehicles had been embarked into landing craft. An hour later, the first boats began returning to *Barnett*, some bearing casualties.

At 10.30, eight hours after *Barnett* had anchored off the French coast, the first LCT came alongside to unload remaining personnel and vehicles. That LCT had already delivered its initial cargo to the beach and was now ready for a second load.[9]

Convoy U-2A1 was due to arrive off Normandy at 02.30, around the same time as the landing ships. This was another slow (5-knot) convoy and included many of the landing craft that would be required for the assault on both parts of Utah Beach. The pace of the convoy had been set by its lead ships, the LCT(A)s, which had struggled in the rough seas. As a result, the front of the convoy arrived at the Transport Area nearly an hour late. Due to its size, the rear of the convoy would not arrive until some three hours later.[10]

Most of the craft had to continue straight on towards the beach. They included twenty-two LCTs, carrying the DD tanks and wading tanks, and eleven gunfire support craft, LCFs, LCG(L)s and LCT(R)s. There were also fifty LCM(3)s, most of which headed for the landing ships to which they had been assigned. Eight of the remaining LCM(3)s reported to LSTs for embarking obstacle clearance personnel.

A group of landing craft in the same convoy that could be overlooked were sixteen LCP(L)s known as 'smokers', which were equipped to create smoke screens for protecting the major warships and landing ships against enemy air attack. They had been towed across the English Channel by larger craft, though in the heavy seas some of the towing craft had to sink their LCP(L)s after the tows repeatedly parted.[11]

Also in Convoy U-2A1 were three LCM(Salvage)s, half of Force U's complement of these craft. Two carried a bulldozer, and later on D-Day, these would rescue over 200 vehicles that had got bogged down on the beach, as well as helping LCTs unbeach. The major part of Convoy U-2A2, which arrived after U-2A1, was 136 LCTs, including seventy-seven belonging to the Royal Navy.[12]

Force U's first amphibious landing took place just after 04.30 (two hours before H-Hour on the main beach), when four LCAs of 552 Assault Flotilla from SS *Empire Gauntlet* landed troops of the US 4th Cavalry Group on the Îles Saint-Marcouf. These craft were escorted by one LCS(S) from USS *Bayfield*, plus control craft PC 484. The landings went smoothly, and the troops confirmed that the islands were not occupied by German forces.[13]

At 05.25, German guns sited inland opened fire at the leading vessels. Some of the smaller craft had become detached from their waves, and control craft assigned them to other waves instead. At around 05.35, the gunfire support craft opened fire on the German defences. They were positioned 500 yards ahead of the craft carrying the first wave of assault infantry. LCG(L)s 5 and 6 were on the outer (northern) flank of the Tare Green boat lane, while LCG(L)s 7 and 893 were in the mirror image position on the southern flank of the Uncle Red boat lane.

The four LCFs were arranged with one craft on either flank of each boat lane: LCFs 18 and 22 for Green, LCFs 27 and 31 for Red. As well as guarding against enemy air attack on the leading waves, once the assault troops had got ashore the LCFs were to fire on any targets of opportunity as would support the troops. LCG(L)s 7 and 893 were shelled by German guns and had to take evasive manoeuvres, with each craft then firing around thirty rounds in return at a range of 4,000 yards which silenced the enemy.[14]

With the lead assault waves still en route for the beach, at around 05.37 the larger warships joined in the shore bombardment. The US Coast Guard rescue craft USCG-16, accompanying the lead waves to Uncle Red, later described the situation at 05.30 (one hour before H-Hour) as 'under severe shelling attacks and with mines going up all around us'.[15]

A 53m-long patrol craft (PC) was the primary control vessel for each half of Utah Beach, assisted by two LCCs as secondary and tertiary controls. They were fitted with navigational equipment to help ensure they could guide waves to the correct beach. At about 05.55, the Uncle Red primary control craft, PC 1261, was engulfed by an explosion, now generally thought to have been caused by a mine, though at least one eyewitness judged it to be from an enemy shell.

The entire Utah Beach landings unintentionally began around 1,500 yards to the south of the planned beaches. The loss of this key control vessel – then at the Line of Departure, 4,000 yards from the beach – is usually given as the main cause of this error. The secondary control vessel for Uncle Red (LCC 80) had been temporarily disabled after fouling a buoy, and while other control craft took measures to replace PC 1261, this took time. However, the absence of control craft on Uncle Red would not explain why the Tare Green waves, which still had a control craft, also landed off course. Veterans from LCC 60 have stated that the main reason was the first wave LCVPs swinging south to avoid swamping the DD tanks with their wash as they passed them.[16]

Smoke and dust caused by the naval and air bombardment may have contributed to the navigational error. Crucially, the landing forces all moved south together, rather than being scattered between the planned and actual landing beaches. Credit for this must go to the Naval Scout Unit on board one of the LCS(S)s escorting Waves 1 and 1A.

There was one of these units for each half of Utah Beach. One of the unit's roles was guiding the DD tanks and the first wave infantry for the final distance between the Line of Departure and the beach. Lieutenant Robert Halperin, in charge of the Scout Unit at Uncle Red, recalled that he tried to ensure the wave kept together after PC 1261 was lost.[17]

Fortunately for the assault forces, both the beach obstacles and the German strongpoints at the new landing site were weaker than at the planned location. Rather than continuing to use the original beach names for the new landing site, Force U moved the codenamed beaches to match the actual landings. These revised beach locations are used below unless otherwise stated. The actual Tare Green landings took place on what had originally been Uncle Red and further south. The revised Uncle Red was completely south of the original one and crossed over into Victor sector (at La Grande Dune).[18]

As the assault waves approached the beach, other fire support was scheduled to come from the army's weapons on board LCTs. Six LCT(5)s carried M7 Priest 105mm self-propelled guns of the 65th Armoured Field Artillery Battalion, which were meant to fire against the beach area on the run-in shoot. In the event, they did not fire due to confusion among the forward observers. The other fire support came from six LCT(A)s that had successfully made the crossing (two more of these craft had not). Each LCT(A) had been fitted with a platform at the bow that would enable two Sherman tanks to fire on the approach to the beach. Each craft carried 150 rounds of additional tank shells for this purpose, so the tanks would land with a full load of their own ammunition.

The Commander Force U later reported that these tanks apparently did not fire from the LCT(A)s. Their orders were to 'be prepared to fire at sea … primarily to the flanks of beach UTAH … Tanks will not fire over heads of leading waves after H−5 minimum, but may fire on targets to the flanks if they can do so without endangering friendly troops.'[19]

From 06.07 to 06.27, medium bombers of the US 9th Air Force bombed the Utah Beach area, ensuring that many of the defenders were still sheltering when the assault troops began landing. Intriguingly, the report of 1st Engineer Special Brigade mentions a plan that some of the bombers would fly low and drop delayed-action bombs to cut lanes through the beach obstacles, which the engineers saw no sign of having been implemented.[20]

The air bombardment overlapped with the LCT(R)s firing their rockets. Only four of the planned five craft were present, as LCT(R) 425 had been disabled on 4 June. Their instructions were to fire at H−2 or when the lead wave of craft was 450 yards from the water's edge. They began firing early, at around 06.08 to 06.10. Each craft targeted a different German strongpoint. As was the case on some other beaches, other personnel seem to have found it difficult to judge the accuracy or effectiveness of the LCT(R) fire, although the Commander Force U assessed it to have been accurate. Reports came back from some of the assault wave boats' crews that LCT(R) fire had fallen on and near both beaches until H+7, resulting in some army and navy casualties.[21]

The final fire-support contribution delivered by landing craft came from twelve LCS(S)s, which were following behind the LCT(R)s. Five of these craft were tasked to Tare Green and the other seven to Uncle Red. They were due to fire when the lead craft carrying assault infantry were 250 yards from the water's edge. Reports from the assault craft praised the LCS(S)s for their accuracy.[22]

The LCS(S)s had crossed the English Channel on board larger ships. These craft continued to support the troops ashore after H-Hour. In the crew of an LCS(S) from USS *Bayfield* was Yogi Berra, the future US star baseball player and coach. As Berra later recalled:

> We went … 300 yards off the beach. We protect[ed] the troops. If they ran into any trouble, we would fire the rockets over. We could fire one rocket if we wanted to, or we could fire off 24 of them, 12 on each side.[23]

THE ASSAULT

The landing craft of Wave 1 had left the Line of Departure on time at H−19 and landed within a minute or two of their planned beaching time of H-Hour. On each of the two sectors of Utah Beach, ten LCVPs were to land two companies from the US 8th Infantry: a total initial assault force of around 620 troops.

The boats carried by a transport ship were not fixed but could be varied according to the operation. As well as the boats carried on davits along the ship's side, additional craft could be carried on its decks. USS *Bayfield*, for example, had a standard complement of twenty-eight craft: twenty-three LCVPs, one LCS(S), two LCP(L)s and two LCM(3)s. A 1946 publication by the Coast Guard's Historical Section stated that for D-Day, *Bayfield* carried nineteen LCVPs, two LCM(3)s and two LCP(L)s, a total of only twenty-three boats. However, other evidence, including archive photographs and veteran accounts, indicates that the ship also carried four LCS(S)s. The LCVPs were used for landing troops, while the LCM(3)s could also land stores or a vehicle. The LCP(L)s were used by boat group commanders, who accompanied at least some waves. Their function was to keep the boats of the wave together and they would not have beached.[24]

Wave 1 landed at H-Hour. On Tare Green, Companies B and C, 1st Battalion, 8th Infantry had loaded from USS *Joseph T. Dickman* onto ten of that ship's LCVPs. The battalion would deal with strongpoint WN-5 at La Grande Dune, then move inland. Initially, there was little German fire, and Captain Robert Crisson, Company C commander, later recalled that the excitable troops had to be reminded to keep their heads down on the LCVP as they drew near the shore. With heavily loaded boats and a flat beach, the craft could not touch down as far up the beach as would have been ideal.[25]

The first wave on Uncle Red comprised ten LCVPs carrying Companies E and F, 2nd Battalion, 8th Infantry, loaded from USS *Barnett*. At least four of the boats came from that ship, but others may have been supplied by other vessels. The first-wave LCVPs 'sprayed the beach with machine gun fire during the assault', as did the accompanying LCP(L)s from *Barnett* carrying boat group commanders. Captain M.C. Adair, a surgeon with 2nd Battalion, reported that the men landed in hip-deep water amid 'heavy' shelling which did not cause many casualties.[26]

At this point, the assault infantry should have been supported by swimming DD tanks, launched from a group of LCTs designated Wave 1A. These tanks were scheduled to beach at H-Hour or as soon as possible afterwards. In practice, they did not land until several more waves had beached – and will be considered at that point.

The landing craft of Wave 2 were due at H+5, carrying part of the reserve companies of the two assault infantry battalions plus obstacle clearance teams and engineers. On each half of Utah there were fifteen

LCVPs, of which nine carried infantry and six contained obstacle clearance personnel. Each fifteen craft were split into two divisions, as fifteen was considered too many for a single boat group commander to lead.

On Tare Green, Companies A and D, 1st Battalion, 8th Infantry, were to land in five and four LCVPs respectively, again having loaded from USS *Barnett*. Companies G and H, 2nd Battalion, 8th Infantry, touched down on Uncle Red in five and four craft respectively.

Taking one battalion as an example, Company D was 1st Battalion's weapons company, which had fewer personnel than the other (rifle) companies such as Company A, and therefore needed fewer boats to carry it. In fact, only part of each company was landing now in Wave 2 – 147 men of Company A and sixty men of Company D. This was 76 per cent and 36 per cent of the two companies' authorised strengths, which were 193 for a rifle company and 166 men for a weapons company. In Company D's four craft there were also a further thirty-one personnel from the two assault companies (B and C). It was common that units and sub-units would be divided up and mixed together like this.[27]

The other twelve LCVPs in Wave 2, divided evenly between the two sectors, had met up with the boats carrying the infantry reserve companies offshore. Naval Combat Demolition Unit (NCDU) men were on eight of the craft, having been loaded from the first five LSTs to arrive off Utah. Despite the name, each NCDU was a mix of eleven naval personnel and five army engineers of 299th Engineer Combat Battalion.

Four more of the twelve LCVPs carried other army engineers (237th Engineer Combat Battalion, also tasked with improving exits for the beach), who had embarked from USS *Barnett*. The Commander Force U reported that only about half of the thirty Wave 2 craft landed on time, with the rest beaching with subsequent waves. The plan was that only minutes after the first wave of assault infantry had landed and begun engaging the defender, navy and army personnel would begin clearing and marking 50-yard-wide paths through the German beach obstacles so that larger landing craft had a better chance of beaching unscathed. Along with their comrades landing at H+17, these men managed to clear the assault area of most obstacles by 08.00.[28]

Wave 2 was accompanied by a single LCVP on each beach, carrying the battalion HQ of 1st and 2nd Battalion, 8th Infantry (on Tare Green and Uncle Red respectively). The 2nd Battalion LCVP was accompanied by another craft carrying Brigadier General Theodore (Teddy) Roosevelt, Assistant Divisional Commander of the US 4th Infantry Division, who had been on board USS *Barnett*. Roosevelt (56) had persuaded the divisional commander that he should be allowed to land with the early waves to inspire the troops and be on the spot to make decisions (he may even have accompanied the first wave). He decided that there should be no attempt to reposition the landings to match the original plan; he is famously said to have declared, 'We'll start the war from right here!'

Whether it would have been possible to divert the long train of landing craft heading for Utah is debatable. At best, it would surely have required hours to move the later waves out to sea, reassemble them and then direct each to its correct landing site. The process of obstacle clearance would have had to have been restarted at the new location. At worst, it would have caused chaos that would have stalled the beach landings and potentially left the US airborne troops without the support from beach-landed troops that they desperately needed. Given his rank, Roosevelt also had an LCT loaded with staff and vehicles, including his jeep, 'Rough Rider', but this would not land until later in the day.[29]

As the infantry began to advance along the coast, they continued to be supported by landing craft, which shelled targets of opportunity. By the end of D-Day, for example, LCG(L) 5 had fired 192 rounds of 4.7in and 420 rounds of 20mm ammunition.

The smallest support craft were also in action. After H-Hour, LCS(S) PA-13-13 proceeded along the coast, firing at a series of enemy positions ahead of the infantry advance. The boat's commander, Ensign Albert Low, was later commended for these actions:

> You ably directed the maneuvering of your boat, while under enemy fire, to support the landing with rocket and machine gun fire and then continued this support from the flank of the beach until assault troops had consolidated their beach position.[30]

★ ★ ★

The next groups of craft to beach will be described wave by wave. According to the plan, they were to come ashore as separate entities, neatly spaced apart in time. In practice, waves mixed together as they landed. Around 06.35 to 06.45, the infantry reserve companies and obstacle clearance teams of Wave 2 (just described) merged with the wading tanks of Wave 3 and the remaining obstacle clearance teams of Wave 4. The DD tanks of Wave 1A landed around 06.50, about twenty minutes late.[31]

The additional obstacle clearance personnel formed the whole of Wave 4, due at H+20 and landing in LCM(3)s and LCVPs. The LCM(3)s had been towed across the English Channel by Royal Navy LCT(4)s, and those LCTs would later land tanks at H+300.

Eight LCM(3)s each carried an army team – a twenty-six-man Beach Obstacle Demolition Party, who had boarded from the LSTs on which they had made the crossing – and 2 tons of explosives. Three LCVPs despatched from LSTs had reserve NCDU teams embarked. Each LCM(3) also carried a handful of men from the 81st Airborne Anti-Aircraft Battalion for anti-aircraft defence of the beach.[32]

The teams landed under mortar and machine-gun fire. Shells struck LCM 109 as it beached, leaving six soldiers as casualties. Two LCM(3)s sank off the beach, one carrying the officer in command of the Utah Beach obstacle demolitions, who, as a result, did not go ashore until 7 June.

The NCDU teams were already tackling the seaward line of obstacles, so the army teams moved on to the next row to landward. Incredibly, the first gaps, at least 50 yards wide and running from the water's edge to near the sea wall at the back of the beach, were created in only five to eight minutes. As the gaps were increased in number and width, they would be valuable for enabling subsequent waves of landing craft to beach without risk of serious damage. This success came at a cost, however, of heavy casualties among the obstacle clearance force.[33]

After landing the obstacle clearance personnel, the LCVPs of Wave 2 and the LCM(3)s of Wave 4 proceeded out to sea, ready to return at H+65 so that the demolition teams could collect more explosives for their work. Four LCT(6)s – LCT 522 and 524 for Tare Green, LCT 810 and 855 for Uncle Red – which were due to land at H+360, also carried 5 tons of additional explosives for the obstacle clearance units among the 150 tons of stores that each LCT carried.[34]

Two waves of craft bearing three companies of 70th Tank Battalion came ashore late at about 06.50. Consequently, the tanks were not able to provide support at H-Hour as intended, but even in their absence the infantry had successfully made the assault.

Companies A and B were equipped with amphibious DD tanks and had crossed to Normandy on eight LCT(6)s. An LCT(6) could carry four DD tanks, whereas the LCT(3)s used to launch DD tanks on the Anglo-Canadian beaches had room for five each.[35]

At 05.47, as the eight LCTs headed for the beach in formation, there was a sudden, shocking explosion. LCT 593 struck a mine that had been laid on the Banc du Cardonnet, which blew the 120ft-long craft in half: the effect of the mine was apparently amplified by the shallow water. Staff Sergeant Gibson, one of the soldiers on board, was thrown into the water but returned to the stern section of the craft and attempted to free a wounded sailor who was caught in the wreckage, but tragically the LCT capsized, taking the wounded man with it. At least five crewmen from LCT 593 were killed, including Ensign Joseph James Schmucker, the officer in charge. Sixteen soldiers of Company A, 70th Tank Battalion also died. The shock of LCT 593 sinking seems to have delayed the other LCTs in this group bound for Uncle Red.[36]

The DD tanks were due to be launched 5,000 yards off the beach. Since the wave was behind schedule and enemy fire was moderate, the officer commanding PC 1176, the Tare Green PC craft, decided that the DD tanks should swim from 3,000 yards instead. Other sources say the distance was 1,500 yards, and indeed, the launching time was probably not the same across the whole wave (06.10 for Tare Green, 06.30 for Uncle Red).

One DD tank was lost at sea, possibly swamped by the blast from an LCT(R) firing, but twenty-seven reached land. DD tanks are often dismissed as being of no value on D-Day. In fact, Utah Beach was the best potential site for their use, though of course, they would have been most effective if they were on time. A US Navy after-action report stated that Utah offered an area of more sheltered water that was suitable for the use of DD tanks. After launching the tanks, the LCTs headed seaward to the Transport Area to help unload larger ships. En route, the now empty LCT 597 was sunk by another mine, with the loss of at least seven crew. Two sinkings and at least thirteen deaths were a heavy loss for a small group of landing craft.[37]

It had been planned that the reserve tank company – Sherman tanks of Company C, 70th Tank Battalion – would hit the beach about fifteen minutes after the DD tanks. They were on board eight LCT(A)s that formed Wave 3, with four craft bound for each half of the beach. Two LCT(A)s had engine trouble and were lost during the crossing to Normandy – LCT(A) 2402, which was destined for Tare Green, and LCT(A) 2301, heading for Uncle Red. The crews of both the landing craft and the tanks were rescued.[38]

There were three Sherman tanks on each LCT(A) – usually, two standard Sherman tanks and one tankdozer with bulldozer blades for helping the obstacle clearance teams. However, one historian states that some LCTs – including at least one of those lost – carried two tankdozers and only a single standard Sherman, and that only four tankdozers successfully reached Utah Beach. All the tanks were equipped to wade through deep water to get ashore. In practice, because the DD tanks were delayed, all three companies landed close together.[39]

None of the six craft that reached Normandy had a smooth landing. Of the Tare Green craft, LCT(A) 2310 took on water during the crossing and lost sections of bulkhead (the sides of the craft). Once the craft beached, it was hit by multiple shells, leaving two crew wounded, fifteen holes in the craft and only one functioning engine. LCT(A)s 2454 and 2478 both sustained damage. On Uncle Red, LCT(A) 2282 was hit by a shell on the beach and had to be towed off, while LCT(A)s 2309 and 2488 sustained lesser damage. Those tankdozers that did get ashore found that the beach obstacles were not fitted with anti-tank mines, so they could quickly drag the obstacles out of the way.[40]

At H+20, personnel of 1106 Engineer Combat Group were due to begin landing. This unit had a very specific role: to open sluice gates that would begin to drain the zone behind Utah Beach that had been flooded by the Germans. At the last minute, the unit's commanding officer discovered that no landing craft had been allocated to land his first four obstacle clearance teams. Taking a chance by putting all his ninety-three men and their explosives into a single LCM(3), he got them ashore.[41]

Waves 5 and 6 were due in quick succession at H+30 and H+37, carrying infantry and engineers. For the H+30 wave, on each half of the beach four boats carried more personnel of the assault infantry battalions: 1st Battalion, 8th Infantry, landing from USS *Joseph T. Dickman* on Tare Green, and 2nd Battalion of the same regiment, which had loaded from USS *Barnett* to land on Uncle Red. Two further boats on each section of beach held more army engineers. In practice, the Tare Green craft beached on Uncle Red by mistake. It is uncertain which ship supplied the boats in both cases.[42]

More LCVPs were due at H+37 but beached late. There were five boats on each half of the beach: three carrying men of the HQs of the same two battalions and two more with army engineers. All originated at the same transport ships as Wave 5.

The five craft heading for Tare Green were a mixture of types and nationalities. Perhaps uniquely for minor landing craft on D-Day, a Royal Navy officer, Sub Lieutenant Roger Lyles RNVR of 552 Assault Flotilla from SS *Empire Gauntlet*, had under his direct command several US Navy LCVPs as well as one or more LCAs from his own flotilla.[43]

Martin J. Perrett was the coxswain on one of USS *Bayfield*'s LCVPs, which probably landed troops at around H+30. The ship and the crews of its landing craft were all members of the US Coast Guard rather than the US Navy. While en route to the beach, Perrett noticed that a US Army lieutenant standing in front of him was looking very white. Moments later, the man vomited over the side of the LCVP but, unfortunately, he was on the windward side and the vomit blew back into Perrett's face, temporarily blinding him. Fortunately, the Motor Machinist's Mate came to his aid:

> So my trusty Motor Mac, seeing my dilemma he reached over and got a bucket of seawater and said, 'Close your eyes Boats', and I said, 'They're already closed. Man, hit me!' So, boy, he hits me with this bucket of seawater and he said, 'Do you want another one?' I said, 'Yes, that was strong medicine'. So he hit me a second time and with this all these kids in the Army, they bust[ed] out laughing ... to probably dispel their fears to the thought that, well if the kid can take this I guess he'll get us in safely.

Perrett recalled how as his wave neared the beach the craft were:

> ... line abreast charging in ... about 50 feet apart ... were you shot at? ... You're darn right we were shot at ... maybe like a city block from the beach I'd see out ahead of me the machine gun bullets hitting the water and cascading ten feet high.

Fortunately, no one on his craft was hit.[44]

Wave 7 (H+50) primarily consisted of the 87th Chemical Mortar Battalion. Though originally conceived as a means of delivering chemical weapons, as its name suggests, this unit's 4.2in mortars would provide mobile, indirect fire support for the infantry, using conventional ammunition until more substantial artillery forces were ashore. The troops had loaded from USS *Joseph T. Dickman* and USS *Barnett* and were delivered by craft from other ships: those on Tare Green from eight Royal Navy LCAs (552 Assault Flotilla, SS *Empire Gauntlet*) and on Uncle Red from eight LCVPs from one of the other transport ships.[45]

Despite some losses of craft due to enemy action or the sea conditions, in general, the small boats in the first waves at Utah Beach had fared well. Certainly, they had fewer losses than the larger LCTs in the first hour. USS *Joseph T. Dickman* reported that the wind was Force 5 strength, resulting in a 'moderate sea', which made loading boats harder and drenched the troops. USS *Barnett* reported that the wind and sea conditions had caused delays in some of the early waves.[46]

Information on boat crew casualties and boat losses is limited. Losses to several LCM(3)s have already been mentioned. Seven LCVPs from

USS *Joseph T. Dickman*'s complement of up to thirty-one craft were lost in the landings, but all managed to put their troops ashore first. Four of these were lost to enemy fire and three were swamped. Two of *Dickman*'s US Coast Guard boats' crew were killed, though it is not clear exactly what time their craft beached: Seaman First Class Stanley A. Glowacki went down with his sunken boat after it received a direct hit and Seaman Second Class Jack E. Rowe died of wounds after being evacuated onto a destroyer.[47]

USS *Bayfield* also had three boats (out of at least nineteen LCVPs) swamped on the beach. The coxswains of *Bayfield*'s lost boats reported that because their craft were so heavily loaded, they took on more water than the pumps could handle. The problem was worsened because they had to travel at high speed to try to keep to schedule. The extra weight of water on board meant that the LCVPs grounded further out on the beach than would otherwise have been the case, and the troops had to land in chest-deep water, but this did not prevent them getting ashore. *Bayfield*'s swamped boats were later recovered and returned to the ship.

USS *Barnett* apparently did not lose any of its craft on D-Day, but two crewmen on one of its LCVPs died: Coxswain Lucio Garcia Garcia and Seaman First Class Harlen Chalmer Murphy. Royal Navy Leading Seaman Percy Frederick Grant from LCA 998 was killed on D-Day. This craft was one of eighteen British craft from 552 LCA Flotilla carried on board SS *Empire Gauntlet*.[48]

There had already been casualties and losses among the larger landing craft, including LCTs 593 and 597 mentioned above. At 06.30, LCF 31 was 800 yards off the beach on the right flank of the Uncle Red boat lanes when it was hit by a German shell, causing the craft to sink immediately. Leonard Lampton was below decks in the LCF's engine room, when suddenly he was knocked unconscious by an explosion. He came round moments later in pitch blackness and climbed a ladder to the upper decks to escape the rising water level. Reaching the emergency hatch at the top of the ladder, he was gripped by a fear that the ship might already be under water but opened it to find himself alone on the empty deck. Abandoning ship, he was saved by a nearby US Coast Guard rescue boat. At least twenty-three of LCF 31's crew of more than sixty men were lost in the sinking (the crew was so large because it included men operating the craft's anti-aircraft guns).

Landing craft were not the only larger vessels being sunk off Utah Beach around the start of the landings. The destroyer USS *Corry* had sunk around 06.33 after being hit by several German shells and possibly also from a mine explosion.[49]

Clearance of the beach obstacles had proceeded so fast that boats from USS *Bayfield*, landing at H+30 or later, reported that they did not encounter any. German artillery was a more persistent problem and continued to shell the beach area for much of D-Day. Often it was not directed by a German forward observer but was simply focused on areas where the Germans predicted Allied forces were likely to be.[50]

An hour after the first landings (H+60), the troops landing in Wave 8 craft had a different role from the majority of those who had come ashore so far. They were army personnel from 1st Engineer Special Brigade (1st ESB), plus sailors of 2nd Naval Beach Battalion, which was attached to that formation. Together, they were to perform a similar role to the Beach Groups on the Anglo-Canadian beaches: organising the vicinity of the beach and ensuring the quick and efficient landings of troops, vehicles and supplies. This included building exits through the sea wall at the back of the beach and clearing mines in areas to be used for troop movement and supply dumps.[51]

Wave 8 comprised four LCVPs and one LCM(3) on each half of Utah Beach. The personnel landed came from USS *Joseph T. Dickman* (for Tare Green) and USS *Barnett* (for Uncle Red); the boats may have been carried by those ships or supplied by another vessel. One of the important roles of the army engineers landing at this point was to mark the flanks of the beaches and the locations of beach exits: this was done with large fabric markers on poles.[52]

Around the same time, the craft of Wave 8A arrived: five or six LCVPs and four LCM(3)s on each half of the beach, scheduled at H+60 on Tare Green and five minutes later on Uncle Red. These craft had already landed obstacle clearance teams as part of Waves 2 (H+5) and 4 (H+17) and were now returning to the beach to provide them with additional explosives.[53]

By now, German resistance on the initial landing beaches had virtually ceased apart from a few snipers. That said, some of the enemy strongpoints were not completely out of action. By about two hours after H-Hour, LCG(L) 893 had fired 60 per cent of its ammunition, while LCG(L)s 5, 6 and 7 continued supporting troops advancing along Green Beach.[54]

★ ★ ★

Controlling and organising landing craft before they beached was as important as the co-ordination work on land. The two primary control vessels were based at the Line of Departure: PC 1176 for Tare Green and the reassigned LCC 60 at Uncle Red. PC 1176, in fact, remained in this role off Utah Beach until 17 June.

After Wave 1 had been put ashore at H-Hour, five LCVPs and four of the accompanying LCS(S)s were available to act as despatch boats, carrying messages and helping to control subsequent landings. Waves were despatched in numerical sequence, but inevitably individual craft became detached, and these were held at the Line of Departure until they could be added to another wave of the same type of landing craft. This orderly process avoided congestion off the beach. Of course, it helped enormously that both beach obstacles and enemy fire were a much lesser threat than at Omaha Beach around the same time. Boat group and wave commanders sent information on beach conditions to HQ ships offshore. Between H+30 and H+60, US Navy Scouts personnel on LCS(S)s started carrying out hydrographic surveys just off the beach, marking cleared channels and any obstructions to navigation.[55]

Two infantry battalions – another 1,500 infantrymen in total – were the next forces to land. One was the third battalion of the assault infantry regiment (3rd Battalion, 8th Infantry, carried on USS *Bayfield*). The second was an additional battalion (3rd Battalion, 22nd Infantry, embarked on SS *Empire Gauntlet*), which had been attached to 8th Infantry for the assault. These troops were accompanied by personnel from supporting units such as 87th Chemical Mortar Battalion, 4th Engineer Combat Battalion, medics and Shore Fire Control Parties (small teams co-ordinating supporting gunfire from warships). Landing on Uncle Red, the new arrivals from 8th Infantry would advance inland, while 3rd Battalion, 22nd Infantry, would head north from Tare Green along the coast, tackling more German strongpoints with the help of tanks from 746th Tank Battalion, which were scheduled to come ashore at H+145.[56] Members of these two battalions came ashore between Wave 9 at H+75 and Wave 12 at H+105.

Several landing craft which were not in the main sequence of waves were allocated to carry commanding officers or HQ parties from infantry battalions or regiments. There was flexibility in when these landed, according to the wishes of the senior officer in each case. Control craft PC 1176 reported that Tare Green Waves 9 to 12 were two hours late leaving the Line of Departure, and the same may well be true for the same waves of craft bound for Uncle Red.[57]

With a capacity greater than an LCVP (double the number of troops or seven times the weight of cargo), LCM(3)s would be extensively used in the coming hours. Most were drawn from the forty-two craft that had crossed the English Channel under their own power in Convoy U-2A1 and did not have a role supporting obstacle clearance teams.

A minority of LCM(3)s had crossed on board larger ships. USS *Bayfield* later reported that LCMs withstood the sea conditions on D-Day better than LCVPs, but the troops on board still got thoroughly soaked during the journey to the beach. LCM(3)s in Waves 9 to 12 encountered 'considerable' fire when they were 1 mile from the beach, and some were nearly hit in cross-fire between the supporting LCG(L)s and German shore batteries.

After the LCM(3)s had landed their first load of troops, the craft began to unload LCI(L)s. Many LCM(3)s in the next waves were loaded with a single M29 Weasel (an open-topped, tracked cargo-carrying vehicle), as well as troops on foot. Each Weasel had to be lowered into the landing craft from a transport ship, a time-consuming process.[58]

The actual landing craft used varied, according to what was available. Describing the planned sequence on Tare Green first, in Wave 9, 3rd Battalion, 22nd Infantry, were to be carried by three LCAs from SS *Empire Gauntlet*, as well as four LCM(3)s. Waves 10, 11 and 12, at H+85, H+95 and H+105, consisted of seven, six and two LCM(3)s respectively. Two additional LCM(3)s would land the commanding officers and their parties from 3rd Battalion and 22nd Infantry respectively, at a time selected by those officers. A single LCT(5) – LCT 447 – came towards the end of this sequence of waves as the regimental commander desired, carrying other 22nd Infantry troops, including three M2 half-tracks, each towing a 105mm howitzer from the regiment's Cannon Company.[59]

The troops of 3rd Battalion, 8th Infantry landed on Uncle Red at the same time in a similar sequence, although the types of craft sometimes varied. Both Waves 9 and 10 (H+75 and H+85) were to be carried on six LCM(3)s. Four LCM(3)s and three LCVPs would form Wave 11 (H+95), followed by two LCM(3)s and one LCVP in Wave 12 (H+105). As on Tare Green, the commanding officers of the battalion and regiment (3rd Battalion, 22nd Infantry) could choose when to come ashore, with their parties in two more LCM(3)s and an LCVP.[60]

Lieutenant Colonel James Batte, commanding officer of 87th Chemical Mortar Battalion, was on board an LCT(6) with the commanding officer of 8th Infantry. An LCT(6) had a ramp at the stern as well as at the bow, to help with unloading vehicles from LSTs. As a result, 'the sea splashed in and washed around on the deck. We spent much time sitting in our jeeps.' The two officers and their staff transferred to an LCVP to land. Batte recounts how, as they landed, a nearby LCVP 'hit a mine and blew up. A soldier in our craft stated, "The lucky bastards, they ain't seasick no more".' Most mines were meant to have been cleared by this point, but apparently some were still present.[61]

The Landings Continue

Due to arrive at H+110 (08.20), Wave 13 marked a change in the types of landing craft arriving at Utah Beach. Since it was expected that there would be a reduced enemy threat by this point, as was the case, more vulnerable and larger types of craft began to land. First, at H+110, a pair of LCT(5)s were due to land on each half of Utah Beach, carrying vehicles of 531st Engineer Shore Regiment. This unit was part of 1st Engineer Special Brigade and would carry out engineering work to improve the beach area and the roads leading inland. LCT 362, one of these craft tasked to land on Uncle Red, was taking on water and drifting in the Transport Area. A Rhino Ferry may have unloaded some of the vehicles before the craft sank in the early hours of D+1, but 531st Engineer Shore Regiment reported that its cargo of bulldozers, trailers and road material was all lost.[62]

Eleven LCT(5)s and LCT(6)s in Wave 14 primarily delivered 29th Field Artillery Battalion, including three batteries of six M7 self-propelled 105mm guns, divided between the two halves of Utah Beach. This wave was scheduled for H+145 (08.55) and most craft probably landed over the next half an hour or so. One of the Tare Green craft did not arrive: around 08.00, LCT 458 was sunk by a mine while crossing the Banc du Cardonnet. At least three of the LCT's crew were killed and thirty-nine of the sixty artillerymen on board (a further twenty troops were wounded).[63]

Among the larger craft in Wave 15 and successive waves over the next nearly two hours were more than forty British-crewed LCT(5)s of 104, 107 and 110 LCT Flotillas, Royal Navy. After the first craft landed in the H+175 wave, the other craft of these British flotillas were due to beach at H+200, H+260 and H+280, with a few remaining LCTs available as spares. A large proportion of the LCTs had on board US Army engineers units which would work on beach exits and roads. Elements of a variety of other army units were also included, such as reconnaissance vehicles from 4 Cavalry Squadron. There was an advance party in jeeps from 359th Infantry: the main force of that infantry regiment, part of US 90th Infantry Division, was not due to land until the afternoon.[64]

On Tare Green, the H+175 craft included LCTs 2056, 2057, 2304, 2331 and 2477. John Mewha on LCT 2304 later described how his craft arrived at the beach, under fire and after tearing its bottom on a beach obstacle. The troops on board were reluctant to go ashore, and he states that the army officer even had to draw his revolver to make the point. Signalman Mike Crumpton on LCT 2331 recalled seeing troops being hit by enemy fire as they advanced up the beach. After one of the trucks on his craft was jammed on the ramp, German shells began falling nearby. Fortunately, the shells did not explode on the wet sand and the troublesome truck was extracted.[65]

Eight Royal Navy LCTs were scheduled to land on Uncle Red at H+175, although LCT 2002 may have had to turn back to the UK due to water leaking into the engine room. Sub Lieutenant Geoffrey Jensen RNVR, commanding officer of LCT 2483, later recalled that his craft arrived late. After struggling with engine trouble, the LCT reached Juno Beach and had to make its way west to Utah. Once at its destination, the first vehicle off was swamped and the LCT was left stranded by the tide before it could complete unloading. After the first of what would turn into six hours of enemy artillery fire, the LCT's crew took shelter ashore. Eventually unbeaching, they managed to return to the UK, despite having one dead engine and two that were temperamental.[66]

The eight British LCT(5)s that formed the core of Wave 16 were due at H+200, but arrived up to an hour late. Four craft beached on each half of Utah Beach, primarily carrying US Army engineers. Three US Navy LCT(6)s also touched down in the same wave: LCTs 580 and 583 on Tare Green and LCT 811 on Uncle Red. The first carried part of 819th Engineer Aviation Battalion and the other two landed vehicles of 4th Medical Battalion.[67]

★ ★ ★

Further convoys arrived off Utah Beach throughout D-Day. The next group of landing craft had reached the Transport Area at 07.30, as part of Convoy U-1B. Its main component was thirty-six LCI(L)s, each with around 200 men on board (including sailors as well as soldiers: for example, men of 2nd Naval Beach Battalion). Now, nine of these LCI(L)s headed for the beach to deliver their troops in Wave 17 at around H+210 (10.00) – and they do appear to have been on time. The wave was led by the Commander Red Assault Group on board LCH 10, a purely naval HQ craft with no army HQ on board. Another LCH – LCH 530 – was an LCI(L) converted for use as a HQ vessel, in this case, for the HQ of 22nd Infantry.[68]

Since Utah Beach had such a shallow gradient, these craft would not hit the beach themselves. Each would close to around 1,000 yards offshore and then unload troops into LCM(3)s, which would take them to the beach. The other LCI(L)s from the same convoy would follow shortly: there were fourteen more in Wave 19 and a further eight in Wave 20. As each of these waves neared the beach, two LCM(3)s were assigned to each LCI(L), following at 100 yards astern and ready to unload troops. Then the LCM(3)s would wait off beach until all three waves had unloaded. The troops from Wave 17 landed rapidly: all were ashore by 10.30.

1st and 2nd Battalion, 22nd Infantry landed in Wave 17 from US Coast Guard-crewed LCI(L)s. 1st Battalion were on board LCI(L)s 319, 320, 321, 322 and 323. Three more craft, LCI(L)s 11, 217 and 218, transported 2nd Battalion of the same regiment, while LCI(L) 229 had been delayed by engine trouble during the Channel crossing. As these troops transferred into LCM(3)s offshore, a few German shells fell nearby, but apparently without disrupting the landings. Once ashore, the two battalions of 22nd Infantry headed north-west through the flooded area behind the beach, to link up with 101st Airborne Division.[69]

Among the three waves of LCI(L)s, Wave 18 (H+220) was formed from eleven US Navy LCT(6)s, delivering two more of US 4th Infantry Division's artillery battalions, including twelve M7 self-propelled howitzers per battalion. The wave was perhaps half an hour late beaching.

Ensign Eugene Pendleton Banks was the officer in charge of LCT 765, lead craft for the five LCTs landing on Uncle Red. As the vehicles disembarked, 'time stood still' as artillery shells fell between the craft. Glancing around the LCT, Banks was annoyed to see that the cook had left the galley, where he was meant to be stationed ready to treat any casualties, apparently in order to watch the landings. After the craft had unbeached, he went to rebuke the cook:

> He didn't say a word but just pointed to a row of holes in the side of the galley. Shrapnel had gone through the 3/8 inch mild steel plating with ease … we fished shell fragments out of our supply of flour and sugar for several days.

Banks also noticed that LCT 620 was slow to unbeach. He learned afterwards that the fuel line on the engine for 620's kedge anchor had been severed by shrapnel. A quick-thinking crewman got the engine working by feeding it directly from a fuel can.[70]

The troops on board the fifteen LCI(L)s of Wave 19 were set to go ashore at H+240 (10.30), but after they had transferred to LCM(3)s, it was around noon before they had all landed. On each half of the beach, four

LCI(L)s carried a battalion of 12th Infantry, the third of US 4th Infantry Division's three infantry regiments to come ashore: 1st Battalion on Tare Green, 2nd Battalion to Uncle Red. In addition, six more LCI(L)s brought troops from various units of 1st Engineer Special Brigade, including the brigade's Dump Section, tasked with setting up supply dumps near the beach, which would soon be called upon to resupply the troops now fighting ashore. LCI(L)s 324 and 96 had US Coast Guard crews, and the remainder were manned by the US Navy. LCI(L)s could only carry troops on foot, so 22nd Infantry's vehicles were scheduled to begin landing from LCTs some two hours later.[71]

The fifteenth vessel of the wave, LCI(L) 214 carried 22nd Infantry HQ personnel and others from the regimental medical detachment, anti-tank and cannon companies. Like many craft in this wave, also on board LCI(L) 214 were members of 320th Anti-Aircraft Balloon Battalion, the first African American unit to land on Utah. There was a three-man team per landing craft who operated a small, fully inflated barrage balloon that had been put on board the vessel by the RAF before leaving the UK. On arrival in France, the team would take the balloon ashore, ballasted with sandbags, for anti-aircraft protection of the beach area.[72]

Generally, this wave landed according to plan, adding another 3,000 personnel to those establishing the beachhead at Utah. Wendell Haire, in the crew of LCI(L) 232, recalled one smaller landing craft being sunk as it approached his vessel to land some of the troops on board. As the LCI(L)s were withdrawing from the beach to the Transport Area, fate intervened again. At around 13.00 and about 5 miles offshore, while passing over the Banc du Cardonnet, LCI(L) 232 hit a mine and sank in five minutes. Nine sailors were rescued by the crews of LCI(L)s 211, 214 and 216, and Ensign F.J. Mueller USNR of LCI(L) 216 was commended for saving two men's lives. However, fourteen of LCI(L) 232's crew were killed in the sinking.[73]

Many of the survivors were seriously injured. Wendell Haire was below decks when the mine struck, 'I had been in the galley and I crawled to the hatch but couldn't get it open. I was in shock.' Fortunately, one of his comrades helped him reach safety:

There was a black fella from North Carolina named Flynt. He came to me. He went and found a lifejacket ... By this time, one side of the ship was much higher than the other. They got the life raft down and seven or eight of us got on it. We didn't get very far and our ship rolled and went right under.[74]

Eight more LCI(L)s were scheduled for H+250 as Wave 20, bringing more infantry: 3rd Battalion, 12th Infantry to Tare Green; 1st Battalion, 401st Glider Infantry to Uncle Red. As its name suggests, the latter was part of US 101st Airborne Division, but had come by sea as there were insufficient gliders to deliver the battalion from the skies. These airborne troops were to make their way inland and rejoin their comrades who had landed by air. Elements of other airborne units landed alongside that battalion, including men from 101st Airborne Division HQ and medics. Like previous LCI(L)s, the troops on these craft disembarked into LCM(3)s for landing.[75]

A mix of nine Royal Navy-crewed LCT(5)s – distinguishable by their '2000-series' pennant numbers – and eight LCT(6)s, manned by the US Navy, formed Wave 21. Divided between the two halves of the beach, this wave was due at H+260 (10.50) and appears to have landed late. Four LCTs carried units of 1st Engineer Special Brigade. Other LCTs carried vehicles of 'teeth' rather than logistical units, including M8 armoured cars from 4 Reconnaissance Troop, and seventeen M5 light tanks from Company D 70th Tank Battalion, as well as support vehicles of the same units. Six LCTs had flexible arrival times depending on circumstances ashore: four were carrying artillery unit support vehicles and two were carrying DUKWs.[76]

August Leo Thomas, coxswain on LCT(6) 663, described what happened slightly earlier in the day at around 09.30, as the US Navy-crewed Wave 21 LCTs used one of the mine-swept lanes across the Banc du Cardonnet:

> There was a terrific explosion, and the LCT 777 seemed to break in half … The skipper [of LCT 663] altered course slightly to avoid running over survivors who were in the water. It was heartbreaking not to be able to stop and render assistance to the men who were so desperately in need of help … some of those men were our friends.

Several naval veterans later recalled that as seven was often considered a lucky number, they expected that LCT(6) 777 should have been an extra-lucky vessel. This proved not to be the case and the Banc du Cardonnet minefield had claimed another vessel. The casualty records are incomplete, but at least seven members of the crew of LCT 777 were killed or later died of wounds, including Ensign Winfield Nelms Kyle Jr USNR (the officer in charge). Others were rescued by neighbouring vessels, including SC 1330 (a US Navy 'submarine chaser' on duty as a control craft), which saved nine men. There were relatively few troops on board and most, if not all, survived to be rescued, though they were all hospitalised.[77]

The next group of twelve LCT(5)s and LCT(6)s (Wave 22) was scheduled to land at H+280, and were less behind schedule at the Line of Departure, so they may have been close to Wave 21. Nine Royal Navy LCT(5)s of 104 LCT Flotilla were accompanied by three US Navy LCT(6)s. They were carrying additional troops and vehicles from 8th and 22nd Infantry, such as half-tracks towing the infantry's own 57mm anti-tank guns or 105mm howitzers. Such weapons would have been little use during the assault but were now being landed in case of an enemy armoured counter-attack.[78]

Fifteen British LCT(4)s were due at H+300 (11.30) in Wave 23, and arrived almost exactly on time. These were the first LCT(4)s to land on Utah, belonging to 50 and 52 LCT Flotillas RN. Eleven LCTs were carrying 746th Tank Battalion. Unlike 70th Tank Battalion, which was already ashore, the majority of this unit was able to land in a single wave, including many supporting vehicles as well as tanks. Landing in over 3ft of water proved no problem for the tanks but was too much for some of the smaller vehicles accompanying them, and there was a delay while the latter were towed off the LCTs.

This was not the first contribution that the LCTs had made on D-Day. US Army engineers had crossed the English Channel on board eight of them before transferring into LCM(3)s, which had been towed by the same craft, to land at H+7 as part of the obstacle clearance teams. The other four LCT(4)s in this wave were mainly carrying army engineer vehicles.[79]

Sixteen more British LCT(4)s arrived as Wave 24: they were due at H+320 (11.50) but they left the Line of Departure forty-five minutes late. The LCTs were probably divided evenly between the two halves of Utah Beach. Units represented in the cargoes of these LCTs included: 12th Infantry; 29th, 42nd and 44th Field Artillery Battalions; 65th Armoured Field Artillery Battalion; 87th Chemical Battalion; 531st Engineer Shore Regiment; and 3207 Quartermaster Service Company.

Ken McCaw of LCT 974 recalled that it was an easy landing, though a lorry landing from another LCT nearby was blown up by a mine on the beach. After their craft dried out on the beach, Wireman Mick Jennings and his comrades from LCT 795 went ashore to shelter from German artillery fire. He was able to use a foxhole that was also occupied by a US soldier, who shared a chocolate bar with him.[80]

Wave 25 was a group of LCT(4)s and LCT(5)s of the Royal Navy, which were designated as spares, in reserve in case other LCTs were disabled, for example, by mechanical problems. Indeed, two other craft in this group are believed to have been used for that purpose: LCT 2226 carried troops but then broke down itself and had to turn back to the UK, while LCT 2331 landed men of 238th Engineer Combat Battalion in the H+175 wave. The remainder of this group were presumably used to unload various larger ships off Utah Beach and therefore individual craft might perhaps have been added to other LCT waves rather than landing as a complete wave.[81]

Eleven US Navy LCT(6)s formed Wave 26. Five of the LCTs were each carrying 150 tons of ammunition: LCTs 522 and 524 on Tare Green, and LCTs 812, 854 and 855 on Uncle Red. The other six craft each carried 150 tons of engineer stores, much of which would be used for road-building in the beachhead area and similar tasks: LCTs 527, 528 and 529 on Tare Green, and LCTs 810, 851 and 852 on Uncle Red. 1st and 2nd Battalions, 531st Engineer Shore Regiment were due to unload these craft. Four of the LCTs had reserve supplies of explosives for the obstacle demolition teams, some of which could be transferred to smaller craft before the LCTs beached. LCTs 530 and 853 accompanied the wave as spare craft: one of these might have been loaded as a twelfth stores craft.[82]

The supplies carried by the LCTs of Wave 26 would tide the troops over until supply dumps had been established, stocked and got running ashore. These were the only landing craft to land on Utah Beach on D-Day that were not combat-loaded, in other words, not needing assistance from other vehicles such as cranes to unload. Force U's after-action report states that the Beachmaster delayed Wave 26 until the Second Tide of D-Day (in other words, after the next low tide, which was due around 17.00). 1st Engineer Special Brigade reported that only six pre-loaded LCTs beached on D-Day, all on the Second Tide, and one of them was lost along with most of its cargo when hit by an enemy shell. This craft may have been LCT 524, which was lost at some point during June 1944. Two more of these LCTs were hit by shells and were unable to beach, but their loads were transferred to other LCTs for landing on 7 June.[83]

Eleven LCI(L)s carried 1st and 3rd Battalions, 359th Infantry to go ashore on Uncle Red and Tare Green respectively. This group apparently did not have a wave number. Part of the US 90th Infantry Division, these troops had been attached to the US 4th Infantry Division for D-Day to provide additional infantry.

The two battalions were accompanied by some regimental HQ and medical personnel, as well as men from 2nd Naval Beach Battalion and 1st Engineer Special Brigade. These were on board a mix of US Coast Guard and US Navy craft. They had been anchored in the Transport Area since around 07.45 and did not have a set landing time but would beach according to the situation. Around 14.00, the Commander Red Assault Group had signalled that these craft should beach, and LCI(L) 552's records state that it beached at 17.25, leading a group of these craft. The gentle beach gradient near low tide meant that the LCI(L)s could not get far up the shore and the troops landed in deep water: some discarded their packs and even their rifles.[84]

Other LCI(L)s from this group seem to have unloaded into smaller craft without beaching at all. First Lieutenant J.Q. Lynd of 1st Battalion, 359th Infantry, described landing from an LCM(3), into which his men had transferred from their LCI(L):

> Almost immediately as our group started the run toward the beach, the [LCM] to our right blew [up]: a brilliant flash, thunderous crack explosion ... Utah Beach was a confused array of metal obstacles, scrambled barbed wire, columns of thick black smoke, the pungent odor of burning rubber, crumped bodies of dead and wounded soldiers.[85]

The movements of ships and landing craft at Utah Beach had not finished for the day. Convoys were still arriving. Sixteen more LSTs (referred to as the Second Tide LSTs), towing between them six Rhino Ferries, had arrived at 14.30 in Convoy U-3, for example.

Between them, these LSTs carried a great variety of vehicles and units, including more from the infantry regiments and tank battalions that had already landed; 90mm anti-aircraft guns and radar from 116th Anti-Aircraft Artillery Battalion; more elements of 1st Engineer Special Brigade; fifty-five DUKW amphibious vehicles; medics and more. As their unit names indicate, 603 Quartermaster Graves Registration Company and 23 Ordnance Bomb Disposal Squad were among those arriving who had particularly specialist roles. There were even several L4 aircraft, which were meant to be assembled and flown off the beachhead for artillery observation.[86]

At 16.30, Convoy U-5 reached the Transport Area after crossing the English Channel at the slow speed of 4 knots, bringing with it a selection of vessels not yet seen off Utah Beach – landing barges. On paper, this convoy included eighteen LBVs (each carrying 50 tons of stores), twenty LBOs, three LBWs (carrying fuel and water respectively), four LBEs for repairing other craft, as well as twenty LCM(3)s and supporting ships. More landing barges arrived in Convoy U-6 at 10.30 on D+1, including eighteen LBVs, four LBEs and two LBKs. 1st Engineer Special Brigade later reported, however, that some barges were delayed or went to Omaha Beach by mistake, and others never arrived. Some barges were only unloaded after D-Day.[87]

Clearly, many ships were starting to gather off Utah Beach, which needed to unload. The officer commanding LST Division 58, consisting of four Second Tide LSTs, expressed frustration in his after-action report that the waiting LSTs had not been able to take the opportunity to beach in daylight on D-Day, as he could see a 'practically clear' beach. Instead, as other convoys arrived, the anchorage became overcrowded.[88]

The officer in question did not have the full picture that lay before the senior commanders at Utah. Rear Admiral Don P. Moon USN, Commander Force U, was aware that the minefield on the Banc du Cardonnet had already claimed a number of ships and landing craft. It had the potential to inflict serious losses to vessels such as the LSTs. Minesweepers would later find 124 bottom mines and seventy-seven moored mines in the area. From his perspective as the naval commander, the best option was to pause the landings and sweep again for mines. The army commander, General J. Lawton Collins of US VII Corps, took a different view. Now the landings had begun, it was essential to get troops, vehicles and supplies ashore as fast as possible. He persuaded Moon that the landings must continue uninterrupted.[89]

★ ★ ★

The initial lift of forces continued to arrive on 7 June, or D+1. Convoy U-4 arrived at Utah around 09.00. It included nine more LSTs, many towing pontoon causeways to speed up unloading. The convoy had crossed the English Channel in company with the larger-sized Convoy B-3, which was bound for Omaha Beach (together, the two convoys were designated Convoy ECL-1). These latest arrivals were the Third Tide LSTs at Utah.

The unloading of all the LSTs that had arrived so far (First, Second and Third Tide ships) was progressing slowly due to difficulties in marrying LSTs to ferry craft. From 10 June onwards, as many as fifteen LSTs were dried out on the beach to unload at once, rather than the slower but less risky process of unloading using ferry craft.[90]

The army began to make demands for priorities in unloading. In the early hours of 7 June, the Commander Force U passed on an army request that LSTs 284 and 499 be unloaded that night on Uncle Red. In particular, the army wanted the four 155mm howitzers that were on board each LST.[91]

Up to eight dumb barges arrived between 7 and 9 June in Tows UB-1, UB-2 and UB-3. These were much larger barges than those designated 'landing barges', such as LBVs, and were loaded with stores, particularly ammunition. As the name 'dumb' implies, they were also unpowered and had to be towed across the English Channel. It appears that they were not meant to be unloaded except at times when normal unloading was impossible, such as during a storm.[92]

★ ★ ★

The dangers and difficulties of the Utah Beach landings are often overlooked. Whether the risk was from naval mines off the coast, obstacles on the beach or enemy artillery, landing craft and their crews were certainly exposed to danger as much as the troops going ashore. Joseph Balkoski argues, '[f]rom the naval perspective, the Utah assault was the most hazardous of the five D-Day invasions'. He acknowledges that exact naval casualties are difficult to calculate but estimates that landing craft crew casualties of all types (not deaths), British as well as American, numbered around 100.[93]

Certainly over sixty named landing craft crewmen have been identified as having died there on D-Day, including some who were classed as missing at the time. Not all the Allied dead are associated with a specific landing craft or other unit, so it is difficult to identify every single crewman. The majority died in the losses of LCTs 458, 593, 597 and 777, plus LCI(L) 232 and LCF 31. Several others died on unknown craft of the US Navy's LCT Flotilla 4 or on minor landing craft. Nearly 90 per cent of the dead are known to have been lost due to the minefield of the Banc du Cardonnet, and the majority were from major landing craft which had larger crews, rather than minor landing craft types.[94]

7

Omaha Beach

The shells tore into the troop compartment ... There was no such thing as a minor wound ... unloading was stopped because it was impossible to get past the pile of dead and wounded.

Lieutenant (j.g.) Coit T. Hendley Jr, USCGR, officer in charge of LCI(L) 85[1]

Omaha was not a site that you would choose for an amphibious landing unless you had to, but the Allies did have to land there. The addition of Utah Beach, when the Allied commanders decided to land on five not three beaches, made Omaha even more essential to avoid Utah being entirely isolated from the Anglo-Canadian landings to the east. Although the landings on Omaha were on a much greater length of beach than the other D-Day beaches (over 4 miles), many features aided the German defenders. Around 300 yards separated the low and high tide marks, so there would be a large, exposed area for the attackers to cross. On the gently sloping, sandy beach there was little cover for the assault troops. Further inland, rough ground turned into steep slopes, usually referred to as bluffs, up to 65 yards in height, which were impassable to vehicles. Five narrow valleys (draws) led inland through the bluffs at points referred to as exits. Areas either side of the main landing beach were unsuitable for landing because of cliffs and offshore rocks.[2]

As on other beaches, German defences were centred on strongpoints (each known as a *Wiederstandnest*) at intervals along the coast, guarding the exits. Shorter-range mortars, as well as strong artillery forces further inland, could also fire on the beach. In March 1944, the well-equipped German 352nd Infantry Division took over the area, but units of the lower-quality 716th Infantry Division remained there too. On 9 April 1944, Allied aerial reconnaissance photos first showed obstacles being constructed on Omaha Beach. Responding to this new threat, Allied planners added many more engineers alongside the assault troops.[3]

The American plan was broadly similar to those on other beaches, though with some variations in details, such as types of vehicles and equipment used. West to east, Omaha was divided into Charlie (where few troops were tasked to land because of cliffs), Dog, Easy and Fox sectors. All troops landing on Omaha were under the command of the US 1st Infantry Division, but one of the two assaulting regimental combat teams (RCT) came from the US 29th Infantry Division. This arrangement was intended to avoid 1st Infantry Division's own troops being spread too thin in the initial landings.

In the western half of Omaha, 116th RCT from US 29th Infantry Division would mostly land on Dog Green, Dog White, Dog Red and Easy Green, aiming to seize exits D1 and D3 in Dog sector, at Vierville and Les Moulins. To the east, 16th RCT of US 1st Infantry Division would mainly assault Easy Red to the west and Fox Green to the east, with exits E1, E3 and F1 (confusingly, exit E3 was on Fox, not Easy). These three exits led to St Laurent, Colleville and Cabourg. The assault on a coastal gun battery at Pointe du Hoc, 4 miles to the west, was also part of the Omaha Beach landings.

H-Hour on Omaha was at 06.30, just like Utah, and nearly an hour ahead of Gold and Sword. The first ships of Force O (also known to the US Navy as Task Force 124) began to anchor in the transport area, around 11 miles off the beach, at 03.00 on D-Day. The long lengths of the convoys meant that vessels would continue to arrive for some time.

Assault Groups O1 and O2 (Task Forces 124.3 and 124.4) were the naval forces for the eastern and western halves of the beach respectively. The convoys across the English Channel contained ships of both Assault Groups together and had identical names: for example, fast Convoy O-1, which included all fifteen landing ships.

At the Anglo-Canadian beaches, the landing ships anchored 7 miles off the French coast, whereas the anchorage off Omaha Beach was 11 miles out to reduce the potential threat from German shore batteries shelling the ships. This meant that the assault troops for Omaha boarded their landing craft in complete darkness and faced a long journey to the beach.

For each half of Omaha, three landing ships – two American APAs and one British LSI(L) – carried many of the troops who would land on

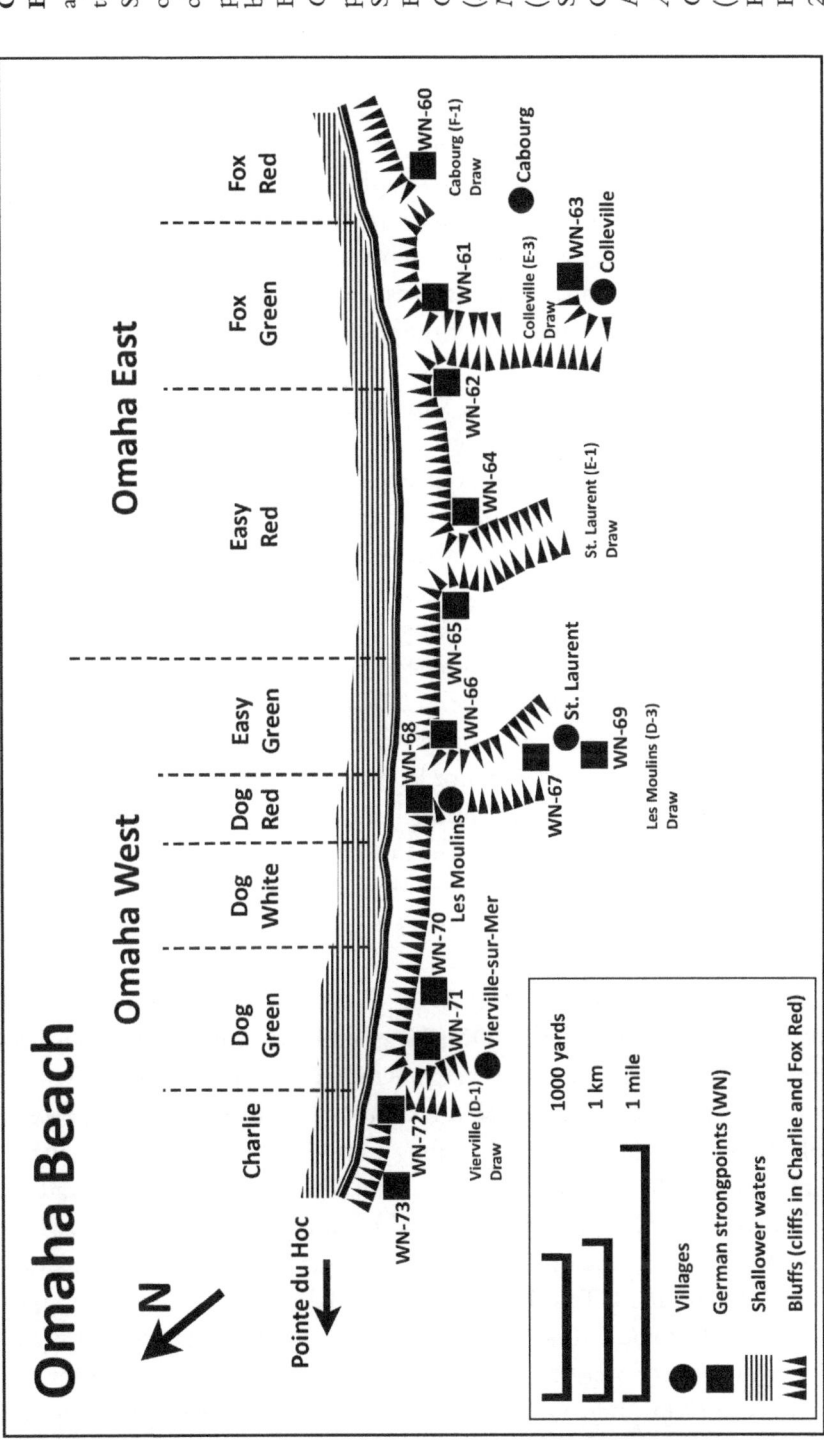

Omaha Beach

Omaha Beach: Map approximately to scale. Some details omitted for clarity. (Map primarily based on: Balkoski, *Omaha*, p.46); Badsey, Stephen & Bean, Tim, *Omaha Beach (Battlezone Normandy)* (Stroud: Sutton, 2004); Chazette, Alain et al., *Atlantikwall Omaha Beach* (Vertou: Histoire & Fortifications, 2014).

Omaha West

Omaha East

Pointe du Hoc

Charlie

Dog Green

Dog White

Dog Red

Easy Green

Easy Red

Fox Green

Fox Red

Vierville (D-1) Draw

Les Moulins (D-3) Draw

St. Laurent (E-1) Draw

Colleville (E-3) Draw

Cabourg (F-1) Draw

WN-73
WN-72
WN-71
WN-70
WN-68
WN-67
WN-66
WN-65
WN-64
WN-62
WN-61
WN-60
WN-69
WN-63

Vierville-sur-Mer
Les Moulins
St. Laurent
Colleville
Cabourg

1000 yards
1 km
1 mile

● Villages
■ German strongpoints (WN)
▤ Shallower waters
▨ Bluffs (cliffs in Charlie and Fox Red)

N

foot in the assault. In each case, craft from an American and a British ship landed two of each RCT's three battalions in three waves from H+1 to H+40. More troops from both ships would follow on, beginning with a wave at H+50, this time carried by small boats 'lent' by other ships whose own troops were not landing immediately. The third battalion of each RCT would land from the second APA in three waves, at H+70 to H+90.

It would typically take nearly two hours for a landing ship to despatch its first three waves of craft. After that, the American ships began to hoist light vehicles from their holds into landing craft alongside. Still more troops remained on board the transports and would land over subsequent hours. The craft that would carry them to the beach would then be on their second journey.[4]

Three more American landing ships were part of Assault Group O3 (Task Force 124.5). They were designated XAPs because their facilities for disembarking troops were not quite as extensive as the APAs'. Whereas troops on each APA could board its landing craft at deck level, most craft on the XAPs had to be lowered into the water before troops could embark. These ships had on board the two reserve RCTs that would follow on from the assault troops, later in the morning. The six transport vessels not yet mentioned were all British and belonged to Assault Group O4 (Task Force 124.6), mostly carrying 2nd and 5th US Rangers.

The head of the huge, slow Convoy O-2 was due off Omaha at 02.30. It included ten LSTs, over 170 major landing craft, including gunfire support craft, and at least seventy minor landing craft (not counting those embarked on larger vessels). Near the head of the convoy were the LCTs carrying amphibious DD tanks and wading tanks that would land around H-Hour, but further back there were craft carrying troops who were due to land hours later.

LSTs began anchoring around 03.00, just to seaward of the anchored transports, and swiftly launched DUKW amphibious trucks, which will feature below. Each LST was also towing a Rhino Ferry and tug, which would be used to land other vehicles. Each LST had been fitted with extra davits, enabling them to carry six minor landing craft which would take part in the assault: in total, these formed a considerable addition to the assault craft.[5]

Sixteen LCT(6)s – carrying a total of sixty-four amphibious DD Sherman tanks – led the first waves of landing craft. These tanks were due to launch from the LCTs at H−65 (05.25), 6,000 yards from land, swim to the beach and provide tank support as the assault troops touched down.

The rough seas posed the question of whether it was advisable for the DD tanks to swim such a distance – that decision had been placed in the hands of the young army officers on board these craft. They made two different decisions: one regiment would swim their tanks while the other would be taken to the beach by the LCTs. The fates of these tanks will be covered below.

Ten LCS(S)s, most of which had crossed the English Channel on the davits of LSTs, were to escort the swimming tanks the remaining distance to the shore. In the event, some of the LCS(S)s were delayed. Twenty-eight LCP(L)s also accompanied the DD tanks to lay a smokescreen if the tanks came under fire while swimming.

At 05.30, sixteen minutes after first light, a number of US warships returned fire against German guns that began firing from near Port-en-Bessin. Twenty minutes later, the Allied naval bombardment of the Omaha Beach area began. Journalist Don Whitehead of the Associated Press was on board an LCVP carrying troops of 16th Infantry. He later wrote:

> I noticed that everyone in our boat appeared to be trembling violently. I knew everyone was scared – but not that scared. And then I realized that the appearance of trembling was caused by the concussion from the big guns of the navy.

The aerial bombing that was expected between H–25 and H–5 all fell inland, missing the German defences, because the airmen feared hitting the first waves of landing craft.[6]

The landing craft also played their role in the bombardment, though not two of the five LCG(L)s, which accidentally crossed to Utah Beach. The other three LCG(L)s opened fire with their 4.7in guns at around 06.10. With the task of 'approaching [the] beach as closely as possible', some eventually closed to around 1,000 yards from the shore. From a range of 6,000 yards and closing, LCG(L) 424 fired sixty-six rounds at a pillbox in WN-71 on the east side of the Vierville Draw. After H-Hour, the LCG(L)s were to fire on targets of opportunity from their positions on the flanks. Seven LCFs provided additional defence against air attack and would also fire on targets of opportunity.[7]

Further fire support was provided by the army's 105mm self-propelled guns firing from LCT(5)s off the beach. The plan was that the guns would begin firing at H–30 minutes when the LCTs were 8,000 yards from land, continuing to adjust range as the craft approached the beach, until they reached the 3,000 yards point at H–5, when they would turn out to sea. The actual firing times differed, with guns on LCT 276 (lead craft on Omaha East) firing between 06.15 and 06.25, for example. During this run-in shoot, the fire of the US artillery was controlled from the LCTs carrying the guns, whose view could rapidly become obscured by smoke and dust. In contrast, the fire of British and Canadian artillery was directed by observers much closer to shore on board LCS(M)s. Another complication affecting the artillery's aim was that the LCTs had to steer to the west to counteract the strong easterly current.[8]

Sixteen LCT(A)s each carried three Sherman tanks, two of them on a ramped platform so they would have a good field of fire on the approach to the beach. On at least some of the LCT(A)s present – of which, more below – the tanks did fire from 06.15 onwards, starting at a range of 3,000 yards from the shore. At H–15, the twelve LCS(S)s escorting the swimming DD tanks or the LCTs carrying them fired their rockets against the beach from just a few hundred yards offshore. These small craft combined scout, control and gunfire support roles on D-Day.[9]

The final touch in the fire support would come from seven LCT(R)s across the entire width of Omaha, set to fire their rockets at H–2 from 3,000 yards out to sea, when the LCT(A) wave only was 300 yards from the beach. The actual firing times were between H–7 and H+2, and in some cases, the first-wave assault craft were as close as 200 yards from the shore at the time of firing. The target of the rockets was the German defences on the bluffs, not the beach as many observers seemed to believe.[10]

We will now look at the assault on Omaha Beach, beginning with Pointe du Hoc.

THE ASSAULT ON POINTE DU HOC

One of the most famous and dramatic incidents of D-Day was the capture of the German coastal gun battery at Pointe du Hoc. In fact, the battery's guns had been moved inland, but the 2nd Rangers had been assigned to assault the battery from the sea at the start of D-Day.

Pointe du Hoc was a headland projecting out into the sea with cliffs on the west and east sides forming natural defences. The Rangers were not the first troops to go ashore at Omaha Beach but will be considered at this stage so as not to interrupt the narrative for the main landing beaches.

The 2nd Rangers were scheduled to land at the foot of the cliffs at 06.30 (H-Hour on Omaha Beach). The assault force of elite American troops was in twelve LCAs of the Royal Navy: five from 522 Assault Flotilla (SS *Amsterdam*), carrying Company D and two-thirds of Company E; five from 520 Assault Flotilla (SS *Ben-My-Chree*), carrying battalion HQ, the remainder of Company E and Company F. An additional LCA from each landing ship carried supplies.

Close-in fire support would be provided by LCS(M)s 91 and 102, respectively from SS *Prince Baudouin* and HMS *Prince Leopold*. Finally, US Navy LCT(5) 413 had embarked four DUKWs fitted with Merryweather extending fire-escape ladders, sourced from the London Fire Brigade. These ladders were intended to help the Rangers to scale the cliffs. LCT 413 launched the DUKWs at 4,000 yards from the shore and then went to help unload ships off the main Omaha landing beaches. The amphibious vehicles, meanwhile, accompanied the LCAs.[11]

Problems began to develop well before H-Hour. The control craft guiding the LCAs had an electrical problem that disabled its navigational equipment and it led the force too far to the east, mistaking another promontory – Pointe et Raz de la Percée – for Pointe du Hoc. This meant that the LCAs arrived at their objective about forty minutes late, and rather than making assault on both the west and east sides of the headland, all craft beached to the east.

Not all the vessels had survived the journey. LCA 860 sank with the loss of four Rangers drowned and the remaining troops could no longer contribute to the assault. LCA 914 sank with the loss of all four Royal Navy crew and the supplies on board, including much of the Rangers' spare ammunition. The other supply craft, LCA 1003, only managed to stay afloat by jettisoning its cargo. LCS(M) 91 took on water and sank, as did one of the DUKWs. These problems were probably as much to do with the craft being overloaded for the sea conditions as to any inherent unseaworthiness.[12]

The Rangers' assault was successful and the LCAs managed to unbeach. At 07.50, HMS *Prince Charles*, SS *Prince Baudouin* and HMS *Prince Leopold* moved closer to the beach to be in a better position to recover the small craft. This was a wise move: on many LCAs, the crews were using their steel helmets to bail out water. On two occasions that evening, several LCVPs were sent to evacuate wounded from the battery by sea, as the Ranger force was still isolated from the main landing beaches. However, enemy fire drove them off.

On 7 June, two LCVPs from USS *Ancon* landed a small party of Rangers and did manage to evacuate some wounded personnel, while LCT 580 delivered ammunition and food.[13]

We will now look at the assault on the main landing beaches, beginning with the western side of Omaha Beach and including 5th Rangers, who were also due to arrive at Pointe du Hoc.

Omaha West: From H-Hour to H+110

Omaha West comprised (west to east) Charlie, Dog Green, Dog White, Dog Red and Easy Green sectors. The plan directed that the first troops to arrive here would be the swimming DD tanks of Companies B and C, 743rd Tank Battalion, at H–5 on Dog Green and Dog White. Lieutenant Dean L. Rockwell USNR, senior naval officer on the eight LCT(6)s carrying the thirty-two DD tanks, had contacted his army opposite number by tank radio. The two men agreed that the sea was too rough to launch the tanks and instead the LCTs would deliver them to the shore. The craft touched down only a few minutes later than the planned time of H–5 (06.25).[14]

As four LCT(6)s delivered Company B's tanks to Dog Green they came under devastating fire from nearby German strongpoints. LCTs 590 and 713 were both hit several times by anti-tank guns, while 590's crew returned fire with the craft's 20mm Oerlikon guns. Although all four LCTs got off the beach again, several LCT crew were killed or left mortally wounded.

Technician Fifth Grade Robert Jarvis was assistant gunner on one of the tanks. Soon after landing, he glanced outside the tank through a periscope, 'As I was watching, the surf rolled a body of a sailor alongside our tank. I recognized the sailor as being one of the crew of our LCT.'

Four LCT(6)s landing Company C's tanks on Dog White also met heavy fire from machine guns and larger weapons. Some of these eight LCTs were reported to have later lost their ramps due to shell damage.[15]

Each LCT carried its DD tanks along the centre of the tank deck. On either side were other troops and jeeps from a wide selection of units, which would land later. Despite this unexpected beaching, they did not land – Omaha around H-Hour was no place for jeeps. Seven of the eight LCTs then proceeded to larger ships offshore to collect further troops and vehicles that were intended to land at H+215. Because of crew casualties already suffered, LCT 590 did not carry out this second landing and was replaced by an LCT from the H+60 wave.[16]

The next group of landing craft due to arrive were nine LCT(A)s, carrying Company A, 743rd Tank Battalion. This was the third company from that battalion to land, but unlike the first two companies, which were equipped with DD tanks, Company A's Sherman tanks were equipped to wade in deep water but could not swim. For simplicity, all craft in this wave will be referred to here as LCT(A), but they were a mix of armoured LCT(A)s plus unarmoured LCT(HE)s and LCT(5)s.

LCT(A)s on the British and Canadian beaches carried Centaur tanks, which fired on approach to the beach from the craft's ramped platform. On Omaha, however, each LCT(A) carried two Sherman tanks on the platform instead. Behind them on the tank deck was a Sherman tankdozer for use in clearing beach obstacles. Had all gone to plan, twenty-four more Shermans would have joined the thirty-two DD Shermans that should already have landed on Omaha West.[17]

The LCT(A)s were to beach on Dog Green, Dog White, Dog Red and Easy Green at H-Hour. They had a difficult crossing, and only five of the eight craft reached the shore roughly on time, around 06.30 to 06.38, overlapping with the assault infantry. Those craft generally did not come under fire until they reached the beach, when the enemy unleashed a heavy fusillade from mortars, machine guns and anti-tank guns.[18]

LCT(A)s 2273 and 2227 were tasked to land at Dog Green. After LCT(A) 2227 had successfully landed its tanks, the crew struggled to withdraw from the beach. Ensign Victor Hicken, the officer in charge, reported, 'We were all huddled down in the wheelhouse, which was armoured, listening to machine gun bullets hitting. A mortar shell blew off the ramp.'

At that point, the landing craft carrying 116th Infantry began to beach and the Germans switched their fire to those craft. This gave the crew of LCT(A) 2227 some respite and they managed to unbeach their craft at 06.50 without any casualties.

During the Channel crossing, the sea had partly flooded the tank deck of LCT(A) 2273, disabling the port engine and causing the craft to list. The craft eventually landed its tanks on Dog Red at 16.00.[19]

On Dog White, LCT(HE) 2050 beached roughly on time despite engine trouble, but with only one of the three engines operational the crew struggled to unbeach. The other craft for that beach, LCT(HE) 2275, began taking on water on the morning of 5 June, which caused it to list and put the starboard engine out of action. After several unsuccessful attempts to beach, LCT(HE) 2275 landed its tanks in the late afternoon of D-Day, but even at this late stage in the day it was hit by enemy fire.[20]

Arriving late off the coast, LCT(A) 2124 struggled to identify the correct location to beach (Dog Red), partly as smoke was obscuring visibility. The two tanks on the LCT(A)'s platform fired at German defences on the run-in, and the craft beached at 06.38 about 50 yards short of the first beach obstacles. As the first two tanks hit the beach they were engaged by German gunfire.

The third, dozer-equipped Sherman remained on board the LCT for a further ten minutes, managing to silence an enemy gun with its fire.

During this engagement, LCT(A) 2124 was hit by ten shells, but none of the crew became casualties. The craft unbeached at 07.05 but had to be towed to the Transport Area as seawater had entered its fuel tanks through shell holes. The loss of LCT(HE) 2229, also due to land on Dog Red, has been described in Chapter 5.[21]

LCT(HE)s 2075 and 2307 were bound for Easy Green. Despite some troubles finding the correct location, LCT(HE) 2075 successfully landed its tanks around the correct time, at 06.38, and withdrew with casualties among the crew. LCT(HE) 2307 had suffered some damage during the crossing and was then hit by machine-gun fire at 1,000 yards from the beach. Its three tanks fired twenty or more rounds each in return. The craft beached at around 06.40, at which point it came under fire from German anti-tank guns.

This seems to have led to a ten-minute delay in the first tanks landing. The officer on the second tank was unwilling to land, believing the water to be too deep, but the LCT(HE) could not be moved closer inshore. Enemy shells wounded some of the LCT(HE)'s crew and severed the ramp cable and chain. Meanwhile, the crew fired fifteen magazines of 20mm Oerlikon ammunition at German defensive positions that were visible on the bluffs.

At 08.00, the craft unbeached with two tanks still on board. Unable to raise its ramp and with only one of its three engines working, it had to be towed stern-first to the Transport Area. With its pumps out of action, the craft began listing and the LCT crew and remaining troops were taken off. Around 18.00 on D-Day, LCT(HE) 2307 capsized and was lost.[22]

It was planned that the assault infantry would hit the beach at H+1, following immediately after the DD tanks at H−5 and the LCT(A)s at H-Hour. As has been described, in practice, the LCT(DD)s and LCT(A)s varied slightly from their intended times and landed simultaneously with the assault infantry (and the obstacle clearance teams, who will be considered in a moment).

At Omaha West, the assault was led by 116th Infantry. One company of that regiment's 1st Battalion would land on Dog Green and three companies from 2nd Battalion would land across Dog White, Dog Red and Easy Green. They did so within minutes of the correct time (around 06.30 to 06.35). However, they were often not in the right place.[23]

The German defenders ignored these small craft until they were about 150 yards from the beach, at which point they were targeted by artillery and machine-gun fire. Five LCAs of 551 Assault Flotilla (from SS *Empire Javelin*) brought Company A, 116th Infantry to the correct location at Dog

Green. A sixth craft had been damaged while being lowered from *Javelin* and sank before reaching the shore (the troops were rescued).

These LCAs were commanded by Sub Lieutenant George 'Jimmy' Green RNVR. The army had asked him to beach three LCAs on each side of the Vierville Draw. He later recalled that the craft touched down 100 yards short of the nearest obstacles and no more than 30 yards from the water's edge. German machine guns on the bluffs opened fire as the infantry advanced. In the coming battle, nearly 100 of Company A's 155 soldiers who had just landed would be killed and most of the rest wounded. Among the dead were nineteen men who later became known as the 'Bedford Boys' after their hometown of Bedford, Virginia, now remembered as the US town that suffered the highest per capita losses of its citizens in the Second World War.[24]

Two other LCAs from 501 Assault Flotilla (HMS *Prince Charles*) landed at the correct location, to the west of the Vierville Draw, with men of Company C, 2nd Rangers, who were scheduled to arrive at H+3 on Charlie sector. Though the troops on both craft were part of the same Ranger battalion, which was about to scale the cliffs at Pointe du Hoc, these men had a different mission. They were also the westernmost of the assault infantry wave to land on the main part of Omaha Beach.

The two craft landed at the foot of a cliff and almost immediately, LCA 418 'disintegrated' after being hit four times by enemy fire. Sub Lieutenant Jimmy Green took his LCA back in to rescue the crew of this destroyed craft. After landing, the Rangers moved further west along the beach, then climbed the cliffs and attacked German strongpoints from the rear – also assisted by one boat carrying men of Company B, 116th Infantry, who landed here by mistake.[25]

Further east, men of Companies G, F and E of 116th Infantry were to land at H+1 on Dog White, Dog Red and Easy Green respectively. They were on board eighteen LCVPs – six per company – from USS *Thomas Jefferson*. The tide pushed most of these craft further east than planned, with none landing on Dog White because Company G's six LCVPs were swept east to Dog Red and Easy Green. The craft carrying Company F landed around the same area. The Germans held their fire initially then targeted the infantry as they headed up the beach, rather than the landing craft and their crews.

Two LCVPs carrying Company E, 116th Infantry were swept by the current around 1,000 yards to the east of their planned landing site of Easy Green. The four craft carrying the remainder of that company landed over a mile to the east. This took them into Omaha East, and they would fight alongside 16th Infantry there.[26]

Each of the eight craft in the LCT(A) wave, which had been due to land at H-Hour, had towed an LCM(3) across the English Channel for one of the Gap Assault Teams (GAT) to use in their obstacle-clearance role. The teams needed the carrying capacity of the 50ft-long LCM(3)s for their explosives and other equipment, which had been preloaded before leaving the UK. Crossing the English Channel on such craft was risky, however, so while the LCM(3)'s crew had remained on board for the crossing, the GAT personnel crossed on the LCT(A). Then, off the beach, in the darkness and rough seas, the GAT personnel would make the hazardous transfer from the larger craft into the LCM(3)s.

The teams had only been added to the assault in April 1944, in response to the increasing numbers of mined beach obstacles that the Germans were placing on Omaha Beach. Each team had the initial task of clearing a 50-yard-wide gap in the beach obstacles in the first hour of the landings to enable larger landing craft to deliver their cargoes to the water's edge once the rising tide began to submerge many of the obstacles. It was planned that gaps would be at 200-yard intervals and the teams would continue to expand them. Each forty-one-man team comprised a fourteen-strong Naval Combat Demolition Unit (nine sailors plus five soldiers) for underwater demolition work, and twenty-seven army engineers to work on the beach. There were also three command LCM(3)s.

Across the whole of Omaha Beach, nearly 1,000 obstacle-clearance personnel would land in the first waves; over a third would become casualties on D-Day. Considering the difficulties experienced by the LCT(A)s during the crossing, it is impressive that only two of the GAT LCM(3)s did not reach the beach on time: most landed within a few minutes of their intended time of H+3. Some craft had been released early during the crossing due to the towing LCT(A)s struggling in the rough seas. Many of the GAT craft were as much as a mile out of position as they too were swept east by the tide.[27]

Several teams could not fulfil their mission because of casualties and one LCM(3) was hit by artillery. Only a couple of gaps could be cleared. Five minutes behind the first LCM(3)s, at H+8, were four more LCM(3)s carrying the Gapping Support Teams. These boats had been loaded with the same explosives and other equipment as the previous wave of LCM(3)s. Each had been towed across the English Channel by an LCG(L) then, before H-Hour, had loaded obstacle-clearance personnel from SS *Princess Maud*. One team landed on time, but the remainder were twenty or more minutes late.[28]

At least one crewman on the LCM(3)s was killed: Motor Machinist's Mate Third Class Dean M. Bakka, from one of the Gapping Support craft landing at H+8 (it is not certain whether his craft operated on Omaha West or East). Bakka's commanding officer, Ensign E.W. Hyman USNR wrote to Bakka's mother:

> Everything went well until we hit the beach. The Germans opened fire on us and put the boat out of commission so we jumped into the water. We were swimming out to sea … when Dean was hit.

The final components of the obstacle-clearance force at Omaha West were six further LCM(3)s: five reserve craft, preloaded with clearance equipment and available as replacements, and one command craft.[29]

Twenty-five LCVPs and LCAs were scheduled to land the next wave of assault troops on Omaha West at H+30, followed at H+40, H+50 and H+57 by further minor landing craft. Many of these troops were loaded from landing ships which had already despatched some or all of their own craft to the beach, so they were collected by small boats from other ships. In the H+30 wave, on each of the four sectors of Omaha West, one craft landed troops of the same company of 116th Infantry that had landed at around H+1. Another two boats carried men from the supporting heavy weapons company (part of Company D, 1st Battalion, on Dog Green, and the whole of Company H, 2nd Battalion, spread across Dog White, Dog Red and Easy Green), equipped with heavy machine guns and 81mm mortars. Anti-aircraft teams also landed by LCVPs.[30]

Across the whole of Omaha West, the majority of H+30 and H+40 boats did land around 07.00 and 07.10 respectively, as planned, although a few were late. At Dog Green, six of the eight H+30-wave LCAs carrying Company B, 116th Infantry beached slightly late at 07.08 on either side of the Vierville Draw, with the other two a few minutes later.

Observing enemy fire on the beach, three other LCAs, led by Sub Lieutenant T.E. Arlidge RNVR, altered course over 1,000 yards to the east and found a safer landing site on Dog White. The craft carrying Company B were met with mortar and machine-gun fire. Soaked to the skin and surrounded by vomiting comrades (he himself did not succumb to seasickness), Private Robert Sales recalled, 'As the ramp lowered, enemy machine guns opened up, firing directly into our boat … I caught my heel in the ramp and fell sideways, out of the path of that MG-42 [German machine gun], and this undoubtedly saved my life'. Two of *Empire Javelin*'s LCAs were lost: LCA 1063 became stuck on the beach obstacles and LCA 1069 sank while returning to the ship.[31]

One LCM(3) carrying army engineers and ten LCAs were scheduled to land ten minutes later, at H+40. Four of the LCAs were from 551 Assault Flotilla (SS *Empire Javelin*). They were mostly carrying HQ personnel of 1st Battalion, 116th Infantry plus men of 149th Engineer Combat Battalion. The LCM and three of *Empire Javelin*'s LCAs landed ten minutes late at 07.20. LCA 853 hit a mined obstacle, killing many troops on board. The crew of LCA 1068 got their waterlogged craft to the beach but then had to abandon it; one of them was killed.

The other six H+40 craft bound for Dog Green were LCAs of 519 Assault Flotilla from SS *Princess Maud*, carrying troops of Company D, 116th Infantry who had embarked from SS *Empire Javelin*. On one craft, a German shell blew off the watertight doors (situated just behind the raised ramp), killing Company D's commander and wounding troops and sailors in the craft. Three LCAs headed further west in an attempt to avoid enemy fire and beached at the base of the cliffs to the west of the Vierville Draw. The troops remained pinned down there for hours.[32]

The final part of 1st Battalion, 116th Infantry disembarked from SS *Empire Javelin* to land on Dog Green at H+50. On board seven LCVPs from USS *Thurston* were Company C and the HQ of 1st Battalion, 116th Infantry. A single LCM(3) from USS *Charles Carroll* carried troops of 121st Engineer Combat Battalion. An unknown officer, perhaps on one of the control craft, had decided to halt the landings on Dog Green due to the very heavy casualties and uncleared obstacles there. They therefore moved east to Dog White, where they still suffered nearly 10 per cent casualties from rifle, machine gun and artillery fire as they came ashore. At least one boat capsized when it was thrown against a beach obstacle, the troops losing all their heavy equipment.[33]

Simultaneously with the above, seventeen LCVPs formed the remainder of the H+30 wave, carrying troops from USS *Thomas Jefferson* to Dog White, Dog Red and Easy Green. Twelve were *Thomas Jefferson*'s own LCVPs, supplemented by five LCVPs from an LST. On board, across the three sectors, were anti-aircraft teams from 397th Anti-Aircraft Artillery Battalion, and men of Company H, 116th Infantry (2nd Battalion's heavy weapons company). Other troops from 2nd Battalion were also part of this wave, plus miscellaneous small parties such as navy and army teams co-ordinating fire support. Most landed only a few minutes late and under fire near the Les Moulins exit, which was close to the boundary between Dog Red and Easy Green. Four of *Thomas Jefferson*'s LCVPs flooded and had to be abandoned by their crews on the beach.[34]

Scheduled ten minutes later, at H+40, across the same three sectors, were three LCM(3)s carrying army engineers and five LCVPs, primarily carrying 81st Chemical Weapons Battalion, a unit equipped with 4.2in mortars (despite its name, its role here did not involve chemical weapons). Some of the H+40 craft had collected troops from *Thomas Jefferson* but the boats were supplied by USS *Charles Carroll* and an LST.

Private First Class A. Cvitanovitch of 112th Engineer Combat Battalion was on one of the LCM(3)s in the H+40 wave. Many in his boat were badly seasick. About 300 yards from Easy Green, they began to hear firing and assumed they were American weapons:

> Some of our boys said, 'The 29th [Division] is on the ball; they are really going to town …' A few minutes later … as the ramp went down all of us got panicky. The boys who were sick weren't sick anymore.

Several of Cvitanovitch's comrades became casualties in the first moments after landing.[35]

The reserve battalion – 3rd Battalion, 116th Infantry – was due to land on Dog White, Dog Red and Easy Green at H+50 (07.20). The troops were carried by twenty LCVPs from USS *Charles Carroll*, which beached a few minutes late. Many landed between the Les Moulins and St Laurent draws. The LCVP carrying battalion HQ hit a mined obstacle which blew off the craft's ramp, sinking it and killing some of the troops. In shoulder-deep water, the survivors had to abandon much of their equipment.

On another LCVP carrying Company L the ramp jammed in the raised position. One of the crew managed to resolve this by shooting the cable in half with his pistol, a move which had all the troops looking in vain for a place to shelter from ricochets.[36]

The final portion of 116th Infantry and supporting troops were due to land at H+57. Company M (3rd Battalion's heavy weapons company) was on six LCVPs bound for Dog Red, alongside three other LCVPs carrying the regimental HQ and other small army and navy parties. They disembarked from USS *Charles Carroll*, probably onto the ship's own boats. These craft landed only minutes later than planned, but had strayed onto Easy Red, beaching just to the west of the St Laurent Draw. Due to land at the same time were Company B, 81st Chemical Weapons Battalion, who loaded from SS *Empire Javelin* onto four LCVPs from another ship. Since their target beach, Dog Green, was closed to landings, they headed east. Two LCVPs were sunk by enemy fire and the men had to transfer to a passing LCT. The surviving four craft beached several hours later, on Easy Green at the opposite end of Omaha West.[37]

Eight LCT(6)s beached around their scheduled time of H+60 (07.30), across Omaha West, carrying vehicles of 6th Engineer Special Brigade and 116th Infantry priority vehicles. The craft suffered considerable damage. Five of the LCTs were from LCT Flotillas 12 and 26 USN, and among that group, two were badly hit by German shells, one of them having to be towed off the beach, one struck a mine and had to be abandoned ashore and the other two unbeached successfully.

Several LCVPs also landed at this time, one of which was rammed and sunk by an unbeaching LCT. A particularly important LCVP touched down on Dog Red, carrying troops from USS *Charles Carroll*. On board were two men who would play key roles in galvanising US troops to advance off the beach, along with their staff: Brigadier General Norman D. Cota, second in command of US 29th Infantry Division, and Colonel Charles Canham, commanding officer of 116th Infantry. The beach obstacles were now nearly covered by the rising tide and their craft was pushed by the waves against a mine-topped wooden pole with such force that the mine was dislodged – fortunately without exploding.[38]

The 116th Infantry and supporting troops were ashore by roughly H+60, as planned, but with heavy casualties and many had landed in the wrong place. Facing strong defences, they had little option but to make a frontal attack against heavy fire. That these troops managed to tip the balance towards victory was one of the key achievements on Omaha. At this stage, landing craft crew casualties and losses of craft were significant, but they did not approach the terrible losses suffered by the army. Seventeen small boats were already lost, including six from SS *Empire Javelin*, six from USS *Charles Carroll* and up to four from USS *Thomas Jefferson*.[39]

The next force to land on Omaha West would play a key role in the struggle to gain victory there. Ranger Force C comprised Companies A and B, 2nd Rangers, and the whole of 5th Rangers. They were on board twenty LCAs, which had been launched around 05.40 from three Royal Navy landing ships that were at anchor at the western end of Force O's Transport Area.

The force's intended role was to reinforce Companies D, E and F of 2nd Rangers, which had landed at Pointe du Hoc earlier. If that assault succeeded, the craft would be summoned to Pointe du Hoc by radio or signal flares. Since the initial Ranger landing force was behind schedule, the message was not sent in time and the reinforcements adopted their alternative plan: to land alongside 116th Infantry.[40]

First to land were Companies A and B, 2nd Rangers, beaching at 07.35 (H+65) on Dog Green, from five LCAs of 501 Assault Flotilla (HMS *Prince Charles*), near the German strongpoint WN-70. As the LCAs beached amid nearly submerged beach obstacles, LCA 401 set off a mine which blew off the craft's bows and killed the coxswain, Able Seaman John Barkley of the South African Naval Forces. The coxswain of LCA 458 was apparently also killed and then that craft's engines flooded. Sub Lieutenant Hilaire Benbow RNVR of LCA 458 led a group of about sixteen survivors from several wrecked British craft, who eventually made their way back to the UK.[41]

Lieutenant Colonel Max Schneider, commanding Ranger Force C, observed the reception given to 2nd Rangers. Hoping to avoid landing in front of WN-70, he agreed with the Royal Navy officer commanding the next wave of LCAs to take the remainder of the force half a mile further to the east onto Dog White. The 5th Rangers came ashore there at about 07.50 to 07.55 in fourteen LCAs. Seven LCAs from 504 Assault Flotilla (HMS *Prince Leopold*) carried Companies A, B and E. Six LCAs of 507 Assault Flotilla (HMS *Prince Baudouin*) transported Companies C, D and F; a seventh craft from that flotilla had taken on water earlier and the troops on board were transferred to an LCT, landing later. An additional LCA from HMS *Prince Charles* carried Schneider and Ranger Force C HQ.

The craft also had to manoeuvre between semi-submerged obstacles and came under artillery fire at the water's edge, but managed to beach in an area partly screened from German view by drifting smoke. This was an area where men of Companies B and C, 116th Infantry had landed over the course of the past hour. A single LCM followed the 5th Rangers to the beach, carrying troops from Company D, 116th Infantry. They had been due to land at H+40 but they managed to transfer to the LCM after their LCA was swamped.[42]

Around the time the Rangers landed on Dog Green and White, a small group of much larger landing craft delivered troops to Omaha West. Three US Coast Guard LCI(L)s were scheduled to beach at H+70 (07.40), each carrying nearly 200 men, many of them army engineers and 7th Naval Beach Battalion personnel. Beaching these large and vulnerable craft so early on D-Day, in the face of uncleared beach obstacles and heavy German fire, was to have tragic consequences.

Also due at H+70 were LCT(6)s 705 and 775, carrying vehicles of 116th Infantry, engineers and others, but it is not clear when they landed. A single LCM(3) from USS *Charles Carroll*, carrying HQ Company person-nel of 116th Infantry, was also scheduled, and arrived five minutes late.[43]

As LCI(L) 91 approached Dog White on time, the officer in charge, Lieutenant (j.g.) Arend Vyn Jr USCGR, observed to one of the army officers that, as a coastguardsman, he had expected to spend the war protecting the eastern coast of the USA but was now taking part in his third amphibious landing.

Without a clear gap, the craft had to beach among the obstacles. The troops 'disembarked reluctantly over both ramps in the face of heavy enemy machine gun and rifle fire'. As the tide came in, the crew had to move the LCI(L) further up the beach to keep it properly grounded. At one point, an enemy bullet ignited the fuel tank on the back of a flame-thrower operator, instantly turning him into a human torch. The man dove into the sea to quench the flames. After twenty minutes, the crew unbeached the craft as it was drifting close to beach obstacles, but it hit a mine, which wounded several troops and created a 2ft hole in the ship's bows above the water line.[44]

Some seventy troops remained on LCI(L) 91 and Vyn's crew moved the craft 100 yards to the west. The disembarkation continued under artillery fire. Suddenly, there was a violent explosion from another mine or a shell, which penetrated the fuel tanks. Immediately, the deck was a mass of fire.

Many troops jumped over the ship's side to escape the flames. Vyn could see significant damage to the ship's hull and bulkheads, and with insufficient water pressure from the ship's pumps to fight the fire, he gave the order to abandon ship. The crew (as well as a few remaining troops) were rescued by smaller craft that came alongside. Five of the crew of LCI(L) 91 were killed, in addition to deaths among the troops on board.[45]

To the east, LCI(L) 94 touched down on Dog Red only seven minutes late. After successfully unloading, the craft fouled an LCVP then was struck by German shells, including three which hit the pilot house. Three coastguardsmen were killed and others wounded. LCI(L) 94 remained on the beach for nearly an hour, only unbeaching at 08.37. Also on board as the craft withdrew was a new passenger, war photographer Robert Capa, who after taking what would become the most famous photographs of D-Day on Easy Red sector, now needed a passage home. Back at sea, Capa photographed the crew treating wounded men on deck.[46]

The third craft, LCI(L) 90, would fare better but still had a difficult landing on Easy Green. Only on the second attempt did the crew manage to beach between the obstacles, around the correct time. Three-quarters of the troops had landed when the stern anchor cable ran off its winch and the craft began to broach-to (swing parallel to the shore), which threw the ramps off their mounts. The craft unbeached and the remaining troops were taken off by LCVPs.[47]

Half an hour later, another LCI(L) landed on Dog White at around its scheduled time of H+100 (08.10). It was LCH 92: an LCI(L) that had been converted into a HQ vessel. On the approach to the beach, those on board – a mix of engineers, 7th Naval Beach Battalion, Military Police, signal personnel and medics – witnessed the ominous sight of LCI(L) 91 beached and on fire to the west.

In fact, the crew aimed to use smoke from the burning craft to cover their approach. As the vessel weaved through the beach obstacles, all at once it came under fire. Photographer's Mate Third Class Seth Shepard recorded that he was suddenly thrown to the deck as 'a terrifying blast lifted the whole ship upward with a sudden lurch from the bow. A sheet of flame and steel shot out from the forward hold.' The impact of this first shell covered the forward deck with burning fuel.

The enemy now began to target LCH 92 with artillery, mortars and machine guns. The forward compartment was partly empty as many troops had already moved up on deck ready to disembark, but the army still suffered heavily from this onslaught. The crew later reported that forty-one men had lost their lives.

LCH 92 had run aground on a runnel and its ramps could not be lowered due to damage from the shelling, so the troops began to disembark by ladders over the port side, where there was less enemy fire. Meanwhile, the crew tried to control the fire.

Once the troops had unloaded, officer in charge Lieutenant Robert M. Salmon USCGR decided that submerged obstacles posed too great a risk to withdraw from the beach and the crew continued to fight the flames. Around 14.00, some six hours after first beaching, Salmon gave the order to abandon ship. The receding tide had removed the water supply for firefighting. Some of LCH 92's crew had been wounded but none were killed.[48]

The army was keen to land its own artillery as early as possible, rather than the navy being the only source of fire support. At H+90, five LCT(5)s were due to beach on Dog White carrying between them eighteen M7 self-propelled 105mm guns of 58th Armoured Field Artillery Battalion, plus supporting vehicles. Although these guns had some armour, they were not intended for close combat, so their landings were postponed until later, but even then, most experienced great difficulties.

Of the five craft, LCTs 332 and 364 beached at similar times (09.40 to 10.00) and both struck mined beach obstacles. LCT 332 had its ramp and a 25ft section of bow blown off, while LCT 364 had a 10ft-square hole in its hull and was also hit by a shell which knocked out the engines. LCT 29 may have experienced similar difficulties as it was apparently abandoned on the beach with the vehicles still on board, its tank deck swamped.

LCT 197 made several beaching attempts from 10.00 onwards, and also suffering major hull damage from striking beach obstacles. The craft and its crew received a Navy Unit Citation for this action. Just before 21.00 the crew and troops abandoned ship, and shortly afterwards, LCT 197 rolled over and slowly sank. One of the crew, Ensign Shadrach Whittis Boaz, was missing, later presumed dead.

The fifth craft, LCT 207, landed its vehicles on Dog Red at 16.00. By 18.30, 58th Armoured Field Artillery Battalion had eleven of its guns set up ashore. The battalion history observed, 'Looking back, it seems a miracle that any of the guns ever got ashore.'[49]

DUKW amphibious vehicles were used in an attempt to land towed 105mm howitzers and 57mm anti-tank guns at H+110. The DUKWs had launched from LSTs over four hours earlier, some 7 miles off the beach. Each DUKW carried one wheeled gun, precariously balanced on the back of the vehicle. Simply launching the heavily loaded DUKWs from the LSTs proved challenging, and many sank immediately. Four DUKWs beat the odds and managed to stay afloat until it was time to beach, but despite the efforts of the troops, only a single gun eventually reached the shore and many personnel were also lost.[50]

OMAHA EAST: FROM H-HOUR TO H+110

The assault on Omaha East was to be made by 16th RCT, the third occasion when this veteran regiment had led US 1st Infantry Division in an amphibious landing. There were many parallels between events here and the landings of 116th RCT to the west. One early difference related to the first troops who were due to arrive on the beach – the amphibious Sherman DD tanks of Companies B and C, 741st Tank Battalion, bound for Easy Red and Fox Green respectively on eight LCT(6)s.

Whereas on the western half of the beach, the army had decided that the weather was too rough for the tanks to swim, 741st Tank Battalion's officers made the decision to launch the tanks into the sea 6,000 yards from the shore at about H−50. Many tanks sank, some immediately and others after several miles.

All of Company C's sixteen tanks sank before reaching the beach and only two from Company B swam all the way. On LCT 600, after launching the first tank, the canvas screens on the other tanks had been damaged and they could no longer float. LCT 600 therefore proceeded to land these three tanks on the beach at 06.45, meaning that in total five DD tanks eventually reached Easy Red. Like the LCTs carrying DD tanks on Omaha West, all eight of these LCTs had additional troops and jeeps positioned along either side of their tank decks who were not intended to land at this point. After launching the DD tanks, the LCTs made their way to the landing ships USS *Henrico* and USS *Samuel Chase* to collect more troops.[51]

Just as on Omaha West, on board each of eight LCT(A)s, LCT(HE)s or LCT(5)s, here referred to as a group as LCT(A)s, there were two standard Sherman tanks and one tankdozer. These vehicles belonged to Company A, 741st Tank Battalion.

Not all craft headed for Easy Red made the full journey. LCT(HE) 2049 suffered major damage from a mine around 20 miles off the French coast, and all personnel on board transferred onto the LCM that was under tow. LCT(HE) 2339 reached the beach on time, despite having engine trouble during the crossing. Nearing the beach, all three tanks on board – including the tankdozer – fired at 'targets of opportunity' ashore, beginning at a distance of 3,000 yards. At 150 yards from shore, the defenders began responding with machine guns, mortars and artillery. The tanks were landed successfully, but several of the LCT's crew were wounded by shrapnel from enemy fire. LCT(HE)s 2425 and 2287 apparently both landed their tanks successfully.[52]

Several of the Fox Green LCT(A)s experienced problems of water ingress due to poor seals on the armour plating on the crafts' sides, as well as engine malfunctions, both common problems for this type of craft on D-Day. One of LCT(A) 2037's bulwarks collapsed during the crossing to France. Despite this, the crew were able to land their cargo of tanks only a few minutes late, at 06.45.

LCT(A) 2043 shipped water into its engine room during the crossing, and as a result, arrived late at the beach at 06.55. While beached, the craft was hit ten times by mortar bombs as well as by artillery shells and machine-gun fire, in some cases below the water line. The third, dozer-equipped tank was hit and disabled before it could be put ashore. As the craft withdrew it had a 15-degree list to starboard, but the crew still found time to tow LCT(A) 2307 off Easy Red, as that craft's engines had broken down.

LCT(A) 2008 already had engine trouble when, at 6 miles from the beach, the chains supporting its ramp broke and the ramp dropped to the lowered position. Temporary repairs twice failed and this delayed the craft's arrival at Fox Green until 08.00, so its tanks were not available to support the assault. While landing its tanks, the craft lost its ramp entirely.[53]

The fourth vessel, LCT(5) 210, was a last-minute replacement for LCT(A) 2228, which on 4 June had been discovered to have a defective engine. Being a stand-in, unlike the others, it was not fitted with a platform on its tank deck. The craft left the UK three and a half hours late after its own engines were replaced but managed to catch up with the rest of its convoy. At 06.33, LCT 210 was the first Allied craft to beach on Fox Red, at the extreme east end of Omaha Beach. No following troops were meant to land on Fox Red, so LCT 210 had apparently gone astray. As the LCT beached, four crewmen were in the bows ready to lower the ramp. Two of them were killed as the vessel was hit by heavy fire from anti-tank guns and machine guns. The other two men were seriously wounded by a shell, but still managed to lower the ramp, enabling the tanks on board to go ashore. By the time LCT 210 withdrew from the beach at 06.55, it had been hit by eight shells and one mortar bomb and had lost its ramp and anchor.[54]

The tanks carried by these LCT(A)s had the role of supporting 16th Infantry and the obstacle-clearance teams, who were due to arrive at H+1 and H+3 respectively. These landings did not all run to time, however, and the current swept many of the boats further east than planned.

Twelve LCVPs from USS *Henrico* carried Companies E and F of that regiment's 2nd Battalion to Easy Red. *Henrico*'s after-action report noted that several of its boats shipped considerable water on the way to the beach, and once there, they found 'heavy surf and undertow and tidal currents [that] paralleled the beach'.[55]

Only one of Company E's six boats landed on Easy Red. The thirty-two troops on board, commanded by 2nd Lieutenant John Spalding, suffered twelve casualties as they crossed the beach. The survivors would go on to find a route up the bluffs behind the beach and played a key role in beginning to break open the German defences here.

The other five craft were swept east onto Fox Green. They came ashore on the 'wrong' (eastern) side of the Colleville Draw, intermixed with the boats carrying Company F. First Sergeant L. Fitzsimmons of Company E later reported, 'The men kept yelling at the coxswain: "You're going left!" He ignored them and kept on the same course.'

Six boats of 116th Infantry also landed here, far adrift from their landing beaches on Omaha East. Captain Edward Wozenksi, commander

of Company E, described the difficult conditions faced by the troops
on landing:

> The boats were hurriedly emptied, the men jumping into the water
> shoulder-high under intense machine gun and antitank fire. No sooner
> was the last man out than the boat received two direct hits from an
> antitank gun, and was believed to have burned and blown up. Now all
> the men in the company could be seen wading ashore into the field of
> intense fire from machine guns, rifles, antitank guns and mortars.[56]

'Our assault section leaders said, "load rifles". A few minutes later, we
hit with a shudder – France!', recalled Private Elmer E. Matekintis of
Company F:

> The Navy boy tried to bring in the boat closer to shore but it was no
> good. We were stuck on a sand bar. I could hear the pinging of bullets
> against the side and front of our boats … All of a sudden the ramp came
> down and we started to come out. The sea was so rough we could hardly
> keep our balance … we were floundering and I started to realise just how
> much equipment we had. It was too much … I finally got off the boat
> and the water was up to my neck.

Matekintis got ashore but remembered seeing several landing craft hit or
sinking nearby. Landing craft crew from *Henrico* later received awards for
their bravery in this landing and other trips to the beach over the following hours.[57]

The troops who were scheduled to land on Fox Green at H+1 were
Companies I and L, 3rd Battalion, 16th Infantry. They were carried by
twelve LCAs of 550 Assault Flotilla from SS *Empire Anvil*. Again, the
craft drifted to the east and beached much later than planned. One of
Company L's craft was swamped several miles offshore. The remaining
five LCAs landed twenty to thirty minutes late, just before 07.00. They
touched down not on Fox Green but on Fox Red, the furthest to the east
that any troops landed on Omaha on D-Day. Ahead of them there was
a bluff 130ft high and the German strongpoint WN-60, which guarded
the Cabourg Draw.

Enemy fire – from artillery to rifles – took its toll on the infantry as they
came ashore. Sergeant William J. Philbin of Company L recalled one of
the crew of his LCA lying flat on the stern of the craft, providing covering
fire for the coxswain. Private First Class John Sweeney later recalled, 'The

carnage and destruction were unbelievable – bodies in the water, destroyed landing craft, confusion.' A series of well-known photographs show infantrymen clustered at the base of a 15ft-high cliff there, dazed from their experiences. Under the leadership of men like Lieutenant Jimmy Monteith of Company L, the troops of that company and other units that had landed there managed to move west and successfully assault WN-60.[58]

The LCAs carrying Company I approached the beach over 1 mile east of their intended landing site. Such navigational errors created a dilemma for the army officers on the spot. Clearly, it was best if troops landed at the correct time and location, so they could carry out the mission for which they had been briefed. Landing in the wrong place risked confusing the troops and could mean that not all the intended objectives would be attacked at the start of the assault. On the other hand, if the assault troops had all landed nearly simultaneously, they stood a greater chance of overwhelming the German defences. If little groups of boats landed piecemeal, the defenders could pick them off in turn.

In this case, there was little option as the beach was backed by vertical cliffs. Company I's commander insisted that the six craft moved west and landed his men closer to their intended landing site. In a journey that was described by the commander of Assault Group O1 as one of 'extreme hardship and difficulty', two craft were swamped and sank, although the personnel were rescued. At 07.00, the company commander radioed the battalion commander to inform him of the delay, and the latter ordered Company K (in the H+30 wave, meaning that it was on the point of landing) to lead the assault instead. The remaining four Company I boats beached around 08.00, some ninety minutes late. Four sailors from landing craft of 550 Assault Flotilla died on D-Day, two each from LCA 849 and LCA 913. It is not certain whether they were lost at this point or in landings made by other craft from SS *Empire Anvil* at H+30 and H+230. Overall, about six of that flotilla's eighteen craft were lost on D-Day.[59]

Scheduled to land at H+3, two minutes after the first infantry, were the Gap Assault Teams (GATs) with the same composition as those landing on Omaha West. Each was to land from an LCM(3) which had been towed across the English Channel by an LCT(A), with the team's personnel boarding from the towing craft to the LCM(3), a few miles off the French coast. Six GATs were to land on Easy Red.

Most did land roughly on time, but many were out of position. Team 10 managed to create a 100-yard gap near the St Laurent Draw, but it was not fully marked. Team 12 cleared a partial gap, though tragically, a German mortar round prematurely set off the explosives that the team had placed on the obstacles, killing and wounding fourteen team members as well as troops nearby. The remaining teams made little progress, suffering further casualties.

In several cases, one of the rubber boats carrying the teams' explosives was hit by German fire, inflicting losses on the men of the teams. It seems almost certain that some of the crews of the LCM(3)s were killed or wounded, but their names are not known. Second Lieutenant Phil Wood of Team 14 reported that after his unit's explosives were hit by German artillery, 'fire enveloped the LCM. The coxswain was blasted off the vessel.'

The remaining two teams were destined for Fox Green. Both had hits from enemy shells, one on the team's LCM(3) and the other on an explosives-laden rubber boat. The resulting casualties and troops sheltering behind obstacles prevented either team from clearing any obstacles in the first hours of the landing.[60]

The Gapping Support Teams were to land at H+8 from four LCM(3)s, which had been towed to Normandy by LCG(L)s and LCT(R)s. They landed twenty to sixty minutes behind schedule, with three teams on Easy Red and the fourth on Fox Green. A further five LCM(3)s carrying reserve equipment had made the crossing towed behind LCFs and were due off the beach at H+25, to be summoned as required.

The rapidly rising tide would soon call a temporary halt to the work of the GATs. In the first hours of the landings, demolition teams were able to create more gaps in the obstacles on Omaha East than was possible on the western half of the beach – no reflection of the bravery of the obstacle-clearance personnel who landed in the first waves. This would naturally have an impact on larger landing craft beaching later on D-Day.[61]

The follow-up companies of the assault infantry were to land at H+30 (07.00). On board seven LCVPs from USS *Henrico* were Company G and part of HQ Company, 2nd Battalion, 16th Infantry, all heading for Easy Red. A further six LCVPs from LST 357 delivered members of 397th Anti-Aircraft Artillery Battalion and other supporting units. These boats landed roughly on time.

Captain Joseph Dawson, commander of Company G, later reported that some of his troops stumbled and fell into the water as they exited the landing craft because they had been sitting in cramped positions on board for so long. Although they experienced heavy fire as they landed, the men of Company G would soon be advancing over the bluffs as they had discovered a blind spot in the German defences.[62]

At the same time, six LCAs of 550 Assault Flotilla (SS *Empire Anvil*) were to land Company K, 16th Infantry, plus supporting personnel, on Fox Green at H+30. These were the remainder of *Empire Anvil's* LCAs, after the twelve craft that had landed in the previous wave. On board one of them, Able Seaman Wally Fraser and another crewman were taking turns on a hand pump as the craft took on water. The troops were sitting in almost 2ft of water for much of the journey and most were seasick. Many of *Empire Anvil's* LCAs suffered from similar problems and they landed thirty-five minutes late at 07.35. Six LCVPs from LST 314 landed more anti-aircraft troops.[63]

Amid the chaos, a lone LCVP arrived off the beach at 07.00. On board were personnel who had loaded from SS *Empire Anvil*, belonging to HQ Company, 3rd Battalion, 16th Infantry, plus a party from the HQ of 62nd Field Artillery Battalion and a Naval Shore Fire Control Party. Equipped with several radio sets, the men on board would soon act as spotters, directing the fire of destroyers against the German defences. The personnel on board later went ashore on Easy Red.[64]

The final wave of the assault infantry was due at H+47, consisting of each battalion's weapons company. More of USS *Henrico's* boats were due to land troops on Easy Red: six LCVPs delivered Company H, 2nd Battalion, 16th Infantry. They were roughly on time, although they were swept east and landed on Fox Green near WN-62. The men found themselves under rifle, machine gun, mortar and artillery fire as soon as they landed. Captain Lawrence Bour of the battalion's HQ Company was on board one of these craft, 'The living lay sprawled from the shingle to a yard or two from the water's edge; the dead floated in the shallows just beyond.'[65]

Also landing at this time was an LCM(3) carrying just over 100 men, mostly medics and engineers, including the Assistant Battalion Surgeon, Captain C.N. Hall. As a doctor, Hall noted that the seasickness pills that had been issued to the troops only seemed to have worked in 40 per cent of cases. With the LCM heading for the shore, he was particularly struck by how hard it was to tell what was going on. He could hear explosions and saw tracers fly across the top of the craft, but it was still quieter than during the rehearsals. After landing, he joined the many other troops sheltering against the shingle bank at the top of the beach.[66]

On Fox Green, at around 07.25 to 07.30, a few minutes later than their scheduled time of H+47, six LCVPs landed Company M, 3rd Battalion, 16th Infantry and its HQ Company. The landing craft came from USS *Dorothea L. Dix*, but they had loaded the troops from

SS *Empire Anvil*. They beached on the eastern side of the beach, the troops wading ashore in knee- to waist-deep water, amid heavy enemy fire and many beach obstacles.

Three boats were lost on the beach, mostly swamped, although one may have hit a mine, and one crewman was killed. The surviving crew went ashore and sheltered at the top of the beach. They remained there until late evening and helped the army by carrying stretchers. Despite the coxswain's protestations, on one LCVP the army officers insisted their craft headed for Easy Red, rather than their designated beach of Fox Green. Around the same time, a single LCM from USS *Dorothea L. Dix* landed around ninety medics and engineers on Fox Green.[67]

The following wave of craft were to land a mere three minutes later, at H+50. They carried a mixture of troops who had disembarked from USS *Henrico*: members of 81st Chemical Weapons Battalion and engineers. Eight LCVPs from USS *Dorothea L. Dix* were scheduled for Easy Red and eight for Fox Green.

It appears that three craft from *Dorothea L. Dix* landed under fire at 07.30, with the troops losing some of their 4.2in mortars in the process. In addition, an LCM(3) delivered 16th Infantry's Advanced Command Post from *Henrico*. Eight more LCVPs were to beach on Fox Green at the same time: three from *Dorothea L. Dix*, the rest from other ships.

After consulting with the army officers on board, the crews of the three *Dorothea L. Dix* boats decided it was too dangerous to land, and in fact, did not beach until 15.35 onwards. The other five LCVPs may also have held off from landing until later.

At this point in the plan, two of 16th Infantry's three battalions should have landed, plus supporting troops. Although at least elements of all those units had got ashore, many could not carry out their intended roles fully, due to enemy fire and the resulting casualties or because they had landed in the wrong location. Many more waves of landing craft were due to beach soon.[68]

Eight LCT(6)s were due to land army engineers and other personnel of 5th Engineer Special Brigade with their vehicles and equipment at H+60 (07.30). Some of these troops were tasked with opening up the beach exits, but that would not be possible for some time. Five craft would land on Easy Red and three on Fox Green.

The tide had now risen to the point that the obstacles were partially submerged. One soldier described the many LCTs 'milling about', as their crews searched for clear gaps where they could beach, while the 'whole cliff was spouting fire … right left and centre'. While some of this group of LCTs were able to beach around the planned time, at least one did not put its troops ashore until 16.00.[69]

Half an hour earlier, as one of these craft, LCT 540, was around 900 yards off the beach, a German shell had mortally wounded the officer in charge, Lieutenant (j.g.) Frederick Nye Moses USNR. As the relief officer (second in command), Ensign William L. Wilhoit USNR took over and the craft continued towards the shore it was hit by eight more enemy shells. Although the LCT beached, the crew could not lower the ramp because a shell had destroyed the ramp motor, and after ten minutes the craft unbeached. Six more crewmen had been wounded, while among the troops, three were killed and twenty-seven wounded.

After the ramp motor was repaired, the LCT put its troops ashore later in the day. For his bravery and leadership, Wilhoit was awarded the Navy Cross, and LCT 540 became one of only two landing craft to receive a Presidential Unit Citation at Normandy.[70]

More 5th Engineer Special Brigade forces, including army engineers and 6th Naval Beach Battalion, were to land at H+65 (07.35) from LCI(L) 88 on Easy Red and LCI(L) 493 on Fox Green. Just as on Omaha West, beaching these large craft so early on D-Day was a gamble.

Both were on time, with the US Navy-crewed LCI(L) 493 heading for an alternative landing spot at Fox Red instead. That craft apparently had a better landing than LCI(L) 88, which beached in the intended sector. A number of DUKWs were due to land around the same time with stores for use by the same troops, having swum to the beach from LSTs further out.[71]

On board LCI(L) 88 was the distinctly unmilitary figure of 39-year-old *New Yorker* journalist Abbott Joseph ('A.J.') Liebling. Shortly after the craft began to put its passengers ashore, it came under heavy German machine gun and artillery fire. Flattening himself against the pilot house to take advantage of the slight cover it offered, Liebling observed at the ship's stern 'a tableau that was like a recruiting poster' as three of the US Coast Guard crew, one an African American wardroom steward, returned fire with a 20mm Oerlikon gun. Enemy fire killed three of the crew and seriously wounded others on board, also dislodging the starboard ramp. Quickly the officer in charge backed his craft off the beach so that the wounded could be cared for.[72]

Infantry played an essential part in an amphibious assault. The next few waves on Omaha East between H+70 and H+90 on Easy Red would see the arrival of 1st Battalion, 16th Infantry, the third battalion of that regiment to come ashore. The battalion and supporting personnel from other units were embarked on some thirty-two LCVPs, many of them with US Coast Guard crews from USS *Samuel Chase*, the ship which was also transporting 1st Battalion.

The twelve LCVPs of the H+70 wave from *Samuel Chase* arrived twenty minutes late, around 08.00, carrying Companies A and C. Approaching the beach, for coxswain Robert Adams, the dominant sensations were the smell of cordite and the sound of machine-gun fire.

On one of these boats was US Coast Guard Chief Photographer's Mate Robert F. Sargent, who would be responsible for some of the most iconic images of D-Day. Approaching the beach, he photographed an adjacent LCVP on which a bullet had set off a soldier's hand grenade, starting a fire. Coxswain Delba L. Nivens put the troops ashore before the crew put out the blaze.

Once the troops on his own LCVP had disembarked, Sargent took another photograph which was later titled 'Into the Jaws of Death'. It shows a view along the craft's empty hold, as soldiers advance through the waves towards the looming bluffs ahead.[73]

1st Battalion's Company B and HQ Company were due at H+80 (07.50) but arrived in twelve more LCVPs about five minutes before the previous wave. The third wave of craft carrying 1st Battalion was to land from eight LCVPs at H+90. In one of these craft, Technical Sergeant James Montague of 37th Engineer Combat Battalion had expected the beach to be free of small-arms fire but heard 'the whine of machine gun slugs' hitting the side of the LCVP as it neared the land. The troops landed in neck-deep water.[74]

The final element of 16th Infantry to land around this time was one LCM(3) and one LCVP, due at H+95 but actually arriving around 08.15, carrying the regimental rear command post and associated personnel such as medics and liaison teams from other units. On board was Colonel George Taylor, commanding officer of 16th Infantry who, after landing, would inspire his men and play a key role in organising the advance off the beach.

A radio operator in Taylor's HQ, Technician Fifth Grade John Pinder, was later awarded the Medal of Honor for repeatedly going back into the water to recover floating radio equipment and setting it up on the beach, despite being wounded twice from heavy enemy fire, until he was hit again and killed.

Probably also on the same craft as Taylor was another man who was responsible for some of the most famous photographs of D-Day: journalist Robert Capa. Eleven photographs survive from the time Capa spent ashore, showing troops striding through the waves or sheltering behind beach obstacles. Historians debate the exact time Capa landed or how much time he spent ashore (before departing via Omaha West as mentioned above), but the drama of those images is undeniable.[75]

A group of five LCT(5)s were due on Fox Green at H+90, carrying eighteen M7 self-propelled 105mm guns and other vehicles of 62nd Field Artillery Battalion. The beach was clearly no place for these valuable yet vulnerable vehicles. The LCTs waited off the beach until conditions were more suitable, variously landing between 15.00 and 22.00. More artillery was due to land at H+105 and H+110, on the back of DUKW amphibious vehicles that were swimming to the beach from LSTs offshore, as was attempted on Omaha West around the same time. Twelve DUKWs carrying guns of 7th Field Artillery Battalion were due to land first but half sank with their artillery pieces. The second group of DUKWs carried artillery and regimental HQ personnel from 16th Infantry. Those DUKWs that survived waited off the beach until later in the day.[76]

At H+110 (08.20), eight more DUKWs were due. More importantly, three craft carrying personnel from the HQ of US 1st Infantry Division were also scheduled to land: two LCM(3)s and an LCVP from USS *Anne Arundel*, which had collected their passengers from USS *Samuel Chase*. The senior officer of this party was Brigadier General Willard Wyman, divisional second in command.

The LCMs, including Wyman, landed slightly late at 08.39, but the LCVP remained afloat to observe the beach from offshore until the afternoon. Don Whitehead of the Associated Press was also in Wyman's craft. With several amphibious landings under his belt as a war reporter already, Whitehead's first thoughts on landing were that this time, the landings had failed. It was too early to tell if he was correct.[77]

THE LANDINGS CONTINUE: OMAHA WEST AND EAST FROM H+120

By H+120 (08.30), 116th and 16th Regimental Combat Teams (RCT) were ashore on Omaha West and East respectively. Some landing craft were waiting off the beach and others would be arriving in the coming hours, according to when conditions on the beach were judged suitable for the troops they carried.

The plans for the landings on the two halves of Omaha Beach were not an exact mirror image for the rest of the day. At any one time, the craft scheduled to land in the east and west were often of different types. The uncleared beach obstacles and continued German resistance on much of the beach were very different from the situation that planners had expected at this point, so many landing craft were delayed from their scheduled time.

The following will mainly describe the landings in the order of the planned timings, rather than their messy, actual sequence on the day. Where the revised beaching times of craft or waves are known, that will be indicated.

The next wave on both halves of the beach was at H+120. On Omaha West, a total of nine LCT(5)s plus three LCT(6)s were to land, spread across all four sectors. Many of the craft were carrying half-track-mounted guns of the 467th Anti-Aircraft Artillery Battalion, plus other vehicles, including those of army engineers. A couple carried vehicles from HQ 2nd Rangers.

Some LCTs tried to beach immediately but were unable to find a clear path through the obstacles and withdrew in the face of heavy enemy fire. LCT(5) 294 struck a mine, which exploded under the crew's quarters, then it was struck by shells and was unable to beach. As the craft's engine room flooded and it began to sink by the stern, the crew of LCT(5) 20 towed it further out to sea, then manoeuvred their craft to face LCT 294 bow to bow and unloaded 294's vehicles onto their own tank deck. The salvage tug USS *Pinto* could not save LCT 294, so the craft was scuttled using explosive charges, but without loss of any personnel or the vehicles carried. Several other LCTs were also damaged.[78]

Some of the craft did not manage to put their vehicles ashore until late afternoon or early evening. One of them, LCT(5) 147, was singled out for criticism by Admiral John L. Hall (Commander Force O), somewhat unfairly, it would seem, as the crew's actions and experiences were comparable to those of many other LCTs at Omaha Beach around this time. Admiral Hall noted:

> The action of the Officer-in-Charge in delaying beaching and unloading was erroneous. The Landing Attack Plan was part of an order and as such should have been obeyed implicitly unless circumstances made obedience impossible. Such was not the case here. If every officer in charge of landing craft is to disregard the Force Commander's order, and decide for himself when to land, the chances for a successful assault are small.

After several unsuccessful attempts in the morning, LCT 147 had landed the last of its vehicles around 16.20.[79]

Several publications describe how the crew of LCT(5) 30 grew tired of waiting, charged through the obstacles and beached, followed by

LCT(6) 554 and other craft. By demonstrating that major landing craft could ram the obstacles, LCT 30 is said to have enabled 18th Infantry – who would be coming ashore soon – to beach with relatively few losses. Historians, including Robert D. Blegen, who served on LCT 149 in the same wave, have since cast doubt on this narrative. The story was apparently introduced in a 1984 War Department publication, *Omaha Beachhead, American Forces in Action Series*, which also refers to LCI(L) 544 – though no such craft existed. It is certain that LCT 30 did manage to land its vehicles, but it came under heavy fire which knocked out the engines and forced the crew to abandon ship. One crewman was killed: Motor Mechanic's Mate First Class John Emanuel Anderson USNR. The LCT and its crew were awarded a Presidential Unit Citation for this action.[80]

Meanwhile, at H+120 on Omaha East, a variety of craft were to land. Although they were all scheduled to land at the same time, they will be described in groups for clarity – even though confusion was more evident than clarity at the time.

As LCT 199 approached the beach at about 08.30, there were twenty to thirty LCTs 'milling about, 50–100 yards from high water'. It was able to beach almost immediately, but others did not do so until the afternoon.[81]

Nine LCT(5)s were to land half-tracks of the 197th Anti-Aircraft Artillery Battalion on Easy Red and Fox Green. The LCTs had difficulties due to obstacles and enemy fire: landing craft were wrecked, vehicles swamped, personnel became casualties or were pinned down at the water's edge. LCT 25, for example, beached at 08.50 but found that the water was too deep for vehicles to get ashore. Beaching again at 09.40, the LCT hit an obstacle and its engine room flooded. Two of the crew were killed by German fire and the surviving crew had to abandon the craft with many of the vehicles still on board. Mortar hits set the LCT alight and it was still burning at 18.00.[82]

Three US Coast Guard-manned LCI(L)s were also timetabled to arrive at H+120 on Omaha East. They were all carrying Engineer Special Brigade personnel and army engineers attached to US 1st Division or US V Corps, with other personnel such as medics and quartermaster troops mixed in. LCI(L)s 85 and 89 were to land on Easy Red, and beached on the correct sector roughly on time.

Lieutenant (j.g.) Coit T. Hendley Jr USCGR, officer in charge of LCI(L) 85, tried to select a landing site that avoided the remaining beach obstacles. As the craft neared the shore, 'the thud of underwater obstacles could be felt on the bottom and sides of the ship. As the bow grounded, a mine exploded, ripping a hole in the forward part of the ship.' Troops began landing on one of the craft's two ramps, but almost immediately, German artillery and machine guns focused on the ship's bow. Hendley continued:

> The shells tore into the troop compartment. They exploded on the exposed deck. They smashed through the massed men trying to get down the ramp ... Men were hit and mutilated. There was no such thing as a minor wound ... unloading was stopped because it was impossible to get past the pile of dead and wounded. Finally a hit finished off the ramp.

The crew moved LCI(L) 85 off the beach and unwounded personnel were transferred to smaller craft to go ashore. The damage control party managed to put out three fires, as army and coast guard medics treated the forty wounded; there were also about fifteen troops dead. Four of the craft's crew were wounded.

The scene was truly shocking, 'The deck was so slick with blood and cluttered with bits of flesh and dead and mutilated men that it was difficult to move from one part of the ship to another.' After transferring the wounded to a transport ship, LCI(L) 85 began to sink, and the crew transferred to a tug. A final demolition charge was needed to sink the craft to avoid it being a hazard to other shipping. The other craft, LCI(L) 89, apparently escaped unscathed.[83]

The third craft, LCI(L) 83, tried three times to beach on Fox Green, beginning at 08.30, but could not find a gap in the obstacles. Thirty-six personnel were able to transfer to an LCVP to go ashore. Next, a shell hit the LCI(L), killing and wounding sixteen men.

At 11.00 the officer in charge, Lieutenant G.F. Hutchinson USCGR decided to make another attempt at beaching, selecting Fox Red as the landing site. As a precaution, he moved the personnel onto the craft's upper deck, where they were less vulnerable to mines. This proved to be a wise choice, as LCI(L) 83 did strike a mined obstacle while beaching and also began to be hit by German artillery. Some troops were wounded, but the unwounded personnel could now disembark. The crew abandoned ship, taking their wounded passengers with them, and dug in below a small cliff.

Once the tide had receded, around 13.00, the crew were able to return to their ship. Using plywood and mattresses, they repaired some of the holes caused by mines and shells, except for one that was 7ft wide and 13ft high, meaning one compartment of the ship remained partly flooded.

After a marathon pumping effort, LCI(L) 83 managed to return to the UK the following day.[84]

Two LCVPs from an LST were to land on Easy Red around H+120, carrying US V Corps HQ personnel. Eight DUKWs launched from LSTs – the majority carrying 16th Infantry's Cannon Company – were to land at the same time on Fox Green. However, Fox Green was still closed to landings, so they probably went elsewhere.[85]

Seven LCT(6)s were due on Easy Red at H+130. Most carried a variety of vehicles. The wave was driven back four times by enemy fire, but most managed to beach on the fifth attempt. Four LCVPs from USS *Dorothea L. Dix* were to beach five minutes after those LCTs, carrying troops of 20th Engineer Combat Battalion, who they had collected from HMS *Empire Anvil*.

Also present in the lead boat was the war correspondent Ernest Hemingway. When the craft reached Fox Green, the army lieutenant on board refused to land, so the LCVPs waited off the beach. They finally beached at 13.15 on the Easy Red/Fox Green boundary and still encountered uncleared obstacles, artillery, mortar and small-arms fire. *Dorothea L. Dix*'s records note, 'Army lieutenant refused to leave the boat until shamed into doing so by Mr Hemingway'.[86]

More craft were due soon after. On Omaha West, LCI(L) 84, carrying medics, engineers and Engineer Special Brigade personnel, was due to beach at H+150. It would seem that the craft landed roughly on time – around 09.00 – since just over an hour later, thirty wounded were taken off LCI(L) 84, suggesting the vessel beached under fire.[87]

The next forty-five minutes, roughly H+180 to H+225 (09.30 to 10.15), saw very different groups of landing craft scheduled to beach on each half of Omaha. On Omaha West, a large number of LCTs were scheduled to beach. Some craft may have landed approximately on time, but it is likely that many were held off the beach until later in the day.

Some of the LCTs had already despatched part of their cargo of troops. They had been carrying amphibious Sherman DD tanks which, in most cases, had been landed on the beach rather than being launched into the sea as originally planned. The DD tanks had occupied the centre of the crafts' tank decks, but at either side were other troops who remained on board until now. These included vehicles from 81st Chemical Weapons Battalion.

Meanwhile, the LCTs had collected additional troops from landing ships offshore to take the place of the DD tanks. They were LCT(6)s, apart from one LCT(5). Six LCTs were to land on Dog Green, with a mixture of personnel and vehicles on board, including from 2nd and 5th Rangers and 116th Infantry. A further three LCTs were scheduled to land on Dog White, with a similarly mixed load of vehicles, also including a few from 743rd Tank Battalion and 58th Field Artillery Battalion.

Three more LCTs were due to land troops on Dog Red, among others, carrying personnel from HQ US 29th Infantry Division, 58th Field Artillery Battalion and engineers. Also landing at this beach were twelve DUKWs, launched from an LST and carrying ammunition. Eighteen more DUKWs with similar cargoes were to land on Easy Green, plus a single LCT.[88]

Six LCM(3)s reached both halves of Omaha Beach around this time. They were equipped for salvaging landing craft. A few more LCT(5)s and LCT(6)s were to arrive on Omaha West at H+225: two each on Dog White and Dog Red, with vehicles from a similar range of units to the LCTs that were timetabled to land shortly before. Again, there is evidence that the actual beaching time of at least some of these craft was early afternoon. One of them was LCT(5) 413 which, earlier in the day, had launched the DUKWs equipped with fire engine ladders for use by 2nd Rangers at Pointe du Hoc; this had presumably embarked additional troops from a landing ship.

A proportion of the LCTs landing over this forty-five-minute period each had on board a team from 320th Barrage Balloon Battalion, which was the only African American unit to land on D-Day, on Utah as well as Omaha. Each team was four men as standard, but sometimes even smaller. On foot, they manhandled the reduced-sized Very Low Altitude balloon off each LCT and took it ashore as part of the anti-aircraft defences of the beachhead.[89]

In the middle of the sequence of landings mentioned above, the next major unit scheduled to land was 18th Regimental Combat Team. This was the second infantry regiment to arrive on Omaha East, following on from 16th RCT. The first of its three infantry battalions was due at H+195 (09.45).

General Wyman, second in command of the US 1st Infantry Division, was able to send messages to the Force O HQ ship, USS *Ancon*, and thus influence some degree of control. At 09.50, Wyman reported that there were too many vehicles on the beach and combat troops on foot were most urgently needed. Twenty minutes later, he communicated that reinforcements were needed on Easy Red, in particular – which was, in fact, where the 18th Infantry were tasked to land. In practice, the regiment began to go ashore around 10.30, forty-five minutes later than planned. Unlike the assault troops who had arrived earlier, 18th Infantry had not been reorganised into boat teams but retained their standard unit organisation.[90]

First to land was 2nd Battalion, 18th Infantry on eighteen LCVPs from USS *Anne Arundel*, possibly also two LCM(3)s from the same ship and on LCI(L) 489. At first, the LCVPs hesitated to beach due to enemy fire and the absence of a clear route through the numerous beach obstacles. The Beachmaster instructed the craft to land on the right flank of Easy Red.

The eighteen LCVPs were divided into three divisions of six craft each. The first managed to find a landing site that was clear of obstacles and beached at about 10.45, despite machine-gun fire at the water's edge and sporadic mortar fire on the beach. The boat division commander's report noted that LCTs from the H+140 and H+150 waves were still waiting off the beach at this point.

The remaining LCVPs arrived up to forty-five minutes later. In total, ten of *Anne Arundel*'s eighteen LCVPs were lost in this beaching, most from collisions with submerged obstacles as the tide was now near its highest point. Despite that, the only crew casualties were one man, who was seriously wounded.

One of the LCM(3)s arriving at the same time hit five to ten unmined obstacles, but these did not cause significant damage. One 18th Infantry soldier, Private Carlton Barrett, had landed earlier with 16th Infantry as part of a small reconnaissance team. He was awarded the Medal of Honor for assisting casualties after landing and then, as 18th Infantry's boats began to arrive, for going out to them to provide information.[91]

The first LCVPs beached at the same time as LCI(L) 489, which had battalion HQ personnel on board. As it approached the beach, the larger craft came under fire and received damage from collisions with beach obstacles.

As the troops began to land using the LCI(L)'s two ramps, Seaman Second Class Travis Wilton 'Al' Allen USNR took a lifeline ashore to help the heavily loaded soldiers who were struggling through the waves under their heavy loads. Allen then carried wounded soldiers back onto the craft for treatment. Pharmacist's Mate First Class James R. Argo set up a makeshift casualty station in the LCI(L)'s mess hall and later also went onto the beach to aid the wounded. After a while, the craft seems to have unbeached, returning to the shore a few hours later to land the remaining troops.[92]

Nine more LCI(L)s were due at Easy Red fifteen minutes after the above wave, at H+210 (10.00), although this was a nominal beaching time, and their actual landing time had always been likely to be varied according to operational circumstances. These carried the other two-thirds of 18th Infantry – 1st and 3rd Battalions. One vessel, LCI(L) 493, was delivering its second load of the day, having first landed troops at H+65. Subsequently, it had collected personnel of the regimental HQ from USS *Anne Arundel*, so they could go ashore around the same time as the rest of that unit.

The LCVPs from the H+195 wave were instructed to remain off the beach after landing their first loads and to help unload the LCI(L)s. Not all did so, but other small boats – LCVPs and LCM(3)s – were available to transfer some of these soldiers ashore.

Among them was an LCVP crewed by US Coast Guardsman Emil Baschschmidt from USS *Samuel Chase*. After putting ashore 18th Infantry troops, he and his comrades had to abandon the boat on the beach. Two hours later, they were taken off the beach on an LCT, but that, in turn, was mined while unbeaching, so Baschschmidt's crew had to go ashore again. It was nearly 16.00 before they managed to get off the beach on an LCI(L).[93]

The nine LCI(L)s landed over a period of time: 1st Battalion, 18th Infantry began to land around 12.23 and 3rd Battalion from 13.30 onwards. Both groups of craft approached the beach to the east of the St Laurent Draw, with 1st Battalion the furthest east of the two.

Captain Edward McGregor of 1st Battalion later described how gaps in the obstacles were 'few and narrow', while the beach was 'under heavy shell fire, plunging [machine gun] fire, and murderous sniper fire'. A 3rd Battalion officer, Captain J.F. Gurka, recounted how most personnel had transferred to smaller craft to go ashore because of the presence of beach obstacles. Two LCI(L)s hit mined obstacles when some 150 yards offshore, but the troops on board were able to wade ashore from that point.

Overall, the soldiers suffered considerable casualties. For example, on LCI(L) 487, which was struck by several shells. The damage to that craft was so great that the officer in charge, Lieutenant Stewart F. Lovell USNR gave the order for most of the crew to abandon ship while he and a few men remained behind in the hope of salvaging their vessel later on.

At this time, LCI(L) 93 had beached nearby with a second load of troops (including Engineer Special Brigade personnel) which had embarked from USS *Samuel B. Chase*. Many of LCI(L) 487's crew, now without their own craft, ran to LCI(L) 93 seeking rescue from the beach, but that craft now became the target of the German guns. As LCI(L) 93 struggled to withdraw from the beach due to a sandbank, it was hit by ten shells in quick succession, two of them passing through the pilot house. Seven of the crew were wounded, two of them seriously, and there were also casualties among the relatively small number of troops still on board.[94]

One of the wounded crew on LCI(L) 93 was Steward's Mate John Noble Roberts, one of the craft's two African American crewmen. Roberts was acting as a messenger because the ship's internal phones had been disabled. He was carrying a message from the officer in charge to the engine room, to reverse the engines in an attempt to get the craft off the beach, when he was severely wounded. As Roberts described:

A shell came through the bulkhead and exploded right underneath me. I knew I'd lost my leg before the medic got to me. The foot was gone, all the muscle, just the skin and bone hanging from my knee down; and my other leg was burning like I was in a fire or something. I thought I wouldn't make it.[95]

Roberts' comrades saved his life by applying a tourniquet and one of them accompanied him when he was evacuated.

After landing their initial load, the H+210 wave LCI(L)s were tasked to return to the Transport Area to collect more personnel from the landing ships USS *Anne Arundel*, USS *Dorothea L. Dix* and USS *Thurston*. One of those that collected a second load from *Thurston* was LCI(L) 497. On this second beaching, that vessel hit mined obstacles and may have been hit by enemy shells also, leading to the crew having to abandon their ship on the beach.[96]

The nine LCI(L)s described above were carrying a major part of 18th RCT's infantrymen, but the vehicles associated with that regiment were still to come ashore. The first of these were due to land on Omaha East in a series of waves totalling twenty-two LCT(5)s and LCT(6)s, to beach from H+220 (10.10) to H+250. Twelve LCTs were to arrive on Easy Red, half of which had launched DD tanks before H-Hour but still had further troops on board that had loaded in the UK, particularly jeeps and trailers. The craft had then collected more troops to replace the DD tanks from USS *Samuel Chase*, USS *Henrico* and SS *Empire Anvil*, and landed the entire load.

The process of loading these additional troops was delayed by the LCT(DD)s arriving at the ship behind schedule and then the need to unload the wounded from those craft before the extra troops could board. It was H+330 by the time the troops from all three ships had been embarked.

The other six of those twelve LCTs were landing their first load of troops. Units carried included members of 18th Infantry's Medical Detachment and Anti-Tank Company, plus others, such as engineers.[97]

Inevitably, for such a large number of craft, the LCTs ended up beaching over a range of times. LCT(5)s 7 and 202 did not beach until 17.35 and 18.00 respectively, while LCT 22 did not beach until 13.30 on 7 June (before that, its landing had been postponed because it did not carry tracked vehicles). Ten LCTs were scheduled to land at Fox Green, of which eight had carried DD tanks earlier in the day. On board the ten craft were a mixture of members of 16th RCT ('overstrength' personnel – in other words, additional to the authorised strength of the regiment and available as replacements for casualties), 5th Engineer Special Brigade, 741st Tank Battalion and 7th Field Artillery Battalion, all units which had begun landing several hours ago. As LCT(6) 856 headed for the beach, the craft was hit by a shell which wounded several of the crew. After abandoning the vessel on the beach, the crew later returned and spent the night on board.[98]

On Omaha West, the equivalent unit to 18th RCT was 115th RCT. Like the assault troops for the western beaches, 116th Infantry, this was another of the US 29th Infantry Division's three infantry regiments. 115th RCT were to land, when ordered by the commander of US V Corps, on the eastern side of Omaha West, in Dog Red and Easy Green sectors. At 06.32 on the morning of D-Day, 115th RCT were given H+240 (10.30) as the start time for their landings.

The timing for these troops to land was presumably issued at such a late stage in case changes in circumstances required some alteration to the plan. All the landing craft carrying 115th RCT had originally been assigned to Follow-Up Force B, but those carrying the infantry had been transferred into Force O, so the troops could be brought ashore earlier in the day if needed. Craft carrying 115th RCT's vehicles remained in Force B.

At the last minute, the location of the landings was revised: 2nd and 1st Battalions, 115th Infantry had been scheduled to land on Dog Red and Easy Green respectively at H+240. Each battalion was carried on four LCI(L)s, one company per craft, along with some supporting troops. Four more of the same type of craft would bring the regimental HQ and 3rd Battalion of 115th Infantry to Dog Red half an hour later. Instead, 115th RCT's arrival was switched to Easy Red, where it was judged they were most needed. The 1st Battalion landed to the east of 2nd Battalion, both beginning to land at just before 11.00.

Not all craft were able to land simultaneously. LCI(L) 408, for example, hit a sandbar and had to withdraw and rebeach, meaning its troops could not start landing for an additional forty-five minutes. On that vessel, Ship's Cook Second Class Raymond James Aubin was mortally wounded by a shell fragment while manning one of the guns and died two days later.

The 3rd Battalion came ashore at around 12.00, in between the previous two battalions. Those LCI(L)s also came under fire as they beached. Lieutenant Colonel John Cooper, commanding officer of 110th Field Artillery Battalion, was descending one of the ramps of LCI(L) 411 when 'a sound like a riveting machine went off over our heads' as a German machine gunner targeted the troops. LCI(L) 553 was unable to get off the beach and began to be accurately shelled by German artillery, so the crew abandoned ship. Motor Machinist's Mate Third Class Robert Leach of LCI(L) 553 was sheltering under a half-track when soldiers advised him to move as it was loaded with ammunition. He later found an LCVP that took him and some fellow crewmembers off the beach.[99]

The Deputy Commander Assault Force O-2 had arrived off the beach on LCH 86 at 11.00. His report later described Omaha West at that time. Around ten LCI(L)s and LCTs were abandoned on the beach. Many LCTs and DUKWs were 'milling about' at 1,000 yards off the coast and further out. He began contacting control craft by loudhailer but could not get in touch with the Beachmasters ashore by radio. He noted that the remaining beach obstacles and high tide were making further landings very difficult. The loss of many LCTs carrying road matting, which had been intended to be laid above the high-water mark, meant that wheeled vehicles would have found it very difficult to move on the beach. In fact, without beach exits open, there was nowhere for vehicles to go.[100]

Between H+230 and H+330 there were a series of waves scheduled to land at Easy Red and Fox Green, each of a relatively small number of craft, but like the previously mentioned waves they were no doubt often delayed and intermixed. At H+230 (10.20), fourteen LCVPs would deliver troops collected from USS *Henrico* and five LCAs would bring personnel from SS *Empire Anvil*.

At H+240, three Rhino Ferries were to land with vehicles from LSTs. Four more Rhinos were set to land mostly lighter vehicles from LSTs at H+240 on Omaha West, one on each of the four sectors. The vehicles included trucks, jeeps and weapons carriers from units such as the engineers, medics and artillery. There was even a detachment from 834th Engineer Aviation Battalion, who were to survey a site for a landing strip for artillery observation planes. The timing for these beachings is unclear, but certainly the large and unwieldy Rhinos were held back due to conditions on the beach. Even at 14.20 there were too many obstacles on the beaches for Rhinos to be able to land. It was possible to unload vehicles from Rhinos off the coast onto LCTs for the final journey to the beach, but it is not clear if this took place. Many LCTs had not yet delivered their initial cargo and LCTs were also needed to unload the landing ships so those vessels could return to the UK.[101]

The following were all scheduled to arrive on Omaha West. Three LCT(5)s would deliver US 1st Infantry Division troops at H+250, including Signals and Military Police, plus vehicles from the divisional HQ. Six LCVPs would bring men of 16th Infantry: these were 'over-strength' personnel.

From around H+250, forty-eight DUKWs were available to be called ashore when required, having swum in from LSTs off the coast. Each of these amphibious trucks was carrying ammunition for the troops. At H+265, two LCTs were due, carrying vehicles of 18th RCT and 348th Engineer Combat Battalion. At H+270, the wave consisted of three LCTs and one LCI(L) carrying US 1st Infantry Division HQ Company and Signals Company personnel, among others.

At H+300, five more LCTs were to deliver to Easy Red the Ground Controlled Interception and Group Control Centre of 85 Group RAF, a British unit that would set up radar equipment for use ashore. Appropriately, two of the LCTs were the only two Royal Navy LCT(4)s in Force O: LCTs 562 and 628. At the same time, four LCTs would arrive at Fox Green, carrying 5th Engineer Special Brigade vehicles and supplies: LCT(6)s 548, 626, 637 and 638.

LCT 637 had a struggle to beach its cargo of engineering equipment. The vessel developed a list on D-Day and then hit a mine on 9 June, but eventually beached several days later. The craft and crew received a Navy Unit Commendation for their efforts. The officer in charge, Ensign Charles Lilly USNR later recalled that before departing the UK, he had to stop the army loading his craft with 250 tons of cargo when it could only transport 180 tons – the LCT may still have been overloaded.

The fourth H+300 craft due on Fox Green was LCT 638 with 160 tons of ammunition. The officer in charge, Ensign Joseph D. Graham USNR, recalled that he was ordered not to beach due to the risk of explosion if the LCT was hit. LCT 638 anchored overnight, away from the rest of the fleet in case of an air raid and beached for the first time at 10.00 on 7 June 1944. After unloading a truck carrying small-arms ammunition and some personnel, the craft unbeached due to sniper fire. They landed the remain-der of their cargo that afternoon and on the following day.[102]

Seven LCTs plus a single LCI(L) were to beach on Easy Red at H+310 (11.40) with vehicles and personnel of 18th RCT. As there were now so many LCTs and LCI(L)s that were struggling to find suitable places to beach, at 12.00, twenty-five LCVPs from USS *Samuel Chase* and USS *Henrico* were sent to Easy Red to help unload personnel from the larger craft.

Meanwhile, on Omaha West there had not been any landings scheduled between H+240 and H+330, although many craft would have landed during this period as they were delayed from their planned landing time. At H+330, three LCT(6)s were due, each carrying 150 tons of stores, mostly ammunition. The plan was that the LCTs would beach and be gradually unloaded to provide the troops ashore with what would be their most important supplies. The three craft had not beached by 16.25 and were sent further out to sea so they would not be a hazard to other craft if hit by enemy fire.[103]

As the afternoon began, the Commander of LCT Flotillas 12 and 26 USN (Lieutenant Commander William Leide USNR) estimated that 60 per cent of the LCTs in the assault forces had not yet beached, 'Many craft were foolishly trying to manoeuvre in the strong wind and heavy surf within 1,000 yards of the beach. This was suicidal.'

Omaha Beach continued to be under German artillery fire during the afternoon. As the Commander Force O put it, the shelling was 'neither heavy not sustained, [but] was deadly accurate'. The Deputy Commander Assault Group O2 reported that the afternoon of D-Day was 'longest eight hours I had ever experienced'. The loss of vehicles landed over the period from 16.00 to 20.00 was a 'terrible thing to see'. He praised the destroyers and gunfire support craft for duelling with German shore batteries with no thought of their own safety. However, both types of ship could not provide full support to the troops ashore, as they were uncertain of the exact location of friendly troops. In the early afternoon, the Commander Gunfire Support Craft asked permission to fire rockets from an LCT(R) against German positions, but both army and navy commanders believed there was too much danger to US troops.[104]

The period up to H+330 (12.00) on Omaha Beach was known as the First Tide. According to the plan, both the assault and the follow-up RCTs would be ashore by the end of this phase, plus supporting troops. Beginning at H+360, roughly the point when the tide began to recede from the high-tide mark, the landings entered the Second Tide. There were so many waves of craft on Omaha East due to land over the following hour and a half that giving an account of them risks becoming a simple list.

The next waves were bringing personnel and vehicles of 18th RCT and 5th Engineer Special Brigade. At H+360, twenty-six LCVPs and two

LCM(3)s arrived as well as two LCTs. Five minutes later, thirty LCVPs and two LCM(3)s, and at H+370, another thirty LCVPs and two LCM(3)s. Ten minutes further on, twenty-one LCVPs and two LCM(3)s, as well as a Rhino Ferry carrying vehicles from an LST, and an LCT carrying vehicles of US V Corps HQ arrived.

At H+400, twenty LCVPs and one LCM(3) were to deliver 18th RCT forces, while five LCT(6)s would deliver vehicles of 5th Engineer Special Brigade and 3275 Quartermaster Company. Twenty minutes later, the wave consisted of twenty-six LCVPs, three LCM(3)s carrying 18th RCT troops, and five LCT(6)s with 5th Engineer Special Brigade vehicles.[105]

As with previous waves, what happened did not closely match the original plan. Three waves of craft despatched from USS *Thurston* were timetabled to beach at H+370 to H+400, but their actual landing times were H+390 to H+495. While it was not unusual that troops were delayed in landing, depending on which craft were available, they were sometimes able to beach earlier than planned.

According to the plan, many of the landing craft just referenced would have been making their second or third trip to the beach, having landed an initial cargo earlier in the morning. Of course, it was impossible for planners to know how many craft might have been lost in these earlier waves, so the actual composition of these waves was likely to vary. Force O's plan stated that, if available, LCTs and LCI(L)s should be used rather than the smaller craft. Some of the cargoes at this stage included jeeps, and while it was possible to lower a jeep from a transport ship into one of the small boats, it was much easier to use an LCT.[106]

By 13.00, US troops had been ashore at Omaha for six and a half hours and were gradually finding weak spots in the German defences. Communications were being established between naval forces and the troops ashore, enabling the ships' firepower to be better co-ordinated with the assault. Despite these developments, it would be wrong to assume that beaching had now become safer and more straightforward for landing craft crews.

Ensign Joseph A. Sullivan USNR led twelve LCVPs carrying jeeps loaded from USS *Anne Arundel* to Easy Red. The Beachmaster instructed that no more than five craft should land at once, so Sullivan formed the wave into three divisions of four and led the first of these to the beach at about 13.00. They faced heavy machine gun and mortar fire as they approached and as Sullivan's craft beached a stake pierced the bottom of the boat. After putting the jeep ashore, although the Beachmaster suggested he abandon the LCVP, Sullivan and his crew spent two hours repairing its bottom with the only spare materials at hand – the wood and nails from the craft's wave sign (a signboard indicating the wave number). They stuffed lifejackets into the remainder of the hole and the coxswain managed to get the craft off the beach. Their craft was recovered onto USS *Thurston* around 18.00. Two other LCVPs of their small wave had been lost.[107]

The landings slowed for several hours around 16.00–18.00, when the tide was at its lowest. One exception was a group of twenty LCM(3)s, which had crossed the English Channel on board the LSD HMS *Oceanway*. This unusual ship, one of two LSDs present on D-Day, had a large hold which could be flooded to admit smaller craft and then drained while the vessel made a sea voyage. Loaded onto each LCM(3) was a Sherman tank of Company B, 745th Tank Battalion. *Oceanway* was ordered to anchor close to the beach and despatch these craft. The tanks were ashore on Fox Green by 17.15, if not sooner, and went on to support 16th Infantry.[108]

HMS *Oceanway* had arrived in Convoy B-2. This was part of Force B, the follow-up naval force for both American beaches, although the majority of vessels were to go to Omaha. Also in that convoy were twelve LCI(L)s plus the flotilla leader, LCH 414, carrying the third infantry regiment of US 1st Infantry Division: 26th Infantry.

At 16.40 these landing craft were ordered to beach to the east side of Easy Red, rather than on Dog Red as planned (one or more may even have beached on Fox Green). The landing was made under intermittent German artillery fire, but it was judged that there was less fire on the eastern half of Omaha than in the west. Several craft grounded on sandbars, which meant the vessel was too far from the shore and the water too deep for the troops on board to easily get to the land.

On LCI(L) 537, the soldiers began descending the craft's ramps before one of the crewmen had set up the lifeline for them to hold when wading ashore. Around twenty soldiers got into trouble in deep water and one man drowned. The craft withdrew and beached twice more, trying to get into shallower water to help the troops. In total, about three hours passed from the first beaching until all the soldiers had been unloaded from LCI(L) 537, and by the end, the craft had been hit by shrapnel in several places and its barrage balloon had been shot down.[109]

LCI(L) 415 had an even more difficult landing. Under artillery fire, one of the crew – Electrician's Mate First Class Arthur Virgil Shields – had volunteered to carry the lifeline ashore to aid the troops as they landed. However, as soon as he stepped off the ramp, he sank into deep water and was recovered by his comrades. The officer in charge, Lieutenant (j.g.)

John Forby Schereschewsky tried to drive the craft up the beach with the engines, but to no avail. The senior soldier on board expressed his frustration at being stuck in this position under fire. Seeing several soldiers struggling in the water nearby, Shields – who had only just been rescued himself – swam to rescue them. He succeeded, but his absence had not immediately been noted, and at the same time, LCI(L) 415 had withdrawn out to sea and then rebeached further down the coast, where the troops were at last put ashore. The crew last saw Shields sheltering behind a tank.

As LCI(L) 416 was beaching, the craft struck a mined obstacle which damaged the ship's screws and prevented it from withdrawing out to sea again. The troops on board landed safely. They included the commander of US 29th Infantry Division, General Charles H. Gerhardt.

As the craft came under fire, the officer in charge gave the order to abandon ship, but moments later, one crewman was wounded by shrapnel. At this point, Shields from LCI(L) 415 boarded the craft, looking for a ride home. He assisted two of LCI(L) 416's crew in moving the wounded man onto the beach. Once ashore, Shields was mortally wounded by shrapnel and died that evening. He was awarded the Navy Cross for his actions in saving the lives of his comrades. His commanding officer noted that he had joined the US Navy on the day after the Japanese attack on Pearl Harbor. One of LCI(L) 416's crew was also killed by shrapnel on the beach.

By 22.30, the other eleven of the twelve LCI(L)s had successfully unbeached. As with the two infantry regiments that had landed from LCI(L)s earlier in the day, the regiment's complement of vehicles would land later from LCTs and LSTs.[110]

The 26th Infantry's vehicles were on board LSTs and Royal Navy LCT(4)s in Convoy B-1, recently arrived. Those LCTs were formed into Q LCT Squadron, comprising 54, 56, 57 and 59 LCT Flotillas. The delays in the landings at Omaha meant that the LCTs would not land their cargoes – which included tank and artillery units that were needed ashore – on the evening of D-Day as planned, but the following day.

Although the newly arrived LSTs could not yet put their cargoes ashore, even by Rhino Ferry, they did send over 100 LCVPs to the beach to evacuate casualties. Some of these LSTs would, in fact, not land their cargoes until 8 June. At daylight on 7 June, all LCT(4)s of Force B that were carrying tanks were sent to the beach to meet the army's needs.[111]

After the low tide, the landings at Omaha were scheduled to resume at H+12 hours (18.30). Between that time and H+18 hours 10 minutes (22.40), nineteen Rhino Ferries were due to beach, carrying 18th RCT vehicles from LSTs, some of them accompanied by a small number of

LCVPs. By 18.00, perhaps only one Rhino had beached. Others attempted to land but found the surf difficult or were driven off by enemy fire. During the night of D-Day, the Rhino crews attempted to continue unloading and it was midday on 7 June before they could be relieved.[112]

Despite the Allies' enormous logistical arrangements, vast manufacturing capabilities and past experience of amphibious warfare, even when the enemy threat was reduced, the landings did not run smoothly. Naval commanders attempted to create order among the chaos. In the late afternoon of D-Day, LCI(L) 89 and 90 were set up as additional control vessels for small craft on the east and west sides of the beach respectively. The Deputy Assault Group Commander O1, on board LCI(L) 492, spent the night of D-Day going round the anchored landing craft, directing those who were uncertain what to do, and attempting to locate and land priority material such as blood plasma, hospital dressings and ammunition requested by the army. He had no records indicating on which craft these were located, so had to go round checking, one by one. His craft also guided other landing craft to the beach, 'It was practically impossible for ferry craft to distinguish any one particular beach during darkness, much less the channels into the beach.'[113]

As on the other beaches, barges were one component of the landing force that is often overlooked. Convoy UB-1 included six 1,000-ton-capacity ammunition barges for Omaha Beach. While some records indicate that this convoy was to arrive in the evening of 7 June, the Commander Force O reported that the barges reached Normandy on the afternoon of D-Day. Their cargoes were intended to form a reserve supply, for use if bad weather delayed unloading.

Two convoys composed primarily of landing barges also arrived. Convoy O-4 was due at H+12 hours on D-Day and Convoy O-5 at 07.00 on 7 June (both were about twelve hours late). Each had thirty-six LBVs with supporting LBWs, LBOs and LBEs, plus two LBKs in the second convoy. Around a third of the LBVs went to the wrong beach or were delayed. Between the two convoys, there were also nearly 100 LCM(3)s in total.[114]

Convoy EBP-1 arrived at Omaha Beach in the early morning of 7 June. This included four personnel ships or troop transports: USS *Susan B. Anthony*, USAT *George W. Goethals*, USAT *Borinquen* and USAT *George S. Simonds* (the last three were US Army Transports, as indicated by the letters 'USAT'). All four did not carry their own landing craft, so they needed assistance from ferry craft to land the troops they carried (nearly

1,500 men on *Borinquen*, 2,300 on *Susan B. Anthony* and around 2,000 on the other two vessels).

Soon after arriving, *Susan B. Anthony* struck a mine and sank at 10.10. The troops on board were transferred to LCTs and several destroyers, averting what could have led to many deaths. Including the ship's crew, 2,689 men were rescued, which is said to be the largest number rescued from a ship without loss of life.[115]

Around 09.00 on 7 June, Convoy B-3 arrived with thirty-one LSTs for Omaha Beach, while a further nine headed for Utah. Troops carried included 175th Infantry, the remaining infantry regiment from US 1st and 29th Infantry Divisions. The naval authorities sought to land the regiment as fast as possible. Many of its units were on board ten LSTs, which anchored 2,000 yards off Dog Green and hailed small boats for unloading the personnel.

One LST developed a particular technique to speed up unloading. The ship's crew offered hot meals to passing craft and then loaded those craft with troops while their crews were preoccupied with the food. When the army said the cargo carried by LST 133 was 'desperately needed' ashore, it was beached at 13.30: a practice which was strongly discouraged because of the perceived risk of damage to the ship. However, for the rest of 7 June, other LSTs continued to be unloaded by Rhino Ferry or LCT, which proved to be much slower.[116]

Within days, drying out LSTs soon became a standard technique, as it proved possible without serious damage. This freed up Rhino Ferries and LCTs of the ferry service to unload MT (Motor Transport) ships instead, as those vessels were unable to beach.

Through the bravery, initiative and determination of the troops – and often lower-ranking personnel at that – US forces had managed to carve out a beachhead at Omaha by the end of D-Day. Those characteristics had also been evident in the actions of the landing craft crews. They played a vital role in ensuring that, despite everything that went wrong at Omaha Beach on D-Day, enough went right to enable the landings there to succeed.

8

Gold Beach

Together with casualties on the beach, the shell[s] landing, smoke, fire etc., it looked to me as if the landing had failed.[1]

Bill Page, crew of LCT(4) 555

The two landing beaches here were King in the east and Jig in the west. Further west lay Item sector, including the small port of Arromanches. Troops did not land on Item in the assault, but the Allies aimed to open it as soon as possible, since before long, one of the two Mulberry Harbours would be laid out there. Adjoining King to the east was Love sector, part of Juno Beach, which, in fact, was a firmer beach but lacked suitable exits and was not used during the initial assault.[2]

King sector was around 2,000 yards long and included the villages of La Rivière on the coast and Ver-sur-Mer, which was slightly inland. Most of the coast along King was marshland, which stretched up to 500 yards inland, backed by a low ridge. King was divided into King Green in the west and King Red to the east.

The other landing sector – Jig – was some 3,000 yards long and included Le Hamel and Asnelles. Popular seaside resorts in peacetime, the coastal hotels and villas of both settlements had been fortified by the German defenders. Jig was further subdivided into Green and Red. An individual beach, such as Jig Green, was sometimes subdivided into Jig Green West and East.

There were patches of peat and clay along the majority of Jig and King, just short of the high-tide mark. Deep runnels in the sand would, when covered by the tide, create sudden areas of deeper water. These were a particular issue on Jig, to the extent that the naval officer in charge of Gold later reported that Jig 'proved to be a bad beach along its whole length, except for one short section in JIG/GREEN'. These characteristics would complicate the unloading of vehicles and stores.[3]

The assault troops found that there were more beach obstacles here than the reconnaissance photographs had shown, including mined stakes, Element C and tetrahedra. The German defenders were a mixture of troops from 716th Infantry Division, a static coastal defence unit, and 352nd Infantry Division, a better equipped and more mobile formation. On D-Day, the assault troops faced the strongest resistance from 352nd Infantry Division troops around Le Hamel on the western side of Gold. Further east, near Ver-sur-Mer, the less-motivated Eastern European troops of 441st Ost Battalion (part of 716th Infantry Division) offered less resistance.[4]

H-Hour on Gold Beach was set for 07.25. As at other beaches, the question arose as to whether conditions were suitable for launching amphibious DD tanks at sea. The Deputy Senior Officer Assault Group (DSOAG) for each half of Gold Beach decided, in consultation with the relevant DD tank unit officers, that the conditions were too rough to launch the DD tanks at 6,000 yards out to sea as planned and the tanks would continue towards the beach on their LCTs. The LCT(DD) momentarily turned aside to let the LCTs carrying the breaching teams of AVREs and flail tanks – LCT(AVRE) – go ahead.[5]

Bound for Jig were eight LCT(3)s of 15 LCT Flotilla, carrying the DD tanks of the Sherwood Rangers Yeomanry. They were accompanied by LCH 317, with the DSOAG on board, eight LCP(L)s and two LCP(Sy)s. All together, these craft were designated Group 3.

A similar group of craft were heading for King, and were designated Group 4: eight LCT(3)s of 12 LCT Flotilla, carrying the DD tanks of 4th/7th Dragoon Guards; LCH 275, with the DSOAG King Red on board; eight LCP(L)s and two LCP(Sy)s. The LCP(L)s were mostly from 708 Assault Flotilla, but four of their number were LCP(A)s on loan from 700 Assault Flotilla, operated by 708 Flotilla's crews.

The LCP(A) was an LCP(L) fitted with some armour and navigation equipment. The role of the LCP(L) was to provide smoke to screen the swimming DD tanks, if necessary, though in the event, this role was not required, and the craft's smoke equipment had been damaged by the rough seas. The LCP(Sy)s were to assist with navigation in the final approach by the DD tanks to the beach. Also part of Groups 3 and 4 were fire-support landing craft, of which more in a moment.[6]

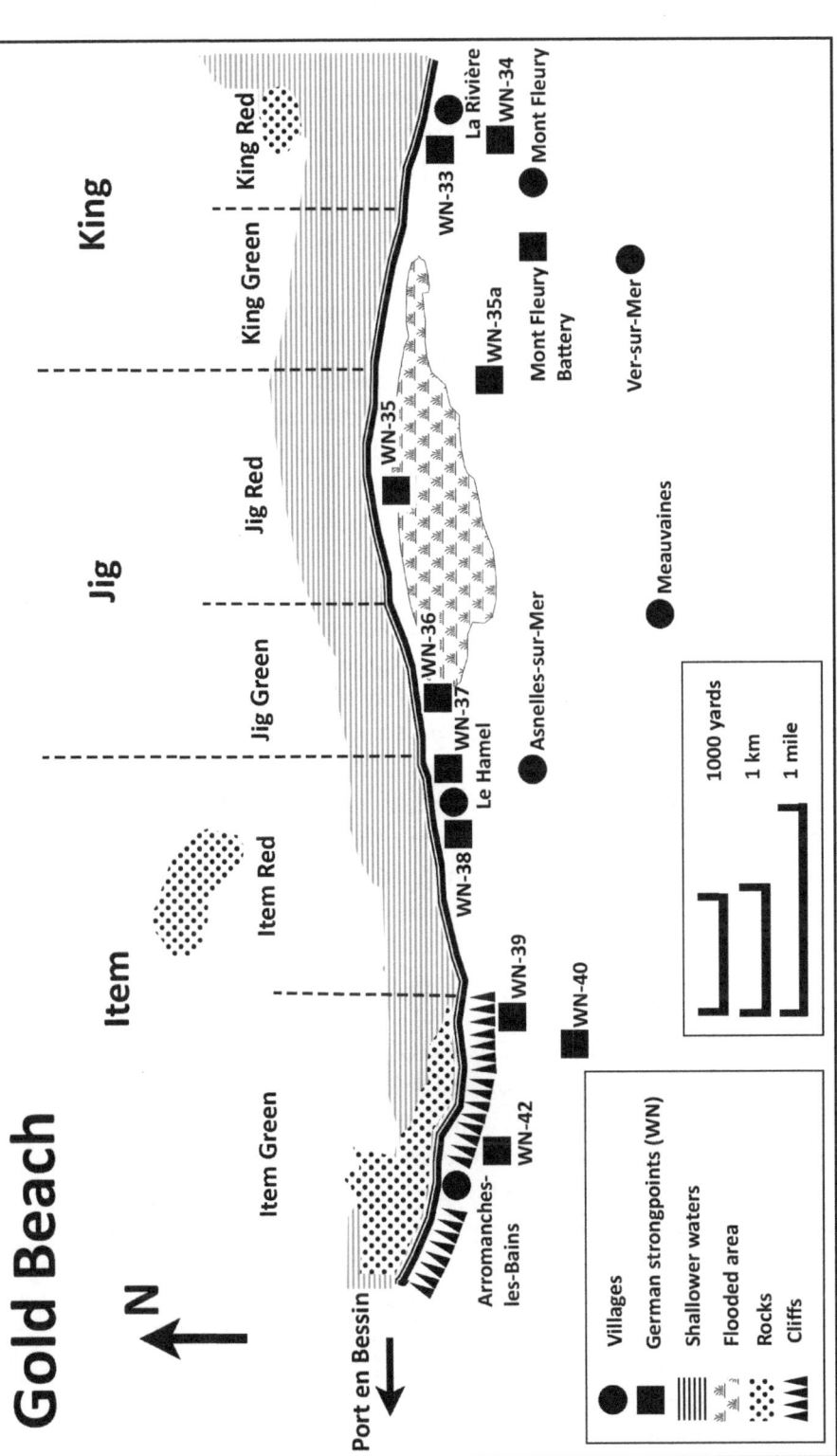

Gold Beach: Map approximately to scale. Some details omitted for clarity. (Map primarily based on: Trew, Simon, *Gold Beach (Battlezone Normandy)* (Stroud: Sutton, 2004); Chazette, Alain et al., *Atlantikwall Gold – Juno – Sword* (Vertou: Histoire & Fortifications, 2013))

Some LSIs were carrying between one and three LCMs, which were lowered into the water with the second and third flights of LCAs around 06.15 to 06.35. Some of these craft held several light vehicles as an advance party for infantry battalion or brigade HQs and were due to meet the relevant LCHs around H-Hour so that at the appropriate time, HQ personnel from the LCH could board the LCM and go ashore. Other LCMs carried stores for use on the beach.[7]

Various fire-support craft would provide the important next stage of the assault. The majority of these fire support craft were from 332 Support Flotilla, which consisted of six LCG(L)s and seven LCFs. Also off King were LCS(L)s 258 and 259, both from 310 Support Flotilla. The LCFs had crossed in convoy with the LCT(AVRE)s, while the other craft had crossed with the LCT(DD)s.

Planners had considered the possibility that conditions might prevent the DD tanks from swimming and that consequently the AVREs would need to land without the DD tanks there to engage the German defences. When the LCG(L)s and LCS(L)s observed that the DD tanks had not launched at sea, they closed on the beach at maximum speed so that they could shell the enemy defences for as long as possible before the LCT(AVRE)s touched down. They opened fire on King Beach at 06.44, while the support craft at Jig were slightly delayed and began firing at 07.00.[8]

Each support craft had been allocated specific targets, and once satisfied that those were destroyed or suppressed, could then fire on any other sections of the defences. The support craft ventured close to the beach to ensure their fire was accurate and to spot for targets – as close as 1,200 yards for the LCG(L)s and 400 yards in the case of the LCS(L)s. Some of the crew of LCS(L) 259 even fired on enemy troops using Lewis guns and rifles in addition to the LCS(L)'s main guns. Meanwhile, the LCFs were on the flanks of the LCT(AVRE)s, and as that group of craft closed the beach, they also fired on the defences, proceeding to within 1,000 yards of the shore and continuing until 07.34.[9]

The army also contributed, with the fire of the Sexton self-propelled guns of three Royal Artillery (RA) field regiments, carried on six LCT(4)s per regiment. There were four guns per LCT, making a total of seventy-two guns between the three regiments.

At Jig, 90th and 147th Field Regiments RA were on LCT(4)s of 33 LCT Flotilla, which included five craft attached from 49 LCT Flotilla (all part of Group 7). At King, six LCT(4)s of 24 LCT Flotilla carried 86th Field Regiment RA, part of Group 8. One craft – LCT 1027, carrying guns of 147th Field Regiment RA – was absent due to engine trouble.

The gunners opened fire at H–33 (06.52), when the LCTs were 11,000 yards from the beach. In what was known as a 'run-in shoot', the craft continued towards land at a rate of 200 yards per minute, with the gunners adjusting their fire to take this into account.[10]

Each regiment was controlled by a radar-equipped Fairmile motor launch with a Forward Observation Officer (FOO) on board, who would radio instructions to the guns to adjust their fire as required. The motor launch for 147th Field Regiment RA had been delayed by engine failure, so the remaining motor launch at Jig directed 147th Field Regiment to fire on 90th Field Regiment's targets at Jig Green East. It was not a perfect arrangement. Because 147th Field Regiment's radios were set to a different frequency, the motor launch had to pass range corrections by loudhailer to LCT 879, and then the army's radio on that craft communicated these instructions to the rest of 147th Field Regiment's guns. While the target on Jig Green East (German strongpoint WN-36) received double the planned weight of shells as a result, 147th Field Regiment's intended target of WN-37 on Jig Green West was not bombarded by the artillery.[11]

Lieutenant Tony Gregson of 147 Regiment RA was on board LCT 708, and was the gun position officer, observing and controlling the fire of the regiment's A Troop. He describes the moment of opening fire:

> The noise and concussion of four guns so close together and fitted with muzzle brakes, was terrific. Wreathes of smoke appeared on the beaches and inland … We repeated the five-rounds gunfire again and again until the paint began to blister on the gun barrels.

After firing five rounds, the troop would adjust fire on Gregson's orders. At H–7, the guns lifted their fire to avoid hitting the assault troops and ceased firing at H+5, by which time the LCTs were 3,400 yards from the beach.[12]

These initial bombardments were no doubt terrifying and sometimes deadly for the German defenders, but many defenders survived. Two LCG(L)s and LCS(L) 258 fired on what they thought was a pillbox; in fact, it was a shelter used in peacetime by people waiting for the train service that ran along the seafront. It survived intact, despite also being fired on by two destroyers, and is now known as 'Stan Hollis' shelter' as it bears a plaque commemorating the D-Day Victoria Cross winner. This structure was not designed to resist bombardment and its survival was presumably down to luck – and perhaps the effect of dust and smoke from the bombardment in obscuring the target.

LCG(L) 2 and LCS(L) 259 fired on the 88mm gun at the west end of La Rivière (part of strongpoint WN-33), as did other craft later on, but as its gun embrasure faced west and was protected by a strong concrete wall facing seaward, it was almost impossible to knock out from the sea. In the end, it was neutralised by troops ashore.

From H-30 to H-Hour, US B-17 heavy bombers supplemented the naval bombardment by attacking a range of targets. Low clouds hampered bombing accuracy and bombs intended for Le Hamel mainly fell to the south of the town. At Asnelles, however, later analysis judged that bombs had destroyed some pillboxes on the seafront.[13]

The LCT(AVRE)s were now leading the waves of assault craft towards the beach. These should have been accompanied by sixteen LCT(A)s carrying Centaur support tanks. Had things gone to plan, there would have been thirty-two Centaurs firing from raised platforms on the decks of the LCT(A)s, beginning at H-30, at a distance of 4,000 yards from the shore. However, at Jig, only two of the LCT(A)s carrying Centaurs arrived on time, while at King, all of the LCT(A)s were delayed by the rough seas and were unable to take part in the assault. Their story will be told below.[14]

Rocket-firing landing craft contributed the final part of the naval bombardment. There were eight LCT(R)s from 322 LCT(R) Flotilla, evenly divided between Jig and King. They had crossed the Channel as part of Groups 7 and 8, along with the LCTs carrying self-propelled guns. The LCT(R)s at Jig opened fire around 07.15, while those off King began firing around 07.21.

The LCT(R) firing did not all go according to plan. Off Jig, at the western end of La Rivière, LCS(L) 259 had to alter course to avoid being hit by rockets falling around it. At Jig, many rockets fell short of their target and it seems that all rockets fired at Asnelles fell into the sea. At Le Hamel, the rockets fell on the western half of town and missed the strongpoint on the eastern side. The tail fins of some rockets were damaged by previous salvos fired from the same craft, which led to rockets colliding and exploding immediately after launch. The after-action report of LCT(R) 440 suggests the weapon could be used accurately, however. The crew noticed German guns firing inland from the beach and altered course so they could fire a concentrated burst of four salvos at three-second intervals against that location. They then fired at five-second intervals against their original target to spread their fire more widely as originally planned.[15]

Next to fire, only moments after the LCT(R)s – at 07.24 at King Beach, for example – were the rocket ships' smaller cousins, the LCA(HR)s, or at least, those craft that were present did so. The plan called for eighteen

LCA(HR)s of 591 LCA(HR) Flotilla to be towed across the Channel behind the LCFs and LCT(AVRE)s of Groups 5 and 6, with three LCTs towing two LCA(HR)s each.

The LCA(HR) crews had very difficult experiences on D-Day. During the crossing, tow ropes or cables often snapped, five times in succession in the case of LCA(HR) 966. The Royal Navy crews of the LCA(HR)s had to decide whether to abandon their craft and transfer to the larger towing vessel or to cast off the tow and continue under their own power. Both LCA(HR)s 961 and 1108 were swamped during the Channel crossing, the former while under its own power and the latter while being towed. Several of the crew were saved but four men drowned between the two craft. Both LCA(HR)s 962 and 972 also sank during the crossing, but crews were rescued by the towing craft and went on to assist the LCT crew – for example, manning the Oerlikon guns.[16]

In total, nine LCA(HR)s crossed in time to fire, although one was unable to fire due to a malfunction. One LCA(HR) arrived an hour late, seven were sunk or rammed on their way to the beach and one had to turn back to the UK. LCA(HR) 1106 was at the point of firing when it was struck by LCT 899 and capsized with the loss of all four crew.

The Force G Naval Commander reported afterwards that the shallow beach gradient and the state of the tide meant that bombs from the LCA(HR)s could not reach the top of the beach and set off mines there, since the range of the bombs was 400 yards. While they had not worked quite as intended, the LCA(HR)s had performed a useful role in setting off mines on some of the beach obstacles, making them safer for the troops landing.[17]

Compared to the barrage produced by the Allies, there was only limited return fire from the German guns, though two batteries near Arromanches did fire on landing craft when they were not being shelled by the fleet. At 07.20, shortly before beaching, the leading LCTs came 'under fairly heavy fire', including from small arms. Many German defensive positions on Gold Beach had received little damage and would resist strongly. These included several anti-tank guns that covered the landing sectors.[18]

H-Hour was 07.25. The tide was higher up the beach than the Allies had forecast, possibly due to strong westerly winds. This meant that the most seaward beach obstacles already had about 1ft of water at their base at H-Hour, and there were only about 100 yards of dry beach below the high-water mark, not 300 yards as expected. While there were advantages to the assault troops of having a shorter distance of beach to cross while under enemy fire, these would be outweighed by the disadvantages of the beach obstacles rapidly becoming covered with water and therefore much harder, if not impossible, to avoid. The assaults on Jig and King took place simultaneously but will be considered in turn.[19]

The Assault on Jig Beach, H-Hour to H+120

The first troops ashore of 231st Infantry Brigade on Jig should have been the DD tanks at H−5, so that they could suppress German defences while the obstacle-clearance teams on foot and in tanks landed at H-Hour, and the assault infantry followed up at H+7. Since the DD tanks had not been launched as planned due to the rough seas, they were behind schedule.

It is always difficult to say with absolute certainty which unit was the first to land at any beach, since anyone who was there had limited visibility and would mostly have been preoccupied with the tasks at hand. The Naval Commander Force G reported that the LCT(AVRE) were 'the first craft to approach the beach'. However, the two LCAs carrying the Landing Craft Obstacle Clearance Unit (LCOCU) teams were just behind them, and being smaller craft, they touched down further inshore, so the LCOCU were the 'first units of Force "G" to land'. Their exact time of landing seems to have been moments before 07.25 (H-Hour).[20]

Nos 9 and 10 LCOCU were on board LCA(OC) 1159 (559 Assault Flotilla) and LCA(OC) 1209 (554 Assault Flotilla) respectively, both craft from HMS *Glenroy*. Each LCOCU consisted of two officers and thirty other ranks. Since floating obstacles were expected some 500–600 yards from the high-water mark at both Jig and King, each LCOCU offloaded two rubber dinghies from their landing craft which were filled with explosive charges. In the event, they did not discover any floating obstacles.

At Jig, events made the LCOCUs' already demanding job even more difficult to achieve. At the water's edge, 9 and 10 LCOCU immediately came under heavy German fire and suffered casualties, which forced them to take cover in the water until tanks came onto the beach and began suppressing enemy defences. As the tide was coming in apace, this meant that the LCOCUs were unable to clear obstacles at this stage of the assault as had been planned.[21]

As soon as more landing craft began to put troops ashore, diving and obstacle demolition became impossible for the LCOCUs. The LCA(OC)s had grounded some distance from the water's edge and carrying charges from them through the heavy surf was also very difficult. As D-Day continued, 9 and 10 LCOCU were amalgamated and began clearing Jig using demolition charges and bulldozers, then abandoned Jig and focused on clearing the adjacent beach of Item Red.[22]

Next to arrive on the beach were the breaching teams carried on board six LCT(4)s of 28 LCT Flotilla. Along with eight LCT(A)s (of which, more in a moment), LCH 100 and one ML (navigation leader), these craft were designated Group 5. Also in that group were eleven LCP(L)s of 706 Assault Flotilla, whose main role was to lay smokescreens to protect other craft, although they did not perform this role on D-Day. As mentioned above, some of the LCTs in this group were towing LCA(HR)s, which fired just before H-Hour.[23]

The LCTs carrying breaching teams touched down within a few minutes of 07.25. Leading Seaman Coxswain Rex Milbourne, in the wheelhouse of LCT 808, recalled that he had the port and starboard deadlights closed, meaning that his only view of the outside world was through the forward porthole. His commanding officer had instructed him, in the absence of other instructions, to aim for a concrete roadway visible on land:

> The clear order I got down the voicepipe was – Full Ahead Both and the CO rang a further 100 Revs from the bridge. We were I suppose doing 12 knots with a nasty starboard quarter wind and rather turbulent sea, which was pushing us to port all the time … the noise … it sounded like the whole of the German Army were firing at us … it was deafening![24]

The objective of the troops they carried was to clear beach obstacles from two 250-yard-wide stretches of Jig Green by H+60 (08.25), and construct exits from the beach. All would suffer heavy casualties on D-Day.

The vehicle components of the breaching teams consisted of AVRE tanks from 82 Assault Squadron RE, Sherman Crab flail tanks of B Squadron, Westminster Dragoons, and three bulldozers or angledozers of the Royal Engineers. As it exited each LCT, the lead AVRE pushed a Roly-Poly carpet, which was meant to help the vehicles cross any boggy ground.[25]

As they approached Jig Green West, three of the LCTs came under enfilading fire from a German anti-tank gun in WN-37 at Asnelles. The craft that suffered the most was LCT(4) 886, which was struck by multiple shells, inflicting around twenty-eight casualties among the troops on board and the LCT's crew.

The first AVRE tank to land from LCT 886 jammed on the ramp and was flooded by the sea. More shells hit the LCT's engine room, wounding the crew there and stopping the engines. A shell struck the bridge, and while it did not penetrate the armour, it killed two soldiers as well as wounding other troops and sailors. Also on board LCT 886 was the crew of the sunken LCA(HR) 963, who went ashore and began destroying beach obstacles using explosives provided by the Royal Engineers.

Its engines disabled, LCT 886 drifted and became broached-to, with most of the troops still on board, having been holed ten times striking mined beach obstacles. The remaining tanks on board LCT 886 were unable to land until early afternoon, when they were able to begin beach clearance work.[26]

Meanwhile the DSOAG Jig Green on board LCH 100 directed close support and LCS(L) 251 engaged WN-37 to try to suppress enemy fire. Fire from that strongpoint was preventing much progress by the three western-most breaching teams, and many tanks were knocked out or bogged down.

The other three LCTs carrying breaching teams beached too far to the east due to the strong cross-tide, on Jig Red rather than Jig Green East as intended. This put them out of position and hampered their efforts to clear exit routes from the beach but did mean they were less vulnerable to fire from WN-37 at Asnelles, to the west.

LCT 749 was hit by several shells which destroyed the starboard bow winch, meaning the crew could not raise the ramp. About 1 mile off the beach, the crew managed to raise the ramp by running a spare cable to the stern anchor winch. They celebrated with a jar of rum that the Royal Engineers had left on board, but witnessed several AVREs on the beach burst into flames as they were struck by enemy fire.[27]

Also on board the LCTs carrying AVREs were Royal Engineers on foot who would work with the AVREs for obstacle clearance. Most personnel (six sections) from 73 Field Company RE, who had successfully landed on time, were on Jig Red West where they only faced machine-gun fire, with three more sections on Jig Green East and one section at Jig Green West. This would mean that fewer obstacles would be cleared on Jig Green in the early part of D-Day.

On each LCT, 73 Field Company RE had two army folboats (wooden-bottomed, canvas-sided, folding boats), which carried most of their explosive charges, as well as two handcarts. The folboats were to be towed ashore by the last AVRE to leave each LCT, but most were damaged in the process or capsized in the surf.[28]

As mentioned above, the LCT(AVRE)s at Jig should have been supported by six LCT(A)s, each carrying two Centaur tanks of 2nd Royal Marine Independent Armoured Support Battery. As the craft approached the shore before H-Hour, the tanks could provide additional fire support by firing from a raised platform on each LCT's tank deck. However, only two of these craft – LCT(A)s 2233 and 2442 of 108 LCT Flotilla – arrived roughly on time, around 07.30. The Centaurs did not fire before beaching and seem to have landed almost immediately, along with a Sherman tank and a Crusader anti-aircraft tank that were also on these craft. Almost all these tanks were soon knocked out by enemy fire or mines or bogged down. The Naval Commander Force G later reported that the Centaurs would have been very useful for counter-fire against German mortars concealed behind terrain. Without them, mortars could only be silenced by the infantry capturing their positions.[29]

The assault infantry were due at H+5 (07.30) and began landing five to ten minutes after the LCT(AVRE) and LCT(A), within five minutes of their planned time. Ten LCAs of 553 Assault Flotilla (carried by SS *Empire Crossbow*) put ashore A and B Companies of 1st Battalion, The Hampshire Regiment (1st Hampshires) plus twenty-five men of 295 Field Company RE, who were to open exits from the beaches.

They came ashore 500 yards further east than their intended landing beach of Jig Green West. Rather than assaulting WN-37 and WN-38 at Le Hamel and Asnelles, by arriving on Jig Green East they faced WN-36, the objective of the neighbouring assault troops, 1st Battalion, The Dorsetshire Regiment (1st Dorsets). They encountered mortar and machine-gun fire as they landed, but A Company were able to capture WN-36 relatively quickly from the stunned defenders. When trying to advance to the west along the dunes, 1st Hampshires would face heavy casualties due to fire from WN-37. The DD tanks had still not arrived, and the breaching teams were pinned down, so the infantry had no tank support.[30]

No.231 Brigade's other assault battalion, 1st Dorsets, were also due to land at H+5 (07.30) to the east of 1st Hampshires, on Jig Green West. The ten LCAs of 525 Assault Flotilla (SS *Empire Spearhead*) were carried just over half a mile further east by the current and instead touched down at Jig Red West, with A Company to the west of B Company, landing at 07.25 and 07.37 respectively. Like 1st Hampshires, they were accompanied by men of 295 Field Company RE for establishing beach exits. As with the adjacent battalion, they did not have tank support when they landed, although the LCTs carrying three breaching teams were in the process of landing on Jig Red. While shelling and mortaring was the main enemy resistance, it caused casualties, particularly among officers and senior NCOs. The LCGs and LCS(L)s were praised by the DSOAG Jig Red for their close-in fire support.[31]

Accompanying the LCAs of 1st Dorsets and 1st Hampshires were several LCS(M)s. Being small craft based on the LCA hull, they could provide

fire support from very close to the beach, on the flanks of the LCAs landing the infantry. The Naval Commander Group G1 later reported that the
LCS(M)s 'did quite useful work in silencing machine gun posts'. While
supporting 1st Dorsets, LCS(M) 99 was hit astern by a shell and sunk.
Three of the ten-man crew were killed outright, while another died while
being evacuated and was later buried at sea.[32]

Following soon behind the first waves of assault infantry were the other
two companies of both battalions: the reserve infantry companies. They
were due at H+20 (07.45) but actually landed about five minutes after that.
Ten LCAs from 524 Assault Flotilla (SS *Empire Arquebus*) landed C and D
Companies of 1st Hampshires as well as men of 295 Field Company RE,
Royal Artillery Command and FOO personnel and others including the
Assistant Beachmaster. They were due on Jig Green West, but like the first
two companies of that battalion they actually landed on Jig Green East.[33]

Major David Warren, commander of C Company, 1st Hampshires,
described the landing:

> During the last half mile of the run-in there was mortar and light artil-
> lery fire coming down on the sea, together with limited small arms fire,
> which in the last hundred yards could be heard striking and passing
> over the LCA. Mortar fire burst close to the craft but it seemed to be on
> fixed lines and not observed, for at this stage the beach would have been
> a more effective target … The obstacles were no real trouble and the
> LCA beached on a runnel about thirty yards from the waterline. Small
> bursts of small arms fire coming from the direction of LE HAMEL and
> LES ROQUETTES were seen on the surface of the water, which at first
> came well up to the thighs.[34]

As his troops landed, the beach was swept with machine gun and mortar fire.

Horace Stone was operating the ramp on one of 524 Assault Flotilla's
craft, and watched many of the troops who left his craft fall on the beach.
A soldier fell wounded before even getting off the ramp and Stone pulled
him on board before jumping into the water with another crewman to
push the LCA back out to sea.[35]

As the 1st Hampshires attacked WN-37 at Le Hamel, the battalion lost
many officers and senior NCOs. This would be a long fight.

LCS(L) 251 now engaged WN-37 'from the closest possible range',
which may have lessened that strongpoint's fire against troops ashore.
That LCS(L) remained close to the shore, engaging WN-37 at point-blank
range until it had to withdraw with a broken recoil cylinder on its gun.

The DSOAG Jig Green also praised LCG(L)s 17 and 18, which fired on a German battery near Arromanches. Destroyers also fired in support from not far off the beach.

Seeking another approach, the Hampshires attacked the strongpoint from the rear. They would reach the centre of Asnelles around 15.00 to 17.00. From the naval commanders' point of view, the situation was 'exasperating'. They could see that the infantry were meeting strong resistance, yet they were not receiving requests for help. Without clear information as to the position of friendly troops in a built-up area, the supporting vessels dared not fire.[36]

The communications breakdown was caused by both the battalion commander and second-in-command of 1st Hampshires becoming casualties (the latter landed at H+120). Nor did naval commanders have any contact from the FOOs accompanying these infantry. Meanwhile, LCG(L)s and destroyers fired on the Arromanches Battery and other opportunity targets instead, which, although useful, did not directly aid the Hampshires. 1st Dorsets' FOOs did make calls for fire to which destroyers responded.[37]

Had the DD tanks landed on time and had more than two LCT(A)s delivered their Centaur tanks around H-Hour, those vehicles might have helped suppress the Le Hamel strongpoint much sooner. Later in the day, several armoured vehicles (including AVRE, flail and DD tanks, plus self-propelled guns) would contribute to the capture of Asnelles and Le Hamel.[38]

Also due at H+20 (07.45), the reserve companies (C and D) of 1st Dorsets, plus elements of supporting units, landed to the east of 1st Hampshires at 07.45 and 07.50 respectively. The troops were on board ten LCAs, which were drawn from two different landing ships and had rendezvoused off the beach before being led in by ML 131. Approaching the beach, the LCAs passed mini-submarine X-20, which had been lying submerged off the coast for several days, and was now providing a final navigation point for the incoming waves of assault craft.

To Sub Lieutenant Ben Sullivan RNVR, in command of the five LCAs of 553 Assault Flotilla (SS *Empire Crossbow*) carrying C Company, the many landing craft heading for Gold Beach on either flank seemed to be 'roaring in like a wave of surf'. Minutes before touchdown, he was surprised when the troops in his craft asked him for permission to smoke. He later commented that, in a post-war career as a toastmaster, he had often given that same permission, 'but never so emotionally as on that day'.[39]

Sullivan determined his craft's position relative to the distinctive wreck of a wooden ship and saw that they were some 400 yards astray to the east.

Consulting with Major Robert Nicoll of 1st Dorsets on his craft, and with a vision of the losses the troops were likely to suffer if they had to make their way along the beach, Sullivan ordered the ten craft to turn to starboard until they reached the correct point. Thus, C Company landed in the correct place, on Jig Green East. They would face little opposition.

D Company arrived further east than intended and behind B Company, beaching on Jig Red from five LCAs of 525 Assault Flotilla (SS *Empire Spearhead*). D Company would suffer heavy casualties from shell and mortar fire, while one of the five LCAs was lost on a mined obstacle.[40]

Most of both assault battalions had now landed. Still to land were both battalion HQs, each on board one LCM, which had crossed the Channel on an LSI (that of 1st Hampshires was on board SS *Empire Arquebus*, and 1st Dorsets' was on SS *Empire Spearhead*). Their landing time was to be chosen at the discretion of the battalion commanding officers, both of whom landed alongside the rest of their men.[41]

At H+35 (08.00), two LCT(3)s of 15 LCT Flotilla delivered various units, including the duplicate HQ of each assault battalion. Most of the remainder of this flotilla was carrying the DD tanks of the Sherwood Rangers Yeomanry, who were still to land. Also on board the two LCTs were three Churchill Crocodile flamethrowing tanks of 141st Regiment RAC (two to accompany 1st Hampshires, one with 1st Dorsets), although all three vehicles drowned while beaching. The LCTs also carried other troops, including three bulldozers from 235 Field Park Company RE, twenty-three men of 200 Field Ambulance RAMC and seven men of 21 Beach Signal Section.[42]

Roughly on time at H+30 (07.55), the beachmasters for Jig Green West and East landed with other Beach Group HQ personnel on each beach in two LCAs from 524 Assault Flotilla (SS *Empire Arquebus*). Their initial role was to carry out reconnaissance ahead of the remainder of the beach group landing. Members of the Royal Navy Beach Commando also began landing around now. For the moment, they were ordered to remain dug in and not yet put up beach signage to guide in landing craft.[43]

A report by personnel of 25 Beach Recovery Section REME described how as they reached Jig Beach at around H+40, they landed:

> … with craft exploding underwater mines around us … all obstacles under water … most of craft that came in at this stage sat on obstacles … immediately in front of us was a sea wall … breached in 2 places only and foot of wall was awash … bad stretch of clay running laterally 30 ft from wall under water. Vehicles landing at this stage then, either

landed in water too deep (including armour) or landed straight into clay or found they could not get off beach owing to the crush for the exits.[44]

To resume our chronological progress throughout the landings on Jig, the DD tanks finally came ashore at 07.58, nearly forty minutes late, having been delivered to the beach by the eight LCT(3)s of 15 LCT Flotilla. Some tanks did swim the final 50 yards to dry land, a sensible precaution, given that the LCT(3) carrying them had a deeper draught than an LCT(4) and risked getting stuck on the beach. B Squadron of the Sherwood Rangers Yeomanry landed on Jig Green West and C Squadron of the same regiment on Jig Green East (with some possibly straying further east onto Jig Red).[45]

Artillery or mortar shells fell around the LCTs as they beached. Midshipman Stan Smith was first lieutenant of LCT 442:

My job was to supervise the lowering of the ramp, then to stand on the end of it … and measure the depth of the water with a sounding pole. It was sufficiently shallow here to allow the first three tanks to swim a few yards before touching down on the sand. Then a mortar bomb exploded about thirty feet behind me on the tank deck. I was unhurt, but one of my sailors was wounded, and the flotation screens of the two remaining tanks were ripped. The [LCT's] captain therefore had to drive the landing craft in closer so that these tanks could leave dry-shod. As they did so, another mortar bomb exploded alongside the last tank.[46]

Several of the Yeomanry had been wounded, as well as Able Seaman 'Cookie' Laurence, LCT 442's cook, who regularly entertained the crew while on shore leave with his skills as a pianist. German shells, rough seas and clay patches on the beach all contributed to the Sherwood Rangers Yeomanry losing seven tanks while landing.

LCT 442 had also struck a mined beach obstacle which, as Smith recounts, 'had blown a 10-foot hole in the port side, opened up the plating of the port bow and twisted the port rudder hard-a-starboard'. Next, the craft was hit on the port side by another LCT which, as well as taking away some of the stanchions holding up the bridge, cut 442's stern anchor wire. The LCT struggled to get off the beach on the engines alone without being able to haul off the beach using the kedge hook. The crew used an axe to cut away the trailing kedge anchor cable and plugged shrapnel holes in the craft's side with wooden wedges and cotton waste. The LCT(3)s that had carried DD tanks then had orders to report to the landing ships at the Lowering Point so they could ferry further personnel ashore.[47]

It was not yet an hour since the first British troops landed on Jig, and the assault units were still fighting to establish a foothold. But Allied D-Day objectives were not limited to gaining control of the beach: other units had to strike out inland and prepare the way for further advances on successive days. This was the intended role of the reserve infantry battalion, the third and final battalion from 231st Infantry Brigade – 2nd Battalion, The Devonshire Regiment. 2nd Devons were to advance south-west down the valley of la Gronde Ruisseau towards Ryes, some 2 miles from the coast. Each wave of two companies was accompanied by men of 295 Field Company RE, who were to join their comrades from the same unit developing beach exits.[48]

Due at H+45 (08.10), 2nd Devons landed in two waves and were all ashore by 08.30. The men beached in twenty Royal Marine-crewed LCAs of 554 and 559 Assault Flotillas from HMS *Glenroy*. The intention was that 2nd Devons would follow on behind 1st Hampshires, but since the latter had come ashore out of position, the Devons were the first infantry to land on Jig Green West and actually slightly further to the east than the plan directed. They found the adjacent German defences at Asnelles still active, with 'spasmodic gunfire and mortar fire'.

The first two companies did not get clear of the beach until 09.15. With the second half of 2nd Devons was one LCA of 524 Assault Flotilla (SS *Empire Arquebus*) containing men of 90 Field Company RE and others. A single LCM that had been carried on the deck of HMS *Glenroy* also accompanied this wave, holding two jeeps from 61 Reconnaissance Regiment and 2nd Devons (plus that battalion's commanding officer) and others.[49]

Around 08.25 (H+60), most of Jig Green was still under fire and the DSOAG judged Jig Green West to be 'untenable'. Enemy fire was preventing obstacle clearance on Jig Green West and following the initial assault, there were no further landings there until 16.00.

Most of the LCOCUs or Royal Engineers teams intended for Jig Green West had landed on Jig Red West and began clearing obstacles there. These two factors led naval commanders to modify the plan and open Jig Red for landings. 295 Field Company RE judged that the uncleared obstacles also led landing craft to beach further out, meaning more vehicles were swamped by the sea as they came ashore. By around H+90, only two of the planned six exits through the minefields were clear (both on Jig Red). The extra high tide also caused vehicle congestion on the beach.[50]

At H+60, the priority vehicles of 231st Infantry Brigade were due to land on Jig Green East from three LCT(4)s, which were part of Group 11.

The cargo of these craft included vehicles from the infantry battalions of the brigade and from No.9 Beach Group operating on the whole of Jig. Six universal carriers of the 1st Dorsets each towed a 6-pounder anti-tank gun, while eight more of the same vehicles each had a 3in mortar team from one of the infantry battalions.

From 51 Mechanical Equipment Section RE there were six D7 Bulldozers which would be useful for a variety of tasks in improving the beach area. Sixty men of 90 Field Company RE came ashore too. As well as assisting with obstacle clearance, they had the role of improving vehicle beach exits and laying trackway running along the back of the beach to aid vehicles in moving inland. Unloading the vehicles proved to be a slow process.[51]

The first self-propelled guns to land on Jig – twelve guns or three troops from each of the 90th and 147th Field Regiments RA – did so within a few minutes of 08.25. They were carried by six LCT(4)s from 33 LCT Flotilla, including several attached from 49 LCT Flotilla (part of Group 7). The LCTs touched down at full speed, earning praise from the naval officer commanding Group 7 for their 'great determination' and ensuring that the guns were all landed 'practically dryshod' on Jig Green.

All the LCTs in this wave were holed by obstacles and mines, but most were able to return to the UK. Around H+60, several landing craft were due to deliver command and control personnel. These included FOO parties on board LCS(M)s that had already played a significant role by directing the self-propelled artillery firing from on board LCTs. Now they went ashore so they could continue to spot for these artillery regiments on land.[52]

At 09.05 an LCM landed twenty-four men from the tactical HQ of 231st Infantry Brigade, which commanded the three infantry battalions that had now landed on Jig. This LCM had crossed the Channel on board HMS *Glenroy* and was lowered ahead of that ship's LCAs. It then reported to HMS *Nith* so that it could collect the brigade commander. As it approached the shore, the LCM struck a mine on a beach obstacle and sank with the loss of much of the HQ equipment, including wireless sets.[53]

Also on board that LCM was the war correspondent Howard Marshall, famous before the war for his cricket commentaries and by now the BBC's Director of War Reporting. Despite being wounded in the hand from the mine explosion, he was able to continue his duties. He returned to the UK soon after, and that same evening, with his clothes still damp from the landing, he recorded a description of what he had seen, which was broadcast on the BBC Home Service around 21.30. This was the first eyewitness account of landing on the Normandy beaches to be heard by a British audience. Marshall described seeing shells burst along and behind the beach as the LCM headed for the shore.[54]

Three other LCMs were due at H+60, carrying preloaded stores (probably for the Royal Engineers). The craft had been carried on the decks of the LSIs. The LCM from SS *Empire Spearhead* (probably LCM 128) broke down and was abandoned in a sinking condition, while the craft from SS *Empire Crossbow* could not be hoisted out as the ship had lost its derrick; those stores were later landed by LCT(3).[55]

Many of the vehicles that were part of or supporting 231st Infantry Brigade (including the Beach Group) were still to land. A significant proportion of them were due to land at H+90 (08.55) from twenty LCT(4)s (designated part of Group 11), bringing tracked vehicles. Ten of these craft were from 23 LCT Flotilla, and tasked to land on Jig Green West, they were presumably diverted to Jig Red as Jig Green was closed to landings. They actually beached around 09.05.

On the way in, the flotilla officer was reassured to see two LCG(L)s 'steaming slowly across the approach to the beach from left to right very close in and engaging the enemy'. All ten LCTs sustained at least some damage, although most vehicles arrived on shore. Four craft (LCTs 555, 576, 1162 and 1164) seem to have been abandoned on the beach or sunk. Signalman Ron Turner on LCT 555 later recalled that his craft was hit by a shell and then was holed under the engine room by a mined obstacle, causing the craft to sink. Fortunately, there were no casualties, and once the tide receded, the troops on board were able to unload safely.[56]

Wireman Bill Page on LCT 555 recalled an incident of the sort that would be entirely overlooked in the official accounts of D-Day but was clearly significant to those involved. As the first vehicle exited the craft, it suddenly drove the ramp into the sand. In the port winch housing, one of the sailors had connected his winch handle ready for raising the ramp. The movement of the ramp caused this handle to spin round, breaking the arms of both sailors who were waiting to carry out that duty.[57]

The other ten LCT(4)s beaching in the H+90 wave were on Jig Green East and part of 53 LCT Flotilla. These carried a variety of tracked vehicles from and supporting 231st Infantry Brigade, including vehicles from 8th Armoured Brigade HQ and twenty-four Sherman tanks and supporting vehicles from A Squadron, Sherwood Rangers Yeomanry. 'Beaches incredibly congested' was the description in the war diary of the latter unit, which continued with British understatement, 'at one period the situation appeared rather difficult'.

To land their vehicles, 53 LCT Flotilla's craft had to 'increase speed and ram the beach obstructions' as there were no clear routes through the obstacles. Mines attached to the obstacles generally caused minor but not critical damage to the LCTs. Unbeaching proved to be more troublesome as some vessels had 'impaled' themselves on beach obstacles and had to be towed off by another craft.[58]

While the LCTs were still on the beach, the crews observed LCAs carrying 47 Royal Marine Commando, which began to beach alongside them. The commandos were due to land at H+120 (09.25), but their actual landing time was around 09.50. Their unique mission was to circle westwards, assaulting and seizing the small port of Port-en-Bessin from the landward side. The commandos were on board fourteen LCAs: six craft of 508 Assault Flotilla (SS *Victoria*) and eight from 502 Assault Flotilla (HMS *Prinses Josephine Charlotte*). Both ships and their accompanying LCA flotillas were part of Force J and were on loan to Force G for D-Day.

One LCA was sunk by enemy fire on the run-in to the beach, and while beaching, four craft were sunk and seven more damaged by collisions with beach obstacles. The LCAs beached along a 1-mile stretch of coast.[59]

LCT 1079 of 53 LCT Flotilla had already landed its vehicles when signalman Ray Fletcher witnessed the arrival of 47 RM Commando's LCAs, although it soon became apparent that his own craft had problems:

Two on our starboard bow blew up in short order before they hit the beach, bodies being thrown in all directions … a report came in that our engine room was flooding. I went belting down and found the stoker with his feet on the control panel with about 2½ feet of water sloshing around him. I also saw a chunk of iron rail sticking up through [the] deck!

The stoker reassured him that the engines would still function, so Fletcher and some of his crewmates helped the commandos:

We joined in and managed to pull five or six chaps out of the surf which was very heavy at the time, but there were others we weren't able to help in time and it was heart-breaking to see some of them drowning in front of your eyes.

Later, as the tide went out, they could examine further damage that their LCT had suffered, 'The port bow had a hole in it about seven feet by three feet, and was turned back like a sardine can … we were lying on a hump on the beach which had buckled the craft amidships.' After some work by a repair party, LCT 1079 was able to return to Portland under its own power.[60]

Many of the commandos had to abandon their weapons and equipment and swim ashore. Bill Page on LCT 555 witnessed these troops arriving as his craft was leaving the beach. As the LCTs unbeached, Page saw some of the commandos crushed between LCTs. As he later recalled, 'together with casualties on the beach, the shell[s] landing, smoke, fire etc., it looked to me as if the landing had failed'.

The confused landings meant that the commandos had to spend two hours rallying in the beach area, delaying the rest of the plan. Despite these setbacks, 47 RM Commando seized its objective a day later than planned, in an assault supported by two LCG(L)s as well as HMS *Emerald*, Typhoon aircraft and 147th Field Regiment RA.[61]

The next group of landing craft to beach were six LCT(4)s, designated part of Group 7, carrying the other half of the two regiments of self-propelled artillery of the 90th and 147th Field Regiments. A seventh LCT carried a variety of vehicles – mostly jeeps, universal carriers and half-tracks – from 231st Infantry Brigade. This entire wave of craft had been due at H+120 (09.25).

Those carrying 90th Field Regiment RA seem to have landed on time. The craft carrying 147th Field Regiment did not land until 11.00 and may have been held back due to vehicle congestion on the beach; they also had to beach on Jig Red not Jig Green due to craft that were broached-to and obstructing the beach. Like the craft that had delivered the H+60 wave of self-propelled guns, many of these LCTs were damaged but most returned home.[62]

For many troops landing around this time, their first impression must have been of a scene of chaos, but the overall plan was unfolding as intended. We will now go back to around H-Hour to look at the assault on King Beach.

THE ASSAULT ON KING BEACH, H-HOUR TO H+120

The plan for the assault by 69th Infantry Brigade on King Beach, delivered by craft of Group G2, had many similarities with that on Jig. There were some slight differences in the timings, with the assault infantry due to land here at H+7.5 minutes and the reserve infantry companies at H+25, rather than H+7 and H+20, for example, although such subtleties were likely to be lost in the chaos of battle.

As on Jig, the decision was made that the LCT(DD)s would deliver the DD tanks onto the beach as the sea was too rough for them to swim. Rather than letting the following waves overtake them, the LCT(DD)s joined formation with the LCT(AVRE)s, taking the place of the LCT(A)s, which had been delayed. The result was that, despite the change in plan for delivering the DD tanks, those vehicles, the breaching teams, LCOCU personnel and assault infantry landed in quick succession and were able to support each other. This still did not mean that all aspects of the plan worked smoothly, however. 541 Assault Flotilla carrying assault infantry reported that the LCT(DD)s had blocked their approach to the beach, leading to a ten-minute delay.[63]

As on Jig, the LCT(AVRE)s reached the beach first, but the two small craft carrying the LCOCU teams – LCA(OC)s 1210 and 1211 – grounded further inshore. This meant that the LCOCUs were the first to land, giving them a few minutes to carry out their obstacle-clearance work without other troops getting in their way. The time was around 07.25, H-Hour. They found the most seaward obstacles were already in about 1ft of water, reinforcing the urgency of their work ahead of the oncoming tide.

Initially, there was no enemy fire. No.4 LCOCU reported that the nine-man team had destroyed five obstacles and prepared six for demolition when 'heavy opposition was started with mortar and M.G. [machine gun] fire and two men were badly wounded'. No.3 LCOCU had a similar experience.[64]

The six LCT(AVRE)s of 34 LCT Flotilla (part of Group 6) carrying the breaching teams touched down around 07.25, with three craft each in the west and east of King. As on Jig, as well as tanks – Churchill AVREs of 81 Assault Squadron RE and Sherman flail tanks of C Squadron, Westminster Dragoons – and bulldozers, each LCT carried two sections of 280 Field Company RE, whose task was to clear gaps in the obstacles on land.

The tanks landed in water around 4ft deep. The process of unloading did not go smoothly, with several LCTs swinging nearly parallel to the beach, causing at least one AVRE to drown. The Roly-Poly matting deployed by the first AVRE as the tanks beached did not work well. However, several AVREs were soon helping 280 Field Company RE by dragging obstacles aside to begin creating a gap, while AVREs and Crabs would soon support the assault infantry at WN-35 on the west side of King and at WN-36 at La Rivière in the east.

Also part of Group 6 were LCFs 25, 26 and 36 (a fourth, LCF 38, had broken down). These craft fired in support of the LCT(AVRE)s from as close as 1,000 yards from the shore until 07.34. As the LCFs ceased fire, the first wave of LCAs were approaching.[65]

Eight LCT(3)s of 12 LCT Flotilla (designated Group 4) delivered the twenty DD tanks of B and C Squadrons, 4th/7th Dragoon Guards to King Green and King Red beaches respectively, with the tanks beaching alongside the LCT(AVRE)s. The war diary of 4th/7th Dragoon Guards states that this unit's tanks landed at 07.20, five or more minutes before the breaching teams, and Lieutenant Jim Ruffell RNVR, commander of one of the LCT(DD)s, believed that his was 'the first LCT to hit the beach'. In contrast, the captain commanding Group G2 reported that the DDs landed alongside the breaching teams at H+2 (07.27). It is perhaps enough to say that DDs and breaching teams clearly landed near simultaneously.

Once on the beach, the DD tanks faced little immediate opposition and were able to advance with the assault infantry, who landed shortly after they did. Accompanying the LCT(DD)s were fire-support landing craft – LCG(L)s 1, 2 and 3 as well as LCS(L)s 258 and 259. After firing at the seafront before the LCTs landed, these craft moved to the left flank and continued to engage any signs of the enemy. The LCS(L)s engaged snipers from close inshore.[66]

The final group of craft scheduled to arrive around H-Hour was the eight LCT(A)s of 109 LCT Flotilla, each carrying two Centaur tanks of 1st Royal Marine Independent Armoured Support Battery plus other vehicles. Apart from one craft, which was left behind due to engine trouble, the LCT(A)s set off from the UK in company with the LCT(AVRE)s, but as mentioned above, they struggled to make the crossing due to flooding. In many cases, water entered through gaps behind the craft's armour plating, leading to engine rooms and tank decks flooding. Three LCT(A)s – 2236, 2225 and 2291 – arrived late, between 08.50 and 09.50. Three other craft – LCT(A)s 2048, 2345 and 2453 – had to be towed back to the UK due to flooded engine rooms.

Another was lost during the Channel crossing. LCT(A) 2039 began listing due to water ingress, to the point where most of the crew were taken off the vessel at 01.00 on D-Day. Four crew remained on board to move the craft clear of other shipping, and forty-five minutes later, they abandoned ship. As they did so, they saw the Sherman tank at the rear of the tank deck break free from its tie-down points and the LCT(A) capsized and sank. Two of the crew and up to three Royal Marines manning or supporting the tanks did not survive.[67]

The assault infantry formed the next wave, arriving roughly at their due time of H+7.5 (07.32). Their LCAs approached the beach 'on a slant westwards', with an LCS(L) positioned inshore of them to provide covering fire. 6th Battalion, The Green Howards (6th Green Howards) were to land on King Green and 5th Battalion, The East Yorkshire Regiment (5th East Yorks) on King Red. Considering the former first, 6th Green Howards were landed by five LCAs of 541 Assault Flotilla (SS *Empire Mace*), while D Company of the same unit arrived about 250 yards to the east on five LCAs of 540 Assault Flotilla (SS *Empire Lance*). The infantry were accompanied by men of 233 Field Company RE for work on beach exits.[68]

SS *Empire Mace* and SS *Empire Lance* each carried a pair of LCS(M)s, which accompanied the first flight of LCAs from that ship. LCS(M)s 79 and 81 from SS *Empire Lance* operated on the starboard flank of the LCAs, firing at targets of opportunity from H−2 to H+30, then were available for laying smoke if required. Both craft sustained some damage – in the case of LCS(M) 81, due to near misses from shells. LCS(M)s 75 and 76 from SS *Empire Mace* carried out a similar role – but both also had on board a FOO team for the self-propelled artillery and before H-Hour had observed the fire of those guns from a position a few hundred yards offshore. Later that morning, LCS(M) 76 rescued 75's crew after the latter craft sustained damage.[69]

540 Assault Flotilla reported 'a good deal of shelling' on the approach to the beach but without any casualties or damage. Since the LCT(AVRE)s and LCT(DD)s were still on the beach, there was limited space for beaching the LCAs. All of 541 Assault Flotilla's craft came ashore within 30 yards of each other, also hampered by 540 Assault Flotilla beaching further to the west than planned. The troops only got wet up to their knees, the beach obstacles posed no threat as they were beyond the water's edge, and there was 'very little firing'.

The LCAs unbeached successfully. Major R.L. Jackson, who landed with D Company, recalled advancing up the beach once ashore, 'Every step we expected to be fired at, but were not. The lack of opposition became eerie. Then, after about 200 yards, we must have reached a German fixed line for suddenly they threw everything at us.'[70]

Remaining with King Green, on time at about 07.50 (H+25), the reserve companies of 6th Green Howards landed, even further to the west than the assault companies. B Company was the westernmost of the two, landing from five LCAs of 541 Assault Flotilla (SS *Empire Mace*), while C Company was in five LCAs of 540 Assault Flotilla (SS *Empire Lance*). Like the assault companies, these infantry were also accompanied by troops from 233 Field

Company RE, and in addition, a platoon of 2nd Cheshires (69th Infantry Brigade's machine-gun company).

As the LCAs approached the beach, the flotilla officer of *Empire Lance*'s craft decided to beach slightly further to the west than the objective of King Green, which was under mortar fire. The craft managed to avoid any collision damage as they landed among obstacles in 1.5ft of water. Mortar fire was falling around them, and two of 540 Assault Flotilla's craft evacuated wounded soldiers when they withdrew from the beach.[71]

Also due around H+25 were two LCMs to land on the very far eastern edge of King Green (so far east that they were possibly even on the western edge of King Red). Both craft had crossed the Channel on board landing ships. One had orders to collect HQ personnel from LCH 187, including Kenneth Taylor, Signals Officer of 6th Green Howards. He recorded in his diary:

> Eventually approached beach and found things difficult. Kept grounding and hitting obstacles with shells falling in water. Made a few attempts to get close in but failed. Eventually decided to climb out but the ramp refused to go down at first. Shrapnel hitting craft so we jumped for it at 0800hrs and water only up to waist. 27 set [radio] got wet thro' and would not work.[72]

Despite the defenders belatedly opening fire, this did not stop both companies from overcoming German strongpoint WN-35 on the beach (the *Osttruppen* (Eastern Europeans drafted into the German army) defenders offered little resistance) and rapidly advancing inland. The engineers quickly created lanes through the barbed wire and minefield behind the beach, while tanks offered 6th Green Howards valuable support. By 09.30, D Company had secured the Mont Fleury Battery on the ridge overlooking the beach. The British plan was working well there.[73]

Meanwhile, on King Red, two companies of 5th East Yorks came ashore almost simultaneously with 6th Green Howards. In the words of the battalion war diary, 'landing very wet – up to 4' water'. As on King Green, the assault infantry were accompanied by men of 233 Field Company RE, who would demolish obstacles and clear mines. A Company beached from five LCAs of 539 Assault Flotilla (SS *Empire Halberd*), while D Company landed slightly further to the east from five LCAs of 542 Assault Flotilla (SS *Empire Rapier*).

A Company faced little opposition and seized WN-34 at the Mont Fleury lighthouse. D Company had a much more difficult assault, landing under point-blank fire from machine guns in seafront houses and mortars firing onto the beach. The 88mm gun located in WN-33 at the west end of La Rivière hit an AVRE tank, triggering the explosive charges on board, which caused many casualties to the nearby infantry. Faced with this fire-power, many of the infantry sheltered against the sea wall.

LCS(M) 110 from SS *Empire Rapier* had accompanied the first wave of infantry to King Red. The crew opened fire at the German defences to the left of the 88mm gun bunker and continued shooting until the reserve companies had landed and the infantry were starting to advance through the German strongpoint. The craft was hit twice by small-arms fire, but the bullets did not penetrate the craft's armour.[74]

With the craft carrying the assault companies of 5th East Yorks were two more LCAs of 539 Assault Flotilla (SS *Empire Halberd*), carrying Tare RN Beach Commando. These craft did not beach with the assault troops but waited off the beach until they were needed to mark gaps created in the beach obstacles. The craft off La Rivière were sniped at from houses and had to withdraw further to sea, while the DSOAG in LCH 275 directed fire onto those houses. Recce parties of Beach Commando had been due to land at H-Hour from LCT(A)s 2048 and 2039, but those craft were delayed and sunk respectively.[75]

The reserve companies of 5th East Yorks were due at H+25 and, according to the battalion war diary, landed on time. Both were carried by the same flotilla that had landed the assault companies: on the left was C Company on board five LCAs of 542 Assault Flotilla (SS *Empire Rapier*), and on the right, B Company on five LCAs from 539 Assault Flotilla (SS *Empire Halberd*). As with 6th Green Howards, with the reserve companies there were also men of 233 Field Company RE and 2nd Cheshires.

Following behind A Company, which had already subdued the defenders they faced, B Company had a straightforward landing. In contrast, C Company suffered casualties as they faced defenders who were still very active. The battalion war diary recounted how C Company's troops, 'wading through deep water were picked off by small arms fire and were unable to reach shore'. C Company joined D Company under the 3m-high sea wall.[76]

Seeing the plight of C and D Companies, at 08.01 the DSOAG King Red ordered fire-support landing craft of 332 Support Flotilla to lend a hand at La Rivière. LCS(L) 258 closed to 400 yards from the beach and fired on two fortified houses to the east of the 88mm gun and was soon joined at a range of 700 yards by LCG(L) 13, which had been summoned from Jig Beach. At 09.10 both houses collapsed, one with an explosion as stored German ammunition was detonated. LCG(L)s 1, 2 and 3, as well as LCS(L) 259, also fired on La Rivière in support of the infantry.

The senior officer of 332 Support Flotilla reported that 'the most skilful gunnery was necessary as our troops were huddled along the foot of the sea wall'. This action enabled the infantry and supporting AVRE, Crab and DD tanks to overcome WN-33, with one Crab finally knocking out the 88mm bunker. Still, many defenders continued to resist until 11.00 and some even longer. 5th East Yorks suffered the heaviest losses on the beach out of all units of the 69th Infantry Brigade.[77]

Good communications between the army and the DSOAG were key to this effective fire support at King Red. The advantages of this co-operation were apparently not obvious to all involved. An account written in 1947 by Major A. Consitt of 5th East Yorks stated that the support landing craft had not helped and had even caused friendly casualties, '[the] LCS joined in the fun for no apparent reason and starting pouring [heavy] MG fire and 4 [inch] shelling into the houses obliterating the leading [infantry section]. To call this off took about 10 mins.'[78]

In a similar arrangement to King Green, also due to land with the 5th East Yorks reserve companies were a pair of LCMs which had crossed the Channel on board LSIs and were to land to the west of the assault infantry. One (launched from SS *Empire Rapier*) carried RE stores and the other had collected headquarters and signals personnel from 5th East Yorks.[79]

At 08.10 (H+45), the reserve battalion (7th Battalion, The Green Howards or 7th Green Howards) began landing around the junction of King Green and King Red, facing Ver-sur-Mer. This was the third of the 69th Infantry Brigade's infantry battalions. B and D Companies landed in this wave, each from six LCAs, respectively from 539 Assault Flotilla (SS *Empire Halberd*) and 542 Assault Flotilla (SS *Empire Rapier*). As with the assault battalions, on board these LCAs there were also men of 233 Field Company RE. Small parties from other units also landed on the same craft, such as 2nd Hertfordshires (beach security battalion for No.9 Beach Group) and 186 Field Ambulance RAMC (one of 50th Infantry Division's medical units). Again, the LCAs were accompanied by two LCMs which had crossed the Channel on board LSIs and now one landed 6th Green Howards HQ personnel, among others, while the other was probably carrying RE supplies.[80]

One of 539 Assault Flotilla's craft carrying 7th Green Howards was LCA 786. As the LCA was being lowered from the LSI, its steering wheel was torn off. Rather than accepting that the craft was out of action and should simply be rehoisted, the Royal Marine coxswain, Corporal George Tandy, decided to steer it by hanging over the side of the LCA with his foot on the rudder. By this method, he landed his troops on time and safely returned to SS *Empire Halberd*, but it meant he spent hours with his lower body submerged in the sea. He was awarded the Distinguished Service Medal for his efforts.[81]

Perhaps counter-intuitively, these craft had a more difficult landing than those that had landed the 6th Battalion of the same regiment as the assault began. Approaching the beach, the senior naval officer on 542 Assault Flotilla's craft could not identify the planned landing site on King Green due to smoke. The LCAs beached 100 yards further west than intended, missing the gap in the beach obstacles that had been cleared by the LCOCUs. There was a variety of uncleared beach obstacles near the water's edge: hedgehogs and wooden or concrete posts with a shell or mine on top. Craft were able to steer through these as they approached, but it was harder to steer an LCA precisely when unbeaching and many hit obstacles. Four of 542 Assault Flotilla's six craft were lost as a result.[82]

The remainder of the battalion (due at H+47) came ashore some ten minutes later, at least some of them well onto King Green. The beach was under what the infantry described as 'slight' mortar fire. C Company landed from six LCAs of 540 Assault Flotilla (SS *Empire Lance*) and A Company from six LCAs of 541 Assault Flotilla (SS *Empire Mace*). Four of 540 Assault Flotilla's craft were damaged by beach obstacles and later sank, while a fifth suffered damage to its rudder and steering gear and had to be towed back to the *Empire Lance*.

When 541 Flotilla's craft beached, about ten minutes late, some obstacles were completely under water. One craft was damaged and had to be abandoned on the beach, while three others had damage – two were holed by obstacles and one lost its steering – but were able to make their way back to the *Empire Mace*. The remaining two of the six 541 Flotilla craft were damaged and lost on trips to the beach later in the day, carrying further troops ashore. One of these was LCA 1000, whose coxswain, Marine L.S. Mitchell, was praised for making repeated beachings until it struck a mined beach obstacle. Two Royal Marine crew from that craft were killed on D-Day, presumably on that occasion.[83]

Also due to land with the LCAs, but in practice one hour late, was LCM 244, which had crossed the Channel on SS *Empire Lance* and carried HQ personnel of 7th Green Howards. While trying to unbeach, the LCM became trapped between two LCTs and broached-to, then was holed by beach obstacles and sank. Four more LCMs carrying stores were due soon afterwards, at H+60. It is not clear when they actually beached.[84]

The next major force to land was the 'first priority tracked vehicles' from 69th Infantry Brigade and the Beach Group. They were due at H+60 (08.25) but touched down twenty-five minutes late at 08.50. Ten LCT(4)s – five each bound for King Red and King Green – carried vehicles from a wide variety of units. Along with the second- and third-priority vehicles, due at H+90 and H+120 respectively, these LCTs were designated Group 13.

As these three successive waves of LCTs landed, many exploded Tellermines on the beach obstacles, but with apparently no casualties or serious damage to craft or the vehicles carried. The first-priority vehicles included types such as Bren Carriers from the brigade's infantry battalion and machine gun battalion (2nd Cheshires). There were the remaining Sherman tanks of 4th/7th Dragoon Guards plus supporting vehicles – this was the unit that had supplied the DD tanks for King Beach. Beach group units included 2nd Hertfordshires, 89 Field Company RE, D7 armoured bulldozers of 51 Mechanical Equipment Section RE, and 75 Pioneer Company.[85]

The craft carrying the second- and third-priority vehicles were due at H+90 and H+120 respectively. The H+90 wave included three LCT(4)s of 24 LCT Flotilla, carrying the first self-propelled artillery to land on King Beach so far – twelve guns and six Sherman Observation Post tanks of 86th Field Regiment RA. The three LCTs were part of Group 8 and had taken part in the run-in shoot before H-Hour. The remainder of that wave was seven or eight LCT(4)s from Group 13: probably two craft from 24 LCT Flotilla and the remainder from 49 LCT Flotilla. These other craft held tracked vehicles from various units, such as the towed guns of 102nd Anti-Tank Regiment RA, Bren Carriers from the infantry battalions of 69th Infantry Brigade, personnel on foot from 2nd Hertfordshires, 75 Pioneer Company and even one press correspondent.

The three LCTs carrying guns of 86th Field Regiment RA landed half an hour early at about 08.25 (H+60, rather than H+90), to take the place of the Centaur tanks on the LCT(A)s that had failed to arrive around H-Hour. The Centaurs were to have acted as stand-in artillery until the self-propelled artillery had reorganised after the run-in shoot and was ready to beach. The remainder of the H+90 LCTs were delayed until 09.25 (H+120), and consequently, they beached at the same time as the third-priority vehicles that were scheduled to arrive onshore at that moment. The latter were carried on four LCT(4)s, probably more from 24 LCT Flotilla.

Most of the third-priority vehicles belonged to the Beach Group, with a few from 69th Infantry Brigade. Many of them were wheeled, whereas the majority of vehicles landing so far had been tracked and therefore were more able to move around on a beach without getting stuck. The plan had been that by H+120, tracking would have been laid on the beach to make it suitable for wheeled vehicles.[86]

Some, if not all, of the LCTs landing at H+120 were signalled by a destroyer to land on King Green, rather than King Red as planned. The cause of this diversion appears to have been congestion on the beach. It had not been possible to clear as many gaps in the beach obstacles as intended nor to establish exits from the beach on schedule.

German shells fell around the craft as they approached the beach, but none were hit. Two of the five LCTs set off mines on beach obstacles and broached-to, meaning that they remained stranded on the beach after unloading. Wireman Frank Howard was on one of these vessels, LCT 903 (of 49 LCT Flotilla). He recalled that they had a near-perfect landing close to the water's edge. A road a few yards inland enabled their cargo of vehicles to be on their way without delay. However, it turned out to be less than perfect, from the crew's point of view, as they soon realised that a shell had apparently passed through the craft without exploding but caused flooding to the extent that it sank just off the beach.[87]

To a certain degree, the landing times of specific groups of landing craft could be advanced or delayed according to circumstances on the beach. However, the ability of naval officers to exercise control had its limits. Captain W.F.N. Gregory-Smith RN, Principal Beachmaster for King Beach, was observing the landings from offshore. He had noted that vehicle movement off the beach was slowed by a lack of functioning exits, while 'the shallows were now blocked by wrecks and empty craft trying to back off the beach in the teeth of a strong westerly wind'. Seeing the LCTs carrying the third-priority vehicles approaching, he ordered messages to be sent pausing their landings by thirty minutes. 'But they might have been sending their message to the moon for all the good it did, and the third wave of LCTs bulldozed their way through the flotsam and discharged another 200 vehicles which came to a grinding halt behind the waiting queue.' It may be that these LCTs were following contradictory orders from another officer.[88]

Scheduled in between the two waves just mentioned, the remaining twelve self-propelled guns and accompanying vehicles of 86th Field Regiment RA were due to land on King at 09.00 (H+105). They were on board three more LCT(4)s, probably from 24 LCT Flotilla, and appear to have landed on time. Petty Officer Motor Mechanic Mick Shirley served on board LCT 684, in either the H+90 or H+105 waves. His craft put the vehicles ashore safely, apart from a jeep, which was turned over by a wave. While withdrawing from the beach, LCT 684 hit a shell fixed to a beach obstacle, which blew a 3ft-square hole in the side of the engine room, forcing the crew to rebeach to avoid sinking.[89]

By around 10.00, 5th East Yorks and supporting tanks had captured La Rivière, and about half an hour later, 6th Green Howards had gained control of the beach area in the rest of King, further to the west from La Rivière, as well as most of the Meuvaines Ridge, a short distance inland. The eastern half of Gold Beach was now fully in British hands.[90]

The support landing craft were still on the lookout for targets. At about 10.20, three of them – LCS(L)s 258 and 259, and LCG(L) 1 – fired on two small pillboxes some 500 yards east of La Rivière, which were sniping at British forces. Only the LCG(L)'s gun could penetrate the concrete, but it had the desired effect as the garrison emerged with hands aloft in surrender to the landing craft offshore. With a few bursts of machine-gun fire, the crews indicated to them that they should make their way towards Juno Beach to surrender.[91]

The Landings Continue: Jig and King

Now, around 09.30, some two hours after H-Hour, we will continue the story of the landings on both Jig and King simultaneously. Most of the assault infantry brigade and supporting troops including the Beach Group had landed, but a wide variety of support units were still to arrive, as well as the reserve infantry brigade. While an exit was open on Jig Red, exits at Jig Green were not yet available, so craft generally avoided landing at that beach until around 16.00.[92]

As on other beaches, after delivering their first load of troops to the beach, most LCAs were tasked with collecting more personnel, such as members of the Beach Group, either directly from ships offshore or from LCT(3)s that had embarked more troops from the landing ships. Earlier in the day, those LCT(3)s had carried DD tanks and had spent longer in that role than expected as they had taken tanks to the beach rather than launching them offshore. This made them about two and a half hours late reaching the LSIs.

To board an LCT(3) from a landing ship, the troops had to climb down scaling ladders or nets on the side of the ship, which took longer due to the rough seas. LCT(3)s were unsuitable for beaching on gently sloping beaches so the preferred option was for them to be unloaded by smaller craft rather than beaching themselves.

Most of the LCA flotillas did not realise that the bigger craft were running late, and when the latter did not appear, they went back to their LSIs rather than waiting longer. Given the difficult first landings experienced by the LCAs, that does seem understandable. Between them, the five flotillas from the LSI off Jig Beach had lost around fifteen craft, including LCM 128 and LCS(M) 99, with many other craft damaged.

By around 13.00, the DSOAG Jig Green reported that the 'shortage of LCA was being acutely felt'. An hour and a half later, the Naval Officer in Charge (NOIC) Gold noted that there were around thirty wrecked or stranded LCTs or LCI(L)s on the beach, though many were later refloated, as well as other minor landing craft.[93]

High tide was expected around 10.30 (about H+180) but was reportedly one hour early due to the strength of the wind, leaving only some 30 yards of exposed beach. The many remaining beach obstacles were now covered by the sea and therefore at their most dangerous. Smaller craft risked broaching-to and being thrown onto obstacles by the surf.

The most efficient way to land the huge numbers of vehicles that the Allied armies needed ashore was by LST. These large and vulnerable ships had no place on the beach in the first hours of the landings, but they were not far behind. The first two LSTs off Gold Beach were due to arrive at the Lowering Position shortly before H-Hour: LST 25 at Jig and LST 264 at King, both US Navy vessels which arrived in Groups 11 and 13.[94]

During the crossing, LST 25 had got separated from the rest of Group 11 and proceeded alone, towing a Rhino Ferry. At H+30 the LST discharged over twenty DUKWs so they could swim the distance of about 1 mile to the beach, to land at H+120, 1 mile east of Asnelles. LST 264 similarly launched DUKWs to swim ashore to King Beach. These amphibious vehicles carried stores such as ammunition, mostly destined for battalion assembly areas. Like other LSTs later in the day, both ships also launched their LCVPs for use as despatch boats. We will return to the LSTs later.[95]

The next major fighting units to land on Gold Beach were the reserve infantry brigades. 56th Independent Infantry Brigade was due to follow up behind 231st Infantry Brigade on Jig Beach, and 151st Infantry Brigade were to follow 69th Infantry Brigade on King. Small advance parties from the two new brigades were already ashore. The main part of each brigade can be summed up as troops on foot carried on LSIs and vehicles carried by both LCT(4)s and LSTs. In the plans, each wave was neatly separated in both time and space along the beach, but on the day, things were much less tidy. For example, part of 151st Infantry Brigade landed on Jig not King, and 50th Division's plan called for the reserve infantry brigade to land an hour earlier on King than on Jig, but the divisional commander chose to delay its landing so, in practice, the two brigades landed around the same time.

The foot personnel of 151st Infantry Brigade were bound for King Beach on board nine US Navy LCI(L)s, most from Divisions 61 and 62, Group 31, LCI(L) Flotilla 12 (a US Navy flotilla was much larger than the Royal Navy unit with the same name, and was subdivided into groups, each of two or more divisions). Together with HMS *Albrighton*, a Hunt-class destroyer serving as an LSH and carrying the brigade HQ, the nine craft were designated as Group 16.

151st Infantry Brigade comprised three battalions – 6th, 8th and 9th, The Durham Light Infantry, and some were equipped with bicycles. Other troops also landing at this time included personnel from the brigade HQ and 54 Balloon Unit RAF with one barrage balloon per craft, each handled by two airmen on foot. These troops were due to land at H+150 (09.50) but many were delayed over an hour.

The priority vehicles of the same brigade landed just after 12.10, nearly an hour later than the infantry and more than an hour after their intended time of H+210 (10.55). They arrived on five LCT(4)s of 55 LCT Flotilla. The vehicles were mostly Bren Carriers and jeeps from 151st Infantry Brigade's three infantry battalions and from brigade HQ.

The LCTs were ordered to beach on Jig Red. Damaged and broached-to craft made it harder to find space to land, but all vehicles were put ashore safely. LCT 922 hit a mine on the approach and had to be abandoned on the beach. LCT 564 was also mined but the Flotilla Engineering Officer was on board and 'managed to cope with the inflow of water by a quick improvisation of the Engine Cooling System', enabling the craft to unbeach.[96]

Turning to 56th Infantry Brigade at Jig Beach, the vehicles from its infantry battalions, from the brigade headquarters and belonging to brigade troops such as signals personnel, landed around the same time as the foot troops of its infantry battalions. The vehicles were carried on five LCT(4)s of 2nd Division, 55 LCT Flotilla, designated part of Group 11. These LCTs also carried Beach Group personnel. Arriving off the beach at 10.30, about half an hour later, these craft received orders to beach on Jig, presumably doing so around 11.30–11.45.

Although most troops barely got their feet – or vehicle tracks – wet, Lieutenant W.A.G. Pugh RNVR (gunnery officer of U LCT Squadron) on LCT 565 reported, 'The beach was a shambles of wreckage of minor craft and transport'. Shells fell around the five craft as they neared the shore. Most of the LCTs hit mined obstacles. On LCT 565, Stoker 1st Class K.M. Jenkins kept his feet over a hole in the engine room to slow the flooding until his crewmates had plugged it.[97]

56th Infantry Brigade's three infantry battalions were the 2nd Battalions of three different regiments: The South Wales Borderers, The Essex Regiment and The Gloucestershire Regiment. Some of the men were equipped with bicycles to speed up their advance inland. Alongside the infantry came supporting and Beach Group troops, such as personnel of 203 Field Ambulance RAMC. All had crossed the English Channel on board ten LCI(L)s, designated part of Group 15. The Royal Canadian Navy's 264 LCI(L) Flotilla comprised seven of these craft, and the other three were manned by the US Navy. The LCI(L)s had arrived off Jig Green at 09.40 and waited their turn to unload their troops.[98]

It had been planned that off the Normandy coast, the troops would transfer from the LCI(L)s into smaller LCMs that had crossed separately. Those craft were fifteen LCM(1)s of 698 Build-Up Flotilla, of which nine craft were scheduled to have crossed the Channel as part of Group 11 and the other six as part of Group 13. These craft were empty during the crossing, so they had space to take on board troops on arrival off Normandy.

On 5 June 1944, the LCMs struggled, even in the relatively sheltered waters of the Solent, and while some tried braving the crossing, all were forced to turn back as they were shipping water in the rough seas. Six craft had to be taken for repair after this effort, but the remainder made another attempt at the crossing on D-Day itself. The only craft from the flotilla to have taken part in the assault was LCM 193, which had crossed on board SS *Empire Rapier*, and had taken off troops from an LCI(L) during the assault. However, it sank with three casualties, including Marine Robert Henry Chapman, who lost his life.[99]

The planners' intention to land troops by LCMs at this point was presumably to avoid the need to expose the larger and more valuable LCI(L)s to possible enemy fire and the risk of damage from uncleared, submerged obstacles. Since 698 Flotilla's LCMs would not be available on time, the LCI(L)s would have to go all the way into the beach to land their troops. The exception was LCI(L) 255, which was carrying the brigadier commanding 56th Infantry Brigade and his staff: an LCM was found to take them ashore.

Various reports place the LCI(L)s carrying 56th Infantry Brigade's infantry battalions as landing over a period of around half an hour, at 11.58–12.30. Not all craft landed simultaneously because many landing craft were landing several thousand troops over a broad stretch of beach. There was no need to co-ordinate beaching times to the last minute, and each craft took some minutes to unload. Many of the craft landed on Jig Red rather than Jig Green as planned, because of the many remaining obstacles, 'heavy mortar fire' and snipers on the latter beach.[100]

The wartime Royal Canadian Navy history described the landings thus:

> There was a heavy surf running which piled up dangerously on the shallow beach across which the troops had to make their way. Although the distance from the LCIs to shore averaged only 12 feet and the depth of water at the ramps was less than 3 feet, the surf caused some of the troops to hesitate up to 15 minutes before disembarking. The delay made unbeaching more difficult, but there was hardly any firing by this time and it was not until after unbeaching that bullet holes were found in the super-structure of two of the craft.[101]

While neither the troops nor the landing craft crews suffered casualties in landing, it was not a straightforward process. Bill Speake of 2nd South Wales Borderers landed from one of the USN craft. He repeatedly went under water and only managed to get ashore by clinging to a guide rope that had been placed by the craft's crew. As a measure of the difficulty of his landing, out of the 400 cigarettes he brought ashore, a mere twenty (safe in a sealed tin under his helmet) survived the experience.

On landing, many of the LCI(L)s were damaged by obstacles or even wreckage from earlier landings that had been submerged by the high tide. Two RCN craft and all three USN LCI(L)s could not unbeach until late afternoon. While waiting for low water, some of the ratings from LCI(L) 310 went exploring on land, apparently as far as Arromanches, where they are said to have discovered a German officers' mess and brought back various souvenirs.[102]

An RCN history attributed the successful unbeachings by four out of the six Canadian craft to careful adjustment of the crafts' trim using ballast and fuel tanks, so that the bottoms of the craft exactly matched the profile of the beach. The USN vessels were the later type of LCI(L), which had a slightly deeper draft, and this may have contributed to their struggles in unbeaching. At least two of the USN craft broached-to. The LCI(L)s then remained off the beach as ferry craft to help with unloading other ships.[103]

Although 50th Infantry Division's landings and advances inland were behind schedule, with hindsight, they were not critically disrupted. This was not obvious at the time: around H+6 hours (13.25), 74 Mechanical Equipment Section RE reported that there was 'chaos' on Jig Green. Around this time, 50th Infantry Division handed control of the beach area to 104 Beach Sub Area, whose personnel had been arriving from around H-Hour and would continue to develop exits, set up stores dumps and other vital tasks. It had been planned that from H+5.5 hours, 10 Beach Group would start preparing Item Red Beach (on the west side of Le Hamel) so that it could be used in the Second Tide landings and for the expected landing of 7th Armoured Division on the evening of D-Day, at H+12 hours (19.25). Continued German resistance in Le Hamel made this impossible to achieve, although Beach Group personnel did begin to reconnoitre the area.[104]

As the tide began to fall in the early afternoon, it revealed uncleared obstacles which could be dealt with by the Royal Engineers. On Jig, they were assisted by REME personnel and even by German prisoners of war. AVREs and a D7 bulldozer from LCT 886, which had experienced such a traumatic landing at the start of D-Day, were finally able to land around 13.00 and began crushing or towing away obstacles. Obstacles on King had been booby-trapped and had to be cleared by demolition rather than towing.[105]

Many of the landings from around 12.00 onwards were not 'teeth' troops but part of the vital logistical tail (which is not to say those men were not in danger from enemy action). Four LCT(4)s which were part of Group 11 were to land on Jig Green West, but probably landed over a wider area of Gold Beach. They were carrying stores not troops: three were primarily loaded with ammunition and the fourth was mostly full of fuel. Each LCT also had several RASC lorries and a crane on board to help unload, and which subsequently would be used to help with the unloading and management of other stores in the beach area. These LCTs were due at H+3 hours (10.25) but seem to have been delayed due to congestion on the beach: the war diary of 305 GT Company RASC indicates that three of them beached between 12.00 and 14.00. The 6th Borders were to assist with unloading and this was expected to take up to six and a half hours.[106]

Many of the following groups of vessels were either L-Series convoys of LSTs and LCTs that were part of Force L, or GM-Series convoys of landing barges. The Force L convoys had identical numbers to the Assault Groups composing that force, but they were entirely different. For example, all of Force L's LCT(3)s were in Assault Group L2, but they crossed the English Channel in Convoys L-3 and L-4.

As with the convoys described above, they were accompanied by supporting ships such as escorts and rescue craft, which while important, will not be described here. Particularly in the case of LSTs, there are a variety of times associated with these convoys in documents and publications, such as the arrival time at the Lowering Position, over 7 miles from the coast, or the time when they would be ready to unload onto Rhino Ferries, much closer to the beach. Although the convoys are described here one by one and in the sequence that they were scheduled to reach Normandy, in reality, delays meant that convoys overlapped and actual timings are often hard to determine.

The next landings on Gold Beach were of vehicles carried by LSTs. As the tide began to go out, any craft that beached were likely to be stranded until the tide turned (low water was around 18.00). Therefore, the LSTs began landing vehicles by Rhino Ferry rather than beaching themselves.

As mentioned above, the first two LSTs to arrive at Gold Beach were LSTs 25 and 264, which had launched DUKWs at sea earlier in the day. The remainder of both ships' cargoes were then to be unloaded, as several Rhino-loads, due to land later in the day. The first Rhino was recorded landing at Jig Green West at 14.30 (roughly H+7 hours). Both LSTs then returned to the UK, leaving behind their Rhino Ferries to continue unloading other vessels.[107]

Beginning around H+6 hours, the next group of ten US LSTs (designated Group 17) were to start unloading. These ships were scheduled to arrive at the Lowering Position at 10.10. The LSTs carried the vehicles of the two reserve brigades, 56th and 151st Infantry Brigades. It was a long process to land them, which began with more DUKWs swimming ashore from the LSTs. They would unload most of the vehicles they carried onto Rhino Ferries, including the eight Rhinos that had been towed by the whole group. Many Rhinos from these ships began beaching around 15.00–15.30.[108]

Group 18 – twelve more US Navy LSTs, veterans of the Sicily and Salerno landings – would arrive at the Lowering Position at 14.10. They were carrying Second Tide vehicles of 56th and 151st Infantry Brigades. The intention was that they would start unloading via the Rhinos they had towed, all to be complete by 19.55 (H+12.5 hours). In practice, the rough seas hampered the offloading of vehicles onto Rhinos.

While some LSTs were able to land vehicles on D-Day – the 24th Lancers being one example of an army unit that got partly ashore from these ships – others had less success. LST 2, for example, beached at 14.15 on 7 June, dried out, and by 17.20 had unloaded its vehicles onto the beach.[109]

At H+12.5 hours, seven newly arrived LSTs from Convoy L-2, part of Force L, were to be ready to unload onto Rhino Ferries. The majority went to King rather than Jig. DUKWs from some of them came straight ashore. The ships carried a particularly broad selection of units, such as Tactical HQ 30 Corps; 3.7in anti-aircraft guns and radar of the 113th Heavy Anti-Aircraft Regiment RA; Royal Engineers Road Construction Companies, whose initial role would be to build an advanced landing ground for the Allied air forces; and 2 Anti-Aircraft Squadron RAF Regiment to man the guns to defend that new airstrip. There were even eight 155mm M12 self-propelled guns of US 987th Field Artillery Battalion, the only US unit to land on British beaches, provided at British request to give the troops at Gold Beach some long-range, land-based artillery capabilities.[110]

Landing barges were also starting to arrive off Gold Beach. There were several convoys, and the exact arrival times of all barges are unclear, so some may have deviated from the planned arrival times described here. Twelve LBVs, accompanied by five LBFs for protection and forming Convoy GM-1, were due by H+12.5 hours. Five of the LBVs were loaded with petrol, while seven were loaded with other stores including ammunition and Royal Engineers' equipment. These barges would be beached and the stores on board would be added to army supply dumps near the beach. The barges included elements of 4, 14 and 15 LBV Flotillas.[111]

Convoy GM-3 was due at the Lowering Position at H+15.5 hours on D-Day. This included thirty LBVs: three more from 4 LBV Flotilla, the remainder of 15 LBV Flotilla, plus the whole of 13 LBV Flotilla. The barges were a mix of loaded vessels, which would beach and dry out so they could have their cargoes taken off, and unloaded barges, which would immediately be used for unloading larger ships. They were also accompanied by 36 LB (Supply and Repair) Flotilla, with six LBEs, two LBWs and fifteen LBOs. Some of the latter barges were towed by trawlers for the Channel crossing. They supported the LBVs and any other craft that needed repair, additional drinking water or refuelling.[112]

The last group of landing barges, Convoy GM-4, was to arrive on midnight on D-Day. It was formed from the majority of 38 LB (Supply and Repair) Flotilla: six LBEs, two LBWs, five LBOs and two LBKs. Again, the barges would support other landing barges and any other craft that needed their help. Able Seaman Bob V. Parker, the signaller on one of these vessels, LBO 86, recalled that the barge was so heavily loaded with diesel that it only had about 1ft of freeboard (the distance from the waterline to the upper edge of the deck). The two LBKs were particularly welcomed by many crewmen on minor landing craft and landing barges off Gold, as their role was to provide hot meals to the crews of such vessels.[113]

Convoy L-3 was due at H+16.5 hours (23.55) on D-Day. Primarily composed of LSTs bound for Juno Beach, it also included sixteen LCT(3)s for Jig Beach, carrying 22nd Armoured Brigade from British 7th Armoured Division. These craft were expected to dry out on the beach to unload. One of these craft was LCT 7074, now preserved at The D-Day Story, Portsmouth. LCT 7074's first lieutenant, Sub Lieutenant Phillip Stephens, recorded in his diary, 'Near Midnight we arrived off the coast of Normandy ... All night we lay just off the coast, watching the flashing and rumble of heavy guns, the tracer curling into the night sky as enemy aircraft bombed the fleet, the burning ships around us'. This LCT did not put its tanks ashore until after 09.30 on 7 June and then became entangled with several other vessels and had to beach again. This gave some of the crew the chance to visit Asnelles-sur-Mer, where they 'were toasted in champagne in the village restaurant' before the LCT unbeached later that day.[114]

At H+17.5 hours (00.55 on 7 June), more LSTs and LCT(3)s were to arrive. This was Convoy L-4, also known as ETL-1 under the numbering system that would be used for convoys over the months after D-Day. The twelve LSTs would wait until there was space for them to land on the beaches, which was expected to be around H+21 hours (04.25 on 7 June 1944). That would be about ninety minutes ahead of low water, so these latest arrivals would dry out on the beach as the tide receded and could be refloated some three hours later on the rising tide. It was planned that the thirty LCT(3)s beach in two waves, at H+17.5 and H+18.5 hours respectively.[115]

Another build-up convoy, Convoy GM-2, was formed from LCM and LCVP flotillas and was due by nightfall on D-Day. The difficult weather meant that the departures and arrivals of these craft were spread out over a longer time than planned. There were six LCM flotillas in Force G, which were a mix of LCM(1)s and LCM(3)s. Both 607 and 698 Build-Up Flotillas were meant to have taken part in the assault using LCM(1)s.

All of 607 Flotilla were carried across the Channel on board LSs, and one of the crew, Marine Edward William Durn, was killed at some point during the day, while 698 Flotilla had set off under their own power on D-1 but were unable to cross the English Channel because of the weather. By the time they set off on D-Day, the original fifteen craft had been whittled down to seven that were still operational, and one more of those was abandoned during the crossing due to leaks. After arriving at Juno Beach early on 7 June, the remnants of the flotilla reported to Gold Beach at 08.00 and were put to work unloading stores ships.[116]

The LCM(1)s of 609 Build-Up Flotilla and the LCM(3)s of 605, 606 and 654 Build-Up Flotillas were not scheduled to arrive off the Normandy coast until the end of D-Day. Some were preloaded with three 10-ton trucks each, while others were empty. Many of the craft set off from the Solent early on D-Day and arrived at Gold Beach about 22.00 the same day. Most of 654 Flotilla's craft did not arrive off the French coast until late on 9 June, along with six craft of 606 Flotilla, after making several unsuccessful crossing attempts.

Lieutenant (E.) Reg Lindlop RNVR, Flotilla Engineering Officer of 605 Flotilla, fell behind the rest of the flotilla after fixing a fuel blockage on one craft. It was 7 June before he managed to land the jeep his craft was carrying. An army major on the beach asked him to get small arms ammunition from the ships offshore. He reported to the HQ ship, and by the time the LCM had been loaded with ammunition and then returned to the beach, it was dark and the beach was deserted. His crew carried the ammunition boxes ashore, only to come under machine-gun fire – presumably from nervous British personnel holed up for the night in the dunes. For the night of 7 June, Lindlop's craft tied up alongside an LCT whose crew kindly fed him and his men: their first meal since midday on D-Day.[117]

Convoy GM-2 also included all the remaining LCVPs of Force G that had not crossed the English Channel on board LSTs. After leaving the Solent at 05.30 on D-Day, over sixty LCVPs of B Build-Up Squadron arrived at Gold Beach around 22.00–23.00, consisting of 805, 806, 807 and 808 Build-Up Flotillas. During the crossing in these small craft, sea-sickness had been 'rife', and in one flotilla 70 per cent of the Royal Marine crewmen were incapacitated. On arrival in Normandy, the crews had to spend the night in their LCVPs and were reliant on neighbouring larger landing craft to obtain hot drinks. They began work early the next day, helping to unload larger ships and landing craft. Of B Squadron's five LCVP flotillas, only 809 Build-Up Flotilla did not make the crossing at the same time and arrived days later instead.[118]

By the end of D-Day, despite a substantial number of lost and damaged landing craft, around 20,000 troops and some 2,100 vehicles were ashore on Gold Beach. The follow-up forces including 7th Armoured Division were behind schedule, but the Allies had a solid foothold in Normandy.[119]

9

Juno Beach

There did not appear to be any gap in these defences so we went through them.

Lieutenant W.J. Turner RNVR, flotilla officer of 518 Assault Flotilla.[1]

From west to east, the Allied planners had divided Juno Beach into Love (where no troops landed), Mike and Nan sectors. The dividing line between Mike and Nan was formed by the River Seulles, which reached the sea on the western edge of the small port of Courseulles. Mike was 2,100 yards long and split into Mike Green and Mike Red. As a Canadian report described it, this was 'a low, sandy shoreline' with sand dunes along the rear of the beach. Being longer, at 5,600 yards, Nan was divided into Green, White and Red. Here, 'the coast is low and sandy, dotted by numerous villas and summer houses'.[2]

Canadian 3rd Infantry Division led the landings on Juno Beach, with two infantry brigades and supporting forces landing side by side. With H-Hour originally set at 07.35, Canadian 7th Infantry Brigade would land on Mike Green, Mike Red and Nan Green, including on both banks of the River Seulles. These beaches will be referred to here as Juno West.

The naval forces for the western beaches were Assault Group J1, which would arrive in a series of medium-sized convoys, numbered J-1, J-3 and so on. On Juno East, Canadian 8th Infantry Brigade would land on Nan White and Nan Red, delivered and supported by Assault Group J2, their H-Hour being ten minutes later at 07.45.

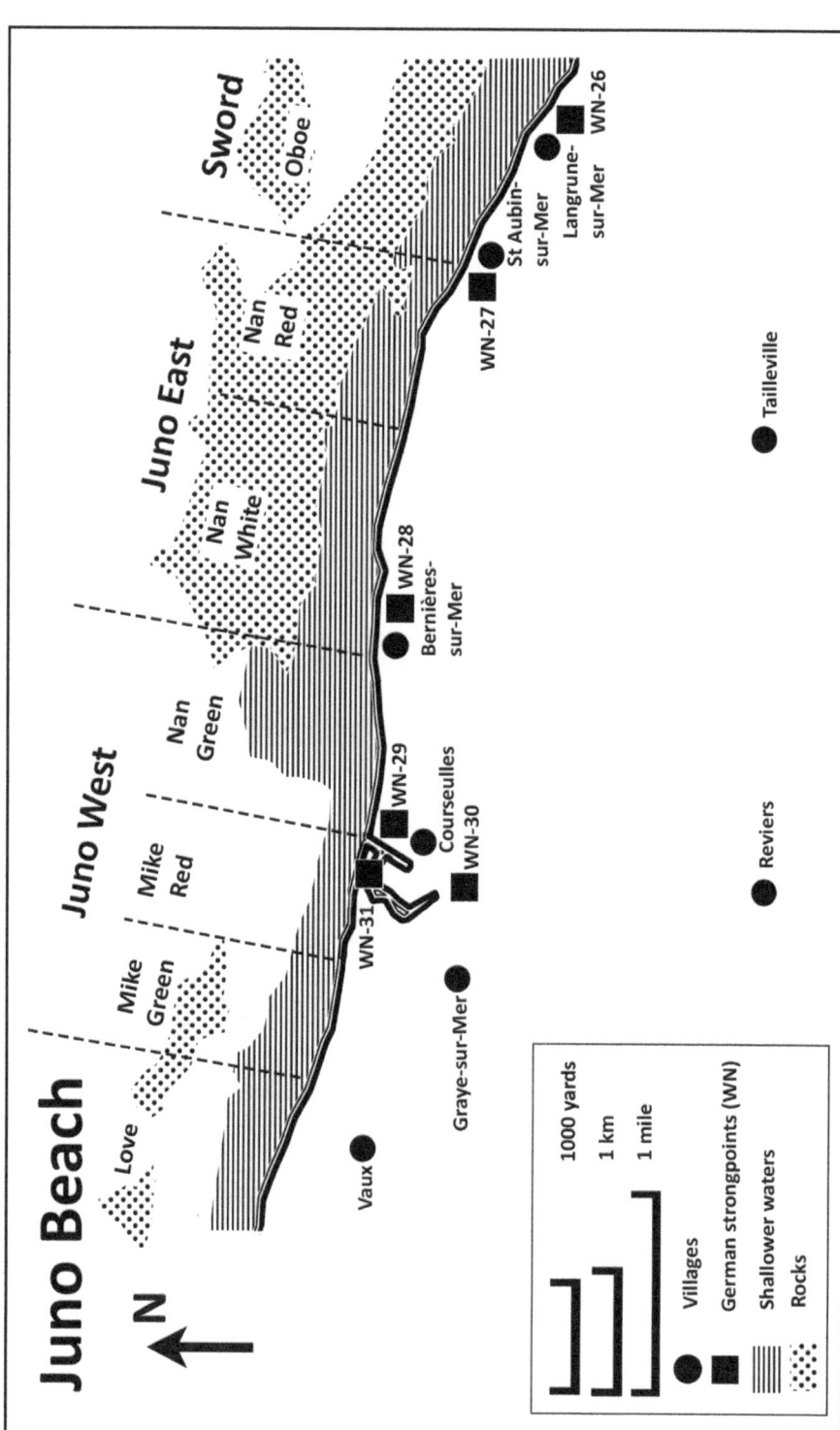

Juno Beach: Map approximately to scale. Some details omitted for clarity. (Map primarily based on: Ford, Ken, *Juno Beach (Battlezone Normandy)* (Stroud: Sutton, 2004); Chazette, *Atlantikwall Gold – Juno – Sword*)

The delayed H-Hour on Juno East – originally twenty minutes later than Gold and Sword Beaches – was designed to ensure that rocks off the beach were sufficiently covered by the tide before the first waves of landing craft had to cross them. H-Hour on the western half of Juno was ten minutes earlier than in the east, to minimise the interval between the assault beginning on Juno compared to the adjacent beaches. However, the timings of both assaults would in fact be adjusted on the day.[3]

Although the terrain at Juno was, at first glance, less intimidating than the bluffs at Omaha Beach, in Nan sector, seafront houses and a sea wall 6–10ft high proved a useful focus for the German defences. The defenders were the German 716th Infantry Division, described by a Canadian report as 'a static formation not distinguished by heroic tradition'. Ahead of D-Day, Canadian 3rd Infantry Division assessed the fighting value of the opposing troops as 40 per cent in a static defensive role compared to the best-trained infantry, or 15 per cent in a counter-attack. Events on D-Day would however show that elements of the German forces were able to strongly resist the Canadians.[4]

The first of Force J's convoys were due to arrive off Juno Beach at H–100 (05.55). At around 06.30, the two senior naval officers decided on a ten-minute delay to H-Hour: it would now be 07.45 for the western side of Juno Beach and 07.55 for the east (the revised times are used below). Some convoys, particularly those containing LCTs, were running behind schedule and the delay would allow craft to regain their places. On the eastern half of the beach, this did enable the LCTs carrying AVREs to catch up.

To the west, the LCTs carrying self-propelled artillery regained their place in the schedule, but the LCT(AVRE)s were even further behind. The Commander Force J ordered the landings to begin without waiting for them. On top of the already late H-Hour, this further delay had the consequence that at the start of the landings, the incoming tide would be even closer to the beach obstacles.[5]

The big troop transports (LSIs) had arrived on time at the Lowering Position, around 7 miles out to sea. Their prompt arrival was important as it would prove difficult to launch their LCAs in the rough seas. SS *Monowai*, which carried the assault companies of the Queen's Own Rifles of Canada, as well as the reserve companies of the Régiment de la Chaudière, arrived at the Lowering Position at 06.20 and lowered its LCAs five minutes later. This allowed the first LCAs ninety-three minutes to reach the beach (including the ten minutes' delay in H-Hour). Some of the assault troops were close to the beach when H-Hour was delayed.

A Company, Regina Rifles, on board the LCAs of 505 Assault Flotilla, were only 1.5 miles offshore when they heard.[6]

By 06.55, the LCTs of 4 and 11 LCT Flotillas carrying the DD tanks for both sides of Juno Beach had arrived offshore, each in a separate convoy. The plan called for the tanks to be launched at H–55, at a distance of 7,000 yards from the beach, so they could swim to the shore, touching down just ahead of the assault infantry. The DD tanks' Launching Position was marked on the western side by mini-submarine X20, which surfaced off the beach after having spent seventy-six hours at sea (the majority of it submerged off the beach to avoid detection).

In fact, visibility was good enough that the landing craft crews could already clearly identify the correct beaches. The DSOAGs for each half of the beach were accompanying the LCTs. Both officers decided that there was too great a risk that the DD tanks would sink in the rough seas. Instead, the LCTs would take the swimming tanks further towards the beach and, if conditions remained unfavourable, would deliver them directly onto the beach. Since an LCT was faster through the water than a DD tank, the craft had to slow down so as not to arrive too early.[7]

As on other D-Day beaches, a variety of fire-support landing craft joined in the naval bombardment. There was a similar but not identical mix of craft on each half of the beach. Off Juno West, there were three LCG(L)s, three LCFs, four LCS(L)s, eight LCT(A)s, one LCT(CB) and four LCT(R)s. Facing Juno East, the support craft were four LCG(L)s, two LCFs, eight LCT(A)s or LCT(5)s, one LCT(CB) and four LCT(R)s.

The LCG(L)s opened fire at about 07.20, some beginning from as far out at 9,000 yards from the beach. As they neared the shore, these craft continued to fire 'in rapid broadsides', as visibility allowed. Closing to 1,000 yards from the shore, they 'cleared the [sea]front [of enemy] to port and starboard', supplementing their 4.7in guns with their 20mm Oerlikons. The accompanying LCFs and the craft of 103 LCT Flotilla that they were escorting also joined in with their Oerlikon and Pom-Pom anti-aircraft guns. To the landing craft crewmen, it must have felt like a formidable barrage. Many German defenders were well protected in the substantial fortifications, however, and would survive to continue the fight.[8]

Once LCG(L) 831 was about 1,000 yards offshore, it was close enough to be hit by enemy mortar fire. Although the crew did not realise it at the time, the craft was also hit eight times by a German anti-tank gun (believed to be a 5cm PAK 38), which penetrated at least one sheet of armour. Fortunately for the crew, the shots hit LCG(L) 831 on the starboard side; had they hit the craft's port side, they might have hit its magazines for

4.7in and 20mm Oerlikon shells, with almost certainly catastrophic results. The mortar bombardment resulted in damage and casualties on board, but sandbags placed on the craft's upper deck prevented a major fire.[9]

One LCT(CB) was present on each half of Juno Beach. Each craft carried two Sherman Firefly tanks on a ramped platform near the vessel's bows. The tanks' 17-pounder guns, more powerful than the 75mm cannon of standard Shermans, would be used against selected strongpoints. LCT(CB) 2041 targeted a German position on Mike Beach at Courseulles, while LCT(CB) 2338 was off Juno East. After firing on the approach to the beach, both craft circled out to sea again with the intention of putting the tanks ashore just after the DD tanks had beached.[10]

At H-30, a total of ninety-six guns in four regiments of self-propelled (SP) artillery were to fire from on board the LCTs carrying them. They were to open fire at 9,000 yards from the beach, continuing the bombardment as the craft steamed towards the shore, known as a run-in shoot. One regiment began firing at 11,000 yards, in response to a request radioed from the craft carrying the infantry. Additional soldiers were carried on the LCTs to pass shells from stacks on the deck to each gun's loader, so that when each gun went ashore, it would still carry a full load of shells.[11]

The 12th and 13th Field Regiments RCA fired on Mike Red and Nan Green respectively, while 14th and 19th Field Regiments RCA fired on Nan White and Nan Red respectively. Each regiment's guns would fire around 100 rounds during the run-in shoot. As the craft advanced, the gunners adjusted the range every two minutes until the LCTs were about 1,800 yards from land, at which point, they turned out to sea again. The guns were shackled to the decks of the LCTs to steady them during the run-in shoot, and the gunners needed time to ready them for disembarkation, as well as clearing away spent shell cases and surplus unfired shells. Lieutenant W.D. Peter Cox and his men of 14th Field Regiment could not bear to dispose of this extra ammunition, so they loaded it onto their guns to the extent that when they landed soon afterwards, they went ashore with the crew literally sitting on stacks of shells.[12]

The 12th Field Regiment's shells fell on target and over an area 500–600 yards deep, while 13th Field Regiment reported that much of their bombardment fell beyond the target. The artillery's bombardment was praised by the general commanding Canadian 3rd Division. However, Force J's report later judged that the damage done by this barrage of fire from warships and landing craft was 'rather disappointing'. Practically every concrete pillbox had signs of being hit, but even the 4.7in shells of the LCG(L)s had done little damage. However, the supporting fire did have an 'excellent' neutralising effect on the enemy; in other words, encouraging the German defenders to take shelter and not fire at the approaching assault craft.[13]

Each artillery regiment's fire was controlled by FOO parties on two LCS(M)s cruising a short distance off the coast. Four of the eight LCS(M)s at Juno Beach were lost on D-Day; LCS(M) 83 sank while being towed across the English Channel by an LCT; and three crew on LCS(M) 47 were killed after the craft simultaneously struck a mine and was hit by a shell at the beach. They included Sub Lieutenant Richard Pirrie RANVR, who is thought to have been the first Australian sailor to die in the Normandy Landings. Four of the crew of LCS(M) 103 also died on D-Day.

Soon after H-Hour, each craft would put its FOO party ashore so that they could continue co-ordinating gunfire from land. The LCS(M)s also provided fire support for the troops ashore from close into the beach.[14]

A major report on fire support on D-Day found that at Nan Red, the FOO was judged to have directed the bombardment slightly high, leading to damage to the upper parts of buildings and suppressing the German defenders, but not directly targeting the main defence positions, just in front. The FOO who directed the fire of 14th Field Regiment RCA reported that the regiment had not received the message delaying H-Hour in time and were unable to delay their bombardment accordingly. The tide carried the LCTs to the east, so the regiment's fire was up to 200 yards to the east of the intended target, as well as about 200 yards beyond it. This meant that the enemy strongpoint at Bernières-sur-Mer was not hit by the fire of the self-propelled guns.[15]

The plan was that half of the eight LCT(R)s off Juno Beach would fire their rockets at H−8 and the other half at H−5. In practice, timings varied by only a few minutes. Each craft targeted the same strongpoints as the self-propelled artillery. The report of 320 LCT(R) Flotilla showed that most of the rocket bombardment was on target, although 103 LCT Flotilla believed that many rockets fell just above high-water mark, short of the German defensive positions that would fire on the assault infantry. Many eyewitnesses off Nan watched as rockets from LCT(R) 437 brought down a passing Typhoon fighter-bomber.[16]

Meanwhile, the LCAs carrying the assault infantry had been steadily closing the 7-mile distance from the Lowering Position to the shore. For most on board, this was not a pleasant experience, but the troops were in good spirits and 556 Assault Flotilla (from SS *Monowai*) reported that the men of the Queen's Own Rifles of Canada were singing on the way in. Those who were seasick 'merely disappeared for a few minutes and came back to join in the songs'. Crewman Ted Busby on LCA 1362 (557 Assault Flotilla, from MV *Llangibby Castle*) recalled:

> We sailed towards the beaches ... The Canadians singing all their ditties ... [some] not too clean and suddenly a voice piped up, 'We shouldn't be singing these dirty songs on a day as this', everything went quiet for a minute or two and then the singing started up again, but not one profane word was used again.[17]

One soldier, Rifleman Andrew Mutch of the Royal Winnipeg Rifles, was lying on the LCA's gunwhale (the narrow deck along the side of the craft) being seasick when a large wave washed him overboard. He was not seen again. The low profile of the assault craft meant that visibility from them was poor. 'It was impossible to see the beach except from the crests of the waves, but in these fleeting moments the assault personnel got glimpses of landmarks that had been made familiar to them by the photographs and diagrams which they had been shown in the briefing.'[18]

The final fire support to be delivered against the beach area at H−3 (or moments after) was due to come from eighteen LCA(HR)s, all from 590 Assault Flotilla. Each craft would fire their 24-spigot mortar bombs in a pattern leading up the beach. These had a shorter range than the rockets fired by an LCT(R) but had the potential to clear a path through mines and obstacles on the beach, as well as giving German troops in the beachfront defences a final encouragement to keep their heads down.

On Juno West, out of nine craft that left the UK only LCA(HR) 1286 reached Normandy on time. The others had been swamped, broke loose from their tows or were cut adrift during the Channel crossing. The problem may have been that the LCG(L)s or LCFs towing each pair of LCA(HR)s had steamed too fast, given the sea conditions. Three of the four crew of LCA(HR) 690 were drowned when that craft sank en route to Normandy.[19]

In contrast, all nine LCA(HR)s reached Juno East on time. Bob Bradshaw was the officer commanding LCA(HR) 671, which fired on Nan Red. His account illustrates how close the craft was to its target. He aimed to hit a gun emplacement and breach the sea wall, to aid the assault troops:

> I was standing forward as far to the port side as possible for the front left bomb with its exposed 16oz fuse was only inches from my shoulder. The coxswain was in his cockpit on the starboard side. As we came on target I waited until we were almost beached and yelled out 'fire' to the

coxswain, who in turn repeated the order down his speaking tube to the engine room and the firing number [another crewman] turned the handle and off went the bombs ... the nearest two went just ahead of the craft and the furthest two went over the promenade hitting houses on the far side.

Bradshaw subsequently realised that while concentrating on hitting his target, he had not allowed enough depth of water under their craft to cushion the downward force from the mortars firing, resulting in damage to the craft, which started to take on water. The naval commander of support craft at Juno judged that the fire of these LCA(HR)s was effective, even though not all were able to get into their planned firing positions.[20]

As on Sword and Gold beaches, the plan was that a series of different units would land on the beach, some on foot and some in vehicles, each making an important contribution to the assault. DD tanks would swim to the beach, coming ashore at H−5. Then at H-Hour, LCTs would deliver AVREs and Sherman flail tanks to deal with bunkers, beach obstacles and minefields, as well as the Centaur tanks of the Royal Marine Independent Armoured Support Batteries. The assault infantry would land at H+5, immediately rushing the first layer of German defences, which the tanks would have spent the last few minutes softening up.

In the event, many troops did not arrive on time, and it remained to be seen what impact this would have on the operation. The assault will be considered for Juno West and East in turn.

Juno West: Mike and Nan Green Beaches, H-Hour to H+60

The DD tanks for Juno West were on board eight LCT(3)s of 4 LCT Flotilla. When a naval officer announced that the DD tanks would not be launched at the intended position at 7,000 yards from the shore, Sergeant Leo Gariepy of B Squadron, 6th Canadian Armoured Regiment (1st Hussars), recalled that the troops 'were fighting mad, but no amount of cursing or pleading would make him change his mind'.[21]

The DSOAG for Mike Red decided that the sea conditions at 1,500 yards offshore were good enough for the DD tanks of A Squadron, 6th Canadian Armoured Regiment to swim the remaining distance. In case of heavy enemy fire, he was concerned to disperse the tanks rather than have them confined on the LCTs.

This manoeuvre involved turning the LCTs into the wind – in other words, parallel to the beach – potentially making the craft a larger target for enemy gunners. Two LCTs launched the tanks successfully. Another LCT only launched one before enemy fire cut the ramp chains, so the LCT's crew had to deliver the remaining four tanks to the shore. This craft struck a mine while on the beach, but still managed to deliver the tanks. The fourth craft, LCT 306, also had damage to its ramp wires and chains (the chains prevented the ramp from opening too far), which prevented the launch of DD tanks at sea but it beached successfully. The crew had to carry out a quick fix, running a spare wire the full length of the LCT and connecting it to the stern capstan so they could raise the ramp enough to land the tanks. At this point, the enemy opened fire, and LCT 306's Oerlikon gunners traded shots with a German machine-gun post to the east.[22]

The four LCT(3)s carrying DD tanks heading for Nan Green were now under the command of the flotilla officer, 4 LCT Flotilla. He decided to swim the DD tanks of B Squadron, 6th Canadian Armoured Regiment from 4,000 yards or less. Nineteen DD tanks managed to get into the sea, though several would be swamped on the way to the shore; one other was stuck on board its carrying craft. The tanks reached the shore just before 08.00. The records of the eight LCTs carrying DD tanks at Juno West are unclear, but at least one craft (LCT(3) 441) was left on the beach, feared to be a total loss.[23]

The DD tanks were in fact the first troops to get ashore on Nan Green, followed soon after by the assault infantry, Regina Rifles. A Company of that regiment landed at 08.09 from five LCAs of 505 Assault Flotilla (SS *Isle of Thanet*). As the LCAs approached the beach there was only 'rather desultory fire'. The coxswains were later praised for the 'great skill and determination' they showed as they weaved between the beach obstacles – a row of stakes 15ft apart with shells on top, then two rows of Element C. A line of hedgehogs were still clear of the water at this point.

As soon as the LCAs' ramps went down there was 'a considerable amount of machine gun fire' from the right and ahead. The flotilla had touched down in front of German strongpoint WN-29 at Courseulles-sur-Mer, and the troops would suffer heavy losses as they advanced. The bowman of one LCA was hit in the leg as he was about to go ashore with the lifeline to guide the troops. Under heavy machine-gun fire, Lieutenant (E.) C.G. Parsons RNVR jumped out of the craft to help the troops ashore. On one craft, six Canadians were hit as soon as the ramp dropped onto the beach, and Captain Ronald Shawcross, second in command of

A Company, pulled the men back onto the craft to save them. When he reached the sea wall at the top of the beach, Shawcross was shocked to find that only four of the men from his LCA were still with him.[24]

Immediately to the east, five LCAs of 510 Assault Flotilla (HMS *Invicta*) were carrying B Company, Regina Rifles. They landed at 08.15, after B Company's commander had requested a short delay to allow the DD tanks to reach the shore and deal with several active pillboxes. On the final approach, the craft had to weave between angled stakes topped with mines. As B Company landed, the troops faced less enemy fire than did A Company alongside them. One LCA was holed by a mine under its engine and sank half an hour after coming off the beach.[25]

Two companies of the Royal Winnipeg Rifles assaulted Mike Red with D Company to the west of B Company. Six LCAs of 516 Assault Flotilla (SS *Lairds Isle*) delivered D Company, who encountered only minor resistance as they landed slightly west of the planned site, at the eastern edge of Mike Green.

B Company came ashore from five LCAs of 509 Assault Flotilla (SS *Canterbury*). Beaching at 07.49 in front of strongpoint WN-31, troops found themselves under heavy shell, mortar and machine-gun fire while their landing craft were still hundreds of yards from land. Many troops were hit while wading ashore and as they made their way up the beach. A fierce close-range fight developed as the Canadians broke into the beach-front defences.[26]

The westernmost assault infantry at Juno were C Company, 1st Canadian Scottish, who had been placed under the command of the Royal Winnipeg Rifles for the assault. They landed at the western side of Mike Green at around 07.50, from five LCAs of 521 Assault Flotilla (HMS *Ulster Monarch*), each of which was flying a white ensign from a jury-rigged mast. At 200 yards from land, an enemy machine gun opened fire, with bullets ricocheting off one craft's bow door, but was silenced by fire from one of the LCAs. There was some sporadic mortar fire from the east. The craft managed to land their troops – some did not even get their feet wet – and withdrew without suffering damage from the beach obstacles.[27]

After H-Hour, the fire-support landing craft continued to look for opportunities to aid the troops ashore. Craft including LCG(L)s 831 and 1007 fired on various targets at and near Courseulles. One crewman on LCG(L) 831 was killed by German fire. Technical Sergeant Richard T. Wright of the US Marine Corps was on board the same craft as an observer, and at one point fired one of the vessel's twin Oerlikon guns at the enemy.[28]

At Mike Green, the assault infantry was accompanied by a small party of British troops, from 8th Battalion, the King's Own Regiment. These were the lead element of the Beach Group troops who, in the coming hours, would clear and organise the beach. The role of the Beach Group was so important that its first personnel landed at this early and dangerous moment.[29]

As on the other D-Day beaches, clearing the obstacles to enable further waves of landing craft to beach was as important as assaulting the enemy defences. LCOCU personnel were due to land with the first wave of assault infantry at H+5 to begin this task. This was a slightly different timetable compared to Sword Beach, where the LCOCUs landed with the reserve companies of the assault battalions at H+20. Each LCOCU was on board an LCA that was designated an LCA(OC), with the last two letters unsurprisingly standing for 'obstacle clearance'.

When No.5 LCOCU in LCA 958 reached Nan Green at 08.05, moments before the first infantry, only the last two rows of obstacles had not yet been covered by the tide: a consequence of the late H-Hour on this beach, plus the effect of the wind. The bulldozers and AVRE tanks were not yet present to help clear obstacles above the water's edge. The LCOCU personnel found that the sea conditions prevented them from diving from the LCAs to deal with obstacles and they were also unable to do much damage to hedgehog obstacles that were out of the water.

LCA 566, carrying No.1 LCOCU, arrived at Mike Red at 08.10, just over ten minutes after the infantry in that sector. Also noting that the beach obstacles were rapidly being covered by the tide, their LCA went west to Mike Green and established that there were fewer obstacles there. Returning to Mike Red, they tried to divert LCTs to Green, but when they were unable to do that, they beached on Mike Green at 08.30. Amid sporadic machine gun and mortar fire, No.1 LCOCU spent the next two hours clearing hedgehogs, working alongside two bulldozers and Royal Canadian Engineer personnel (who landed from LCT(A)s following on after the LCOCUs). By 10.30, the tide had risen to the point where the obstacles were difficult to access and the LCTs were able to beach over the top of them, at which point, the unit returned to HMS *Royal Ulsterman*.[30]

Ten LCT(5)s of 102 LCT Flotilla carried the breaching teams who would begin the army's obstacle-clearance role. These were Churchill AVRE tanks of 26th Assault Squadron RE, accompanied by Sherman Crab mine-clearing flail tanks of B Squadron, 22nd Dragoons. They had been due at H-Hour (07.55) so they could begin their work before the infantry touched down, but they were running late. The naval commander of Assault Group J1 had made the decision to continue with the landings, rather than wait for the arrival of the tanks, which would have meant the tide would have risen higher still. Five LCTs arrived at Mike beach at around 08.00–08.10, while the other five reached Nan Green at 08.15–08.30. Each team was tasked with clearing a gap at a specific location, and many individual LCTs touched down further to the east than planned.[31]

The LCTs were accompanied by LCS(L)s to provide smoke and close support with their 6-pounder guns against enemy strongpoints. The LCS(L)s had their own allocated targets up to H–5, at which point they switched to targets of opportunity.[32]

Another unit scheduled to arrive at H-Hour was the Centaur tanks of 3rd Royal Marine Armoured Support Battery. These were carried in ten LCT(A)s or LCT(HE)s from 103 and 105 LCT Flotillas. Each LCT was fitted with a ramped platform on its tank deck so that two Centaurs positioned side by side could provide fire support. The main difference between these two types, both of which had originated as LCT(5)s, was that the LCT(A)s had extra armour installed, while the LCT(HE)s did not. It is not always clear which type applied to a particular craft, and as a group they are referred to here as LCT(A)s.

Many of these craft also carried a bulldozer and Royal Canadian Engineers troops on foot for obstacle-clearance work. They were accompanied by one LCT(CB), fitted with a similar ramp for two Sherman Firefly tanks. These armoured vehicles were tasked with firing on specific German strongpoints with their powerful 17-pounder guns (hence the designation CB, or Concrete-Buster).

Information about these craft on D-Day is sparse. On Nan Green, at least two LCT(A)s arrived around 08.05 and contributed to the assault: one was LCT(A) 2263, which was left seriously damaged by obstacles and mines. LCT(CB) 2041 accompanied these craft, and the Sherman Firefly tanks fired from the specially fitted platform. Sub Lieutenant Norman Vingoe, the LCT(CB)'s second lieutenant, was supervising the ramp party and was therefore in front of the Fireflies' guns when they fired. He recalled the blast had a considerable effect on his ears. As the craft beached, he heard 'the scrape of the mined obstacles on the hull within a foot or two'. The remainder of the LCT(A) wave bound for Nan Green had struggled to keep up with the rest of their convoy during the Channel crossing and arrived late.[33]

Most of the craft heading for Mike Red and Green were delayed by two hours. However, enough Royal Canadian Engineers personnel on foot had arrived to clear a 50-yard gap in the obstacles by 08.30. Unfortunately for them, it was later blocked by two disabled LCTs.[34]

The remaining companies of the assault infantry battalions were scheduled to land at H+20, accompanied by men of 262 Field Company RE for obstacle-clearance work. Twelve LCAs of 557 Assault Flotilla (MV *Llangibby Castle*) would carry the Royal Winnipeg Rifles to Mike Green. The flotilla's craft shipped water over their bows in the sea conditions, which were described as 'worse than we had ever lowered in before'. The LCAs beached around 08.15 and the coxswains had to manoeuvre through the beach obstacles, but still managed to beach at high speed in order to give the troops the driest landing possible. Several craft were hit by machine gun and mortar fire on the beach or struck mines as they withdrew.

On the other side of Juno West, the Regina Rifles were to land on Nan Green in twelve LCAs: the remaining six craft from 557 Assault Flotilla, plus six others from 511 Assault Flotilla (SS *Mecklenburg*). Despite slowing their speed to avoid arriving early, on reaching Nan Green, 557 Assault Flotilla's six craft found that the assault companies had not yet landed and the troops on board (C Company, Regina Rifles) asked them to delay landing for fifteen minutes until 08.30.

Six LCAs from 511 Assault Flotilla carried D Company of the Regina Rifles in the other half of the Nan Green H+20 wave. The craft had to delay for twenty-five minutes for the AVRE tanks to arrive, after which they made a difficult landing. German small arms and artillery fire fell around the LCAs as they approached the beach. First, the flotilla officer's craft was blown up at about 100 yards from the beach, then two more LCAs had their bottoms ripped open by stakes and sank. The flotilla's surviving craft rescued the crew and troops of these last two craft, who had gathered on the sterns of the LCAs, which were the only parts remaining above water.

The obstacles (many of them mined) were just over an LCA's length apart, and the strong current made it difficult to manoeuvre between them. Many of the soldiers went ashore by climbing over an LCT that had already beached, as this was safer than weaving between the obstacles. Half of 511 Assault Flotilla's six LCAs were lost. Even the surviving craft had multiple holes in their bottoms and only managed to get back to SS *Mecklenburg* with all men on board bailing out the water. One crewman was killed, and three others were wounded. As for the troops, the navy reported that most were 'violently seasick' during the run-in to the beach. Six men had to be taken back on board an LCA 'in a semi-drowned condition' rather than putting them ashore.[35]

However, 557 Assault Flotilla had suffered even worse. A survivor from LCA 1017, which was lost after exploding a mine on a beach obstacle, stated that the men on board the craft had to bail out water with their helmets. He was convinced that the LCA would have sunk, had it not been for the cork built into its sides.

By the end of D-Day, in total less than half of the flotilla's craft were recovered, one sinking as it waited to be recovered, and nine more had been abandoned on the beach due to mortar or mine damage. At least eight and possibly up to eleven of the flotilla's LCA crews were killed on the beach on D-Day, among them Lieutenant Denis St John Batty Atkinson RM.[36]

The next unit to land was the third (reserve) infantry battalion of the Canadian 7th Infantry Brigade – 1st Canadian Scottish (less one company that had landed at H+5). They came ashore on Mike Green from 08.30 onwards, close to their intended landing time of H+45, using twenty-two LCAs drawn from three different troop transport ships: six LCAs from 517 Assault Flotilla (SS *Duke of Argyll*), eight from 526 Assault Flotilla (HMS *Queen Emma*) and eight from Royal Canadian Navy craft of 528 Assault Flotilla (HMCS *Prince Henry*).

Compared to the earlier landings, enemy fire was now mainly limited to mortars, but the conditions on the beach remained treacherous. The LCA crews rigged up lifelines from their craft to the shore to help the heavily laden soldiers get onto land.

As LCA 1372 (commanded by Lieutenant G.E. Nuttall RCNVR, 528 Assault Flotilla) reached the beach, a salvo of German mortar bombs fell in front of it. The soldiers exited the craft swiftly, but he estimated that a third of them had shrapnel wounds. One of the crew, Able Seaman D. Tennant was also wounded in three places by mortar shrapnel but continued about his duties until ordered to rest. The craft had two holes in its bottom from obstacles, but after these were repaired the crew made a second trip to the beach in it.

LCA 1021 was commanded by Leading Seaman Douglas Townson, who had been wounded by shrapnel just before landing. While on the beach, a tracked vehicle pushed the LCA broadside to the shore and cut the kedge anchor line, making it harder for the LCA to withdraw. On withdrawing from the beach, the craft was disabled when it hit a mine which badly wounded the stoker, Leading Stoker Bialowas. Due to the severity of Bialowas's wound, his comrades left him ashore in the care of a medic, having dug a foxhole to shelter him from the continuing mortar fire. The remaining crew of LCA 1021 then boarded an LCT to return to their ship, only to have to transfer to an LCI(L) when that LCT in turn was sunk.[37]

At 08.20 (earlier than their planned landing time of H+60), the remainder of the 6th Canadian Armoured Regiment landed on Mike Green. Two squadrons had landed around H-Hour, operating DD tanks. Equipped with standard Sherman tanks, the third squadron and the HQ squadron landed now from three LCT(4)s of 20 LCT Flotilla. These same three LCTs also carried priority vehicles from the infantry battalions that had already landed.

At 08.30, LCTs 507 and 513 of the same flotilla brought ashore a very different unit: the Inns of Court Regiment, who were tasked with carrying out reconnaissance in depth towards the River Orne and River Odon and blowing up bridges to delay the advance of enemy reinforcements.[38]

Simultaneously with the events described above, the assault had been taking place on Nan Red and White beaches.

JUNO EAST: NAN RED AND WHITE BEACHES, H-HOUR TO H+60

On the eastern half of Juno Beach, H-Hour had been delayed to 07.55. As on Juno West, the initial landings did not exactly follow the intended sequence. With the LCT(DD)s delayed, craft carrying the breaching teams of 'Funnies' were the first to land. These were eight LCT(5)s from 106 LCT Flotilla, delivering Churchill AVRE tanks of 80th Assault Squadron RE and Sherman Crab flail tanks of the 22nd Dragoons.

Some of the LCTs carrying the breaching teams (at Nan Red) are said to have put their tanks ashore around 07.45, while those on Nan White landed around 08.05–08.20. Many were further east than planned, and they faced considerable enemy fire. On Nan White, some craft beached in front of German strongpoint WN-28. The LCTs had to beach among the half-submerged obstacles. Two were later reported as sunk or damaged beyond repair on the beach, and a third was unable to leave the beach without repair.[39]

The LCT(AVRE)s should have been accompanied by three LCMs carrying some 100 men of the Royal Engineers for clearing beach obstacles. The LCMs had crossed the Channel independently and were to collect the troops from MV *Llangibby Castle*. However, in the rough seas the LCMs took longer than expected to cross and the Royal Engineers were an hour late landing.[40]

The LCT(A)s were meant to beach along with the LCT(AVRE)s at H-Hour, but most craft were late, apart from LCT(CB) 2338. The two

Sherman Firefly tanks on board used their 17-pounder guns to good effect, demolishing the corner of a building in the targeted enemy strongpoint on their second salvo. LCT(CB) 2338 beached at 07.55 and the tanks went ashore five minutes later. As it was coming off the beach it was hit by multiple shells from German anti-tank guns which caused major damage, including blowing off the bow ramp. One of the crew attempted to return fire with one of the LCT's 20mm Oerlikons but was badly wounded.

At this point, Wireman R.V. Weston appeared on the LCT(CB)'s bridge and offered the commanding officer, Lieutenant Robert J. Pardington, a milk tin full of petrol. Pardington recalled, 'I asked him what on earth it was for and he replied that he thought the ship was sinking and that I wanted to destroy the confidential books etc! I told him we were in enough trouble already without setting fire to the bloody ship'. The LCT took on water at its bows, and with its propellers almost out of the water, it had to be taken under tow.[41]

The assault infantry landed around 08.10–08.15. On Nan Red, the men of A and B Companies, the North Shore Regiment, arrived in ten LCAs of 558 Assault Flotilla (SS *Clan Lamont*). As they approached the beach, the LCAs had turned away at one point to allow the LCT(AVRE)s to pass and land first. As they drew nearer, their flotilla officer ordered 558 Assault Flotilla to slow to half-speed, as he could see that the DD tanks had not yet landed and the AVREs 'seemed to be in difficulties'. Before long, he ordered the LCAs back to full speed as he realised that delaying would only increase the problem of submerged beach obstacles.

The flotilla officer reported that the troops ducked under the protection of the LCAs' armour as enemy small-arms fire hit the crafts' ramp. One sergeant was hit by a bullet that penetrated the armour, fortunately only winding him. Managing to weave in between the beach obstacles – which included 11ft-high stakes, fitted with mines and interconnected by barbed wire – the LCAs landed the troops in water that was at most 2ft deep.

The Royal Marine crews reported German sniper, machine gun and 'very accurate' mortar fire, though they did not suffer any serious casualties despite several craft being hit. Much of that fire emanated from well-fortified German strongpoint WN-27, which caused many infantry casualties on the beach. It would hold out for hours, with the Canadians having to clear the buildings systematically and parts of the strongpoint only being cleared around 20.00 on D-Day.[42]

On Nan White, A and B Companies, Queen's Own Rifles of Canada (QORC), landed at around 08.15 from ten LCAs of 556 Assault Flotilla (SS *Monowai*). The flotilla hove-to for fifteen minutes off the beaches, but apparently did not realise that H-Hour had been delayed. When 400 yards offshore, an LCP(L) brought a message that the flotilla should let the LCT(A) wave land first. Since those LCTs were over a mile astern, the 556 Assault Flotilla commander and the infantry battalion commander requested permission to carry on, which was granted. There was no German fire at this point, and as one QORC soldier later recalled it, since the Allied fleet was out of sight due to the waves, there was also an air of unreality.

Arriving at the beach, the flotilla found that the tide had risen to the point where they had to weave in between the obstacles. The German mortars and machine guns were recovering from the bombardment and had begun firing. One soldier, Rifleman Doug Hester of B Company, had the sobering experience as his craft approached the beach of hearing the bullets strike the LCA's armour. Minutes later, B Company landed in front of the German strongpoint of WN-28 at Bernières-sur-Mer, in water up to the troops' armpits and 200m further east than planned. Most of the men on Hester's craft were killed or wounded in the shallows or on the beach. As he described, 'A machine gun firing from the second floor window of the hotel focused on our down-ramp. The three in front of me ... were killed. I jumped out between bursts into their rising blood.'[43]

The troops were in danger of being pinned down on the beach, but help arrived through unexpected circumstances involving one of the landing craft carrying B Company. As it approached the beach, one LCA's rudder jammed, sending it further east. As a result, Lieutenant Hank Elliot and his platoon came ashore with little opposition and were able to attack the strongpoint from the flank, eventually leading the German defenders to begin to surrender.

The LCOCUs also landed with the assault infantry. The rising tide and rough seas prevented the LCOCU teams from clearing many beach obstacles.[44]

The landing craft crewmen were also becoming casualties. Major Elliott Dalton of A Company QORC turned round to ask the coxswain of his craft why they were straying to the east, only to realise that the Marine had been killed by a bullet between the eyes and the LCA had been directing itself. At least three crewmen of 556 Assault Flotilla were killed. Five of its ten craft were lost, with much of the damage occurring after the troops had been landed.

As his craft unbeached, the flotilla officer, Captain Geoffrey William Clelland RM, is said to have stood on its gunwhales and fended off from obstacles with a sounding pole. Three LCAs had to be abandoned on the beach, and two more had been holed and sank soon after unbeaching.[45]

The DD tanks of C Squadron, 10th Canadian Armoured Regiment, were on board eight LCT(3)s of 11 LCT Flotilla. The tanks had been launched as close as 500 yards from the shore, in a 'wet wade' rather than swimming. One LCT landed its DD tanks even further west, on Love Beach. On Nan Red, the DD tanks hit the beach shortly after the infantry, while on Nan White, they beached some ten minutes later, around 08.21.[46]

The LCTs came under considerable enemy fire. After LCT 317 hit a mine while near the beach, it was targeted by German anti-tank guns. One shell killed Stoker 1st Class Dennis Purnell, who was working in the engine room, while another killed Ordinary Seaman Sidney Bartley, who was on deck. LCT 354 came under small-arms fire. The port Oerlikon gun could return fire, but the inexperienced gunner took cover. The craft's other gunner, Able Seaman Franks, changed over from the starboard gun and used the port-side weapon to fire dozens of 20mm rounds at a nearby pillbox. Franks was awarded the Distinguished Service Medal for silencing this enemy position.[47]

Fire-support landing craft – the LCFs and LCG(L)s of 331st Support Squadron – were able to assist the assault companies in overcoming German defences along the beachfront. LCF 21 was called in to help at Bernières, with its commander, Lieutenant Sidney Orum, bringing the craft in so close that it 'grounded for a few minutes and engaged these points with very intense and accurate fire. There is no doubt that this fire was of the greatest value to the Assault Companies.' LCF 32 gave similar supporting fire on Nan Red.[48]

At Juno West, eight LCT(A)s and LCT(HE)s of 103 LCT and 105 LCT(A) Flotillas were carrying Centaur tanks for fire support, plus bulldozers and engineers for obstacle clearance. The exact landing time for these craft is unclear. A few may have been only slightly late, while others arrived around 08.50–09.20, an hour or more after the planned beaching time.

On Nan White, the LCT(A)s hit the beach at 'emergency full ahead' speed, landing their tanks in around 4ft of water. They faced considerable enemy fire, particularly because there was a delay in some tanks landing as they had not warmed up their engines (apparently a mistake on the part of the tank crews). The flotilla officer also noted that the tanks' water-proofing prevented them firing from on board the LCT(A) – a puzzling statement, because that was the express purpose of putting Centaur tanks on board these craft. Although the Centaurs could not yet return fire, the LCT crews engaged German machine-gun positions with their 20mm Oerlikon guns. In the gun battle, two unknown Oerlikon gunners were killed on LCT(A) 2283.[49]

LCT(A) 2009 came under fire, including from a German 75mm gun further west. The flotilla coxswain of 103 LCT Flotilla was killed by a bullet that passed through one of the small apertures in the armoured wheelhouse of the craft. A 75mm shell passed through the thin metal side of the same craft and ended up protruding out of the armour of one of the Centaur tanks on board. It was still there when the tank went ashore. LCT(A) 2009 then had its ramp blown off by a mine. Later, it was refitted with the ramp from another LCT that had been abandoned on the beach.[50]

Malcolm Cook, wireman on LCT(HE) 2306, describes the scene as his craft approached the beach:

The roar and exhaust mingling with the smoke created a great sense of urgency … I made my way to the starboard winch house at the bow … We took up station and almost at once came under heavy machine gun fire from the shore. It sounded pretty scary from inside and something came inboard kicking up an almighty ruckus. We both assumed a position of sitting on our haunches with steel helmet and head lowered to protect the chest and lower abdomen.

After landing the tanks, Cook made his way to the wheelhouse, where he found the skipper had come down from the bridge to seek additional protection and the coxswain was bending over in case enemy bullets came through the vision slits:

The craft was perched at the bow onto the obstacles and was stuck there until a wave lifted it off and then dunked it down on the spikes again. The engines were stalling as the props fouled the obstacles. The stokers were desperately trying to restart them, you could hear the THUNK as the starter engaged. In reality the propellers were being torn off and the hull was being punctured on the obstacles.

With the incoming tide, LCT(HE) 2306 drifted to the west with the wind. The skipper called the Oerlikon gunners into the wheelhouse as they had no targets. An explosion on the craft's port side indicated that they had hit a mine and the LCT sank onto the beach. As the tide came up it flooded the tank deck, eventually reaching the mess deck doorway near the stern, where the crew sheltered until the tide went out again. Naval authorities judged the LCT to be unfit for further service.[51]

The reserve companies of the assault infantry battalions – (C and D) of the Queen's Own Rifles of Canada – were due to land on Nan Red and White at H+20 (08.15). In practice, they arrived at 08.30 on Nan White. These troops were in twelve LCAs, six each from 518 Assault Flotilla (SS *Isle of Guernsey*) and from 506 Assault Flotilla (HMS *Duke of Wellington*) and 518 Assault Flotilla reported that LCG(L)s and LCFs maintained 'very accurate and steady fire' from the flanks as they beached.

Charles Bruce was a coxswain on one of 506 Assault Flotilla's craft. As they headed towards the beach, the waves broke over the bow of the LCA and he was soon saturated by the sea water. He describes looking through the vision slit of his coxswain's position:

> I could see the beach very well, the high concrete sea wall, the large bunkers and dead ahead slightly on our port side a thick concrete pill box ... The obstacles near the beach were slightly visible, pieces of old iron triangular protruding above the slight waves, and I began weaving port-starboard-port-starboard, slow engines and thankfully weaving without mishap, with a shout of 'Down doors'. My bowman swung the inner doors and away went the troops, middle row followed by starboard row finally port side.[52]

Bruce's focus on his duties was so intense that he was unaware of the noise of the naval bombardment until his crewmates told him about it later.

On withdrawing from the beach, Bruce's LCA hit two mines and the crew had to abandon the craft, briefly digging in on the beach to keep safe. They tried to escape out to sea on one LCT but were told by its crew that the craft was sinking. After swimming out to another LCT, they managed to get aboard an LSI. A few hours later, he woke up in a hammock after a well-deserved sleep, having just arrived at Southampton.[53]

Although the troops had a safe landing, the two flotillas lost heavily. Half of their twelve LCAs were sunk or too badly damaged to be recovered by their troop transports. Lieutenant W.J. Turner RNVR, the flotilla officer of 518 Assault Flotilla, later reported that they faced several rows of beach obstacles only 20ft apart and to a depth of 30 yards, with some completely submerged, 'There did not appear to be any gap in these defences so we went through them'. The flotilla officer's craft, LCA 710, struck a mine, which blew in the stern of the craft and killed Stoker 1st Class George William Bush, though the troops were able to get ashore safely.

Returning to SS *Isle of Guernsey* with the crews of two other wrecked LCAs on board – LCA 710 and LCA 650 – LCA 835 also rescued the crew of a sinking craft from HMS *Invicta*, and three crewmen from one of HMS *Duke of Wellington*'s LCAs.

Also due at H+20, the reserve companies (C and D) of the North Shore Regiment landed on Nan Red at 08.45 from twelve LCAs, six craft coming from each of 515 Assault Flotilla (HMS *St Helier*) and 513 Assault Flotilla (HMS *Brigadier*). They landed further west than the first companies and escaped the worst of enemy fire on the beach. Beach obstacles were just visible above the water, but the coxswains managed to avoid them.[54]

Able Seaman Bob Hare of 513 Assault Flotilla was coxswain of one of the LCAs from which some of the classic film footage of D-Day was captured:

> About a week before D-Day four of our landing craft were fitted with News Cameras. We had a practice run so that they could be finally adjusted with the lens directed at the ramp, our instructions were for the cox'n to switch on the camera just as we were about to hit the beach, for there were no cameramen on board.[55]

Due to heavy seas and surf on the beach, most of the film was spoiled by sea water but two of the cameras worked.

LCA 522, in 513 Assault Flotilla, carried special navigational equipment. The crew had been told it must not fall into enemy hands. After the craft hit a mined obstacle and had to be abandoned, two of the crew remained on board to dismantle the equipment, and one – Sub Lieutenant Milne Henry McMaster RNVR – was killed by mortar fire, while another crewman was badly wounded.

The next wave of troops – the Régiment de la Chaudière – was the reserve infantry battalion of 8th Canadian Infantry Brigade. They were due to land at H+45 (08.40) on both Nan Red and Nan White. The craft carrying these troops had departed from their LSIs around two hours previously. Six LCAs of 512 Assault Flotilla (SS *Lady of Mann*) touched down on Nan Red about 08.30. The rest of the regiment landed on Nan White roughly on time in eighteen LCAs: six craft each from 544 Assault Flotilla (SS *Monowai*), 529 Assault Flotilla RCN (HMCS *Prince David*) and 558 Assault Flotilla (SS *Clan Lamont*).

As well as the infantry battalion, the LCAs also carried HQ troops, Royal Canadian Engineers, Royal Navy Beach Commandos and others. One LCA from 544 Assault Flotilla carried Royal Marines of 30 Assault

Unit. This specialist unit had the task of capturing special equipment at the German radar station at Douvres-la-Délivrande, a few miles inland on the eastern side of Juno Beach, although, in practice, the radar station resisted until after D-Day.[56]

Considerable enemy fire was aimed at the landing craft offshore and 544 Assault Flotilla had to beach further east than planned. As the craft travelled parallel to the coast through the Nan Red area to get to their correct landing site, they came under small-arms fire from the shore – possibly from WN-27 at St Aubin.

All the LCAs faced rows of partly submerged beach obstacles. The coxswains tried to weave their craft through the obstructions, which meant they could not deploy their kedge anchors to assist in withdrawing from the beach. In the rough surf and heavy current pushing eastwards, many of the LCAs collided with the obstacles, setting off mines or ripping holes in their bottoms. Some LCAs suffered substantial damage and yet most of the men on board survived, though in several cases the troops had to discard their equipment and swim ashore. In all, 544 Assault Flotilla lost five of the six LCAs that had landed the Régiment de la Chaudière. The crews from these craft remained on the beach for two and a half hours, helping medical personnel there. At least two crewmen from these three flotillas died on D-Day.[57]

Also scheduled for H+45, 48 RM Commando landed at St Aubin (Nan Red) slightly late, at 08.43, in six LCI(S)s of 202 LCI(S) Flotilla. The flotilla officer on board LCI(S) 525 was a Belgian, Commander Georges Gustave Charles Louis Timmermans RNR, the senior officer of the Royal Navy Section Belge (Belgian Section). B Company, the North Shore Regiment, had landed here just over half an hour earlier, but the beach was still a battleground. German defenders in strongpoint WN-27 were still putting up strong resistance and the beach obstacles remained uncleared.

The commandos fired their 2in mortars from the landing craft as they approached the beach to cover their approach. Captain Dan Flunder of 48 RM Commando was on the deck of one of these craft as they approached the beach. 'I didn't realise we were under fire until I saw two men collapse and fall over the starboard side ... I later found three bullet holes in my map case – they must have passed between my arm and my body.'[58]

Like the LCAs just mentioned, the wooden-hulled LCI(S)s suffered considerable damage from mined obstacles. Three of the LCI(S)s hit obstacles and two could not break free and became targets for fire from WN-27. Some of the commandos on board tried to swim to shore but were swept away and drowned. Others were rescued from the stricken vessels by other landing craft. Much of Y Troop ended up on an LCT that took them back to the UK despite their determination to get into action.

After the bows of LCI(S) 539 were badly damaged by a mine, the crew managed to successfully beach stern-first. Three of the craft's crew were killed by German fire, and in response, the commanding officer, Sub Lieutenant William J. Edney RNVR returned fire with one of the craft's 20mm Oerlikon guns (mounted midway along the side of the vessel).[59]

As they landed, the commandos suffered heavy casualties from mortars and machine guns, especially those on the flanks. Lieutenant Colonel Buell, commanding the North Shore Regiment, witnessed some of the commandos being hit by enemy fire as they descended one of the ramps of an LCI(S), '[The] poor devils just folded in the middle and fell overboard as though they were a row of wheat sheaves tumbling into the water. The craft then pulled out, leaving its ramp down and those men who had not been hit, jumped into the water.'[60]

At 09.30, the LCFs and LCG(L)s of 331st Support Flotilla along with LCS(L) 257 supported the advance of 48 RM Commando to the east along the coast. At one point, the craft fired in support of the North Shore Regiment instead. The support craft were still aiding the Royal Marine Commandos at 15.20, when they fired a barrage prior to the commandos making an attack. A Royal Marine signaller on board one of the craft helped co-ordinate the fire support.[61]

THE LANDINGS CONTINUE: 09.00 ONWARDS

We will now consider the landings across the whole of Juno Beach, for the remainder of D-Day. By around H+60 (08.55), the planners had expected that the beach area would have been secured and troops who were not part of the initial assault could start to land. They can be loosely divided into personnel who would be organising the beach area and units who would play roles in continuing the advance inland from Juno Beach. The exact timings for the landings over the following hours are often unclear. In some cases, a group of craft did not all land together, as was originally planned: no doubt congestion on the beach was one factor determining this.

On the eastern side of Juno Beach, the next group of craft beached on time. First, at H+60 (09.05), LCT(5)s 2230 and 2232 of 106 LCT Flotilla arrived at Nan Red carrying first-priority vehicles of the North Shore Regiment and 48 RM Commando. At the same time, four LCT(4)s of 36 LCT Flotilla delivered to Nan White, A Squadron, 10th Canadian

Armoured Regiment, plus priority vehicles from other units. Two of these six craft were too damaged in the process to unbeach.[62]

Due five minutes later at H+65, and landing roughly on time, were two more Royal Navy craft, LCI(S)s 526 and 536, carrying HQ, 4th Special Service Brigade to Nan Red. Four Royal Canadian Navy-manned craft were scheduled at the same time, each to deliver 160 or more British and Canadian Beach Group troops, including engineers and pioneers: LCI(L)s 121 and 299 to Nan Red and LCI(L)s 249 and 301 to Nan White.

Faced with rows of beach obstacles, the LCI(L)s aimed to break through them at full speed, 16 knots. Half a mile off the beach, a wave knocked off one ramp from LCI(L) 121, taking with it the first lieutenant, who was then swept under the vessel. He fortunately had the presence of mind to dive clear of the propellers and was later returned to his ship after being fished out of the sea by a passing LCA. LCI(L) 121 continued to the beach, where it struck a mined obstacle that blew a 10ft by 5ft hole in the ship's side, killing at least five soldiers and seriously wounding several more (none of the crew became casualties). LCI(L) 121 remained on the shore under enemy fire for two and a half hours while the wounded soldiers were treated.

LCI(L) 249 also had a hole blown in its bows by a mine, but without any casualties on board. Withdrawing from the beach, the vessel acquired eight more holes from collisions with obstacles, three of them in the engine room. With the engine flooded, the craft had to be taken under tow by LCI(L) 298. The other two LCI(L)s had more straightforward beachings, although LCI(L) 298's bow Oerlikon gunner had traded fire with a German sniper at a house further inland and mortar fire on the beach intensified the longer the LCI(L)s lingered there.[63]

Meanwhile, on the western half of Juno Beach, six LCT(4)s from 20 and 31 LCT Flotillas brought ashore the M7 Priest 105mm self-propelled guns of 12th Field Regiment RCA on Mike Red and Green, with half the craft on each beach. As they came ashore at around their scheduled time of H+75 (09.00), several LCTs set off mines. This left LCT 500 badly damaged and unable to leave the beach for several days until it was repaired. LCT 677 received multiple holes in its bottom, just missing the fuel tanks. Its starboard propeller was damaged, meaning that it had to return to the UK on only one engine. The 12th Field Regiment's guns now gave the army the capability to provide artillery support from units ashore rather than having to rely solely on the navy's guns. On both beaches they were accompanied by another LCT carrying mainly Beach Group and divisional personnel (such as signals troops). They were slow to unload their vehicles and were still hampered by congestion on the beach and the presence of many mined beach obstacles. The artillery was soon in action, firing on enemy positions inland.[64]

Accompanying the LCTs was LCI(L) 117 from 260 LCI(L) Flotilla RCN. The LCI(L) was hit by machine-gun fire, though without any casualties. It took twenty-five minutes to unload the vessel, partly because it had lost one of its two ramps in a collision with another craft as it approached the beach, but also because many of the troops being landed were struggling with bulky, awkward equipment. The troops were mostly Beach Group personnel (such as men from 8th Battalion, the King's Regiment), pioneers, Royal Engineers and Royal Canadian Engineers. Around the same time on Nan Green, LCT 2079 delivered priority vehicles for the Regina Rifles, as well as men of 6th Field Company, Royal Canadian Engineers.[65]

Both regiments of self-propelled artillery on Juno East were scheduled to arrive at the same time of H+75 (09.10). These two units were on board sixteen LCTs. Half of them – eight LCT(4)s of 22 and 30 LCT Flotillas – carried 14th Field Regiment RCA to Nan White. The regiment landed there from 09.25, under some shell and machine-gun fire, and found the beach very congested with vehicles. LCT 524 was recorded as being left damaged beyond immediate repair.[66]

The other eight LCT(4)s from the same two flotillas were bound for Nan Red at H+90, loaded with 19th Field Regiment RCA, plus priority vehicles of the 7th Canadian Infantry Brigade. The first guns of this unit began coming ashore at 09.45, slightly later than planned, and the last landed in mid-afternoon.

The first troops ashore had several casualties from mortars on landing, but the first gun was in action from just behind the beach ten minutes later. LCT(4)s 782, 881 and 882 carried further vehicles to Nan White at H+90, including the 40mm Crusader self-propelled anti-aircraft guns of the 114th Light Anti-Aircraft Regiment.[67]

Despite the Canadian troops flooding ashore, there were still some German troops holding out in the beachfront area on Nan Red (St Aubin). Just before midday, LCT 707, which had delivered vehicles of 19th Field Regiment RCA was broached-to on the beach. German soldiers had infiltrated back into a mortar position only 15 yards from the craft and began firing at it and a dramatic exchange of fire ensued. One mortar bomb landed on the LCT's deck, but Leading Stoker Gamble threw it overboard. Another sailor, Leading Wireman Pettett, engaged the enemy position with the port Oerlikon, but the gun jammed, and he was killed by enemy rifle fire. The LCT's commanding officer, Lieutenant Alfred

William Everton Hollands RNVR, engaged the German troops with the craft's Lanchester submachine gun (LCTs were typically supplied with one of these weapons for emergency use). Hollands was mortally wounded by one of several mortar bombs that struck the craft. The first lieutenant, Midshipman Fowler RNVR, ordered the crew to go ashore, found an army doctor to care for the wounded and sourced a bulldozer to help push the LCT back out to sea. Once successfully under way, Fowler discovered that the craft's steering was not responding (unbeknown to him, both rudders had been sheared off when landing). He managed to steer the LCT back to the Solent using its engines alone.[68]

The second unit of M7 Priest self-propelled guns was now timetabled to land on Juno West: 13th Field Regiment RCA, due to come ashore on Mike Beach at H+105 (09.30). They were on board six more LCT(4)s of 31 LCT Flotilla. Other craft from that flotilla had delivered the 12th Field Regiment at H+75. They were accompanied by LCT(4) 528 and LCI(L) 177, both of which carried Beach Group personnel plus elements of a few units of 7th Canadian Infantry Brigade. Many of these craft landed their cargoes later than planned. Congestion on the beach meant that the first of 13th Field Regiment's three batteries only landed at around 13.38, and came ashore further east than planned, on Nan Green. The other two batteries landed around 15.00. LCI(L) 177 also landed later than planned.[69]

LCT(4) 575 broke its back because of the strain of drying out on the beach. Nearby, Wireman Don Bass of LCT(4) 574 wondered about the buzzing noise he could hear. A Canadian Army officer pointedly told him that the sound was bullets fired by a sniper from a nearby pillbox. The Canadian enlisted nearby troops to deal with this threat.

At some point during the day, LCT(4) 717, from 31 LCT Flotilla, beached next to LCT 574, possibly on Mike Beach – it is not clear what LCT 717 was carrying or when it was scheduled to beach. As the tide receded, LCT 717 settled onto a mine, which exploded under the engine room, killing two men working there: Petty Officer Motor Mechanic Charles Harold Lethbridge and Stoker 1st Class Thomas McCormick. Don Bass volunteered to recover their bodies, 'not realising at first what a gruesome job this was to be'.

Other members of LCT 717's crew were wounded, and for shelter, were brought on board LCT 574. By early afternoon, it was stranded on the beach. Later in the day, a German FW 190 fighter aircraft dropped a bomb alongside the beached vessel, which caused additional casualties, including killing Leading Motor Mechanic Kenneth Roy Johnson of LCT 574. The dead were later buried at sea.[70]

Continued German resistance in places, damage inflicted by remaining German beach obstacles and slower than expected progress in opening exits leading inland led to considerable vehicle congestion along Juno Beach. Five exits off the beach had been established by 10.40 on Nan Red and White, while on Mike Beach one exit was set up by 11.12. At about 10.30, in the eastern half of Juno, craft arriving began to be diverted to Nan White, and at 14.00 Nan Red was closed to landings. Obstacle-clearance teams focused on opening up Nan White.[71]

LCI(L) 285, carrying Beach Group personnel, and seven more LCT(4)s, mostly of 36 LCT Flotilla, were due at H+135 (10.00) on Juno West. The LCTs were transporting Beach Group and 7th Infantry Brigade vehicles. They were almost certainly all delayed due to congestion on the beach. By this point, according to the timetable for the landings, the whole of the 7th and 8th Infantry Brigades should have landed on Juno West and East respectively, along with their supporting units, such as artillery, and the Beach Group personnel under their command.

High tide was over the next few hours, meaning the beach would be very small and there was a risk of landing craft being stranded as the tide started to recede, so according to the timetable, there was a pause in the scheduled landings. In practice, some landing craft seem to have continued beaching because they were behind schedule, as the need to put their cargoes ashore outweighed the risk that the craft might get stranded on the beach.

At least one of the seven LCTs was left on the beach by the receding tide. The first lieutenant of LCT(4) 770, Sub Lieutenant Henry Smith RNVR later recalled how the whole crew gathered around the engines, hoping that their bulk would offer some additional protection in case of enemy fire.[72]

There was still an enormous amount of activity offshore, however. Now the Canadians had gained a foothold ashore, the waters off Juno Beach were safer, but the troop transports (LSI) were too deep-draughted and too valuable to be brought near the beach. Personnel still on board were to be unloaded from the LSIs and landed by LCAs or LCTs but may have been put ashore by LCI(L)s instead, and three LCMs were also to be available. Some of these were craft that would remain off the French coast for weeks after D-Day, as part of the Ferry Service. Others made one or two more trips, before returning to the UK later on D-Day or the next day.

This stage of the landings could not be planned in such detail. It was, of course, impossible to forecast which landing craft might be out of action after their first trip to the beach, so whichever craft became available for ferrying duties were allocated to land the next serial of troops according to whatever was judged the highest priority. Several of the ships had substantial numbers of troops on board, in proportion to their size – over 700 on SS *Monowai*, for example.

In Assault Group J2, by 10.30 only two LCI(S)s and one LCT had reported for ferry duties and been allocated to unload ships. Later, three LCTs that had lost their bow doors reported for duty but were not used for ferrying troops as their tank decks were awash. All of that group's remaining troops had been disembarked from their ships by 14.30. Some LCTs that were to collect troops from larger ships first had to offload wounded, further delaying the operation. MV *Llangibby Castle* reported that it was unable to use its lower sally ports to load troops onto ferry craft as the LCTs were rising and falling so much in the rough seas.[73]

Troops landed in these later waves from the LSI included many Beach Group personnel, including from Royal Engineer Field Companies, Pioneer Corps companies and 5th Royal Berkshires, one of the Beach Group protection battalions. Other units represented included men from Ordnance Beach Detachments, Detail Issuing Depots and Petrol Depots: these unit names hint at their essential logistical functions that would be vital to sustaining the advance from Juno Beach.

British airborne troops were also landed here, for example, from 4 Airlanding Anti-Tank Battery and 195 Airlanding Field Ambulance. Not all airborne soldiers could be landed by air on D-Day. These men had to make their way over land to the landing zones of British 6th Airborne Division, once Juno and Sword beaches had been linked up to create a route through.

The reserve infantry brigade group, based around the 9th Canadian Infantry Brigade, next started to arrive. This was the third of 3rd Canadian Division's three infantry brigades and was embarked on the naval force Assault Group J3, which was divided into several convoys. Convoy J-13 included the LSI(H) HMS *Royal Ulsterman*, carrying HQ staff of British I Corps, of Canadian 3rd Infantry Division and of Canadian 9th Infantry Brigade. This ship was available as a standby HQ ship, in case one of the other HQ ships was out of action. The troops on board were put ashore by the end of the morning, using the ship's own LCAs (555 Assault Flotilla).

Also in Convoy J-13 were eleven LCI(L)s and twenty LCT(4)s of 35 and 37 LCT Flotillas, carrying respectively the 9th Canadian Infantry Brigade Group's foot personnel and vehicles. Four LCT(3)s mainly carried stores, LCFs 24 and 29 provided additional anti-aircraft defence and one LCT(R) carried rockets to reload the LCT(R)s that had fired just before H-Hour. Two further convoys formed from LSTs would arrive later.[74]

The brigade's three infantry battalions were scheduled to land at H+150 (10.25) on Juno East from eleven LCI(L)s of 262 LCI(L) Flotilla, manned by the Royal Canadian Navy. On D-Day, the troops began landing about an hour later than this and were all ashore by around 11.50. The Stormont, Dundas and Glengarry Highlanders had to land on Nan White, alongside the other two battalions, rather than on Nan Red as planned due to continuing German resistance there. The brigade's objective was to strike inland as fast as possible, not to subdue the coastal defences. The Highland Light Infantry of Canada and the North Nova Scotia Highlanders came ashore alongside them.[75]

The flotilla's commanding officers drove their craft well up the beach to land the troops as safely and quickly as possible. In fact, although five sailors received shrapnel wounds from enemy fire, there were apparently no casualties to the troops during the landing. The high tide meant there was only a narrow beach, leading to – as the war diary of the Highland Light Infantry of Canada described it – 'an awful shambles' as troops waited to move inland through the limited exits. It often took thirty minutes or more to unload, partly because on some craft the troops had over 100 bicycles, which had to be landed via the LCI(L)s' side ramps.[76]

All but one of the flotilla's eleven LCI(L)s were damaged as they beached or unbeached. Four craft had major damage and flooded engine rooms and had to spend two days on the beach carrying out repairs, before they were able to return to the UK. On the beach, the crews managed to repair the holes caused by mines by stuffing them with blankets, mattresses and gas capes, even using cement and timber to patch them up. In a spare moment, the crews had a game of baseball.

At high tide, around 23.00 on 8 June, bulldozers operating on the beach helped the LCI(L)s get afloat again.[77] One of these craft was LCI(L) 270. Arriving at the beach on D-Day, it hit five obstacles, resulting in a 4ft-wide hole in its bows. The craft's commanding officer had wisely brought the troops on deck rather than keeping them in the troop space, as he judged that there was more risk to the soldiers from the craft hitting a mine than from enemy fire on deck. As a result, there were no casualties among the troops. While the crew carried out repair work to the craft, the Royal Engineers cleared forty-three shells and mines from obstacles within 25 yards of the craft.

As LCI(L) 270 left the beach on 8 June, after spending sixty hours stranded ashore, German aircraft dropped anti-personnel bombs in the area, one of which struck 270 near the bridge, slightly wounding four of the crew. The four craft anchored off Normandy until the afternoon of 9 June. Their crews had burned their signals books and charts in case of an enemy counter-attack while they were on the beach, so they had to borrow charts for the return journey. Finally, they reached the UK at 10.20 on 10 June 1944.[78]

A variety of supporting vehicles were due to land on Juno East at or from H+180. Six LCT(4)s of 35 LCT Flotilla were to carry priority vehicles of the Canadian 9th Infantry Brigade and Canadian 3rd Infantry Division to Nan Red but were moved to Nan White instead. These troops were extremely varied and from dozens of units, ranging from two men with a handcart, to jeeps, universal carriers equipped with mortars or a 6-pounder anti-tank gun, to 3-ton or 15-cwt general service lorries and even a few M10 self-propelled anti-tank guns.

Twelve more LCTs (mostly from 37 LCT Flotilla) were to land vehicles at Nan White. Nine of these vessels carried the 27th Canadian Armoured Regiment, which was to support the 9th Canadian Infantry Brigade's infantry units. The other three had embarked vehicles from the Canadian 9th Infantry Brigade and Canadian 3rd Infantry Division. An additional two LCT(4)s – LCT 781 and 761 – delivered an RAF fighter direction unit. By 14.00 all these vehicles were ashore. To anyone with time to spare to watch the stream of landings, it must have seemed a bewildering variety of troops and vehicles.[79]

Four LCT(3)s, each carrying 190 tons of stores, were due to land across the whole of Juno Beach from H+240 (11.55): LCTs 302 and 413 in the west and LCTs 474 and 7011 to the east. The supplies they would deliver were for use until supply depots had been established on land and they would be unloaded by RASC vehicles. As the Canadian 8th Infantry Brigade had instructed its units, 'Ammunition is the priority store on D-Day'. Units of the brigade were ordered to land with enough other stores and supplies for the first two days, so this was more of an emergency reserve. Bert Poole, who served on LCT 7011, recalled that it took several days to unload fully.[80]

Efforts continued to clear substantial gaps in the beach obstacles and establish more beach exits. Landing craft – mainly LCTs – were allowed to beach in the gaps between obstacles. Nan Red remained closed to landings completely at 14.00, and obstacle-clearance efforts were focused on Nan White. At 15.30, Mike was declared clear of obstacles.

Another factor was the falling tide (low water would be around 18.00). At 15.00 the DSOAG Mike Red decided to beach the maximum number of LCTs on the falling tide and leave them to dry out on the beach, accepting that it was more important to unload them promptly than to ensure they had a speedy return to the UK. From around 12.00, as the tide began to go out, a key concern was to unload the LSTs that were beginning to arrive. In anticipation of the LSTs' arrival, the LCP(Sy) which had arrived at the start of D-Day with the DD tanks began surveying for the most suitable places to beach these ships at high water.[81]

The twelve LSTs towing Rhino Ferries were due off the beach at 10.30 as Convoy J-15. In fact, their arrival was delayed about fifty minutes but the Rhino Ferries had survived the crossing. Convoy J-16 consisted of ten more LSTs and two Rhino Ferries. It arrived on time around 13.30, having lost one Rhino during the crossing.

As these larger ships began to arrive they were directed to mine-swept anchorages. The strong wind led to the tows to some Rhinos parting or caused some LSTs to drag their anchors. As more LSTs arrived, congestion in the LST anchorage became problematic. LSTs began to be unloaded by Rhino Ferry, with the Rhinos setting off for the beach at 15.00 off Nan and at 15.45 off Mike.[82]

Corporal John Bright, a wireless operator in the Royal Corps of Signals attached to the Canadian 3rd Division, described the scene as he came ashore on a Rhino around this time near Bernières-sur-Mer, 'Crippled landing craft at odd angles, abandoned tanks and vehicles, bodies on the beach and floating in the water, smoke and fires everywhere and above it all the noise, noise, noise [of gunfire]'.[83]

The first convoy from the follow-up forces (Force L) was due around 15.00. Designated Group L1 (expressed by the US Navy in the phonetic alphabet as the romantically titled 'Love One Convoy'), it was primarily carrying vehicles of British 51st (Highland) Infantry Division. The convoy included thirteen LSTs, which were carrying LCVPs that would be left at Normandy – though not necessarily all at Juno Beach – for use with the ferry service. Several of these carried HQ staff from the British Second Army and the 21st Army Group. An additional LST (LST 981, US Navy) was part of Group L1 but had hit a mine during the journey to Normandy. The ship managed to return to Portsmouth. Also in the convoy were seven LCI(L)s, the LSD HMS *Northway*, carrying forty-six DUKWs loaded with stores, and four preloaded stores coasters for Juno Beach.[84]

Convoy L-3, the second convoy from follow-up Force L, arrived off Juno Beach just before midnight on D-Day and anchored about 1.5 miles off the beach. It included ten LCI(L)s and fifteen US Navy-manned LSTs, as well as three British-built LST(1)s. A group of LCT(3)s that crossed with the convoy were to go to Gold Beach. The commander of L-3 was keen to dry the LSTs out to speed up unloading, but the Force J staff wanted to continue unloading by Rhino.[85]

The process of unloading from LSTs proved to be very slow, partly because some Rhinos dried out on the beach, had engine breakdowns or broached-to (many of the accompanying Rhino tugs, which helped steer the larger ferries, had been lost in the crossing). The first Rhinos headed for the beach at 15.00, but by 16.30 there were now thirty-five LSTs awaiting to unload, carrying over 8,000 personnel and over 2,000 vehicles. Low water at around 18.00 imposed another pause in beachings.

When high water arrived, at 23.00, only two LSTs waiting off Juno had been fully unloaded. An air raid and smoke covering the area hampered the work of the Rhinos. At 23.11, poor weather halted the unloading from Rhinos on Nan Green, and by the next morning, several Rhinos had broached-to on Juno Beach.

In the final hour of D-Day, the slowness of unloading from LSTs led the army to make priority requests for the tanks and HQ of Canadian 2nd Armoured Brigade and anti-tank guns. Both were needed to meet the anticipated German counter-attack against Juno Beach. This caused further disruption to the sequence of landings.[86]

Around 19.00, a new type of vessel was due off Juno Beach, in Convoy JM-1 – landing barges. This convoy comprised nine LBVs, preloaded with 450 tons of stores, escorted by four LBFs for protection against air attack. The main component of Convoy JM-2 was ferry craft for use in unloading larger ships and was due at 21.30. It consisted of ninety-six LCMs, and eighty LCVPs, which were relatively small craft to cross the Channel independently. More ferry craft were due at 22.30 in Convoy JM-3: twenty-four loaded LBVs and nine unloaded LBVs, six LBEs, two LBWs and eighteen LBOs.

Most of the barges in these convoys were delayed and arrived overnight. The Commander Force J judged the landing barges' crossing to be 'a very fine performance'. Some craft and crews were lost in the difficult conditions. Overnight, as they would also do on subsequent nights, LCP(L)s of 703 and 705 Assault Flotillas made smoke to screen the Juno anchorage during an air raid. There were 'night defence lines' around the anchorage, with German E-boats operating beyond.[87]

The work of the LCP(Sy)s continued into D+1, with LCP(L) assisting, for example by carrying buoys. On D-Day, after surveying for places to beach LSTs, they marked with buoys a channel off both Mike and Nan beaches that avoided the rocky outcrops off the coast. They also marked a channel for DUKWs to use from Nan White to the coaster anchorage and buoyed-out the Gooseberry anchorage. Next, they marked the position for the Gooseberry itself: in other words, the positions where a line of ships would be sunk to form a sheltered anchorage off the beach. Then they surveyed and marked a channel into the small port of Courseulles, anticipating its use for unloading.[88]

Force J's report on Operation Neptune refers to the 'unexpectedly feeble effort of the enemy coast and beach defences', which reminds the reader that Force J's landing craft crews could have faced an even tougher challenge. Whether considering the threat from beach obstacles or enemy actions, 'unexpectedly feeble' was probably not a phrase many of the crews or the troops they put ashore would have used, however. The tally of lost landing craft tells a clear story: of the 168 LCAs used at Juno, thirty-six craft (21 per cent) were lost or damaged; the figures for LCTs of all types was forty-two out of 150 (28 per cent). In many cases, these losses did not prevent the troops on board being put ashore, and some of these craft could be recovered and repaired. Almost every incident would have been a traumatic one for the crew concerned, however, even if they did not become casualties.[89]

Men of the Canadian 9th Infantry Brigade board LCI(L) 276 using the ramps by which they would land on Juno Beach at H+150. LCI(L) 252 is in the background: both were Royal Canadian Navy craft from 262 LCI(L) Flotilla. (Gilbert Alexander Milne/Canada Dept of National Defence/Library and Archives Canada/PA-132811)

Landing craft crews often got to know the troops they carried after spending several days together in a confined space before D-Day, and sometimes in joint training. Here, a US Coast Guardsman (left) entertains troops of the US 90th Infantry Division with his gramophone. (US National Archives 205578570/026-G-037-020-001)

Wrecked vehicles on Omaha Beach (including RAF Crossley trucks), probably on 7 June 1944. The uncleared German beach obstacles hint at the challenge faced by landing craft crews in touching down through these defences. An LST is beached in the distance. (US Naval History & Heritage Command, NH 80-G-45714)

Common in German coastal defences, 5cm anti-tank guns like this one at Ver-sur-Mer (Gold Beach) were a threat to both tanks and landing craft. The bunker's concrete wall to seaward (left) sheltered the gun from Allied naval bombardment, but it could fire along the beach in both directions. (IWM B 5252)

One of the most famous photographs of D-Day: 'Into the Jaws of Death' by Chief Photographer's Mate Robert F. Sargent USCGR. Men of the 1st Battalion, US 16th Infantry wade ashore at Omaha Beach, seen from the coxswain's position on an LCVP of USS *Samuel Chase* at about 08.00. (US Naval History & Heritage Command, NH 26-G-2343)

Canadian troops, some with bicycles, come ashore from LCI(L) 299 of the Royal Canadian Navy at Bernières-sur-Mer on the morning of D-Day. Soldiers are steadying themselves on the two lifelines that crewmen have taken ashore. (Gilbert Alexander Milne/Canada Dept of National Defence/ Library and Archives Canada/PA-122765)

LCT(4) 1006 and a second LCT(4) on D-Day just off Nan White, Juno Beach, still carrying vehicles of the 27th Canadian Armoured Regiment and the North Nova Scotia Highlanders, to land at H+180. (Gilbert Alexander Milne/Canada Dept of National Defence/Library and Archives Canada/ PA-137018)

Men of 47 RM Commando land on Jig Green from an LCA of 502 Assault Flotilla (HMS *Prinses Josephine Charlotte*) around 09.50 on D-Day. The commandos had a difficult landing, with many casualties and craft lost. LCT(4) 858 behind was still stuck on the beach after landing at about 08.25. (IWM B 5245)

The battle-damaged US Coast Guard-crewed LCI(L) 85 off Omaha Beach on D-Day. After beaching on Easy Red around 08.30, the craft was hit by machine-gun fire and shells. The many casualties were transferred to another ship before the LCI(L) sank. (US National Archives 205578816/026-G-038-030-001)

US troops board an LCVP while it is hoisted on the davits of an attack transport ship. Known as rail-loading, this was much easier than if the men had to climb down a net into the craft. The coxswain's position can be seen on the left. (US National Archives 205578419/026-G-036-017-001)

M7 Priest self-propelled guns of the 13th Field Regiment RCA come ashore from LCT(4) 574 at Juno Beach: note the uncleared beach obstacles. Scheduled to beach at H+105 (09.30), this craft probably landed later on D-Day. Several dried-out LCTs can just be seen beyond the obstacles. (The D-Day Story, Portsmouth, 2014/147/8)

US troops come ashore from US Navy LCM(3)s at Tare Green, Utah Beach, on 8 June 1944. This illustrates the flat terrain of Utah, with few landmarks, apart from a single house in this case. (US Naval History & Heritage Command/US National Archives, NH 80-G-252624)

A US Navy LCT(5) ferries US Army jeeps ashore from a larger transport ship, possibly the one visible behind. This is clearly after D-Day, since the LCT's 20mm Oerlikons are covered over and the crew seem relaxed about enemy threats. (Conseil Régional de Basse-Normandie/US National Archives)

LCT(A) 2008 ferries foot troops ashore after 6 June 1944. On D-Day, this craft was delayed from its planned beaching time of H-Hour, then lost its ramp while landing wading Sherman tanks of the 741st Tank Battalion on Omaha Beach. (US Naval History & Heritage Command/US National Archives, NH 80-G-252719)

A GMC truck transfers from LCT(6) 535 of the US Navy to a pontoon causeway at Normandy, days after D-Day. NL pontoons like this one were assembled from the same components as Rhino Ferries but were connected to the shore. (Conseil Régional de Basse-Normandie/US National Archives)

British vehicles including a Sherman tank of HQ 8th Armoured Brigade transfer from US Coast Guard LST(2) 21 onto a Rhino Ferry, off the Normandy coast. Using the Rhino meant the LST did not need to beach, and therefore could unload more rapidly. (US Naval History & Heritage Command/US Coast Guard Collection at US National Archives, NH 26-G-2370)

Royal Navy LCT(5) 2130 alongside a Spud pierhead at the Mulberry Harbour at Arromanches. A crane is unloading stores from the LCT onto waiting trucks, which would carry them inland. The Mulberry Harbour sped up unloading, though not all Allied naval commanders were in favour of it. (The D-Day Story, Portsmouth, 2005/135)

Crewmen take a break on LCT(5) 2130, amid piles of stores on the craft's tank deck, presumably unloaded from a large ship offshore, in August 1944. At least one group of landing craft crew who went ashore in Normandy were arrested by Military Police for being improperly dressed. (The D-Day Story, Portsmouth, 2005/143)

A crane unloads netted stores from US Navy LCT(6) 583, dried out on a Normandy beach, 15 June 1944. Hinged 'Mulock extensions' can be seen on the end of the LCT's ramp: these decreased its angle for easier unloading of vehicles. (US Naval History & Heritage Command/US National Archives, NH 80-G-253001)

The various units organising the beaches were essential to receive and manage everything the landing craft put ashore. Here, personnel of the Uncle Red Beach HQ at La Grande Dune, Utah Beach, line the back of the beach. Beach Exit 2 is on the right. (Conseil Régional de Basse-Normandie/ US National Archives)

US forces arrive at the St Laurent exit on Easy Red, Omaha Beach, soon after D-Day. DUKWs and LCTs of various types can be seen near the beach, while larger ships are at anchor off the coast. (US Naval History & Heritage Command/US Army Signal Corps Collection at US National Archives, NH SC 193082)

On 2 August 1944, a Sherman tank of the French 2nd Armoured Division lands on Utah Beach from LST(2) 517, which has beached at the water's edge. Planners had been reluctant to risk LSTs drying out on the beach, but they proved tough enough to do so. (Conseil Régional de Basse-Normandie/ US National Archives)

An international gathering of LCI(S) officers at Buckingham Palace shortly after
VE-Day, when Commander Georges Timmermans RNR (centre, with his wife,
Marie-Louise) was decorated with the DSC for service at Normandy, including
command of 202 LCI(S) Flotilla. He later became the first commodore of the post-war
Belgian Navy. Commander Rupert Curtis RNVR (left) was similarly decorated for
leading 200 LCI(S) Flotilla and went on to document the wartime role of these craft.
Lieutenant Nigel Cromar RNVR (second from left) had survived the explosion of his
craft LCI(S) 524 off Sword Beach on D-Day. Lieutenant Chris Berg RNZVR (right)
had been the commanding officer of LCI(S) 505. (The D-Day Story, Portsmouth,
1992/275/276/80)

Landing diagrams and more detailed landing tables form the basis for the D-Day section of this book. This example shows 16th Regimental Combat Team on Omaha East. Each line is a different wave, each symbol represents an individual landing craft. (John William Boehne III Collection, AFC/2001/001/31844, Veterans History Project, US Library of Congress)

10

Sword Beach

All hell let loose with L.C.I.(S)s strewn about at all angles and troops storming beach.

Petty Officer Motor Mechanic J.E. Burton, LCI(S) 535[1]

H-Hour on Sword Beach was set for 07.25. Around two hours before that, three German torpedo boats had burst through the smokescreen that low-flying Allied aircraft had laid to screen Force S from the German gun batteries at Le Havre. Approaching Force S from the east, they fired eighteen torpedoes, one of which struck HMNoS *Svenner* and the destroyer sank with the loss of forty-three crew. Several other torpedoes narrowly missed other vessels, including the Force S HQ ship HMS *Largs*. Accompanying *Largs* were the six LSIs transporting the assault infantry brigade and supporting troops. Damaging these vulnerable ships could have seriously disrupted the landings.[2]

Queen sector of Sword Beach was 3,000 yards wide, but the assault would be launched against a frontage of only 1,600 yards, in turn divided into Queen Red in the east and Queen White in the west. The landing beach was relatively narrow because sandbanks to the east and low cliffs to the west made adjacent areas unsuitable. Consequently, the British 3rd Infantry Division landed on a one-brigade front, rather than a two-brigade one like Juno, Gold and Omaha beaches. Along with Utah, Sword was one of the two beaches added in early 1944, when the newly appointed Allied commanders expanded the COSSAC plan from three to five assault divisions.

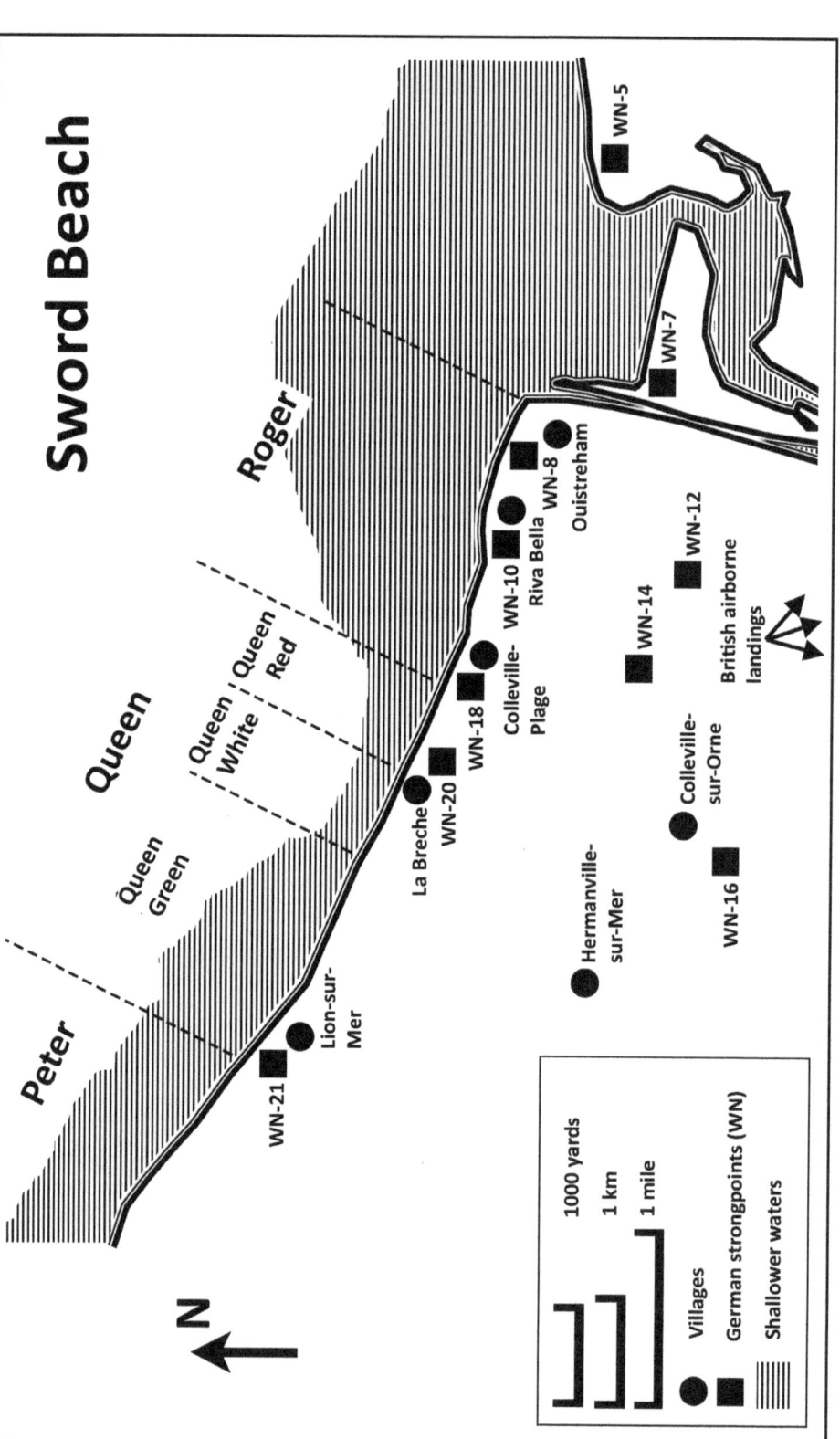

Sword Beach: Map approximately to scale. Some details omitted for clarity. (Map primarily based on: Ford, Ken, *Sword Beach (Battlezone Normandy)* (Stroud: Sutton, 2004); Chazette, *Atlantikwall Gold – Juno – Sword*)

The core of the first group of craft was designated Group 1 (not to be confused with the convoy numbers for Sword Beach, which began with 'S'). It included eight LCT(3)s of 14 LCT Flotilla carrying DD tanks. Also with this group were three LCG(L)s and three LCS(L)s to provide close-in fire support. Marking the Launching Position for DD tanks was mini-submarine X23, which had surfaced 7,000 yards out after spending forty-eight hours submerged off the French coast. Faced with rough seas, the naval commander decided that it was too risky to launch the DD tanks at the planned distance from the beach. Instead, the tanks would launch from closer in, at 5,000 yards, which they did at around 06.15.[3]

Next came Group 2, which were the first landing craft intended to deposit their cargoes on the beach. This group comprised the main body of the assault troops who, at H-Hour, would fight their way ashore. With the assistance of the DD tanks that were due to have landed seven and a half minutes before H-Hour, if all went well, they would subdue the enemy's beach defences. Twenty LCAs carrying the assault infantry formed the core of this assault wave.

One infantry battalion was to land on each beach: 1st Battalion, South Lancashire Regiment (1st South Lancs), on Queen White and 2nd Battalion, East Yorkshire Regiment (2nd East Yorks), on Queen Red. Each battalion had two of its four companies in the first assault wave and two following soon after in the next wave. A and C Companies of 1st South Lancs were carried by 535 Assault Flotilla from HMS *Glenearn*. A and B Companies of 2nd East Yorks would be landed by 536 Assault Flotilla from SS *Empire Cutlass*.[4]

Supporting the assault infantry in Group 2 were ten LCTs carrying AVREs and flail tanks to deal with bunkers, beach obstacles, minefields and other defences on and behind the beach. Scheduled to accompany them were eight LCT(A)s or LCT(HE)s and one LCT(CB), all of which carried tanks to provide fire support from on board the craft. Two LCFs escorted the group to guard against air attack.

It had been planned that the LCAs would rendezvous with these supporting LCTs off the beach. Six LCT(A)s and the lone LCT(CB) were late but generally managed to get into formation before touchdown. The remaining two LCT(A)s did not arrive in time for the assault. The LCAs of 536 Assault Flotilla were also initially delayed but managed to make up time before beaching.[5]

1st South Lancs were allowed to stand up for the first part of passage to the beach, while there was minimal danger from enemy fire, and 'the men kept cheerful singing songs in chorus'. As the assault wave made its way to the water's edge, a barrage of gunfire was directed at the beach, including from fire-support landing craft. As well as the LCT(A)s, LCT(CB) and LCA(HR)s just mentioned, there were three LCG(L)s, three LCS(L)(2)s, five LCT(R)s and eighteen LCTs carrying self-propelled guns. Each type was in a specific position relative to the assault troops, began firing at a specific time and had its own targets. In the absence of enemy air attack at this point, the LCFs were also potentially available for supporting fire but were not used.[6]

First of the support craft to fire were LCG(L)s 9, 10 and 11 with their 4.7in guns. They were due to begin firing from H−45. However, at H−65 (06.20), the LCG(L)s opened fire with a few rounds after they were fired on from a large house to the east of the beach. From H−55 to H−15, two of these craft fired against Queen White and the third at Queen Red. They were using high-explosive shells as their main aim was to help suppress the defenders.

To avoid hitting the assault troops, they transferred their fire to German defences on the flanks, now switching to armour-piercing ammunition for greater effect against concrete emplacements, as well as firing remaining high-explosive ammunition indirectly at targets behind the beachfront houses, which could not be reached by direct fire. They could only fire in brief intervals when the smoke along the beach cleared to reveal their targets. They were said to have destroyed 'a strong point centred in a field and a pill box', while LCG(L)s 9 and 10 responded to small-arms fire in the Ouistreham area.[7]

Then, at about 06.48, the 7th, 33rd and 76th Field Regiments RA contributed shells from their self-propelled guns to the barrage. They were still on board their LCT(4)s: eighteen craft from 32 and 38 LCT Flotillas, together designated Group 4 with each regiment on six LCTs. The 76th Field Regiment fired on Queen White and the other two regiments shelled Queen Red, conducting what was known as the run-in shoot. After ranging shots at 10,000 yards or more, their bombardment began with the LCTs closing steadily on the beach all the time. The fall of shot was to be observed by FOOs in LCP(L)s nearer the shore. After a pause at H−10, for five minutes before H-Hour the guns fired at targets further inland. The LCTs then turned back out to sea as the guns would land later in the morning.[8]

The fire of each Royal Artillery regiment was directed by a FOO on an LCP(L) closer to shore, though they were hampered because the rough seas had knocked out their navigational equipment. Two of these craft, LCP(L)s 309 and 312, carrying the FOOs of the 76th and 33rd Field

Regiments respectively, were destroyed by shells early on D-Day. They were, in fact, part of the most numerous group of landing craft in these first two groups.

With Group 1, there were around twenty LCP(L)s, from 704 and 707 LCP(L) Flotillas. These small and easily overlooked craft were jacks of all trades. One of their main roles – smoke-laying – was not called for on D-Day, but they did play an important role in rescuing the crews of sunken DD tanks. Two were designated LCP(L)(N), the 'N' standing for Navigation, as their role was to lead the swimming DD tanks to Queen White or Queen Red.[9]

Next, it was the turn of the pair of Centaur tanks of the 5th Royal Marine Independent Armoured Support Battery which were on board each LCT(A) or LCT(HE) to fire, and from around H–30 they targeted specific bunkers. The tanks on the accompanying LCT(CB) 2337 apparently did not fire while approaching the beach.

Three LCS(L)s – numbers 253, 256 and 260 – formed a line ahead of the line of LCTs carrying DD tanks, and then accompanied the DD tanks once launched. From H–20 to H-Hour they fired their 6-pounder and 20mm Oerlikon guns at targets of opportunity, such as pillboxes along the beaches. At H+20, all three craft moved to the eastern side of Sword to suppress small-arms fire that was enfilading the landings.

Not everything went smoothly for the fire-support craft. An enemy shell knocked out LCG(L) 9's port engine but the damage was soon repaired. By H+180, both of LCG(L) 9's 4.7in guns were out of action due to mechanical failure, though one continued firing with a screwdriver replacing the broken part.[10]

The dust and smoke caused by the bombardment made it impossible to direct the fire of individual guns. There seems to have been many occasions when German mortar or artillery fire falling around landing craft was mistaken for part of the fire-support craft's bombardment falling short. In the ten minutes before H-Hour, the five LCT(R)s of Group 3 fired their rockets over the top of the assault troops in their LCAs, targeting an area 1,400 yards wide and 300 yards deep in the vicinity of the beach and immediately behind it. In a two-row formation, they began firing at 3,500 yards from the target, at 07.15 and 07.21 respectively.[11]

Meanwhile, the LCAs carrying the assault troops neared the beach. They had been afloat for nearly two hours, a trying experience in the rough seas for both their crews and the troops on board. The noise and sight of the naval bombardment provided a welcome boost to morale, as Marine Edward Neale of 535 Assault Flotilla recounts:

Our journey to the beach was anything but comfortable. With such high waves and buffeting winds the craft was making very heavy going, every wave crashing into the bows caused the craft to [come to] a shuddering halt, shipping gallons of water into the well deck soaking everyone to the skin. The troops were really feeling the effects of being thrown about and many were violently sick which did little to help matters ... My first inkling that this was not our usual exercise was when a salvo of 16 inch shells went screaming overhead like 'Banshees' out of Hell. Almost at the same moment we happened to pass a Rocket ship as she let go of her rockets in batches of about twenty. The noise was indescribable! We just watched in awe as they cascaded onto the beach like a giant firework display.[12]

As Group 2 neared the beach, the craft changed into the formation they would use for the assault landing, moving from line astern (columns) into a line abreast, parallel to the beach. The LCT(AVRE)s were in the centre, flanked on the left (east) by four LCT(A)s plus, on the far left, LCT(CB) 2337, and on the right by the remaining two LCT(A)s. Following behind this line of craft were the twenty LCAs carrying the assault infantry, flanked on either side by an LCF.

The LCT(A)s had set off from the UK each towing one of nine LCA(HR)s, which would fire their spigot mortars at the beach to destroy mines just before the infantry landed. However, the rough seas meant that all but one – LCA(HR) 976 – had been lost or abandoned in the crossing. That craft's commanding officer, Lieutenant F.H. Penfold RNVR, reported that he fired its mortar bombs up the beach as intended, setting fire to one of the houses at the rear. He believed some of the assault infantry followed the path of the mortars, which in theory would have set off any mines buried on the beach.[13]

Following in the wake of the bombardment, it was time for the assault, with H-Hour at 07.25. At sea there was 'appreciable swell' and waves of 4–5ft high. The tide was higher up the shore than expected, with around 250 rather than 400 yards of beach still exposed. Some beach obstacles were already sitting in water 2–4ft deep.[14]

Not all of the assault forces were able to land exactly on time, but despite the long journey and rough seas, the majority arrived close to their allotted time. Only a minority failed to arrive during the assault at all.

The core of the assault was the assault infantry: A and C Companies of the 1st South Lancs landed on Queen White, and A and B Companies of the 2nd East Yorks on Queen Red. Two sections of 246 Field Company

RE landed on each beach with the infantry, as well as a handful of personnel from other units. For clarity, the events over the thirty minutes or so after H-Hour will be considered separately for the two beaches.

The Assault on Queen White, H-Hour to H+45

The two assault companies of 1st South Lancs were carried by LCAs of 535 Assault Flotilla from HMS *Glenearn*. The craft encountered 'practically no opposition until craft beached, when small arms and mortar fire began'. They arrived on the western edge of Queen White, but part of A Company landed further east than intended, in front of German strongpoint Cod (WN-20), and as they advanced up the beach they suffered losses including the A Company commander. C Company attacked Cod.

Although all craft successfully returned to the *Glenearn*, it was not an easy landing for the Royal Marine crews, with some wounded.[15] As his LCA approached the beach, Marine Edward Neale ducked down into the craft to avoid bullets flying overhead. After unloading their troops, one of the engines of Neale's craft became choked with sand and the crew were unable to unbeach. A near-miss from a shell damaged the LCA, 'We were half filled with water, but as the craft was packed with cork she remained afloat, but was acting rather like a waterlogged Hippo'. As they returned to *Glenearn*, Neale's crew were all bailing out desperately and he thought he was going to die, but with another LCA giving them a tow they regained the safety of *Glenearn*.[16]

The assault infantry was meant to have been preceded seven and a half minutes earlier by the DD tanks of A Squadron, 13th/18th Hussars. In practice, the DD tanks beached on Queen White around the same time but slightly further to the west than the infantry. Sixteen of the twenty DD tanks reached the beach: one sank after launching and three were run down by LCTs. It took the tanks a few minutes to drop their canvas screens before they could fire their guns, by which time the infantry was already in action.[17]

The five LCT(4)s of 45 LCT Flotilla carrying the breaching teams landed at 07.30–07.40, roughly simultaneously with the infantry as planned. On board were AVRE tanks of 77 Assault Squadron RE and flail tanks of 22nd Dragoons. They were intended to establish a route for vehicles off the beach that was clear of mines and had a firmer surface, courtesy of the log carpet laid by the AVREs. This was their primary mission, but they could also tackle the German defenders (though not necessarily simultaneously: the flail tanks had to reverse their turrets to clear mines, for example).[18]

LCT 947 was the first craft of the flotilla to hit the beach and came under heavy fire. The second vehicle (a flail tank) was hit by an anti-tank shell as it was about to exit the craft. Sub Lieutenant Lambton Burn RNVR described what happened, 'There is a sudden jerk as our bows hit the beach. Down goes the ramp, with Sub Lieutenant Monty Glengarry, RNZNVR, and his party working like madmen at the bows.'

The first tank exited the LCT and then:

> ... enemy fire is now concentrated on us. There are bursts on both sides and then – snap – two direct hits on our bows followed by a third snap like a whip cracking over the tank hold. The First Lieutenant is flung sideways against a bulkhead and lies stunned.[19]

The second tank was jammed in place on the bow door, preventing further vehicles from unloading. Further enemy fire was directed at the LCT, sometimes described as mortar bombs but possibly further anti-tank gun-fire. This triggered the explosion of Bangalore torpedoes that were carried on one of the AVREs, killing three soldiers, including Lieutenant Colonel Arthur Cocks, commanding the 5th Assault Regiment RE, and leaving four more soldiers wounded. Remarkably, none of the LCT's crew were killed. The LCT had to return to the UK with its bow door jammed open, allowing the sea to flood in and making for a slow and fraught crossing.

The other LCTs successfully landed their tanks, which were immediately pitched into a close-range exchange of fire with German gun positions along the beach. From the landing craft point of view, the tanks at least drew some of the enemy fire away from them.[20]

Two LCTs of 100 LCT Flotilla – LCT(A)s 2334 and 2433 – also landed on Queen White around 07.30, about the same time as the LCT(AVRE)s and to the west. These craft had come under mortar fire at 3,000 yards from the beach and then machine-gun fire as they drew nearer.

The load of each LCT(A) included two Centaur tanks, which were now intended to provide the army with indirect fire until their own self-propelled guns were ashore. Once ashore, the Centaurs supported with direct fire but received no indirect fire targets. The LCT(A)s suffered heavy enemy fire on the beach and after unbeaching, LCT(A) 2334 lost its bow door due to damage to the hinges.[21]

The next group of eighteen LCAs (part of Group 5) arrived on time at H+20. They were accompanied by LCF 42, which was hit several times by enemy fire on D-Day and may have served to draw fire from the smaller craft it was escorting. To the east, ten LCAs of 537 Assault Flotilla (SS *Empire Battleaxe*) carried HQ and D Company, 1st South Lancs, part of the reserve companies of the same battalion that had landed at H-Hour. Major Adrian Roose of the 1st South Lancs described the moment:

> Out of the haze of smoke the underwater obstacles loomed up ... we weaved in between iron rails and ramps and pickets with tellamines [Tellermines, anti-tank mines, fixed on posts] ... The noise was so continuous that it seemed almost like a siren. The seamanship was magnificent. The LCAs weaved in and out of the obstacles and we almost had a dry landing ... Mortar fire was coming down on the sands, an 88mm gun was firing along the line of the beach and there was continuous machine-gun and rifle fire. Immediately ahead of us a DD tank, its rear end enveloped in flames ... continued to fire its gun.[22]

Shrapnel passed through the engine compartment of LCA 611 and out the other side, killing the stoker. The armour plate along the side of an LCA protected the troop space but did not extend further to the stern to cover the engine compartment. Three other men on board were wounded.

To the right of Queen White, eight LCAs of 536 Assault Flotilla (SS *Empire Cutlass*) carried B Company, 1st South Lancs. These last craft faced poor visibility due to dust and smoke and were swept to the left by the current, but at nearly the last moment they altered course to land at the intended location. LCA 791 had become waterlogged and sank on approach to the beach, but the troops and crew safely transferred to a passing empty LCA.[23]

The LCAs of 536 and 537 Assault Flotillas also carried other supporting troops, including personnel from 629 Field Squadron RE, Fox RN Beach Commando, 8 Field Ambulance RAMC, 5 Beach Group and No.7 Landing Craft Obstacle Clearance Unit (LCOCU). The RN Beach Commando and Beach Group personnel were to start the arrangements for organising the beach – from a navy and army perspective respectively. The RN Beach Commandos reported that they had to abandon much of their equipment due to deep water and beach obstacles.

The engineers and LCOCU personnel were to deal with beach obstacles above and below the waterline respectively. Working with the AVRE tanks, their objective was to clear lanes through the beach obstacles before they were covered by the tide. No.7 LCOCU, on board LCA 780 of 537 Assault Flotilla, rapidly found their work hampered by heavy surf and the rapidly rising tide. The LCOCU waited offshore until they saw beach exit markers put out by 629 Field Squadron RE, and then buoyed one route to seaward on Queen White and used a loudhailer to direct approaching landing craft. They were unable to carry out any underwater demolition of obstacles due to the rough seas which exhausted the men or swept them away. The LCOCU divers also risked being hit by further craft arriving at the beach. The whole task was carried out under fire from enemy machine gunners in beachfront houses. At 08.30, the RE squadron leader decided that further obstacle clearance was impossible for the moment and clearance efforts would focus on the routes off the beaches.[24]

Two other LCAs from 537 Assault Flotilla (LCAs 779 and 1215) landed men of 629 Field Squadron RE on Queen White at the same time. Some of the engineers' supplies (for demolishing beach obstacles) remained on board the two craft, which waited off the beach and delivered them an hour later.[25]

By 08.10, opposition on much of Queen White had been overcome, except for the occasional sniper. However, at the junction with Queen Red, the fighting to subdue Strongpoint Cod would continue until 10.00.[26]

The Assault on Queen Red, H-Hour to H+45

At Queen Red, the assault forces landed around H-Hour, with the LCT(AVRE)s apparently beaching a few minutes before the swimming DD tanks and the LCAs carrying the assault infantry. The AVRE tanks of 77 Assault Squadron RE and the flail tanks of the 22nd Dragoons were carried by five LCT(4)s of 45 LCT Flotilla (the other half of the flotilla that had landed similar vehicles on Queen White). Several LCTs were hit by enemy fire but carried on and the sailors did not suffer any casualties.[27]

A and B Companies of 2nd East Yorks came ashore from the ten craft of 536 Assault Flotilla (SS *Empire Cutlass*). At 200 yards from the beach, the craft faced mortar and machine-gun fire from the defenders, which proved to be heavier than on Queen White. At the request of the army officers, the Royal Marine crews returned fire with the Lewis guns mounted in the port-side forward positions on the LCAs. Two of the ten LCAs were lost and two more sank while returning to *Cutlass*, and at least one crewman was wounded. The infantry immediately assaulted strongpoint Cod and suffered many casualties as soon as they left their landing craft.[28]

The DD tanks of B Squadron, 13th/18th Hussars, were slightly later than their planned beaching time of H−7.5. On LCT(3) 467, the lead DD tank tore its flotation skirt while preparing to launch, meaning that it would have sunk. Rather than pushing it off the ramp, the LCT's commanding officer decide to land all five tanks directly on the beach, and they ended up beaching at H+40. LCT 465 was unable to launch its fifth DD tank due to damage to the chains supporting its ramp, so the vehicle had to be taken back to the UK.

This left fourteen of the original twenty DD tanks swimming to shore. By the time they had dropped their flotation screens and were ready to fight, the infantry had been in action for several minutes. Many of the tanks had landed further west than the infantry, so they were less well positioned to support the latter.[29]

Among the landing craft, the five LCT(A)s of 100 LCT Flotilla bore the brunt of enemy fire. Carrying Centaur tanks of 5th Royal Marine Independent Armoured Support Battery, as well as other vehicles, the first craft beached about five minutes late, at H+5, and the remainder just minutes later. LCT(CB) 2337 was positioned furthest east, with LCT(A) 2191 and LCT(HE) 2012 adjacent, and LCT(A) 2052 and LCT(HE) 2123 further to the west.[30]

After landing its tanks, LCT(A) 2191 was hit by several mortar bombs. The port Oerlikon gunner opened fire on a German anti-tank gun that he had spotted between two of the seafront houses. The gun's first shell hit the bow, killing Sub Lieutenant Sidney Green RNVR (on board as an observation officer) and Wireman Edward Trendell.

The LCT swung round so that the stern faced the beach. A second shell killed the two officers on the bridge and set the craft on fire. Signalman Peter Hutchins was also on the bridge and was seriously wounded, 'It felt like a giant pair of cymbals had been used each side of my head'. Able Seaman Robert 'Geordie' Bryson and Leading Stoker Vic Orme were sheltering in the wheelhouse when it was hit, and both men were badly wounded in the legs so that they could not move. Despite his severe wounds, Hutchins pulled Orme onto the deck but could not do the same for Bryson because the latter's braces caught on the jagged edges of damaged metal at the wheelhouse door. Hutchins decided to go over the side of the LCT with a lifebelt to try to get help. Washed up on the beach, he was cared for by soldiers who found him.[31]

LCT(A) 2191 now drifted some 400 yards along the beach. Still on board, Vic Orme was unable to pull Geordie Bryson out of the wheelhouse. As they comforted each other, an explosion in the wheelhouse killed Bryson and stunned his comrade. When Orme came to, the deck was hot from the fires burning below. Deciding that he would rather die from drowning than fire, Orme managed to get into the water and float ashore, where he was rescued. Six of the crew had been killed and most of the survivors were wounded.[32]

LCT(A) 2052 also managed to land its tanks but was hit by enemy shells, killing Able Seaman Norman Hannah and wounding five crewmen. The commanding officer, Lieutenant C. Woodham RNVR later reported that German shells had left holes about 5in in diameter, and he believed enemy fire had targeted the craft's bridge and wheelhouse. Like LCT(A) 2191, it was left a wreck on the beach.[33]

Furthest to the east of this group was LCT(CB) 2337. In fact, this craft landed the furthest east of the entire Allied landing force on D-Day: a dubious position for an unarmoured craft. Its exposed position meant it drew considerable enemy fire as it approached the beach. The craft developed a list to starboard, probably because the heavy load on board had led to the sea partly flooding its tank deck. The LCT(CB) successfully landed its vehicles – most importantly, the two Sherman Firefly tanks with their powerful guns. As the LCT turned out to sea it was hit by shell and mortar fire, which mortally wounded one of the Oerlikon gunners, Able Seaman Edward Mills, who died the following day.

LCT(CB) 2337 eventually reached the UK early on 8 June, after a long crossing due to engine room power problems and damage from the shell hits on D-Day. The craft was still towing LCT(A) 2334, which it had rescued from the beach; 2334 had lost its bow door and had engine trouble. Sub Lieutenant R.W. Rawlings RNVR, 2337's commanding officer, had remained at his post for the return crossing, despite his wounds, and was later awarded the Distinguished Service Cross for his courage.[34]

Next to beach on Queen Red were LCI(S)s 523 and 527, part of 201 LCI(S) Flotilla, carrying Free French Commandos. They were due to land at H+30 but beached five minutes early at 07.50. These troops had a symbolic as well as a tactical role: they were the only Free French unit to land on the beaches on D-Day. They landed at the far east side of Queen Red, further right than the assault infantry (2nd East Yorks) had done at H-Hour. This meant that they encountered German defenders, who had not yet faced assault troops at close quarters.

At around 1,000 yards from the beach, the craft came under machine gun and mortar fire. They had to beach between intact beach obstacles. LCI(S) 523 managed to land its troops without loss but had one of its two landing ramps blown away and suffered a hole in its bottom from a mined obstacle. The craft's commanding officer, Sub Lieutenant J.H.W. Berry RNVR recounted later that his philosophy was to land his craft as far up the beach as possible, in the hope of minimising casualties amongst the troops. Therefore, he beached his craft at emergency speed, 'so hard that we were dry abeam of the bridge'.[35]

Meanwhile, LCI(S) 527 had lost both ramps before reaching the beach, making it very difficult for its troops to land. LCI(S) 523 came alongside so the commandos on 527 could transfer on board, then LCI(S) 523 beached again to deliver them to shore using its one remaining ramp, despite continued shelling. At 08.20 the crew of LCI(S) 523 started operating the craft's pumps, a task they would perform continuously for the next twenty-four hours.[36]

As on Queen White, on Queen Red, the craft carrying the reserve companies of the assault infantry were scheduled to arrive for H+20 (07.45): twenty-two LCAs in total, part of Group 5. The eight craft of 538 Assault Flotilla (SS *Empire Broadsword*) did not wait for other craft, which were running late, and landed on Queen Red five minutes early. Four of the craft carried personnel of 5 Beach Group and two held men of 629 Field Squadron RE. The remaining two LCAs carried Fox RN Beach Commando and 76 Field Regiment RA respectively, as well as 8 Field Ambulance personnel on both. Their landing went smoothly and only one craft (LCA 1381) had to be abandoned on the beach due to damage suffered on landing.

The rest of the twenty-two H+20-wave craft reached the shore about fifteen minutes late. They included twelve LCAs of 543 Assault Flotilla (HMS *Glenearn*). Ten of the twelve carried the reserve companies of the assault battalion (HQ, C and D Companies of the 2nd East Yorks) and the other two had on board further personnel from 629 Field Company RE. Another two LCAs from HMS *Glenearn*'s other flotilla – 535 Assault Flotilla – brought No.8 LCOCU and Fox RN Beach Commando respectively.

LCF 34 escorted the LCAs to the beach. The battalion bugler of the 2nd East Yorks played during the journey to the shore, which was said to have kept the troops cheerful. Smoke and dust made it hard to identify landmarks until close in. The flotilla touched down further east than planned, and the troops faced accurate enemy fire that caused significant casualties. The LCAs suffered considerable damage, and some of the crew spent three days and two nights on the beach until they had repaired two craft. Five LCAs from the flotilla were damaged by obstacles or shelling.[37]

The next craft to land were carrying No.4 Commando, who landed in two waves at the army's request. Along with the two LCI(S)s just mentioned, these craft were designated Group 6. The first wave comprised eight LCAs of 500 Assault Flotilla (HMS *Prinses Astrid*), followed by six

LCAs of 514 Assault Flotilla (SS *Maid of Orleans*). The two flotillas touched down on Queen Red around their scheduled times of H+30 and H+33 (07.55 and 07.58) respectively.[38]

As they neared the shore, both flotillas were hit by 'fairly severe machine gun and mortar fire', which caused casualties to the troops. This was probably coming from the La Breche strongpoint (WN-18), which the commandos would have to assault after landing. When 500 Assault Flotilla beached its LCAs between two damaged LCTs (presumably two of the LCT(A) wave) it provided some useful cover from enemy fire.

All of the flotilla's craft managed to unbeach, but despite the efforts of their crews, half of the eight LCAs sank while returning to HMS *Prinses Astrid*, due to damage from beach obstacles or, in one case, from shell fire. The crews from the sinking LCAs (as well as various stores) were rescued by other craft in the flotilla and by a passing LCM, and the flotilla suffered no casualties on D-Day. Back at their landing ship, the LCA crews were so exhausted from their efforts that the flotilla engineering officer, Lieutenant (E) L.B. Jenness RNZVR leapt on board each craft to help them hook on so they could be recovered onto the davits.[39]

514 Assault Flotilla touched down to the west of the other flotilla carrying No.4 Commando and tried to take advantage of the cover provided by LCTs on the beach. Even before they left the craft, there were casualties among the commandos. Signalman H. Conley on one of the LCAs noticed that the force of a mortar bomb hit had knocked out the commando padre's false teeth: after fishing them out of the mixture of sea water and blood in the craft's scuppers, the padre replaced them in his mouth.

Another mortar shell destroyed the bows of one of the six LCAs, which had to be abandoned on the beach. The other five craft managed to return to SS *Maid of Orleans*, with the last one arriving at 10.30, four hours and twenty minutes after launching. When Conley got back on board the ship, he was welcomed by one of the ship's crew, 'An elderly merchant seaman came over and put his arms round my neck and cried'.[40]

THE LANDINGS CONTINUE, H+45 ONWARDS

British forces had now gained a foothold on Sword Beach, but it was still a dangerous place for landing craft and their crews. The remainder of this chapter will look at the whole beach. Group 7 was the next wave to touch down, on time at around 08.10 (H+45), on both Queen Red and Queen White. This comprised thirteen LCT(4)s of 41 LCT Flotilla, carrying a variety of vehicles. Among the troops on the LCTs were the other half of the 13th/18th Hussars, whose comrades had landed around H-Hour in amphibious DD tanks. These troops would come ashore in tanks equipped only for wading in relatively shallow water.

Other troops on the LCTs were mainly priority vehicles such as Bren Carriers with anti-tank guns or mortars from the assault infantry battalions. There were also M10 self-propelled anti-tank guns and self-propelled Crusader 40mm light anti-aircraft guns (each with a towed 40mm anti-aircraft gun) belonging to the infantry's parent unit, 8th Infantry Brigade. These troops bolstered the beach area defences in case of enemy tank or air attack. Vehicles of Beach Group units also landed from these LCTs and their personnel would work on clearing the exits from the beach, setting up communications and more.[41]

The new arrivals still came under enemy fire. At 400 yards from the shore, some of the LCTs were targeted by machine-gun fire, though this caused no serious problems. Nearing the water's edge, they encountered a chaotic scene. Army personnel and burning tanks were scattered across the beach and many half-submerged beach obstacles remained in position. The majority of the LCTs were able to land their cargoes successfully, despite mortar and occasional machine-gun fire. At least seven of the craft were seriously damaged, though none to the degree that they could not return to the UK, and there were crew casualties on five vessels. Just after LCT 898 touched down, it was hit several times by shells, killing Able Seaman Lawrence Batty and seriously injuring four others, as well as badly damaging the LCT's bow door.[42]

To Wireman Denis Garrod, it seemed impossible that LCT 980 would not collide with the beach obstacles. The commanding officer, Sub Lieutenant Peter Gurnsey RNZVR, aimed the craft directly at one mined obstacle. This blew a hole in the ramp, but being directly in the centre of the ramp, the hole did not impede the vehicles' tracks as they disembarked.

Next, Garrod moved from the port side winch at the LCT's bow to the kedge anchor on the stern. His place was taken by LCT 980's first lieutenant, Sub Lieutenant John Bruce Tait RNZVR. Seconds later, a mortar bomb exploded to starboard, and a piece of shrapnel killed Tait instantly. Then the LCT hit a mined obstacle, which stopped both engines. The crew managed to return to the UK but had to steer by varying the engine speeds, as the explosion had disabled the rudders.[43]

Beaching some fifteen minutes later in an LCA on Queen White, Sub Lieutenant James Leslie RNVR witnessed a brave LCT crewman operating a 20mm Oerlikon gun – normally a two-man job:

> He fought with his Oerlikon with enemy riflemen concealed in the roofs and what was left of the upper stories of shattered houses. We could see him changing magazines all by himself and he was such a 'shorty' he had difficulty doing this, but we couldn't help him. I hope he survived.[44]

LCT 610 remained on the beach for an hour while attempts were made to start a Sherman tank, but in the end, it had to unbeach with the tank still on board. LCT 854 was hit by German mortar bombs, which detonated a supply of British mortar bombs carried by vehicles on board. This caused a fire that burnt out three Bren Carriers belonging to the 2nd East Yorks. The crew only succeeded in extinguishing the flames when an LCI(L) came alongside and passed them its hose, because the explosion had destroyed the pipes on the tank deck that the LCT's crew would have used to put out the fire. The shelling had also killed and wounded some of the troops on board. One unwounded soldier had refused to go ashore and was taken back to the UK. LCT 854's wireman, William Joyce, later recalled that the crew had to wash what he described as 'mincemeat' off the front of the bridge after the incident.[45]

While unbeaching, LCT 945 became entangled with a mined beach obstacle. Midshipman Craddock Jones RNVR courageously dealt with the mine so it could get clear, but in the process was left behind. His comrades believed he had drowned, but he is now buried in Normandy with the date of death as 22 June 1944. It is unclear what happened to him over the subsequent weeks but he was mentioned in despatches for his actions.[46]

As their craft pulled away from Sword Beach, for the crews of Group 7's LCTs this had been a brief but violent episode. William Joyce of LCT 854 later remembered how 'the most thrilling point in my life was when as we went in on "D" DAY we hoisted our Battle Ensign'. However, he continued, 'When we came off [the beach] it was full of holes'.[47]

The next wave of landing craft were Group 8, tasked to land at H+60 (08.25) carrying 1st Battalion, Suffolk Regiment (1st Suffolks), which was the third reserve battalion of 8th Infantry Brigade. They were following up to support the brigade's other two battalions, 1st South Lancs and 2nd East Yorks, who had landed at H-Hour. This wave was led by three craft of 261 LCI(L) Flotilla: LCI(L)s 130, 131 and 183. Each carried around

200 troops. These were relatively large and vulnerable craft to be landing so early on D-Day.

Behind the LCI(L)s were eighteen LCAs carrying the rest of 1st Suffolks: eight from 537 Assault Flotilla (SS *Empire Battleaxe*) and ten from 538 Assault Flotilla (SS *Empire Broadsword*). Once on the beach, it took time for the big LCI(L)s to unload their troops, whereas the smaller LCAs following behind them were able to land their troops rapidly, possibly aided by the fact that the larger LCI(L)s seemed to have drawn enemy fire away from them.[48]

As the LCAs approached the beach it was at first covered by smoke. At 1,000 yards out, the exact position could be identified, which was the junction between Queen Red and Queen White beaches, slightly to the east from where the three LCI(L)s were about to touch down, and close to German strongpoint Cod (WN-20). All eighteen LCAs touched down together in knee-deep water and roughly on time.

A post-action report described the scene, '... burning vehicles and houses, and there was a tremendous smell of explosives and burnt metal. The noise was shattering'. The commanding officer of 537 Assault Flotilla described enemy shell fire landing in the sea 300 yards offshore to his right, 'sporadic' machine-gun fire from the beachfront houses and mortar fire against nearby LCTs that was coming from behind a large house (probably in WN-20).[49]

One of the LCAs that was hit by enemy fire was carrying the FOO supporting 1st Suffolks. Five LCAs of 537 Assault Flotilla returned to their landing ship, some with damage but not enough to sink them. LCA 611 received several direct hits while beached, killing the stoker driver, Marine Gerald Pike, and causing so much damage that the LCA was abandoned on the beach. LCAs 1252 and 584 were also lost on or near the beach.[50]

LCA 870 was hit by a mortar shell, which disabled the craft as well as killing two men from 538 Assault Flotilla: 870's coxswain, Corporal Gerald Dean, and Marine Albert Alfred Gale, who was nearby on LCA 673. Sub Lieutenant James W.C. Leslie RNVR recalled that after unbeaching, he and his crew had to transfer from the sinking LCA 796 to another vessel of their flotilla, LCA 1341. A mile or two out at sea, LCA 1341 was travelling at speed to get out of range of enemy fire and suddenly went nose-down into the swell. The craft was flooded at the bow and both crews were forced up onto the stern and then into the water. Leslie swam to the surface and threw off his equipment to help him stay afloat.

As he discarded his steel helmet, he briefly glimpsed the photo of his infant son tucked into its crown. Both crews were eventually rescued, but Corporal Eric James Smith of LCA 796 and Marine Edward Henry Charles Scaplehorn of LCA 1341 were both missing after D-Day and may have died during these events.

The rough seas made it hard for SS *Empire Broadsword* to recover the surviving vessels of 538 Assault Flotilla. Aiming to create an area of sheltered water, *Broadsword* raised anchor and went ahead at slow speed while turning gradually. Finally, the ship's captain ordered surplus oil to be pumped overboard to help calm the waves. Together, these measures made it easier to recover the LCAs.[51]

As the three LCI(L)s carrying the remainder of 1st Suffolks approached the beach, the senior naval officer – Lieutenant Commander C.R. Wall RNVR, on LCI(L) 130 – had led the craft to the eastern end of Queen White, hoping to avoid German mortar fire. The three vessels beached on time at 08.25, at a speed of 10 knots and driving up onto the beach so the troops landed in only a couple of feet of water. In the centre of the three vessels, LCI(L) 183's port ramp was disabled by a shell which also wounded some of the soldiers. The crew fitted an emergency ladder instead. Two of the Royal Navy crew (the telegraphist and a seaman rating), whose names are unknown, were killed by another shell which hit the craft soon afterwards.[52]

Immediately to the east, as the crew of LCI(L) 130 lowered its ramps, both struck obstacles and were thrown off their rollers. The troops (which included the rear HQ of 1st Suffolks) had to disembark using scrambling nets and ladders. This was a slow process, made worse because the army officers on board would not organise the troops to speed up the landing, so the ship's naval officers had to do this.

Enemy shells caused damage to the craft as well as wounding several soldiers. Even after LCI(L) 130 had been on the beach for an hour, most of the soldiers were still on board. The craft was taking on water and listing to port due to a shell hole below the water line. The crew then unbeached and the remaining troops were transferred to LCI(S) 516 for landing. The crew of LCI(L)130 managed to keep pumping out the craft during the return to Portsmouth, where they were received as 'heroic survivors' on entering the harbour.[53]

The third craft, LCI(L) 131, beached just to the west. The crew successfully landed the army's hand carts, which must have been tricky to manoeuvre down the narrow ramps. Peter Houghton, flotilla leading signalman, who was on board LCI(L) 131, described the scene:

Germans open fire on flotilla … strong smell of cordite in the air … noise terrible, shells and bullets everywhere splashing around in the sea, finally hit above the waterline by several 88mm shells, one of which penetrated the armour plating on the bridge, offensive shell [was] thrown overboard, several others remained locked in the deckhead.

Both the craft's ramps were carried away by enemy fire, so the troops had to disembark using ladders instead. The first lieutenant was wounded by enemy fire and would have fallen overboard had Houghton not caught hold of him.

Although still under heavy shell fire, the remaining 100 or so troops on LCI(L) 131 were reluctant to go ashore using scrambling nets and ladders. To complicate matters, all the army officers had gone ashore and of the three naval officers, only the commanding officer remained unwounded. The craft unbeached and later transferred the remaining soldiers to LCAs for landing. One crew member, Ordinary Seaman Butler, had taken a line onto the beach to assist the troops in unloading and apparently had to be left ashore when the craft unbeached, although as far as is known, he survived.[54]

Around H+65 (08.30), the commander of the Royal Engineers squadron on Sword decided that the tide had risen to the point that it was no longer possible to do obstacle-clearance work and so for now, the obstacle-clearance teams' personnel and vehicles would focus on keeping the beach exits clear. This meant that landing craft had to take their chances with the obstacles which were increasingly submerged by the tide. The LCOCU had only buoyed one channel through the obstacles and were now ashore because working in the shallows was proving too difficult.[55]

Eight LCM(3)s of 653 Build-Up Flotilla landed thirty-five minutes late at 08.30, with the craft divided equally between Queen White and Queen Red. These LCMs carried Bren Carriers loaded with explosives for obstacle demolition by 263 Field Company RE. Its personnel had crossed the English Channel on board HMS *Prinses Astrid*, but the LCMs had been late to the rendezvous to collect them. As the LCMs were late, the personnel embarked on two LCI(L)s instead, which beached ninety minutes late, so the LCMs ended up landing their cargoes first. On the beach, LCM 1088 was hit by a shell, and at least one other craft hit a mine. In total, two of the Royal Marine crewmen were killed and four wounded.[56]

Before H-Hour, the three Royal Artillery field regiments (7th, 33rd and 76th) had fired their guns from on board eighteen LCT(4)s of 32 and 38 LCT Flotillas on the run-in shoot. Those craft had headed back out to sea but now it was time for them to beach. First to land was 76th Field Regiment at 08.35, five minutes before the planned time of H+70. The regiment came ashore from six LCTs (three each on Queen White and Queen Red), which were designated Group 4. Each LCT carried one troop of four self-propelled guns plus an Observation Post Sherman tank and half-tracks. Vehicle congestion meant that the guns had to make their first land-based shoots of D-Day from the shallows on the beach.[57]

Two of the LCTs had particularly difficult landings. At 100 yards from the beach, LCT 532 was hit by a mortar shell, which set fire to three self-propelled guns at the rear of the craft. The remaining vehicles on board were put ashore, and although the LCT's crew extinguished the fire, there were now no unwounded gunners on board to check whether the three guns could be landed, so they were taken back to the UK. On 532's return journey to the UK, both its engines failed as a shell had holed the fuel tank, allowing sea water to mix with the fuel, and another LCT had to take it in tow.[58]

On reaching the beach, LCT 750 hit a Teller mine, which blew a large hole in the ramp and caused other damage to the wires and door chains supporting it. Although two guns managed to land, a half-track got jammed on the ramp. As LCT 750 unbeached, with the intention of clearing the half-track from the ramp and then returning to the beach to unload the remaining vehicles, the engine room was either hit by a shell or struck a mined beach obstacle. This left the craft drastically listing to port. Later, the LCT was swept onto the beach and that afternoon, the remaining vehicles were unloaded. LCT 750 had to be abandoned on the beach.[59]

Several commando units were due to land at H+75 (08.40). They were carried on twelve LCI(S)s of 200 LCI(S) Flotilla, plus two attached craft from 201 LCI(S) Flotilla, together designated Group 9. The highly trained commandos knew these landing craft crews well after several months of training together. Each craft carried around 100 troops, with the exceptions of LCI(S) 508, which was a rescue craft, and LCI(S) 510, which acted as a hospital ship.

The first seven LCI(S)s landed No.6 Commando and HQ 1st Special Service Brigade on Queen Red at 08.41, one minute late. Led by the flotilla officer, Lieutenant Commander Rupert Curtis RNVR, 200 LCI(S) Flotilla was aiming at the eastern side of the landing area because the commandos' objectives ashore lay in that direction.

At first, little enemy fire was directed at the craft. Travelling at 12 knots, they passed LCI(S) 527 towing LCI(S) 523, which had rope around its propeller: these two vessels had just delivered the Free French Commandos and were now heading back out to sea. As they neared the shore, the crews could see beach obstacles projecting some 2ft above the water.[60]

The LCI(S)s came under considerable German fire at the moment of beaching, from anti-tank guns and machine guns on the flanks, probably from German strongpoints WN-20 to the west and WN-18 to the east, as well as mortars from just inland. The commandos lay down on the upper decks of the LCI(S)s, protecting themselves using the crafts' bulletproof coamings, or remained below decks. Rupert Curtis described the final moments before LCI(S) 519 touched down:

> The smallest detail seemed to assume a microscopic clarity ... I felt I could discern a clear path through the menacing stakes. It looked a bit of a zig-zag but I backed my instinct and took 519 through with rapid helm orders. We emerged unscathed and I called for more power from the engine room to thrust our bows hard on to the beach to ensure as dry a landing as possible. Then we kept both engines running at half ahead to hold the bows in position.

The commandos were able to land in only 2–3ft of water. This was fortunate as the men were heavily loaded and, on some craft, had with them up to sixty bicycles.[61]

German shells pierced the gun shield of LCI(S) 519's port Oerlikon gun, fortunately continuing on their way without hitting either the gunners or the ship. Other shells hit and disabled the starboard engine of LCI(S) 502, beached immediately to port of 519, and four hit its fuel tanks. Mortar bombs killed some of the commandos on board the craft as well as some who had just landed. In the confusion under fire, LCI(S) 505's ramps were misaligned and had to be jettisoned, with troops instead using scrambling nets to disembark. The crews of LCI(S)s 516 and 521 returned fire with their 20mm Oerlikon guns against seafront houses, with LCS(L)s to the east also providing supporting fire.[62]

At about 08.45, 41 RM Commando landed from five craft in the second group of LCI(S)s. The commandos should have landed on Queen White as their objectives lay on the west side of Sword Beach. In fact, they landed on Queen Red, some 300m adrift. The commandos had to wade 200 yards to dry land under fire from German strongpoint WN-20.

As LCI(S) 531 unbeached, a flooded engine room caused the craft to drift off to the east and the crew were taken on board LCI(S) 506, which had also landed Royal Marine Commandos. As Lieutenant Stanley Tasker RNVR of LCI(S) 531 went below to save the craft's confidential books, his opposite number on 506, Lieutenant F.J. Backlog RNVR, urged him to hurry with the words, 'Hurry up Stanley, I'm sinking too'.[63]

LCI(S) 524 had been badly shot up on the beach by mortars and anti-tank guns, and there was a fire in the craft's engine room, but the crew managed to get out to sea again. Several of the crew were wounded, including Ordinary Seaman Harold Barton, who had lost a foot but asked that other casualties be treated first. At about 2 miles off the coast, LCI(S) 524 exploded 'in a sheet of flame'. The craft was said to have received a direct hit from an enemy gun, although it may simply be that the fire had spread to and ignited its fuel tanks. Twelve of the crew died, including Barton and the first lieutenant, Sub Lieutenant Frank Hastings Hardy RNVR; both men received mentions in despatches for their actions on D-Day.

Incredibly, 524's commanding officer, Lieutenant Nigel Cromar RNVR, and three of his crew survived. They were rescued by US Coast Guard Cutter No.35, which was accompanying the LCI(S)s as a rescue ship. The US Coast Guard crew descended the vessel's scrambling nets to pluck the British sailors from the sea at the centre of a pool of burning fuel.[64]

The next scheduled landings were due at H+105 (09.10), by No.3 Commando and 45 RM Commando. In total, they were carried by ten LCI(S)s from 201 LCI(S) Flotilla, designated Group 9A, with each commando unit on five different craft. In the event, No.3 Commando landed at least five minutes early, while 45 RM Commando came ashore on time. These vessels began receiving enemy fire when they were 3 miles from the beach.

Around this time, the troops on LCI(S) 509 suffered their first casualty: an army officer hit as he was descending the ladder from the bridge. Both commando units were bound for Queen Red because, just like Nos 4 and 6 Commando, who had landed earlier, their objectives were on the eastern side of Sword Beach. Unfortunately, several LCTs were broached-to in the centre of Queen Red, blocking that immediate area's use by other craft.[65]

Petty Officer Motor Mechanic J.E. Burton was manning the starboard engine below decks on LCI(S) 535, carrying men of No.3 Commando. Through the hull he could feel the shockwaves as shells exploded nearby, 'One shell dropped very close to the port side of the engine room and when it exploded all the tins of paint, grease, etc. shot off a shelf and the stoker on the port engine leapt across the engine room and into my arms'. Once the craft touched down, the two men remained in the engine room, waiting anxiously for the signal to unbeach. Burton peeked out of the engine room hatch to see what was happening nearby and 'all hell let loose with LCI(S)s strewn about at all angles and troops storming beach'.[66]

LCI(S) 509 set off a mine on a beach obstacle which left the craft dead in the water just off the beach. Several commandos on board were killed because the forward troop spaces in which they were waiting were flooded as the explosion blasted a hole in the craft's bottom: some were apparently stunned or wounded and drowned before they could be rescued. LCI(S) 512 also hit a mine but successfully landed its troops then, despite taking on water, came alongside 509 and took its troops to shore as well. After landing them, LCI(S) 512 also became unmanoeuvrable and broached-to. Its crew went ashore, led by the commanding officer, Lieutenant P. Whitworth RNVR, who was apparently wielding a Tommy gun. LCI(S) 518 took off the upper-deck crew from the wrecked LCI(S) 509 to replace casualties on board. Meanwhile, 509's two officers had also gone ashore.[67]

Back on LCI(S) 535, it only managed to unbeach when the engine room crew applied emergency power full astern. Noticing that the engine room floor was beginning to slope towards the bow rather than the stern as would normally be the case, Burton realised that the craft was taking on water forward because of hitting mined obstacles on the beach. Most of the crew were taken off by another vessel, but some remained on board and the LCI(S) was towed back to the UK. Of the five craft that had landed No.3 Commando, only LCI(S) 501 remained undamaged.[68]

The landing craft that delivered 45 RM Commando at 09.10 also came under heavy fire. LCI(S) 518, commanded by the flotilla officer, Lieutenant Commander Jack Deslandes RNVR, was hit by several shells. An armour-piercing shot killed Able Seamen Cecil Norman Giles and Louis Eric Milne, who were in an exposed position on the craft's deck, manning the ramps. A mortar bomb hit near the bridge and exploded some of the commandos' ammunition, killing and wounding both crew and commandos; three other crew later died. Deslandes said that the deck of his craft 'was like a butcher's shop'.

LCI(S) 528 escaped lightly, despite being hit by a shell. LCI(S) 517 sank just after unbeaching and the crew were rescued by LCI(S) 516. LCI(S) 517's coxswain, Bill Binding, recalled that he managed to abandon ship carrying his suitcase, which contained two precious bottles of rum. Out of the five craft that landed 45 RM Commando, only two escaped with light or no damage and no casualties.[69]

In total, twenty-eight LCI(S)s had landed the commandos – which includes four spare or hospital craft – out of which five had been lost and three-quarters of the remainder had damage, mainly to rudders and propellers. Four craft had such damage that they returned to the UK immediately and two of these arrived 'in a sinking condition'. In the case of LCI(S) 535, it was at a 45-degree angle in the water, with its propellers in the air. Lieutenant Commander Rupert Curtis later observed that if the German defenders had fired incendiary or high-explosive shot at the LCI(S)s, rather than solid shot, many craft might have exploded due to hits in their vulnerable, non-sealing fuel tanks. He estimated that this could have led to half of the commando brigade becoming casualties.[70]

The next self-propelled artillery regiment to land on Sword Beach, 33rd Field Regiment RA, came ashore on time at H+105 (09.10). They were on board six LCT(4)s of 32 LCT Flotilla (designated Group 4A). They were meant to land on both Queen Red and Queen White, but all landed on White. With the beach exits still very congested, the regiment's guns joined those of 76th Field Regiment RA in firing from the shallows at targets inland. At the water's edge, several LCTs were hit by enemy shells or collided with obstacles and there was also occasional sniping and machine-gun fire. LCTs 889 and 597 both had to be towed off the beach. After hitting obstacles while putting its cargo ashore, LCT 593 had to return to the beach to avoid sinking and while there, a shell killed Stoker Thomas E. Beatson and wounded two of his crewmates. LCT 593 remained on the beach for repairs until 9 June and was later towed back to the UK.[71]

Next, eleven LCT(4)s of 43 LCT Flotilla (designated Group 10) landed across both Queen White and Queen Red, on time at H+120 (09.25). Nine of these craft were carrying vehicles: what were classed as second-priority vehicles for 1st Suffolks and its parent unit, 8th Infantry Brigade, as well as for the Beach Group and a wide range of other units. Like many earlier craft, these LCTs also came under fire, particularly from mortars. LCT 1125 had to use its Oerlikons to silence sniping from a beachfront house.

At least three LCTs found that the first vehicles to be landed became bogged down, which blocked the exit from the craft, so the crew had to unbeach the LCT and come ashore in a new position, and it took an hour or more to land all their vehicles. Several craft also sustained damage from now-submerged mined beach obstacles.[72]

Two LCT(4)s – 1011 and 1013 – accompanying this group, each carried 200 tons of stores, particularly ammunition, as well as Beach Group vehicles, and took hours to unload. During the first twenty-four hours of the landings, this ammunition would form the initial supply that units could draw on when needed. The stores were destined for four Sector Stores Dumps, which were to be 100–200 yards inland from the beach. To move these stores to the dumps, each LCT carried five 3-ton trucks and the personnel to operate them.[73]

By around 10.00, the beach assault phase was complete: the vast majority of the 8th Infantry Brigade group had landed, except for a few administrative vehicles that would follow later. This roughly coincided with high tide. The incoming tide meant that the beach was only about 30ft wide, leaving little room for vehicles, and some wheeled vehicles had got stuck in the sand. The 2nd East Yorks managed to finish clearing German strongpoint WN-20; however, larger enemy guns were still firing from further inland.[74]

The next major army formation to land was 185th Infantry Brigade, which was the intermediate brigade: the second of British 3rd Infantry Division's three brigades to come ashore. The brigade HQ landed from an LCI(S) at 10.00. The craft originally allocated for this role, LCI(S) 524, had exploded about half an hour earlier, as mentioned above. The brigade's three infantry battalions were due to start landing at H+150 (09.55), each from three LCI(L)s of 263 LCI(L) Flotilla, designated Group 11. 1st Battalion, Norfolk Regiment (1st Norfolks) came ashore five minutes early, on Queen Red. The remaining two battalions may have landed nearer 10.10: 2nd Battalion, Warwickshire Regiment (2nd Warwicks) on Queen White, and 2nd Battalion, The King's Shropshire Light Infantry (2nd KSLI) on Queen Red.

Two of the craft carrying 2nd Warwicks and one of those carrying the 2nd KSLI were hit by German shell or mortar fire, which inflicted some casualties among the troops before they landed. 2nd KSLI's war diary described the battalion landing in 4–5ft of water, noting that 'it was NOT an easy landing'. However, it was a fast landing: as little as seven minutes in many cases.[75]

LCI(L) 300 was one of the craft carrying 1st Norfolks. The craft's commanding officer, Lieutenant Sidney Henry RNVR, described how his craft beached in front of an enemy-occupied building resembling a hotel which:

> ... was now full of Germans firing down on us from the windows ... I ran on to a submerged beach obstacle which holed the engineroom and detonated a mine under No. 2 troopspace – then holes started appearing in the decks where the mortars were hitting. The explosions stunned everyone momentarily then we all shook ourselves and swung into action. The Oerlikon gunners started blasting the hotel.

After unbeaching, the crew removed the effects of the dead troops on board and buried them at sea using sections of the dismantled galley stove to weight the bodies down.[76]

On LCI(L) 179, crewman Joshua Skinner and his messmate, Jonny Seldon, had saved several tots of rum which they were keeping in Seldon's locker. Both men were on damage-control duty, and after a near-miss by a shell, they decided to sample the rum, only to find that a piece of shrapnel had passed through the locker and smashed the jar. More seriously, one of the crew was badly wounded in the arm.[77]

While LCI(L) 126 was still landing its troops, the crew welcomed on board two officers from LCI(S) 509, Lieutenant Tommy Twiddle RNVR and Lieutenant Herbert Langley RNVR. As described earlier, they had been forced to abandon their craft on the beach after it was holed by a beach obstacle while landing troops of No.3 Commando about forty-five minutes earlier. With shells still bursting around, LCI(L) 126's first lieutenant set them up in the wardroom with a drink to help them recover from their ordeal. Moments later, a German shell hit the wardroom and wounded both men.[78]

Meanwhile, 185th Infantry Brigade, with supporting tanks and other troops, had the D-Day objective of capturing the city of Caen, about 10 miles inland. Although this would prove to be overly ambitious, their day began well as the infantry were ashore promptly. The next requirement was tanks to accompany them to Caen. Due at H+185 (10.30) were eleven LCT(4)s of 40 LCT Flotilla (Group 12), carrying tanks of the Staffordshire Yeomanry (part of British 27th Armoured Brigade) as well as two troops of flail mine-clearing tanks of the Westminster Dragoons, part of 17 and 253 Field Companies RE, and three Valentine Scissors Bridge tanks. These vehicles landed on Queen White and were to support the 185th Infantry Brigade in its advance on Caen. Some Beach Group vehicles were also on these craft.

The tanks landed on time but faced congestion on the beach, which was not helped by the fact that it was close to high tide and the extent of dry beach had now greatly reduced. From the LCTs' point of view, it was a relatively simple landing, although under fire. LCT 958 was hit by a shell and had to be towed back to the UK by another craft from the same flotilla.[79]

The next troops to land were from the third self-propelled artillery regiment, 7th Field Regiment RA. The guns were carried in six LCT(4)s of 32 LCT Flotilla (designated Group 4B), who were due to beach at H+195 (10.40) and were about five minutes late. Their landing on Queen White was not without incident. LCT 859 exploded a succession of mined beach obstacles while landing, which fatally wounded Petty Officer Motor Mechanic Robert Swinney Elliott Stafford and rendered the flotilla officer, Lieutenant Commander Whitehead unconscious as he was inspecting the damage from a previous explosion. This broke the craft's back and the crew had to abandon it on the beach. At least one crewman on another craft was also wounded.[80]

Six LCI(L)s of the US Navy's LCI(L) Division 8, Flotilla 2 (Group 13) landed personnel on Queen White within five minutes of their intended time of H+215 (11.05). These craft and many of their crews had served in the Mediterranean theatre before returning to the UK to take part in Operation Neptune. They were followed soon after by eight more LCI(L)s, which landed at the junction of Queen White and Queen Red, about five minutes later than their due time of 11.25 (H+230). Designated Group 14, four of these were the remainder of LCI(L) Division 8, Flotilla 2, US Navy, and the other four were part of the Royal Navy's 251 LCI(L) Flotilla. These two groups of LCI(L)s were primarily carrying members of 5 Beach Group, such as personnel from the defence battalion (5th Battalion, Kings Regiment), Pioneer companies, Ordnance Beach Detachment personnel and more. Lead elements of 6 Beach Group also began landing.[81]

As Group 13's six craft approached the beach, the crews saw shells bursting along Queen Red and Queen White. The plan had been that three craft would land on each beach, but at 10.40, orders were issued that all six should land on Queen White. They left intervals of 100 yards between craft. Despite the shellfire continuing around them, Group 13 had little or no damage to craft or casualties among the crews and troops, and had unbeached by 11.40.[82]

Group 14's craft also landed under fire but did not escape so lightly. Damage to LCI(L) 174 knocked out its port propeller and the craft broached-to, leading to it being stuck on the beach until the afternoon, when it was towed back to the UK. LCI(L) 116 was hit by two shells after unbeaching but did not suffer serious damage.

LCI(L) 111's Oerlikon gunners returned fire at the beachfront houses, where there were still some German defenders active. A German shell hit LCI(L) 111 in the hull before it could beach, causing casualties to the troops and flooding. While still on the beach, crew members including Alan Higgins entered the troop space to remove the dead and wounded. Shrapnel from the shell had passed straight through the craft, and Higgins recounts that although the flooding was not deep, it was enough to put the wounded at risk of drowning. He applied morphine to several seriously wounded men and the crew later transferred some to a destroyer offshore for treatment. Lightly wounded troops were still landed, and Higgins remembered one wounded man being helped ashore by comrades, 'His left foot and boot as one, a mangle of flesh and leather. I shall never forget the almost apologetic look he gave me as he passed by.' The damage did not prevent LCI(L) 111 returning to the UK under its own power.[83]

At H+250 (11.35), a large wave of craft was due. It included sixteen LCT(4)s formed from the majority of 42 and 48 LCT Flotillas, except for four craft on other duties, and was designated Group 15. They carried priority vehicles for the 185th Infantry Brigade from a variety of units, including the brigade HQ and its three infantry battalions, 2nd KSLI, 2nd Warwicks and 1st Norfolks, as well as various supporting units such as the Royal Artillery, Royal Engineers and more.

The craft arrived off the beaches on time but were faced with vehicle congestion on shore. They began to land on both beaches as planned and some had touched down on Queen White when those on White were ordered to withdraw and the whole group landed further east, almost on Queen Red.

The LCTs began unloading but congestion on the beach hampered the process. Sub Lieutenant Frederick E. Naylor RNVR, commanding officer of LCT 953, recalled that rather than unloading in a matter of minutes, as he was accustomed, the LCT was on the beach for an hour as the unloading of the troops on board was delayed due to high tide and a vehicle traffic jam, 'It was a severe test of nerves just to sit there'. When unbeaching, his craft exploded a mine on a beach obstacle, which destroyed the craft's propellers and broke its back, although fortunately there were no casualties among the crew. At this point, while adrift just off the French coast, Naylor had 'a panoramic view of five miles of coast with fires, smoke, and explosions everywhere, which lives with me to this day'. Eventually, the craft was towed back to Portsmouth.[84]

In his role as signalman on board LCT 821 in the same flotilla, Signalman Eric J. Loseby was on the bridge with the commanding officer. As the craft landed its cargo of vehicles, the two men kept their heads down after a bullet passed close by them. Mortar bombs were landing further along the beach. Loseby was puzzled as to why there seemed to be a group of mugs floating near the water's edge, but then realised that they were attached to the packs still worn by the semi-submerged bodies of troops who had been killed earlier in the day.

After unloading, the crew realised 'with a sickening reality' that the LCT's kedge anchor cable had parted after fouling on a beach obstacle, so their craft would not be able to unbeach immediately but would have to wait for the tide to come in again and refloat them. The LCT's engines had to be shut down when the receding tide soon deprived them of essential cooling water. This, in turn, meant that there was no lighting on board.

'The craft became a dark, silent bulk except for the occasional rattle of flying debris against the hull.' At least the crew could use their coal stove to make a hot drink and Loseby also took the opportunity to have a shave.[85]

Two other LCTs were also part of Group 15 and had arrived off France at around the same time but waited until the afternoon of D-Day before beaching. Like two similar LCTs of 43 LCT Flotilla, which had beached at H+120 as described above, LCTs 1026 and 1070 each carried 200 tons of stores, mainly Royal Engineers' stores and ammunition, for issuing to units on D-Day. The beaching of these two craft was postponed until the afternoon, presumably because enemy shelling and vehicle congestion on the beach made it an unsuitable place to bring ashore LCTs loaded with ammunition. As it was, when the two LCTs beached later on D-Day, Sub Lieutenant Alan Richardson RNVR of LCT 1026 remembered 'a somewhat nail-biting hour when the enemy got the mortar range of our section of beach and pounded the beach for about an hour. Thankfully we were not hit.'[86]

The orders of the British 9th Infantry Brigade state that stores from each LCT were to be unloaded into a separate Sector Stores Dump ashore, close to the beach. The planners' intention was that each infantry brigade would use a separate dump for resupply, with the fourth dump in reserve. This arrangement bought time for the longer-term infrastructure of storage dumps (the Beach Maintenance Area) to be created slightly further inland, which would come into operation when they were sufficiently stocked.

The fighting troops also had their own vehicles carrying stores, which they drew on before turning to any of the dumps. Preparing these dumps was so essential that the brigade's orders threatened that any troops who diverted DUKWs for other tasks would be liable to trial by court martial.[87]

The next wave of craft was apparently due to beach at either H+270 or H+330 (11.55 or 12.55) – sources disagree – but in any case, they seem to have landed at 11.55. This next wave was designated Group 16 and comprised nine LCI(L)s, six of them from 266 LCI(L) Flotilla and three from 265 LCI(L) Flotilla. The main forces on board were the reserve infantry brigade: British 3rd Infantry Division's third brigade, the 9th Infantry Brigade. This comprised 2nd Battalion, Lincolnshire Regiment (2nd Lincolns), 1st Battalion, King's Own Scottish Borderers (1st KOSB) and 2nd Battalion, Royal Ulster Rifles (2nd RUR). The craft also carried other personnel such as medical and signals units.[88]

After departing the Lowering Position, the group received a warning that Queen Red was currently too congested for use, so the three craft that were due to land there joined the rest of the group in landing on the western end of Queen White. As they beached, the craft had to weave between beach obstacles that were showing above the water as the tide fell. There was 'sporadic rifle and mortar fire, some from the houses along the beach and a few bombs were dropped to the westward by enemy aircraft'. Some of the troops had a dry landing, but on LCI(L) 375, for example, the troops were wading through the sea up to their necks, and the senior army officer asked the commanding officer to rebeach, which he complied with, although the water was now only chest high, and the troops did not attempt to land the bicycles that they were carrying.[89]

The landing craft crews did not suffer any casualties, but four vessels had damage from beach obstacles or could not refloat for other reasons. It took around an hour for the troops carried by LCI(L)s 388 and 291 to unload, by which time both craft had been left aground as the tide receded. Both crews went ashore.

Since snipers in beachfront houses were causing 'a lot of trouble', some of the two crews used the ships' small arms as well as weapons they had found on the beach and entered the houses, along with some soldiers. They reportedly drove off seven snipers and returned with an 18-year-old Pole in German service, who said he was the last of his unit alive. At the request of an army captain, the crew of 388 fired a few bursts of Oerlikon fire at other houses and this seemed to reduce the sniping.

Both craft unbeached later. In the case of LCI(L) 388, this was at mid-morning on 7 June, since at the first high tide the crew discovered that the port side propeller had been damaged by a beach obstacle and had to carry out repairs.[90]

While still on the beach, LCI(L) 375's engine room quickly flooded due to a 6in hole. The delay on the beach did however mean that the troops who had already landed could return about an hour later to collect their bicycles. It was the evening of 7 June before the crew could repair the damage and the craft could be refloated, and it only returned to the UK on 10 June.

LCI(L) 387 also had flooding in its engine room. After the first lieutenant, Sub Lieutenant A. Pickles RNVR, had spent forty-five minutes sitting on an oakum pad to block the hole, the crew realised that they would have to beach again immediately. They made repairs, and late on the evening of D-Day managed to unbeach. Arriving back at Portsmouth at 13.00 on 7 June, the commanding officer, Sub Lieutenant S.F. Williams RNVR, was unable to get a response to his signal requesting help, so he beached his craft on Southsea beach. He reported that by this point, the crew had been operating a bucket chain for fifteen hours to cope with flooding, because the portable fire pumps had overheated shortly after unbeaching.[91]

At 12.45, the navy paused the landings for half an hour to allow time to clear away some of the debris on the beach. The next wave was twelve LCT(4)s of 39 LCT Flotilla, designated Group 18. They were ordered to hold off the shore at first, and beached about 14.15, some forty minutes after their scheduled time of H+330, on both parts of Sword Beach. They came under German artillery fire as they headed for the beach, and the falling tide had revealed many beach obstacles. Space on the beach was so limited due to submerged vehicles that LCT 612 reported having to beach over the top of obstacles, relying on the craft's speed to reach the shallows.

The first tank off LCT 612 opened fire at beachfront buildings to deal with suspected enemy snipers and machine gunners. Most prominent among the troops now landing were 1st East Riding Yeomanry, which was the third tank regiment of 27th Armoured Brigade. Their role was to advance rapidly inland towards Caen, supporting 9th Infantry Brigade. Also on board the LCTs were part of 27th Armoured Brigade's HQ and some priority vehicles of the three infantry battalions of 9th Infantry Brigade.[92]

Group 19's landing craft had also been delayed from their intended landing time of H+360. These were twelve LCT(4)s of 47 LCT Flotilla, carrying priority vehicles and stores for 9th Infantry Brigade, which went ashore on Queen Red. As they approached the beach, the craft were shelled, apparently from the Le Havre direction. This firing was ineffective but still worrying for at least some of the personnel on board the LCTs. Most of the craft landed on Queen Red.

As LCT 627 neared the shore, Midshipman Arthur Walters RNVR, the craft's first lieutenant, recalled passing floating bodies and a drifting, disabled LCT with 'a vacant, flattened, smoking quarterdeck, where there used to be a wheelhouse, wardroom, and bridge superstructure – and no sign of life'. Walters was at the LCT's bow, with the role of supervising the raising and lowering of the bow door and the troops going ashore. He had been told that when his craft beached there was a likelihood that the Germans would be counter-attacking the beachhead. He carried a revolver, 'I had orders to wear it and to use it against any unauthorised person who might attempt to board whilst we were beached … not only the enemy, but any "friends" who might be tempted to beat a hasty retreat'.[93]

By the time the LCTs of Groups 18 and 19 were ready to unbeach, the rapidly falling tide had left many of them stranded, as well as sometimes revealing beach obstacles or drowned vehicles that blocked their retreat. No.47 LCT Flotilla reported that many craft had sustained damage to their undersides from mines attached to beach obstacles and four out of the flotilla's twelve craft were unable to immediately return to the UK after unloading. John Dennis of LCT 1065 describes that his commanding officer 'gave the order to abandon [ship] and take the Lanchester Guns and pitch in with the Army' (LCTs carried Lanchester submachine guns for defence).[94]

Also landing around this time were eighty-eight DUKW amphibious trucks preloaded with ammunition. They had arrived off the beaches on the first LSTs to reach Sword Beach: five LST(2)s of 1 LST Flotilla. These vessels had crossed in a small convoy (Assault Group S13), which was scheduled to arrive off Sword Beach at H+240 (1125). Due to the size and vulnerability of the LSTs, it was never planned that they would beach at this point on D-Day. Instead, the DUKWs from 101 General Transport Company RASC were launched from the LSTs several miles out to sea. The LSTs also carried other vehicles, which would land later via one of the Rhino Ferries that each LST had towed across the Channel. The DUKWs would make further trips to unload any other ships – particularly coasters – as required.[95]

This ended the First Tide landings, as the tide fell to the point where it was judged impractical to attempt to land. The next series of landings, beginning as the tide started to rise, would be classed as the Second Tide. No doubt, in practice, it was not quite as neat as this sounds. On paper, the First Tide landings included 110 LCTs, which were to land 1,210 vehicles, not including the vehicles on board the first five LSTs.[96]

★ ★ ★

Events on the beaches after the initial assault tend to be overlooked today. As the above accounts indicate, it was clearly far from safe. Norman Moss was a crewman on an LCA from SS *Empire Battleaxe*, who had landed troops within the first hour of the landings. However, it was his second trip to the beach in mid- or late morning, carrying further troops from *Battleaxe*, that really made an impact on him:

> This was to be a journey from hell and to this day gives me nightmares … As we neared the beach, all sorts of craft lay stranded on the beach, tanks, artillery guns … dead bodies lying in the water and on the beach. We were all seeing the true horrors of war.[97]

Different vessels could be used during the Second Tide landings compared to the preceding hours. Since German defences along the beach and in the immediate coastal area were, in theory (and mostly in practice), overcome, there was no need to divide personnel up between the many minor landing craft such as LCAs that had been used in the first hours (the assault phase). Larger and more vulnerable vessels could be used instead to maximise the volume of personnel, vehicles and stores that were landed. Therefore, a major part of the Second Tide landings were vehicles landed from LSTs, which would anchor offshore, using Rhino Ferries to move those vehicles (and their associated personnel) the last few miles to the beach. The Rhinos were able to unload some vehicles from the LSTs on D-Day before darkness drew a halt.

As the afternoon wore on, the beach was gradually cleared of wreckage and the beach exits were developed to the point where they could cope with the arrival of the many vehicles on board the LSTs. At 15.35, Captain E.W. Bush RN (Captain Group S3) went ashore and found that the beach was becoming clearer of craft but there were still more than twenty-four major landing craft such as LCTs and LCI(L)s dried out on shore. He also recorded continuous mortar fire and an attack by seven German Ju 88 aircraft.[98]

The next wave of landings involved the five LSTs that had arrived several hours ago and had already discharged DUKWs. These remained anchored offshore, but now unloaded the lighter vehicles carried on their top decks using the Rhino Ferry that each ship had towed across the Channel. The Rhinos were scheduled to land their first load of vehicles at 14.25 (H+420) but were delayed until around 16.55 (H+570).

The troops landed from these five LSTs were from a great variety of units. There were too many to list in full detail here, but a representative sample will illustrate the point: in most cases they were not the 'teeth' arms that had by now already landed, but the large and essential logistical and support 'tail' without which the more front-line troops would soon have run out of supplies. Many were Beach Group troops (part of 101 Beach Sub Area), which would help organise and protect the landing beach and the supply depots that were being created immediately behind it. For example, personnel from 84 Field Company RE would work on beach exits and beach clearance – most of this unit had already landed – and 91 Field Company RE would be responsible for transit and assembly areas. There were reconnaissance parties from units whose main bodies would land later, such as from 103rd Heavy Anti-Aircraft Regiment and 73rd Light Anti-Aircraft Regiment, which would provide anti-aircraft defence of the beach area.[99]

The other group of units landing from these first LSTs were part of the British 3rd Infantry Division and attached forces. There were in total more than twenty Bren Carriers from three of the infantry battalions of 9th and 185th Infantry Brigades. No.101 Anti-Tank Battery, 20th Anti-Tank Regiment RA brought ashore twelve 6-pounder anti-tank guns towed by Bren Carriers (the self-propelled guns of that regiment had already landed). There were Light Aid Detachments (LADs) to support the self-propelled guns and tanks of units that had already landed: 7th and 33rd Field Regiments RA, plus the three tank regiments of 27th Armoured Brigade – as well as an RASC company to support the latter. From or attached to the various commando units that had landed at Sword earlier in the day there were thirty jeeps, including several FOO parties.

Advanced elements of 6 Beach Group had already landed, but the majority were due to land at H+11.5 hours (18.55), although they landed slightly later. These troops were landed by eight LCI(L)s, of which five were drawn from 265 LCI(L) Flotilla, two from 261 LCI(L) Flotilla and one from 266 LCI(L) Flotilla. Units from this beach group were to pass through 5 Beach Group, set up assembly areas and the beach maintenance area. The craft were ordered to land on Queen Red, but on approaching the beach the flotilla officer observed two Rhinos blocking part of that beach and decided to go ashore further east, on Queen Green. Here, the uncleared German beach obstacles threatened to damage the LCI(L)s. Combined with heavy surf at the water's edge, a strong tidal current and deep water due to the shallow beach gradient, the conditions here were unsuitable.

Seeking a better landing site, all eight LCI(L)s moved to parts of Queen Red that were not blocked by Rhinos. The conditions were not much better, and three of the crew of LCI(L) 383 dived into the water to rescue two soldiers who were at risk of drowning (both men were subsequently taken back to the UK on the craft, rather than landing in Normandy). The commanding officer of the same craft reported landing the troops' eight handcarts by lashing them all together and pitching them over the side so a bulldozer could recover them.

Some craft later moved to Queen White to unload. Several of the LCI(L)s had lost one or both ramps and had to unload via another LCI(L) or an LCM that had come alongside. It took two hours or more for some of the troops to be put ashore.[100]

The lengthy process of landing troops from these LCI(L)s overlapped with the landing of vehicles from nine more LST(2)s. They had reached Normandy around H+12 hours (19.25) in convoys S-14A and S-15B, with four of the LSTs towing one Rhino Ferry each. These ships were split between Queen White (five LSTs, three Rhinos) and Queen Red (four LSTs, one Rhino). First the LSTs launched sixty-six DUKWs, which were to beach around H+12.5 hours. Then the remaining vehicles would be landed by Rhino, including those Rhinos that had arrived earlier in the day once they had emptied their own wave of LSTs. Included in this group of LSTs were several that were medically equipped, meaning they had been converted to be able to take wounded troops in stretchers on their return to the UK.[101]

At 23.25 (H+16.5 hours), three LSTs were due to arrive. Among their cargoes were sixteen 5.5in guns of 53rd Medium Regiment RA and twelve guns of 93rd Light Anti-Aircraft Regiment RA (half of them were triple 20mm on self-propelled Crusaders, and half towed triple 20mm guns). Originally, it had been planned that these vessels would dry out on the beach to unload, but a late decision was made to unload them using the Rhinos that were already at Sword Beach once they had finished their earlier tasks.[102]

It was not yet twenty-four hours since the first troops had come ashore at Sword Beach. At 05.25 on 7 June (H+22 hours), five more LST(2)s arrived off the beach. They were part of Force L, specifically Group L5, and had crossed with other ships also bound for Gold and Juno beaches in Convoy ETM-1. These ships launched sixty-six DUKWs, which swam ashore. The LSTs were not towing Rhino Ferries, so they would have to wait for Rhinos that had been brought over by earlier LSTs before they could unload their remaining vehicles (the intention was that this would be around H+24).[103]

One group of vessels that are often overlooked when telling the story of D-Day are those belonging to the Build-Up and Landing Barge Flotillas. At Sword Beach, these numbered around 200 vessels of which seventy-two were landing barges and the remainder minor landing craft. Royal Marine crews operated six flotillas of sixteen LCVPs each: 803, 810, 811, 812, 813 and 814 Build-Up Flotillas. Two others – 602 and 603 Build-Up Flotillas – had LCM(1)s, while 653 Build-Up Flotilla was equipped with LCM(3)s. The latter has already had a passing mention above: eight LCM(3)s of 653 Build-Up Flotilla had crossed earlier than the rest to land Royal Engineer equipment about an hour after H-Hour.

This early arrival was the exception, however, and most landing barge and build-up vessels arrived at Sword later on D-Day or on D+1. They would spend weeks (or longer) at Normandy, acting as ferry craft and helping to unload larger vessels. The landing barges had Royal Navy crews. As their names suggest, 5 and 6 LBV Flotillas were equipped with the LBVs. Some LBVs were carrying stores that would be unloaded for use by the troops ashore, while others crossed empty. No.35 Landing Barge (Supply and Repair) Flotilla had a mix of support craft: one LCE, six LBEs, one LBK, ten LBOs and two LBWs. No.30 Landing Barge (Supply and Repair) Flotilla primarily operated at Juno Beach but seems to have supplied three LBEs, one LBK, six LBOs and two LBWs to operate off Sword. These were the flotilla compositions on paper, but lost or delayed craft would have altered the exact numbers.[104]

Records of what these craft carried across the English Channel are incomplete. Most of the minor landing craft arrived roughly when expected, but bad weather delayed some barges by twelve hours or more, while others had to turn back or were lost during the crossing. It was planned that Convoy SM-1 (five LBFs and nine laden LBVs) would arrive off Sword Beach at H+13.5 hours. These nine LBVs carried 450 tons of stores, including 82 tons of ammunition, 232 tons of Royal Engineers stores, 101 tons of petrol, lubricants and oil and 25 tons of water. The Royal Engineers stores included bridging materials which bridging company lorries that had landed on the first tide would return as soon as possible to collect.[105]

Convoy SM-2 (all the LCM and LCVP flotillas listed immediately above) were due to arrive off Sword before the end of D-Day. Due around the same time were the landing barges of Group SM3, including twenty-seven LBVs (six laden, twenty-one empty), three LBEs, two LBWs and twelve LBOs.

Convoy SM-4 consisted of some of the landing barges from the Supply and Repair Flotillas (six LBEs, two LBWs, four LBOs and two LBKs) and did not depart the UK until the early morning of 7 June 1944, with an arrival time of 23.00 that day. Until the LBKs arrived on D+1 with the means to provide the crews of minor landing craft with hot meals, they had to go without a decent meal. Six of the LBVs that would be available to be unloaded on D+1 (it is not clear which convoy they arrived in) would together provide 300 tons of stores: 20 tons of ammunition, 50 tons of smoke-generating materials, 102 tons of Royal Engineers stores and 128 tons of other army supplies.[106]

Landing barges could dry out on the beach for ease of unloading. Similarly, the preloaded LCMs were reported to have beached on arrival and then at first light on 7 June, they began unloading stores and motor transport from coasters moored off the beach.

Landing barge crews remembered the voyage to Sword Beach as 'very hairy', 'horrendous' and 'grim'. Stoker Alf Bairstow on LBV 42 recalled that soon after they arrived at Sword Beach a German shell destroyed their craft's wheelhouse and engines, so they had to be towed everywhere. Since they were carrying a cargo of petrol, they were forbidden to smoke or strike a match.[107]

In an extreme case, LBV 201 took twelve days to reach its destination. The barge set off in convoy from the Solent area at 07.30 on 5 June but had engine trouble and ended up beached on the Isle of Wight alongside LBE 32, which was suffering from similar problems. After some maintenance work, both barges set off again at 14.00 on D-Day, although the LBE had to turn back two hours later with more engine problems. The LBV continued and for a while was towed by a convoy until the towing ship went to action stations and had to cast them adrift in order to speed up. About an hour later, another passing convoy opened fire on LBV 201, but ceased fire when signalled the 'V' sign. One engine was out of action for hours from 03.00.

At 06.00 the crew sighted the French coast but there was no sign of Allied shipping, and without a compass they could only head east and then follow a southbound convoy. A passing trawler informed them they were off Sword Beach, and around 20.00 on 7 June, a fleet minesweeper took them under tow, eventually reaching Omaha Beach on 8 June. After some persuasion, an LBE repaired their engines and LBV 201 managed to reach Sword Beach on 18 June, twelve days late.[108]

With the approach of dusk on D-Day, a group of craft moved to the east flank of the landing beaches to form the Trout Line. This was a defensive line of support landing craft and other vessels, such as motor launches and motor torpedo boats, which was intended to protect the anchorage against German attacks from the east – for example, E-boats sortieing from Le Havre.

Royal Marine Buck Taylor was part of the crew of LCF 24, which had spent most of D-Day off Juno Beach. Around 20.00, they moved to join the Trout Line and were in position by 22.00. It was a busy night, as Allied shipping fired in response to a German air raid around midnight, in which he counted twenty bombs falling in the water, 'The sky is covered with flares and tracer fire, all ships seem to be putting up anything they have got'. At 03.00 there was an E-boat warning, though no attack materialised, and forty-five minutes later there was another air raid.[109]

The above accounts have been about landings that did take place, but at 20.30, the decision was made by Allied commanders to cancel a pair of amphibious assaults. Operations Frog and Deer were commando landings that had been planned in case they were needed to destroy the German gun batteries at Houlgate, Benerville and Villerville. These were major batteries located to the east of the River Orne and beyond the Allied landing area, which could have seriously interfered with the landings. The troops who would have carried out this landing were 46 RM Commando, embarked on board two LSIs, HMS *Prins Albert* and SS *Princess Margaret*. The two ships carried respectively eight LCAs from 503 Assault Flotilla and six LCAs of 523 Assault Flotilla.[110]

Twenty-four hours after H-Hour, at 07.25 on 7 June, nine LCI(L)s delivered foot troops from units including the 12th Battalion, Devonshire Regiment (part of the 6th Airborne Division) as well as 420 reinforcements who could be used to replace casualties in units that were already ashore. These craft had crossed the English Channel in Convoy ETM-1. At 08.55 (H+25.5 hours), eight motor transport (MT) coasters arrived carrying vehicles from a variety of units such as the 3rd Infantry Division, the 12th Devonshires and the Beach Groups. The ships anchored at the Lowering Position and would be unloaded by ferry craft.

Around the same time, a single LCI(L) delivered personnel of 1028 and 1056 Port Operating Companies RE. Two more MT coasters were due at 19.55 on D+1 (H+36.5 hours), which would again anchor offshore and transfer their cargo of vehicles into ferry craft. These last arrivals on the evening of D+1 brought an end to the landings of the British 3rd Infantry Division, but more convoys would continue to arrive over the following days bringing further troops, vehicles and supplies.[111]

The casualties among the troops landing on Sword Beach indicate the severity of the fighting there on D-Day. A wartime report attempted to compare the losses on each beach. For the assault battalions on Sword Beach, these were estimated at 22.5 per cent and 28 per cent for Queen White and Queen Red respectively. These figures exclude fighting further inland and are necessarily an estimate because the exact location of all casualties was hard to determine. The next highest figures on the other Anglo-Canadian beaches were 16 per cent on King Red (Gold Beach) and 15 per cent on both Nan White and Nan Red (Juno Beach).[112]

The Commander Force S pithily summed up the German defences on Sword with the phrase, 'Too much concrete, too little morale'. The above accounts show that putting the troops ashore on Sword Beach was much more challenging that this might suggest.[113]

11

After D-Day

D-Day was only the beginning of a long campaign: the Allies needed a constant flow of fresh troops and supplies in order to expand the newly won bridgehead. Losses and crew casualties on D-Day clearly had an impact on later operations. Complete losses of ships and landing craft were lower than predicted, but as the following table shows, an unexpectedly large number – particularly of LCTs and smaller craft – had been damaged (see ddaylandingcraft.net for a Roll of Honour of landing craft crewmen).[1]

Number of craft:	Total / Lost or badly damaged on D-Day					
	Utah	Omaha	Gold	Juno	Sword	Total
LCT (all types) inc. LCT(A)/(HE)	158 / 11+	144 / 20+	148 / 34	150 / 42	141 / 18	741 / 125+
LCI(L) & LCH	49 / 11	37 / 10+	27 / 0	27 / 4	54 / 9	194 / 34+
LCI(S)				11 / 7	28 / 15	39 / 22
LCM inc. LCM(Salvage)	73 / 2+	151 / 8?	96 / 10	96 / 2	48 / 7	464 / 29+
LCA	18 / 1?	76 / 14	148 / 52	168 / 36	92 / 29	474 / 132
LCVP (excluding ferry craft)	65 / 43	124 / 40+				189 / 83+
LCP(L) & LCP(Sy)	18 / 7?	36 / 0	38 / 2	42 / 0	20 / 3	154 / 12+

After D-Day, landing craft operated in the Shuttle or Ferry service. Those in the Shuttle service, primarily LSTs, LCI(L)s, LCT(3)s and LCT(4)s, made repeated crossings of the English Channel, alongside other shipping. With their sizeable carrying capacity, LSTs underpinned the build-up period, as post-D-Day operations were known. 'Medically fitted' LSTs, with racks for stretchers along the sides of the tank deck and extra medical staff, were also vital for evacuating the many wounded from the land battle. Channel crossings 'could be idyllic on velvet star-studded nights when there was no wind, the air was warm, the sea calm … in the moonlight even an LCT took on a certain beauty …' 'Starlight' convoys to Normandy (each identified with the addition of a sequential number) were intended to travel at night so that darkness would hide the convoy's approach. Return convoys were designated 'Bluesky': a daytime return trip aimed to avoid the threat of nighttime attacks by E-boat (fast German torpedo boats). Operation Neptune ended on 30 June, when, as the Admiralty described it, Neptune 'merged into the larger operation – "Overlord" – of which it had been the naval preliminary'. Yet the Shuttle service was still running a year later, though with many fewer craft. [2]

Some 1,500 ferry craft remained based on the Normandy coast, tasked with 'ferrying' troops and other cargoes the last few miles to the beach from larger ships. They included LCT(5)s and LCT(6)s – which were specially designed to unload LSTs – landing barges, DUKWs, Rhinos and many minor landing craft. The process was directed by a variety of naval officers and units, working with the Allied armies. Landing craft crews, especially on ferry craft, experienced spartan living conditions. Royal Navy Signalman G.R. Cooper on LCT(5) 2226 recalled that over time the crew's clothing became worn out: 'we wore any gear we found on the beach. Pretty soon we had a signal telling us that any person found wearing a piratical rig would be severely dealt with.' [3]

The two Mulberry artificial harbours were assembled soon after D-Day, to provide a means of speeding up unloading. Mulberry A at Saint-Laurent-sur-Mer (Omaha Beach) was abandoned after being critically damaged by the storm of 19–21 June. Some of its components were used to repair damage to Mulberry B at Arromanches (Gold Beach), which continued in use well beyond the end of the Normandy campaign. MT ships and LSTs using the Mulberry could unload six times faster than drying out on the beach. Though the US Navy were sceptical of the value of the Mulberries, historian Christopher Yung points out that the period immediately following the storm, when disembarkation could only take place over the beaches, demonstrates that the Allies could not have achieved a sufficient unloading rate without the Mulberry harbours. Naval lighter pontoons proved useful for speeding up the landing of vehicles from LCTs and LSTs, particularly as a means of crossing patches of clay on the beach. Although both Mulberries and the Gooseberries (breakwaters formed from sunken merchant ships) provided valuable shelter, the storm left some 800 landing craft lost or damaged. It was only on 8 July – at the next spring tides – that 600 of these now repaired craft could be refloated.[4]

To resolve the interruption in unloading caused by the storm, increasing numbers of LSTs and even coasters were dried out on the beach: the vessel would be stranded by the falling tide, so its cargo could be more easily unloaded. This technique was initially discouraged for fear of hull damage and because it risked delays. An LST would have an eighteen-hour turn-around time if it was dried out and it waited to be refloated by the tide, compared to four hours if unloaded by Rhino – assuming a Rhino was immediately available. Drying out became common practice to unload LSTs, LCTs, LBVs and smaller craft.[5]

The Mulberry harbours were the Allies' solution to the problem that ports in Normandy were unlikely to be immediately available due to damage and German sabotage. The smaller ports came into use soon after D-Day, with LBVs and minor landing craft unloading some 1,000 tons of supplies per day at both Courseulles (Juno Beach) and Port-en-Bessin (Gold Beach). By August, barges and landing craft were among the vessels delivering cargoes to the newly opened port of Cherbourg. The vast majority of personnel and vehicles were landed via the beaches, however, (including Mulberry B) rather than at ports.[6]

There are various incomplete sets of figures for the numbers of landing craft and landing ships lost during the whole Normandy campaign. For the period from D-Day to D+30 (6 July 1944), the Admiralty list 168 major and minor landing craft, ships and barges lost, and 502 damaged. These figures appear only to cover the Eastern Task Force (ETF), off the British Canadian beaches. For the entire period of June and July 1944, the ETF reported 448 landing craft lost; at least 80 per cent were minor landing craft, among them 186 LCAs, fifty-eight LCVPs and eighty LCMs. Only twenty-five LCTs, three LCI(L)s and LCHs, three LCG(L)s, and thirty-six barges of all types are on this list.[7]

From D-Day to D+25 (1 July 1944), figures for the Western Task Force (WTF, operating off the US beaches) record twenty-two LSTs and 160 major landing craft lost or damaged (minor landing craft are excluded). The roughly equivalent figures for the ETF were twenty-six LSTs and 361 major landing craft (though over five additional days, up to D+30). The major landing craft figure is significantly higher for the ETF, which probably mainly reflects differing definitions of 'damaged'. Enemy attack was a relatively low threat: only twenty-three of those 160 WTF major landing craft were lost to the enemy, of which nineteen were from mines. The impact of the storm can be illustrated by the fact that sixty-nine of that same group of 160 craft were lost or damaged during the three days of the storm, forty-one on D-Day, thirty-nine over the period D+1 to D+4, and the remaining eleven on other days up to D+25.[8]

Though responsible for a comparatively small proportion of losses, German forces did remain a threat. Sword Beach was under regular artillery fire from the east, and on 15 June five beached US LSTs and two other ships were hit by German shells. In the daytime, LCG(L)s often patrolled the eastern flank to provide counter-battery fire and draw off enemy shells. Aerial bombing and minelaying were also ongoing threats, particularly at night. German air raids on the anchorage on the night of 7–8 June killed several Royal Navy sailors of B Build-Up Squadron, and destroyed four LCVPs. Every evening up to forty British support craft, such as LCFs and LCG(L)s, moored in a line along the eastern edge of the landings – the 'Trout Line' – as protection against attacks by small German craft, such as explosive motor boats and human torpedoes. LCP(L)s and LCVPs sometimes also patrolled as part of these defences, and motor torpedo boats and motor launches formed an outer screen. Around 100 crewmen were killed during Trout Line duties, which continued until the end of August 1944.[9]

Though a relatively small proportion of landing craft and ships were lost to enemy action, this was little consolation for the crews concerned. Several incidents are described below; other ships were also lost over the same period. At 01.15 on 8 June 1944, LCT(4) 875 of the Royal Navy was torpedoed by an E-boat with the loss of eleven crew. Just a few hours later, up to eight E-boats fought a forty-minute battle with torpedoes and gunfire against a British convoy of fourteen LCTs and three LCI(L)s heading for France. Both LCI(L) 105 and LCT(3) 390 were torpedoed and sank swiftly, killing seven and eight Royal Navy crew respectively. Troops on board the LCI(L) who also died included a reconnaissance party of fourteen RAOC officers. LCT(4) 608 had its bows blown off, but was later successfully towed back to the UK. As well as the single motor launch escort, LCT(3) 372's crew exploded an E-boat at 200 yards' range with their 2-pounder Pom-Pom guns.[10]

Later that day, thirteen US sailors died when LST 499 was sunk by a mine off Utah Beach. E-boats struck again in the early morning of 9 June, sinking two US Navy LSTs. LST 314 sank rapidly with the loss of some sixty-six crew, while LST 376 was heavily damaged (at least forty-seven crew were killed) and had to be scuttled a few hours later. There were also losses amongst the embarked troops. Over the next ten days, two more US Navy LSTs were badly damaged and a third sunk (one by a torpedo, two by mines), with the deaths of at least fifty-nine sailors in total. Thirty-five Royal Navy sailors died when LCH 185 was sunk by a mine on 25 June. Around half of the post-D-Day landing craft crew deaths in June were on the above six LSTs alone, reflecting the large crews of such ships. Total crew deaths were lower in July, but rose again in August, particularly due to the death of sixty-seven Royal Navy sailors and Royal Marines in the loss of LCF 1 on 17 August while on the Trout Line.[11]

Over the period 7–30 June, the arrivals of troop-carrying shipping at Normandy amounted to 905 LSTs, 1,442 LCTs and 372 LCI(L)s, as well as over 1,500 ships of other types. These crossings delivered 850,000 troops, 485,000 tons of stores and 153,000 vehicles. Support personnel and bases in the United Kingdom played an essential role in these efforts. From the Royal Navy's Portsmouth Command, for example, 95,762 personnel and 13,299 vehicles had been embarked before D-Day, while over the period from D-Day to 4 July, a further 208,742 personnel and 48,439 vehicles were despatched. Various inter-service bodies co-ordinated the movement of Allied forces to France. BUCO (Build Up Control Organisation) matched the army's requirements for shipping with the available vessels. A TURCO (Turn Round Control Organisation) at each major embarkation point identified the arriving vessels and ensured each was ready to make another Channel crossing. MOVCO (the Movement Control Organisation) timetabled the movement of troops from concentration areas inland to embarkation sites.[12]

Up to 3 July 1944, repairs had been carried out afloat to 1,021 landing craft in the Gosport and Calshot areas of the Solent. A further thirty LCTs had been beached near Gosport for repairs below the waterline, often involving rudder or hull damage. More substantial repair work was carried out at bases that had repair facilities, or at private yards. With his eye for detail, the serviceability status of LCTs was a subject on which British Prime Minister Winston Churchill demanded regular reports during the months after D-Day.[13]

Some landing craft from Normandy were later used in operations elsewhere, including the landings in the South of France (Operation Dragoon) on 15 August 1944, and the Walcheren landings in the Netherlands (Operation Infatuate) on 1 November. From August, some major landing craft and their crews began to be urgently prepared for the Far East: the craft were 'tropicalised', or fitted with additional equipment for hot environments. Horace Ely of 524 Assault Flotilla, a veteran of the North Africa, Sicily and Salerno landings as well as Normandy, found himself transferred to the British Army and sent to Burma: 'I remember going through a big tent [in] Liverpool and getting my Navy discharge papers in one hand and Army call up in the other one.'[14]

With the war at an end, most landing craft were soon scrapped or sold off, for example as houseboats. A handful still survive as museum ships, such as LCT(3) 7074 at The D-Day Story, Portsmouth, UK, and LST 325 and LST 393 at Evansville, Indiana, and Muskegon, Michigan, respectively. The former LST 510 – now renamed MV *Cape Henlopen* – still operates as a passenger ferry across Long Island Sound, USA.[15]

For most landing craft veterans, their service at Normandy was a formative and memorable part of their lives, but one that was difficult to discuss with non-veterans. Many, like Raymond C. Oram of LCT(4) 1046, drew positive lessons from their service: 'To keep fit, to be alert, to see and appreciate what goes on around you ... Never to forget those with whom I trained and served who did not survive to enjoy the happy and long life that I have experienced.' Many carried physical or mental scars. LCA crewman Norman Moss wrote his wartime memoirs for the LST and Landing Craft Association, concluding: 'For some fifty years I lived with this memory and spoke very little of my time at war. It often provoked nightmares. Now at the ripe old age of 83 ... it might help me to lay down some memories to peace at last.'[16]

The D-Day landing craft story has not come to an end. Veterans' stories sometimes continue through their children. Growing up, Tom Carter and his siblings regularly looked at the D-Day diary of their father, US Navy veteran Luke Carter of LCT(6) 614: 'We grew up knowing the difference between a 20mm and a quad 40 the way other kids grew up knowing the difference between a tricycle and a bicycle.' In 2016 the remains of an unknown serviceman buried at the Normandy American Cemetery were identified through research and DNA testing as those of Motor Machinist's Mate Class John Emanuel Anderson USN of LCT(5) 30, a craft lost at Omaha Beach. Anderson's remains were reinterred at his home town of Willmar, Minnesota, some seventy-four years after he had left.[17]

Order of Battle

This order of battle represents landing craft in their units (squadrons, flotillas, groups and divisions, within assault groups), which were partly for administrative purposes. US flotillas were comparable in size to British/Canadian squadrons; US groups were comparable to British/Canadian flotillas.

On D-Day, not all craft operated alongside the rest of the same unit. The craft are not listed below in the convoys they formed on D-Day to cross the English Channel. This Order of Battle is based on the 'Green List', dated 6 June 1944, produced by the Royal Navy and including a supplement listing US Navy landing craft, but supplemented by many other sources. After D-Day, the order of battle changed due to craft being damaged or lost.[*]

The exact composition of the minor landing craft carried by landing ships – the various types of LSIs and APAs – was not fixed, and sometimes slight variations were made for D-Day compared to the craft shown in the 'Green List'. The order of battle below shows the actual craft carried on D-Day, as far as could be determined.

---

[*] The main source for this section was the 'Green List', including US craft section, at the National Archive (TNA), ADM 210/8. Various threads on the different beaches on WW2Talk.com by Mike ('Trux') and other forum members were also particularly useful on points of detail. Many other files from TNA and Fold3 were also used to compile this list, as were other sources, including but not limited to: RAN, Admiralty, *Battle Summary*; TNA, ADM 179/458; TNA, ADM 199/1563; TNA, ADM 199/1564; TNA, ADM 199/1568. Veterans' memoirs were also used to confirm certain details.

There are many issues that may obscure certain details. For example, many APAs (US landing ships) carried several more LCVPs than their standard allowance. In addition to those that landed troops, there were often a couple of craft for use by boat commanders, which wartime records do not always mention (those extra craft are included below). As mentioned in previous chapters, many LSTs were towing Rhino Ferries, and some were towing pontoon causeways – neither are listed here. Fuelling trawlers accompanying landing barges are also not listed. A small number of minor landing craft carried on board other types of ships, including LSTs, FDTs and LSEs are not included or not listed in detail. Despite best efforts, there are undoubtedly errors in this list, and the author will be glad to hear more via ddaylandingcraft.net.

The wide variety of vessels other than landing craft are not listed here, which of course is not to suggest that they did not play a vital role in Operation Neptune. For more information on other vessels, see:

Benbow, Tim (ed.), *Operation Neptune: The D-Day Landings, 6 June 1944* (Solihull: Helion, 2015).

Williams, Greg H., *The US Navy at Normandy: Fleet Organization and Operations in the D-Day Invasion* (Jefferson, NC: McFarland, 2020).

Winser, John de S., *The D-Day Ships* (Kendal: World Ship Society, 1994).

Key

[*A]	This craft was an alternative, last-minute replacement (for example, due to engine failure on another craft).
[*C]	Craft 'on call', without an exact landing time.
[*L]	Craft lost shortly before D-Day; naturally, that meant that such craft were not present on D-Day, but they are included in this list as they may be referred to in planning documents (craft lost on D-Day are not specifically identified here).
[*N]	Craft was not operational, not allocated to assault duties or otherwise not present on D-Day.
[*RM]	Crew of craft indicated – one or more LCS(M)s – were primarily or entirely Royal Marines, whereas remainder of flotilla had Royal Navy crews.

[*SP]   Spare craft held in reserve as last-minute replacements and probably did not sail on D-Day but were used in later crossings.

[???]   Landing craft pennant or hull number not known, typically because a landing craft was replaced shortly before D-Day.

[number] x [landing craft type]

The quantity of that type of craft, pennant/hull numbers not known, so '18 x LCAs 655, 657 ...' means eighteen LCAs, including LCA 655, LCA 657, etc.

'?'   Indicates uncertainty.

Service (RN, RM, USN, USCG)

Indicates the service to which the majority of crew members belonged.

Note: LCHs were sometimes described as LCI(L)s, which was the type of craft they were converted from. LCT(A) units might include a mix of LCT(A)s, LCT(HE)s, LCT(CB)s and LCT(5)s.

Force U (Task Force 125, USN)

Carrying US 4th Infantry Division and supporting forces.

Green Assault Group (Task Group 125.4, USN)

Divided between Red and Green Assault Groups: 8th, 12th and 22nd Regimental Combat Teams of US 4th Infantry Division and supporting forces (including two battalions of 359th Infantry Regiment, US 90th Infantry Division):

LCH 530 (SOAG Green).
USS *Joseph T. Dickman* (APA 13), USCG: 31 x LCVPs, 4 x LCS(S)s, 2 x LCM(3)s. Crews USCG, except for LCS(S)s, which have USN crews.
552 Assault Flotilla, RN (SS *Empire Gauntlet*, LSI(L)): 18 x LCAs 666, 727, 734, 799, 800, 846, 912, 923, 942, 943, 955, 957, 959, 991, 992, 998, 1042, 1135; LCP(L)s 41, 47.

LST Flotilla 10, USN
Group 29, Division 57, USN: LST(2)s 47, 48, 281, 501.
Group 29, Division 58, USN: LST(2)s 49, 50, 283, 491, 492.

Group 32, Division 63, USN: LST(2)s 57, 290, 500, 508, 539.
Group 32, Division 64, USN: LST(2) 351.
[These LSTs were carrying additional LCVPs, which were used in the assault and later as ferry craft.]

LCI(L) Flotilla 10, USN
LCI(L) Group 30, Division 59, USCG: LCI(L)s 319, 320: LCH 321 (DSOAG Green); LCI(L)s 322, 323, 324.
LCI(L) Group 30, Division 60, USCG: LCI(L) 96.

LCI(L) Flotilla 11, USN
LCI(L) Group 32, Division 63, USN: LCI(L)s 513, 514, 515, 516, 517.
LCI(L) Group 32, Division 64, USN: LCI(L)s 517, 521, 522, 523, 524 [★C], 525, 526.
LCI(L) Group 33, Division 65, USN: LCI(L)s 527, 528, 529, 551, 552.

LCT Flotilla 4, USN
LCT Group 10, Division 19, USN: LCT(5)s 447, 456, 457, 458, 459, 497.
LCT Group 11, Division 22, USN: LCT(6)s 522, 524, 527, 528, 529, 530.
LCT Group 12, Division 23, USN: LCT(6)s 525, 526, 532, 533, 534.
LCT Group 12, Division 24, USN: LCT(6)s 515, 516, 517, 518, 519, 520.

LCT Flotilla 17, USN
LCT Group 49, Division 67, USN: LCT(6)s 580, 581, 583, 584, 585.
LCT Group 49, Division 70, USN: LCT(6)s 592, 593, 594, 595.

G LCT Squadron, RN
52 LCT Flotilla, RN: LCT(4)s 512, 646, 793, 795, 798, 799, 822, 837, 977, 996, 997, 1050.

O LCT Squadron, RN
104 LCT Flotilla, RN: LCT(5)s 2045, 2189, 2194, 2226, 2261, 2331, 2440. [Presumed to have been in Green Assault Group. One more craft of this flotilla, which is listed below in Red Assault Group, Force U, may in fact have been in Green Assault Group.]
107 LCT Flotilla, RN: LCT(5)s 2011, 2053, 2056, 2057, 2073, 2074, 2186, 2235, 2269, 2292, 2302, 2304, 2427, 2477, 2485.

LCM Flotilla 2, USN: 26 x LCM(3)s, including 3 x LCM(3)s of LCM Salvage Flotilla, USN; 4 x LCM(3)s with Gap Assault Team reserve/explosives.
LCCs 60, 70.

Red Assault Group (Task Group 125.5, USN)

Divided between Red and Green Assault Groups: 8th, 12th and 22nd Regimental Combat Teams of US 4th Infantry Division and supporting forces (including two battalions of 359th Infantry Regiment, US 90th Infantry Division):

LCH 10 (SOAG Red); LCI(L) 217 (DSOAG Red).
USS *Bayfield* (APA 33), USCG: 19 x LCVPs, 2 x LCM(3)s, 2 x LCP(L)s, 4 x LCS(S)s. USCG crews for all except LCS(S)s, which have USN crews.
USS *Barnett* (APA 5), USN/USCG: 25 x LCVPs, 2 x LCP(L)s, 2 x LCM(3)s, 4 x LCS(S)s. Ship's crew, and probably also landing craft crews, were a mix of USN and USCG.

LST Flotilla 10, USN
Group 29, Division 57, USN: LST(2)s 230, 282.
Group 32, Division 64, USN: LST(2)s 46, 58, 294, 509, 515.
Group 32, Division 66, USN: LST(2)s 311, 346, 371, 380, 382, 400.
These were carrying additional LCVPs, which were used in the assault and later as ferry craft.

LCI(L) Flotilla 2, USN
LCI(L) Group 5, Division 7, USN: LCI(L)s 3, 4, 5, 8.
LCI(L) Group 5, Division 9, USN: LCI(L)s 11, 218, 219, 229, 232.
LCI(L) Group 5, Division 10, USN: LCI(L)s 211, 212, 213, 214, 216, 231, 215.

LCI(L) Flotilla 10, USN
LCI(L) Group 30, Division 60, USCG: LCH 95 [later Ferry Control HQ]; LCI(L)s 96, 325, 326, 349, 350.

LCI(L) Flotilla 11, USN
LCI(L) Group 32, Division 63, USN: LCH 419.

LCT Flotilla 4, USN
LCT Group 10, Division 20, USN: LCT(5)s 443, 474, 475, 486, 489, 495.
LCT Group 11, Division 21, USN: LCT(5)s 3, 362, 476, 492; LCT(6)s 510, 511.
LCT Group 12, Division 23, USN: LCT(6) 531. [Rest of division is in Green Assault Group.]

LCT Flotilla 17, USN
LCT Group 50, Division 99, USN: LCT(6)s 620, 621, 662, 763, 764, 765.
LCT Group 50, Division 100, USN: LCT(6)s 663, 766, 777, 809, 810, 811.
LCT Group 50, Division 101, USN: LCT(6)s 851, 852, 853, 854, 855, 812.
LCT Group 51, Division 102, USN: LCT(6)s 664, 709, 710, 778, 779, 780.
LCT Group 49, Division 70, USN: LCT(6)s 596, 597. [Rest of Division in Green Assault Group.]

G LCT Squadron, RN
44 LCT Flotilla, RN: LCT(4)s 651, 753 [*SP], 755 [*SP], 756, 758, 800 [*SP], 954, 965, 966, 967, 969 [*SP], 970 [*SP]. [Only five of these LCTs present on D-Day?]
50 LCT Flotilla, RN: LCT(4)s 645, 691, 794, 797, 801, 824, 833, 836, 920, 956, 974, 975.

O LCT Squadron, RN
104 LCT Flotilla, RN: LCT(5)s 2002, 2046, 2055, 2130, 2131, 2272, 2303; LCT(6) 3628. [One craft listed here may in fact have been in Green Assault Group, Force U.]
110 LCT Flotilla, RN: LCT(5)s 2004, 2040, 2135, 2138, 2188, 2363, 2421, 2423, 2424, 2429, 2437, 2483, 2484, 2498 [*L]; LCT(6) 3627.
LCM Flotilla 2, USN: 26 x LCM(3)s [including 3 x LCM(3)s of LCM Salvage Flotilla, USN; 4 x LCM(3)s with Gap Assault Team reserve/explosives].
LCCs 80, 90.

Force U Support Group (Task Group 125.7, USN)

LCH 209.
LCG(L)s 5, 6, 7, 893.
LCFs 18, 22, 27, 31.

LCT(A)s 2282, 2301, 2309, 2310, 2402, 2454, 2478, 2488.
LCT(R)s 368, 425, 439, 448, 481.
12 x LCS(S)s 1, 2, 3, 4, 5, 6, 7, 8, 9, 10, 11, 12 [listed above, under the APAs that transported them across the English Channel].
16 x LCP(L)s 85, 86, 88, 95, 97, 98, 118, 137, 145, 146, 149, 150, 240, 245, 246, 269 [towed across the English Channel].

Build-Up Flotillas (Becomes Far Shore Service Group, Force U; Task Group 125.10, USN)

X LB Squadron, RN
8 LBV Flotilla, RN: LBV(2)s 5, 9, 14, 15, 16, 21, 30, 51, 65, 73, 82, 83.
19 LBV Flotilla, RN: LBV(2)s 29, 31, 35, 50, 63, 72, 87, 113, 118, 121, 137, 174.
20 LBV Flotilla, RN: LBV(2)s 151, 154, 157, 170, 175, 181, 184, 186, 187, 210, 212, 230.
33 LB (Supply and Repair) Flotilla, RN: LBEs 12, 30, 32; LBOs 13, 21, 24, 26, 77, 79, 82, 92, 95, 96; LBW 6.
34 LB (Supply and Repair) Flotilla, RN: LBEs 28, 33, 34, 37, 52, 55; LBKs 3, 8; LBOs 6, 11, 30, 44, 54, 63, 69, 87, 88, 89; LBWs 1, 4.
LCM Flotilla 2, USN: 16 x LCM(3)s.

Force O (Task Force 124, USN)

Carrying US 1st Infantry Division (plus one regimental combat team of US 29th Infantry Division) and supporting forces.

Assault Group O1 (Task Group 124.3, USN)

Carrying US 16th Regimental Combat Team and supporting forces.

Transport Division 1
USS *Samuel Chase* (APA 26), USCG: 27 x LCVPs, 1 x LCS(S), 2 x LCM(3)s.
USS *Henrico* (APA 45), USN: 25 x LCVPs, 2 x LCM(3)s.
550 Assault Flotilla, RN (SS *Empire Anvil*, LSI(L)): 18 x LCAs 655, 657, 725, 787, 788, 849, 852, 913, 1028, 1030, 1074, 1079, 1080, 1081, 1082, 1088, 1134, 1144; LCP(L)s 28, 37.

LST Flotilla 10, USN (Including Attached Divisions from LST Flotilla 12)
Group 34, Division 68, USN: LSTs 314, 357, 374, 376.
Group 35, Division 69, USN: LSTs 309, 373.
[Small boats carried by these included a total of 5 x LCS(S)s plus LCVPs.]

LCI(L) Flotilla 10, USN
LCI(L) Group 28, Division 56, USN: LCI(L) 493.
LCI(L) Group 29, Division 57, USCG: LCI(L)s 83, 85; LCH 87;
LCI(L) 88.
LCI(L) Group 29, Division 58, USCG: LCI(L) 89.

LCT Flotilla 26
LCT Group 36, Division 71, USN: LCT(6)s 598, 599, 600, 601, 602, 603.

LCT Flotilla 18
LCT Group 52, Division 103, USN: LCT(5)s 18, 20.
LCT Group 53, Division 105, USN: LCT(5)s 25, 199, 200, 201.
LCT Group 53, Division 106, USN: LCT(5)s 195, 271, 305.
LCT Group 54, Division 108, USN: LCT(5)s 206, 209, 213, 276, 293.

LCT Flotilla 19
LCT Group 55, Division 109, USN: LCT(6)s 537, 538, 539, 540, 541, 542.
LCT Group 55, Division 110, USN: LCT(6)s 543, 544, 545, 546, 547, 548.
LCT Group 55, Division 111, USN: LCT(6)s 549, 550, 623, 624, 625, 626.
LCT Group 56, Division 112, USN: LCT(6)s 637, 638.

Provisional LCT Flotilla 26
LCT Group 76, Division 152, USN: LCT(6)s 814, 815, 856.
LCT Group 77, Division 153, USN: LCT(6) 769.
Control craft, USN: LCCs 10, 20.
18 x LCM(3)s.

Assault Group O2 (Task Group 124.4, USN)

Carrying US 115th and 116th Regimental Combat Teams and supporting forces.

Transport Division 3
USS *Charles Carroll* (APA 28), USN/USCG: 29 x LCVPs, 2 x LCM(3)s.

USS *Thomas Jefferson* (APA 30), USN: 32 x LCVPs, 2 x LCP(L)s, 1 x
LCS(S), 2 x LCM(3)s.
551 Assault Flotilla, RN (SS *Empire Javelin*, LSI(L)): 18 x LCAs 724, 730,
832, 839, 853, 879, 910, 911, 922, 924, 1012, 1063, 1066, 1067, 1068,
1069, 1075, 1076; LCP(L)s 20, 115.

LST Flotilla 10, USN (Including Attached Divisions from LST Flotilla 12)
Group 34, Division 67, USN: LSTs 310, 315, 316, 317, 332.
Group 35, Division 69, USN: LST 372.
[Small boats carried included 5 x LCS(S)s plus LCVPs.]

LCI(L) Flotilla 10, USN
LCI(L) Group 29, Division 57, USCG: LCI(L) 84; LCH 86.
LCI(L) Group 29, Division 58, USCG: LCI(L)s 90, 91; LCH 92; LCI(L) 94.
LCI(L) Group 34, Division 66, USN: LCI(L)s 409, 410, 553, 554, 555, 557.
LCI(L) Group 34, Division 67, USN: LCI(L)s 408, 411, 412, 413, 540, 541.

LCT Flotilla 12, USN
LCT Group 34, Division 68, USN: LCT(6)s 535, 536, 612, 613, 614, 615.
LCT Group 35, Division 69, USN: LCT(6)s 586, 587, 588, 589, 590, 591.
LCT Group 34, Division 97, USN: LCT(6)s 616, 703, 704, 705, 775, 776.
LCT Group 34, Division 98, USN: LCT(6)s 617.

LCT Flotilla 18, USN
LCT Group 52, Division 103, USN: LCT(5)s 29, 364.
LCT Group 52, Division 104, USN: LCT(5)s 80, 149, 197, 207, 214, 332.
LCT Group 53, Division 106, USN: LCT(5)s 27, 147, 153.
LCT Group 54, Division 107, USN: LCT(5)s 30, 244, 294.

Provisional LCT Flotilla 26, USN
LCT Group 36, Division 72, USN: LCT(6)s 569, 570, 571, 572, 573, 622.
LCT Group 76, Division 151, USN: LCT(6)s 713, 714, 767.
LCT Group 76, Division 152, USN: LCT(6)s 665, 666, 813.
Control craft, USN: LCCs 30, 40, 50.
18 x LCM(3)s.
[HMS *Oceanway* (LSD) sometimes shown as part of Assault Group O2,
but was in Force B.]

Assault Group O3 (Task Group 124.5, USN)

Carrying US 18th Regimental Combat Team and supporting forces.

Transport Division 97
USS *Anne Arundel* (XAP 76), USN: 26 x LCVPs, 2 x LCM(3)s.
USS *Thurston* (XAP 77), USN: 22 x LCVPs, 2 x LCM(3)s.
USS *Dorothea L. Dix* (XAP 67), USN: 24 x LCVPs, 2 x LCM(3)s.

LST Flotilla 10, USN (Including Attached Divisions from LST Flotilla 12)
Group 30, Division 59, USN: LSTs 51, 133, 134, 285, 286, 502.
Group 34, Division 68, USN: LSTs 6, 375.
Group 34, Division 67, USN: LST 75.
Group 35, Division 69, USN: LSTs 157, 347, 350.

LCI(L) Flotilla 10, USN
LCI(L) Group 28, Division 55, USN: LCI(L)s 487, 488, 489, 490, 491;
LCH 492.
LCI(L) Group 28, Division 56, USN: LCI(L)s 494, 495, 496, 497, 498.
LCI(L) Group 29, Division 58, USCG: LCI(L) 93.

LCT Flotilla 12, USN
LCT Group 34, Division 98, USN: LCT(6)s 618, 619, 706, 707, 708.

LCT Flotilla 18, USN
LCT Group 52, Division 103, USN: LCT(5)s 431, 434.
LCT Group 53, Division 105, USN: LCT(5)s 7, 22.
LCT Group 54, Division 107, USN: LCT(5)s 415, 460.
LCT Group 54, Division 108, USN: LCT(5) 202.

LCT Flotilla 19, USN
LCT Group 56, Division 112, USN: LCT(6)s 639, 640, 641, 642.
LCT Group 57, Division 113, USN: LCT(6)s 611, 643[*N], 644, 645,
646, 647, 555, 648.
LCT Group 57, Division 114, USN: LCT(6)s 651, 652, 857, 653, 650, 649.

Provisional LCT Flotilla 26, USN
LCT Group 76, Division 151, USN: LCT(6)s 711, 712, 768.
LCT Group 77, Division 153, USN: LCT(6)s 657, 658, 659, 667, 715.
LCT Group 77, Division 154, USN: LCT(6) 654.

Q LCT Squadron, RN (Part)
57 LCT Flotilla [lent to Force O]: LCTs 562, 628. [Remainder of
57 LCT Flotilla was in Force B.]

Assault Group O4 (Task Group 124.6, USN)

Carrying US 2nd and 5th Rangers:

507 Assault Flotilla, RN (SS *Prince Baudouin*, LSI(S)): 7 x LCAs 521, 554,
577, 578, 670, 863, 1377; LCS(M) 91 [*RM].
501 Assault Flotilla, RN (HMS *Prince Charles*, LSI(S)): 8 x LCAs 401,
418, 421, 441, 458, 626, 750, 1038.
504 Assault Flotilla, RN (HMS *Prince Leopold*, LSI(S)): 7 x LCAs 550,
568, 570, 571, 622, 623, 1045; LCS(M) 102 [*RM].
522 Assault Flotilla, RN (SS *Amsterdam*, LSI(H)): 6 x LCAs 668, 858,
860, 861, 862, 914.
520 Assault Flotilla, RN (SS *Ben-my-Chree*, LSI(H)): 6 x LCAs 722, 883,
884, 887, 888, 1003.
519 Assault Flotilla, RN (SS *Princess Maud*, LSI(H)): 6 x LCAs 649, 662,
837, 843, 857, 882.

LCT Flotilla 18, USN
LCT Group 54, Division 107, USN: LCT(5) 413.

Force O Gunfire Support Group

LCI(L) Group 34, Division 66, USN: LCH 520.
LCG(L) Group 1, Division 1, USN: LCG(L)s 424, 426, 449, 687, 811.
LCF Group 1, Division 1, USN: LCFs 3, 5, 6, 7, 9, 11, 12.
LCT(A) & LCT(5) Group 1, Division 1, USN: LCT(A)s 2008, 2124,
2227, 2273, 2037, 2043, 2275; LCT(5) 210 [*A]; LCT(A) 2228 [*N].
LCT(5) Group 3, Division 4, USN: LCT(A) 2049; LCT(HE)s 2050,
2075, 2229, 2287.
LCT(5) Group 3, Division 5, USN: LCT(HE) 2307, LCT(5) 2297,
LCT(HE) 2339, LCT(HE) 2425, LCT(5) 2487.
LCT(R) Group 1, Division 1, USN: LCT(R) 366, 423, 447, 450, 452,
464, 473, 482, 483.
LCP(L)s 3, 43, 84, 85, 102, 110, 114, 128, 160, 162, 163, 198, 200, 211,
230, 231, 232, 235, 236, 237, 238, 239, 241, 242, 243, 244, 245, 247,
248, 294, 295, 313.

Build-Up Flotillas Force O

Y LB Squadron, RN

7 LBV Flotilla, RN: LBV(2)s 3, 11, 23, 53, 67, 70, 76, 101, 153, 206, 214, 225.

9 LBV Flotilla, RN: LBV(2)s 98, 100, 132, 140, 141, 156, 161, 172, 176, 211, 228, 239.

10 LBV Flotilla, RN: LBV(2)s 2, 26, 49, 68, 78, 79, 81, 103, 105, 131, 150, 192.

11 LBV Flotilla, RN: LBV(2)s 8, 27, 61, 69, 84, 89, 95, 104, 106, 124, 191, 232.

12 LBV Flotilla, RN: LBV(2)s 12, 33, 42, 64, 66, 92, 94, 109, 160, 203, 209, 229.

18 LBV Flotilla, RN: LBV(2)s 7, 37, 39, 55, 62, 80, 93, 102, 129, 136, 149, 168.

32 LB (Supply and Repair) Flotilla, RN: LBEs 26, 31, 57, 58, 60; LBK 5; LBOs 10, 16, 18, 37, 46, 56, 57, 84, 97; LBWs 7, 8.

39 LB (Supply and Repair) Flotilla, RN: LBEs 8, 10, 17, 25, 27, 29, 41, 46; LBK 7; LBOs 27, 68, 93, 98; LBWs 15, 18, 20.

Force G

Carrying British 50th Infantry Division and supporting forces.

Assault Group G1

Carrying British 231st Infantry Brigade Group and supporting forces.

524 Assault Flotilla, RN (SS *Empire Arquebus*, LSI(L)): 15 x LCAs 602, 654, 656, 663, 733, 920, 921, 926, 1005, 1008, 1009, 1010, 1026, 1254, 1384; LCS(M)s 78, 109, 112 [*RM].

553 Assault Flotilla, RN (SS *Empire Crossbow*, LSI(L)): 15 x LCAs 500, 917, 954, 956, 997, 1023, 1032, 1050, 1053, 1058, 1061, 1152, 1158, 1174, 1385; LCS(M)s 108, 113, 114 [*RM].

525 Assault Flotilla, RN (SS *Empire Spearhead*, LSI(L)): 15 x LCAs 732, 949, 951, 952, 994, 1013, 1024, 1043, 1046, 1047, 1048, 1055, 1060, 1148, 1149; LCS(M)s 77, 80, 99 [*RM].

554 Assault Flotilla, RM (HMS *Glenroy*, LSI(L)): 11 x LCAs 737, 793, 847, 915, 929, 1029, 1083, 1086, 1095, 1130; LCA(OC) 1209; LCS(M) 74.

559 Assault Flotilla, RM (HMS *Glenroy*, LSI(L)): 11 x LCAs 175, 190, 339, 348, 380, 404, 490, 546, 658, 703; LCA(OC) 1159; LCS(M) 73. HQ craft: LCHs 100, 317.

Support Squadron, RN
332 Support Flotilla, RN (part): LCFs 19, 20, 35; LCG(L)s 13, 17, 18. [RM gunnery personnel.]
108 LCT Flotilla, RN (part): LCT(A)s 2005, 2233, 2238, 2262, 2266, 2426, 2442, 2499.
322 LCT(R) Flotilla, RN: LCT(R)s 434, 435, 436, 438.
591 Assault Flotilla, RN: LCA(HR)s 960, 961, 962, 963, 966, 968, 969, 970, 972, 1101, 1103, 1104, 1105, 1106, 1108, 1109, 1110, 1287.

D LCT Squadron, RN
15 LCT Flotilla, RN: LCT(3)s 442, 468, 469, 470, 471, 472, 476, 7006, 7007, 7008, 7009, 7013.
23 LCT Flotilla, RN: LCT(4)s 543 [*N], 546, 555, 571, 576, 577, 604, 635, 901, 1041, 1162, 1164.
28 LCT Flotilla, RN: LCT(4)s 598, 599, 600, 647, 749, 803, 805, 807, 808, 809, 810, 886.
33 LCT Flotilla, RN: LCT(4)s 631, 640, 664, 678, 708^, 718, 719, 720, 733^, 783, 857, 858, 878, 879, 897, 905^, 1073^, 1027^ [^ = craft attached to this flotilla from 49 LCT Flotilla].
53 LCT Flotilla, RN: LCT(4)s 710, 737, 902, 928, 1009, 1034, 1074, 1076, 1078, 1079, 1118, 1119.
25 LBF Flotilla, RN: LBFs 1, 3, 6, 7, 12, 13, 14, 15.

Assault Group G2

Carrying British 69th Infantry Brigade Group and supporting forces.

539 Assault Flotilla, RM (SS *Empire Halberd*, LSI(L)): LCAs 282, 350, 358, 367, 393, 502, 510, 543, 591, 786, 907, 909, 1112, 1136, 1153, 1154, 1155, 1156.
540 Assault Flotilla, RN (SS *Empire Lance*, LSI(L)): LCAs 279, 613, 636, 731, 771, 930, 984, 999, 1011, 1041, 1065, 1132, 1133, 1147, 1210, 1380; LCS(M) 79, 81 [*RM].
541 Assault Flotilla, RM (SS *Empire Mace*, LSI(L)): LCAs 345, 372, 383, 466, 501, 628, 749, 798, 1000, 1027, 1052, 1056, 1062, 1139, 1141, 1143; LCS(M)s 75, 76.

542 Assault Flotilla, RM (SS *Empire Rapier*, LSI(L)): LCAs 409, 434, 588, 614, 789, 797, 848, 871, 928, 947, 1094, 1211, 1212, 1213, 1214, 1374, 1378; LCS(M) 110.
HQ craft: LCHs 187, 275.

Support Squadron, RN
332 Support Flotilla, RN (part): LCFs 25, 26, 36, 38; LCG(L) 1, 2, 3. [RM gunnery personnel.]
109 LCT Flotilla, RN (part): LCT(A)s 2039, 2048, 2121, 2225, 2236, 2291, 2345, 2453.
322 LCT(R) Flotilla, RN: LCT(R)s 362, 440, 459, 460.
310 Support Flotilla, RN: LCS(L)s 251, 252 [*N], 258, 259. [RM gunnery personnel] [part of flotilla, attached from Force J.]

L LCT Squadron
12 LCT Flotilla, RN: LCT(3)s 427, 428, 429, 430, 432, 433, 451, 453, 454, 463, 475, 7012.
24 LCT Flotilla, RN: LCT(4)s 502, 503, 511, 520, 521, 533, 643, 644, 683, 684, 883, 884.
34 LCT Flotilla, RN: LCT(4)s 519, 726, 727, 762, 763, 765, 766, 896, 899, 929, 930, 931.
49 LCT Flotilla, RN: LCT(4)s 704, 730, 735, 903, 1045 [*N], 1072. [These craft were designated 1st Division, 49 LCT Flotilla. The flotilla's other craft, designated 2nd Division, were for D-Day attached to 33 LCT Flotilla, D LCT Squadron, Assault Group G1.]
51 LCT Flotilla, RN: LCT(4)s 1028, 1030, 1031, 1032, 1033, 1038, 1039, 1077, 1097, 1098, 1099, 1163.
26 LBF Flotilla, RN: LBFs 2, 4, 5, 8, 9, 10, 11.

Assault Group G3

Carrying British 151st and 56th Infantry Brigade Groups and supporting forces.

LST Flotilla 4, USN
LST Group 11, Division 22, USN: LST(2)s 1, 359, 519.

LST Flotilla 10, USN
LST Group 28, Division 55, USN: LST(2)s 30, 52, 264, 287, 493, 503.
LST Group 28, Division 56, USN: LST(2)s 44, 229, 279, 280, 293.

LST Flotilla 11, USN
LST Group 33, Division 65, USN: LST(2)s 2, 308, 312, 344, 345, 370.

LST Flotilla 17, USN
LST Group 51, Division 101, USN (except for two ships which were USCG): LST(2)s 17^, 21^, 25, 72, 73, 520 [^ = USCG crew]. [On D-Day, these ships were under the administrative control of LST Flotilla 11, Group 33.]
264 LCI(L) Flotilla, RCN: LCI(L)s 255, 288, 295, 302, 305, 310, 311.

LCI(L) Flotilla 11, USN
LCI(L) Group 31, Division 61, USN: LCI(L)s 499, 500, 501, 502, 505, 506.
LCI(L) Group 31, Division 62, USN: LCI(L)s 507, 508, 509, 510, 511, 512.
LCI(L) Group 35, Division 70, USN: LCI(L)s 75, 400, 421.

U LCT Squadron
55 LCT Flotilla, RN: 1st Division: LCT(4)s 564, 922, 924, 926, 1121.
55 LCT Flotilla, RN: 2nd Division: LCT(4)s 565, 711, 923, 1120, 1122; LCT(4)s 732 [*N], 907 [*N].

Not Attached to Assault Groups

LCH 245.
700 Assault Flotilla, RM: LCP(L)s 165^, 168, 176^, 199^, 208^, 273, 275, 278, 283, 284, 288, 296 [^ = armoured craft, on D-Day lent to 708 Assault Flotilla].
706 Assault Flotilla, RM: LCP(L)s 229, 298, 299, 300, 301, 302, 303, 304, 305, 306, 307, 308.
708 Assault Flotilla, RN: LCP(L)s 4, 7, 13, 23, 31, 34, 40, 44, 46, 53, 151, 161 [on D-Day, this flotilla lent four of the craft, pennant numbers not identified, to 700 Assault Flotilla in exchange for craft borrowed from that flotilla].

Commando Lift

508 Assault Flotilla, RN (SS *Victoria*, LSI(H)): LCAs 579, 586, 592, 593, 594, 859.
502 Assault Flotilla, RN (HMS *Prinses Josephine Charlotte*, LSI(S)): LCAs 290, 320, 349, 412, 431, 442, 503, 509.

Build-Up Flotillas Force G

B Build-Up Squadron
805 Build-Up Flotilla, RM: LCVPs 1017, 1215, 1216, 1217, 1218, 1219, 1220, 1221, 1222, 1223, 1224, 1225, 1226, 1227, 1228, 1230.
806 Build-Up Flotilla, RM: LCVPs 1045, 1048, 1050, 1107, 1108, 1112, 1113, 1131, 1134, 1136, 1138, 1142, 1149, 1150, 1151, 1156.
807 Build-Up Flotilla, RM: LCVPs 1160, 1162, 1163, 1164, 1165, 1166, 1167, 1168, 1169, 1172, 1173, 1174, 1175, 1176, 1177, 1178.
808 Build-Up Flotilla, RM: LCVPs 1022, 1052, 1103, 1152, 1183, 1186, 1187, 1188, 1189, 1190, 1191, 1192, 1193, 1194, 1195, 1196.
809 Build-Up Flotilla, RM: LCVPs 1179, 1180, 1182, 1185, 1197, 1198, 1199, 1200, 1201, 1202, 1203, 1204, 1205, 1206, 1207, 1210.

E Build-Up Squadron
605 Build-Up Flotilla, RM: LCM(3)s 541, 557, 573, 940, 1075, 1114, 1138, 1245, 1246, 1280, 1284, 1285, 1288, 1292, 1390, 1391.
606 Build-Up Flotilla, RM: LCM(3)s 524, 526, 531, 535, 560, 563, 576, 577, 582, 1080, 1090, 1190, 1191, 1192, 1193, 1196.
607 Build-Up Flotilla, RM: LCM(1)s 128, 164, 165, 239, 244, 251, 281, 314, 365, 387, 409, 425, 426, 431, 443, 444. [All of this flotilla's craft were carried on LSIs on D-Day.]
609 Build-Up Flotilla, RM: LCM(1)s 77, 114, 138, 242, 247, 249, 321, 340, 363, 382, 386, 407, 408, 423, 424, 465.
654 Build-Up Flotilla, RM: LCM(3)s 530, 587, 625, 629, 1056, 1127, 1188, 1219, 1220, 1221, 1239, 1296, 1297, 1298, 1392, 1393.
698 Build-Up Flotilla, RM: LCM(1)s 193, 203, 231, 240, 241, 246, 270, 274, 303, 313, 364, 369, 372, 373, 374, 381.

Z LB Squadron
13 LBV Flotilla, RN: LBV(2)s 110, 133, 143, 152, 159, 165, 166, 189, 196, 197, 198, 236.
14 LBV Flotilla, RN: LBV(2)s 144, 162, 163, 164, 179, 185, 188, 194, 213, 217, 222, 227.
15 LBV Flotilla, RN: LBV(2)s 138, 142, 148, 167, 177, 178, 190, 204, 205, 208, 216, 240.
36 LB (Supply and Repair) Flotilla, RN: LCE 23; LBEs 18, 23, 38, 49, 50, 51; LBK 4; LBOs 9, 14, 17, 23, 39, 53, 55, 73, 75, 80; LBWs 10, 17.
38 LB (Supply and Repair) Flotilla, RN: LCE 24; LBEs 3, 5, 13, 14, 24, 48; LBK 1; LBOs 3, 19, 22, 60, 70, 71, 72, 76, 81, 86; LBWs 11, 19.

Force J

Carrying Canadian 3rd Infantry Division and supporting forces.

499 Ancillary Flotilla, RN (HMS *Hillary*, LSH): LCP(L)s 504, 528, 534, 761, 853, 854.

Assault Group J1

Carrying Canadian 7th Infantry Brigade Group and supporting forces.

557 Assault Flotilla, RM (MV *Llangibby Castle*, LSI(L)): 18 x LCAs 303, 590, 642, 830, 989, 1016, 1017, 1036, 1037, 1089, 1090, 1093, 1096, 1124, 1131, 1146, 1173, 1382.
528 Assault Flotilla, RCN (HMCS *Prince Henry*, LSI(M)): 8 x LCAs 736, 850, 856, 925, 1021, 1033, 1371, 1372.
526 Assault Flotilla, RM (HMS *Queen Emma*, LSI(M)): 8 x LCAs 228, 411, 512, 538, 556, 557, 1031, 1336.
509 Assault Flotilla, RM (SS *Canterbury*, LSI(H)): 6 x LCAs 596, 647, 824, 1039, 1040; LCA(OC) [???].
517 Assault Flotilla, RN (SS *Duke of Argyll*, LSI(H)): 6 x LCAs 692, 706, 818, 834, 836, 1025.
510 Assault Flotilla, RN (HMS *Invicta*, LSI(H)): 5 x LCAs 774, 775, 807, 808, 809; LCS(M) 47.
505 Assault Flotilla, RN (SS *Isle of Thanet*, LSI(H)): 5 x LCAs 520, 643, 644, 763, 767; LCA(OC) [???].
516 Assault Flotilla, RN (SS *Lairds Isle*, LSI(H)): 6 x LCAs 598, 661, 772, 831, 838, 875.
511 Assault Flotilla, RN (SS *Mecklenberg*, LSI(H)): 6 x LCAs 684, 810, 815, 816, 819, 823.
521 Assault Flotilla, RN (HMS *Ulster Monarch*, LSI(H)): 5 x LCAs 583, 721, 885, 886, 889; LCS(M) 44.

K LCT Squadron
HQ craft: LCHs 98, 168.
4 LCT Flotilla, RN: LCT(3)s 302, 303, 306, 311, 372, 390, 399, 411, 413, 422, 441, 7010.
20 LCT Flotilla, RN: LCT(4)s 500, 506, 507, 508, 509, 510, 513, 514, 517, 522, 528, 531.

31 LCT Flotilla, RN: LCT(4)s 566, 569, 574, 575, 629, 677, 706, 709, 712, 717, 781, 876.
102 LCT Flotilla, RN: LCT(5)s 2044, 2047; LCT(HE) 2076; LCT(5)s 2077, 2079, 2243, 2246, 2270, 2296, 2336, 2343, 2399.

1st Support Squadron, RN
333 Support Flotilla, RN: LCFs 1, 33, 37; LCG(L)s 831, 1007, 1062; LCT(CB) 2041. [LCFs and LCG(L)s had RM gunnery personnel.]
105 LCT(A) Flotilla, RN: LCT(A) 2009; LCT(HE) 2010; LCT(A) 2014; LCT(HE) 2120; LCT(A)(HE) 2263; LCT(A)s 2283, 2428 [*L], 2455.
320 LCT(R) Flotilla, RN: LCT(R)s 337, 359, 363, 367, 378, 398, 405, 437.
900 Support Flotilla, RN: LCS(L)s 202, 203, 204, 205. [RM gunnery personnel.]
703 Assault Flotilla, RN: LCP(L)s 127, 130, 131, 132, 133, 134, 135, 143, 144, 148, 153, 158.

Assault Group J2

Carrying Canadian 8th Infantry Brigade Group and supporting forces.

558 Assault Flotilla, RM (SS *Clan Lamont*, LSI(L)): 17 x LCAs 523, 530, 609, 659, 667, 805, 869, 916, 978, 1084, 1087, 1129, 1142, 1253, 1339, 1340, [???]; LCS(M)s 103, 105.
544 Assault Flotilla, RM (SS *Monowai*, LSI(L)): 10 x LCAs 197, 208, 280, 289, 462, 683, 1035, 1057, 1091, 1092.
556 Assault Flotilla, RM (SS *Monowai*, LSI(L)): 10 x LCAs 565, 728, 729, 851, 918, 919, 946, 948, 1034, [???].
529 Assault Flotilla, RCN (HMCS *Prince David*, LSI(M)): 7 x LCAs 1059, 1137, 1138, 1150, 1151, 1373, 1375; LCS(M) 101.
513 Assault Flotilla, RN (HMS *Brigadier*, LSI(H)): 6 x LCAs 522, 713, 717, 817, 820, 821.
506 Assault Flotilla, RM (HMS *Duke of Wellington*, LSI(H)): 6 x LCAs 416, 467, 519, 525, 768, 803.
518 Assault Flotilla, RN (SS *Isle of Guernsey*, LSI(H)): 6 x LCAs 650, 710, 835, 841, 844, 881.
512 Assault Flotilla, RN (SS *Lady of Mann*, LSI(H)): 6 x LCAs 581, 595, 705, 714, 814, 826.
515 Assault Flotilla, RN (HMS *St Helier*, LSI(H)): 6 x LCAs 563, 691, 735, 827, 833, 878.

[Under tow by major landing craft during crossing of the English Channel:]
LCS(M) 83 [formerly 529 Assault Flotilla, RCN, on HMCS *Prince David*].
LCS(M) 89 [formerly 509 Assault Flotilla, RM, on SS *Canterbury*].
LCS(M) 105 [formerly 558 Assault Flotilla, RM, on SS *Clan Lamont*].

N LCT Squadron
HQ craft: LCHs 167, 239.
11 LCT Flotilla, RN: LCT(3)s 313, 317, 318, 320, 324, 341, 345, 354, 382, 384, 474, 7011.
22 LCT Flotilla, RN: LCT(4)s 501, 516, 518, 524, 525, 526, 529, 530, 716, 767, 804, 885.
30 LCT Flotilla, RN: LCT(4)s 602, 630, 637, 707, 715, 723, 724, 782, 855, 856, 881, 882.
106 LCT Flotilla, RN: LCT(4)s 2013, 2038, 2193, 2230, 2232, 2286, 2289, 2295, 2436, 2439, 2441, 2479.

2nd Support Squadron
331 Support Flotilla, RN: LCFs 21, 32; LCG(L)s 680, 681, 764, 939. [RM gunnery personnel.]
103 LCT Flotilla, RN: LCT(HE)s 2051, 2078, 2150, 2234, 2240, 2285, 2306; LCT(HE) 2313.
590 Assault Flotilla, RN: LCA(OC)s 566^, 738^, 958^, 985#; LCA(HR) 671, 686, 690, 708, 712, 716, 873, 874, 876, 880, 965, 1002, 1071, 1072, 1102, 1107, 1285, 1286 [^ = two of these craft were possibly on SS *Canterbury* with 509 Assault Flotilla and on SS *Isle of Thanet* with 505 Assault Flotilla] [# = craft on HMCS *Prince David* with 529 Assault Flotilla].
702 Assault Flotilla, RN: LCP(L)s 166, 170, 173, 175, 186, 187, 188, 191, 192, 195, 207, 234.

Assault Group J3

Carrying Canadian 9th Infantry Brigade Group and supporting forces.

555 Assault Flotilla, RN (HMS *Royal Ulsterman*, LSI(H)): 6 x LCAs 338, 463, 517, 518, 540, 748.
2 LST(2) Flotilla, RN: LST(2)s 323, 368, 404, 405, 409, 410, 413, 425; LCP(R)s 584, 606, 639, 815, 822, 895, 929, 952, 958, 979.

4 LST(2) Flotilla, RN: LST(2)s 8, 11, 62, 65, 159, 160, 199, 416; LCP(L)s 537, 852; LCP(R)s 641, 644, 767, 964, 971, 972, 976.
9 LST(2) Flotilla, RN: LST(2)s 80, 180, 215, 238, 239, 402, 421; LCP(R)s 645, 725, 818, 899, 960, 988, 1013; LCVP 1258.
LST(2) 401 [★N]. [Under repair on D-Day.]

P LCT Squadron
260 LCI(L) Flotilla, RCN: LCI(L)s 117, 121, 166, 177, 249, 266, 271, 277, 285, 298, 301.
262 LCI(L) Flotilla, RCN: LCI(L)s 115, 118, 125, 135, 250, 252, 262, 263, 270, 276, 299, 306.
35 LCT Flotilla, RN: LCT(4)s 632, 636, 652, 667, 669, 670, 671, 679, 721, 759, 760, 761.
36 LCT Flotilla, RN: LCF 24; LCT(4)s 534, 541, 672, 673, 768, 769, 770, 932, 933, 934, 935, 936.
37 LCT Flotilla, RN: LCF 29; LCT(4)s 634, 639, 700, 729, 937, 938, 940, 941, 943, 1006, 1008, 1315.
705 Assault Flotilla, RN: LCP(L)s 167, 171, 172, 178, 179, 196, 202, 265, 266, 268, 270, 274.
Detached from 103 LCT Flotilla: LCT(CB) 2338.

Assault Group J4 (Commando Lift)

523 Assault Flotilla, RN (SS *Princess Margaret*, LSI(H)): 6 x LCAs 890, 891, 892, 893, 894, 895.
503 Assault Flotilla, RN (HMS *Prins Albert*, LSI(S)): 8 x LCAs 392, 444, 457, 483, 486, 527, 529, 1337.

Support Squadron, RN
202 LCI(S) Flotilla, RN: LCI(S)s 513, 514^, 515, 520, 525, 526, 533, 536, 537, 539, 540 [^ = lent from 200 LCI(S) Flotilla].
[Note: The Green List of 6 June 1944 shows 200 & 201 LCI(S) Flotillas, RN, as being part of Force J, but here they are listed under Force S, which both operated with on D-Day. In addition, the following craft from this flotilla are listed under Force S because they were lent to 201 LCI(S) Flotilla: LCI(S)s 509, 522 and 538.
310 Support Flotilla, RN: LCS(L)s 254, 255, 257. [RM gunnery personnel.] [Part of flotilla, remainder attached to Forces G and S.]
701 Assault Flotilla, RN: LCP(L)s 19, 94, 119, 120, 122, 124, 125, 129, 147, 152, 155, 158.

Not Attached to Assault Groups, Force J

712 Assault Flotilla, RN: LCP(SY)s 154, 177, 190, 201, 281, 290, 291, 292.
LSE 2

Build-Up Flotillas, Force J

A Build-Up Squadron
800 Build-Up Flotilla, RM: LCVPs 1005, 1006, 1007, 1008, 1009, 1010, 1011, 1012, 1014, 1015, 1023, 1024, 1025, 1026, 1027, 1055.
801 Build-Up Flotilla, RM: LCVPs 1028, 1029, 1030, 1031, 1032, 1033, 1034, 1035, 1036, 1037, 1038, 1039, 1041, 1042, 1043, 1211.
802 Build-Up Flotilla, RM: LCVPs 1013, 1074, 1075, 1076, 1077, 1078, 1079, 1080, 1081, 1082, 1083, 1086, 1092, 1097, 1208, 1209.
804 Build-Up Flotilla, RM: LCVPs 1123, 1124, 1125, 1126, 1127, 1128, 1129, 1130, 1140, 1143, 1144, 1146, 1263, 1264, 1265, 1266.

F Build-Up Squadron
600 Build-Up Flotilla, RM: LCM(1)s 248, 262, 265, 267, 290, 316, 317, 333, 334, 335, 336, 337, 338, 342, 344, 345.
601 Build-Up Flotilla, RM: LCM(1)s 166, 168, 180, 199, 216, 226, 229, 238, 256, 266, 276, 298, 330, 339, 346, 383.
604 Build-Up Flotilla, RM: LCM(1)s 154, 171, 217, 223, 236, 306, 307, 308, 311, 320, 359, 360, 362, 368, 380, 422.
650 Build-Up Flotilla, RM: LCM(1)s 1100, 1164, 1197, 1212, 1213, 1214, 1215, 1216, 1234, 1235, 1236, 1240, 1241, 1242, 1277, 1278.
651 Build-Up Flotilla, RM: LCM(1)s 1051, 1053, 1054, 1055, 1057, 1058, 1059, 1060, 1106, 1163, 1201, 1222, 1224, 1225, 1226, 1279.
652 Build-Up Flotilla, RM: LCM(1)s 1065, 1132, 1144, 1146, 1161, 1162, 1172, 1179, 1180, 1184, 1189, 1200, 1227, 1233.

W LB Squadron
1 LBV Flotilla, RN: LBV(2)s 19, 20, 28, 34, 45, 90, 97, 116, 123, 126, 128, 130.
2 LBV Flotilla, RN: LBV(2)s 4, 18, 22, 38, 40, 46, 57, 71, 86, 115, 127, 235.
3 LBV Flotilla, RN: LBV(2)s 6, 25, 47, 48, 52, 54, 74, 107, 120, 122, 223, 231.
4 LBV Flotilla, RN: LBV(2)s 17, 36, 41, 58, 60, 91, 125, 139, 169, 183, 215, 224.

16 LBV Flotilla, RN: LBV(2)s 145, 146, 147, 155, 171, 173, 180, 193, 195, 202, 221, 237.

30 LB (Supply and Repair) Flotilla, RN: LCE 15; LBEs 2, 4, 16, 36, 43, 47; LBK 10; LBOs 32, 33, 34, 38, 40, 41, 45, 48, 64, 90; LBWs 5, 14.

31 LB (Supply and Repair) Flotilla, RN: LCE 16; LBEs 6, 9, 21, 22, 39, 54; LBK 4; LBOs 4, 7, 8, 20, 28, 43, 47, 49, 66, 83; LBWs 2, 9.

37 LB (Supply and Repair) Flotilla, RN: LCE 19; LBEs 15, 19, 20, 44, 45, 54; LBK 2; LBOs 1, 2, 29, 35, 36, 58, 59, 61, 67, 78; LBWs 3, 16.

Force S

Carrying British 3rd Infantry Division and supporting forces.

Assault Group S1

Carrying British 9th Infantry Brigade Group and supporting forces.

LST Squadron, RN, Force S
1 LST(2) Flotilla, RN: LST(2)s 9, 302, 303, 304, 320, 324, 361, 363; LCP(L)s 523, 525, 529, 756, 857; LCP(R)s 581, 582, 927.
3 LST(2) Flotilla, RN: LST(2)s 322, 367, 408, 419, 420, 423, 427, 428; LCP(L)s 520, 855; LCP(R)s 657, 924, 931, 932, 935, 961.
5 LST(2) Flotilla, RN: LST(2)s 162, 163, 164, 364, 365, 412, 415, 430; LCP(L)s 510, 524, 856; LCP(R)s 586, 933, 974, 981, 983

T Squadron, RN
265 LCI(L) Flotilla, RN: LCI(L)s 374, 381, 382, 383, 385, 386, 389, 390.
266 LCI(L) Flotilla, RN: LCI(L)s 241, 375, 376, 384, 387, 388, 391.
39 LCT Flotilla, RN: LCT(4)s 539, 609, 611, 612, 666, 675, 682, 787, 788, 851, 852, 864, 1015, 1080, 1083 [*N].
47 LCT Flotilla, RN: LCT(4)s 627, 674, 754 [*N], 828, 900, 944, 1003, 1017, 1019, 1020, 1022, 1023, 1065, 1067, 1068.

Assault Group S2

Carrying British 185th Infantry Brigade Group and supporting forces.

I Squadron, RN
251 LCI(L) Flotilla, RN: LCI(L)s 111, 116, 136, 174, 175, 210, 244, 246, 313.

263 LCI(L) Flotilla, RN: LCI(L)s 126, 164, 165, 169, 171, 179, 181, 300, 377, 378, 379, 380.

40 LCT Flotilla, RN: LCT(4)s 641, 649, 650, 668, 748, 752, 892, 952, 958, 959, 960, 961.

42 LCT Flotilla, RN: LCT(4)s 545, 751, 802, 821, 829, 894, 953, 964, 968, 1042.

48 LCT Flotilla, RN: LCT(4)s 568, 950, 1024, 1025, 1026, 1066, 1069, 1070, 1071, 1095, 1096, 1168.

LCI(L) Flotilla 2, USN
LCI(L) Group 4, Division 8, USN: LCI(L)s 9, 12, 13, 14, 15, 16, 33, 35, 193, 238.

Assault Group S3

Carrying British 8th Infantry Brigade Group and supporting forces.

535 Assault Flotilla, RM (HMS *Glenearn*, LSI(L)): 12 x LCAs 171^, 223, 318, 352^, 471, 604, 664, 782, 784, 804, 868, 872 [^ = craft on loan to 543 Assault Flotilla, which was on the same ship].

543 Assault Flotilla, RM (HMS *Glenearn*, LSI(L)): 12 x LCAs 337, 601, 896, 897, 899, 900, 901, 904, 979, 1216, 1383, 1491.

537 Assault Flotilla, RM (SS *Empire Battleaxe*, LSI(L)): 18 x LCAs 429, 496, 524, 584, 611, 653, 770, 778, 779, 780, 781, 792, 840, 898, 1215, 1251, 1252, 1338.

538 Assault Flotilla, RM (SS *Empire Broadsword*, LSI(L)): 18 x LCAs 387, 424, 635, 637, 638, 651, 652, 665, 673, 796, 870, 903, 905, 906, 1341, 1376, 1379, 1381.

536 Assault Flotilla, RM (SS *Empire Cutlass*, LSI(L)): 18 x LCAs 341, 344, 485, 572, 589, 704, 757, 777, 791, 795, 866, 867, 902, 993, 1015, 1113, 1157, 1256.

E Squadron, RN
HQ craft: LCH 269
261 LCI(L) Flotilla, RN: LCI(L)s 130, 131, 134, 180, 183, 291.

41 LCT Flotilla, RN: LCT(4)s 608, 610, 789, 790, 853, 854, 863, 898, 945, 946, 978, 979, 980, 1084^ [^ = craft on loan to 43 LCT Flotilla].

14 LCT Flotilla, RN: LCT(3)s 431, 443, 444, 455, 456, 461, 462, 465, 466, 467.

43 LCT Flotilla, RN: LCT(4)s 676, 728, 731, 942, 1011, 1013, 1014, 1018, 1125, 1126.

45 LCT Flotilla, RN: LCT(4)s 909, 947, 951, 981, 1010, 1016, 1082, 1092, 1093, 1094.

Support Squadron, RN
HQ craft: LCH 185
330 Support Flotilla, RN: LCFs 30, 34, 39, 42; LCG(L)s 9, 10, 11.
32 LCT Flotilla, RN: LCT(4)s 504, 544, 558, 593, 597, 665, 685, 739, 784, 785, 786, 814, 859, 887, 889, 812, 1051.
38 LCT Flotilla, RN: LCT(4)s 523, 532, 750, 813, 826, 827, 860, 861, 891.
100 LCT Flotilla, RN: LCT(A)s 2012, 2042, 2052, 2123, 2191, 2334, 2432, 2433; LCT(CB) 2337.
321 LCT(R) Flotilla, RN: LCT(R)s 331, 334, 419, 457, 458.
592 Assault Flotilla, RM: LCA(HR)s 709, 719, 776, 829, 976, 977, 1001, 1064, 1070.
704 LCP(L) Flotilla, RM: LCP(L)s 21, 22, 51, 121; LCP(SY)s 139, 289.
707 LCP(L) Flotilla, RM: LCP(L)s 189, 197, 272, 279, 280, 282, 285, 286, 309, 310, 311, 312.
200 LCI(S) Flotilla, RN: LCI(S)s 502, 503, 504, 505, 506^, 507, 508, 510, 516, 519, 521, 529, 531 [^ = lent from 201 LCI(S) Flotilla. In addition, the following craft from this flotilla were lent to other LCI(S) flotillas: LCI(S) 514 was lent to 202 LCI(S) Flotilla; LCI(S) 517 was lent to 201 LCI(S) Flotilla.]
201 LCI(S) Flotilla, RN: LCI(S)s 501, 509^, 512, 517^, 518, 522#, 523, 524, 527, 528, 530, 532, 534, 535, 538# [^ = lent from 200 LCI(S) Flotilla; # = lent from 202 LCI(S) Flotilla. In addition, the following craft from this flotilla were lent to other LCI(S) flotillas: LCI(S) 506 was lent to 200 LCI(S) Flotilla; LCI(S) 531 was lent to 200 LCI(S) Flotilla.]
310 Support Flotilla, RN: LCS(L)s 253, 256, 260. [RM gunnery personnel.] [Part of flotilla attached from Force J.]
Note: The 'Green List' of 6 June 1944 shows 200 & 201 LCI(S) Flotillas, RN, as being part of Force J, but both are listed here under Force S with which they operated on D-Day.

Build-Up Flotillas, Force S

C Build-Up Squadron
803 Build-Up Flotilla, RM: LCVPs 1099, 1100, 1110, 1114, 1115, 1116, 1117, 1118, 1119, 1120, 1121, 1122, 1259, 1260, 1261, 1262.
810 Build-Up Flotilla, RM: LCVPs 1016, 1044, 1046, 1047, 1049, 1051, 1053, 1054, 1056, 1057, 1058, 1059, 1245, 1246, 1247, 1248.

811 Build-Up Flotilla, RM: LCVPs 1084, 1085, 1087, 1088, 1089, 1090, 1091, 1093, 1094, 1236, 1238, 1241, 1242, 1243, 1244, 1249.
812 Build-Up Flotilla, RM: LCVPs 1095, 1096, 1098, 1101, 1102, 1104, 1105, 1106, 1109, 1251, 1252, 1253, 1254, 1255, 1256, 1257.
813 Build-Up Flotilla, RM: LCVPs 1060, 1062, 1063, 1111, 1132, 1133, 1135, 1137, 1139, 1141, 1145, 1147, 1235, 1237, 1239, 1240.
814 Build-Up Flotilla, RM: LCVPs 1064, 1065, 1067, 1148, 1153, 1154, 1155, 1157, 1158, 1159, 1161, 1170, 1171, 1181, 1184, 1250.

D Build-Up Squadron
602 Build-Up Flotilla, RM: LCM(1)s 184, 191, 245, 250, 289, 312, 318, 347, 348, 349, 350, 353, 354, 355, 377, 384.
603 Build-Up Flotilla, RM: LCM(1)s 202, 268, 269, 319, 351, 352, 356, 357, 358, 361, 378, 379, 385, 419, 420, 421.
653 Build-Up Flotilla, RM: LCM(3)s 561, 627, 1050, 1088, 1128, 1175, 1176, 1208, 1232, 1244, 1282, 1287, 1289, 1290, 1293, 1371.

U LB Squadron
5 LBV Flotilla, RN: LBV(2)s 10, 13, 24, 32, 59, 75, 77, 85, 96, 108, 114, 238.
6 LBV Flotilla, RN: LBV(2)s 1, 43, 44, 88, 99, 111, 117, 119, 135, 199, 200, 201.
35 LB (Supply and Repair) Flotilla, RN: LCE 13; LBEs 1, 7, 35, 40, 42, 53; LBK 6; LBOs 5, 12, 15, 25, 31, 42, 50, 51, 52, 35; LBWs 12, 13.

Commando Lift, Attached to Force S from Force J

514 Assault Flotilla, RN (SS *Maid of Orleans*, LSI(H)): 6 x LCAs 715, 812, 822, 825, 828, 877.
500 Assault Flotilla, RN (HMS *Prinses Astrid*, LSI(S)): 8 x LCAs 360, 419, 422, 468, 476, 494, 535, 1098.

Force B (Task Force 126, USN)

Assault Group B1 (Task Group 126.2, USN)

LST Flotilla 10, USN
LST Group 10, Division 60, USN: LST(2)s 53, 288, 325, 494, 495, 504, 505.

LST Flotilla 11, USN
LST Group 31, Division 61, USN: LST(2)s 54, 55, 289, 291, 496, 511.
LST Group 31, Division 62, USN: LST(2)s 56, 292, 497, 498, 506, 512.

Q LCT Squadron, RN
54 LCT Flotilla, RN: LCT(4)s 656, 689, 690, 692, 796, 832, 921, 957, 998, 999, 1046, 1047.
56 LCT Flotilla, RN: LCT(4)s 515, 638, 757, 815, 838, 1000, 1001, 1048, 1049, 1106, 1170, 1171.
57 LCT Flotilla, RN: LCT(4)s 703, 713, 925, 927, 1002, 1035, 1037, 1040, 1123, 1166.
59 LCT Flotilla, RN: LCT(4)s 573, 875, 904, 1043, 1081, 1085, 1086, 1087, 1088, 1124, 1127, 1169.

Assault Group B2 (Task Group 126.3, USN)

LCI(L) Flotilla 12, USN
Group 35, Division 68, USN: LCI(L)s 401, 403, 537, 538, 539, 556.
Group 35, Division 69, USN: LCH 414; LCI(L)s 415, 416, 417, 418, 420, 542.
20 x LCM(3)s, USN, on board HMS *Oceanway* (LSD) ['sailing independently' but joined B-2].

Assault Group B3 (Task Group 126.4, USN)

LST Flotilla 11, USN
LST Group 35, Division 70, USN: LST(2)s 7, 306, 331, 391, 392, 393.
LST Group 35, Division 97, USN: LST(2)s 59, 510, 516, 523, 532, 533.
LST Group 36, Division 71, USN: LST(2)s 5, 61, 307, 335, 355, 369.
LST Group 36, Division 72, USN: LST(2)s 336, 337, 338, 356, 388, 389.

LST Flotilla 4, USN
LST Group 12, Division 23, USN: LST(2)s 16^, 27^, 28, 212, 262^, 266, 538 [^ = USCG crew].

Not in Assault Groups

LST Flotilla 4, USN
LST Group 12, Division 23, USN: LST(2)s 326^, 197, 381^
[^ = USCG crew].

[These three LSTs arrived just too late to participate on D-Day, but joined the operation soon after.]

Force L

Assault Group L1

HMS *Northway* (LSD).
7 LST(2) Flotilla, RN: LST(2)s 214, 237, 301, 319, 321, 366, 406
8 LST(2) Flotilla, RN: LST(2)s 63, 165, 198, 200, 403, 161.
[These carried LCP(R)s.]

LST Flotilla 4, USN
LST Group 11, Division 22, USN: LST(2)s 377, 378, 379.
LST Group 52, Division 21, USN: LST(2)s 327^, 384, 385, 386, 540, 360, 383 [^ = USCG crew].

LST Flotilla 17, USN
LST Group 49, Division 98, USN: LST(2)s 60, 137, 295, 517, 534, 535.
LST Group 49, Division 102, USN: LST(2)s 175, 176^, 208, 209, 261^, 530 [^ = USCG crew].
LST Group 50, Division 99, USN: LST(2)s 138, 139, 524, 527, 536, 537.
LST Group 50, Division 100, USN: LST(2)s 521, 522, 528, 529, 541, 542.

LST Flotilla 18, USN
LST Group 52, Division 103, USN: LST(2)s 543, 682, 980, 981, 982, 983.

Assault Group L2

V LCT Squadron, RN
16 LCT Flotilla, RN: LCT(3)s 7057, 7058, 7063, 7064, 7065, 7068, 7077, 7090, 7097, 7098, 7099.
18 LCT Flotilla, RN: LCT(3)s 7034, 7036, 7039, 7053, 7054, 7070, 7072, 7073, 7075, 7100, 7102.
19 LCT Flotilla, RN: LCT(3)s 7044, 7046, 7047, 7050, 7078, 7085, 7087, 7088, 7089, 7096, 7101.

H LCT Squadron, RN
6 LCT Flotilla, RN: LCT(3)s 7035, 7043, 7045, 7048, 7049, 7080, 7082, 7083, 7084, 7086, 7091, 7092.
17 LCT Flotilla, RN: LCT(3)s 7051, 7052, 7066, 7067, 7069, 7071, 7074, 7076, 7079, 7081.

Assault Group L3

Maracailbo class: HMS *Misoa*, HMS *Bachaquero*, HMS *Tasajera*.

A LCI(L) Squadron, RN
252 LCI(L) Flotilla, RN: LCI(L)s 109, 122, 123, 127, 129, 172, 176, 242, 243, 256.
253 LCI(L) Flotilla, RN: LCI(L)s 103, 104, 105, 106, 110, 178, 182, 268, 307.

Roll of Honour

The number of Allied landing craft crewmen who died in the Normandy campaign is a grim measure of the dangers that they were exposed to. Those killed on D-Day alone were over 250 (at time of writing). A Roll of Honour for crewmen killed in the entire campaign, associated with this book, is available at:

ddaylandingcraft.net.

Further information on individuals who died, submitted via the website, would be greatly appreciated.

The complexities of compiling a Roll of Honour include the fact that not all deceased landing craft crewmen are identified as such. The records of the Commonwealth War Graves Commission associate some British and Commonwealth crewmen with a shore base, such as HMS *Copra*, rather than with a specific landing craft or flotilla. 'Copra' stood for 'Combined Operations Pay Records & Accounts' and was the base responsible for keeping records of Royal Navy personnel serving with Combined Operations. For example, Corporal Eric James Smith RM was the coxswain of LCA 796 (538 Assault Flotilla, SS *Empire Broadsword*, Force S) and died on D-Day after his craft was sunk by a beach obstacle. At the time of writing, the Commonwealth War Graves Commission record him under HMS *Copra*.*

---

* www.combinedops.com/COPRA.htm. Smith's landing craft can be identified from TNA: ADM 199/1650; DEFE: 2/420; Lund & Ludlam, *War of the Landing Craft*, pp.151–53.

Several websites based on official records list Ensign George Robert Edwards USN of 'LCI-5, Flotilla 1', who died on D-Day. In fact, he was not serving on an LCI(L) but on LCT(6) 663, LCT Flotilla 17, Force U.* This is not meant as a criticism of organisations and websites that commemorate the war dead, but reflects sometimes incomplete wartime records. Information gathered in the research for this book will be passed on to relevant organisations should it be useful for updating their existing records.

---

* www.naval-history.net/WW2UScasaaDB-USNBPbyNameD.htm; www.honorstates.org/profiles/36706/; Fold3, US Naval Advanced Base 12, Utah.

Notes

Introduction: 'Ugly and Unorthodox ...'

1. DDS, 1992/275/80: Rupert Curtis scrapbook.
2. (Marshall) Teheran Conference Transcript, quoted in Balkoski, Joseph, *Omaha Beach: D-Day, June 6, 1944* (Mechanicsburg, PA: Stackpole, 2004), p.19; (Eisenhower) McGee, William L., *The Amphibians Are Coming! Emergence of the 'Gator Navy and its Revolutionary Landing Craft* (Santa Barbara, CA: 2000), p.xxiv.
3. Roskill, Stephen W., *The War at Sea, Vol. III: The Offensive, Part II: 1 June 1944–14 August 1945* (London: HMSO, 1961), p.19; Ellis, Lionel Frederic, *Victory in the West, Vol. 1: The Battle of Normandy* (London: HMSO, 1962), p.507; Fold3, CB 04385A, Report by the Allied Naval Commander-in-Chief Expeditionary Force on Operation Neptune, Vol. 1, p.121; Commander US Naval Forces in Europe, 'The Invasion of Normandy: Operation Neptune', *United States Naval Administration in World War II*, Vol. V (1948), p.292, downloaded from US Naval History and Heritage Command (history.navy.mil).
4. www.history.navy.mil/research/histories/ship-histories/danfs/l/lst-921.html (accessed 20/5/2023).
5. Robert D. Blegen, 'LCT(5) Flotilla 18 at Omaha Beach, D-Day, June 6, 1944' at ww2lct.org/history/stories/flot_18_at_omaha.htm (accessed 18/3/2023).

1. Landing Craft Types: Origins, Design and Construction

1. Mowry, George, 'Landing Craft and the War Production Board, April 1942 to May 1944' in *Historical Reports on War Administration: War Production Board, Special Study No. 11* (Washington DC: Civilian Production Administration, 1944), via books.google.com, p.1.

    Sources used throughout this chapter include: Brown, D.K. (ed.), *The Design and Construction of British Warships 1939–1945* (London: Conway Maritime Press,

1996), pp.40–80; Ladd, J.D., *Assault from the Sea 1939–45: The Craft, the Landings, the Men* (London: David & Charles, 1976); Baker III, A.D. (ed.), *Allied Landing Craft of World War Two* (London: Arms & Armour, 1985); Winser, John de S., *The D-Day Ships* (Kendal: World Ship Society, 1994); Buffetaut, Yves, *D-Day Ships: The Allied Invasion Fleet, June 1944* (London: Conway, 2004); TNA, ADM 239/242; TNA, ADM 239/354; WW2Talk.com, threads on all five beaches by Mike ('Trux'). Other sources are referenced under particular types of craft.

2. DHH, 81-520-1250, Box 72: RALB (Rear Admiral Landing Craft and Bases) Temporary Memoranda; TNA, AIR 20/5017; DDS, 1992/275/135, H.F.J. Higgs, 'Notes on Major LC'; Fold3, USS *Dorothea L. Dix*, Report on Operations, North Coast of France.

3. Captain Todhunter RN, quoted in Baker, Rowland, 'Notes on the Development of Landing Craft' in A.D. Duckworth (ed.), *Transactions of the Institution of Naval Architects*, Vol. 89 (London: Institution of Naval Architects, 1947), pp.218–58; Furer, Julius Augustus, *Administration of the Navy Department in World War II* (Washington, DC: Naval History Division, 1959) p.232 (viewed at www.ibiblio.org).

4. Friedman, *US Amphibious Ships*, p.94.

5. Doyle, David, *US Landing Craft of WWII, Vol. 1: The LCP(L), LCP(R), LCV, LCVP, LCS(L), LCM and LCI* (Atglen, PA: Schiffer, 2019); Friedman, Norman, *US Amphibious Ships and Craft: An Illustrated Design History*. (Annapolis, MD: Naval Institute Press, 2002), pp.75–86.

6. TNA, DEFE 2/420.

7. Doyle, *US Landing Craft, Vol. 1*; Roberts, Charles C., *The Boat that Won the War: An Illustrated History of the Higgins LCVP* (Barnsley: Seaforth, 2017); Friedman, *US Amphibious Ships*, pp.208–12.

8. Doyle, *US Landing Craft, Vol. 1*, p.26.

9. Robert J. Dolan quoted in Witter, Robert E., *Small Boats and Large Slow Targets: Oral Histories of United States Amphibious Forces Personnel in WWII* (Missoula, MT: Pictorial Histories, 1998), pp.46–54; Fold3, Report of Commander, Task Group 124.3, pp.7–8. Unsurprisingly, LCV stood for Landing Craft, Vehicle.

10. TNA, WO 193/489; TNA, DEFE 2/1165; Fold3, CB 04385A, Report by the Allied Naval Commander-in-Chief Expeditionary Force on Operation Neptune, Vol. 1, p.121; DDS, 1995/100/1, Robert Adams' account (original at the Eisenhower Center).

11. Fold3, USS *Anne Arundel*, Report on Operations, Normandy; Fold3, LST Flotilla 12, Action Report on Operations, Normandy.

12. Lavery, Brian, *Assault Landing Craft: Design, Construction and Operations* (Barnsley: Seaforth, 2009).

13. Fold3, CB 04385A, Report by the Allied Naval Commander-in-Chief Expeditionary Force on Operation Neptune, Vol. 1, p.121.

14. Doyle, *US Landing Craft, Vol.1*, pp.52–73.

15. (Obstacles) Fold3, USS *Anne Arundel*, Report on Operations, Normandy; (rough seas) Fold3, USS *Joseph T. Dickman*, Report on Operations, Normandy.

16. (Ferry craft) TNA, DEFE 2/417; (salvage) United States Fleet, *Amphibious Operations: Invasion of Northern France* (COMINCH P-006) (Washington DC:

Navy Department, 1944), ch.5, p.32, via Naval Academy Library at usna.edu/ Library (accessed, 16/02/2021).

17. Doyle, *US Landing Craft, Vol. 2*, pp.6–35; Friedman, *US Amphibious Ships*, pp.111–22, pp.134–36.

18. Quote from TNA, WO 193/395.

19. Fold3, Commander-in-Chief Atlantic Fleet, Administrative History, pp.562–69; Fold3, CB 04385A, Report by the Allied Naval Commander-in-Chief Expeditionary Force on Operation Neptune, Vol. 1, p.121; Fold3, Commander 11th PHIBFOR, Report by Commander Force O on Operations, June 1944, pp.118–19; (number built) Doyle, *US Landing Craft, Vol. 2*, p.6.

20. TNA, ADM 1/17022.

21. Fold3, Commander Task Force 122, Report on Naval Operations, Invasion of Normandy, p.518.

22. Lund, Paul, & Harry Ludlam, *The War of the Landing Craft* (London: W. Foulsham, 1976), p.142; Anderson Jr., Richard C., *Cracking Hitler's Atlantic Wall: The 1st Assault Brigade Royal Engineers on D-Day* (Mechanicsburg, PA: Stackpole, 2010), p.27.

23. (Makeshift arrangement) United States Fleet, *Amphibious Operations*, ch.2, p.25; TNA, DEFE 2/427.

24. Rottman, Gordon L., *Landing Craft, Infantry and Fire Support*, New Vanguard Series, 157 (Oxford: Osprey, 2009); USS LCI National Association, *USS LCI, Vol. I* (Paducah, KY: Turner Publishing, 1993); Friedman, *US Amphibious Ships*, pp.139–48; (three LCMs) Fold3, LCI(L) 528, Report on Operations in Normandy; (gradients) TNA, DEFE 2/420; (curtains/piano/facilities) Lund & Ludlum, *War of the Landing Craft*, pp.61–62; (mobility) Fold3, Commander 11th PHIBFOR, Report by Commander Force O on Operations, June 1944, p.119; (Niedermair) McGee, *The Amphibians are Coming!*, pp.195–97.

25. DDS, 2014/58/149, Alan Villiers, 'The Story of the Lice', *Ships and the Sea*, 1952.

26. (Preferred appointment) Lund & Ludlum, *War of the Landing Craft*, pp.136–37.

27. TNA, ADM 179/516.

28. Fold3, Commander Gunfire Support Craft, Force O, Action Report, July 1944.

29. TNA, DEFE 2/417.

30. Friedman, *US Amphibious Ships*, pp.223–25, pp.278–81; Palmer Jr, William H.P., *We Called Ourselves Rocketboatmen* (GoToPublish, 2018).

31. Fold3, COMPHIBBASES (Commander Amphibious Bases), UK.

32. TNA, ADM 239/242; TNA, DEFE 2/416; TNA, DEFE 2/427.

33. TNA, DEFE 2/417.

34. TNA, ADM 202/449.

35. TNA, DEFE 2/733.

36. TNA, ADM 179/506.

37. TNA, DEFE 2/433.

38. Jarman, W.D. 'Jim', *Those Wallowing Beauties: The Story of the Landing Barges in World War II* (Lewes: Book Guild, 1997); Gustav Milne, 'London's Lightermen at D-DAY Invasion of Normandy', www.citizan.org.uk/blog/2020/Jun/03/ londons-lightermen-d-day-invasion-normandy.

39. TNA, AIR 20/5017.

40. Fold3, CB 04385A, Report by the Allied Naval Commander-in-Chief Expeditionary Force on Operation Neptune, Vol. 1, p.0122–24; TNA, ADM 179/506.

41. TNA, DEFE 2/419.

42. WW2Talk.com, thread on Sword Beach by Mike ('Trux'); Fold3, Commander Task Force 122, Report on Naval Operations, Invasion of Normandy, p.518; TNA, ADM 179/506; Fold3, Commander 11th PHIBFOR, Report by Commander Force O on Operations, June 1944, pp.15–16; Fort Wayne Engineers Club, *Engineers News*, Vol. 6, No.5 (January 1944). Downloaded from fortwayneengineersclub.org (accessed 15/3/2023); DDS, 2022/82, 'American Steel Dredge Company Inc, Packing and Shipping Instructions, Design 349B. Bolted Section Steel Barges for Gasoline and Dry Cargo' (1943); Symonds, Craig, *Neptune: The Allied Invasion of Europe and the D-Day Landings* (Oxford: Oxford University Press, 2014), p.311.

43. Macdermott, Brian, *Ships without Names: The Story of the Royal Navy's Tank Landing Ships of World War Two* (London: Arms & Armour, 1992); Rottman, Gordon L., *Landing Ship, Tank (LST) 1942–2002*, New Vanguard Series, 115 (Oxford: Osprey, 2005); Doyle, *US Landing Craft, Vol.2*.

44. Symonds, *Neptune*, p.166.

45. (Capacity) TNA, DEFE 2/427.

46. Winser, *The D-Day Ships*, pp.34–42; Baker, *Allied Landing Craft*.

47. Baker, *Allied Landing Craft*, Supplement No.1, p.63.

48. The design was by Captain John N. Laycock (US Navy Seabee Museum article, 'Captain John N. Laycock', at www.history.navy.mil/content/history/museums/seabee/explore/civil-engineer-corps-history/john-n-laycock.html).

49. Frank A. Blazich Jr, 'Inventors and Innovators: Naval Lighterage and Anglo-American Success in the Amphibious Invasions of German-Occupied Europe' in *The Northern Mariner*, 31, No.2 (Summer 2021), pp.125–72.

50. Zaloga, Steven, *The Devil's Garden: Rommel's Desperate Defense of Omaha Beach on D-Day* (Mechanicsburg, PA: Stackpole, 2013), p.183; Ladd, J.D., *Assault from the Sea 1939–45*, pp.155–67; TNA, AIR 20/5020.

51. TNA, CAB 102/539; Furer, *Administration of the Navy*, p.261.

52. Kepher, Stephen C., *COSSAC: Lt Gen Sir Frederick Morgan and the Genesis of Operation Overlord* (Annapolis, MD: Naval Institute Press, 2020), pp.171–72.

53. TNA, CAB 102/539; Moore, George, *Building for Victory: The Warships Building Programmes of the Royal Navy 1939–1945* (Kendal: World Ship Society, 2003), pp.8, 82; Postan, Michael M., *British War Production* (London: HMSO, 1952), pp.283–87, 442 (viewed at www.ibiblio.org).

54. TNA, CAB 102/539.

55. Lindberg, Michael, & Daniel Todd, *Anglo-American Shipbuilding in World War II: A Geographical Perspective* (Westport, CT: Praeger, 2004), pp.122–23.

56. Todman, Dan, *Britain's War. A New World 1942–1947* (London: Penguin Random House, 2020), pp.477–78; Pritchard, James, *A Bridge of Ships: Canadian Shipbuilding During the Second World War* (Montreal: McGill-Queen's University Press, 2011), p.288; www.saltscapes.com/roots-folks/3066-the-d-day-minca-barges.html (accessed 17/9/2023); TNA, ADM 229/32.

57. Furer, *Administration of the Navy Department*, pp.213–16, 239–42, 246, 252–53, 261; Mowry, *Landing Craft*, p.7.

58. Fold3, CinC Atlantic Fleet, Administrative History, pp.562–69.

59. Postan, *War Production*, pp.365, 406; Moore, *Building for Victory*, p.90.

60. TNA, CAB 102/539; Postan, *War Production*, p.218; J.W. Smith & T.S. Holden, *Where Ships are Born* (1946, republished 1953 by Wear Shipbuilders Association), p.131: www.searlecanada.org/sunderland/sunderland116.html#index (accessed 13/10/2021); Imperial War Museum, IWM 20164, interview with Lilly Errington.

61. Clark, Andrew L., *A Cornfield Shipyard* (Evansville, IN: MT Publishing, 1991); University of Southern Indiana, Archives and Special Collections, Edward Klingler (OH 0035), Manson Reichert (OH 0047), John Koch Jr (OH 0050) interviews.

62. Lund & Ludlum, *War of the Landing Craft*, p.67; DDS, 2014/58/57, Paul Motte-Harrison account.

63. Yung, Christopher D., *Gators of Neptune: Naval Amphibious Planning for the Normandy Invasion* (Annapolis, MD: Naval Institute Press, 2006), pp.33–36.

64. For example: *Lessons of Operation Torch* in TNA, DEFE 2/716; Yung, *Gators*, pp.6–7, 36–40. TNA, DEFE 2/716; Lorelli, John A., *To Foreign Shores: US Amphibious Operations in World War II* (Annapolis, MD: Naval Institute Press, 1995), pp.71–83, 146–51.

65. Fold3, USS *Charles Carroll*, Report on Operations, Normandy.

2. Allied Strategy and Landing Craft Production

1. Eisenhower Library, Diary of Dwight D. Eisenhower January–July 1943, entry 22 January 1942, at www.eisenhowerlibrary.gov/research/online-documents/diaries-dwight-d-eisenhower, viewed 27/10/2023.

2. Furer, *Administration of the Navy Department*, p.261; Postan, *War Production*, p.247.

3. DDS, 1992/275/150, The Evolution and Development of Combined Operations Technique and Material, CR 2627/45 (3.1946); TNA, DEFE 2/696.

4. Moore, *Building for Victory*, pp.35, 45–62; DDS, 1992/275/150, The Evolution and Development of Combined Operations Technique and Material, CR 2627/45 (3.1946); Postan, *War Production*, pp.283–87.

5. Fold3, CinC Atlantic Fleet, Administrative History, pp.562–69; Friedman, *US Amphibious Ships*, p.113; Moore, *Building for Victory*, pp.35–38, 40–41.

6. Friedman, *US Amphibious Ships*, pp.20–21.

7. Friedman, *US Amphibious Ships*, pp.117–20; Ellis, *Victory*, p.512.

8. Stoler, *Allies*, pp.28, 61–63; Todman, Dan, *Britain's War: Into Battle 1937–1941* (London: Penguin Random House, 2016) pp.201–02; GDP figure from www.thebalancemoney.com/us-gdp-by-year-3305543.

9. O'Brien, Phillips Payson, *How the War was Won* (Cambridge: Cambridge University Press, 2015), p.207; DDS, 1992/275/150, The Evolution and Development of Combined Operations Technique and Material, CR 2627/45 (3.1946).

10. Stoler, *Allies*, pp.61–69; TNA, DEFE 2/696; Friedman, *US Amphibious Ships*, pp.151–57, 219–20.

11. Friedman, *US Amphibious Ships*, pp.219–20; Leighton, Richard, & Robert Coakley, *Global Logistics and Strategy 1943–1945* (Washington DC: Center of Military History, 1989), p.11.

12. Commander US Naval Forces in Europe, 'The Invasion of Normandy: Operation Neptune', *United States Naval Administration in World War II, Vol. V* (1948), pp.11–12.

13. Kepher, *COSSAC*, pp.3–4; Yung, *Gators of Neptune*, p.44; TNA, DEFE 2/696; Commander US Naval Forces, *Neptune*, pp.19, 51–63.

14. Kepher, *COSSAC*, pp.36–38.

15. *Ibid.*, pp.26–35.

16. Mowry, *Landing Craft*, pp.7–8, 23.

17. Leighton & Croakley, *Global Logistics*, p.17; Mowry, *Landing Craft*, p.2.

18. www.navsource.org/archives/10/18/18idx.htm (accessed 24/2/2022); Mowry, *Landing Craft*, pp.5, 9–14, 21–22.

19. Stoler, *Allies*, pp.66–69; Todman, *Britain's War: A New World*, p.213; Kepher, *COSSAC*, p.6.

20. Symonds, *Neptune*, p.100; Friedman, *US Amphibious Ships*, p.220; TNA, DEFE 2/696; DDS, 1992/275/150, The Evolution and Development of Combined Operations Technique and Material, CR 2627/45 (3.1946); Fold3, CinC Atlantic Fleet, Administrative History, pp.555–60.

21. Todman, *Britain's War: A New World*, p.299.

22. Friedman, *US Amphibious Ships*, p.220; Symonds, *Neptune*, pp.148, 157–58; Mowry, *Landing Craft*, p.21; Postan, *War Production*, p.201.

23. Kepher, *COSSAC*, pp.8–9, 179.

24. Herman, Arthur, *Freedom's Forge: How American Business Produced Victory in World War II* (New York, NY: Random House, 2012), pp.192–99; Furer, *Administration of the Navy Department*, pp.242–44, 291–92; Mowry, *Landing Craft*, pp.21–22.

25. Mowry, *Landing Craft*, p.23.

26. TNA, DEFE 2/696; O'Brien, *How the War was Won*, pp.224–25.

27. Commander US Naval Forces, *Neptune*, pp.20–23; Stoler, *Allies*, pp.86–91; DDS, 1992/275/150, CR 2627/45 (3.1946); Fold3, Commander-in-Chief Atlantic Fleet, Administrative History, pp.562–69; TNA, CAB 102/539.

28. TNA, WO 193/395; TNA, WO 193/488.

29. Kepher, *COSSAC*, pp.99–100.

30. Kepher, *COSSAC*, p.95; Fold3, Trident Conference, Washington, May 1943: Papers and Minutes of Meetings, pp.224–29, 260–62. These figures do not include 'unallocated' craft which are in addition to these figures, e.g. thirteen unallocated LSTs in January 1944, growing to sixty-one by May 1944.

31. DDS, 1992/275/150, CR 2627/45 (3.1946); TNA, DEFE 2/696; Commander US Naval Forces, *Neptune*, pp.105–06; TNA, WO 193/488.

32. Fold3, Commander-in-Chief Atlantic Fleet, Administrative History, pp.575–77; TNA, WO 193/488.

33. Kepher, *COSSAC*, pp.40, 52–55, 103; quote by Commodore John Hughes-Hallett on being appointed representative to COSSAC of the Royal Navy's Commander-in-Chief, Portsmouth, quoted in Kepher, *COSSAC*, p.48.

34. Kepher, *COSSAC*, pp.81–92.

35. Eisenhower Library, Ray Barker interview, pp.91, 98; TNA, WO 193/488 (20 per cent of the UK's total naval shipbuilding capacity was now taken up by landing craft); CARL, N7370-B, Operation Overlord: Appendices to COSSAC plan.

36. Kepher, *COSSAC*, pp.168–69, 182.

37. Mowry, *Landing Craft*, pp.25–27.

38. Mowry, *Landing Craft*, pp.2, 33–35, 62.

39. Summary report of conversations with General Charles H. Bonesteel III, USA Retired, US Army War College, pp.161–62. With thanks to James Holland for directing me to this source.

40. TNA, ADM 1/17022.

41. TNA, DEFE 2/460; TNA, BT 87/123; TNA, DEFE 2/460; Postan, *War Production*, pp.262–64; TNA, ADM 1/17022.

42. CARL, N7370-B, Operation Overlord: Appendices to COSSAC plan.

43. TNA, DEFE 2/460.

44. Mowry, *Landing Craft*, pp.39–42, 56; Commander US Naval Forces, *Neptune*, pp.105–06.

45. TNA, ADM 1/17022; Moore, *Building for Victory*, p.92; TNA, BT 87/123. One of the LCT(3★)s built was LCT 7074, now on display at The D-Day Story, Portsmouth (in partnership with the National Museum of the Royal Navy).

46. TNA, CAB 102/539; Moore, *Building for Victory*, p.92; Postan, *War Production*, p.296–98.

47. Quote from Kepher, *COSSAC*, p.204; Dan Todman, *Britain's War: A New World*, pp.486–89; Commander US Naval Forces, *Neptune*, pp.105–06.

48. Mowry, *Landing Craft*, pp.30–31, 39; TNA, WO 193/488.

49. Fold3, Commander-in-Chief Atlantic Fleet, Administrative History, pp.562–69; Postan, *War Production*, p.243.

50. TNA, ADM 229/32.

51. Mowry, *Landing Craft*, pp.35, 51–52.

52. Bedell Smith, quoted in Kepher, *COSSAC*, p.210.

53. Kepher, *COSSAC*, pp.211–12; letter from Montgomery to Lieutenant General Sir Oliver Leese, 22 January 1944 in Stephen Brooks, *Montgomery and the Battle of Normandy* (Stroud: The History Press, 2008), p.38; Yung, *Gators of Neptune*, p.75; Ellis, *Victory in the West*, pp.32–33. COSSAC's views on the best landing beaches are given in CARL, N7370-B, Operation Overlord: Appendices to COSSAC plan, pp.107–08.

54. Kepher, *COSSAC*, p.214.

55. Letters between Montgomery and Eisenhower, 21 February 1944, in Brooks, *Montgomery*, pp.47–48; Kepher, *COSSAC*, pp.215–16.

56. Letter by Montgomery to Eisenhower, 23 February 1944, in Brooks, *Montgomery*, pp.51–52.

57. Montgomery diary notes, 11 February 1944, in Brooks, *Montgomery*, pp.43–44.

58. TNA, DEFE 2/696; Yung, *Gators of Neptune*, pp.66–71; Ellis, *Victory*, pp.33–34.

59. Yung, *Gators of Neptune*, pp.64–66, 72–74.
60. Ellis, *Victory*, p.35; Commander US Naval Forces, *Neptune*, pp. 108–10, 118–19; TNA, DEFE 2/696; Yung, *Gators of Neptune*, pp.72–74; Commander US Naval Forces, *Neptune*, pp.369–70; War TNA, AIR 20/5020; Fold3, COMLANCRAB (Commander, Landing Craft Bases) 11th PHIBFOR, pp.1–3.
61. TNA, AIR 9/299.
62. TNA, WO 229/64; Fold3, Commander, Transports, 11th PHIBFOR, Diary June 1944, pp.4–6; Commander US Naval Forces, *Neptune*, pp.110–16.
63. Commander US Naval Forces, *Neptune*, pp.108–10, 118–19.
64. Yung, *Gators of Neptune*, p.75.
65. DDS, 1992/275/150, The Evolution and Development of Combined Operations Technique and Material, CR 2627/45 (3.1946).
66. TNA, CAB 102/539.

3. FORGING THE WEAPON: LANDING CRAFT CREWS, BASES AND TRAINING

1. DHH, 81-520-1250, Box 79, File 2, Vol. 2, correspondence regarding training.
2. DDS, 2014/58/172, anonymous account.
3. DDS, 2014/58/285, Reg Deighton account; DDS, 2014/58/107, Raymond Shone account.
4. Lund & Ludlum, *War of the Landing Craft*, pp.14–17, 22.
5. DDS, 2014/58/187, Alan Higgins account; DDS, 2014/58/273, Robert Thompson account.
6. DDS, 2014/58/57, Paul Motte Harrison account; DDS, 2014/58/191, Buck Taylor account.
7. Lund & Ludlum, *War of the Landing Craft*, pp.78–80.
8. *Ibid.*, pp.82–91.
9. DDS, 2014/58/72, Raymond Oram account.
10. Lund & Ludlum, *War of the Landing Craft*, pp.136–37.
11. TNA, ADM 179/508; TNA, DEFE 2/696; DDS, 2014/58/165 Eric Holderness account; TNA, ADM 202/448.
12. TNA, ADM 179/508.
13. McGee, *Amphibians*, pp.9, 34–35; Lorelli, *To Foreign Shores*, pp.39–41.
14. Symonds, *Neptune*, p.155; Fold3, Commander, Gunfire Support Craft, Force O, Action Report, July 1944, pp.5–7.
15. DDS, 2014/58/149, Alan Villiers, 'The Story of the Lice', *Ships and the Sea*, 1952.
16. DDS, 2014/58/104, Edward Zealley account; DHH, 81-520-1250, Box 79, File 3, Vol. 4, pp.144–45.
17. DHH, 81-520-1250, Box 72, File 2, Vol. 3, Rear Admiral Landing Craft and Bases at Combined Operations HQ, temporary memoranda; Lund & Ludlum, *War of the Landing Craft*, pp.136–37; DDS, 2014/58/57, Paul Motte-Harrison account; DDS, 2014/58/37, Andrew Marchant account.
18. DDS, 2014/58/114, Joe Graham account.
19. DDS, 2014/58/154, D.G. Woodford account.

20. DDS, 2014/58/300, Stan McGowan account; France, John, 'The Final LCI Assault of Omaha Beach', *Elsie Item*, November 2016, pp.10–28.

21. DDS, 2014/58/172, anonymous account.

22. DDS, 2014/58/154, D.G. Woodford account; DDS, 2014/58/65a, Bill Page account.

23. DDS, 2014/58/50, Reg Dean account; DDS, 2014/58/12, Raymond C. Oram account.

24. DDS, 2014/58/7, S.W. (Bill) Havill account; DDS, 2014/58/3, E.J. Loseby account.

25. DDS, 2014/58/61, A.H. (Harry) Eddy account.

26. DDS, 2014/58/152, R. Wild account; DDS, 2014/13, Norman Moss account; DDS, 2014/58/171, Bob Bradshaw account.

27. TNA, DEFE 2/696.

28. DDH, 81-520-1250, Box 79, File 3, Vol. 4, pp.4, 32, 85, 123; TNA, DEFE 2/696.

29. TNA, WO 193/395; TNA, DEFE 2/696.

30. TNA, DEFE 2/696.

31. *Ibid.*

32. TNA, ADM 1/17813.

33. TNA, ADM 179/508.

34. *Ibid.*

35. *Ibid.*; TNA, DEFE 2/696.

36. *Ibid.*; TNA, ADM 179/516; Yung, *Gators of Neptune*, p.155.

37. TNA, ADM 179/516; Yung, *Gators of Neptune*, p.155.

38. Fold3, 1st Engineer Special Brigade, Notes, Utah Beach, pp.19–26; Yung, *Gators of Neptune*, pp.156–62; Royal Canadian Navy Historical Section, *The RCN's Part In The Invasion of France* (London: Royal Canadian Navy, 1945) from navsource. org/archives/10/15/15000002.htm, p.28 (accessed 16/2/2021); Caddick-Adams, Peter, *Sand and Steel: A New History of D-Day* (London: Penguin Random House, 2014), pp.200–03.

39. DDS, 2014/13, Norman Moss account.

40. DDS, ADM 202/449; TNA, DEFE 2/416.

41. TNA, ADM 199/1560.

42. DDS, 2014/58/51, Roy Nelson account.

4. The Plan

1. DEFE 2/427; United States Fleet, *Amphibious Operations*, ch.5, pp.2–4.

2. TNA, DEFE 2/696; TNA, DEFE 2/529.

3. DDS, 2005/1412, Anon., 'A Wren's Eye View by Two Slant O' (1945), pp.16–19. The author was a Second Officer WRNS (Assistant Staff Officer in charge of Landing Ships and Craft) on the staff of COSSAC then ANCXF.

4. CARL, N7379, Amendment No.3 to Neptune, Initial Joint Plan (NJC 1004, dated 1/2/1944), pp.77, 89.

5. TNA, DEFE 2/427; Lieutenant Commander William Leide, LCT Flotillas 12 and 26, Action Report, 29 June 1944: ww2lct.org/history/actionreports/table1. htm (accessed 18/3/2023).

6.	DDS, 1992/275/150, The Evolution and Development of Combined Operations Technique and Material, CR 2627/45 (3.1946); Commander US Naval Forces, *Neptune*, pp.274–75; Fold3, Commander Task Force 122, Report on Naval Operations, Invasion of Normandy, p.511.

7.	TNA, ADM 210/8; (breaching teams) Anderson, *Cracking*, p.117.

8.	TNA, ADM 210/8.

9.	TNA, DEFE 2/427; United States Fleet, *Amphibious Operations*, ch.5, pp.2–4.

10.	(Statement in Neptune Initial Joint Plan) CARL, N7379, Amendment No.3 to Neptune, Initial Joint Plan (NJC 1004, dated 1/2/1944), p.77; United States Fleet, *Amphibious Operations*, ch.5, pp.2–4.

11.	Lieutenant Commander William Leide, LCT Flotillas 12 and 26, Action Report 29 June 1944: ww2lct.org/history/actionreports/table1.htm (accessed 18/3/2023); TNA, ADM 210/8.

12.	Commander US Naval Forces, *Neptune*, pp.377–78.

13.	TNA, ADM 199/1560; CARL, N7374-A, Annexes 22–26 to First Army Operations Plan, Neptune: Mounting (25 Feb 1944), p.13. The author is grateful for the work done by members of WW2Talk.com forum, especially Mike ('Trux') and Michel Sabarly, in compiling and making public the information extracted from landing tables.

14.	The LCT that had engine trouble may have been LCT 600. United States Fleet, *Amphibious Operations*, ch.5, p.8; TNA, DEFE 2/419; DDS, 2014/58/214, Bill Kiss account.

15.	McManus, John C., *The Dead and Those Who are About to Die: D-Day: The Big Red One at Omaha Beach* (New York, NY: Caliber, 2014), p.37; Gawne, Jonathan, *Spearheading D-Day: American Special Units in Normandy* (Paris: Histoire & Collections, 2001), pp.84–90.

16.	Fold3, Commander Task Group 124.4/SS *Empire Javelin* Report.

17.	DDS, 1995/100/45, Oscar Rich account (original kept at the Eisenhower Center).

18.	Fold3, Commander Task Force 122, Report on Naval Operations, Invasion of Normandy, pp.502–03.

19.	TNA, DEFE 2/427.

20.	TNA, DEFE 2/416; Fold3, LST Flotilla 12, Action Report on Operations, Normandy, Report of Deputy Commander, Assault Group O2; (Commander TG 125.7) United States Fleet, *Amphibious Operations*, ch.2, p.19.

21.	Balkoski, *Omaha*, pp.47–51.

5. Embarkation, Departure and Crossing

1.	DDS, 1990/1314/2, ONEAST/J2; DDS, 2014/58/162, D. Scott account.

2.	DDS, 2014/58/186, Peter Denham account; WW2Talk.com, thread on Omaha Beach by Mike ('Trux').

3.	Lund & Ludlum, *The War of the Landing Craft*, pp.144, 146; TNA, ADM 179/506.

4. Fold3, USS *Thurston*, War History; Fold3, COM 11th PHIBFOR, War Diary, May 1944; Fold3, Commander 11th PHIBFOR, Report by Commander Force O on Operations, June 1944, pp.5–7.

5. Commander US Naval Forces, *Neptune*, pp.275–78, 305–06. Force O, U and B figures taken from Fold3, 1st US Army, Annex 2, pp.224–26 – personnel/vehicle figures are mostly planning figures not those actually loaded; Force L figures from TNA, ADM 199/1560.

6. Fold3, CB 04385A, Report by the Allied Naval Commander-in-Chief Expeditionary Force on Operation Neptune, Vol, 1, p.3268; Commander US Naval Forces, *Neptune*, pp.275–78, 305–06; Fold3, CB 04385A, Report by the Allied Naval Commander-in-Chief Expeditionary Force on Operation Neptune, Vol. 1, XFNP Naval Plan, p.3270.

7. TNA, ADM 179/405; TNA, DEFE 2/420.

8. TNA, DEFE 2/419; United States Fleet, *Amphibious Operations*, ch.5, pp.4–5; (LCT 2498) Commander US Naval Forces, *Neptune*, pp.375–80.

9. Fold3, USS *Samuel Chase*, Report, War Operations, Normandy, 6–7 June 1944; United States Fleet, *Amphibious Operations*, ch.1, p.16.

10. TNA, ADM 179/508. At a late stage in planning, Forces O, U and B had not allocated loads to a total of eight LST(2)s, fifty-six LCTs and fourteen LCI(L)s, although no doubt changes meant some of these were used on D-Day after all (Fold3, 1st US Army, Annex 2, pp.224–28). In Force J, as 100 per cent of craft were available, there were spare craft and two extra LCT(5)s were loaded with AVRE tanks (TNA, ADM 179/506).

11. DDS, 2014/58/204, Alf Twelftree account.

12. DDS, 2014/58/169, Charles Bruce; Eugene Pendleton Banks' account at www. jstor.org/stable/community.35123267?seq=1; Ken Hawkins, quoted in Jarman, *Those Wallowing Beauties*, p.118.

13. DDS, 2014/58/191, Lieutenant Colonel G.R. Perkins, 'Royal Marines in Major Landing Craft on D-Day' (Royal Marines Historical Society); TNA, DEFE 2/416.

14. DDS, 2014/58/236, Bill Schumacker account; DDS, 2014/58/294, Roland John Tracey account.

15. DDS, 2014/58/68, Albert [no surname] account; DDS, 2014/58/248, Frederick E. Naylor account.

16. DDS, 2014/58/13, Norman Moss account; DDS, 2014/58/190, Malcolm Cook account; DDS, 2014/58/286, Ron Wilson account.

17. Balkoski, *Omaha*, p.61; DDS, 2014/58/99, John Andrews; DDS, 2014/58/6, John Lambourne account.

18. TNA, ADM 179/506; DDS, 2010/19, Menu of LST 522 for week beginning 5 June 1944.

19. DDS, 2014/58/191, Buck Taylor account.

20. DDS, 2014/58/224, Derek Brightman account.

21. Hugill, John Antony Crawford, *The Hazard Mesh* (London: Hurst & Blackett, 1946), p.15.

22. United States Fleet, *Amphibious Operations*, ch.1, p.10; Fold3, Report, LCM Flotilla 2; Benbow, *Operation Neptune*, p.107.

23. DDS, 2014/58/139, Rex Eye account; DDS, 2014/58/128, Ken McCaw account.

24. Fold3, CB 04385A, Report by the Allied Naval Commander-in-Chief Expeditionary Force on Operation Neptune, Vol. 1, pp.564–66.

25. Balkoski, *Omaha*, pp.57–61; COMTRANS, 11th PHIBFOR, Action Report, Force B (Fold3, Commander, Transports, 11th PHIBFOR, Diary June 1944, pp.4–6); TNA, ADM 199/1560; Fold3, CB 04385A, Report by the Allied Naval Commander-in-Chief Expeditionary Force on Operation Neptune, Vol. 1, p.667, Commander Force U Report.

26. Fold3, Commander Gunfire Support Craft, Force O, Action Report, Normandy.

27. (5 miles) Fold3, CB 04385A, Report by the Allied Naval Commander-in-Chief Expeditionary Force on Operation Neptune, Vol. 1, p.3251; Lund & Ludlum, *War of the Landing Craft*, p.149.

28. Balkoski, *Omaha*, pp.62–63; DHH, 81-520-8000, Box 265, HMCS *Prince Henry*; DDS, 2014/58/3, E.J. Loseby account.

29. (Leaking) TNA, DEFE 2/416; Fold3, Sinking of LCT(A) 2229 en route to Normandy; Williams, Greg H., *The US Navy at Normandy. Fleet Organization and Operations in the D-Day Invasion* (Jefferson, NC: McFarland, 2020), pp.149, 215–19.

30. DDS, 2014/58/259, Michael Irwin account.

31. DDS, 2014/58/177, R.M. Crumpton account, pp.9–10.

32. (Pills) TNA, DEFE 2/419; TNA, ADM 199/1560; Lund & Ludlum, *War of the Landing Craft*, p.163.

33. TNA, ADM 199/1560.

34. TNA, DEFE 2/427; Fold3, Commander, Gunfire Support Craft, Force O, Action Report, Normandy.

35. Palmer, *We Called Ourselves Rocketboatmen*, p.66.

36. DDS, 2014/58/21, Edward Neale account.

37. Fold3, USS *Samuel Chase*, War History; WW2Talk.com, thread on Utah Beach by Mike ('Trux'); TNA, ADM 179/506.

38. DDS, 2014/58/67, Reg Hodgson account.

39. Fold3, CB 04385A, Report by the Allied Naval Commander-in-Chief Expeditionary Force on Operation Neptune, Vol. 1, XFNP, p.3252. These sweeps could apparently be quite effective (Elliott, Peter, *Allied Minesweeping in World War II*, pp.92–93).

40. Fold3, USS *Thurston*, Action Report, Bay of Seine, Normandy, 6 June 1944; TNA, ADM 199/1560.

41. Fold3, USS *Anne Arundel*, Report, Operations, May–June 1944, Report from Assistant Despatching Officer, Primary Control Vessel PC 564; Fold3, USS *Anne Arundel*, Report, Operations Normandy, 5–7 June 1944; DND, Reginald H. Roy, 'Canadian Participation in the Operations in North-West Europe, 1944, Part 1: The Assault and Subsequent Operations of 3 Canadian Inf Div and 2 Canadian Armed Bde 6–30 June 1944', AHQ Report 54 (1952), p.43; the control organisation did not always work smoothly, particularly due to congestion.

42. DND, Reginald Roy, 'Canadian Participation', pp.31–32; DHH, 81-520-8000, Box 265, HMCS *Prince Henry*.

43. DDS, 2014/58/186, Peter Denham account; TNA, ADM 199/1560.

44. Martin Perrett account from history.uscg.mil/Our-Collections/Oral-Histories-Memoirs/Marvin-Perrett/ (accessed 10/3/2023).

45. Account by Jimmy Green at www.bbc.co.uk/history/ww2peopleswar/stories/68/a1929468.shtml (accessed 20/5/2023).

46. Balkoski, *Omaha*, pp.329–31; TNA, DEFE 2/416.

47. I am grateful to Dr Simon Trew, formerly of the Royal Military Academy, Sandhurst, for first bringing this point to my attention through his research.

48. TNA, DEFE 2/491.

49. TNA, DEFE 2/433.

50. DDS, 1990/1308, Allied Naval Commander-in-Chief Expeditionary Force, Operation Neptune Orders (10 April 1944); Balkoski, *Omaha*, p.327.

51. Fold3, CB 04385A, Report by the Allied Naval Commander-in-Chief Expeditionary Force on Operation Neptune, Vol. 1, XFNP, pp.3223–25.

52. TNA, ADM 179/506.

53. TNA, ADM 202/449; DDS, 2014/58/171, Bob Bradshaw account.

54. TNA, ADM 202/449.

55. Yung, *Gators of Neptune*, p.75; TNA, ADM 199/1560; Commander US Naval Forces, *Neptune*, p.305; TNA, DEFE 2/427.

56. DDS, 2014/58/154, D.G. Woodford account.

57. Chandler, David, & James L. Collins (eds), *The D-Day Encyclopaedia* (Oxford: Helicon, 1994), pp.382–85.

58. DDS, 2005/852, 'Erkennungstafel Landungsboote Feindmächte' (German Landing Craft Recognition Manual); McManus, *The Dead and Those Who are About to Die*, p.49; Kenyon, David, *Bletchley Park and D-Day: The Untold Story of How the Battle of Normandy was Won* (London: Yale University Press, 2019) pp.1–2.

6. Utah Beach

1. Martin Perrett account from history.uscg.mil/Our-Collections/Oral-Histories-Memoirs/Marvin-Perrett/ (accessed 10/3/2023).

2. Balkoski, Joseph, *Utah Beach: The Amphibious Landing and Airborne Operations on D-Day, June 6, 1944* (Mechanicsburg, PA: Stackpole, 2005), p.xiv.

3. TNA, ADM 199/1568.

4. Fold3, 1st Engineer Special Brigade Notes, Utah Beach, pp.48–51.

5. DDS, 1990/167, Commander Task Force 122, *Neptune Monograph* (April 1944); Fold3, 1st Engineer Special Brigade Notes, Utah Beach, pp.48–51; TNA, ADM 199/1568.

6. Balkoski, *Utah Beach*, pp.29, 297–98.

7. (Transport area) Fold3, Commander Task Force 122, Report on Naval Operations, Invasion of Normandy, p.567.

8. Fold3, CB 04385A, Report by the Allied Naval Commander-in-Chief Expeditionary Force on Operation Neptune, Vol. 1, p.666, Commander Force U Report. The LSTs were 47, 48, 230, 281 and 282.

9. Fold3, USS *Barnett*, Action Report, Operations, Normandy, 5–17 June 1944; Fold3, USS *Bayfield*, Report on Operations, Normandy, 5–17 June 1944.

10. Fold3, CB 04385A, Report by the Allied Naval Commander-in-Chief Expeditionary Force on Operation Neptune, Vol. 1, p.667, Commander Force U Report; Williams, *The US Navy at Normandy*, pp.165–66.

11. Fold3, CB 04385A, Report by the Allied Naval Commander-in-Chief Expeditionary Force on Operation Neptune, Vol. 1, p.666, Commander Force U Report; (LCMs) TNA, ADM 199/1568. In total 42 LCM(3)s in Convoy U-2A1 went to assigned transports to load (Fold3, Report, LCM Flotilla 2). One LCT(R) and two LCT(A)s had not crossed successfully and are not included in these figures. (LCP(L)s) TNA, ADM 199/1568; Fold3, COM TASK UNIT 125.7.1, Report.)

12. Fold3, CB 04385A, Report by the Allied Naval Commander-in-Chief Expeditionary Force on Operation Neptune, Vol. 1, pp.667, 676, Commander Force U Report; (half) TNA, ADM 199/1568; Williams, *The US Navy at Normandy*, pp.169–71.

13. Fold3, Report, Commander Task Group 125.5.1; Balkoski, *Utah*, pp.173–77.

14. Fold3, Report, Commander Task Unit 125.4.6, PC 1176; Fold3, COMTASK-GROUP 125.5; TNA, ADM 199/1568; Fold3, COM TASK UNIT 125.7.1, Report; Williams, *The US Navy at Normandy*, pp.221–22.

15. Fold3, Report, Commander Task Group 125.5.1.

16. Fold3, Report, Commander Task Group 125.5.1; Fold3, CB 04385A, Report by the Allied Naval Commander-in-Chief Expeditionary Force on Operation Neptune, Vol. 1, p.667, Commander Force U Report; Fold3, Report, Commander Task Unit 125.4.6, PC 1176; Fold3, COMTASK-GROUP 125.5; Balkoski, *Utah*, pp.181, 184; Williams, *The US Navy at Normandy*, pp.228–29; Gawne, *Spearheading D-Day*, p.151.

17. TNA, ADM 199/1568; Gawne, *Spearheading D-Day*, p.80; Balkoski, *Utah*, pp.181–82; TNA, DEFE 2/427.

18. Fold3, 1st Engineer Special Brigade Notes, Utah Beach, pp.55, 60, 64; Fold3, US Army Corps of Engineers, Chronology of Events, p.3586; also Fold3, 1st Engineer Special Brigade Notes, Utah Beach, p.59; Fold3, CB 04385A, Report by the Allied Naval Commander-in-Chief Expeditionary Force on Operation Neptune, Vol. 1, p.667, Commander Force U Report. Originally, there had been an intervening space between Sugar Red and Tare Green, but the revised beaches were immediately adjacent (Fold3, 1st Engineer Special Brigade Notes, Utah Beach, pp.167–68).

19. Gawne, *Spearheading D-Day*, p.179; Fold3, CB 04385A, Report by the Allied Naval Commander-in-Chief Expeditionary Force on Operation Neptune, Vol. 1, p.655; CARL, 70th Tank Battalion, '"Soixante-Dix": a history of the 70th Tank Battalion, 1940–1945', p.235; WW2Talk.com, thread on Utah Beach by Mike ('Trux'). The LCTs were: 443, 474, 475, 484, 486 and 495.

20. Williams, *The US Navy at Normandy*, p.220; Fold3, 1st Engineer Special Brigade Notes, Utah Beach, p.58.

21. Williams, *The US Navy at Normandy*, p.166; TNA, ADM 199/1568; Fold3, CB 04385A, Report by the Allied Naval Commander-in-Chief Expeditionary Force

on Operation Neptune, Vol. 1, p.654; Fold3, Report, Commander Task Group 125.5.1; (targets) TNA, ADM 199/1568.

22. (Distance from the water's edge) TNA, ADM 199/1568.

23. From allhands.navy.mil/Stories/Article/2512337/ americas-pastime-and-its-naval-history.

24. Friedman, *US Amphibious Ships*, p.190; United States Coast Guard, *The Coast Guard at War. Landings in France, XI*, p.29 (US Coast Guard Headquarters, 1946) downloaded from history-uscg-mil,; photo shows LCS(S) PA 33-27 (*Bayfield* was APA-33). The US Navy photo 80-G-252688 from history.navy.mil confirms *Bayfield* had four LCS(S)s on board (Palmer, *We Called Ourselves Rocketboatmen*, pp.64, 72). Wave numbers are generally straightforward to determine for Utah Beach and will be given in this chapter. For some other beaches they are less certain and are omitted.

25. (H–19) TNA, ADM 199/1568; Balkoski, *Utah*, pp.174, 186, 191, 198–99; Fold3, Report, Commander Task Unit 125.4.6, PC 1176.

26. A comment in *Barnett*'s log about 'the four [of *Barnett*'s] LCVPs of the first wave' implies that the other six LCVPs may have been supplied by another ship. Fold3, USS *Barnett*, Action Report, Operations, Normandy, 5–17 June 1944; Fold3, Report, Commander Task Group 125.5.1; (Adair) Balkoski, *Utah*, p.191.

27. It is not certain which ship these LCVPs came from.

28. Fold3, CB 04385A, Report by the Allied Naval Commander-in-Chief Expeditionary Force on Operation Neptune, Vol. 1, p.666, Commander Force U Report; TNA, ADM 199/1568; Fold3, US Army Corps of Engineers, Chronology of Events, p.3588.

29. Balkoski, *Utah*, pp.177, 179; WW2Talk.com, thread on Utah Beach by Mike ('Trux').

30. Williams, *The US Navy at Normandy*, pp.232–33; Palmer, *We Called Ourselves Rocketboatmen*, pp.80–85, reproduction of letter from Admiral Harold Stark to Ensign Low, p.90.

31. (Wave 2 and Wave 4 at least land 'almost simultaneously' 06.35–06.45) 'The Corps of Engineers: The War Against Germany' p.333.

32. www.history.navy.mil/research/library/online-reading-room/title-list-alphabetically/ d/d-day-the-normandy-invasion-combat-demolition-units.html (accessed 18/3/2023); TNA, ADM 199/1568. 81st Airborne AA Battalion was part of US 101st Airborne Division (WW2Talk.com, thread on Utah Beach by Mike 'Trux').

33. Fold3, Report, LCM Flotilla 2; 'The Corps of Engineers: The War Against Germany', p.333, history.army.mil/html/reference/Normandy/TS/COE/ COE15.htm (accessed 23/6/2023); Balkoski, *Utah*, p.211; CMH_Utah Beach to Cherbourg, pp.47–48; Fold3, US Army Corps of Engineers, Chronology of Events, p.3587.

34. (H+65) Fold3, Report, LCM Flotilla 2; TNA, ADM 199/1568; Fold3, US Army Corps of Engineers, Chronology of Events, p.3588.

35. The LCT(DD)s were: 510, 531, 592, 593, 594, 595, 596 and 597 (Williams, *The US Navy at Normandy*, pp.171–72; DDS, 2014/60/2: Tony Chapman, 'Utah Beach, D-Day Normandy'.

36. Balkoski, *Utah*, pp.204–05, 322; Joseph Suozzo, report on LCTs at Utah (ww2lct.org/history/stories/JSuozzo_report.htm); Ensign Donald Eidemiller of LCT(6) 594, quoted in 'PROJECT CARDONNET: Report of WW2 Wrecks of the Banc du Cardonnet, Normandy' (Southsea Sub-Aqua Club, BSAC Branch 0009, December 2017); Williams, *The US Navy at Normandy*, p.246; Balkoski, *Utah*, p.204; (the delay) Fold3, CB 04385A, Report by the Allied Naval Commander-in-Chief Expeditionary Force on Operation Neptune, Vol. 1, p.654; www.naval-history.net/WW2UScasaaDB-USNBPbyDate1944.htm (accessed, 20/5/2023); Fold3, US Naval Advanced Base 11, Omaha, Diary, July 1944.

37. (LCT 593) Fold3, Report, Commander Task Unit 125.4.6, PC 1176; Fold3, CB 04385A, Report by the Allied Naval Commander-in-Chief Expeditionary Force on Operation Neptune, Vol. 1, p.654; Napier, Stephen, *The Armoured Campaign in Normandy, June–August 1944* (Stroud: History Press, 2017), p.66; United States Fleet, *Amphibious Operations*, ch.2, p.4; (LCT 597) www.naval-history.net/WW2UScasaaDB-USNBPbyDate1944.htm (accessed 20/5/2023); Fold3, US Naval Advanced Base 11, Omaha, Diary, July 1944.

38. Joseph Suozzo, report on LCTs at Utah (ww2lct.org/history/stories/JSuozzo_report.htm); Fold3, Commander Gunfire Support Craft, Force O, Action Report, Normandy.

39. TNA, ADM 199/1568; Gawne, *Spearheading D-Day*, pp.162–63; Joseph Suozzo, report on LCTs at Utah (ww2lct.org/history/stories/JSuozzo_report.htm); (The battalion's history states that the DD tank companies landed first, but this may have been based on the plan rather than what actually happened) CARL, 70th Tank Battalion, '"*Soixante-Dix*": a history of the 70th Tank Battalion, 1940–1945', p.10; TNA, ADM 199/1568.

40. Joseph Suozzo, report on LCTs at Utah (ww2lct.org/history/stories/JSuozzo_report.htm); Robert D. Blegen, 'LCT(5) Flotilla 18 at Omaha Beach, D-Day, June 6, 1944' at ww2lct.org/history/stories/flot_18_at_omaha.htm (accessed 18/3/2023); Fold3, 1st Engineer Special Brigade Notes, Utah Beach, p.63.

41. Fold3, 1st Engineer Special Brigade Notes, Utah Beach, p.65; 'The Corps of Engineers: The War Against Germany', pp.333–34, history.army.mil/html/reference/Normandy/TS/COE/COE15.htm (accessed 23/6/2023).

42. (Both beaches) WW2Talk.com, thread on Utah Beach by Mike ('Trux'); (Tare Green) Fold3, Report, Commander Task Unit 125.4.6, PC 1176; TNA, ADM 199/1568.

43. (Information superseded) WW2Talk.com, thread on Utah Beach by Mike ('Trux'); Fold3, Report, Commander Task Unit 125.4.6, PC 1176; TNA, ADM 199/1568; Roger Lyles' account, at counties.britishlegion.org.uk/media/6539746/65-years-on.pdf. With thanks to David Lyles for assistance about his father's experiences.

44. Martin Perrett account from history.uscg.mil/Our-Collections/Oral-Histories-Memoirs/Marvin-Perrett/ (accessed 10/3/2023).

45. TNA, ADM 199/1568; Gawne, *Spearheading D-Day*, p.175.

46. Fold3, USS *Joseph T. Dickman*, War History; Fold3, Report, Commander Task Group 125.5.1; Fold3, USS *Barnett*, War Diary, June 1944.

47. history.uscg.mil/Browse-by-Topic/Conflicts/World-War-II/D-Day-June-6-1944-Normandy/D-Day-KIA/; Fold3, USS *Joseph T. Dickman*, Report on Operations, Normandy; Fold3, USS *Joseph T. Dickman*, War Diary, June 1944.

48. Fold3, USS *Joseph T. Dickman*, Report on Operations, Normandy; Fold3, USS *Joseph T. Dickman*, War History; Fold3, USS *Bayfield*, Report on Operations, Normandy, 5–17 June 1944; (P.F. Grant) cwgc.org/find-records/find-war-dead/; Fold3, USS *Barnett*, Action Report, Operations, Normandy, 5–17 June 1944. LCA 998 was lost in June or July 1944 and may well have been lost on D-Day itself.

49. TNA, ADM 199/1568; Williams, *The US Navy at Normandy*, pp.224–29; www.northernexpress.com/news/feature/lucky-larry-lampton-75-years-after-d-day/; Fold3, Commander Gunfire Support Craft, Force O, Action Report, Normandy. (USS *Corry*) Balkoski, *Utah*, p.213.

50. Fold3, US Army Corps of Engineers, Chronology of Events, p.3589; Fold3, 1st Engineer Special Brigade Notes, Utah Beach, p.62; Fold3, USS *Bayfield*, Report on Operations, Normandy, 5–17 June 1944.

51. Gawne, *Spearheading D-Day*, pp.226–65; Fold3, 1st Engineer Special Brigade Notes, Utah Beach, pp.30, 34

52. WW2Talk.com, thread on Utah Beach by Mike ('Trux'); TNA, ADM 199/1568; Fold3, 1st Engineer Special Brigade Notes, Utah Beach, pp.57, 63, 65, 70.

53. TNA, ADM 199/1568.

54. Fold3, 1st Engineer Special Brigade Notes, Utah Beach, p.63; Williams, *The US Navy at Normandy*, p.221; Fold3, COM TASK UNIT 125.7.1 Report.

55. Fold3, Report, Commander Task Unit 125.4.6, PC 1176; Fold3, CB 04385A, Report by the Allied Naval Commander-in-Chief Expeditionary Force on Operation Neptune, Vol. 1, p.654; TNA, ADM 199/1568. At 09.28, PC 484 was assigned as the new Primary Control for Uncle Red (Fold3, COMTASK-GROUP 125.5).

56. WW2Talk.com, thread on Utah Beach by Mike ('Trux'); Balkoski, *Utah*, pp.221–24.

57. Fold3, Report, Commander Task Unit 125.4.6, PC 1176.

58. TNA, ADM 199/1568; Fold3, USS *Bayfield*, Report on Operations, Normandy, 5–17 June 1944; Fold3, Report, LCM Flotilla 2.

59. (Landing diagram) TNA, ADM 199/1568; WW2Talk.com, thread on Utah Beach by Mike ('Trux'); DDS, 2014/60/2, Tony Chapman, 'Utah Beach, D-Day Normandy'.

60. (Landing diagram) TNA, ADM 199/1568; WW2Talk.com, thread on Utah Beach by Mike ('Trux').

61. Balkoski, *Utah*, p.226.

62. DDS, 2014/60/2, Tony Chapman, 'Utah Beach, D-Day Normandy'; TNA, ADM 199/1568; (531st Engineer Shore Regiment Report) Balkoski, *Utah*, p.239; Williams, *The US Navy at Normandy*, p.223; Fold3, CB 04385A, Report by the Allied Naval Commander-in-Chief Expeditionary Force on Operation Neptune, Vol. 1, p.653.

63. (Landing diagram) TNA, ADM 199/1568; Balkoski, *Utah*, p.228; CARL, N2146.40-3, Armor in Operation Neptune (Establishment of the Normandy Beachhead) (Fort Knox, KY: The Armored School), pp.26, 50; Balkoski, *Utah*, pp.224, 226–27; (landing diagram) TNA, ADM 199/1568; (LCT 486) Fold3, CB

04385A, Report by the Allied Naval Commander-in-Chief Expeditionary Force on Operation Neptune, Vol. 1, p.686, Commander Force U Report. The craft were: LCTs 458, 459, 497 and 511 on Tare Green; LCTs 443, 474, 475, 486, 489 and 495 on Uncle Red (DDS, 2014/60/2, Tony Chapman, 'Utah Beach, D-Day Normandy'; Williams, *The US Navy at Normandy*, pp.171–76. LCT 486 would be sunk by a mine on 7 June 1944 with the loss of several crew.

64. WW2Talk.com, thread on Utah Beach by Mike ('Trux').

65. DDS, 2014/58/74, John Mewha letter; (Mewha) www.combinedops.com/LCT%202304.htm (accessed 6/7/2023); (Crumpton) www.combinedops.com/LCT%202331.htm (accessed 6/7/2023).

66. DDS, 2014/60/2, Tony Chapman, 'Utah Beach, D-Day Normandy'; (LCT 2002) Williams, *The US Navy at Normandy*, p.174; (LCT 2483) Lund & Ludlum, *War of the Landing Craft*, p.172. The other craft were LCTs 2004, 2272, 2310, 2423, 2429 and 3627 (WW2Talk.com, thread on Utah Beach by Mike 'Trux').

67. WW2Talk.com, thread on Utah Beach by Mike ('Trux'); DDS, 2014/60/2, Tony Chapman, 'Utah Beach, D-Day Normandy'; Fold3, CB 04385A, Report by the Allied Naval Commander-in-Chief Expeditionary Force on Operation Neptune, Vol. 1, p.653. These craft were: LCTs 2011, 2074 and 2302 plus one other on Tare Green; LCTs 2138, 2188, 2437 and one other vessel on Uncle Red. The two unknown craft would have been drawn from a pool of spare LCTs, and were replacements for LCT 2269, which missed D-Day as it was under repair, and LCT 2498, which had capsized while under tow on 4 June 1944 (WW2Talk.com, thread on Utah Beach by Mike 'Trux').

68. Fold3, Commander Task Force 122, Report on Operations, Normandy; Fold3, Report, Commander, Task Unit 125.5.3, Report on Operations, Normandy; Fold3, CB 04385A, Report by the Allied Naval Commander-in-Chief Expeditionary Force on Operation Neptune, Vol. 1, p.681, Commander Force U Report; (the tide) DDS, 1990/167, Commander Task Force 122, *Neptune Monograph* (April 1944). Different sources are contradictory on whether there were thirty-six or forty-five LCI(L)s in this convoy.

69. (10.30) Balkoski, *Utah*, p.233; TNA, ADM 199/1568; Fold3, Report, Commander Task Unit 125.4.6, PC 1176; WW2Talk.com, thread on Utah Beach by Mike ('Trux'); Fold3, COMTASK-GROUP 125.5; Fold3, Report, Commander, Task Unit 125.5.3, Report on Operations, Normandy; United States Coast Guard, *The Coast Guard at War*, pp.143, 145; Fold3, USS *Bayfield*, Report on Operations, Normandy, 5–17 June 1944.

70. Fold3, Report, Commander Task Unit 125.4.6, PC 1176. LCTs 525, 532, 533, 536 and 534 carried the 44th Field Artillery Battalion to Tare Green. LCTs 620, 621, 662, 763 and 765 carried the 42nd Field Artillery Battalion to Uncle Red. LCT(5) 3 and a single LCVP were also standing by at this point for use by the Commanding General, 4th Infantry Division Artillery and staff (WW2Talk.com, thread on Utah Beach by Mike 'Trux'); (Banks) PDF: JSTOR_community.35123267_Wake Forest Uni Faculty WW2, downloaded from www.jstor.org/stable/community.35123267?seq=1.

71. (Noon) Balkoski, *Utah*, p.234; WW2Talk.com, thread on Utah Beach by Mike ('Trux'); Fold3, 1st Engineer Special Brigade Notes, Utah Beach, p.69. The craft

in this wave were: LCI(L)s 96, 211, 212, 213, 214, 215, 216, 219, 232, 324, 513, 514, 517, 525, 526. (WW2Talk.com, thread on Utah Beach by Mike 'Trux'.)

72. WW2Talk.com, thread on Utah Beach by Mike ('Trux'); Gawne, *Spearheading D-Day*, pp.187–93; Fold3, CB 04385A, Report by the Allied Naval Commander-in-Chief Expeditionary Force on Operation Neptune, Vol. 1, p.655.

73. Fold3, COMTASK-GROUP 125.5; Fold3, Report, Commander Task Unit 125.5.3, Report on Operations, Normandy; (Wendell Haire) navy. togetherweserved.com/usn/servlet/tws.webapp.WebApp?cmd=ShadowBoxPro file&type=Person&ID=813677 (accessed 20/4/2023); Williams, *The US Navy at Normandy*, pp.267–68.

74. (Wendell Haire) navy.togetherweserved.com/usn/servlet/tws.webapp.WebApp? cmd=ShadowBoxProfile&type=Person&ID=813677 (accessed 20/4/2023). Haire says that there were thirteen survivors from a crew of twenty-eight. LCI(L) 232 would usually have had a crew of twenty-four (Garner Area Historical Society page on Facebook, z-p3-upload.facebook.com/GarnerHistory/posts/1154562351815086, accessed 30/6/2023).

75. The craft were: LCI(L)s 516, 521, 522 and 523 at Tare Green; LCI(L)s 3, 4, 5 and 8 at Uncle Red (WW2Talk.com, thread on Utah Beach by Mike 'Trux').

76. The 1st ESB units were delivered by LCTs 519, 520, 663 and 766. Other units were carried by LCTs 515, 517, 2040, 2135, 2427 and 2485 – LCT 2424 was to have been part of this wave but had to turn back to the UK due to a water leak (DDS, 2014/58/242, Roy Green account). Craft with flexible timings were LCTs 2073, 2186, 2421 and 2484, carrying vehicles of artillery units, and LCTs 518 and 777, carrying DUKWs (WW2Talk.com, thread on Utah Beach by Mike 'Trux').

77. Grant, James A., *777: The voyage of a D-Day LCT*, 2019, from Scribd.com); Fold3, COMTASK-GROUP 125.5; Fold3, SC 1330, Report on Operations, Normandy; History of 479 Amphibian Truck Company at www.loc.gov/item/afc2001001.0290 2/?ID=pm0001001&page=1.

78. (The delay) Fold3, Report, Commander Task Unit 125.4.6, PC 1176; WW2Talk. com, thread on Utah Beach by Mike ('Trux'); DDS, 2014/60/2, Tony Chapman, 'Utah Beach, D-Day Normandy'. British LCT(5)s 2045, 2053, 2261 and 2440, plus LCT(6) 3628 were on Tare Green, accompanied by a sole US-manned vessel, LCT 585. On Uncle Red, LCT(5)s 2046, 2055, 2131 and 2303 of the Royal Navy beached alongside US Navy craft, LCT(5) 476. LCT(6)s 584 and 764, and LCT(5) 2363 carried HQ personnel with more flexibility about when they landed.

79. CARL, N2146.40-3, 'Armor in Operation Neptune (Establishment of the Normandy Beachhead)' (Fort Knox, KY: The Armored School), pp.46–47, 68; LCTs carrying 746th Tank Battalion were: 512, 646, 837, 997 and 1050 on Tare Green; 691, 797, 801, 824, 836 and 956 on Uncle Red. LCTs 793, 794 and 975 were mainly carrying army engineer vehicles. LCT 833 carried additional vehicles of the 70th Tank Battalion (WW2Talk.com, thread on Utah Beach by Mike 'Trux').

80. The sixteen craft were LCTs 645, 651, 756, 758, 795 , 798, 799, 822, 920, 954, 965, 966, 967, 974, 977 and 996. Fold3, Report, Commander,Task Unit 125.4.6, PC 1176; WW2Talk.com, thread on Utah Beach by Mike ('Trux');

DDS, 2014/60/2, Tony Chapman, 'Utah Beach, D-Day Normandy'; DDS, 2014/58/128, Ken McCaw account; DDS, 2014/58/55, Mick Jennings account.

81. These craft were LCTs 753, 755, 800, 969, 970, 2189, 2194 and 2292. Control craft PC 1176, off Tare Green, did report five craft of Wave 25 leaving the Line of Departure thirty-five minutes late, which may have been some of these LCTs (WW2Talk.com, thread on Utah Beach by Mike 'Trux'); (LCT 2226) DDS, 2014/60/2, Tony Chapman, 'Utah Beach, D-Day Normandy'; (LCT 2331) DDS, 2014/58/177, R.M. Crumpton account; Fold3, Report, Commander Task Unit 125.4.6, PC 1176.

82. Fold3, 1st Engineer Special Brigade Notes, Utah Beach, pp.32, 57; Transcript of Demolition Plan from APPENDIX THREE TO ANNEX 'GEORGE' to OPERATION ORDER No.3-44, from: www.6juin1944.com/assaut/utah/en_page.php?page=00344 (accessed 25/6/1944).

83. (Late) Fold3, Report, Commander Task Unit 125.4.6, PC 1176; WW2Talk.com, thread on Utah Beach by Mike ('Trux'); Fold3, CB 04385A, Report by the Allied Naval Commander-in-Chief Expeditionary Force on Operation Neptune, Vol. 1, p.654, Commander Force U Report; Fold3, 1st Engineer Special Brigade Notes, Utah Beach, pp.68, 136.

84. These were: US Coast Guard craft LCI(L)s 325, 326, 349 and 350; US Navy craft LCI(L)s 524, 527, 528, 529, 551 and 552; Fold3, COMTASK-GROUP 125.5; WW2Talk.com, thread on Utah Beach by Mike ('Trux'); (tide) DDS, 1990/167, Commander Task Force 122, *Neptune Monograph* (April 1944); Fold3, LCI(L) 552, Action Report, Invasion of Normandy.

85. Williams, *The US Navy at Normandy*, p.165; Balkoski, *Utah*, pp.298–99.

86. WW2Talk.com, thread on Utah Beach by Mike ('Trux').

87. Fold3, CB 04385A, Report by the Allied Naval Commander-in-Chief Expeditionary Force on Operation Neptune, Vol. 1, p.658; Fold3, Commander Task Force 122, Report on Operations, Normandy; Fold3, 1st Engineer Special Brigade Notes, Utah Beach, pp.136, 140; Fold3, Commander Task Force 122, Report on Operations, Normandy; Fold3, 1st Engineer Special Brigade Notes, Utah Beach, p.77.

88. Williams, *The US Navy at Normandy*, pp.181–82.

89. Balkoski, *Utah*, pp.217–18.

90. Benbow, *Operation Neptune*, p.286; Fold3, LST Flotilla 4, War Diary, 6 June 1944; Fold3, 1st Engineer Special Brigade Notes, Utah Beach, p.83; Fold3, CB 04385A, Report by the Allied Naval Commander-in-Chief Expeditionary Force on Operation Neptune, Vol. 1, p.655, p.674, Commander Force U Report; Fold3, COMTASK-GROUP 125.5; Fold3, 1st Engineer Special Brigade Notes, Utah Beach, p.82.

91. Fold3, COMTASK-GROUP 125.5.

92. Fold3, COMTASK-GROUP 125.5; Fold3, 1st Engineer Special Brigade Notes, Utah Beach, p.136.

93. Balkoski, *Utah*, pp.322–23, 328. Balkoski's casualty figures here do not include the crew of PC 1261, Naval Combat Demolitions Unit personnel or naval shore fire-control parties.

94. See the Roll of Honour at ddaylandingcraft.net for the most up-to-date research on deaths of landing craft crewmen.

7. Omaha Beach

1. United States Coast Guard, *The Coast Guard at War*, p.173. The author is grateful for the work done by members of WW2Talk.com forum, especially Mike ('Trux') and Michel Sabarly, in compiling and making public information extracted from landing tables at ww2talk.com/index.php?threads/omaha-beach.69555/, which has been useful for this chapter.
2. Fold3, CB 04385A, Report by the Allied Naval Commander-in-Chief Expeditionary Force on Operation Neptune, Vol. 1, p.508.
3. Badsey, Stephen, & Tim Bean, *Omaha Beach. (Battlezone Normandy)* (Stroud: Sutton, 2004), pp.27–34; Balkoski, *Omaha*, p.140; DDS, 1990/167, Commander Task Force 122, *Neptune Monograph* (April 1944); Lewis, Adrian, *Omaha Beach: A Flawed Victory* (London: University of North Carolina, 2001), pp.276–82. 352nd Infantry Division's troops were not temporarily present on an anti-invasion exercise, as sometimes stated.
4. Fold3, Commander Task Group 124.3 (Assault Group O1), Report, p.2.
5. Benbow, Tim (ed.), *Operation Neptune*, p.282; WW2Talk.com, thread on Omaha Beach by Mike ('Trux'); (six davits) TNA, ADM 210/8.
6. Balkoski, *Omaha*, p.83.
7. Williams, *The US Navy at Normandy*, pp.209, 239; WW2Talk.com, thread on Omaha Beach by Mike ('Trux'). The LCFs were 3, 5, 6, 7, 9, 11 and 12.
8. WW2Talk.com, thread on Omaha Beach by Mike ('Trux'); Williams, *The US Navy at Normandy*, p.272. A study afterwards found less evidence of self-propelled artillery having fired at Omaha (TNA, DEFE 2/491). Guns on LCTs 206, 209, 213, 276 and 293 fired on Fox Green; those on LCTs 29, 197, 207, 332 and 364 fired on Dog White.
9. (LCT(A)) Fold3, LCT(A) 2339, Report, Normandy; Badsey, *Omaha*, p.57; (LCS(S)) Fold3, COM TASK GROUP 124.4, Operations and Lessons.
10. Balkoski, *Omaha* pp.80, 84–85; United States Fleet, *Amphibious Operations*, ch.2, pp.5, 20; Fold3, COM GUNFIRE SUPPORT, Report on Operations, Normandy.
11. Robert D. Blegen, 'LCT(5) Flotilla 18 at Omaha Beach, D-Day, June 6, 1944' at ww2lct.org/history/stories/flot_18_at_omaha.htm (accessed 18/3/2023).
12. Fold3, Commander Assault Group 4/HMS *Prince Charles*; Fold3, USS *Charles Carroll*, Report on Operations, Normandy; Caddick-Adams, *Sand and Steel*, p.615.
13. Fold3, LST Flotilla 12, Action Report on Operations, Normandy; Williams, *The US Navy at Normandy*, p.246.
14. Williams, *The US Navy at Normandy*, pp.146–47; Napier, *The Armoured Campaign*, pp.48–51; WW2Talk.com, thread on Omaha Beach by Mike ('Trux').
15. Williams, *The US Navy at Normandy*, pp.147, 154, 255–56; WW2Talk.com, thread on Omaha Beach by Mike ('Trux'); Fold3, USS *Charles Carroll*,

War Diary, June 1944; (tank crew quote) Balkoski, *Omaha*, p.108. The four LCT(DD)s on Dog Green were 588, 590, 591 and 713. The 743rd Tank Battalion later reported that one LCT had been sunk, but this was incorrect (Fold3, Commander Task Group 124.4, Operations and Lessons, pp.8–9; Williams, *The US Navy at Normandy*, p.147). The four LCT(DD)s on Dog White were 535, 586, 587 and 589.

16. Operation Order BB-44 at ww2lct.org/history/actionreports/force_o.htm (accessed 18/3/2023); Fold3, USS *Thomas Jefferson*, Report on Operations, Normandy; Lieutenant Commander William Leide, LCT Flotillas 12 and 26, Action Report, 29 June 1944, at ww2lct.org/history/actionreports/table1.htm (accessed 18/3/2023).

17. Badsey, *Omaha*, p.62; Williams, *The US Navy at Normandy*, pp.149, 214, 235; Fold3, Commander Task Group 124.4, Report on Operations, June 1944, p.2; Balkoski, *Omaha*, pp.97, 105, 107.

18. Balkoski, *Omaha*, p.106. Many of the LCT(A) wave were swapped between beaches in the final days before D-Day, so the following is a best attempt to match craft to beaches.

19. WW2Talk.com, thread on Omaha Beach by Mike ('Trux'); Balkoski, *Omaha*, pp.106, 196; Fold3, SS *Empire Javelin*, Report on Operations, Normandy; Fold3, LCT(A) 2273 Report, Normandy.

20. Fold3, LCT(A) 2050, Report on Operations, Normandy; Fold3, LCT(A) 2275, Report on Operations, Normandy 02.

21. Fold3, LCT(A) 2124.

22. Fold3, LCT(A) 2075, Report on Operations, Normandy; Fold3, LCT(A) 2307, Report on Operations, Normandy; Williams, *The US Navy at Normandy*, pp.235–37.

23. Williams, *The US Navy at Normandy*, p.214; Fold3, USS *Thomas Jefferson*, Report on Operations, Normandy; Fold3, SS *Empire Javelin*, Report on Operations, Normandy; Fold3, COM TASK GROUP 124.4, Report on Operations, June 1944.

24. www.bbc.co.uk/history/ww2peopleswar/stories/68/a1929468.shtml (accessed 4/12/2022); (Green quote) Balkoski, *Omaha*, pp.111, 119–22.

25. Balkoski, *Omaha*, pp.113–17; Fold3, SS *Empire Javelin*, Report on Operations, Normandy; www.bbc.co.uk/history/ww2peopleswar/stories/68/a1929468.shtml (accessed 5/3/2023); Balkoski, *Omaha*, pp.213–17. The unit led by Tom Hanks in *Saving Private Ryan* is based on the story of Company C, 2nd Rangers.

26. Fold3, USS *Thomas Jefferson*, Report on Operations, Normandy; Balkoski, *Omaha*, pp.123–28; Gawne, *Spearheading D-Day*, pp. 126–53.

27. McManus, *The Dead and Those Who are About to Die*, pp.49–51; Balkoski, *Omaha*, pp.145, 148, 152; Report of Naval Combat Demolition Units at www.history. navy.mil/research/library/online-reading-room/title-list-alphabetically/d/d-day-the-normandy-invasion-combat-demolition-units.html.

28. WW2Talk.com, thread on Omaha Beach by Mike ('Trux'); Balkoski, *Omaha*, pp.148–49; Williams, *The US Navy at Normandy*, p.206. The six LCAs from SS *Princess Maud* loaded troops from SS *Empire Javelin*.

29. Letter published in the *Roland Record*, the local paper in Bakka's home town of Roland, Iowa, 20 July 1944, on newspaperarchive.com.

30. WW2Talk.com, thread on Omaha Beach by Mike ('Trux'); Balkoski, *Omaha*, p.242.

31. Balkoski, *Omaha*, pp.160–61; DDS, 1995/100/52, John R. Slaughter, 'Wartime Memories of J. Robert Slaughter and Selected Men of the 116th Infantry, 29th Division, 1941–1945' (original at the Eisenhower Center); Fold3, SS *Empire Javelin*, Report on Operations, Normandy.

32. WW2Talk.com, thread on Omaha Beach by Mike ('Trux'); Fold3, SS *Empire Javelin*, Report on Operations, Normandy. Sub Lieutenant Jimmy Green describes Wheeldon's death at www.bbc.co.uk/history/ww2peopleswar/stories/68/a1929468.shtml; Balkoski, *Omaha*, pp.160, pp.324–25; DDS, 1995/100/52, Robert Sales quoted in John R. Slaughter, 'Wartime Memories of J. Robert Slaughter and Selected Men of the 116th Infantry, 29th Division, 1941–1945' (original at the Eisenhower Center); Bernard Latakas quoted in *Ibid*.

33. WW2Talk.com, thread on Omaha Beach by Mike ('Trux'); Balkoski, *Omaha*, pp.168–70.

34. WW2Talk.com, thread on Omaha Beach by Mike ('Trux').

35. WW2Talk.com, thread on Omaha Beach by Mike ('Trux'); Fold3, USS *Thomas Jefferson*, Action Report, Operations, Normandy; Fold3, USS *Charles Carroll*, War Diary, June 1944; DDS, 1995/100/109, A. Cvitanovitch account (original at the US National Archives).

36. Balkoski, *Omaha*, pp.182–83, 185, 232.

37. WW2Talk.com, thread on Omaha Beach by Mike ('Trux').

38. Lieutenant Commander William Leide, LCT Flotillas 12 and 26, Action Report, 29 June 1944 at ww2lct.org/history/actionreports/table1.htm (accessed 18/3/2023). The five LCTs in question were 536, 612, 613, 622 and 703. Fold3, USS *Thomas Jefferson*, Action Report, Operations, Normandy; Balkoski, *Omaha*, p.231.

39. Balkoski, *Omaha*, pp.191–97; Fold3, COM TASK GROUP 124.4, Operations and Lessons, p.2; Fold3, USS *Thomas Jefferson*, Action Report, Operations, Normandy; Williams, *The US Navy at Normandy*, p.213.

40. Fold3, Commander Assault Group 4/HMS *Prince Charles*.

41. Balkoski, *Omaha*, pp.171–73, 192, 221; Fold3, Commander Assault Group 4/HMS *Prince Charles*, 501 Flotilla Report.

42. Balkoski, *Omaha*, pp.172–76, 224–25; Fold3, COM Assault Group O4, Report on Operations, Normandy, 17 June 1944: Fold3, Commander Assault Group 4/HMS *Prince Charles*.

43. (LCI(L)s) Balkoski, *Omaha*, p.176; (LCTs and LCVP) Operation Order BB-44 at ww2lct.org/history/actionreports/force_o.htm (accessed 18/3/2023); Williams, *The US Navy at Normandy*, p.151; Fold3, USS *Charles Carroll*, Report on Operations, Normandy.

44. Fold3, COM 11th PHIBFOR, LCI(L) 91 Report on Operations, Normandy; Balkoski, *Omaha*, pp.179–80.

45. Original at Fold3, COM 11th PHIBFOR, LCI(L) 91 Report on Operations, Normandy; Balkoski, *Omaha*, p.179; DDS, 1995/100/43, Debs Peters' account (original at the Eisenhower Center); www.history.uscg.mil/Browse-by-Topic/Conflicts/World-War-II/D-Day-June-6-1944-Normandy/D-Day-KIA/ (accessed 27/5/2023).

46. www.history.uscg.mil/Browse-by-Topic/Conflicts/World-War-II/D-Day-June-6-1944-Normandy/D-Day-KIA/ (accessed 27/5/2023); Williams, *The US Navy at Normandy*, pp.251–52; WW2Talk.com, thread on Omaha Beach by Mike ('Trux'); MMM1c Clifford Lewis quoted in Balkoski, *Omaha*, p.180. On board LCI(L) 94 was US Coast Guard Chief Photographer's Mate David Ruley, who shot motion picture footage of the vessel as it beached.

47. WW2Talk.com, thread on Omaha Beach by Mike ('Trux').

48. Balkoski, *Omaha*, pp.180–81; Williams, *The US Navy at Normandy*, pp.140, 249–50; original at Fold3, COM 11th PHIBFOR, LCI(L) 91 Report on Operations, Normandy. The army casualties may be an overestimate.

49. WW2Talk.com, thread on Omaha Beach by Mike ('Trux'); Williams, *The US Navy at Normandy*, pp.151, 252–53, 278; Operation Order BB-44 at ww2lct.org/history/actionreports/force_o.htm (accessed 18/3/2023); Robert D. Blegen, 'LCT(5) Flotilla 18 at Omaha Beach, D-Day, June 6, 1944' at ww2lct.org/history/stories/flot_18_at_omaha.htm (accessed 18/3/2023); Fold3, LCT Flotilla 18, Damage to Craft on D-Day. Based on those sources, the five LCTs are believed to have been 29, 197, 207, 332 and 364. (Battalion history) Balkoski, *Omaha*, p.305. (citation) www.history. navy.mil/research/library/online-reading-room/title-list-alphabetically/n/navy-mc-awards-manual-rev1953/pt2-unit-awards.html (accessed 21/6/2023).

50. Balkoski, *Omaha*, pp.239–40; Fold3, LST Flotilla 12, Action Report on Operations, Normandy; Fold3, LST Group 34, Report on Invasion of Normandy; WW2Talk.com, thread on Omaha Beach by Mike ('Trux'); 29thdivisionassociation.com/29th-division-111th-field-artillery/#:~:text=The%20entire%20regiment%20suffers%20in,still%20prove%20to%20be%20high, (accessed 27/5/2023).

51. Williams, *The US Navy at Normandy*, pp.132, 146–47; Balkoski, *Omaha*, pp.100–04; WW2Talk.com, thread on Omaha Beach by Mike ('Trux'); Napier, *The Armoured Campaign*, pp.39–48. The four LCT(DD)s on Fox Green were 549, 598, 601 and 602. The four LCT(DD)s on Easy Red were 537, 599, 600 and 603 (WW2Talk.com, thread on Omaha Beach by Mike 'Trux').

52. Fold3, LCT 2049, Report on Mining, Normandy; Fold3, LCT(A) 2339, Report, Normandy; Fold3, USS *Dorothea L. Dix*, report on operations, North Coast of France.

53. Fold3, LCT(A) 2037, Report Normandy; Fold3, LCT(A) 2043, Report, Normandy; Fold3, LCT(A) 2008, Report, Normandy.

54. Fold3, LCT 210, Report, Normandy.

55. Fold3, USS *Henrico*, Report on Operations, Normandy.

56. Balkoski, *Omaha*, pp.136, 138; Fold3, USS *Henrico*, Report on Operations, Normandy. Quote from Balkoski, *Omaha*, p.137.

57. DDS, 1995/100/124, Elmer Matekintis account (original at US National Archives); Fold3, USS *Henrico*, War History.

58. Fold3, COM TASK GROUP 124.4, Operations and Lessons, p.2; DDS, 1995/100/126, William J. Philbin account (original at the US National Archives); Balkoski, *Omaha*, pp.132–34, 207–09.

59. Balkoski, *Omaha*, p.132; Fold3, Commander Task Group 124.3 (Assault Group O1), Report, p.2; Fold3, USS *Thomas Jefferson*, Report on Operations, Normandy, Report of US Liaison Officer on Board SS *Empire Anvil*.

60. Anderson, *Cracking*, pp.189–91; Balkoski, *Omaha*, pp.149–52.

61. Report of Naval Combat Demolition Units at www.history.navy.mil/research/library/online-reading-room/title-list-alphabetically/d/d-day-the-normandy-invasion-combat-demolition-units.html (accessed 3/6/2023); Balkoski, *Omaha*, p.152.

62. Balkoski, *Omaha*, pp.167–68; WW2Talk.com, thread on Omaha Beach by Mike ('Trux'); Fold3, LCT(A) 2037, Report, Normandy.

63. Balkoski, *Omaha*, p.165; WW2Talk.com, thread on Omaha Beach by Mike ('Trux'); Anvil's boats landed at 07.35 (Fold3, Commander, Task Group 124.3 (Assault Group O1), Report, p.2).

64. Fold3, USS *Dorothea L. Dix*, Report on Operations, North Coast of France; WW2Talk.com, thread on Omaha Beach by Mike ('Trux').

65. Fold3, Commander Task Group 124.3 (Assault Group O1), Report, p.2; Balkoski, *Omaha*, pp.165–66; landing diagram at Balkoski, *Omaha*, p.164.

66. WW2Talk.com, thread on Omaha Beach by Mike ('Trux'); DDS, 1995/100/114, C.N. Hall account (original at the US National Archives); Balkoski, *Omaha*, pp.152–54.

67. (Janowicz) Fold3, USS *Dorothea L. Dix*, Report on Operations, North Coast of France; www.mlive.com/news/bay-city/2014/06/military_items_personal_effect.html (viewed 20/4/2023).

68. (Easy Red) Fold3, Commander Task Group 124.3 (Assault Group O1), Report, p.2; Fold3, USS *Dorothea L. Dix*, report on operations, North Coast of France; Balkoski, *Omaha*, p.166.

69. LCTs 538, 539, 540, 541 and 542 were to land on Easy Red, LCTs 543, 544 and 545 on Fox Green (WW2Talk.com, thread on Omaha Beach by Mike 'Trux'); (milling about) DDS, 1995/100/106, L.A. Conroe account (original at US National Archives); Balkoski, *Omaha*, p.156.

70. Williams, *The US Navy at Normandy*, pp.222, 237–38, 247; valor.militarytimes.com/hero/21628 (accessed 21/6/2023); www.history.navy.mil/research/library/online-reading-room/title-list-alphabetically/n/navy-mc-awards-manual-rev1953/pt2-unit-awards.html (accessed 21/6/2023). The other craft to receive a Presidential Unit Citation at Normandy was LCT 30.

71. WW2Talk.com, thread on Omaha Beach by Mike ('Trux').

72. Balkoski, *Omaha*, pp.176–77; Timothy Gay, 'A.J. Liebling on D-Day', *American Heritage*, Spring 2019, Vol. 64, Issue 2 (www.americanheritage.com/aj-liebling-d-day).

73. WW2Talk.com, thread on Omaha Beach by Mike ('Trux'); Fold3, 77826, USS *Samuel Chase* War Diary, June 1944; DDS, 1995/100/1, Robert Adams

account (original at the Eisenhower Center); (Nivens) www.history.navy.mil/
our-collections/photography/wars-and-events/world-war-ii/d-day/26-G-2342.
html (accessed 21/6/2023); (Sargent) United States Coast Guard, *The Coast Guard
at War*, pp.63, 65; Balkoski, *Omaha*, p.186; Fold3, Commander Task Group
124.3 (Assault Group O1), Report, p.2.

74. Balkoski, *Omaha*, p.189.
75. *Ibid.*, pp.198–200, 211; www.iwm.org.uk/history/robert-
     capa-and-omaha-beach; medium.com/exposure-magazine/
     alternate-history-robert-capa-on-d-day-2657f9af914.
76. Williams, *The US Navy at Normandy*, pp.134, 22; Robert L. Hembree account
     in Lefebvre, Laurent, *They Were On Omaha Beach: 194 Eyewitnesses* (Chatenay-
     Malabry: Laurent Lefebvre, 2003) p.180; WW2Talk.com, thread on Omaha
     Beach by Mike ('Trux'). The LCTs were 206, 209, 213, 276 and 293 (ww2lct.
     org). (DUKWs) Balkoski, *Omaha*, pp.239–40; Fold3, Operation Neptune,
     Engineer Combat Battalions Reports, p.216.
77. Balkoski, *Omaha*, p.247; Fold3, USS *Anne Arundel*, Report, Operations
     Normandy, 5–7 June 1944; WW2Talk.com, thread on Omaha Beach by
     Mike ('Trux').
78. The LCTs and their planned beaching locations were: on Dog Green LCTs 27,
     214; on Dog White LCTs 147, 153; on Dog Red LCTs 80, 149, 615, 616, 776;
     on Easy Green LCTs 30, 244, 294 (WW2Talk.com, thread on Omaha Beach by
     Mike 'Trux'); TNA, ADM 199/1564. The 10 July Report of Loss of Landing
     Craft US LCT(5) 197, LCT(5) 294, by Commander, LCT Flotilla 18, in Robert
     D. Blegen, 'LCT(5) Flotilla 18 at Omaha Beach, D-Day, June 6, 1944' at ww2lct.
     org/history/stories/flot_18_at_omaha.htm (accessed 18/3/2023); Fold3, LCT
     149, Report on Operations, Normandy.
79. Robert D. Blegen, 'LCT(5) Flotilla 18 at Omaha Beach, D-Day, June 6, 1944'
     at ww2lct.org/history/stories/flot_18_at_omaha.htm (accessed 18/3/2023);
     Williams, *The US Navy at Normandy*, p.263.
80. Robert D. Blegen, 'LCT(5) Flotilla 18 at Omaha Beach, D-Day, June 6, 1944'
     at ww2lct.org/history/stories/flot_18_at_omaha.htm (accessed 18/3/2023);
     Williams, *The US Navy at Normandy*, p.263; Fold3, LCT Flotilla 18, Damage to
     Craft on D-Day; (Presidential Unit Citation) www.history.navy.mil/research/
     library/online-reading-room/title-list-alphabetically/n/navy-mc-awards-manual-
     rev1953/pt2-unit-awards.html (accessed 21/6/2023).
81. Williams, *The US Navy at Normandy*, p.259.
82. Balkoski, *Omaha*, p.243; ww2lct.org/history/stories/flot_18_at_omaha.htm. The
     craft were: LCTs 25, 199, 200, 201, 271, 546 and 547 on Easy Red; LCTs 18,
     20, 195 and 305 on Fox Green (ww2lct.org; TNA, ADM 199/1564). Report of
     Damage to Landing Craft due to Enemy Action by Commander LCT Flotilla 18,
     11 July 1944, in Robert D. Blegen, 'LCT(5) Flotilla 18 at Omaha Beach, D-Day,
     June 6, 1944' at ww2lct.org/history/stories/flot_18_at_omaha.htm (accessed
     18/3/2023); Fold3, LCT 25, Report, Normandy; Fold3, LCT Flotilla 18,
     Damage to Craft on D-Day.
83. United States Coast Guard, *The Coast Guard at War*, pp.171–75, 297; Balkoski,
     Omaha, p.177; WW2Talk.com, thread on Omaha Beach by Mike ('Trux').

84. United States Coast Guard, *The Coast Guard at War*, pp.151–59; interview with Leroy C. Bowen Jr, 7/18/2004, tile.loc.gov/storage-services/service/vhp/0171/017142/sr0001.xml (accessed 30/6/2023).

85. WW2Talk.com, thread on Omaha Beach by Mike ('Trux'); Fold3, USS *Dorothea L. Dix*, Report on Operations, North Coast of France.

86. H+130: Williams, *The US Navy at Normandy*, p.137; WW2Talk.com, thread on Omaha Beach by Mike ('Trux'). These craft were: LCTs 550, 623, 624, 625, 814, 815 and 2487 (ADM 199_1564-082). (H+135) WW2Talk.com, thread on Omaha Beach by Mike ('Trux'); (boat crew reports) Fold3, USS *Dorothea L. Dix*, Report on Operations, North Coast of France.

87. Fold3, USS *Anne Arundel*, Report on Operations Normandy, 5 –7 June 1944, Report of Assistant Boat Group Commander Wave 20.

88. WW2Talk.com, thread on Omaha Beach by Mike ('Trux'); Williams, *The US Navy at Normandy*, pp.151–52; Report, LCTs O2: Lieutenant Commander William Leide, LCT Flotillas 12 and 26, Action Report 29 June 1944 at ww2lct.org/history/actionreports/table1.htm (accessed 18/3/2023); Fold3_LCT(A) 2487, Report, Normandy; Fold3, LCT(A) 2297, Report, Normandy. The thirteen craft scheduled to land on Omaha West were probably: on Dog Green LCT(5) 2297, plus LCT(6)s 590, 591, 713, 714, 767; on Dog White LCT(6)s 535, 570, 587; on Dog Red LCT(6)s 586, 589, 617; on Easy Green LCT(6) 588. Some LCTs were swapped between beaches just before D-Day, so the identities are not absolutely certain.

89. TNA, ADM 199/1564. The four LCTs were: on Dog White, LCT(6)s 571, 572; on Dog Red, LCT(5) 413, LCT(6) 573 (TNA, ADM 199/1564). (320th) WW2Talk.com, thread on Omaha Beach by Mike ('Trux'); Gawne, *Spearheading D-Day*, pp.187–93.

90. Balkoski, *Omaha*, pp.248–51.

91. Balkoski, *Omaha*, pp.250–52 (including interviews), 187–88; WW2Talk.com, thread on Omaha Beach by Mike ('Trux'); Williams, *The US Navy at Normandy*, p.240; Fold3, USS *Anne Arundel*, Report Operations Normandy, 5–7 June 1944: Report of Boat Group Commander Wave 20, Report of Assistant Boat Group Commander Wave 20, Report of Boat Division Leader, Boat Division C; Fold3, USS *Anne Arundel*, Action Report, Operations Normandy, June 1944.

92. Balkoski, *Omaha*, pp.250–56; (Chuck Phillips account) Lefebvre, *They Were on Omaha Beach*, pp.204–06, 237–38; (Karl Bischoff account) *ibid.*, p.206; (James Argo account) *ibid.*, pp.206–07.

93. Fold3, USS *Anne Arundel*, Action Report, Operations Normandy, June 1944; United States Coast Guard, *The Coast Guard at War*, pp.67, 69.

94. Balkoski, *Omaha*, pp.252, 263–64; Fold3_USS Anne Arundel rept ops Ndy 1944-06-05to07_81741_03 -_04; usslci.org/the-story-of-the-lcil-93-and-lcil-487-at-normandy/; Williams, *The US Navy at Normandy*, pp.274–75. The nine LCI(L)s carrying the 18th RCT were: Regimental HQ, LCI(L) 490; 1st Battalion, LCI(L)s 488, 494, 496, 498; 3rd Battalion, LCI(L)s 93, 487, 495 and 497 (TNA, ADM 199/1564).

95. (Roberts account) www.mycg.uscg.mil/News/Article/2409301/the-long-blue-line-into-the-jaws-of-deathsm2-john-roberts-and-lci-93-at-omaha-b/ (accessed 17/6/2023).

96. Fold3, USS *Thurston*, Action Report, Bay of Seine, Normandy, 6 June 1944; Norman Lockert account, Lefebvre, *They Were on Omaha Beach*, pp.117, 326–27.

97. TNA, ADM 199/1564; WW2Talk.com, thread on Omaha Beach by Mike ('Trux'); Williams, *The US Navy at Normandy*, p.156; Fold3, Commander Task Group 124.3 (Assault Group O1), Report, pp.2–3.

98. Fold3, LCT 22, Report, Normandy; Action Report, 13 July 1944, in Robert D. Blegen, 'LCT(5) Flotilla 18 at Omaha Beach, D-Day, June 6, 1944' at ww2lct. org/history/stories/flot_18_at_omaha.htm (accessed 18/3/2023); Williams, *The US Navy at Normandy*, pp.260–62. The Easy Red craft included LCTs 7, 22, 202, 415, 431, 434, 618, 619, 706, 707, 708. The Fox Green craft were LCTs 537, 549, 598, 599, 600, 601, 602, 603, 769, 856 (TNA, ADM 199/1564).

99. TNA, ADM 199/1564; Balkoski, *Omaha*, pp.250–58; Fold3, COM TASK GROUP 124.4, Report on Operations, June 1944; (John Cooper account) Balkoski, *Omaha*, pp.259–60; (Robert Leach account) Lefebvre, *They Were on Omaha Beach*, pp.213–14. The craft landing 115th RCT in the H+240 and H+270 waves were: 1st Battalion, LCI(L)s 411, 412, 413 and 554; 2nd Battalion, LCI(L)s 408, 409, 410 and 553; 3rd Battalion, LCI(L)s 540, 541, 555 and 557.

100. Fold3, LST Flotilla 12, Action Report on Operations, Normandy; Fold3, USS *Anne Arundel*, Action Report, Operations Normandy, June 1944, PC 564. The Deputy Commander, Assault Force O-2 was on LCH 86. There are some errors in the report, which refers to 115th RCT as 118th RCT and says the unit landed on Fox Beaches, in the early afternoon.

101. WW2Talk.com, thread on Omaha Beach by Mike ('Trux'); Fold3, USS *Thomas Jefferson*, Report on Operations, Normandy; United States Coast Guard, *The Coast Guard at War*, p.299. H+240 on Omaha West: landing vehicles from LSTs 310, 315, 316 and 317. At least one Rhino carrying vehicles from LST 6 (TNA, ADM 199/1564).

102. WW2Talk.com, thread on Omaha Beach by Mike ('Trux'); Fold3, Operation Neptune, Engineer Combat Battalions, Reports, pp.214, 216; (Charles Lilly account) Caddick-Adams, *Sand and Steel*, p.365; (LCT 637) www.history.navy. mil/research/library/online-reading-room/title-list-alphabetically/n/navy-mc-awards-manual-rev1953/pt2-unit-awards.html (accessed 21/6/2023); (Joseph Graham account) Lefebvre, *They Were on Omaha Beach*, pp.118, 199–200, 249–50.

103. The H+310 LCTs were 460, 639, 640, 641, 652, 653 and 657 (US Library of Congress, Veterans History Project, AFC/2001/001/31844, John William Boehne III Collection); Fold3, Operation Neptune, Engineer Combat Battalions Reports, p.217; Fold3, Commander, Task Group 124.3 (Assault Group O1), Report June–July 1944, p.2; Lieutenant Commander William Leide, LCT Flotillas 12 and 26, Action Report, 29 June 1944 at ww2lct.org/history/ actionreports/table1.htm (accessed 18/3/2023). The three H+330 LCTs were 665, 666, 813 (TNA, ADM 199/1564).

104. Lieutenant Commander William Leide, LCT Flotillas 12 and 26, Action Report, 29 June 1944, at ww2lct.org/history/actionreports/table1.htm (accessed

18/3/2023); Fold3, Commander 11th PHIBFOR, Report by Commander Force O on Operations, June 1944, pp.8–11; Fold3, LST Flotilla 12, Action Report on Operations, Normandy; United States Fleet, *Amphibious Operations*, ch.2, pp.21–2.

105. Fold3, Operation Neptune, Engineer Combat Battalions Reports, pp.217, 218; TNA, ADM 199/1565; WW2Talk.com, thread on Omaha Beach by Mike ('Trux').

106. Fold3, USS *Thurston*, Action Report, Bay of Seine, Normandy, 6 June 1944; (earlier) Fold3, USS *Dorothea L. Dix*, War Diary, June 1944; Fold3, USS *Dorothea L. Dix*, report on operations, North Coast of France.

107. Fold3, USS *Anne Arundel*, Action Report, Operations Normandy, June 1944; Fold3, USS *Anne Arundel*, Report, Operations Normandy, 5–7 June 1944, Report of Wave 29 Commander.

108. United States Coast Guard, *The Coast Guard at War*, p.300; Balkoski, *Omaha*, pp.315–16.

109. Fold3, LCI(L) Flotilla 12, War Diary, June 1944; Fold3, LST Flotilla 12, Action Report on Operations, Normandy; Williams, *The US Navy at Normandy*, pp.271–73; France, John, 'The Final LCI Assault of Omaha Beach', *Elsie Item*, November 2016, pp.10–28. The craft were LCI(L)s 401, 403, 415, 416, 417, 418, 420, 537, 538, 539, 542, 556 plus LCH 414.

110. Fold3, LCI(L) Flotilla 12, War Diary, June 1944; France, John, 'The Final LCI Assault of Omaha Beach', *Elsie Item*, November 2016, pp.10–28; Fold3, Commander, Transports, 11th PHIBFOR, Diary, June 1944, Force B Report, pp.4, 11.

111. Fold3, Commander, Transports, 11th PHIBFOR, Diary, June 1944, Force B Report, p.7; Fold3, LST Flotilla 12, Action Report on Operations, Normandy; WW2Talk.com, thread on Omaha Beach by Mike ('Trux').

112. Fold3, Operation Neptune, Engineer Combat Battalions Reports, pp.214, 218; Fold3, LST Flotilla 12, Action Report on Operations, Normandy; DDS, 1995/100/104, Stanley Bach account (original at the US National Archives).

113. United States Coast Guard, *The Coast Guard at War*, pp.299–300.

114. Benbow, *Operation Neptune*, p.283; Fold3, Commander 11th PHIBFOR, Report by Commander Force O on Operations, June 1944, pp.120–21; United States Coast Guard, *The Coast Guard at War*, p.301; WW2Talk.com, thread on Omaha Beach by Mike ('Trux').

115. Winser, *The D-Day Ships*, pp.34–42; Fold3, Commander 11th PHIBFOR, Report by Commander Force O on Operations, June 1944, pp.11–15.

116. Fold3, LST Flotilla 4, War Diary, 6 June 1944; Fold3, LST Flotilla 12, Action Report on Operations, Normandy.

8. Gold Beach

1. DDS, 2014/58/65, Bill Page account. The author is grateful for the work done by members of WW2Talk.com forum, especially Mike ('Trux') and Michel Sabarly, in compiling and making public information extracted from landing

tables at ww2talk.com/index.php?threads/gold-beach.56252/, which has been useful for this chapter.

2. TNA, DEFE 2/416.

3. TNA, DEFE 2/416.

4. TNA, DEFE 2/416; TNA, DEFE 2/490; Trew, Simon, *Gold Beach (Battlezone Normandy)* (Stroud: Sutton, 2004), pp.15–21.

5. TNA, DEFE 2/416.

6. WW2Talk.com, thread on Gold Beach by Mike ('Trux'); TNA, ADM 202/449; TNA, DEFE 2/417.

7. TNA, DEFE 2/416.

8. TNA, DEFE 2/416. Those supporting the landings at Jig were LCG(L)s 13, 17 and 18, plus LCFs 19, 20 and 35, while those at King were LCG(L)s 1, 2 and 3, and LCFs 25, 26, 36 and 38. LCF 38 arrived fifty minutes late due to engine trouble (TNA, DEFE 2/416).

9. TNA, DEFE 2/416.

10. Michel Sabarly at ww2talk.com/index.php?threads/147th-field-regiment-ra-lct.89682/ (accessed 7/1/2023); TNA, DEFE 2/416.

11. TNA, DEFE 2/416; Townend, Will, & Frank Baldwin, *Gunners in Normandy: The History of the Royal Artillery in North-West Europe, January 1942 to August 1944* (Cheltenham: History Press, 2020), p.150.

12. Lund & Ludlum, *War of the Landing Craft*, pp.164–66. For some reason, Gregson says the troop began firing at H–20 and 5,000 yards, which is contradicted by the report of ML 136, TNA, DEFE 2/416.

13. Trew, *Gold Beach*, p.117; TNA, DEFE 2/416; (air bombardment) TNA, DEFE 2/416; TNA, DEFE 2.490.

14. TNA, DEFE 2/416. Unlike on Juno and Sword, the group of LCT(A)s did not include an LCT(CB).

15. Around 07.15 (TNA, DEFE 2/416). Firing on Jig were LCT(R)s 434, 435, 436 and 438. Firing on King were LCT(R)s 362, 440, 459 and 460 (TNA, DEFE 2/416; TNA, DEFE 2/490).

16. TNA, DEFE 2/416.

17. *Ibid.*; DDS, 2014/58/259, Michael Irwin account. The eight craft that were able to fire their bombs on time were LCA(HR)s 968, 969, 970, 1101, 1103, 1104, 1110 and 1287 (TNA, DEFE 2/416; DDS, 2014/58/259, Michael Irwin account).

18. TNA, DEFE 2/416; Trew, *Gold Beach*, pp.51–52, 54.

19. TNA, DEFE 2/416; TNA, DEFE 2/417.

20. *Ibid.*

21. *Ibid.*

22. *Ibid.*

23. TNA, ADM 202/449. The breaching teams were on board LCTs 647, 749, 805, 807, 808 and 886. There were twelve craft in 706 Assault Flotilla but it seems that one did not cross to Normandy for D-Day.

24. DDS, 2014/58/189, Rex Milbourne; Anderson, *Cracking*, p.52.

25. TNA, DEFE 2/416; TNA, DEFE 2/490; Anderson, *Cracking*, pp.52, 151; WW2Talk.com, thread on Gold Beach by Mike ('Trux').

26. TNA, 2/416; TNA, DEFE 2/490; TNA, DEFE 2/426; Anderson, *Cracking*, pp.166, 176–78; IWM photo A23948, viewed at www.iwm.org.uk/collections/item/object/205155958 (LCT 886 can be seen beached just east of Asnelles facing out to sea and with the wording 'All looters will be shot. You have been warned' painted on its port side).

27. TNA, DEFE 2/416; TNA, DEFE 2/490; Trew, *Gold Beach*, p.137; DDS, 2014/58/62, Jack Booker.

28. Anderson, *Cracking*, p.179; TNA, DEFE 2/490.

29. Anderson, *Cracking*, p.181; TNA, DEFE 2/490; TNA, DEFE 2/417.

30. Trew, *Gold Beach*, p.55, p.137; Anderson, *Cracking*, pp.180–81; TNA, DEFE 2/490; TNA, DEFE 2/416; 295 Field Company RE War Diary in Winter, Paul, *D-Day Documents* (London: Bloomsbury, 2014), p.432. Sources disagree on the 1st Hants' landing time (07.30: TNA, DEFE 2/490; 07.35: DSOAG Jig Green, TNA, DEFE 2/416).

31. (Landing times, casualties) TNA, DEFE 2/490; Trew, *Gold Beach*, pp.55, 137; TNA, DEFE 2/416.

32. TNA, DEFE 2/416.

33. WW2Talk.com, thread on Gold Beach by Mike ('Trux'); Trew, *Gold Beach*, p.120.

34. Warren quoted in Anderson, *Cracking*, p.180.

35. DDS, 2014/58/279, Horace Stone account.

36. TNA, DEFE 2/416; Anderson, *Cracking*, p.174; Trew, *Gold Beach*, pp.138–39, 142–46; TNA, DEFE 2/417; TNA, DEFE 2/416.

37. TNA, DEFE 2/416; TNA, ADM 179/516; TNA, DEFE 2/416.

38. TNA, DEFE 2/416; Anderson, *Cracking*, pp.180–81.

39. WW2Talk.com, thread on Gold Beach by Mike ('Trux'); 1st Dorsets War Diary in Winter, *D-Day Documents*, p.419; DDS, 2014/58/124, Ben Sullivan.

40. DDS, 2014/58/124, Ben Sullivan; WW2Talk.com, thread on Gold Beach by Mike ('Trux'); DDS, 2014/58/160d confirms which flotilla carried which company; (landing site) Trew, *Gold Beach*, p.140; TNA, DEFE 2/490.

41. 1st Dorsets' CO landed at 07.50 with D Coy (Winter, *D-Day Documents*, p.410). The 1st Hants' CO landed just behind the assault companies (Jary, Christopher, et al., *D-Day Spearhead Brigade: The Hampshires, Dorsets and Devons on 6th June 1944* (Bristol: Semper Fidelis, 2019), p.62.

42. WW2Talk.com, thread on Gold Beach by Mike ('Trux'); War Diary 141st Regiment RAC, TNA, WO 171/877.

43. TNA, DEFE 2/417; WW2Talk.com, thread on Gold Beach by Mike ('Trux'); TNA, DEFE 2/416.

44. TNA, DEFE 2/490.

45. Holland, James, *Brothers in Arms: One Legendary Tank Regiment's Bloody War from D-Day to VE-Day* (London: Penguin Random House, 2021), p.39.

46. DDS, 2014/58/25, Stanley Smith.

47. DDS, 2014/58/25, Stanley Smith; Holland, *Brothers in Arms*, p.30.

48. Trew, *Gold Beach*, p.135.

49. TNA, DEFE 2/490; Trew, *Gold Beach*, p.140; WW2Talk.com, thread on Gold Beach by Mike ('Trux').

50. TNA, DEFE 2/416; TNA, DEFE 2/490; Anderson, *Cracking*, p.183; Trew, *Gold Beach*, p.56; Report of 295 Field Company RE, quoted in TNA, DEFE 2/490.

51. WW2Talk.com, thread on Gold Beach by Mike ('Trux').

52. TNA, DEFE 2/416; War Diary of 90th Field Regiment RA, in Winter, *D-Day Documents*, p.426; Lund & Ludlum, *War of the Landing Craft*, p.166.

53. WW2Talk.com, thread on Gold Beach by Mike ('Trux'); Trew, *Gold Beach*, p.56; 231 Infantry Brigade HQ War Diary in Winter, *D-Day Documents*, p.411.

54. Howard Marshall biog and transcript of War Report programme on D-Day from www.bbc.com/historyofthebbc/100-voices/ww2/war-report.

55. TNA, DEFE 2/416.

56. TNA, DEFE 2/416; DDS, 2014/58/252, Ron Turner account. The craft from 23 LCT Flotilla were LCTs 546, 555, 571, 576, 577, 604, 635, 1041, 1162, 1164 (TNA, DEFE 2/416).

57. DDS, 2014/58/65, Bill Page account.

58. WW2Talk.com, thread on Gold Beach by Mike ('Trux'); Sherwood Rangers Yeomanry War Diary, quoted in TNA, DEFE 2/490; SRY War Diary in Winter, *D-Day Documents*, p.448; TNA, DEFE 2/416.

59. Trew, *Gold Beach*, p.154; Anderson, *Cracking*, p.182; TNA, DEFE 2/490.

60. DDS, 2014/58/84, Ray G. Fletcher.

61. DDS, 2014/58/65, Bill Page account; Trew, *Gold Beach*, pp.56, 153–54.

62. WW2Talk.com, thread on Gold Beach by Mike ('Trux'); Townend & Baldwin, *Gunners in Normandy*, p.166; TNA, DEFE 2/416; 90th Field Regiment War Diary, WO 171/982. Report by senior officer Group 7 on SP Artillery also says the second division landed at H+125 (TNA, DEFE 2/416). The craft were probably from 33 LCT Flotilla, including some attached from 49 LCT Flotilla.

63. TNA, DEFE 2/416; Trew, *Gold Beach*, p.60.

64. TNA, DEFE 2/417; Anderson, *Cracking*, p.152; TNA, DEFE 2/416.

65. TNA, DEFE 2/416; Anderson, *Cracking*, pp.152–59.

66. TNA, DEFE 2/416; 4th/7th Dragoon Guards War Diary in Winter, *D-Day Documents*, p.450; TNA, DEFE 2/490; Ruffell, quoted in Lund & Ludlum, *War of the Landing Craft*, p.162.

67. TNA, DEFE 2/416; cwgc.org/find-records/find-war-dead/. The landing times of tanks on King Beach mentioned in the War Diary of 1 RM Armoured Support Regiment seem to indicate that one LCT(A) arrived around 08.50, one at 09.30 and a third at 09.50. The first craft to arrive was probably LCT(A) 2236, followed by LCT(A)s 2225 and 2291 (war diary in Winter, *D-Day Documents*, p.485). TNA, DEFE 2/416, Report FO 109 LCT Flotilla, says LCT(A) 2236 beached at 08.10. This contradicts the Captain Group G2, who reported that only one LCT(A) arrived at King Beach on D-Day. (Later on D-Day) Trew, *Gold Beach*, p.65.

68. TNA, DEFE 2/416; Trew, *Gold Beach*, p.118; TNA, WO 171/1302; TNA, DEFE 2/490. (The 6th Green Howards' landing time) The DSOAG King Red stated that they landed 'shortly' after the DD tanks and both LCA flotillas gave their time of beaching as five minutes after the AVREs. Both accounts would put that time at about 07.30. The 6th Green Howards, however, recorded their time of landing as 07.37.

69. TNA, DEFE 2/416; TNA, ADM 202/449; DDS, 2005/1376, Commander Force G, *Force G Orders for Operation 'Neptune'* (short title: ONEAST/G).
70. TNA, DEFE 2/416; Jackson quoted in Trew, *Gold Beach*, pp.119–20. Jackson was seriously wounded in the leg by a mortar round which also killed his radio operator and his military policemen (who would have aided him in his role as the 6th Green Howards' landing officer). He lay on the beach for a considerable time and was only saved from drowning in the incoming tide when he was rescued by one of his comrades.
71. TNA, DEFE 2/416; Trew, *Gold Beach*, p.120.
72. WW2Talk.com, thread on Gold Beach by Mike ('Trux'); patricktaylor.com/war-diary-1.
73. Trew, *Gold Beach*, pp.67, 120–22, 126; Anderson, *Cracking*, p.16.
74. TNA, WO 171/1398, War Diary 5th East Yorks; TNA, ADM 202/449.
75. TNA, DEFE 2/416.
76. TNA, WO 171/1398, War Diary 5th East Yorks. TNA, DEFE 2/490 confuses B and C Coys.
77. TNA, DEFE 2/416; TNA, DEFE 2/490; Trew, *Gold Beach*, pp.63–64; Anderson, *Cracking*, pp.160–61, 184.
78. TNA, DEFE 2/416; Major Consitt account at www.normandywarguide.com/archives/the-landing-of-5-east-yorks-1944-june (accessed 20/1/2023).
79. Major Consitt account at www.normandywarguide.com/archives/the-landing-of-5-east-yorks-1944-june (accessed 20/1/2023); WW2Talk.com, thread on Gold Beach by Mike ('Trux').
80. WW2Talk.com, thread on Gold Beach by Mike ('Trux'); DDS, 2005/1376, Group G2 Assault Landing Table.
81. DDS, 2005/1376, Group G2 Assault Landing Table; account by Kevin Tandy (son of George Tandy), www.bbc.co.uk/history/ww2peopleswar/stories/72/a2844272.shtml (accessed 30/1/2023). Don Howard, who crewed another craft carrying Green Howards, says Tandy was in 'the next boat but one' to his, thus confirming Tandy's craft carried the 7th Green Howards (DDS, 2014/58/277, Don Howard account).
82. TNA, DEFE 2/416; TNA, WO 171/1303, 7th Green Howards War Diary.
83. TNA, WO 171/1303, 7th Green Howards War Diary; WW2Talk, Gold thread; TNA, DEFE 2/416.
84. WW2Talk, Gold thread; TNA, DEFE 2/416; DDS, 2005/1376, Commander Force G, Force G Orders for Operation 'Neptune' (ONEAST/G).
85. TNA, DEFE 2/416; WW2Talk, Gold thread (see for comprehensive list of vehicles); Anderson, *Cracking*, p.164. The ten LCTs may have been from 51 LCT Flotilla.
86. The LCT(4)s due at H+90 were apparently to land at King Red from 1st Division, 49 LCT Flotilla, and at King Green from 24 LCT Flotilla (see WW2Talk.com, thread on Gold Beach by Mike ('Trux')); DDS, 2005/1376, Commander Force G, Force G Orders for Operation 'Neptune' (ONEAST/G); DDS, 2014/58/301, Lynn Shirley account. A photograph (National Army Museum, 1975-03-63-18-33), taken on King Beach later in the day showing an LCT of 24 LCT Flotilla bearing an LTIN from the H+120 wave, suggests that the craft carrying third-priority vehicles at H+120 were from that flotilla, but

this is not certain. Other sources are 86th Field Regiment War Diary in Winter, *D-Day Documents*, p.480 and TNA, DEFE 2/416.

87. DDS, 2014/58/108, Frank Howard account.

88. Lee, David, *Beachhead Assault: The Story of the Royal Naval Commandos in World War II* (London: Greenhill, 2004), p.147.

89. 86th Field Regiment War Diary in Winter, *D-Day Documents*, p.480; Townend & Baldwin, *Gunners*, p.166; DDS, 2014/58/301, Lynn Shirley account. That 86th Field Regiment RA's guns were carried by 24 LCT Flotilla is partly deduced from Shirley's account, but is not absolutely certain.

90. Anderson, *Cracking*, p.161 (quotes TNA, DEFE 2/490); Trew, *Gold Beach*, p.126.

91. TNA, DEFE 2/416.

92. TNA, DEFE 2/416.

93. WW2Talk.com, thread on Gold Beach by Mike ('Trux'); TNA, DEFE 2/416.

94. TNA, DEFE 2/416; (LSTs 25 and 264) Fold3, LST Group 33, June 1944.

95. WW2Talk.com, thread on Gold Beach by Mike ('Trux'); Fold3, LST Flotilla 4, War Diary 6 June 1944; TNA, WO 171/2515, 705 Company RASC War Diary.

96. TNA, DEFE 2/416. The five LCTs carrying 151st Infantry Brigade's vehicles were 564, 922, 924, 926 and 1121.

97. TNA, DEFE 2/416. The five LCTs carrying 56th Infantry Brigade's vehicles were 565, 711, 923, 1120 and 1122.

98. Royal Canadian Navy Historical Section, *The RCN's Part in the Invasion of France* (London: RCN, 1945) p.107. The RCN craft of 264 LCI(L) Flotilla were 255 (HQ craft, did not beach), 288, 295, 302, 305, 310 and 311. The three US Navy craft were LCI(L)s 400, 421 and 511, from LCI(L) Flotilla 12, Group 35, Division 62.

99. TNA, DEFE 2/416; TNA, ADM 202/449.

100. (Landing times) TNA, DEFE 2/416; Royal Canadian Navy, *The RCN's Part*, p.107; War Diaries of the 2nd SWB, the 2nd Glosters and the 2nd Essex in Winter, *D-Day Documents*, pp.476–78. TNA, DEFE 2/490, based on 2nd Essex War Diary says that the battalion landed on Jig Green.

101. Royal Canadian Navy, *The RCN's Part*, p.107.

102. Holborn, Andrew, 'The Role of 56th (Independent) Infantry Brigade During the Normandy Campaign June–September 1944', PhD Thesis, University of Plymouth (2009), p.126, at pearl.plymouth.ac.uk/handle/10026.1/1996, (accessed 17/10/2022); TNA, DEFE 2/416; Royal Canadian Navy, *The RCN's Part*, p.108.

103. TNA, DEFE 2/416; Royal Canadian Navy, *The RCN's Part*, p.107.

104. Trew, *Gold Beach*, p.66; TNA, DEFE 2/490; WW2Talk.com, thread on Gold Beach by Mike ('Trux').

105. TNA, DEFE 2/490; TNA, DEFE 2/416.

106. (Beaching times) TNA, WO 171/2433, 305 Company RASC War Diary; WW2Talk.com, thread on Gold Beach by Mike ('Trux').

107. WW2Talk.com, thread on Gold Beach by Mike ('Trux'); TNA, DEFE 2/490; Fold3, LST 25, War History; DDS, 2005/1376, Commander Force G, Force G Orders for Operation 'Neptune' (ONEAST/G); Gold Beach Landing Tables, 231st Bde_from 6juin1944.com.

108. TNA, DEFE 2/416; Fold3, LST Group 33; TNA, WO 171/2433, 305 Company RASC War Diary; TNA, DEFE 2/416; DDS, 2005/1376, Commander Force G, Force G Orders for Operation 'Neptune' (ONEAST/G); landing tables at 6juin1944.com. The US LSTs were as follows (the first two were manned by the US Coast Guard, the rest by the US Navy): LSTs 17, 21, 72, 73, 308, 312, 344, 345, 370 and 520 from LST Flotilla 11, Group 33, Division 65, and LST Flotilla 17, Group 51, Division 101 (Fold3, LST Group 33).

109. Fold3, US LST 2, Report on Operations, Normandy; 24th Lancers War Diary in Winter, *D-Day Documents*, p.451. The LSTs were 1, 2, 44, 52, 229, 280, 293, 359, 493 and 503 (ww2talk.com/index.php?threads/gold-area-ltin-hull-number-matches-for-us-lst.54035/).

110. DDS, 2005/1376, Commander Force G, Force G Orders for Operation 'Neptune' (ONEAST/G), Appendix B, Diagram of Arrivals on D-Day; TNA, WO 171/2515, 705 Company RASC War Diary; Benbow, *Operation Neptune*, p.281; WW2Talk.com, thread on Gold Beach by Mike ('Trux'); Townend & Baldwin, *Gunners*, p.111.

111. Benbow, *Operation Neptune*, p.280; Jarman, *Those Wallowing Beauties*, pp.236–37.

112. Benbow, *Operation Neptune*, p.280; Jarman, *Those Wallowing Beauties*, pp.236–37; WW2Talk.com, thread on Gold Beach by Mike ('Trux').

113. Benbow, *Operation Neptune*, p.280; Jarman, *Those Wallowing Beauties*, pp.236–37.

114. WW2Talk.com, thread on Gold Beach by Mike ('Trux'); Phillip Stephens quoted in Evans, George, *The Landfall Story* (Liverpool: G. Evans, 1992), p.63. LCT 7074 was rescued and conserved by, and is owned by, the National Museum of the Royal Navy.

115. Benbow, *Operation Neptune*, p.281; WW2Talk.com, thread on Gold Beach by Mike ('Trux'); DDS, 2005/1376, Commander Force G, Force G Orders for Operation 'Neptune' (ONEAST/G), Appendix B, Diagram of Arrivals on D-Day; (tides) 1990/1308, Allied Naval Commander-in-Chief Expeditionary Force, Operation Neptune Orders (ON) (10 April 1944).

116. (607 Flotilla) TNA, DEFE 2/416; TNA, ADM 202/449. Besides LCM 391, which had earlier crossed to Normandy on board SS *Empire Rapier*, 698 Build-Up Flotilla consisted of LCMs 203, 231, 240, 241, 246, 270, 274, 303, 313, 364, 369, 372, 373, 374 and 381.

117. Benbow, *Operation Neptune*, p.280; TNA, DEFE 2/416; TNA, ADM 202/449; Jarman, *Those Wallowing Beauties*, pp.119–20.

118. (B Build-Up Squadron) TNA, DEFE 2/416; (806 & 805 Flotillas) TNA, ADM 202/449.

119. Trew, *Gold Beach*, pp.83–84.

9. Juno Beach

1. TNA, ADM 179/506. The author is grateful for the detailed information on landings at Juno Beach, including landing table information, compiled by Mike ('Trux') at ww2talk.com/index.php?threads/juno-beach.51316/, and the landing

table spreadsheet by Michel Sabarly at ww2talk.com/index.php?resources/
landing-table-3-canadian-infantry-division-brigade-groups.102/, which were
both useful for this chapter.

2. DND, Reginald Roy, 'Canadian Participation', pp.22–23.
3. TNA, ADM 179/506.
4. DND, Reginald Roy, 'Canadian Participation', pp.23–24.
5. (06.30) TNA, ADM 179/516; (delays) TNA, ADM 179/506.
6. TNA, ADM 179/506; TNA, ADM 202/449.
7. (DDs launch time) DDS, 1990/1314, Commander Force J, Operation 'Neptune',
   Force 'J' Naval Operation Orders (19 May 1944); TNA, ADM 179/516; TNA,
   ADM 179/506; Zuelhke, *Juno Beach: Canada's D-Day Victory, June 6, 1944*
   (Vancouver: Douglas & McIntyre, 2004) p.164; DND, 2nd Canadian Armoured
   Brigade Memo quoted in Reginald Roy, 'Canadian Participation', p.33.
8. TNA, ADM 179/179; Ford, Ken, *Juno Beach (Battlezone Normandy)* (Stroud:
   Sutton, 2004), p.34.
9. DDS, 2014/58/191, Lieutenant Colonel G.R. Perkins, 'Royal Marines in Major
   Landing Craft on D-Day' (Royal Marines Historical Society).
10. Zuehlke, Mark, *Juno Beach*, p.163.
11. *Ibid.*, pp.158–60; TNA, ADM 179/506.
12. TNA, DEFE 2/433; TNA, ADM 179/506; DDS, 2014/58/287, Gordon
    Kimmins, 2014/58/288, George Shrimpton account; Zuehlke, *Juno Beach*,
    pp.158–61.
13. Zuelhke, *Juno Beach*, p.160; TNA, ADM 179/506.
14. TNA, ADM 179/506; DHH, 81-520-8000 Box 263, HMCS *Prince David*; www.
    keymilitary.com/article/absent-friends (accessed 1/7/2023).
15. TNA, DEFE 2/433.
16. TNA, ADM 179/506.
17. DDS, 2014/58/69, Ted Busby account.
18. TNA, ADM 202/449; DND, 'A Canadian naval account', quoted in Reginald
    Roy, 'Canadian Participation', pp.76, 81.
19. TNA, ADM 179/506.
20. DDS, 2014/58/171, Bob Bradshaw account; TNA, ADM 179/506.
21. The LCTs carrying DD Tanks were 303, 306, 311, 372, 390, 422, 441 and 7010.
    They were led by LCH 168 and accompanied by a number of LCP(L)s, some to
    provide smoke if needed. Leo Gariepy, quoted in Miller, Russell, *Nothing Less
    Than Victory: An Oral History of D-Day* (London: Michael Joseph, 1993), p.324.
22. TNA, ADM 179/506; Napier, *The Armoured Campaign*, pp.33–34; Anderson,
    Cracking, p.136; Zuelhke, *Juno Beach*, pp.170–72, 178.
23. TNA, ADM 179/506; TNA, ADM 199/1650; Napier, *The Armoured Campaign*,
    pp.34–36.
24. TNA, ADM 179/506; Zuelhke, *Juno Beach*, pp.191, 193.
25. TNA, ADM 179/506; Ford, *Juno Beach*, p.42.
26. Zuehlke, *Juno Beach*, pp.183, 187, 189–90.
27. TNA, ADM 179/506; Jack Fawcett account in Miller, *Nothing Less*, p.329;
    Zuehlke, *Juno Beach*, p.184; Royal Winnipeg Rifles War Diary in Winter, *D-Day
    Documents*, p.289.

28. 'Newsmen Were Closest Marines to Normandy Landings' by Herbert C. Merillat USMC, in *Fortitudine*, Spring 1994, www.marines.mil/. Also see account written jointly by Captain Herbert C. Merillat USMC, who was on board LCG(L) 1007 and TSgt Richard T. Wright USMC on LCG(L) 831: TNA, ADM 202/449.

29. Anderson, *Cracking*, pp.138–39.

30. TNA, ADM 179/506 (No.5 LCOCU document says 08.50 but numbers are clearly transposed, should be 08.05; Anderson, *Cracking*, p.136 confirms).

31. TNA, ADM 179/506; Anderson, *Cracking*, pp.120–23, 132–35; DDS, 2014/58/182, Norman Vingoe account.

32. DDS, 2014/58/191, Lieutenant Colonel G.R. Perkins, 'Royal Marines in Major Landing Craft on D-Day' (Royal Marines Historical Society).

33. WW2Talk.com, thread on Juno Beach by Mike ('Trux'); Anderson, *Cracking*, p.138; TNA, ADM 179/506.

34. WW2Talk.com, thread on Juno Beach by Mike ('Trux'); Anderson, *Cracking*, pp.139–40; LCT(A) 2428 capsized off Selsey Bill (wreck found in 2008 by Southsea Sub-Aqua Club: southseasubaqua.org.uk); TNA, DEFE 2/490.

35. Zuehlke, *Juno Beach*, pp.195–97; TNA, ADM 202/449; TNA, ADM 179/506; WW2Talk.com, thread on Juno Beach by Mike ('Trux').

36. WW2Talk.com, thread on Juno Beach by Mike ('Trux'); TNA, ADM 199/1650; TNA, ADM 179/506; TNA, ADM 202/449; Zuehlke, *Juno Beach*, p.196.

37. TNA, ADM 179/506; DHH, 81-520-8000 Box 265, HMCS *Prince Henry*.

38. (H+20) LCTs 506, 517 and 522 (WW2Talk.com, thread on Juno Beach by Mike 'Trux'); WW2Talk.com, Force J landing table spreadsheet by Michel Sabarly; Winter, *D-Day Documents*, p.361.

39. Anderson, *Cracking*, pp.120–22; Reginald Edwards account in Lund & Ludlum, *War of the Landing Craft*, p.158; TNA, ADM 179/506. The craft were LCT(5)s 2013, 2038, 2193, 2286, 2289, 2436, 2441 and 2479.

40. TNA, ADM 202/449. The LCMs may have been LCM(3)s from 652 Build-Up Flotilla.

41. DDS, 2014/58/170, Robert Pardington account; DDS, 2014/58/272, Robert Pardington account; Zuehlke, *Juno Beach*, p.180.

42. (North Shores War Diary) Winter, *D-Day Documents*, p.308; Anderson, *Cracking*, p.124; TNA, ADM 179/506; Zuehlke, *Juno Beach*, pp.173, 198–203; Ford, *Juno Beach*, pp.52–53.

43. QORC War Diary in Winter, *D-Day Documents*, p.308; TNA, ADM 179/506; Liddle, Peter, *D-Day By Those Who Were There* (Barnsley: Pen & Sword, 2004) p.157; Zuehlke, *Juno Beach*, pp.173, 175, 210–14; Ford, *Juno Beach*, p.48.

44. TNA, ADM 179/506.

45. Zuehlke, *Juno Beach*, p.214; TNA, ADM 179/506. Captain Clelland was awarded the DSC for D-Day (Lund & Ludlum, *War of the Landing Craft*, p.157).

46. TNA, ADM 179/506; Napier, *The Armoured Campaign*, pp.29–30; Anderson, *Cracking*, p.129.

47. TNA, ADM 179/506; Lund & Ludlum, *War of the Landing Craft*, p.163.

48. TNA, ADM 179/506; DDS, 2014/58/191, Lieutenant Colonel G.R. Perkins, 'Royal Marines in Major Landing Craft on D-Day' (Royal Marines Historical Society).

49. Anderson, *Cracking*, p.130; TNA, ADM 179/506. Several reports written by senior officers mistakenly label 105 LCT(A) Flotilla as 106 LCT Flotilla. LCT(A) 2455 apparently had engine trouble and did not reach Juno Beach on D-Day (DDS, 2014/58/37, Andrew Marchant account; TNA, ADM 179/506).

50. TNA, ADM 179/506. The anonymous flotilla coxswain of 103 LCT Flotilla was accompanying his flotilla officer on board a craft of 105 LCT(A) Flotilla for D-Day.

51. DDS, 2014/58/190, Malcolm Cook account; TNA, ADM 179/506.

52. DDS, 2014/58/169, Charles Bruce account.

53. (518 Flotilla losses) TNA, ADM 179/506; DDS, 2014/58/169, Charles Bruce account.

54. (QORC) TNA, ADM 179/506.

55. DDS, 2014/58/167, Bob Hare account.

56. 30 Assault Unit: TNA, ADM 179/506.

57. TNA, ADM 179/506; Ford, *Juno Beach*, pp.53–54.

58. (Timmermans) www.unithistories.com/officers/RNR_officersT.html (accessed 15/7/2023); Miller, *Nothing Less*, p.322.

59. Lund & Ludlum, *War of the Landing Craft*, p.155; DDS, 2014/58/135, Anon., 'Operation Overlord. The LCIs In The Assault on Normandy'; TNA, ADM 179/506; 48 RM Commando War Diary in Winter, *D-Day Documents*, p.364.

60. Zuehlke, *Juno Beach*, p.208.

61. TNA, ADM 179/506; DDS, 2014/58/191, Lieutenant Colonel G.R. Perkins, 'Royal Marines in Major Landing Craft on D-Day' (Royal Marines Historical Society); TNA, ADM 179/516; (LCG(L)s) TNA, ADM 179/506; 48 RM Commando War Diary in Winter, *D-Day Documents*, pp.364–66.

62. TNA, ADM 179/506. Craft landing the 10th Canadian Armoured Regiment were LCTs 541, 672, 932 and 934 (WW2Talk.com, Force J landing table spreadsheet by Michel Sabarly).

63. Royal Canadian Navy, *The RCN's Part*, p.99.

64. TNA, ADM 179/506; Zuehlke, *Juno Beach*, p.252; Ford, *Juno Beach*, p.41; (LCT 500) article in *Navy News* D-Day Supplement, 1994; DDS, 2014/58/287, Gordon Kimmins. The craft carrying the 12th Field Regiment RCA were LCTs 500, 508, 514, 569, 677 and 709; also LCTs 509 and 510 carrying other personnel (WW2Talk.com, Force J landing table spreadsheet by Michel Sabarly).

65. Royal Canadian Navy, *The RCN's Part*, pp.101–02.

66. TNA, ADM 179/506; 14th Field Regiment RCA War Diary in Winter, *D-Day Documents*, p.328; Townend & Baldwin, *Gunners*, p.163. The eight LCTs carrying 14th Field Regiment RCA were: LCT 516, 524, 525, 530, 637, 716, 855 and 885 (WW2Talk.com, Force J landing table spreadsheet by Michel Sabarly).

67. Townend & Baldwin, *Gunners*, p.164; TNA, ADM 179/506. The eight LCTs carrying the 19th Field Regiment RCA were 501, 518, 526, 529, 602, 707, 767 and 804 (WW2Talk.com, Force J landing table spreadsheet by Michel Sabarly).

68. TNA, ADM 179/506.

69. Townend & Baldwin, *Gunners*, pp.158, 163; WW2Talk, Juno; Royal Canadian Navy, *The RCN's Part*. The six craft carrying the 13th Field Regiment RCA were LCTs 574, 575, 629, 706, 781 and 876 WW2Talk.com, Force J landing table spreadsheet by Michel Sabarly).

70. DDS, 2014/58/96, E. Bentley account; TNA, ADM 179/506; Don Bass account in Buckenham, Colin, *The Kedge Hook Files: 25 Years of the L.S.T. & Landing Craft Association* (Diss: DataTech DTP, 2011), pp.206–11. According to Bass, there were six dead in total from LCTs 574 and 717 in this incident, but if so, not all their identities are known. LCT 712 may also have beached near the other craft of 31 LCT Flotilla at some point on D-Day.

71. Anderson, *Cracking*, pp.127, 147.

72. The seven LCT(4)s were 531, 534, 768, 770, 933, 935 and 936 (WW2Talk.com, Force J landing table spreadsheet by Michel Sabarly). Henry Smith's account from www.thesasig.com/blog/blog-30/ (accessed 9/6/2023).

73. TNA, ADM 179/506; TNA, ADM 202/449; DDS, 1992/275/153, Copy of Force J Loading Document.

74. WW2Talk.com, thread on Juno Beach by Mike ('Trux'); DDS, 1990/1314/2, Commander Force J, Operation 'Neptune', Force 'J' Naval Operation Orders (19 May 1944). George Saunders account at www.combinedops.com/HMS%20Royal%20Ulsterman.htm (accessed 9/8/2023).

75. TNA, ADM 179/506; Anderson, *Cracking*, p.142; War Diary, HQ Canadian 9th Infantry Brigade in Winter, *D-Day Documents*, p.311.

76. TNA, ADM 179/506; Anderson, *Cracking*, p.142; quote from Winter, *D-Day Documents*, p.314. The craft were: LCI(L)s 115, 118, 125, 135, 250, 252, 262, 263, 270, 276, 306.

77. TNA, ADM 179/506; Anderson, *Cracking*, p.142; DHH, 8000-411-262, Box 400, Report of 262nd LCI(L) Flotilla for June 1944; Royal Canadian Navy, *The RCN's Part*, pp.103–04.

78. DHH, 81-520-8000, Box 317, Landing Craft, Infantry; Royal Canadian Navy, *The RCN's Part*, pp.103–04.

79. WW2Talk.com, thread on Juno Beach by Mike ('Trux'). The LCTs scheduled for Nan Red were 632, 636, 667, 669, 679 and 721. Those scheduled for Nan White were LCTs 634, 639, 670, 700, 759, 937, 938, 940, 941, 943, 1006, 1008 (WW2Talk.com, Force J landing table spreadsheet by Michel Sabarly).

80. WW2Talk.com, thread on Juno Beach by Mike ('Trux'); HC, T-7620, 8th Canadian Infantry Brigade Admin Order, May 1944; DDS, 2014/58/161, Bert Poole account.

81. (Mike clear) Anderson, *Cracking*, pp.127, 141; (low tide, drying out) TNA, ADM 179/506.

82. DDS, 1990/1314/2, Commander Force J, Operation 'Neptune'. Force 'J' Naval Operation Orders (19 May 1944); Benbow, *Operation Neptune*, p.281; TNA, ADM 179/506; DDS, 1990/1314/2, Commander Force J, Operation 'Neptune'. Force 'J' Naval Operation Orders (19 May 1944); WW2Talk.com, thread on Juno Beach by Mike ('Trux'); HC, T-7620, 8th Canadian Infantry Brigade Admin Order, May 1944. Convoy J-15 included LSTs 8, 62, 159, 180, 199, 215, 238, 239 and 416. Convoy J-16 included LSTs 80, 323, 402, 404, 405, 409, 410, 413 and 425.

83. Liddle, *D-Day by Those Who Were There*, p.172.

84. DDS, 1990/1314, Commander Force J, Operation 'Neptune'. Force 'J' Naval Operation Orders (19 May 1944); TNA, ADM 179/506. LST 981 – during the crossing it hit a mine and was left behind (TNA, ADM 179/506). TNA,

WO 171/92, BUCO West War Diary; WW2Talk.com, Force J landing table spreadsheet by Michel Sabarly.

85. DDS, 1990/1314, Commander Force J, Operation 'Neptune'. Force 'J' Naval Operation Orders (19 May 1944); Fold3_LST GR 49_war diary 1944_06_84538-01 -02. The US-crewed LSTs were 360, 383, 384, 385, 517, 529, 543, 682, 980, 982, 983 (Fold3, LST Flotilla 17, War Diary, June 1944).

86. TNA, ADM 179/506.

87. DDS, 1990/1314, Commander Force J, Operation 'Neptune'. Force 'J' Naval Operation Orders (19 May 1944); TNA, ADM 179/506.

88. Assault Force 'J'. Survey (WW2Talk.com, Force J landing table spreadsheet by Michel Sabarly).

89. TNA, ADM 179/506.

10. Sword Beach

1. DDS, 1992/275/165, 'D-Day 6 June 1944. Some recollections of Petty Officer Motor-Mechanic J.E. Burton P/MX500209, L.C.I.(S) 535'. The author is grateful for the detailed information on landings at Sword Beach including landing table information, compiled by Mike ('Trux') at ww2talk.com/index.php?threads/ sword-beach.38764/page-4, and Force S landing table spreadsheet by Michel Sabarly: ww2talk.com/index.php?resources/landing-table-3-british-infantry- division-group-first-tide.39/, which were useful for this chapter. Landing tables for Sword Beach survive at TNA, WO 219/3075 (first tide), and DDS, 1995/72/3 to 1995/72/5, '3 British Infantry Division. Landing table. Second tide. Operation Overlord', '[…] Third Tide […]' and '[…] Fourth Tide […]'.

2. (Svenner) uboat.net/allies/warships/ship/712.html (accessed 19/9/2022); DDS, 1992/275/133, Sword Beach Report.

3. DDS, 1992/275/133, Sword Beach Report; Fold3, Naval Operation Orders for the Invasion of Normandy, p.1000, copy of ONEAST/S7B; TNA, DEFE 2/490; TNA, DEFE 2/419; (DD tanks) TNA, ADM 179/506. The LCT(DD)s were 443, 444, 455, 456, 461, 465 and 467 (WW2Talk.com, thread on Sword Beach by Mike 'Trux').

4. Some wartime documents and, as a result, some more recent publications, incorrectly swap these two flotillas between LSIs.

5. TNA, DEFE 2/420; TNA, DEFE 2/419.

6. (1st South Lancs) TNA, DEFE 2/420; TNA, DEFE 2/419.

7. TNA, DEFE 2/420; TNA, DEFE 2/419.

8. TNA, DEFE 2/420. On Gold and Juno Beaches, FOOs in this role were on board LCS(M)s but apparently none were available for Sword Beach. The LCTs carrying artillery were as follows: 7th Field Regiment, LCTs 665, 685, 784, 859, 786 and 814; 33rd Field Regiment, LCTs 544, 593, 597, 887, 889 and 1051; 76th Field Regiment, LCTs 532, 750, 826, 827, 860 and 861 (TNA, DEFE 2/420).

9. (QH) TNA, DEFE 2/419.

10. (LCT(CB) 2337) John Brooke account from ddnf.org.uk/memories/j_brooke/ (accessed 8/2/2023); (LCG(L)) TNA, DEFE 2/419; TNA, DEFE 2/420.

11. LCT(R)s 419, 334 and 457 in the first row, 458 and 351 to their rear (TNA, DEFE 2/420).

12. DDS, 2014/58/21, Edward Neale account.

13. TNA, DEFE 2/419; DDS, 2001/1536/333, Frank and Joan Shaw Collection, F.H. Penfold account.

14. DDS, 1992/275/133, Sword Beach Report; TNA, DEFE 2/420.

15. TNA, DEFE 2/420; Ford, Ken, *Sword Beach (Battlezone Normandy)* (Stroud: Sutton, 2004); Anderson, *Cracking*.

16. DDS, 2014/58/21, Edward Neale account.

17. Napier, *The Armoured Campaign*, p.19.

18. Anderson, *Cracking*, p.104. The LCTs were LCT 947, plus four of these craft: 909, 951, 981, 1010, 1016, 1082, 1092, 1093 and 1094 (the other five landed on Queen Red).

19. Anderson, *Cracking*, p.96; Burn, Lambton, *'Down Ramps!' Saga of the Eighth Armada* (London: Carroll & Nicholson, 1947), pp.213–14.

20. Anderson, *Cracking*, pp.96–97; TNA, DEFE 2/420; DDS, 2021/80, Ron Smith oral history.

21. TNA, DEFE 2/420; DDS, 1992/275/133, Sword Beach Report.

22. TNA, DEFE 2/420; Adrian Roose account in Anderson, *Cracking*, p.107.

23. DDS, 1992/275/133, Sword Beach Report; TNA, DEFE 2/419; TNA, DEFE 2/420.

24. DDS, 1992/275/133, Sword Beach Report; TNA, DEFE 2/420; TNA, DEFE 2/419.

25. TNA, DEFE 2/420.

26. DDS, 1992/275/133, Sword Beach Report.

27. DDS, 1992/275/133, Sword Beach Report; TNA, DEFE 2/420. The LCT(AVRE)s were five of these craft: 909, 951, 981, 1010, 1016, 1082, 1092, 1093 and 1094 (the other five landed on Queen White).

28. TNA, DEFE 2/420; Craggs, Tracy, 'An "Unspectacular" War? Reconstructing the History of the 2nd Battalion East Yorkshire Regiment During the Second World War', PhD Thesis, University of Sheffield (2013), p.123, at etheses. whiterose.ac.uk/3626/ (accessed 17/10/2022).

29. DDS, 1992/275/133, Sword Beach Report; Anderson, *Cracking*, pp.102, 104.

30. TNA, DEFE 2/420; DDS, 1992/275/133, Sword Beach Report.

31. The enemy gun was described by a surviving crew member as a self-propelled 88mm, but may have been a fixed-position 75mm gun. DDS, 2014/58/30, Sheila Orme, widow of Vic Orme; DDS, 2014/58/79, M.E. Mawson account.

32. TNA, DEFE 2/420; DDS, 2014/58/27, Peter Hutchins; Anderson, *Cracking*, p.102; WW2Talk.com, thread on Sword Beach by Mike ('Trux').

33. TNA, DEFE 2/420; DDS, 2014/57/59, John Royce account; TNA, ADM 199/1650.

34. TNA, DEFE 2/420; John Brooke account from ddnf.org.uk/memories/j_brooke/ (accessed 8/2/2023); DDS, 2014/58/101, Jim Brooker account.

35. DDS, 2014/58/101, Jim Brooker account; TNA, DEFE 2/420; DDS, 1992/275/144, Letter from J.W. Berry of LCI(S) 523 to Rupert Curtis 2/4/1979 and notes.

36. TNA, DEFE 2/420.
37. TNA, DEFE 2/420; DDS, 1992/275/133, Sword Beach Report.
38. TNA, DEFE 2/420.
39. TNA, DEFE 2/420.
40. TNA, DEFE 2/420; DDS, 2014/58/63, H. Conley account; DDS, 2014/59/10, letter from Captain K. Wright in Curtis, Rupert, 'Chronicles of D-Day'.
41. WW2Talk.com, thread on Sword Beach by Mike ('Trux'); TNA, DEFE 2/420.
42. TNA, DEFE 2/420; TNA, DEFE 2/419; DDS, 1993/14, photos by Sub Lieutenant Philips William Doleman Winkley RNVR (CO LCT 979, 41 LCT Flotilla) show Queen White at this point.
43. TNA, DEFE 2/420.
44. Lund & Ludlum, *War of the Landing Craft*, p.155.
45. TNA, DEFE 2/420; DDS, 2014/58/282, Eric Crees account.
46. TNA, DEFE 2/420; cwgc.org/find-records/find-war-dead.
47. DDS, 2014/58/282, Eric Crees account.
48. TNA, DEFE 2/420.
49. TNA, DEFE 2/420; TNA WO 171/1381, WAR DIARY 1st Suffolks. Depending on different accounts, the 1st Suffolks seem to have landed either two minutes early at about 08.23 (H+58) or on time at 08.25 (H+60). The 1st Suffolks War Diary says the landing was five minutes late, but also states that H-Hour was 07.20, which probably means they landed on time! DDS, 1992/275/133, Sword Beach Report; TNA, DEFE 2/420.
50. TNA WO 171/1381, War Diary 1st Suffolks; TNA, DEFE 2/420.
51. TNA, DEFE 2/420; Lund & Ludlum, *War of the Landing Craft*, pp.152–53; cwgc. org/find-records/find-war-dead/ records Scaplehorn's date of death as 7 June for some reason; (recovery) DDS, 2014/58/90, diary of Obs Lt G.A.D. Bourne, in notes by Brian Bignell.
52. TNA, DEFE 2/420.
53. TNA, DEFE 2/420; DDS, 2014/58/268, Harry Lancashire; DDS, 1992/275/131, Curtis, Rupert, 'D-Day – We landed the Commandos'.
54. TNA, DEFE 2/420; DDS, 2014/58/168, Peter Houghton (it is likely that the shell was a smaller calibre than 88mm).
55. TNA, DEFE 2/420; TNA, DEFE 2/419; DDS, 1992/275/133, Sword Beach Report.
56. DDS, 1992/275/133, Sword Beach Report; TNA, DEFE 2/420. These LCM(3)s were also part of Group 6.
57. WW2Talk.com, thread on Sword Beach by Mike ('Trux').
58. TNA, DEFE 2/420.
59. TNA, DEFE 2/420; War Diary of 76th Field Regt RA, in Winter, *D-Day Documents*, p.214.
60. TNA, DEFE 2/420; DDS, 2014/58/135, Anon., 'Operation Overlord. The LCIs In The Assault on Normandy'; DDS, 1992/275/131, Curtis, Rupert, 'D-Day – We landed the Commandos'.
61. (Fire from both flanks) DDS, 2014/58/101, Jim Brooker account; Derek Mills-Roberts account in Anderson, *Cracking*, p.110; DDS, 1992/275/131, Curtis, Rupert, 'D-Day – We landed the Commandos'; DDS, 1992/275/101/2, Lieutenant Langley, 'LCI/S/ 509 in the Normandy Invasion'.

62. TNA, DEFE 2/420; DDS, 1992/275/131, Curtis, Rupert, 'D-Day – We landed the Commandos'; DDS, 2014/58/135, Anon., 'Operation Overlord. The LCIs In The Assault on Normandy'.

63. DDS, 1992/275/133, Sword Beach Report; Ford, *Sword Beach*, p.56; DDS, 1992/275/131, Curtis, Rupert, 'D-Day – We landed the Commandos'; DDS, 1992/275/164, Log of LCI(S) 529.

64. cwgc.org/find-records/find-war-dead/; TNA, DEFE 2/420; DDS, 1992/275/131, Curtis, Rupert, 'D-Day – We landed the Commandos'; TNA, DEFE 2/419; L. Rupert Curtis, 'Wacco, America!', US Naval Institute Proceedings Vol. 71 (1945) from www.usni.org/magazines/proceedings/1945/december/wacco-america (accessed 22/4/2023).

65. TNA, DEFE 2/420; DDS, 1992/275/101/2, Lieutenant Langley, 'LCI/S/ 509 in the Normandy Invasion'.

66. DDS, 1992/275/165, 'D-Day 6 June 1944. Some recollections of Petty Officer Motor-Mechanic J.E. Burton P/MX500209, L.C.I.(S) 535'.

67. DDS, 1992/275/131, Curtis, Rupert, 'D-Day – We landed the Commandos'; DDS, 1992/275/101/2, Lieutenant Langley, 'LCI/S/ 509 in the Normandy Invasion'.

68. DDS, 1992/275/165, 'D-Day 6 June 1944. Some recollections of Petty Officer Motor-Mechanic J.E. Burton P/MX500209, L.C.I.(S) 535'.; TNA, DEFE 2/420.

69. DDS, 1992/275/131, Curtis, Rupert, 'D-Day – We landed the Commandos'; TNA, DEFE 2/420; DDS, 2001/1536/45, Frank and Joan Shaw Collection, Bill Binding account.

70. DDS, 1992/275/101/2, Lieutenant Langley, 'LCI/S/ 509 in the Normandy Invasion'; DDS, 2014/58/135, Anon., 'Operation Overlord. The LCIs in the Assault on Normandy'; DDS, 1992/275/131, Curtis, Rupert, 'D-Day – We landed the Commandos'.

71. TNA, DEFE 2/420; cwgc.org/find-records/find-war-dead/ records Beatson's date of death as 9 June 1944, but TNA, DEFE 2/420 gives the impression he died on D-Day.

72. TNA, DEFE 2/420.

73. WW2Talk.com, thread on Sword Beach by Mike ('Trux'); TNA, DEFE 2/420; DDS, 1992/275/133, Sword Beach Report; DDS, 1995/72/2, 6 Beach Group Op/Admin Order.

74. Anderson, *Cracking*, p.111. Predicted high tide at Arromanches was 10.00–11.00 and would have been perhaps 20–30 minutes later on Sword Beach (DDS, 1990/1308, Allied Naval Commander-in-Chief Expeditionary Force, Operation Neptune Orders (ON), 10 April 1944, Tidal Predictions).

75. Winter, *D-Day Documents*, p.200; TNA, DEFE 2/420. Those craft believed to have been in the H+150 wave are LCI(L)s 126, 164, 169, 300, 378 and 380 (WW2Talk.com, Force S landing table spreadsheet by Michel Sabarly and TNA, WO 219/3075), plus three more LCI(L)s, probably drawn from the rest of 263 LCI(L) Flotilla: LCI(L)s 165, 171, 181, 377 and 379. LCI(L) 179 apparently accompanied the group as a rescue craft, and in fact did rescue some survivors from the sunken destroyer HNoMS *Svenner* (DDS, 2014/58/138, Joshua Skinner account), and one or more additional empty craft from the flotilla may have accompanied the rest as rescue or hospital vessels.

76. Lund & Ludlum, *War of the Landing Craft*, p.153.

77. DDS, 2014/58/138, Joshua Skinner account.

78. DDS, 1992/275/101/2, Lieutenant Langley, 'LCI/S/ 509 in the Normandy Invasion'.

79. Winter, *D-Day Documents*, pp.205, 233; TNA, DEFE 2/420. The H+185 LCTs were 650, 952 and 958, and all but one of the following craft: LCTs 641, 649, 668, 748, 752, 892, 959, 960 and 961.

80. TNA, DEFE 2/420.

81. WW2Talk.com, thread on Sword Beach by Mike ('Trux'); DDS, 1992/275/133, Sword Beach Report. The H+215 craft were LCI(L)s 9, 12, 14, 15, 16 and 33 (all US Navy). The H+230 craft were LCI(L)s 13, 35, 193 and 238 (US Navy); LCI(L)s 111, 116, 174 and 175 (Royal Navy) (WW2Talk.com, thread on Sword Beach by Mike ('Trux') and other sources).

82. TNA, DEFE 2/420.

83. TNA, DEFE 2/420; DDS, 2014/58/187, Alan Higgins account; DDS, 2014/58/122, K.J. Tuppen account.

84. WW2Talk.com, thread on Sword Beach by Mike ('Trux'); DDS, 2014/58/284, Frederick Naylor account.

85. DDS, 2014/58/3, E.J. Loseby account.

86. These two craft were officially due at H+240 – DDS, 1992/275/133, Sword Beach report; DDS, 2014/58/70, Alan Richardson; DDS, 2014/58/290, Alan P. Daines account.

87. TNA, WO 171/616, HQ 9th Infantry Brigade War Diary, May 1944.

88. TNA, DEFE 2/420; WW2Talk.com, Force S landing table spreadsheet by Michel Sabarly; Fold3, Naval Operation Orders for the Invasion of Normandy, p.1000, copy of ONEAST/S7B. The craft were LCI(L)s 385, 389 and 390 of 265 LCI(L) Flotilla, and LCI(L)s 375, 376, 384, 387, 388 and 391 of 266 LCI(L) Flotilla.

89. Fold3, Naval Operation Orders for the Invasion of Normandy, p.1000, copy of ONEAST/S7B; TNA, DEFE 2/420.

90. TNA, DEFE 2/420.

91. TNA, DEFE 2/420; DDS, 2014/58/234, J.H. Willis account.

92. (Pause) Anderson, *Cracking*, p.113; TNA, DEFE 2/420. The Group 18 LCTs were 539, 609, 611, 612, 675, 787, 788, 851, 852, 864, 1015 and 1080 (TNA, DEFE 2/420).

93. TNA, DEFE 2/420. The Group 19 LCTs were 627, 674, 944, 1003, 1017, 1019, 1020, 1022, 1023, 1065, 1067 and 1068 (TNA, DEFE 2/420; DDS, 2014/58/164, Arthur Walters).

94. TNA, DEFE 2/420; DDS, 2014/58/253, John Dennis account.

95. WW2Talk.com, thread on Sword Beach by Mike ('Trux'); TNA, DEFE 2/420. LST 324, 361 and three others.

96. TNA, DEFE 2/420.

97. DDS, 2014/58/13, Norman Moss account.

98. TNA, DEFE 2/419.

99. This and the following paragraphs are sourced from WW2Talk.com, thread on Sword Beach by Mike ('Trux'); DDS, 1995/72/3, '3 British Infantry Division. Landing table. Second tide. Operation Overlord'.

100. TNA, DEFE 2/420. The craft were: from 261 LCI(L) Flotilla – LCI(L)s 134 and 180; from 265 LCI(L) Flotilla, LCI(L)s 374, 381, 382, 383 and 386; from 266 LCI(L) Flotilla, LCI(L) 241 (TNA, DEFE 2/420).

101. 1990/1308, Allied Naval Commander-in-Chief Expeditionary Force, Operation Neptune Orders (ON), 10 April 1944; DDS, 1995/72/3, '3 British Infantry Division. Landing table. Second tide. Operation Overlord'; TNA, DEFE 2/419 (1990/1308 shows nine LST(2)s towing four Rhinos, beaching at H+11.75hrs by Rhino, also three LST(2)s at H+16.25hrs, which could bring the number to 12?) 1990/1308 says three LST(2)s landed at H+11.75hrs, unloaded by Rhino. 1995/72/3 says five LSTs towing three Rhinos for White, four LSTs towing one Rhino for Red, with seventy DUKWs between them (likely to be most up-to-date figures).

102. DDS, 1995/72/3, '3 British Infantry Division. Landing table. Second tide. Operation Overlord'.

103. DDS, 1995/72/4, '3 British Infantry Division. Landing table. Third tide. Operation Overlord'; 1990/1308, Allied Naval Commander-in-Chief Expeditionary Force, Operation Neptune Orders (ON), 10 April 1944, mentions 5 LSTs. The LSTs were 162, 163, 164, 415 and 430 (Winser, *D-Day Ships*, p.91).

104. Jarman, *Those Wallowing Beauties*, p.250, says there were sixty-four landing barges at Sword; TNA, ADM 210/8; Benbow, *Operation Neptune*, p.222.

105. Benbow, *Operation Neptune*, pp.151, 274; 1990/1308, Allied Naval Commander-in-Chief Expeditionary Force, Operation Neptune Orders (ON), 10 April 1944 (TNA, ADM 179/405).

106. DDS, 1995/72/2, Overlord: 6 Beach Group Op Order/Admin Order; TNA, WO 171/616, HQ 9th Infantry Brigade War Diary, May 1944; TNA, DEFE 2/420; Benbow, *Operation Neptune* pp.151, 274; 1990/1308, Allied Naval Commander-in-Chief Expeditionary Force, *Operation Neptune orders* (ON), 10 April 1944.

107. TNA, DEFE 2/420; Jarman, *Those Wallowing Beauties*, pp.128–30.

108. TNA, DEFE 2/420.

109. DDS, 2014/58/191, Buck Taylor account.

110. TNA, ADM 199/1644; TNA, DEFE 2/419.

111. DDS, 1995/72/4 to 1995/72/5, '3 British Infantry Division. Landing table. Third tide. Operation Overlord' and '[…] Fourth Tide […]'; WW2Talk.com, thread on Sword Beach by Mike ('Trux'). These LCILs were craft of 252 and/or 253 LCI(L) Flotilla.

112. TNA, DEFE 2/490.

113. TNA, DEFE 2/419.

11. After D-Day

1. These figures are an estimate based on a variety of sources, but exact numbers are difficult to determine. Only selected types of craft are shown. The figure for sunk/lost and badly damaged craft is combined, as these categories could be hard to distinguish at the time (some damaged craft were no doubt later repaired).

'+' indicates that the true lost/damaged figure may be higher. LCMs in the ferry role are included in the totals for each type of craft (though some in fact arrived later than D-Day). LCTs and LCI(L)s in Follow-on Forces B and L are not included. RAN, Admiralty, *Battle Summary*, pp.36–37, 109; Anderson, *Cracking*, pp.115, 147, 185, 208, 220; TNA, DEFE 2/427; TNA, ADM 179/516; United States Fleet, *Amphibious Operations*, pp.1–6, pp.1–14; TNA, ADM 199/1650 & ADM 199/1651, HM Ships and Vessels Lost: Survivor's reports.

2. TNA, ADM 179/508; TNA, DEFE 2/696; RAN, Admiralty, *Battle Summary*, p.152; Lund, *War*, p.193; TNA, ADM 179/506; TNA, ADM 179/508; Fold3, LST Group 35 Action Report.

3. Commander US Naval Forces, *Neptune*, p.312; DDS, 2014/58/243, G.R. Cooper.

4. Yung, *Gators*, p.215; TNA, DEFE 2/427; TNA, ADM 179/516; RAN, Admiralty, *Battle Summary*, p.141.

5. TNA, ADM 179/506.

6. TNA, ADM 179/516; CARL, N16117-B, Cherbourg. D + 20–D+177, 26 June to 30 November.

7. (ETF, D-Day to D+30) RAN, Admiralty, *Battle Summary*, p.132: figures only include ships and craft reported in difficulties and which received assistance, but do not include those that did not report damage, or that returned to the UK under own power; includes LSTs but not other types of landing ships. (June–July 1944) *Ibid.*, pp.125–29 (figures include a few craft lost while on loan to US forces).

8. Fold3, Western Task Force, Commander Task Force 122, Report on Invasion of Normandy.

9. TNA, DEFE 2/420; TNA, DEFE 2/419; Fold3, LST 2, Report on Operations, Normandy; Fold3, USS *Bayfield*, War Diary, June 1944; RAN, Admiralty, *Battle Summary*, p.144; DDS, 2014/58/191, Lt Col G.R. Perkins, 'Royal Marines in Major Landing Craft on D-Day' (RM Historical Society).

10. In addition to those otherwise noted, sources used for the following paragraphs were navalhistory.net (viewed 29/10/2023) for US deaths, and cwgc.org. uk (viewed 29/10/2023) for British and Commonwealth deaths. (Convoy battle) TNA, ADM 179/506; TNA, ADM 53/119687; (RAOC) www. warmemorialsonline.org.uk/memorial/100339 (viewed 29/10/2023).

11. (LSTs 314 and 376) Fold3, LST Group 34, Report on Invasion of Normandy; Bill Hochman account, wikimapia.org/16557855/Wreck-of-USS-LST-376 (viewed 23/10/2023). (LST 280) Fold3, LST 287, War History; Fold3, LST 280, AA Action Report English Channel, 15/6/1944. (LST 133) United States Coast Guard, *Coast Guard*, p.165. (LST 523) Fold3, USS *Bayfield* War Diary June 1944. (LCH 185) wrecksite.eu/wreck.aspx?270357 (viewed 26/10/2023). (LCF 1) DDS, 2021/88, Norman Kenneth White.

12. TNA, DEFE 2/427; RAN, Admiralty, *Battle Summary*, p.120; Edwards, Kenneth, *Operation Neptune* (Stroud: Fonthill, revised edition 2013), pp.78–79; Commander US Naval Forces, *Neptune*, pp.312–13; TNA, DEFE 2/427.

13. Ellis, *Victory*, pp.90–91; TNA, ADM 179/508; (Churchill) TNA, ADM 1/15631.

14. DDS, 2014/58/107, Raymond Shone; DDS, 2014/58/279, Horace Ely.

15. (MV *Cape Henlopen*) www.longislandferry.com/Common/Help.aspx?page=fleet (viewed 21/10/2023). Surviving but deteriorating craft include: LCT(4) 728 (Force S on D-Day) and a second LCT(4), sunk as a makeshift breakwater in Poole Harbour (UK) in 1950, citizan.org.uk/blog/2017/Dec/06/poole-harbour-d-day-tank-landing-craft-last-dying-breed/ (viewed 21/10/2023); LCH 269 (also Force S, and later bought by a New Jersey firm), barely visible on satellite imagery of the waterways near Atlantic City, New Jersey, njmaritimemuseum.org/historic-treasure-in-the-atlantic-city-mud/ (viewed 21/10/2023).

16. DDS, 2014/58/12, Raymond Oram; DDS, 2014/13, Norman Moss.

17. Tom Carter, *Beachhead Normandy: An LCT's Odyssey*, preface (viewed on Google Books, 03/05/2023). www.findagrave.com/memorial/56641851/john-emanuel-anderson (viewed 18/11/2023); Anderson's name also remains on the Tablets of the Missing at the Normandy American Cemetery.

Bibliography and Sources

SELECT BIBLIOGRAPHY

Adcock, Al, *WWII US Landing Craft in Action: Warships No. 17* (Carrollton, TX: Squadron/Signal, 2003).

Anderson Jr, Richard C., *Cracking Hitler's Atlantic Wall: The 1st Assault Brigade Royal Engineers on D-Day.* (Mechanicsburg, PA: Stackpole, 2010).

Badsey, Stephen, & Tim Bean, *Omaha Beach (Battlezone Normandy)* (Stroud: Sutton, 2004).

Badsey, Stephen, *Utah Beach (Battlezone Normandy)* (Stroud: Sutton, 2004).

Baker, Rowland, 'Notes on the Development of Landing Craft' in A.D. Duckworth (ed.), *Transactions of the Institution of Naval Architects, Vol. 89* (London: Institution of Naval Architects, 1947).

Baker, Rowland, 'Ships of the Invasion Fleet' in A.D. Duckworth (ed.), *Transactions of the Institution of Naval Architects*, Vol. 89 (London: Institution of Naval Architects, 1947).

Baker III, A.D. (ed.), *Allied Landing Craft of World War Two* (London: Arms & Armour, 1985).

Balkoski, Joseph, *Omaha Beach: D-Day, June 6, 1944* (Mechanicsburg, PA: Stackpole, 2004).

Balkoski, Joseph, *Utah Beach: The Amphibious Landing and Airborne Operations on D-Day, June 6, 1944* (Mechanicsburg, PA: Stackpole, 2005).

Benbow, Tim (ed.), *Operation Neptune: The D-Day Landings, 6 June 1944* (Solihull: Helion, 2015).

Brooks, Stephen, *Montgomery and the Battle of Normandy* (Stroud: The History Press, 2008).

Brown, D.K. (ed.), *The Design and Construction of British Warships 1939–1945* (London: Conway Maritime Press, 1996).

Buckenham, Colin, *The Kedge Hook Files: 25 Years of the L.S.T. & Landing Craft Association* (Diss: DataTech DTP, 2011).

Buffetaut, Yves, *D-Day Ships: The Allied Invasion Fleet, June 1944* (London: Conway, 2004).

Burn, Lambton, *'Down Ramps!': Saga of the Eighth Armada* (London: Carroll & Nicholson, 1947).

Caddick-Adams, Peter, *Sand and Steel: A New History of D-Day* (London: Penguin Random House, 2014).

Chandler, David, & James L. Collins (eds), *The D-Day Encyclopaedia* (Oxford: Helicon, 1994).

Chazette, Alain, et al., *Atlantikwall: Utah Beach* (Vertou: Histoire & Fortifications, 2012).

Chazette, Alain, et al., *Atlantikwall: Gold–Juno–Sword* (Vertou: Histoire & Fortifications, 2013).

Chazette, Alain, et al., *Atlantikwall: Omaha Beach* (Vertou: Histoire & Fortifications, 2014).

Clark, Andrew L., *A Cornfield Shipyard* (Evansville, IN: MT Publishing, 1991).

Commander US Naval Forces in Europe, *The Invasion of Normandy: Operation Neptune, United States Naval Administration in World War II, Volume V* (1948).

Craggs, Tracy, 'An "Unspectacular" War? Reconstructing the History of the 2nd Battalion East Yorkshire Regiment During the Second World War' (PhD Thesis, University of Sheffield, 2013) at etheses.whiterose.ac.uk/3626/ (accessed 17/10/2022).

Doyle, David, *US Landing Craft of WWII, Vol. 1: The LCP(L), LCP(R), LCV, LCVP, LCS(L), LCM and LCI* (Atglen, PA: Schiffer, 2019).

Doyle, David, *US Landing Craft of WWII, Vol. 2: The LCT, LSM, LCS(L)(3) and LST* (Atglen, PA: Schiffer, 2020).

Dunphie, Christopher, & Garry Johnson, *Normandy: Gold Beach, Inland from King, June 1944*, Battleground Europe series (Barnsley: Pen & Sword, 1999).

Dyer, George C., *The Amphibians Came to Conquer: The Story of Admiral Richmond Kelly Turner, Volume 1* (US Marine Corps FMFRP 12-109-I, no date, downloaded from www.marines.mil).

Edwards, Kenneth, *Operation Neptune* (Stroud: Fonthill, revised edition, 2013).

Elliott, Peter, *Allied Minesweeping in World War II* (Cambridge: Patrick Stephens, 1979).

Ellis, Lionel Frederic, *Victory in the West, Vol. 1: The Battle of Normandy* (London: HMSO, 1962).

Evans, George, *The Landfall Story* (Liverpool: G. Evans, 1992).

Fergusson, Bernard, *The Watery Maze: The Story of Combined Operations* (London: Collins, 1961).

Ford, Ken, *Juno Beach (Battlezone Normandy)* (Stroud: Sutton, 2004).

Ford, Ken, *Sword Beach (Battlezone Normandy)* (Stroud: Sutton, 2004).

Friedman, Norman, *U.S. Amphibious Ships and Craft: An Illustrated Design History* (Anapolis, MD: Naval Institute Press, 2002).

Furer, Julius Augustus, *Administration of the Navy Department in World War II* (Washington, DC: Naval History Division, 1959) viewed at www.ibiblio.org.

Gawne, Jonathan, *Spearheading D-Day: American Special Units in Normandy* (Paris: Histoire & Collections, 2001).

Herman, Arthur, *Freedom's Forge. How American Business Produced Victory in World War II* (New York: Random House, 2012).

Holborn, Andrew, 'The Role of 56th (Independent) Infantry Brigade During the Normandy Campaign June–September 1944' (PhD Thesis, University of Plymouth, 2009). Accessed at pearl.plymouth.ac.uk/handle/10026.1/1996.

Holland, James, *Brothers in Arms: One Legendary Tank Regiment's Bloody War from D-Day to VE-Day* (London: Penguin Random House, 2021).

Hugill, John Antony Crawford, *The Hazard Mesh* (London: Hurst & Blackett, 1946).

Jarman, W.D. 'Jim', *Those Wallowing Beauties: The Story of the Landing Barges in World War II* (Lewes: Book Guild, 1997).

Jary, Christopher, et al., *D-Day Spearhead Brigade: The Hampshires, Dorsets and Devons on 6th June 1944* (Bristol: Semper Fidelis, 2019).

Kenyon, David, *Bletchley Park and D-Day: The Untold Story of How the Battle of Normandy was Won* (London: Yale University Press, 2019).

Kepher, Stephen C., *COSSAC: Lt Gen Sir Frederick Morgan and the Genesis of Operation Overlord* (Anapolis, MD: Naval Institute Press, 2020).

Kilvert-Jones, Tim, *Normandy: Omaha Beach: V Corps Battle for the Beachhead*, Battleground Europe series (Barnsley: Leo Cooper, 1999).

Kilvert-Jones, Tim, *Normandy: Sword Beach: 3rd British Infantry Division's Battle for the Normandy Beachhead 6th June–10th June 1944*, Battleground Europe series (Barnsley: Leo Cooper, 2001).

Ladd, J.D., *Assault from the Sea 1939–45: The Craft, the Landings, the Men* (London: David & Charles, 1976).

Lavery, Brian, *Assault Landing Craft: Design, Construction and Operations* (Barnsley: Seaforth, 2009).

Lee, David, *Beachhead Assault: The Story of the Royal Naval Commandos in World War II* (London: Greenhill, 2004).

Lefebvre, Laurent, *They Were on Omaha Beach: 194 Eyewitnesses* (Chatenay-Malabry: Laurent Lefebvre, 2003).

Leighton, Richard, & Robert Coakley, *Global Logistics and Strategy 1943–1945* (Washington DC: Center of Military History, 1989) downloaded from US Army Center of Military History (history.army.mil).

Lewis, Adrian, *Omaha Beach: A Flawed Victory* (London: University of North Carolina, 2001).

Liddle, Peter, *D-Day by Those Who Were There* (Barnsley: Pen & Sword, 2004).

Lindberg, Michael, & Daniel Todd, *Anglo-American Shipbuilding in World War II: A Geographical Perspective* (Westport, CT: Praeger, 2004).

Lorelli, John A., *To Foreign Shores: U.S. Amphibious Operations in World War II* (Anapolis, MD: Naval Institute Press, 1995).

Lund, Paul, & Harry Ludlam, *The War of the Landing Craft* (London: W. Foulsham, 1976).

Macdermott, Brian, *Ships Without Names: The Story of the Royal Navy's Tank Landing Ships of World War Two* (London: Arms & Armour, 1992).

McGee, William L., *The Amphibians Are Coming! Emergence of the 'Gator Navy and its Revolutionary Landing Craft* (Santa Barbara, CA: 2000).

McManus, John C., *The Dead and Those Who are About to Die: The Big Red One at Omaha Beach* (New York: Caliber, 2014).

Miller, Russell, *Nothing Less Than Victory: An Oral History of D-Day* (London: Michael Joseph, 1993).

Moore, George, *Building for Victory: The Warships Building Programmes of the Royal Navy 1939–1945* (Kendal: World Ship Society, 2003).

Mowry, George, *Landing Craft and the War Production Board, April 1942 to May 1944, Historical Reports on War Administration: War Production Board, Special Study No.11* (Washington DC: Civilian Production Administration, 1944) via books.google.com

Napier, Stephen, *The Armoured Campaign in Normandy, June–August 1944* (Stroud: History Press, 2017).

O'Brien, Phillips Payson, *How the War was Won* (Cambridge: Cambridge University Press, 2015)

Palmer Jr, William H.P., *We Called Ourselves Rocketboatmen* (GoToPublish, 2018).

Postan, Michael M., *British War Production* (London: HMSO, 1952) viewed at www.ibiblio.org

Pritchard, James, *A Bridge of Ships: Canadian Shipbuilding During the Second World War* (Montreal: McGill-Queen's University Press, 2011).

Ramsey, Winston G. (ed.), *D-Day Then and Now, Vols 1 & 2* (London: After the Battle, 1995).

Roberts, Charles C., *The Boat that Won the War: An Illustrated History of the Higgins LCVP* (Barnsley: Seaforth, 2017).

Roskill, Stephen W., *The War at Sea, Volume III: The Offensive, Part II: 1 June 1944– 14 August 1945* (London: HMSO, 1961).

Rottman, Gordon L., *Landing Ship, Tank (LST) 1942–2002*, New Vanguard Series, *115* (Oxford: Osprey, 2005).

Rottman, Gordon L., *Landing Craft, Infantry and Fire Support*, New Vanguard Series, *157* (Oxford: Osprey, 2009).

Royal Canadian Navy Historical Section, *The RCN's Part in the Invasion of France* (London: Royal Canadian Navy, 1945) from navsource.org/archives/10/15/15000002.htm (accessed 16/2/2021).

Saunders, Tim, *Normandy: Gold Beach. Jig Sector and West*, Battleground Europe Series (Barnsley: Leo Cooper, 2002).

Shilleto, Carl, *Normandy: Utah Beach, St Mère Eglise*, Battleground Europe Series (Barnsley: Leo Cooper, 2001).

Stoler, Mark A., *Allies in War: Britain and America Against the Axis, 1940–1945* (London: Hodder, 2005)

Symonds, Craig, *Neptune: The Allied Invasion of Europe and the D-Day Landings* (Oxford: Oxford University Press, 2014).

Todman, Dan, *Britain's War: Into Battle 1937–1941* (London: Penguin Random House, 2016).

Todman, Dan, *Britain's War. A New World 1942–1947* (London: Penguin Random House, 2020).

Townend, Will, & Frank Baldwin, *Gunners in Normandy: The History of the Royal Artillery in North-West Europe January 1942 to August 1944* (Cheltenham: History Press, 2020).

Trew, Simon, *Gold Beach (Battlezone Normandy)* (Stroud: Sutton, 2004).

United States Coast Guard, *The Coast Guard at War: Landings in France, XI* (US Coast Guard Headquarters, 1946) downloaded from history-uscg-mil

United States Fleet, *Amphibious Operations: Invasion of Northern France* (COMINCH P-006) (Washington DC: Navy Department, 1944). Accessed via US Naval Academy Library at usna.edu/Library.

USS LCI National Association, *USS LCI*, Vol. I (Paducah, KY: Turner Publishing, 1993).

Williams, Greg H., *The US Navy at Normandy: Fleet Organization and Operations in the D-Day Invasion* (Jefferson, NC: McFarland, 2020).

Winser, John de S., *The D-Day Ships* (Kendal: World Ship Society, 1994).

Winter, Paul, *D-Day Documents* (London: Bloomsbury, 2014).

Witter, Robert E., *Small Boats and Large Slow Targets: Oral Histories of United States Amphibious Forces Personnel in WWII* (Missoula, MT: Pictorial Histories, 1998).

Yung, Christopher D., *Gators of Neptune: Naval Amphibious Planning for the Normandy Invasion* (Anapolis, MD: Naval Institute Press, 2006).

Zaloga, Steven, *The Devil's Garden: Rommel's Desperate Defense of Omaha Beach on D-Day* (Mechanicsburg, PA: Stackpole, 2013).

Zuehlke, Mark, *Juno Beach: Canada's D-Day Victory, June 6, 1944* (Vancouver: Douglas & McIntyre, 2004).

ARCHIVAL REFERENCES
(REFERRED TO IN NOTES BY THEIR ABBREVIATIONS)

RAN: Royal Australian Navy website, World War II Naval Staff Histories

(From www.navy.gov.au/media-room/publications/wwii-naval-staff-histories, accessed 27/06/2022).

Admiralty, *Battle Summary No.39, Operation 'Neptune'. Landings in Normandy. June, 1944. CB.3081.* (1947)

CARL: Ike Skelton Combined Arms Reference Library at the US Army Command and General Staff College, USA

(From cgsc.contentdm.oclc.org/digital, accessed 31/12/2022).

'70th Tank Battalion, "*Soixante-Dix*": A History of the 70th Tank Battalion, 1940–1945'.

N2146.40-3: 'Armor in Operation Neptune (establishment of the Normandy Beachhead)'. Fort Knox, KY: The Armored School.

N7370-B, Operation Overlord. Appendices to COSSAC plan.

N7374-A: Annexes 22–26, 'First Army Operations Plan, Neptune: Mounting' (25 February 1944).

N7379: Amendment No.3, 'Neptune: Initial Joint Plan' (NJC 1004, dated 1 February 1944).

N16117-A: Mulberry B. D +4–D +147, 10 June to 31 October.
N16117-B: Cherbourg. D +20–D+177, 26 June to 30 November.

DDS: The D-Day Story, Portsmouth, UK

(Documents within larger collections are described individually in the notes.)

1990/167: Commander Task Force 122, 'Neptune Monograph', April 1944.
1990/1308: Allied Naval Commander-in-Chief Expeditionary Force, 'Operation Neptune Orders' (short title: ON) 10 April 1944.
1990/1314/2: Commander Force J, 'Operation "Neptune": Force "J" Naval Operation Orders', 19 May 1944.
1992/275: Rupert Curtis collection.
1995/72: H.A. Redburn collection.
1995/100: Russell Miller collection (includes copies of some originals held at the Eisenhower Center, New Orleans, and at the US National Archive).
2001/1536: Frank and Joan Shaw collection.
2005/1412: Anon, 'A Wren's Eye View by Two Slant O' (1945).
2010/19: Menu of LST 522 for week beginning 5 June 1944.
2005/852: '*Erkennungstafel Landungsboote Feindmächte*' (German Landing Craft Recognition Manual).
2005/1376: Commander Force G, '*Force G Orders for Operation Neptune*' (short title: ONEAST/G).
2014/58, 2014/59, 2014/60: LST and Landing Craft Association collection.
2022/82, *American Steel Dredge Company Inc, 'Packing and Shipping Instructions: Design 349B, Bolted Section Steel Barges for Gasoline and Dry Cargo'* (1943).

DHH: Directorate of History and Heritage, Canada

81-520-1000, Box 11, Landing Craft.
81-520-1250, Boxes 72 & 79, Training.
81-520-8000, Boxes 263–65, HMCS *Prince David*, HMCS *Prince Henry*.
81-520-8000, Box 317, Landing Craft.
8000-411, LCA and LCI(L) Flotillas.

DND: Department of National Defense, Canada

(Accessed 3/4/2021.)
Army Headquarters Reports downloaded from www.canada.ca/en/department-national-defence/services/military-history/history-heritage/official-military-history-lineages/reports/army-headquarters-1948-1959.html.

Steiger, A.G., 'The Campaign in North-West Europe: Information from German Sources, Part 1: German defence preparations in the West', AHQ Report 40 (1951).
Corry, G.D., 'The German Defences in the Courseulles – St Aubin Area of the Normandy Coast', AHQ Report 41 (1950).

Hunter, T.M., 'Preliminary Planning for Operation "Overlord"' AHQ Report 42 (1952).

Roy, Reginald H., 'Canadian Participation in the Operations in North-West Europe, 1944, Part 1: The Assault and Subsequent Operations of 3 Canadian Inf Div and 2 Canadian Armed Bde 6–30 June 44', AHQ Report 54 (1952).

Canadian Military Headquarters Reports downloaded from www.canada.ca/en/department-national-defence/services/military-history/history-heritage/official-military-history-lineages/reports/military-headquarters-1940-1948.html.

Graham, G.S., 'OPERATION "OVERLORD" and its Sequel: Canadian Participation in the Operations in North-West Europe, 6 June–31 July 1944 (Preliminary Report)', CMHQ Report 131 (1945).

Fold3: US National Archives

(Accessed via Fold3.com.) All are US Navy units unless stated.

Reports, War Diaries of PC (Patrol Craft): 484, 552, 564, 568, 617, 618.

Reports, War Diaries of SC (Submarine Chaser): 1232, 1252, 1307, 1330.

Reports, Commander, Task Group/Unit: COMTASK-GROUP 124.4 (SS *Empire Javelin*); COMTASK-GROUP 125.5; COMTASK-GROUP 125.10; COMTASK-UNIT 125.5.1; COMTASK-UNIT 125.5.3; COMTASK-UNIT 125.7.1.

Reports, War Diaries, War Histories of landing ships: HMS *Prince Baudouin*★; Commander Assault Group 4/HMS *Prince Charles*★ (including ML 304); HMS *Prince Leopold*★; SS *Empire Javelin*; USS *Anne Arundel*; USS *Barnett*; USS *Bayfield*; USS *Charles Carroll*; USS *Dorothea L. Dix*; USS *Henrico*; USS *Joseph T. Dickman*; USS *Samuel Chase*; USS *Thomas Jefferson*; USS *Thurston*. (★ Royal Navy ships.)

Reports, LCI(L)s and LCHs: 3, 4, 5, 8, 9, 83, 91, 92, 95, 96, 229, 231, 319, 321, 322, 323, 324, 325, 326, 349, 350, 401, 419, 490, 491, 492, 494, 495, 496, 497, 499, 513, 527, 528, 537, 551, 552.

Reports/War Diaries, LCI(L) Flotillas: 11, 12.

Reports, LCI(L) Groups: 28, 31, 32, 33, 34.

Reports, LCM Flotilla 2.

Reports, LCTs and LCT(A)s: 7, 18, 22, 25, 80, 147, 149, 195, 199, 201, 202, 207, 209, 210, 214, 244, 271, 276, 293, 415, 431, 434, 460, 644, 645, 646, 647, 648, 649, 651, 652, 653, 715, 857, 2008, 2037, 2043, 2049, 2050, 2075, 2124, 2227, 2239, 2273, 2275, 2282, 2297, 2307, 2310, 2402, 2487.

Reports, LCT Groups: 55, 56.

Reports, LCT Flotillas: 18, 19.

Reports, War Diaries, War Histories of LSTs: 1, 2, 17, 21, 25, 30, 51, 52, 57, 75, 133, 229, 279, 280, 286, 287, 309, 312, 344, 345, 360, 373, 377, 378, 379, 503, 520.

Reports, War Diaries of LST Groups: 11, 12, 29, 30, 31, 32, 33, 34, 35, 36, 49, 50, 51, 52.

War diaries, LST Flotillas: 4, 10, 12, 17, 18.

Other US Navy Documents

CinC Atlantic Fleet, Administrative History.

Commander, Force O, Action Report, Assault on Colleville-Vierville.
Commander, 11th PHIBFOR (11th Amphibious Force) War Diary, January–June 1944.
Commander, 11th PHIBFOR, Report by Commander Force O on Operations, June 1944.
Commander, 11th PHIBFOR, Report USCG Rescue Flotilla 1.
COMLANCRAB (Commander, Landing Craft Bases), 11th PHIBFOR.
COMPHIBBASES (Commander, Amphibious Bases), UK.
Commander, Task Force 127, Report on Operations, June 1944.
Commander, Task Group 126.4 (LST Flotilla 18).
Commander, Transports, 11th PHIBFOR.
Commander, Gunfire Support Craft, Force O.
Commander, Task Group 124.3 (Assault Group O1).
Commander, Task Group 124.4 (Assault Group O2).
Commander, Group 2, 11th PHIBFOR, War Diary.
Commander, Task Force 122 (Western Task Force).
Commander, Task Unit 125.4.6.
Commander, Task Unit 125.5.3.
Commander, Task Unit 125.2.3, Naval Combat Demolition Units.
Commander, Task Unit 125.7.1.
US Naval Advanced Amphibious Base, Southampton, War Diary, June 1944.
US Naval Advanced Base 11, Omaha.
US Naval Advanced Base 12, Utah.
Naval Combat Demolition Units, Force O.
Operation Neptune, Naval Operational Orders (short title: ON) 10 April 1944.
Operation Neptune, Engineer Combat Battalions, Reports.
CB 04385A, Report by the Allied Naval Commander-in-Chief Expeditionary Force on Operation Neptune, Vol. 1.
USS *Bannock*, War Diary.

US Army Documents

1st Engineer Special Brigade, Notes, Utah Beach.
1st Army, Report on Operation Neptune.
Transportation Corps, 'Invasion: The History of the Transportation Corps in the European Theater of Operations', Vol. III, April–June 1944.
US Assault Training Center, Training Schedules.
US Army Corps of Engineers, Historical Report: European Theater of Operations.
US Army Corps of Engineers, Chronology of Events.

Other Documents

Trident Conference, Washington, May 1943: Papers and Minutes of Meetings.

HC: Héritage Canadiana

War Diaries at heritage.canadiana.ca (accessed 10/10/2022).
T-7620: 8th Canadian Infantry Brigade.

LOC: Library of Congress

John William Boehne III Collection, AFC/2001/001/31844: Veterans History Project.

TNA: The National Archives, UK

Files are referenced in the notes only under their TNA reference number. (Not listed: selected British and Canadian Army War Diaries were also consulted.)

ADM 1/13192: Fuel and Water Supply Arrangements for Landing Craft During Operation Overlord.

ADM 1/15631: First Lord's Weekly Reports to Prime Minister on Condition and Whereabouts of LCTs Used in Operation Overlord.

ADM 1/17022: Discussions on Landing Craft Production Situation with Regard to Operation Overlord.

ADM 1/17813: Embarkation Hards for Landing Craft and Ships: Design Requirements, Construction, Approaches and Site Code Letters.

ADM 116/4760: Technical History of Landing Craft, Tank (Rocket).

ADM 116/4852: Landing Craft: Future Construction Programme, 1943.

ADM 179/405: Operation Neptune: Eastern Task Force Naval Plan.

ADM 179/458: Allocation of Ships and Craft of Western Task Force.

ADM 179/472: Details of Sailing Programme of Assault Forces for Operation Neptune.

ADM 179/506: Operation Neptune: Report of Proceedings of Force J.

ADM 179/507: Operation Neptune: Reports of Proceedings not Included Elsewhere.

ADM 179/508: Operation Overlord: Report on Part Played by Landing Craft Bases, Portsmouth Command.

ADM 179/516: Operation Neptune: Report of Naval Commander Eastern Task Force, Relating to Proceedings.

ADM 199/1559: Eastern Task Forces – Force J: Orders and Memoranda.

ADM 199/1560: Eastern Task Forces – Force L: Orders and Memoranda.

ADM 199/1563: Western Task Force: Operation Plans, Orders, etc.

ADM 199/1565: Western Task Force: Operational Orders etc.

ADM 199/1566: Western Task Force: Operation Plan and Orders.

ADM 199/1567: Western Task Force: Operation Orders.

ADM 199/1568: Western Task Force: Operation Orders, Instructions, etc.

ADM 199/1570: Western Task Force: Operation Orders.

ADM 199/1644: Operation Neptune: Landings, Engagements, Actions, etc: Reports.

ADM 199/1645: Operation Neptune: Landings, Engagements, Actions, etc: Reports.

ADM 199/1650: HM Ships and Vessels Lost: Survivors' Interrogation Reports, etc.

ADM 199/1651: HM Ships and Vessels Lost: Survivors' Interrogation Reports, etc.

ADM 202/448: Training losses, Observations and Conclusions (Landing Craft Reports).

ADM 202/449: Normandy Area (Landing Craft Reports).

ADM 210/8: Lists of Landing Ships, Craft and Barges, June–July 1944 (Green List).

ADM 210/9: Lists of Landing Ships, Craft and Barges, August–September 1944 (Green List).

ADM 229/31: Reports, Director of Naval Construction, August–October 1943.

ADM 229/32: Reports, Director of Naval Construction, October 1943–January 1944.

ADM 239/242: Development of Landing Ships and Craft.

ADM 239/354: Details of Combined Operations Major and Minor Landing Craft, Landing Barges, Small Boats and Amphibians.

AIR 20/5017: Combined Operations: Landing Craft, 1943.

AIR 20/5019: Combined Operations: Landing Craft, 1943–44.

AIR 20/5020: Combined Operations: Landing Craft, 1944.

AIR 20/5021: Combined Operations: Landing Craft, 1944.

AIR 20/5023: Combined Operations: Landing Craft, 1945–50.

AIR 9/299: Mediterranean: Landing Craft Problems.

AIR 9/418: Landing Ships and Craft: Loading Capacities.

AN 2/6: Landing Craft, Eastleigh Works, 1940–42 (Railway Executive Committee).

BT 87/123: Production of Landing Craft, 1943–44 (Ministry of Production).

CAB 102/539: Memorandum on Naval Production, 1939–45, with special reference to landing craft.

DEFE 2/1114: Landing Ships and Craft: Requirements and Production, 1943–45.

DEFE 2/1165: Modifications of Landing Craft for Use in Surf: Investigations and Reports.

DEFE 2/1327: Historical Notes on the Development of Landing Craft.

DEFE 2/1328: Proposals Regarding the Writing of a History of Combined Operations.

DEFE 2/1430: Training and Drafting of Landing Craft Officers and Ratings other than LCTs.

DEFE 2/1917: USA Chief of Combined Operations Representative Bulletins, No.28 (April 1944).

DEFE 2/416: Report by Naval Commander, Force G.

DEFE 2/417: Report by Naval Commander, Force G.

DEFE 2/419: Report by Naval Commander, Force S.

DEFE 2/420: Report by Naval Commander, Force S.

DEFE 2/426: Admiralty Summary of Lessons Learned in Operation Overlord.

DEFE 2/427: Admiralty Summary of Lessons Learned in Operation Overlord.

DEFE 2/433: Report of Special Observer Party Investigating the Effect of Fire Support.

DEFE 2/459: Mounting of the Operation and Availability of Forces, 1943–44.

DEFE 2/460: Availability and Manning of Landing Ships and Craft, 1943–44.

DEFE 2/489: Lessons Learned from Use of New Equipment, 1944.

DEFE 2/490: Opposition Encountered on the British Beaches in Normandy on D-Day.

DEFE 2/491: Comparison of British and American Areas in Normandy in Terms of Fire Support and its Effects.

DEFE 2/527: Operation Rankin, 1943–44.

DEFE 2/529: Rattle Conference, Part 1, 1943.

DEFE 2/696: Notes for Compilation of Narrative of the Development of the Combined Operations Organisation, 1940–45.

DEFE 2/716: Establishments, Units, Ships, etc: Monthly Progress Reports, 1941–44.

DEFE 2/733: Combined Operations Headquarters: Monthly Information Summaries, Vol. 1, 1942–43.

DEFE 2/734: Combined Operations Headquarters: Monthly Information Summaries, Vol. 2, 1943–44.

DEFE 2/735: Combined Operations Headquarters: Monthly Information Summaries, Vol. 3, 1944–45.

DEFE 2/736: Experimental Establishments: Trials Reports, 1942–44.

DEFE 2/780: Histories and Accounts of Chief of Combined Operations Representative Washington.

WO 193/395: Landing Craft and Combined Training, 1943–44.

WO 193/396: Landing Craft and Combined Training, 1944–45.

WO 193/488: Landing Craft: Production and Requirements, 1943.

WO 193/489: Landing Craft: Production and Requirements, 1944–45.

WO 199/1213: Operation Overlord, Hants Sub-District Instructions, 1943.

WO 199/1372: Operation Neptune, Outline Movement Plan.

WO 219/3075: Operation Neptune, Landing Tables: British 3rd Infantry Division Group, First Tide.

WO 219/3076: Operation Neptune, Landing Tables: British 7th Armoured Division, Second and Third Tide; British 3rd Infantry Division Second Tide.

WO 219/3077: Operation Neptune, Landing Tables: British 56th, 69th, 151st and 231st Infantry Brigades; British 4th Special Service Brigade; British 51st Highland Division.

WO 219/3082: Operation Overlord: Availability and Allocation of Landing Craft.

WO 291/1028: Value of Protective Armour for Landing Craft Assault.

US Army War College

Summary report of conversations with General Charles H. Bonesteel III, USA Retired.

Oral History

Eisenhower Library: General Ray Barker.

Imperial War Museum: IWM 20164, interview with Lilly Errington.

The D-Day Story, Portsmouth: 2021/80, Ron Smith.

United States Coast Guard website (accessed 10/3/2023): Martin J. Perrett, history. uscg.mil/Our-Collections/Oral-Histories-Memoirs/Marvin-Perrett/

University of Southern Indiana, Archives and Special Collections (accessed 26/04/2023): Edward Klingler (OH 0035), Manson Reichert (OH 0047), John Koch Jr. (OH 0050), digitalarchives.usi.edu/digital/collection/p17218coll1.

Websites

Landing tables: 6juin1944.com.

combinedops.com.

Commonwealth War Graves Commission: cwgc.org/find-records/find-war-dead/.

honorstates.org.

LCT Flotillas of WWII: ww2lct.org.

US National D-Day Memorial Necrology Project: dday.org/learn/necrology-project/.

naval-history.net: Including US Navy casualty lists.

USS Landing Craft Infantry National Association newsletter, *Elsie Item*: usslci.org/archives.

WW2Talk.com, thread on Utah Beach by Mike ('Trux'): ww2talk.com/index. php?threads/utah-beach-d-day.82917/ (accessed 19/3/2021).

WW2Talk.com, thread on Juno Beach by Mike ('Trux'): ww2talk.com/index. php?threads/omaha-beach.69555/ (accessed 19/3/2021).

WW2Talk.com, thread on Gold Beach by Mike ('Trux'): ww2talk.com/index. php?threads/gold-beach.56252/ (accessed 19/3/2021).

WW2Talk.com, thread on Juno Beach by Mike ('Trux'): ww2talk.com/index. php?threads/juno-beach.51316/ (accessed 19/3/2021).

WW2Talk.com, Force J landing table spreadsheet by Michel Sabarly: ww2talk. com/index.php?resources/landing-table-3-canadian-infantry-division-brigade-groups.102/ (accessed 19/3/2021).

WW2Talk.com, thread on Sword Beach by Mike ('Trux'): ww2talk.com/index. php?threads/sword-beach.38764/page-4 (accessed 19/3/2021).

WW2Talk.com, Force S landing table spreadsheet by Michel Sabarly: ww2talk.com/ index.php?resources/landing-table-3-british-infantry-division-group-first-tide.39/ (accessed 19/3/2021).

WW2Talk.com, thread on Force L by Mike ('Trux'): ww2talk.com/index. php?threads/naval-force-l.52958/ (accessed 19/3/2021).

Index of Landing Craft

Only major landing craft and LSTs are indexed here. Minor landing craft and landing barges are indexed under unit only (e.g. flotilla). Individual landing craft are not indexed in the Order of Battle section, but units such as flotillas are.

LCF
LCF 1: 359
LCF 3: 411n7
LCF 5: 411n7
LCF 6: 411n7
LCF 7: 411n7
LCF 9: 411n7
LCF 11: 411n7
LCF 12: 411n7
LCF 18: 154
LCF 19: 420n8
LCF 20: 420n8
LCF 21: 154, 284
LCF 22: 154
LCF 24: 118, 294, 353
LCF 25: 247, 420n8
LCF 26: 247, 420n8
LCF 27: 154
LCF 29: 294
LCF 31: 154, 164, 177
LCF 32: 284
LCF 34: 329
LCF 35: 420n8
LCF 36: 247, 420n8
LCF 38: 247, 420n8
LCF 42: 324–5
LCG(L)
LCG(L) 1: 248, 252, 256, 420n8
LCG(L) 2: 232, 248, 252, 420n8
LCG(L) 3: 248, 252, 420n8
LCG(L) 5: 154, 165
LCG(L) 6: 154, 165
LCG(L) 7: 154, 165

LCG(L) 9: 320–1
LCG(L) 10: 320
LCG(L) 11: 320
LCG(L) 13: 251–2, 420n8
LCG(L) 17: 239, 420n8
LCG(L) 18: 239, 420n8
LCG(L) 424: 183
LCG(L) 831: 270–1, 276
LCG(L) 893: 154, 165
LCG(L) 1007: 276
LCH
LCH 10: 169
LCH 86: 218
LCH 87: 141
LCH 92: 197
LCH 100: 236
LCH 168: 426n21
LCH 185: 358–9
LCH 187: 86, 250
LCH 275: 228
LCH 414: 222
LCH 530: 169
LCI(L)
LCI(L) 3: 409n75
LCI(L) 4: 409n75
LCI(L) 5: 409n75
LCI(L) 8: 409n75
LCI(L) 9: 434n81
LCI(L) 11: 170
LCI(L) 12: 434n81
LCI(L) 13: 434n81
LCI(L) 14: 434n81
LCI(L) 15: 434n81
LCI(L) 16: 434n81

LCI(L) 33: 434n81
LCI(L) 35: 434n81
LCI(L) 83: 211–2
LCI(L) 84: 212
LCI(L) 85: 179, 210–1, 306
LCI(L) 88: 206
LCI(L) 89: 210–1, 224
LCI(L) 90: 196–7, 224
LCI(L) 91: 196–7
LCI(L) 93: 215–6
LCI(L) 94: 117, 196
LCI(L) 96: 409n71
LCI(L) 105: 358
LCI(L) 111: 86, 343–4
LCI(L) 115: 429n76
LCI(L) 117: 291
LCI(L) 118: 429n76
LCI(L) 121: 290
LCI(L) 125: 429n76
LCI(L) 126: 342
LCI(L) 130: 332, 334
LCI(L) 131: 332, 334–5
LCI(L) 134: 435n100
LCI(L) 135: 429n76
LCI(L) 164: 433n75
LCI(L) 165: 433n75
LCI(L) 169: 433n75
LCI(L) 171: 433n75
LCI(L) 174: 343
LCI(L) 175: 434n81
LCI(L) 177: 91, 292
LCI(L) 179: 342
LCI(L) 180: 435n100
LCI(L) 181: 433n75
LCI(L) 183: 332, 334

LCI(L) 193: 434n81
LCI(L) 211: 171
LCI(L) 212: 409n71
LCI(L) 213: 409n71
LCI(L) 214: 171
LCI(L) 215: 409n71
LCI(L) 216: 171
LCI(L) 217: 170
LCI(L) 218: 170
LCI(L) 219: 409n71
LCI(L) 232: 171, 177
LCI(L) 238: 434n81
LCI(L) 241: 435n100
LCI(L) 249: 290
LCI(L) 250: 429n76
LCI(L) 252: 300, 429n76
LCI(L) 255: 259
LCI(L) 262: 429n76
LCI(L) 263: 429n76
LCI(L) 270: 429n76
LCI(L) 276: 300, 429n76
LCI(L) 270: 295–6
LCI(L) 285: 293
LCI(L) 288: 424n98
LCI(L) 295: 424n98
LCI(L) 298: 290
LCI(L) 299: 290, 304
LCI(L) 300: 341
LCI(L) 301: 290
LCI(L) 302: 424n98
LCI(L) 305: 424n98
LCI(L) 306: 429n76
LCI(L) 310: 424n98
LCI(L) 311: 424n98
LCI(L) 319: 170
LCI(L) 320: 170

LCI(L) 321: 170
LCI(L) 322: 170
LCI(L) 323: 170
LCI(L) 324: 409n71
LCI(L) 325: 410n84
LCI(L) 326: 410n84
LCI(L) 349: 410n84
LCI(L) 350: 410n84
LCI(L) 374: 435n100
LCI(L) 375: 346
LCI(L) 376: 434n88
LCI(L) 377: 433n75
LCI(L) 378: 433n75
LCI(L) 379: 433n75
LCI(L) 380: 433n75
LCI(L) 381: 435n100
LCI(L) 382: 435n100
LCI(L) 383: 350
LCI(L) 385: 434n88
LCI(L) 386: 435n100
LCI(L) 387: 346–7
LCI(L) 388: 434n88
LCI(L) 389: 434n88
LCI(L) 390: 434n88
LCI(L) 391: 434n88
LCI(L) 400: 424n98
LCI(L) 401: 419n109
LCI(L) 403: 419n109
LCI(L) 408: 217
LCI(L) 409: 418n99
LCI(L) 410: 418n99
LCI(L) 411: 218
LCI(L) 412: 418n99
LCI(L) 415: 90–1, 222–3
LCI(L) 416: 223
LCI(L) 417: 419n109
LCI(L) 418: 419n109
LCI(L) 420: 419n109
LCI(L) 421: 424n98
LCI(L) 487: 215
LCI(L) 488: 141, 418n94
LCI(L) 490: 418n94
LCI(L) 492: 224
LCI(L) 493: 206, 214–5
LCI(L) 494: 418n94
LCI(L) 495: 418n94
LCI(L) 496: 418n94
LCI(L) 497: 216
LCI(L) 498: 418n94
LCI(L) 413: 418n99
LCI(L) 511: 424n98
LCI(L) 513: 409n71
LCI(L) 514: 409n71
LCI(L) 516: 409n75
LCI(L) 517: 409n71
LCI(L) 521: 409n75
LCI(L) 522: 409n75
LCI(L) 523: 409n75
LCI(L) 524: 410n84
LCI(L) 525: 409n71
LCI(L) 527: 410n84
LCI(L) 528: 410n84
LCI(L) 529: 410n84
LCI(L) 537: 222

LCI(L) 538: 419n109
LCI(L) 539: 419n109
LCI(L) 540: 418n99
LCI(L) 541: 418n99
LCI(L) 542: 419n109
LCI(L) 551: 410n84
LCI(L) 552: 175
LCI(L) 553: 218
LCI(L) 554: 418n99
LCI(L) 555: 418n99
LCI(L) 556: 419n109
LCI(L) 557: 418n99

LCI(S)
LCI(S) 501: 339
LCI(S) 505: 315, 337
LCI(S) 506: 337–8
LCI(S) 508: 334
LCI(S) 509: 338–9, 342
LCI(S) 510: 334
LCI(S) 512: 339
LCI(S) 516: 334, 337, 339
LCI(S) 517: 339
LCI(S) 518: 339
LCI(S) 519: 17, 315, 337
LCI(S) 521: 337
LCI(S) 523: 328–9, 336–7
LCI(S) 524: 315, 338, 341
LCI(S) 525: 288, 315
LCI(S) 526: 290
LCI(S) 527: 328–9, 336–7
LCI(S) 528: 339
LCI(S) 531: 337–8
LCI(S) 535: 317, 338–40
LCI(S) 536: 290
LCI(S) 539: 289

LCS(L)
LCS(L) 251: 236, 238
LCS(L) 253: 321
LCS(L) 256: 321
LCS(L) 257: 289
LCS(L) 258: 251–2, 256
LCS(L) 259: 230, 232, 252, 256
LCS(L) 260: 321

LCT(3) and LCT(3★)
LCT(3) 302: 296
LCT(3) 303: 426n21
LCT(3) 306: 275
LCT(3) 311: 426n21
LCT(3) 317: 284
LCT(3) 323: 91
LCT(3) 354: 121, 284
LCT(3) 372: 358, 426n21
LCT(3) 390: 358
LCT(3) 413: 296
LCT(3) 422: 426n21
LCT(3) 441: 426n21
LCT(3) 442: 241
LCT(3) 443: 430n3

LCT(3) 444: 430n3
LCT(3) 455: 430n3
LCT(3) 456: 430n3
LCT(3) 461: 430n3
LCT(3) 465: 327, 430n3
LCT(3) 467: 326, 430n3
LCT(3) 474: 296
LCT(3) 7010: 426n21
LCT(3) 7011: 296
LCT(3) 7069: 60
LCT(3) 7070: 90–1, 131
LCT(3) 7073: 118
LCT(3) 7074: 264, 360
LCT(3) 7086: 85

LCT(4)
LCT(4) 500: 290
LCT(4) 501: 428n67
LCT(4) 507: 281
LCT(4) 508: 428n64
LCT(4) 509: 428n64
LCT(4) 510: 428n64
LCT(4) 514: 428n64
LCT(4) 516: 428n66
LCT(4) 518: 428n67
LCT(4) 524: 291
LCT(4) 525: 428n66
LCT(4) 526: 428n67
LCT(4) 528: 292
LCT(4) 529: 428n67
LCT(4) 530: 428n66
LCT(4) 531: 429n72
LCT(4) 532: 336, 430n8
LCT(4) 534: 429n72
LCT(4) 539: 434n92
LCT(4) 544: 430n8
LCT(4) 546: 422n56
LCT(4) 555: 244
LCT(4) 562: 219
LCT(4) 564: 258
LCT(4) 565: 258–9
LCT(4) 569: 428n64
LCT(4) 571: 422n56
LCT(4) 574: 292
LCT(4) 575: 292
LCT(4) 576: 244
LCT(4) 577: 422n56
LCT(4) 593: 340, 430n8
LCT(4) 597: 340, 430n8
LCT(4) 600: 400n14
LCT(4) 602: 428n67
LCT(4) 604: 422n56
LCT(4) 608: 358
LCT(4) 609: 434n92
LCT(4) 610: 147–8, 332
LCT(4) 611: 434n92
LCT(4) 612: 434n92
LCT(4) 627: 434n93
LCT(4) 628: 219
LCT(4) 629: 429n69
LCT(4) 632: 429n79
LCT(4) 634: 429n79
LCT(4) 635: 422n56
LCT(4) 636: 429n79

LCT(4) 637: 428n66
LCT(4) 639: 429n79
LCT(4) 641: 434n79
LCT(4) 647: 104, 421n23
LCT(4) 649: 434n79
LCT(4) 650: 434n79
LCT(4) 665: 430n8
LCT(4) 667: 429n79
LCT(4) 668: 434n79
LCT(4) 669: 429n79
LCT(4) 670: 429n79
LCT(4) 674: 434n93
LCT(4) 675: 434n92
LCT(4) 677: 290
LCT(4) 679: 429n79
LCT(4) 684: 256
LCT(4) 685: 430n8
LCT(4) 700: 429n79
LCT(4) 706: 429n69
LCT(4) 707: 291–2
LCT(4) 708: 231
LCT(4) 709: 428n64
LCT(4) 711: 424n97
LCT(4) 716: 428n66
LCT(4) 717: 292
LCT(4) 721: 429n79
LCT(4) 748: 434n79
LCT(4) 749: 236
LCT(4) 750: 336, 430n8
LCT(4) 752: 434n79
LCT(4) 759: 429n79
LCT(4) 761: 296
LCT(4) 767: 428n67
LCT(4) 768: 429n72
LCT(4) 770: 293
LCT(4) 781: 296, 429n69
LCT(4) 782: 291
LCT(4) 784: 430n8
LCT(4) 786: 430n8
LCT(4) 787: 434n92
LCT(4) 788: 434n92
LCT(4) 789: 148
LCT(4) 794: 173
LCT(4) 795: 173
LCT(4) 804: 119, 428n67
LCT(4) 805: 421n23
LCT(4) 807: 421n23
LCT(4) 808: 119, 235
LCT(4) 809: 118
LCT(4) 814: 430n8
LCT(4) 821: 92, 344–5
LCT(4) 826: 430n8
LCT(4) 827: 430n8
LCT(4) 851: 434n92
LCT(4) 852: 434n92
LCT(4) 854: 332
LCT(4) 855: 428n66
LCT(4) 858: 305
LCT(4) 859: 342–3, 430n8
LCT(4) 860: 430n8

LCT(4) 861: 430n8
LCT(4) 864: 434n92
LCT(4) 875: 358
LCT(4) 876: 429n69
LCT(4) 879: 231
LCT(4) 881: 291
LCT(4) 882: 291
LCT(4) 885: 428n66
LCT(4) 886: 235–6, 261
LCT(4) 887: 430n8
LCT(4) 889: 340, 430n8
LCT(4) 892: 434n79
LCT(4) 898: 331
LCT(4) 899: 233
LCT(4) 903: 255
LCT(4) 909: 431n18,
  431n27
LCT(4) 922: 258
LCT(4) 923: 424n97
LCT(4) 924: 424n96
LCT(4) 926: 424n96
LCT(4) 933: 429n72
LCT(4) 935: 429n72
LCT(4) 936: 429n72
LCT(4) 937: 429n79
LCT(4) 938: 429n79
LCT(4) 940: 429n79
LCT(4) 941: 429n79
LCT(4) 943: 429n79
LCT(4) 944: 92, 434n93
LCT(4) 945: 332
LCT(4) 947: 324
LCT(4) 951: 431n18,
  431n27
LCT(4) 952: 434n79
LCT(4) 953: 344
LCT(4) 958: 342
LCT(4) 959: 434n79
LCT(4) 960: 434n79
LCT(4) 961: 434n79
LCT(4) 974: 119, 173,
  432n42
LCT(4) 979: 432n42
LCT(4) 980: 331
LCT(4) 981: 116,
  431n18, 431n27
LCT(4) 1003: 434n93
LCT(4) 1006: 305,
  429n79
LCT(4) 1008: 429n79
LCT(4) 1010: 431n18,
  431n27
LCT(4) 1011: 340
LCT(4) 1013: 340
LCT(4) 1015: 434n92
LCT(4) 1016: 431n18,
  431n27
LCT(4) 1017: 434n93
LCT(4) 1019: 434n93
LCT(4) 1020: 434n93
LCT(4) 1022: 434n93
LCT(4) 1023: 434n93
LCT(4) 1026: 345
LCT(4) 1027: 230

LCT(4) 1041: 422n56
LCT(4) 1046: 360
LCT(4) 1051: 430n8
LCT(4) 1065: 348
LCT(4) 1067: 434n93
LCT(4) 1068: 434n93
LCT(4) 1070: 345
LCT(4) 1079: 245–6
LCT(4) 1080: 434n92
LCT(4) 1082: 431n18,
  431n27
LCT(4) 1092: 431n18,
  431n27
LCT(4) 1093: 431n18,
  431n27
LCT(4) 1094: 431n18,
  431n27
LCT(4) 1120: 424n97
LCT(4) 1121: 424n96
LCT(4) 1122: 424n97
LCT(4) 1125: 340
LCT(4) 1162: 244
LCT(4) 1164: 244

LCT(5)
LCT(5) 3: 409n70
LCT(5) 7: 217
LCT(5) 18: 417n82
LCT(5) 20: 198, 417n82
LCT(5) 25: 210
LCT(5) 27: 70, 416n78
LCT(5) 29: 411n8
LCT(5) 30: 209–10,
  360, 416n70
LCT(5) 80: 416n78
LCT(5) 147: 209
LCT(5) 149: 20, 416n78
LCT(5) 195: 417n82
LCT(5) 197: 198, 411n8
LCT(5) 199: 210
LCT(5) 200: 417n82
LCT(5) 201: 417n82
LCT(5) 202: 217
LCT(5) 205: 416n76
LCT(5) 206: 411n8
LCT(5) 207: 198, 411n8
LCT(5) 209: 411n8,
  416n76
LCT(5) 210: 200
LCT(5) 213: 411n8,
  416n76
LCT(5) 214: 416n78
LCT(5) 244: 416n78
LCT(5) 271: 417n82
LCT(5) 276: 183, 416n76
LCT(5) 293: 411n8,
  416n76
LCT(5) 294: 209
LCT(5) 305: 417n82
LCT(5) 332: 197, 411n8
LCT(5) 362: 168
LCT(5) 364: 197–8,
  411n8
LCT(5) 413: 417n89
LCT(5) 415: 418n98

LCT(5) 431: 418n98
LCT(5) 434: 418n98
LCT(5) 443: 408n63
LCT(5) 447: 167
LCT(5) 458: 408n63
LCT(5) 459: 408n63
LCT(5) 460: 418n103
LCT(5) 474: 408n63
LCT(5) 475: 408n63
LCT(5) 476: 409n78
LCT(5) 486: 408n63
LCT(5) 489: 408n63
LCT(5) 495: 408n63
LCT(5) 497: 408n63
LCT(5) 612: 347
LCT(5) 627: 347
LCT(5) 458: 168, 177
LCT(5) 2002: 169
LCT(5) 2004: 408n66
LCT(5) 2011: 408n67
LCT(5) 2040: 409n76
LCT(5) 2045: 409n78
LCT(5) 2046: 409n78
LCT(5) 2053: 90,
  409n78
LCT(5) 2055: 409n78
LCT(5) 2056: 168
LCT(5) 2057: 168
LCT(5) 2073: 409n76
LCT(5) 2074: 408n67
LCT(5) 2079: 291
LCT(5) 2130: 136, 311
LCT(5) 2131: 409n78
LCT(5) 2135: 409n76
LCT(5) 2138: 408n67
LCT(5) 2186: 409n76
LCT(5) 2188: 408n67
LCT(5) 2226: 173–4,
  356
LCT(5) 2230: 289
LCT(5) 2231: 174
LCT(5) 2232: 289
LCT(5) 2235: 85
LCT(5) 2261: 409n78
LCT(5) 2269: 408n67
LCT(5) 2272: 408n66
LCT(5) 2302: 408n67
LCT(5) 2303: 409n78
LCT(5) 2304: 168–9
LCT(5) 2310: 408n66
LCT(5) 2331: 168–9
LCT(5) 2363: 409n78
LCT(5) 2440: 409n78
LCT(5) 2421: 409n76
LCT(5) 2423: 408n66
LCT(5) 2424: 409n76
LCT(5) 2427: 409n76
LCT(5) 2429: 408n66
LCT(5) 2437: 408n67
LCT(5) 2477: 168
LCT(5) 2483: 169
LCT(5) 2484: 409n76
LCT(5) 2485: 409n76
LCT(5) 2189: 410n81

LCT(5) 2194: 410n81
LCT(5) 2292: 410n81
LCT(5) 2297: 417n88
LCT(5) 2487: 417n86
LCT(5) 2498: 114,
  408n67

LCT(6)
LCT(6) 510: 406n35
LCT(6) 511: 408n63
LCT(6) 512: 410n79
LCT(6) 515: 409n76
LCT(6) 517: 409n76
LCT(6) 518: 409n76
LCT(6) 519: 409n76
LCT(6) 520: 409n76
LCT(6) 522: 160, 174
LCT(6) 524: 160, 174
LCT(6) 525: 409n70
LCT(6) 527: 174
LCT(6) 528: 174
LCT(6) 529: 174
LCT(6) 530: 174
LCT(6) 531: 406n35
LCT(6) 532: 409n70
LCT(6) 533: 409n70
LCT(6) 534: 409n70
LCT(6) 535: 309,
  412n15, 417n88
LCT(6) 536: 413n38
LCT(6) 537: 414n51,
  418n98
LCT(6) 538: 415n69
LCT(6) 539: 415n69
LCT(6) 540: 206
LCT(6) 541: 415n69
LCT(6) 542: 415n69
LCT(6) 543: 415n69
LCT(6) 544: 415n69
LCT(6) 545: 415n69
LCT(6) 546: 417n82
LCT(6) 547: 417n82
LCT(6) 548: 219
LCT(6) 549: 414n51,
  418n98
LCT(6) 550: 417n86
LCT(6) 554: 210
LCT(6) 570: 417n88
LCT(6) 571: 417n89
LCT(6) 572: 417n89
LCT(6) 576: 417n89
LCT(6) 580: 169
LCT(6) 583: 169, 312
LCT(6) 584: 409n78
LCT(6) 586: 412n15,
  417n88
LCT(6) 587: 412n15,
  417n88
LCT(6) 588: 412n15,
  417n88
LCT(6) 589: 412n15,
  417n88
LCT(6) 590: 186, 417n88
LCT(6) 591: 412n15,
  417n88

LCT(6) 592: 406n35
LCT(6) 593: 160–1,
177, 406n35
LCT(6) 594: 406n35
LCT(6) 595: 406n35
LCT(6) 596: 406n35
LCT(6) 597: 161, 177,
406n35
LCT(6) 598: 414n51,
418n98
LCT(6) 599: 414n51,
418n98
LCT(6) 600: 198–9,
418n98
LCT(6) 601: 414n51,
418n98
LCT(6) 602: 414n51,
418n98
LCT(6) 603: 414n51,
418n98
LCT(6) 612: 413n38
LCT(6) 613: 413n38
LCT(6) 614: 360
LCT(6) 615: 416n78
LCT(6) 616: 416n78
LCT(6) 617: 417n88
LCT(6) 618: 418n98
LCT(6) 619: 418n98
LCT(6) 620: 170
LCT(6) 621: 409n70
LCT(6) 622: 413n38
LCT(6) 623: 417n86
LCT(6) 624: 417n86
LCT(6) 625: 417n86
LCT(6) 626: 219
LCT(6) 637: 219
LCT(6) 638: 219
LCT(6) 639: 418n103
LCT(6) 640: 418n103
LCT(6) 641: 418n103
LCT(6) 645: 410n80
LCT(6) 646: 410n79
LCT(6) 651: 410n80
LCT(6) 652: 418n103
LCT(6) 653: 418n103
LCT(6) 657: 418n103
LCT(6) 662: 409n70
LCT(6) 663: 172, 389
LCT(6) 665: 419n103
LCT(6) 666: 419n103
LCT(6) 691: 410n79
LCT(6) 703: 413n38
LCT(6) 705: 195
LCT(6) 706: 418n98
LCT(6) 707: 418n98
LCT(6) 708: 418n98
LCT(6) 713: 417n88
LCT(6) 714: 186,
417n88
LCT(6) 753: 410n81
LCT(6) 755: 410n81

LCT(6) 756: 410n80
LCT(6) 758: 410n80
LCT(6) 763: 409n70
LCT(6) 764: 409n78
LCT(6) 765: 115, 170
LCT(6) 766: 409n76
LCT(6) 767: 417n88
LCT(6) 769: 418n98
LCT(6) 775: 195
LCT(6) 776: 416n78
LCT(6) 777: 172, 177
LCT(6) 793: 410n79
LCT(6) 794: 410n79
LCT(6) 795: 410n80
LCT(6) 797: 410n79
LCT(6) 798: 410n80
LCT(6) 799: 410n80
LCT(6) 800: 410n81
LCT(6) 801: 410n79
LCT(6) 810: 160, 174
LCT(6) 811: 169
LCT(6) 812: 174
LCT(6) 813: 419n103
LCT(6) 814: 417n86
LCT(6) 815: 417n86
LCT(6) 822: 410n80
LCT(6) 824: 410n79
LCT(6) 836: 410n79
LCT(6) 837: 410n79
LCT(6) 851: 174
LCT(6) 852: 174
LCT(6) 853: 174
LCT(6) 854: 174
LCT(6) 855: 160, 174
LCT(6) 856: 217
LCT(6) 920: 410n80
LCT(6) 954: 410n80
LCT(6) 956: 410n79
LCT(6) 965: 410n80
LCT(6) 966: 410n80
LCT(6) 967: 410n80
LCT(6) 969: 410n81
LCT(6) 975: 410n79
LCT(6) 977: 410n80
LCT(6) 996: 410n80
LCT(6) 997: 410n79
LCT(6) 1050: 410n79
LCT(6) 3627: 408n66
LCT(6) 3628: 409n78
**LCT(A) (also see
LCT(HE))**
LCT(A) 2008: 308
LCT(A) 2009: 285
LCT(A) 2039: 248, 251
LCT(A) 2048: 248, 251
LCT(A) 2052: 116, 328
LCT(A) 2191: 327–8
LCT(A) 2225: 248
LCT(A) 2227: 187
LCT(A) 2233: 237
LCT(A) 2236: 248

LCT(A) 2263: 278
LCT(A) 2273: 187
LCT(A) 2282: 162
LCT(A) 2283: 285
LCT(A) 2291: 248
LCT(A) 2301: 161
LCT(A) 2309: 162
LCT(A) 2310: 162
LCT(A) 2334: 324, 328
LCT(A) 2345: 85, 248
LCT(A) 2433: 324
LCT(A) 2442: 237
LCT(A) 2453: 248
LCT(A) 2454: 162
LCT(A) 2455: 428n49
LCT(A) 2478: 162
LCT(A) 2488: 162
LCT(CB)
LCT(CB) 2041: 278
LCT(CB) 2337: 321–2,
327–8
LCT(CB) 2338: 271,
281–2
**LCT(HE) (also see
LCT(A))**
LCT(HE) 2008:
199–200
LCT(HE) 2037: 199
LCT(HE) 2049: 199
LCT(HE) 2050: 187
LCT(HE) 2075: 188
LCT(HE) 2124: 187–8
LCT(HE) 2229: 120,
188
LCT(HE) 2239: 199
LCT(HE) 2245: 199
LCT(HE) 2275: 187
LCT(HE) 2287: 199
LCT(HE) 2306: 285–6
LCT(HE) 2307: 188
LCT(R)
LCT(R) 362: 420n15
LCT(R) 437: 272
LCT(R) 434: 420n15
LCT(R) 435: 420n15
LCT(R) 436: 420n15
LCT(R) 438: 420n15
LCT(R) 440: 232
LCT(R) 459: 420n15
LCT(R) 460: 420n15
**LST (all indexed are
LST(2))**
LST 1: 425n109
LST 2: 262
LST 8: 429n82
LST 17: 425n108
LST 21: 310, 425n108
LST 25: 257, 262
LST 44: 425n109
LST 52: 425n109
LST 62: 429n82

LST 72: 425n108
LST 73: 425n108
LST 80: 429n82
LST 133: 225
LST 159: 429n82
LST 162: 435n103
LST 163: 435n103
LST 164: 435n103
LST 180: 429n82
LST 197: 83
LST 199: 429n82
LST 215: 429n82
LST 229 425n109
LST 238: 429n82
LST 239: 429n82
LST 264: 257, 262
LST 280: 425n109
LST 284: 176
LST 293: 425n109
LST 308: 425n108
LST 312: 425n108
LST 314: 204, 358
LST 323: 429n82
LST 325: 360
LST 326: 83
LST 344: 425n108
LST 345: 425n108
LST 359: 425n109
LST 360: 430n85
LST 370: 425n108
LST 376: 358
LST 381: 83
LST 383: 430n85
LST 384: 430n85
LST 385: 430n85
LST 393: 360
LST 402: 429n82
LST 404: 429n82
LST 405: 429n82
LST 409: 429n82
LST 413: 429n82
LST 415: 435n103
LST 416: 429n82
LST 425: 429n82
LST 430: 435n103
LST 493: 425n109
LST 499: 176, 358
LST 503: 425n109
LST 507: 44
LST 510: 360
LST 517: 430n85
LST 520: 425n108
LST 522: 117
LST 529: 430n85
LST 531: 44
LST 543: 430n85
LST 682: 430n85
LST 980: 430n85
LST 981: 297
LST 982: 430n85
LST 983: 430n85

Index

Due to space constraints, most individuals who were not landing craft crew or otherwise involved with amphibious vessels are not indexed; the exception being only the most senior officers. Similarly, ships other than landing craft, LSTs and other associated landing ships are not listed. References in italic refer to images or maps.

Adams, Robert 207

Admiralty 27, 66, 76–8, 99

Allen, Seaman Second Class Ravis Wilton 'Al' 214

Amsterdam, SS 184, 371

Andrews, John 117

Anne Arundel, USS 208, 214, 215–6, 221, 370

Anzio Landings: see Operation Shingle

Anderson, Motor Machinist's Mate First Class John Emanuel 210, 360

Area Z (English Channel) *110–1*, 120

Argo, Pharmacist's Mate First Class James R. 214

Arlidge, Lieutenant T.E. 191

Arromanches *112*, *229*, 233, *311*, 356, 260

Asnelles 227, *229*, 232, 235–7, 239, 257, 264

Assault Groups, Allied Naval; B1 385–6; B2 386; B3 387; G1 238, 372–3; G2 373–4; G3 374–5; J1 267, 278, 377–8; J2 267, 378–9; J3 294, 379–80; J4 380; L1 387; L2 387–8; L3 388; S1 382; S2 382–3; S3 383–4

Atkinson, Lieutenant Denis St John Batty 280

Aubin, Ship's Cook Raymond James 217

Bachaquero, HMS 43, 388

Backlog, Lieutenant F.J. 338

Bairstow, Stoker Alf 352

Baker, Rowland 30

Bakka, Motor Machinist's Mate Third Class Dean M. 190–1

Banks, Ensign Eugene Pendleton 115, 170

Barges: see Landing Barges

Barnaby, K.C. 31

Barnett, USS 152–3, 158, 162–3, 165, 365

Bartley, Ordinary Seaman Sidney 284

Barton, Ordinary Seaman Harold 338

Baschschmidt, Emil 215

Bass, Don 292

Batty, Able Seaman Lawrence 331

Bayfield, USS 47, 125, *144*, 149, 152–4, 156, 157, 162, 164–7, 365

Beaches: see under names of individual beaches

Beatson, Stoker Thomas E. 340

Bedell Smith, Lieutenant General Walter 80

Ben-my-Chree, SS 184, 371

Bennett, Seaman 121

Berg, Lieutenant Chris *315*

Bernières-sur-Mer *268*, 272, 283, 297, *304*

Berra, Yogi 156

Berry, Sub Lieutenant J.H.W. 328

Bialowas, Leading Stoker 280–1

Binding, Bill 339

Boaz, Ensign Shadrach Whittis 198

Bombardment, Naval 126–7

Bonesteel, General Charles 76

Borinquen, USAT 224–5

Bradshaw, Bob 130, 273

Briefing: see D-Day, Briefing

Brigadier, HMS 287, 378

Brightman, Midshipman Derek 118

British Army 94, *146* and passim; **21st Army Group** 297; **British Second Army** 297; **Brigades / Brigade Groups**: 8th Armoured Brigade 244, *310*; 8th Infantry Brigade 331–2, 340, 383; 9th Infantry Brigade 345, 347, 382; 27th Armoured Brigade 342, 347, 350; 56th Infantry Brigade 257, 262; 69th Infantry Brigade 246–57, 373; 151st Infantry Brigade 257–8, 262; 185th Infantry Brigade 340–2, 344, 382; 231st Infantry Brigade 234–46, 257, 372; **Battalions and Regiments**: 1st Dorsets 237–40, 243; 1st East Riding Yeomanry 347; 1st Hampshires 237–40; 1st KOSB 345; 1st Norfolks 341, 344; 1st South Lancs 319–20, 322–3, 325; 1st Suffolks 332–4, 340; 2nd Cheshires 249, 251, 254; 2nd Devons 242; 2nd East Yorks 319, 322–3, 329, 340; 2nd Essex 259–60; 2nd Glosters 259–60;

2nd Hertfordshires 252, 254; 2nd KSLI 341, 344; 2nd Lincolns 345; 2nd RUR 345; 2nd South Wales Borderers 259–60; 2nd Warwicks 341, 344; 4th/7th Dragoon Guards 228, 248, 254; 5th East Yorks 37, 250–2, 256; 5th Kings 343; 5th Royal Berkshires 294; 6th Borderers 261; 6th Durhams 258; 6th Green Howards *146*, 249–51, 256; 7th Field Regiment RA 320, 335, 342; 7th Green Howards 252–3; 8th Durhams 258; 8th Kings 277, 291; 9th Durhams 258; 13th/18th Hussars *147–8*, 323, 326, 331; 20th AT Regiment RA 350; 22nd Dragoons 277–8, 281, 323, 326; 33rd Field Regiment RA 320–1, 335, 340; 53rd Medium Regiment RA 350; 73rd LAA Regiment RA 349; 76th Field Regiment RA 320–1, 329, 335–6, 340; 86th Field Regiment RA 230–1, 254–5; 90th Field Regiment RA 230–1, 243, 246; 93rd LAA Regiment RA 350; 103rd HAA Regiment RA 349; 114th LAA Regiment RA 291; 141st Regiment RAC 240; 147th Field Regiment RA 230–1, 243, 246; Inns of Court Regiment 282; Sherwood Rangers Yeomanry 228, 240–1, 244; Staffordshire Yeomanry 342; Westminster Dragoons 235, 247, 342; **Beach Groups and Beach Sub-Areas** 165, 240, 243–4, 252, 254–5, 261, 290, 292–4, 331, 342–3, 349–50; **Commandos, Army** (also see Commandos): 1st Special Service Brigade 336–7; Free French Commandos 328, 336–7; No.3 Commando 338–9, 342; No.4 Commando 329–30; No.6 Commando 336–7; **Corps**: I Corps 292; XXX Corps 121, 263; **Divisions**: 3rd Infantry Division 96–7, 317–54, 382; 6th Airborne Division 294; 7th Armoured Division 261, 264–5; 50th Infantry Division 227–65, 372; 51st (Highland) Infantry Division 297; **Pioneer Corps** 254; **Royal Army Medical Corps** 240, 252, 259, 325; **Royal Army Service Corps** 42,

261, 348; **Royal Electrical and Mechanical Engineers** 240; **Royal Engineers (RE)**: 235–6, 243, 254, 281, 291, 294, 335, 342, 344, 349; 5th Assault Regiment 324; 26th Assault Squadron 277–8; 73 Field Company 236; 77 Assault Squadron 323, 326; 80 Assault Squadron 281; 81 Assault Squadron 247; 82 Assault Squadron 235; 89 Field Company 253; 90 Field Company 243; 233 Field Company 249–52; 246 Field Company 322–3; 235 Field Park Company 240; 262 Field Company 279; 263 Field Company 335; 280 Field Company 247; 295 Field Company 237–8, 242; 629 Field Squadron 325–6, 329; **Royal Signals** 240; Bruce, Charles 115, 286; Bryson, Able Seaman Robert 'Geordie' 327; BUCO (Build Up Control Organisation) 359; Build-Up Craft (see also Royal Navy units; Royal Marine units) 27, 95, 97, 103, *111*, 351, 367, 372, 376, 381, 384–5; Bureau of Ships (US Navy) 43, 70, 78; Burn, Sub Lieutenant Lambton 324; Bursledon 94; Burton, Petty Officer Motor Mechanic J.E. 317, 338–9; Busby, Ted 273; Bush, Captain E.W. 349; Bush, Stoker 1st Class George William 286; Butler, Ordinary Seaman 335; Cabourg 180, *181*; Calshot 359; Canada 45, 59; Canadian Army 118; **Brigades / Brigade Groups**: 7th Canadian Infantry Brigade 267, 291–3, 377; 8th Canadian Infantry Brigade 267, 293, 295, 378; 9th Canadian Infantry Brigade 294–5, *300*, 379; **Divisions**: 3rd Canadian Infantry Division 267–99, 377; **Regiments**: 6th Canadian Armoured Regiment 274–5, 282; 10th Canadian Armoured Regiment 289–90; 12th Field Regiment RCA 271, 290, 292; 13th Field Regiment RCA 271, 292,

306; 14th Field Regiment RCA 271–2, 291; 19th Field Regiment RCA 271, 291; 27th Canadian Armoured Regiment 295, *305;* 1st Canadian Scottish 46, 276, 280; Fort Garry Horse 121; Highland Light Infantry of Canada 295; North Nova Scotia Highlanders 295, *305;* North Shore Regiment 282, 288–9; Queen's Own Rifles of Canada *138*, 269, 272, 282–3, 286 ; Régiment de la Chaudière *138*, 269, 287–8 ; Regina Rifles 269–70, 275–6, 279, 291; Royal Winipeg Rifles 273, 276; Stormont, Dundas and Glengarry Highlanders 295; **Royal Canadian Engineers** 277–9, 287, 291; *Canterbury*, SS 276, 377, 379; Capa, Robert 196, 207–8; Carter, Luke 360; Casualties (also see under each of the five beaches; Landing Craft Crew, Casualties To) 153; Amongst Troops 126, 356, 358; Channel Crossing, English (also see Area Z; Convoys, Individual; D-Day, Postponement; Piccadilly Circus) *110–1*, 118–9, 259, 278; Craft shipping water 120, 248; Deaths during Crossing 120–1, 233, 248, 259, 273; Departure 118; Losses of Craft During Crossing 120, 199, 233, 248, 272–3; Recall, 5 June 1944 118; Speed of Convoys 119; Towing Craft During 120–1; *Charles Carroll*, USS 61, 192–5, 368; Chapman, Marine Robert Henry 259; Chiefs of Staff (British) 69–70, 93; Churchill, Prime Minister Winston 30, 43, 66–7, 70–1, 76, 78–9, 359; *Clan Lamont*, SS 282, 287, 378, 379; Clelland, Captain Geoffrey William 283; Colleville 180, *181*; Collins, General J. Lawton 176; Combined Chiefs of Staff (US/ British) 73; Combined Commanders (British) 69; Combined Operations Command 33, 48, 66, 69, 86, 94, 99

Commandos (also see British
  Army: Commandos, Army;
  Royal Marines: Commandos,
  Royal Marines) 35, 77, 128
Conferences, Allied 71–3, 75,
  78–9, 100
Conley, Signalman H. 330
Convoys, Individual (also see
  Groups; Assault Groups,
  Allied Naval); B-1 223;
  B-2 222; B-3 225; Bluesky
  convoys 356; ECL-1 176;
  EPB-1 224; ETL-1 264;
  ETM-1 351; GM-1 263;
  GM-2 264–5; GM-3 263;
  GM-4 263; J-1 267; J-3 267;
  J-13 294; JM-1 298; JM-2
  298; L-1 297; L-2 263; L-3
  261, 264, 297; L-4 261, 264;
  O-1 180; O-2 119; O-4 224;
  O-5 224; S-14A 350; S-15B
  350; SM-1 352; SM-2 352;
  SM-4 352; Starlight convoys
  356; U-1A 152; U-1B 169;
  U-2A 118; U-2A1 153–4;
  U-2A2 154; U-2B 152; U-4
  176; U-5 175; U-6 175; UB-1
  177, 224; UB-2 177; UB-3
  177
Cook, Wireman Malcolm 284
Cooper, Signalman G.R. 356
Copra, HMS 389
Corry, USS 164
COSSAC staff (Chief of Staff to
  Supreme Allied Commander):
  also see Morgan, Frederick,
  General Sir 72–4, 80, 99–100,
  317
Courseulles 42, *112*, 267, *268*, 271,
  276, 299, 357
Cricket, HMS 94
Cromar, Lieutenant Nigel *315*, 338
Crossing: see Channel Crossing,
  English
Crumpton, Signalman R.M.
  121, 169
Curtis, Commander Rupert 17,
  315, 336–7, 340
D-Day, Briefing 115–7
D-Day, Planning 67–83, 94–5;
  Allocation of troops to
  landing craft 102, 104–5,
  158; Assault Load for D-Day,
  Total 130; Army Plans
  127–9; Assault Force Size
  74–5, 77, 80–3, 132; Beach
  Gradient and Surface 30, 47,
  102, 107; Bombardment,
  Naval 101; Channel crossing
  (also see Channel Crossing,
  English) 101; Convoys (also
  see Convoys, Individual)
  111, 118–9; Date 82; Dawn
  and Daylight 101, 119, 129;

H-Hour, Time of 101, 119;
  Plans and Orders 100–1,
  103, 129; Obstacles, Beach
  101, 190; Tides 81, 101–2,
  129, 348–9; Waves, Landing
  102–3, 405n24
D-Day, Postponement 118–9
Dartmouth *110*, 113
Davies, Lieutenant Ron 104
Dean, Corporal Gerald 333
Dean, Reg 91
Deighton, Able Seaman Len 85
Dennis, John 348
Deslandes, Lieutenant
  Commander Jack 339
Dieppe Raid 61, 93, 95
Disembarkation *303–5, 307,
  309–10, 312–4*
Divisions (US Navy) (see US
  Navy units)
Dolan, Robert J. 26
Dorothea L. Dix, USS 204–5,
  216, 370
Duke of Argyll, SS 46 280, 377
Duke of Wellington, HMS 286–7,
  378
DUKW 48, 61, 198, 208, 213,
  257, 348–51
Dundonald, HMS 87
Dunkirk Evacuation 30
Durn, Marine Edward William
  264
Eastway, HMS 47
Eastern Task Force 35, 97, 100,
  112, 357
Eddy, Harold 92
Edney, Sub Lieutenant William
  J. 289
Edwards, Ensign George Robert
  389
Edwards, J.B. (company) 62
Eisenhower, General Dwight D.
  (Supreme Allied Commander)
  18, 26, 65, 68, 81, 82, 117
Ellis, John *136*
Ely, Horace 359
Emerald, HMS 246
Embarkation and Loading of
  Craft 88, 94, 104, *110*, 114–8,
  147–8, 401n6; After D-Day
  359; Unused Landing Craft
  115, 401n10
Empire Anvil, SS 201–2, 204–5,
  216, 217, 367
Empire Arquebus, SS 328, 240, 372
Empire Battleaxe, SS 117, 325, 333,
  348–9, 383
Empire Broadsword, SS 329, 333–4,
  383, 389
Empire Crossbow, SS 130, 237, 239,
  244, 372
Empire Cutlass, SS 319, 325–6, 383
Empire Gauntlet, SS 152, 154,
  162–4, 166–7, 363

Empire Glenroy, HMS 243, 372,
  373
Empire Halberd, SS 46, 250–3, 373
Empire Javelin, SS 105, 188, 191–4,
  368
Empire Lance, SS 249–50, 253, 373
Empire Mace, SS 249, 253, 373
Empire Rapier, SS 250–2, 259, 374
Empire Spearhead, SS 46, 237, 240,
  244, 372
Exercises, Amphibious Training
  44, 96–7, 120, *146*
Falmouth 113
Far East Theatre 48, 61, 67, 73–4,
  359
Felixstowe *111*, 114
Ferry Service (Landing Craft) 129,
  130, 294, *308, 311–2*, 356
Fletcher, Signalman Ray 245
Flotillas: see Royal Navy Units;
  Royal Marine Units, US Navy
  units, Royal Canadian Navy
Forces, Naval Assault; Force B 97,
  106, *110*, 113, 131, 217, 222–4,
  385–7; Force G 95–7, 102,
  104, 106, *110*, 115, 121, 124,
  227–5, 372–6; Force J 95–7,
  102–3, 106, 109, *110*, 115,
  125, 130, 266–99, 377–82;
  Force L 43, 97–8, 106, *110*,
  117, 121, 131, 263–4, 296–8,
  351, 387–8; Force O 61, 95,
  97, 104–6, *110*, 113, 115, 119,
  179–225, 367–72; Force S
  95–7, 102, 104, 106, *110*,
  114–6, 317–54, 382–5; Force
  U 47, 96–7, 106, *110*, 113–4,
  118–20, *143, 144*, 149–77,
  363–7
Forward Observation Officers
  (FOO) 37, 231, 239, 272,
  320–1
Fowey 113
Fowler, Midshipman 292
Fowler, Sub Lieutenant Leslie *136*
Fraser, Able Seaman Wally 204
Free French ; Commandos 328;
  2nd Armoured Division *314*
Gale, Marine Albert Alfred 333
Gamble, Leading Stoker 291
Garcia, Coxswain Lucio Garcia
  164
Garrod, Wireman Denis 331
German forces; Batteries (see
  German Strongpoints and
  Batteries, Individual) ; Beach
  Obstacles (for obstacle
  clearance, see Allied Obstacles
  and Obstacle Clearance under
  each beach) 128; Bunkers
  127–8, *300*, 256, 270–1;
  Defensive Fire 129, 270–1;
  German Air Force (Luftwaffe)
  113, 131, 264, 292, 295, 349,

353; German Army (Heer) 80, 107, 180, 228, 250, 269, 346, 358; German Navy (Kriegsmarine) 38, 44, 97, 131, 317, 353, 356, 358–9; Mines and minefields *110–1*, 120, 123–4, 149, 357; Strongpoints (also see German Strongpoints and Batteries, Individual) 128

German Strongpoints and Batteries, Individual (For strongpoints not listed here, see the map of each beach); Arromanches Batteries 233, 239; Mont Fleury Battery *229*, 250; WN-5 *151*, 157; WN-18 *318*, 330, 337; WN-20 (Cod) *318*, 323, 326, 333–4, 337, 340; WN-27 *268*, 282, 288; WN-28 *268*, 281, 283; WN-33 *268*, 275; WN-33 *229*, 232, 251; WN-34 *229*, 250; WN-35 *229*, 247, 250; WN-36 *229*, 231, 237, 247; WN-37 *229*, 231, 235–8; WN-38 *229*, 237; WN-60 *181*, 201–2; WN-62 *181*, 204; WN-70 *181*, 195; WN-71 *181*, 183

George S. Simonds, USAT 224

George W. Goethals, USAT 224

Giles, Able Seaman Cecil Norman 339

Glenearn, HMS 123, 319, 323, 329, 383

Glengarry, Sub Lieutenant Monty 324

Glossary 9–15

Glowacki, Seaman First Class Stanley A. 164

Gold Beach 36, 102, 107, *110–2*, 119, 127, 227–65, 356; **Bombardment, Naval** 230–3, 237–9, 249, 251–2, 256; **Casualties**: Amongst Landing Craft Crew 233, 235, 238, 241, 259; Amongst Troops 235, 237, 238, 240, 241, 246, 354; **DD tanks At** 228, 230, 234, 237, 241, 247–8; **Features of** 227–8, *229*; **German Defences** 227, *300*; **Landing Craft Lost At** 233, 238, 240, 245, 248, 253–7; **Map of** *229*; **Obstacles and Obstacle Clearance** 228, 234–6, 238, 240, 242–4, 247, 250, 253, 254; **Plan for Assault** 257, 259

Gooseberry Harbours 26, 299

Gosport *62*, 113–4, *147*, 359

Grant, Leading Seaman Percy Frederick, 164

Green, Sub Lieutenant George 'Jimmy' 126, 188, 189

Green, Sub Lieutenant Sidney 327

Graham, Ensign Joseph D. 219

Guernsey, Sub Lieutenant Peter 331

Haire, Wendell 171

Hall, Admiral John L., 37, 209

Halperin, Lieutenant Robert 155

Hannah, Able Seaman Norman 328

Hardy, Sub Lieutenant Frank Hastings 338

Hare, Able Seaman Bob 297

Harrison, Sub Lieutenant Paul Motte 60, 86

Havill, Bill 91

Hawkins, Ken 116

Hawthorn Leslie (R. & W. Hawthorn, Leslie & Co.) 60

Helder, HMS 66

Hendley, Lieutenant (j.g.) Coit T. 179, 210–1

Henrico, USS 199–201, 203–4, 217, 219, 367

Henry, Lieutenant Sidney 341

Hicken, Ensign Victor 187

Higgins Industries 16, 28, *142*

Higgins, Alan 86, 343

Hillary, HMS 377

Hodgson, Leading Seaman Reg 123

Holderness, Alan 88

Hollands, Lieutenant Alfred William Everton 291–2

Houghton, Leading Signalman Peter 334–5

Howard, Wireman Frank 255

Hugill, John Antony Crawford 118

Hutchins, Signalman Peter 327

Hutchinson, Lieutenant G.F. 211

Hyman, Ensign E.W. 191

Intelligence 105–7

Inter-Service Training and Development Centre 46

Inveraray 88

Invicta, HMS 276, 287, 377

Irwin, Sub Lieutenant Michael, 121

Isle of Guernsey, SS 286–7, 378

Isle of Thanet, SS 275, 377, 379

Japan, Invasion of 79, 83

Jenkins, Stoker 1st Class K.M. 259

Jenness, Lieutenant (E) L.B. Jenness 330

Jennings, Wireman Mick 173

Jensen, Sub Lieutenant Geoffrey 169

Johnson, Leading Motor Mechanic Kenneth Roy 292

Joint Chiefs of Staff (US) 70, 75, 82

Jones, Midshipman Craddock 332

Joseph T. Dickman, USS 152, 157, 162–5, 363

Joyce, Wireman William 332

Juno Beach 36, 47, 102, *110–2*, 119, 266–99, *304–6*, 352–3; **Bombardment, Naval** 270–4, 276, 278, 289; **Casualties**: Amongst Landing Craft Crew 271, 275–6, 279–80, 285–8; Amongst Troops 275–6, 280, 282, 289, 354; **DD tanks At** 270, 274–5, 281–2, 284; **Features of** 267, *268*, 269; **German Defences** 270, 282; **Landing Craft Lost At** 271, 275, 279, 281, 285–8, 299; **Map of** *268*; **Obstacles and Obstacle Clearance** 275, 277–82, 286–7, 290, *306*

King Alfred, HMS 86–7

Kiss, Bill 104

Kyle Jr, Ensign Winfield Nelms 172

La Grande Dune *151*, 155, 157, *312*

La Rivière 227, *229*, 232, 251–2, 256

Lady of Mann, SS 287, 378

Lairds Isle, SS 276, 377

Lambourne, John 117

Lampton, Leonard 164

Landing: see Disembarkation

Landing Barges 41–3, 102, 106, 263–5, 352–3, 357; Dumb barges 42–3; LBE 42, 130; LBF 42, 353; LBK 42, 130, *136;* LBO 42, 130; LBV 42, 88, 114, 130, *140;* LBW 42, 130

Landing Craft and Landing Ships, Themes; **After action reports** 18; **Armour** 25, 27, 32, 35, 38, 270, 282–3; **Army, behaviour on board craft** 121–2; **Bases, Shore** 86–8, 93–4, 359; **Beaching** 125; **Breaking Back, Craft** 31, 344; **Broaching To** 126; **Capacity** 24–5, 82; **Command and Control** 103–4, 122, 124, 154–5, 255; **Communications equipment** 124; **Construction** 27, 28, 31, 33–4, 57–60, *62–3*, 65–83, *133–4*, *135*, 360; locations (map) *62–3*; Raw materials 71–2, 75–6, 78, 80; **Crew**: see Landing Craft Crew; **Definition** 18, 23; **Design** 23–56; **Damage** 113; **Draught** 24–41; **Drying Out On Beach, Craft** 126, 225, *312*, *314*, 357; **Engines**

25–7, 30, 43, 72, 75, 78–9, 93, *134*; **Fire support types** (also see Bombardment, Naval) 36–41, 89; **Flotilla Staff** 92–3; **Food** 39, 42, 116, 117, 118, 121, 123, 225; **Hull Numbers** (see pennant numbers); **Losses of Craft** (also see Landing Craft Lost – under each of the five beaches) 355, 357–9; **Maintenance** (also see Landing Craft and Landing Ships, themes, Repair) 89, 95, 109, *135*, 200; **Manning levels** 87–8, 92–3; **Mine Clearance Sweeps** 123–4; **Modifications** 32, 38, 41, 109; **Mulock Ramp Extensions** 109, *312*; **Naming of Types** 23; **Navigation equipment** 124, 154; **Number built or modified** 27, 28, 33, 38–9, 41, 44, 58, 65–83; **Number of each type per naval force** 106; **Number participating in Operation Neptune** 18–9, 27–8, 33, 35–6, 38–9, 41, 44–5, 60; **Orders and Intelligence issued** 105–7, 117, 123–4; **Pennant Numbers** 9, 31–2, 34; **Radio Countermeasures** 124; **Ramp** 26, 34, 43, 241, 275, 285; **Repair** (also see Landing Craft and Landing Ships, themes: Maintenance) 359; **Specifications** 24–41; **Stores** (Supplies) 113, *145*; **Unbeaching** 26, 126; **Weapons fitted to** 24, 32, 36–41, *139*, *140*, *142*, *135*, 270, 275, 285, 326, 332, 337, 341
Landing Craft Crew; Casualties To 120–1, 355, 389–90; Clothing *311*, 356; Facilities on board 24, 27; Background 85–6; Roles on Board 89–92; Training 85–9, 97–8; Officers 90–2, 115–7; Other Ranks 91, 115–7
Landing Craft Obstacle Clearance Units (see Royal Marines: Landing Craft Obstacle Clearance Units (LCOCU))
Landing Craft Types (due to space limitations, not every reference to each craft type is indexed) See also Landing Ship Types; LCA 26, 27–8, 29, 45–6, *49*, 57–8, 92, 103, 106, 116, 130, 131, *146*, *135*, 273, 355, 357, 286; LCA(HR) 36, 40, 92, 120, 130, *137*,

273–4, 322; LCC 39, 40–1, *143*; LCE 29; LCF 38–41, 81, 116, 120, 230; LCG(L) 38–41, *53*, 74, 81, 116, 120, 127, 131, 230, 271, 276, 320–1, 355, 357, 358; LCG(M) 32; LCH 34, 106, 124, *141*, 355, 357; LCI(L) 33–4, 35, *51*, 63, 68, 70, 72–3, 79, 81, 82, 89, 103–4, 106, 119, 130–1, *141*, *145*, 259–60, 335, 355, 359; LCI(S) 17, 35, *52*, 89, 106, *142*, 355; LCM (all types) 34, 45, 106, 119, 120, 230, 355, 357; LCM(1) 28–9, *50*, 58, 129, 351; LCM(3) 28–9, *51*, 69, 72–3, 113, 129, *145*, *307*, 351; LCM(Salvage) 29; LCP(A) 228; LCP(L) 25, 29, 37, 68, 120, *143*, 228, 321, 355; LCP(Sy) 25–6, 228, 297, 355; LCP(R) 26; LCS(L) 37, 40, *55*, 127, *142*, 230, 278, 319–21; LCS(M) 36, 40, *54*, *139*, 271; LCS(S) 37, 40, 122, *144;* LCT (all types) 30–3, 68, 91–2, 100, 103–4, 106, 113–4, 119, 130, 131, *307*, 357, 359; LCT(1) 30, 66; LCT(2) 30, 58; LCT(3) 30–1, 35, *50*, 58, 62, 68, 73, 102; LCT(3★) 30, 62, 78; LCT(4) 30–1, 35, *50*, 57, 58, 62, 73, 102, *147–8;* LCT(5) 30–2, 35, 44, *51*, 59, 63, 67, 70, 72, 73, 79, 102, 131, *136*, *308;* LCT(6) 30–2, 35, 44, 59, 63, 79, *134;* LCT(8) 83; LCT(A) 32, 70, 81, 102, 120, 124, 127, 236–7, 278, 324, 327; LCT(CB) 32, 102, 127, 271, 278, 281–2, 319–21, 327–8; LCT(HE) 32, 102, 127, 278; LCT(R) 39–41, *54*, 74, 81, 120, 124, 127, *140*, 321–2; LCV 68; LCVP 26–7, 29, 45–6, *49*, 92, 113, 125, 129, 131, *300*, 351, 355, 357; LST: see Landing Ship Types
Landing Ship, Themes 81, 106, 122, 182, 317; Craft carried 157, 363–88; Davits 45, 109, 122; Deck cargo 123; Derricks 45; Loading Landing Craft on Board Ship 122–3, 256, *306*
Landing Ship Types ; APA 46, 96, 106, *142;* ARL 47; FDT 47; LSD 46–7; LSE 47, 73; LSH 47, 106; LSI(H) 45, 77, 82, 294; LSI(L) 45–6, 73, *138*, LSI(M) 46; LSI(S) 46, *56*, 77; LST(1) 43, 66; LST(2) 31, 43–5, 47–8, *55*, 59–61, 63, 67–8, 70, 73, 79, 81–2, 103–4,

106, 119, 129, 131, *133*, *146*, *314*, 357, 359; LST(3) 45, 79, 83; XAP 46, 182
Landing Table Index Number 104
Laney, Lemuel C., Ensign 122
Langley, Lieutenant Herbert 342
Largs 74
Largs, HMS 317
Laurence, Able Seaman 'Cookie' 241
Le Hamel 227–8, *229*, 232, 237–9, 261
Le Havre *111–2*, 317, 347, 353
Leach, Motor Machinist's Mate Third Class Robert 218
Leide, Lieutenant Commander William 101
Lend-Lease 31, 36, 67, 72
Les Moulins 180, *181*
Leslie, Sub Lieutenant James 332–4
Lethbridge, Petty Officer Motor Mechanic Charles Harold 292
Lewis, Motor Machinist's Mate 1st Class Clifford 117
Liebling, Alfred Joseph 206
Lilly, Ensign Charles 219
Lindlop, Lieutenant (E) Reg 265
Little Creek, VA 88
Llangibby Castle, MV *4*, 103, 130, 273, 281, 294, 377
Lloyd, Lieutenant J.G. 39
Loading of Landing Craft: see Embarkation
Lochailort, HMS 86–7
Loseby, Eric J. 120, 344–5
Lovell, Lieutenant Stewart F. 215
Low, Ensign Albert 159
Lowering Position *112*, 122, 126, 152
LST and Landing Craft Association 7, 360
Lund, Midshipman John 113
LVT 48
Lyles, Sub Lieutenant Roger 162
Lynd, First Lieutenant J.Q. 175
McCaw, Ken 119
McCormick, Stoker 1st Class Thomas 292
Maid of Orleans, SS 330, 385
Manatee, HMS 88
Maritime Commission (US) 75, 80
Marshall, George C., General (US) 18, 68
Marshall, Howard 243
Marshalling Areas *110*, 113
McMaster, Sub Lieutenant Henry Milne 287
Mecklenberg, SS 279, 377
Medina, HMS 88
Mediterranean Theatre 61, 67, 73, 77
Merchant Navy, British 46, 86, 330

Mewha, John 168
Milne, Able Seaman Louis Eric
  339
Misoa, HMS 43, 388
Milbourne, Coxswain Rex 235
Mills, Able Seaman Edward 328
Ministry of Production (UK) 77
Mitchell, Marine L.S. 253
Montgomery, Field Marshal Sir
  Bernard 80–2
Monowai, SS *138*, 269, 282, 287,
  294, 378
Moon, Rear Admiral Don P. 176
Morgan, General Sir Frederick
  (see also COSSAC) 71–3, 99
Moses, Lieutenant (j.g.) Frederick
  Nye 206
Moss, Norman 92, 97, 117, 348–9,
  360
Mountbatten, Admiral Lord Louis
  69, 99–100
MOVCO (Movement Control
  Organisation) 359
Mueller, Ensign F.J. 171
Mulberry Harbours 26, *311*, 356–7
Murphy, Seaman First Class
  Harlen Chalmer 164
Naval Lighter (NL) Pontoon 44,
  47–8, 61, *309*
Naylor, Sub Lieutenant Frederick
  E. 344
Neale, Marine Edward 123, 323
Nelson, Donald 71, 76
Nelson, Roy 98
New Forest 114
Newhaven *110*–1, 114
Niedermair, John C. 34, 43, 67
Nith, HMS 243
Nivens, Coxswain Delba L. 207
North Africa Landings: see
  Operation Torch
Northney, HMS 66, 88, 95
Northway, HMS 47, 297, 387
Nuttall, Lieutenant G.E. 280
Obstacle Clearance, Allied 128
Oceanway, HMS 47, 222, 369, 386
Office for War Mobilization
  (US) 79
Omaha Beach (also see Pointe du
  Hoc) 37, 39, 47, 48, *110*–2,
  119, 126, 179–225, *300*, *303*,
  306, *313*, 356; **Bombardment,
  Naval** 183–4; **Casualties**:
  Amongst Landing Craft
  Crew 186, 190–2, 196–7,
  200, 202–3, 210–1, 215, 217;
  Amongst Troops 192–4, 196,
  200, 211; **DD tanks At** 182–3,
  186, 198–9, 212; **Features
  of** 179–80, *181*; **German
  Defences** 179–80, 183–4, *300*;
  Landing Craft Lost At 188,
  190, 192–4, 197, 199, 201, 203,
  209, 210, 214, 215; **Map of**

181; **Obstacles and Obstacle
  Clearance** 180, 190–7, 200,
  202–3, *300*
Operation Anvil 79, 82, 359
Operation Avalanche 70, 74
Operation Bolero 68, 71
Operation Deer 353–4
Operation Dragoon: see
  Operation Anvil
Operation Frog 353–4
Operation Husky 48, 70, 73,
  93, 99
Operation Infatuate 359
Operation Neptune 18–9, 83, 85,
  93–4, 99–100, *110*, 356 and
  passim
Operation Rattle 74
Operation Roundup 69–70
Operation Shingle 74, 83
Operation Skyscraper 69
Operation Sledgehammer 69
Operation Torch 33, 61, 69–72,
  88, 93, 99
Oram, Sub Lieutenant Raymond
  87, 360
Orme, Leading Stoker Vic 327–8
Order of Battle 363–88
Orum, Lieutenant Sidney 284
Pacific Theatre: see Far East
  Theatre
Page, Wireman Bill 227, 244, 246
Pardington, Lieutenant Robert
  J. 282
Parker, Able Seaman Bob V. 263
Parsons, Lieutenant (E) C.G. 275
Penfold, Lieutenant F.H. 322
Perrett, Martin J. 125, 149, 162–3
Pettett, Leading Wireman 291
Photographs and Film of D-Day
  196–7, 202, 207, 286, *303*,
  414n46
Piccadilly Circus 120
Pickles, Sub Lieutenant A. 346
Pike, Marine Gerald 333
Pinto, USS 209
Pirrie, Sub Lieutenant Richard
  272
Planning: see D-Day, Planning
Plymouth *110*, 113
Pointe du Hoc 36, 102, 180,
  184–5, 189, 194, 213
Pontoon Causeway: see Naval
  Lighter (NL) Pontoon
Poole 62, 94, 113
Poole, Bert 296
Porcupine II, HMS 88
Port-en-Bessin *111*–2, 245, 357
Portland *110*, 113
Portsmouth, UK 62, *110*–1,
  113–4, 346
Portsmouth Command, Royal
  Navy 94–6, 99, 115, 359
Prinses Astrid, HMS 329–30, 335,
  385

Prince Baudouin, SS 46, *56*, 185,
  195, 371
Prince Charles, HMS 189, 195, 371
Prince David, HMCS 93, 287,
  378, 379
Prince Henry, HMCS 93, 125,
  280, 377
Prince Leopold, HMS 117, 185,
  195, 371
Princess Margaret, HMS 354, 380
Princess Maud, SS 190, 371
Prins Albert, HMS 354, 380
Prinses Josephine Charlotte, HMS
  245, 305, 375
Pugh, Lieutenant W.A.G. 258
Purnell, Stoker 1st Class Dennis
  284
Quebec, HMS 88
Queen Emma, HMS 46, 130, 280,
  377
Ramsay, Admiral Sir Bertram
  (Allied Naval Commander-
  in-Chief) 42, 82, 99–102
Rawlings, Sub Lieutenant R.W.
  328
Rhino Ferry 43, 44, 47–8, 129,
  218, 257, 262, *310*
Roberts, Steward's Mate John
  Noble 216
Rockwell, Lieutenant Dean L. 186
Roll of Honour 389–90
Roosevelt, President Franklin D.,
  68, 69–70, 78–9
Roosevelt, Brigadier General
  Theodore 158–9
Rosyth 95
Rowe, Seaman Second Class Jack
  E. 164
Royal Air Force (RAF) 219, *302*
Royal Canadian Navy (also see
  under names of individual
  ships) 89, 93, *300*, *304*; 260
  LCI(L) Flotilla 290, 380; 262
  LCI(L) Flotilla 295, *300*, 380;
  264 LCI(L) Flotilla 259–60,
  375; 528 Assault Flotilla 280,
  377; 529 Assault Flotilla
  287–8, 378–9
Royal Corps of Naval
  Constructors 30
Royal Marines (also see Royal
  Navy; Royal Canadian Navy);
  30 Assault Unit 287–8;
  Crews, Royal Marines:
  27, 86–8, 93, 98, 102, *139*,
  253, 323, 351 and passim;
  Commandos, Royal Marine
  (also see Commandos):
  41 RM Commando 337–8;
  45 RM Commando 338–9;
  46 RM Commando 354; 47
  RM Commando 245–6, *305*;
  48 RM Commando 288–9;
  Flotillas RM, Landing

Craft: 506 Assault Flotilla 115, 286, 378; 509 Assault Flotilla 276, 377, 379; 526 Assault Flotilla 130, 280, 377; 535 Assault Flotilla 123, 319, 321–3, 329, 383; 536 Assault Flotilla 319, 325–6, 383; 537 Assault Flotilla 97, 325–6, 333, 348–9, 383; 538 Assault Flotilla 329, 333–4, 383, 389; 539 Assault Flotilla 250–2, 373; 541 Assault Flotilla 247, 249, 253, 373; 542 Assault Flotilla 250–1, 253, 374; 543 Assault Flotilla 329, 383; 544 Assault Flotilla 287–8, 378; 554 Assault Flotilla 234, 242, 372; 556 Assault Flotilla 272, 282–4, 378; 557 Assault Flotilla 4, 103, 130, 273, 279–80, 377; 558 Assault Flotilla 282, 287–8, 378; 559 Assault Flotilla 234, 242, 373; 592 Assault Flotilla 121, 384; 600 Build-Up Flotilla 381; 601 Build-Up Flotilla 381; 602 Build-Up Flotilla 351, 385; 603 Build-Up Flotilla 351, 385; 604 Build-Up Flotilla 381; 605 Build-Up Flotilla 265, 376; 606 Build-Up Flotilla 265, 376; 607 Build-Up Flotilla 264, 376; 609 Build-Up Flotilla 265, 376; 650 Build-Up Flotilla 381; 651 Build-Up Flotilla 381; 652 Build-Up Flotilla 381, 427n40; 653 Build-Up Flotilla 335, 351, 385; 654 Build-Up Flotilla 265, 376; 698 Build-Up Flotilla 259, 264–5, 376; 700 Assault Flotilla 228, 375; 704 Assault Flotilla 321, 384; 706 Assault Flotilla 235, 375; 707 Assault Flotilla 321, 375; 800 Build-Up Flotilla 381; 801 Build-Up Flotilla 381; 802 Build-Up Flotilla 381; 803 Build-Up Flotilla 351, 384; 804 Build-Up Flotilla 381; 805 Build-Up Flotilla 97, 265, 376; 806 Build-Up Flotilla 265, 376; 807 Build-Up Flotilla 265, 376; 808 Build-Up Flotilla 97, 265, 376; 809 Build-Up Flotilla 97, 376; 810 Build-Up Flotilla 351, 384; 811 Build-Up Flotilla 351, 385; 812 Build-Up Flotilla 351, 385; 813 Build-Up Flotilla 351, 385; 814 Build-Up Flotilla 351, 385; **Landing Craft**

Obstacle Clearance Units (LCOCU) 28, 32, 234–5, 247, 277, 283, 325–6, 329, 335; **Royal Marine Independent Armoured Support Batteries**: 1st Battery 248; 2nd Battery 236; 3rd Battery 247, 374; 5th Battery 278; 5th Battery 321, 327; **Squadrons RM, Landing Craft**: A Build-Up Squadron 381; B Build-Up Squadron 265, 376; C Build-Up Squadron 384; D Build-Up Squadron 385; E Build-Up Squadron 376; F Build-Up Squadron 381; Royal Navy Landing Craft Units (also see Royal Marines; Royal Canadian Navy; see under names of individual ships and shore bases) 44; **Flotillas RN, Landing Craft**: 1 LBV Flotilla 381; 1 LST Flotilla 348, 382; 2 LBV Flotilla 381; 2 LST Flotilla 379; 3 LBV Flotilla 381; 3 LST Flotilla 382; 4 LBV Flotilla 263, 381; 4 LCT Flotilla 275, 377; 4 LST Flotilla 380; 5 LBV Flotilla 352, 385; 5 LST Flotilla 382; 6 LBV Flotilla 352, 385; 6 LCT Flotilla 388; 7 LBV Flotilla 372; 7 LST Flotilla 387; 8 LBV Flotilla 367; 8 LST Flotilla 387; 9 LBV Flotilla 372; 9 LST Flotilla 380; 10 LBV Flotilla 372; 11 LBV Flotilla 372; 11 LCT Flotilla 284, 379; 12 LBV Flotilla 372; 12 LCT Flotilla 228, 248, 374; 13 LBV Flotilla 263, 376; 14 LBV Flotilla 263, 376; 14 LCT Flotilla 319, 383; 15 LBV Flotilla 263, 376; 15 LCT Flotilla 228, 240–1, 373; 16 LBV Flotilla 381; 16 LCT Flotilla 387; 17 LCT Flotilla 388; 18 LBV Flotilla 372; 18 LCT Flotilla 387; 19 LBV Flotilla 367; 19 LCT Flotilla 387; 20 LBV Flotilla 367; 20 LCT Flotilla 281, 290, 377; 22 LCT Flotilla 291, 379; 23 LCT Flotilla 244, 373; 24 LCT Flotilla 230, 254–5, 374; 25 LBF Flotilla 373; 26 LBF Flotilla 374; 28 LCT Flotilla 104, 235, 373; 30 LB (Supply & Repair) Flotilla 352, 382; 30 LCT Flotilla 291, 379; 31 LB (Supply & Repair) Flotilla 382; 31 LCT Flotilla 290, 292 368; 32 LB (Supply & Repair) Flotilla 372; 32 LCT

Flotilla 320, 335–6, 340, 342, 384; 33 LB (Supply & Repair) Flotilla 367; 33 LCT Flotilla 230, 243, 373, 374, 422n62; 34 LB (Supply & Repair) Flotilla 367; 34 LCT Flotilla 247, 374; 35 LB (Supply & Repair) Flotilla 352, 385; 35 LCT Flotilla 294–5, 380; 36 LB (Supply & Repair) Flotilla 263, 376; 36 LCT Flotilla 289, 380; 37 LB (Supply & Repair) Flotilla 382; 37 LCT Flotilla 294–5, 380; 38 LB (Supply & Repair) Flotilla 263, 376; 38 LCT Flotilla 320, 335–6, 384; 39 LB (Supply & Repair) Flotilla 372; 39 LCT Flotilla 347, 382; 40 LCT Flotilla 383; 41 LCT Flotilla 331, 383; 42 LCT Flotilla 344, 383; 43 LCT Flotilla 340, 383; 44 LCT Flotilla 366; 45 LCT Flotilla 116, 323, 326, 384; 47 LCT Flotilla 347–8, 382; 48 LCT Flotilla 344–5, 383; 49 LCT Flotilla 230, 243, 254–5, 374, 422n62; 50 LCT Flotilla 173, 366; 51 LCT Flotilla 374, 423n85; 52 LCT Flotilla 173, 364; 53 LCT Flotilla 244–5, 373; 54 LCT Flotilla 223, 386; 55 LCT Flotilla 258, 375; 56 LCT Flotilla 223, 386; 57 LCT Flotilla 223, 371, 386; 59 LCT Flotilla 223, 386; 100 LCT Flotilla 324, 327, 384; 102 LCT Flotilla 368; 103 LCT Flotilla 270, 278, 284–5, 379; 104 LCT Flotilla 167, 364, 366; 105 LCT(A) Flotilla 270, 278, 284–5, 378, 428n49; 106 LCT Flotilla 379, 289, 428n49; 107 LCT Flotilla 167 364; 108 LCT Flotilla 236–7, 373; 109 LCT Flotilla 248, 374; 110 LCT Flotilla 167, 366; 200 LCI(S) Flotilla 17, 315, 336–7, 380, 384; 201 LCI(S) Flotilla 328, 336–40, 380, 384; 202 LCI(S) Flotilla 288–9, 315, 380, 384; 251 LCI(L) Flotilla 343–4, 382; 252 LCI(L) Flotilla 354, 388; 253 LCI(L) Flotilla 354, 388; 260 LCI(L) Flotilla (see Royal Canadian Navy); 261 LCI(L) Flotilla 332–5, 350, 383; 262 LCI(L) Flotilla (see Royal Canadian Navy); 263 LCI(L) Flotilla 340–2, 383; 264 LCI(L) Flotilla (see Royal Canadian Navy); 265 LCI(L) Flotilla 345, 382; 266 LCI(L)

Flotilla 345, 350, 382; 310
Support Flotilla 230–2, 236,
248, 252, 256, 270, 374, 380;
320 LCT(R) Flotilla 270,
378; 321 LCT(R) Flotilla
384; 322 LCT(R) Flotilla
232, 373–4; 330 Support
Flotilla 384; 331 Support
Flotilla 270, 284, 289–379;
332 Support Flotilla 230, 232,
248, 251–2, 256, 373–4; 333
Support Flotilla 270, 378;
499 Ancillary Flotilla 377;
500 Assault Flotilla 329–30,
385; 501 Assault Flotilla 189,
371; 502 Assault Flotilla 245,
305, 375; 503 Assault Flotilla
354, 380; 504 Assault Flotilla
195, 371; 505 Assault Flotilla
270, 275, 377; 507 Assault
Flotilla 195, 371; 508 Assault
Flotilla 245, 375; 510 Assault
Flotilla 276, 377; 511 Assault
Flotilla 279, 377; 512 Assault
Flotilla 287–8, 378; 513
Assault Flotilla 286–7, 378;
514 Assault Flotilla 329–30,
385; 515 Assault Flotilla
378; 516 Assault Flotilla 276,
377; 517 Assault Flotilla 280,
377; 518 Assault Flotilla
267, 286–7, 378; 519 Assault
Flotilla 192, 371; 520 Assault
Flotilla 184–5, 371; 521
Assault Flotilla 276, 377; 522
Assault Flotilla 184–5, 371;
523 Assault Flotilla 354, 380;
524 Assault Flotilla 238, 240,
359, 372 ; 525 Assault Flotilla
237, 240, 372; 528 Assault
Flotilla (see Royal Canadian
Navy); 529 Assault Flotilla
(see Royal Canadian Navy);
540 Assault Flotilla 249–50,
253, 373; 550 Assault Flotilla
201–2, 204, 367; 551 Assault
Flotilla 126, 188, 192, 368; 552
Assault Flotilla 154, 162–3,
363; 553 Assault Flotilla 237,
239, 372; 555 Assault Flotilla
294, 379; 590 Assault Flotilla
273, 379; 591 Assault Flotilla
233, 373; 592 Assault Flotilla
121, 384; 701 Assault Flotilla
380; 702 Assault Flotilla 379;
703 Assault Flotilla 298, 378;
705 Assault Flotilla 298, 380;
708 Assault Flotilla 228, 375;
712 Assault Flotilla 381; 900
Support Flotilla 270, 378;
Supply and Repair flotillas
42; **Royal Navy crews**
27, 97, 102; **Royal Naval
Reserve (RNR)** 90; **Royal**

Navy Beach Commandos
128, 240, 251, 287, 325, 329;
**Squadrons RN, Landing
Craft**: 1st Support Squadron
378; 2nd Support Squadron
379; A LCI(L) Squadron 388;
D LCT Squadron 373; E
LCT Squadron 383; G LCT
Squadron 364, 365; H LCT
Squadron 388; I Squadron
382; L LST Squadron, Force
S 382; K LCT Squadron
377; N LCT Squadron 379;
O LCT Squadron 364, 365;
P LCT Squadron 380; Q
LCT Squadron 223, 371,
386; T LCT Squadron 382;
U LB Squadron 385; U
LCT Squadron 115, 375; V
LCT Squadron 387; W LB
Squadron 381; X LB Squadron
367; Y LB Squadron 372; Z
LB Squadron 376; Support
Squadron, Group G1 373;
Support Squadron, Group G2
374; Support Squadron, Force
J 380; Support Squadron,
Force S 384
Royal Ulsterman, HMS 277, 294,
379
Ruffell, Lieutenant Jim 248
Salmon, Lieutenant Robert M. 197
Samuel Chase, USS 114, *142*, 199,
207, 208, 215–6, 219, *300*, 367
Salerno Landings: See Operation
Avalanche
Sargent, Chief Photographer's
Mate Robert F. 207, *303*
Scaplehorn, Marine Edward
Henry Charles 334
Schereschewsky, Lieutenant (j.g.)
John Forby 90–1, 222–3
Seasickness 118, 121, 158, 191, 272,
279–80
Seldon, Jonny 342
Shepard, Photographer's Mate
Third Class Seth 197
Shields, Electrician's Mate First
Class Arthur Virgil 222–3
Shipbuilding and Shipbuilding
Yards (see: Landing Craft
and Landing Ships (Themes),
Construction)
Shirley, Petty Officer Motor
Mechanic Mick 256
Shone, Sub Lieutenant Raymond
85
Shoreham 114
Shrapnel, HMS 88
Shuttle Service (Landing Craft)
356
Sicily, Invasion of: See Operation
Husky
Skinner, Joshua 342

Slapton Sands 44
Smith, Corporal Eric James 334,
389
Smith, Midshipman Stan 241
Smith, Sub Lieutenant Henry 293
Solent, The 118, 119, *148*
Solomons, MD 88
Southampton 95, *110–1*, 114, 116
Squadrons (see Royal Navy and
Royal Marine Landing Craft
Units; US Navy units)
Squid, HMS 95
St Aubin-sur-Mer *268*, 288
St Helier, HMS 287, 378
St Laurent-sur-Mer 180, *181*, 356
Stafford, Petty Officer Motor
Mechanic Robert Swinney
Elliott 342
Stanswood Bay 114
Stockton Construction Co. 58, 62
Stone, Horace 238
Storm, Great (19–23 June 1944) 42
Stephens, Sub Lieutenant Phillip
264
Stokes Bay 88
Strategy, Allied 65–83
Sullivan, Sub Lieutenant Ben
239–40
Sullivan, Ensign Joseph A. 221
Supreme Allied Commander: see
Eisenhower, General Dwight
D.
Susan B. Anthony, USS 224–5
Sword Beach 35, 36, 37, 102,
110–2, 119, 128, 317–54;
Bombardment, Naval
319–22; **Casualties**: Amongst
Landing Craft Crew 324–8,
331–5, 338–42; Amongst
Troops 324, 330–2, 337–9,
343–4, 354; **DD tanks At**
319, 323, 326–7; **Features of**
317, *318* ; **German Defences**
337, 341, 354; **Landing Craft
Lost At** 326–30, 333–4,
338–40, 342, 344; **Map of**
318; **Obstacles and Obstacle
Clearance** 323, 325–6, 334–6,
339, 348
Tait, Sub Lieutenant John Bruce
331
Tandy, Corporal George 253
Tanks 31–2, 44, 81, 100, 103, 121,
132, *147–8*
Tasajera, HMS 43, 388
Tasker, Stanley, Lieutenant 337–8
Taylor, Buck 86, 353
Thomas, Able Seaman 130
Thomas Jefferson, USS 189, 192–4,
368
Thompson, Robert 86
Thurston, USS 113, 192, 216, 221,
370
Tilbury 114

Timmermans, Commander
  Georges 288, *315*
Tormentor, HMS 66, 95
Torquay *110*, 113
Townson, Leading Seaman
  Douglas 280
Tracey, Midshipman Roland 116
Transport Area: see Lowering
  Position
Troon 87
Trout Line 37, 38, 356, 353, 358–9
Time 21
Training, other than crews (see
  also Exercises, Amphibious
  Training) 77, 96
Trendell, Wireman Edward 327
Troops, experiences on board
  landing craft 27, 121, 125–6,
  148, *300*, *307*
TURCO (Turn Round Control
  Organisation) 359
Turner, Signalman Ron 244
Turner, Lieutenant W.J. 267, 286
Turtle, HMS 94
Twelftree, Sub Lieutenant Alf 115
Twiddle, Lieutenant Tommy 342
Ulster Monarch, HMS 276, 377
US Army 68, 69, 75, 79, 80;
  African American personnel
  171, 213; **Battalion (Bn.)** (for
  Infantry Battalions, see under
  Regiment): 2nd Rangers 182,
  184–5, 188, 194–5, 209, 213,
  371; 4th Engineer Combat
  Battalion 166; 4th Medical
  Battalion 169; 5th Field
  Artillery 105; 5th Rangers
  182, 185, 194–5, 213,371; 7th
  Field Artillery Battalion 208;
  29th Field Artillery Battalion
  168, 173; 37th Engineer
  Combat Battalion 207; 42nd
  Field Artillery Battalion 173;
  44th Field Artillery Battalion
  173; 58th Armoured Field
  Artillery Battalion 197–8, 213;
  62nd Field Artillery Battalion
  204, 208; 65th Armoured
  Field Artillery Battalion 155,
  173; 70th Tank Battalion
  159–61, 173; 81st Airborne
  Anti-Aircraft Battalion 160;
  81st Chemical Weapons
  Battalion 193, 205; 87th
  Chemical Mortar Battalion
  163, 166–7, 173; 112th
  Engineer Combat Battalion
  193; 116th Anti-Aircraft
  Artillery Battalion 175; 121st
  Engineer Combat Battalion
  192; 197th Anti-Aircraft
  Artillery Battalion 210; 149th
  Engineer Combat Battalion
  192; 237th Engineer Combat

Battalion 158; 238th Engineer
  Combat Battalion 174; 299th
  Engineer Combat Battalion
  158; 320th Barrage Balloon
  Battalion 171, 213; 348th
  Engineer Combat Battalion
  219; 397th Anti-Aircraft
  Artillery Battalion 192, 203;
  467th Anti-Aircraft Artillery
  Battalion 209; 741st Tank
  Battalion 198–200; 743rd
  Tank Battalion 186–8, 213;
  745th Tank Battalion 222;
  746th Tank Battalion 166,
  173; 819th Engineer Aviation
  Battalion 169; **Corps**:
  V Corps 210; VII Corps 150,
  176; **Division**: 1st Infantry
  Division 180, 198, 208,
  210, 213, 367; 4th Infantry
  Division 96–7, 150–77, 363,
  365; 29th Infantry Division
  180, 194, 213, 223, 367; 82nd
  Airborne Division 150; 90th
  Infantry Division 150, 168,
  174, *300*, 363, 365; 101st
  Airborne Division 150, 170,
  172; **Obstacle clearance
  teams** 28, 32, 159 (also see
  US Navy: Naval Combat
  Demolition Units); **Other**:
  1st Engineer Special Brigade
  165, 171–2, 174–5; 4 Cavalry
  Squadron 168; 5th Engineer
  Special Brigade 205–6, 217,
  219–21; 6th Engineer Special
  Brigade 194; 23 Ordnance
  Bomb Disposal Squad 175;
  603 Quartermaster Graves
  Registration Company 175;
  1106 Engineer Combat Group
  162; 3207 Quartermaster
  Service Company 173; 3275
  Quartermaster Company
  221; Gap Assault Teams 190,
  202–3; **Rangers** (also see
  US Army Units: Battalions
  under battalion number)
  128; Ranger Force C 194–5;
  **Regiment / Regimental
  Combat Team**: 8th Infantry
  157–8, 162, 173, 166; 12th
  Infantry 171–3, 363, 365;
  16th Infantry 126, 180, 183,
  198, 200–4, 206–8, 211, 222,
  300, 367; 18th Infantry 213–5,
  216–7, 219–21, 223, 370;
  22nd Infantry 166–7, 169–71,
  173, 363, 365; 26th Infantry
  222–3; 115th Infantry 217–8,
  368; 116th Infantry 180,
  187–9, 191–5, 200, 208, 368;
  175th Infantry 225; 359th
  Infantry 168, 174–5, 363,

365; 401st Glider Infantry
  172; 531st Engineer Shore
  Regiment 168, 173–4
US Coast Guard 44, 102, 114, 117,
  142, 154, 195–7, *301*, 338
US Marine Corps 66–7, 276
US Navy 44, 75, 79, 80, 102;
  2nd Naval Beach Battalion
  165, 169, 174; **6th Naval
  Beach Battalion** 206; **7th
  Naval Beach Battalion**
  195, 197; **11th Amphibious
  Force** 119; **African
  American personnel** *145*,
  206, 216; **Atlantic Fleet**
  88; **Commander, Force O**
  (see Hall, John L., Admiral);
  **Divisions USN, Landing
  Craft**: LCF Division 1: 371;
  LCG(L) Division 1: 371;
  LCI(L) Division 7: 365;
  LCI(L) Division 8: 343, 383;
  LCI(L) Division 9: 365;
  LCI(L) Division 10: 365;
  LCI(L) Division 55: 370;
  LCI(L) Division 56: 368, 370;
  LCI(L) Division 57: 368–9;
  LCI(L) Division 58: 368–70;
  LCI(L) Division 59: 364;
  LCI(L) Division 60: 364, 365;
  LCI(L) Division 61: 258, 375;
  LCI(L) Division 62: 259–60,
  375; LCI(L) Division 63:
  364–5; LCI(L) Division 64:
  364; LCI(L) Division 65:
  364; LCI(L) Division 66:
  369, 371; LCI(L) Division 67:
  369; LCI(L) Division 68:
  386; LCI(L) Division 69:
  386; LCI(L) Division 70:
  375; LCT Division 20:
  366; LCT Division 21:
  366; LCT Division 23:
  366; LCT Division 19:
  364; LCT Division 22:
  364; LCT Division 23:
  364; LCT Division 24:
  364; LCT Division 67:
  364; LCT Division 68:
  369; LCT Division 69: 369;
  LCT Division 70: 364,
  366; LCT Division 71:
  368; LCT Division 72:
  369; LCT Division 97: 369;
  LCT Division 98: 369–70;
  LCT Division 99: 366;
  LCT Division 100: 366;
  LCT Division 101: 366;
  LCT Division 102: 366;
  LCT Division 103: 368–70;
  LCT Division 104: 369;
  LCT Division 105: 368,
  370; LCT Division 106:
  368–9; LCT Division 107:

369–71; LCT Division 108: 368, 370; LCT Division 109: 368; LCT Division 110: 368; LCT Division 111: 368; LCT Division 112: 368, 370; LCT Division 113: 370; LCT Division 114: 370; LCT Division 151: 369–70; LCT Division 152: 368–9; LCT Division 153: 368, 370; LCT Division 154: 370; LCT(5) Division 4: 371; LCT(5) Division 5: 371; LCT(A)/LCT(5) Division 1: 371; LCT(R) Division 1: 371; LST Division 21: 387; LST Division 22: 374, 387; LST Division 23: 386; LST Division 55: 374; LST Division 56: 374; LST Division 57: 363, 365; LST Division 58: 363; LST Division 59: 370; LST Division 60: 385; LST Division 61: 386; LST Division 62: 386; LST Division 63: 363; LST Division 64: 364–5; LST Division 66: 365; LST Division 67: 369–70; LST Division 68: 368, 370; LST Division 69: 368–70; LST Division 70: 386; LST Division 71: 386; LST Division 72: 386; LST Division 97: 386; LST Division 98: 387; LST Division 99: 387; LST Division 100: 387; LST Division 101: 375; LST Division 102: 387; LST Division 103: 387; **Flotillas USN, Landing Craft**: LCI(L) Flotilla 2: 343, 365, 383; LCI(L) Flotilla 10: 364–5, 368–70; LCI(L) Flotilla 11: 364–5, 375; LCI(L) Flotilla 12: 386; LCM Flotilla 2: 365–7; LCM Salvage Flotilla 365–6; LCT Flotilla 4: 177 364–5; LCT Flotilla 12: 369–70; LCT Flotilla 17: 364–5, 375, 389; LCT Flotilla 18: 368–71; LCT Flotilla 19: 368, 370; LCT Flotilla 26: 368; LCT Flotilla 26, Provisional 368, 369, 370; LST Flotilla 4: 374, 386–7; LST Flotilla 10: 363, 365, 368–70, 374, 385; LST Flotilla 11: 375; LST Flotilla 12: 258–60, 369; LST Flotilla 17: 375, 387; LST Flotilla 18: 387; **Force O Gunfire Support Group** 371; **Force U**

Support Group 366; **Groups USN, Landing Craft**: LCF Group 1: 371; LCG(L) Group 1: 371; LCI(L) Group 4: 383; LCI(L) Group 5: 365; LCI(L) Group 28: 368, 370; LCI(L) Group 29: 368–70; LCI(L) Group 30: 364–5; LCI(L) Group 31: 258, 375; LCI(L) Group 32: 364–5; LCI(L) Group 33: 364; LCI(L) Group 34: 369, 371; LCI(L) Group 35: 259–60, 375, 386; LCT Group 10: 364; LCT Group 11: 364; LCT Group 12: 364; LCT Group 34: 369–70; LCT Group 35: 369; LCT Group 36: 368–9; LCT Group 49: 364; LCT Group 52: 368–70; LCT Group 53: 368–70; LCT Group 54: 368–71; LCT Group 55: 368; LCT Group 56: 368, 370; LCT Group 57: 370; LCT Group 76: 368–70; LCT Group 77: 368, 370; LCT(5) Group 3: 371; LCT(A)/LCT(5) Group 1: 371; LCT(R) Group 1: 371; LST Group 10: 385; LST Group 11: 374, 387; LST Group 12: 386; LST Group 28: 374; LST Group 29: 363, 365; LST Group 30: 370; LST Group 31: 386; LST Group 32: 363, 365; LST Group 33: 375; LST Group 34: 368, 370; LST Group 35: 368, 370, 386; LST Group 36: 386; LST Group 49: 387; LST Group 50: 387; LST Group 51: 375; LST Group 52: 387; **Naval Beach Battalions** 128; **Naval Combat Demolition Units** 158–9, 190; **Scout and Raider Units** 37, 155, 166; **Shore Fire Control Party** 166, 204; **Task Forces USN**: Task Force 124: 367–72; Task Force 125: 363–7; Task Force 126: 385–7; **Task Groups USN** (also see Assault Groups); Task Group 124.3: 367–8; Task Group 124.4: 368–9; Task Group 124.5: 182, 370–1; Task Group 124.6: 182, 371; Task Group 125.4: 363–5; Task Group 125.5: 365–6; Task Group 125.7: 366–7; Task Group 125.10: 367; Task Group 126.2: 385–6; Task Group 126.3: 386; Task Group 126.4: 386; **Transport Division**: Transport Division

1: 367; Transport Division 3: 368; Transport Division 97: 370

Utah Beach 39, *110–2*, 119, 122, 125, 128, 149–50, *151*, 152–77, 3*14*; **Banc du Cardonnet** 149, *151*, 168, 171, 172, 176; **Bombardment, Naval** 154–6, 159; **Casualties**: Amongst Landing Craft Crew 160–1, 163–4, 168, 171, 172, 177; Amongst Troops 160–1, 168, 172; **Changed Location of Landings** 154, 159; **DD tanks** At 153–61; **Features of** 149–50, *151*, 152, 169–70, *307*, *312*; **German Defences** 152, 154, 155, 158, 176; **Îles Saint-Marcouf** 149, *151*, 154; **Landing Craft Present At** 150, 152–77; **Landing Craft Lost At** 160–2, 164, 168, 171, 172, 177; **Map of** *151*

Obstacles and Obstacle Clearance 158–60, 162, 167–8, 174
Ver-sur-Mer 227–8, *229*, 252, *302*
Victoria, SS 245, 375
Vierville-sur-Mer 180, *181*, 189, 191
Villiers, Alan 34, 89
Vingoe, Sub Lieutenant Norman 278
Vyn Jr, Lieutenant (j.g.) Arend, 196
Walcheren Landings: see Operation Infatuate
Wall, Lieutenant Commander C.R. 334
Walters, Midshipman Arthur 347
War Cabinet, British 30, 78, 82, 93
War Production Board (US) 71–2, 76, 79
Warren, HMS 74
Western Task Force 100, *112*, 357
Weston, Wireman R.V. 282
Weymouth *110–1*, 113, 118
Whitehead, Don 182, 208
Whitehead, Lieutenant Commander 342
Whitworth, Lieutenant P. 339
Wilhoit, Ensign William L. 206
Wilkerson, Ensign Virgil Eugene 120
Williams, Sub Lieutenant S.F. 346
Wilmington, DE 63
Wilson, Charles E. 76
Wilson, Ron 117
Women's Royal Naval Service (WRNS) 96, 100, *135*
Women Construction Workers 60, 89
Woodham, Lieutenant C. 328
Zealley, Able Seaman Edward 89